Political
Power and
Communications
in Indonesia

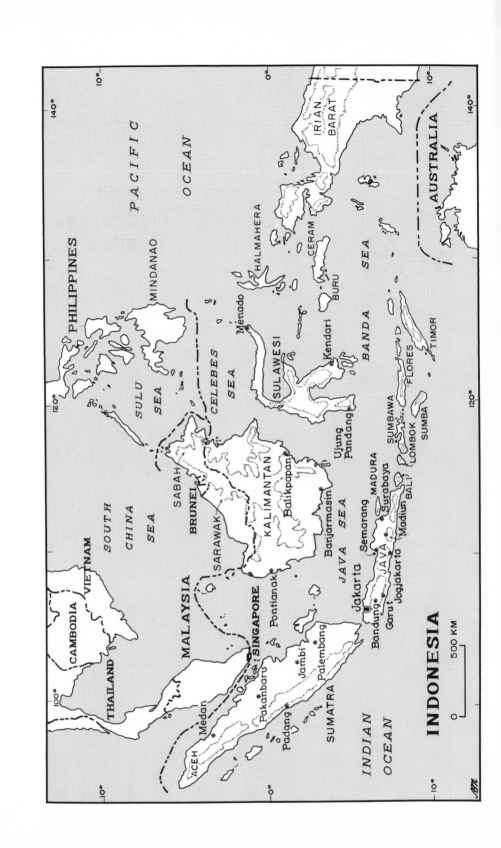

Political Power and Communications in Indonesia

Edited by
Karl D. Jackson
and Lucian W. Pye

University of
California Press
Berkeley
Los Angeles
London

University of California Press
Berkeley and Los Angeles, California

University of California Press, Ltd.
London, England

Copyright © 1978 by
The Regents of the University of California

ISBN 0-520-03303-5
Library of Congress Catalog
Card Number: 76-19976

Printed in the United States of America
Designed by Wolfgang Lederer

To Harold R. Isaacs
Teacher, Colleague, and Friend

Contents

List of Figures and Tables   ix

Contributors   xv

Preface   xix

PART I: Overview

1. Bureaucratic Polity: A Theoretical Framework for the Analysis of Power and Communications in Indonesia   KARL D. JACKSON   3

2. The Political Implications of Structure and Culture in Indonesia   KARL D. JACKSON   23

PART II: Institutions

3. The Military: Structure, Procedures, and Effects on Indonesian Society   ULF SUNDHAUSSEN   45

4. The Bureaucracy in Political Context: Weakness in Strength   DONALD K. EMMERSON   82

5. Indonesia's New Economic Policy and Its Sociopolitical Implications   BRUCE GLASSBURNER   137

6. Participation and the Political Parties   R. WILLIAM LIDDLE   171

7. Conceptions of Politics, Power, and Ideology in Contemporary Indonesian Islam   ALLAN A. SAMSON   196

PART III: Communications and Integration

8. The Mass Communications System in Indonesia   ASTRID SUSANTO   229

9. The Indonesian Press: An Editor's Perspective   NONO ANWAR MAKARIM   259

10. Cartoons and Monuments: The Evolution of
    Political Communication under the New Order
    BENEDICT R. O'G. ANDERSON   282

11. Bureaucratic Linkages and Policy-Making in Indo-
    nesia: BIMAS Revisited   GARY E. HANSEN   322

12. Urbanization and the Rise of Patron-Client Rela-
    tions: The Changing Quality of Interpersonal
    Communications in the Neighborhoods of Bandung
    and the Villages of West Java   KARL D. JACKSON   343

Conclusion

13. The Prospects for Bureaucratic Polity in Indonesia
    KARL D. JACKSON   395

    Bibliography   399
    Index   413

Figures and Tables

FIGURES

Frontispiece
Map of Indonesia ii

Chapter 3
1. KOWILHANs and KODAMs, 1973 63
2. The Organizational Structure of the Department of Defense and Security, 1974 66

Chapter 8
1. Java Television Coverage 244

Chapter 10
1. Frontispiece 283
2a-g. Sibarani Cartoons 287
3a-f. Johnny Hidajat Cartoons 290
4. Petruk 296
5. West Irian Monument 302
6. Mock-Up of National Monument 302
7. Sketch of Tjandi Sumberdjati, Fourteenth-Century Burial Temple 306
8. Gateway at Selecta 306
9. "Barabudur" by Oesman Effendi 309
10. Bayon II 310
11. Udjang 315
12. The Youthful Sultan Hamengkubuwono IX of Jogjakarta ... 316

Chapter 12

1. Perception of Self as Advisor in Response to the Question, "Do People Come to You for Advice or Help or To Pay Respect?": Whole Samples   357

2. Number of Persons Coming for Advice or Help: Elites Only   358

3. Response to the Question, "How Often Do You [the Advisor] Meet with Them?": Elites Only   359

4. Response to the Question, "If You Need Help . . . How Many People Could You Call Up Who Consider You Their Advisor-Patron?": Elites Only   361

5. Response to the Question, "Could You Say that You Are Their Bapak?": Elites Only   362

6. Response to the Question, "Are the People Who Come to You Members or Ex-Members of Organizations You Have Supported or Been a Member of?": Elites Only   364

7. Response to the Question, "Are There People Here You Go to for Advice, Opinions, Help, or just to Pay Respect?": Elites Only   369

8. Number of General Advisors as Indicated by Response to the Question, "How Many People Could You Go to for Advice?": Elites Only   371

9. Response to the Question, "If Your Son Needs a *Hajat* [Religious Festival] for Which You Don't Have the Money, Is There a Man Who Can Give You Help?": Elites Only   372

10. Residence of Financial Benefactor: Elites Only   373

11. Feelings of Moral Obligation toward a Financial Benefactor Indicated by Response to the Question, "If You Felt *Hutang Budi* How Far Would You Go to Repay It?": Elites Only   377

12. Alternative Actions Selected for Pa Dadap: Elites Only   384

13. Willingness of *Anak-Buah* to Follow Their *Haji* Out of an *Aliran*: Elites Only   386

14. Changing Parties for Financial Reward: Elites Only   388

TABLES

Chapter 5

1. Receipts and Expenditures of the Indonesian Central Government, 1966-1974   139

2. Balance of Payments, 1966-1975/76 140

3. Targets in Rice Cultivation for the First Five-Year Plan 143

4. Rice Production in Indonesia, 1968-1973, Revised Data 144

5. Prices of Medium-Quality Rice in Selected Indonesian Cities, 1968-1974 145

6. Production Growth Rates of Selected Agricultural Commodities, 1966-1972 150

7. Tax Receipts of the Indonesian Government, 1973/74, 1974/75, 1975/76 154

8. Expenditures by the Indonesian Government, 1972/73 and 1973/74 158

9. City Growth in Indonesia, 1961-1971 161

10. Planned Sectoral Production Growth Rates for the Second Five-Year Plan 169

Chapter 8

1. The Indonesian Population by Island and Urban-Rural 231

2. Occupation, by Percentage, Designating a Mass Medium as the First Priority Source of Information: Rural West Java 232

3. Respondents Designating a Medium as the Most Important Source of Information: City of Bandung 233

4. Reasons for Listening to Radio Programs among Jakarta Respondents 236

5. Reasons for Listening to Radio Programs among East Javanese Respondents 236

6. Most Popular Programs 237

7. Occupation by Listening Habits in West Javanese Village 238

8. Occupation by Listening Habits for a Semirural Population 238

9. Sources of Information for the Student Radio Station in Bandung 239

10. Occupation of Persons Responding to the Broadcast Questionnaire in Bandung 240

11. Frequency of Listening to Student Radio Station in Bandung 241

12. Average Listening Time for Student Radio Station Audience 241

13. Reasons for Listening to Bandung Student Radio Station
    (Radio IPMI)   242

14. Topics of Greatest Interest to Listeners of Bandung Student
    Radio (IPMI) by Broadcast Interview and Direct Interview
    Samples   242

15. Program Offerings of TVRI in 1971 and 1972   245

16. Occupation of Television-Owning Parents of Bandung
    Elementary School Students   245

17. Reasons for Watching Television in Bandung   246

18. Country of Origin of Films Imported during 1971   247

19. Percentage of Respondents Selecting Various Media as the
    Most Important Source of Information about New Products
    in the City of Bandung   249

20. Why People Read the Newspaper in Bandung   250

21. Percentage of the Total Number of News Items Devoted to
    Election News, Domestic News, and Foreign News by
    Kompas and *Pikiran Rakyat*, April-June 1971   250

22. Percentage of the Total Column Centimeters Used for
    Election News, Domestic News, and Foreign News by
    Kompas and *Pikiran Rakyat*, April-June 1971   251

23. Sources Used by Newspapers for Election News Stories   251

24. Percentage of Total Column Centimeters of Election
    Coverage Devoted to Different Types of Stories by *Kompas*
    and *Pikiran Rakyat*, April-June 1971   252

25. Sources of General Information and Election News among
    Bandung Adults   254

26. Which Newspaper Was Used as the Source of General
    Information and Election News?   255

27. Was the Election News Clear Enough in *Kompas* and
    Pikiran Rakyat?   255

28. Type of Article Most Comprehensible to Respondents   256

29. Opinion Leadership in Five West Java Fishing Villages   257

    Chapter 12

 1. Completed Interviews as Percentage of Total   355

 2. Response to the Question, "Do These People Come for
    Financial Advice Only, Personal Advice, Political Advice,
    Religious Advice, or All Kinds?"   360

3. Overlap Between Role of Advisor and Advisee: Elites Only   368

4. Percentage Affirming that They Have a General Advisor, Financial Advisor, Local Political Advisor, or Outside Political Advisor: Elites Only   370

5. Percentage Possessing an Advisor-Advisee Relationship of 6 to 25 Years' Duration for the General Advisor, Financial Advisor, and Local Political Advisor by Rural and Urban: Elites Only   379

6. Percentage Affirming a Direct Connection between Having an Advisor and Membership in an Organization: Elites Only   381

Contributors

BENEDICT B. R. O'G. ANDERSON, born in China in 1936, is Professor of Government and Asian Studies at Cornell University, Associate Director of the Cornell Modern Indonesia Project, and chief editor of *Indonesia*. His main fields of research are the culture and politics of modern Indonesia. His publications include *Mythology and the Tolerance of the Javanese*; "The Language of Indonesian Politics"; *Java in a Time of Revolution: Occupation and Resistance, 1944-1946*; and "The Idea of Power in Javanese Culture."

DONALD K. EMMERSON, born in Japan in 1940, is Associate Professor of Political Science at the University of Wisconsin, Madison. His main research fields have included symbolism, technology, bureaucracy, and social change in Indonesia. Among his publications are *Students and Politics in Developing Nations* (as editor and coauthor); "Bureaucratic Alienation in Indonesia: The Director General's Dilemma"; "Students and the Establishment in Indonesia: The Status-Generation Gap"; and *Indonesia's Elite: Political Culture and Cultural Politics*.

BRUCE GLASSBURNER, born in Nebraska in 1920, is Professor of Economics at the University of California, Davis, and has been Chairman of the Department of Economics there and Chairman of the Field Staff of the University of California Indonesia Project. He has edited the *Pakistan Development Review* and is a member of the editorial board of the *Bulletin of Indonesian Economic Studies*. His main research fields are Asian economics and macroeconomic theory. Among his publications are "Problems of Economic Policy in Indonesia, 1950-1957"; "High-Level Manpower for Economic Development: The Indonesian Experience"; "Aspects of the Problem of Foreign Exchange Pricing in Pakistan"; "Pricing of Foreign Exchange in Indonesia, 1966-1967"; *The Economy of Indonesia: Selected Readings*; "Government in the Economy of Hong Kong" (with James Riedel); and *Teori Dan Kebijaksanaan Ekonomi Makro* (Theory and Policy of Macroeconomics) (with Aditiawan Chandra).

GARY E. HANSEN, born in Nebraska in 1939, is a Research Associate at the Technology and Development Institute, East-West Center, Honolulu, Hawaii. His main field of interest has been the political economy of rural change in Indonesia and Southeast Asia. Among his publications are *The Politics and*

Administration of Rural Development in Indonesia; Rural Local Government and Agricultural Development in Java; and a forthcoming book, *Agricultural and Rural Development in Indonesia.*

KARL D. JACKSON, born in Massachusetts in 1942, is Assistant Professor of Political Science at the University of California, Berkeley and is Co-Chairperson of the Berkeley Mass Communications Project. His main fields of research are communications and rural politics in Indonesia. His publications include *Communication and National Integration in Sundanese Villages: Implications for Communication Strategy* (with Johannes Moeliono) and "Participation in Rebellion: The Dar'ul Islam in West Java" (with Johannes Moeliono).

R. WILLIAM LIDDLE, born in Pennsylvania in 1938, is Associate Professor of Political Science at Ohio State University and has been Chairperson of the Indonesia Studies Committee of the Association for Asian Studies. His main field of research has been local level politics in contemporary Indonesia. His publications include *Ethnicity, Party, and National Integration: An Indonesian Case Study*; "Modernizing Indonesian Politics"; and "Evolution from Above: National Leadership and Local Development in Indonesia."

NONO ANWAR MAKARIM, born in Indonesia in 1939, is currently completing the doctoral program in law at Harvard University. He has been a member of the Indonesian Parliament and is the former chief editor of the newspaper *Harian Kami.* His main fields of interest are law, the press, and social change in Indonesia. He is the author of numerous articles on Indonesian social, economic, and political events.

LUCIAN W. PYE, born in China in 1921, is a Ford Professor of Political Science at the Massachusetts Institute of Technology. He has done field work in Southeast Asia and Hong Kong and has served in various capacities in scholarly associations and public affairs organizations. He is author of numerous books, including *Guerrilla Communism in Malaya; Politics, Personality, and Nation-Building: Burma's Search for Identity; Aspects of Political Development; China: An Introduction;* and *Mao Tse-Tung: The Man in the Leader.*

ALLAN A. SAMSON, born in Illinois in 1939, is a Research Associate of the Center for South and Southeast Asia Studies, University of California, Berkeley. His major research fields are religion and political development and Indonesian politics. His publications include "Islam in Indonesian Politics"; "Army and Islam in Indonesia"; and "Religious Belief and Political Action in Indonesian Islamic Modernism."

ULF SUNDHAUSSEN, born in 1934 in Germany, is a Lecturer in Government at the University of Queensland, Australia. His main research interests are the military in politics and the politics of developing countries. His publications include "The Military in Research on Indonesian Politics"; "New Guinea's

Army — A Political Role?"; *The Military in Indonesia*; and "Ideology and Nation-Building in Papua New Guinea."

ASTRID SUSANTO, born in Indonesia in 1936, is the Dean of the Faculty of Journalism at the Universitas Pajajaran in Bandung. Her main research fields are mass media and journalism in Indonesia.

Preface

THE EXOTIC CHARMS and cultural mysteries of Indonesia have long fascinated the Western imagination. Since independence, Indonesia has asserted a claim to world attention because of its leadership potential in Southeast Asia and among Third World countries, its status as the largest Islamic country in the world, and its wealth of natural resources, including oil. One would have thought that this combination of intrinsic interest and political and economic importance would have guaranteed extensive and sustained scholarly research. The story of Indonesia's struggle for independence from Holland, the initial halting attempts at parliamentary rule and economic development, and the period of flamboyant rule by Sukarno did produce a shelf of books. But now for more than a decade there has been relative silence about this important country, reflecting in part the faddishness of academic curiosity, and in part a somewhat repressive political climate which has increasingly restricted research.

Among specialists on Southeast Asia and the developing world, there should be continuous discussion as to what theories best explain Indonesian developments. Our theoretical contention is that there have been remarkably enduring qualities in Indonesian politics, and the change from the ideologically verbose Sukarno era to the more austere Suharto period is more apparent than real. By concentrating attention on the basic structural, cultural, and institutional framework of Indonesian politics, we have sought to reveal the distinctive character of power and social communication in a society which has been experiencing both change and cultural reaffirmation. Though at different times Indonesia may seemingly present different faces to the world, it is the scholar's duty to delineate the country's enduring dimensions.

In Part I we present our theory of the "bureaucratic polity" which we feel best explains the persistence of the Indonesian political system. We then examine the general structural and cultural factors that shape it. Finally, from more objective, sociological, and even geographic considerations, we move to interpretations of the subjective, psychological dimensions of power in Indonesia.

Part II deals with the principal institutions of government, with each chapter examining a different key element in the "bureaucratic polity" in light of recent empirical research by mainly younger scholars with extensive field research experience. Because of the commanding role of the military we begin with Ulf Sundhaussen, who has had a unique opportunity to observe and study the Indonesian army. The next key element of power in the Indonesian system is the civilian bureaucracy, analyzed by Donald K. Emmerson, who on two occasions has studied its operations. Although not a separate "institution," the small group of Western-trained economists who have guided much of public policy for the Suharto regime deserve special attention; their policies are evaluated by Bruce Glassburner, who has worked closely with them on a professional basis.

Among Indonesian specialists there is some question as to the actual role of the political parties and the degree to which they represent fully mobilized, enduring social cleavages. In our introductory analysis of the "bureaucratic polity" we tend to discount the influence of the parties, but R. William Liddle, who has studied them firsthand in both Sumatra and Java, assigns them considerably more importance. This is a difference in views which the editors welcome, because at this stage the advancement of Indonesian studies demands not consensus but greater richness in theories and more tolerance for ambiguities. The final chapter in Part II by Allan A. Samson deals with the concept of power in Islamic ideology, and thus provides an appropriate bridge for leaving the study of the power processes in the formal "institutions" of government to enter the area of more general social and communications processes.

To understand Indonesia as a "bureaucratic polity" it is necessary to appreciate the limited influence on politics of general social processes. The Indonesian bureaucratic polity is stable but weak, easy to rule but difficult to modernize. Isolating the peasantry from party politics and fostering a one-way communication system ensures the short-term survival of the regime but substantially inhibits the government's ability to mobilize the peasantry for economic and social development. This is why we have chosen to juxtapose power and communications in the quest for understanding how interests are advanced in the Indonesian political process.

Therefore, Part III is devoted to communications and integration, and appropriately begins with two chapters by Indonesian authors: Astrid Susanto analyzes the structure and the general characteristics of the mass media of Indonesia, and Nono Anwar Markarim provides an intimate, firsthand report of the problems of being an editor in Jakarta. Although the mass media may have limited political influence, this does not mean that there is any lack of political subtlety, as Benedict R. O'G. Anderson demonstrates in his analysis of cartoons and monuments.

The evolution of organizational forms and the mobilization process are confronted in the final two chapters. Gary E. Hansen presents a case study of the Jakarta government's limited ability to mobilize the peasantry even for a program designed to advance their self-interest as rice-growers. Finally, Karl D. Jackson reports data which show how urbanization has altered traditional authority relations toward more self-interest-oriented patron-client ties, a change that helps to explain why urban growth has not been a threat to the system of "bureaucratic polity."

In sum, the picture of Indonesia which emerges from this study is devoid of the optimism that characterized so much of the earlier literature on that country and the rest of the developing world. At the same time the authors give little support to the extreme pessimists who would forecast increasing decay and disintegration. Instead we strive for a better understanding of the forces underlying the durability of Indonesia and its political culture. Forces of change are at work, though their rhythm is not that of the ideological pronouncements or the military directives that have provided the surface drama of recent years.

Only if we revive and sustain scholarly research will we be able in time to understand the processes of change and continuity in a society as complex as Indonesia's. Sound insight into the political and social processes in the Third World requires that our theorizing not be unduly shaped by crisis cases or those countries which at any particular moment may, for one reason or another, be commanding the attention of the headlines. Analysis of the character of the dual phenomena of power and communications in developing countries provides a solid basis for building knowledge.

This study was made possible by a grant to the M.I.T. Center for International Studies from the research office of the United States Information Agency. In particular the project profited greatly from the assistance of Dr. Ralph Greenhouse of the Research Office. In expressing our appreciation for this support, we must also make it clear that the agency has not endorsed this work, nor do the contents reflect official opinion. We would also like to thank Jessie Janjigian of the Center for International Studies; her editorial skills helped to transform the early manuscripts into finished products. We owe thanks to John McBrearty and Larry Rosenthal, who prepared the bibliography. Finally the Committee on Research and the Center for South/Southeast Asia Studies of the University of California, Berkeley, supplied additional support in preparing the manuscript for publication.

PART I: Overview

1

Bureaucratic Polity: A Theoretical Framework for the Analysis of Power and Communications in Indonesia

KARL D. JACKSON

MOST OBSERVERS OF Indonesian politics in the 1970s have condemned in varying degrees its authoritarianism and corruption and doubted whether significant economic development has been achieved. These observers chronicle the restraint of the press, the intimidation of students and intellectuals, the government's manipulation of political parties, and the substantial shortcomings of major development programs. Often implicit in these accounts is a note of surprise that the government of a land of 130,000,000 persons can exist without mass political participation, that President Suharto has ruled longer and more effectively than his charismatic predecessor President Sukarno, and that a system of government suffused with so much corruption can endure so long in the midst of one of the largest and poorest populations in the Third World. To understand how all this has been possible and to foresee probable trends in the future, it is necessary to appreciate the extent to which apparently separate political events can be understood as outcomes of the particular type of political system called "bureaucratic polity."

My major thesis is that at least since 1957, when parliamentary democracy ended with the declaration of martial law, the basic form of government has not changed fundamentally. Although the principal actors and policy emphases have altered and power in the 1970s is more concentrated than ever before in the hands of the president, Indonesia remains a bureaucratic polity — that is, a political system in which power and participation in national decisions are limited almost entirely to the employees of the state, particularly the officer corps and the highest levels of the bureaucracy, including especially the highly trained specialists known as the technocrats.

Although the number of bureaucrats and army officers influencing policy implementation at the local level is much larger, national policies are established

I would like to thank Benedict Anderson, Russell Betts, Suchitra Bhakdi, Jyotirindra Das Gupta, Kenneth Jowitt, Robert Kagan, Dwight King, Martin Landau, Lucian W. Pye, Leo Rose, Lawrence Shrader, and Gunnar Sjoblom, who were kind enough to comment on an earlier draft of this chapter.

by a small ruling circle whose members respond primarily, albeit not exclusively, to the values and interests of less than one thousand persons comprising the bureaucratic, technocratic, and military elite of the country. Although Sukarno's policies brought national economic ruin, adversely affecting the lives of tens of millions of Indonesians, the regime endured as long as a significant proportion of the Jakarta elite remained satisfied (or at least not unified in opposition). Only events as shocking as those surrounding the attempted Communist coup of September 30, 1965 were sufficient to alienate most of the military and bureaucratic elite, including especially the officers directly commanding troops near Jakarta. As a result, Sukarno's ruling circle was replaced by Suharto's, but the bureaucratic polity has endured and competition for power remains restricted to the very highest levels of the Jakarta military and bureaucratic elite.

This chapter will outline the concept of bureaucratic polity and sketch the important modifications of the Suharto era. Chapter 2 will present the structural and cultural variables that account in large part for the continued existence of bureaucratic polity and for the likelihood that bureaucratic polity, under whatever leadership, will continue to be the system of government in Indonesia for the foreseeable future.

BUREAUCRATIC POLITY

The concept of bureaucratic polity is distinguishable from other forms of government by the degree to which national decision-making is insulated from social and political forces outside the highest elite echelons of the capital city. Like islands cut off from the social sea surrounding them, bureaucratic polities are largely impervious to currents in their own societies and may be more responsive to external pressures emanating from the international arena. Yet, in spite of the relative absence of mass participation, in country after country in the Third World such systems exhibit remarkable endurance unless confronted by strong, often externally backed military challenges.

Although it is a truism that the employees of a state wield its power, there is a significant difference in such states as Indonesia and other bureaucratic polities in the developing world. In these cases the military and the bureaucracy are not accountable to other political forces such as political parties, interest groups, or organized communal interests. Actions designed to influence governmental decisions originate entirely within the elite itself without any need for mass participation or mobilization. Power does not result from the articulation of interests from the social and geographic periphery of society. Bureaucratic polities favor neither democratic nor totalitarian forms of mass participation. Parties, to the extent that they exist at all, neither control the central bureaucracy nor effectively organize the masses at the local level. Essentially, bureaucratic polity is a form of government in which there is no regular participation or mobilization of the people. (For descriptions of what has been called bureaucratic polity, see Riggs 1966: 310-96; Linz 1975: 264-306; Scott 1972*b*: 57-91; Willner 1970: 242-306; Huntington 1968: 78-92; Huntington and Nelson 1976.)

Some element of participation must, of course, exist in all polities, but in bureaucratic polities the only form of participation regularly involving large numbers of citizens relates to implementing rather than deciding national policies. Such participation, furthermore, tends to be limited to the local level and consists almost entirely of obtaining individual relief from government regulations or exactions rather than changing offending laws for all citizens. Even this form of local participation tends to be organized by vertical rather than horizontal groupings, that is, through traditional authority and patron-client groupings rather than through groups based on similar social attributes such as class.

Indonesia since Sukarno has been a presidential variant of a bureaucratic polity.[1] The president of the republic, his personal advisors, a group of Western-trained technocrats, the most important generals in HANKAM,[2] members of the cabinet, and a few top bureaucrats exercise decisive power over national policy-making. The country has neither autonomous political parties which can influence decision-making nor a state political party with a coherent ideology and organizational capacity for consistently mobilizing the citizenry. The main arena for political competition is not the country at large, and power is not obtained through the cultivation of mass movements. Instead, meaningful power is obtained through interpersonal competition in the elite circle in closest physical proximity to the president. Elections are held to legitimize, through democratic symbolism, the power arrangements already determined by competing elite circles in Jakarta. The general public consists chiefly of peasants who are neither involved nor greatly affected by the outcome of Jakarta's political struggles, and outside narrow elite circles public opinion on most national issues either does not exist or can safely be ignored.

Whenever mass mobilization has occurred in Indonesia the initiative has come from within the elite. Participation aimed at disciplining the central government has succeeded only if substantial segments of the officer corps and bureaucracy have supported it. From the late 1950s onward, there have been repeated instances in which the general public has failed to support its elected representatives. Likewise, the political parties, with the partial exception of the PKI (the Indonesian Communist party), have been organized from above by elites, and they have not been accountable to the groups they purported to represent (see Lev 1967: 58-61; McVey 1969: 8). These parties have lacked coherent and compelling ideologies, and without the support of mass publics in crisis situations they have been incapable of resisting the pressures of the

---

1. There is nothing peculiarly Third World about bureaucratic polity. The European response to the structural and cultural conditions prevailing in Indonesia was similar, although by no means identical. Colonial government was isolated from the peasantry, incapable of consistent penetration beyond the urban centers, dependent on external (international) support, nonparticipatory, and basically an administrative rather than a political state.

2. HANKAM (*Departmen Pertahanan Keamanan*) is the Indonesian Department of Defense and Security which controls the military services and the national police force. Its role will be discussed in Chapter 3. "The Military: Structures, Procedures, and Effects on Indonesian Society," by Ulf Sundhaussen.

president or the army. Parties representing millions of voters have been outlawed by government fiat, but there has been no massive public outcry. In 1959 President Sukarno dismissed the elected Constituent Assembly when it did not support his desire to return to the Constitution of 1945 (Feith 1963: 358-66); likewise, in 1960 he dismissed the legally elected Parliament when it disagreed with him over the budget (Feith 1963: 343). Further, in 1960 he banned the modernist Muslim party (the Masyumi) and the Socialist party (the PSI). In similar fashion President Suharto outlawed the PKI and imprisoned tens of thousands of its operatives, proscribed former Masyumi leaders from participating in the new Muslim party, the PMI, openly manipulated the leaderships of the legal political parties, and summarily retired powerful generals such as General Sumitro and Sutowo (see Chapter 7 in this book and Sloan 1971: 44-76; Feith 1968; Crouch 1971: 177-92; McIntyre 1972: 283-310; Davies 1974; Starner 1974a). All of these actions, under the Old and the New Order, in the presence and the absence of a charismatic figure, transpired without significant sustained opposition from outside the elite. As one technocrat remarked regarding the austere economic stabilization program of the New Order,

> Oh, people may say this is ignoring the voice of the people, but we simply had more important things to do with our time. We had clear support for our policies from the government, and that was really all that was necessary. When you are in the government, you can do certain things [Weinstein 1972: 630].

THE LIMITS OF PRESIDENTIAL POWER

The chief power-holders under Guided Democracy were President Sukarno and the army; under the New Order power resides with the president, who modulates the competition for power in both the civilian and military bureaucracies (see Feith 1963; Hindley 1962: 915-26; Hindley 1967). Under Guided Democracy only the PKI was a serious extra-elite contender, and it was allowed to exist only so long as it did not threaten the existence of the ruling military and bureaucratic circles. The events of September 30, 1965, in which six senior generals were murdered, implicated the PKI in an overt, violent attempt to overturn the system of politics in which only a narrow elite participated, and as a result even the protection of President Sukarno was insufficient to prevent the PKI's destruction. The crisis extending from September 30, 1965 to Sukarno's final removal in March 1967 was the most formidable one ever faced by the Indonesian bureaucratic polity (Hindley 1970: 23-66). Sukarno's ouster illustrates that a bureaucratic polity is not a one-man, sultanistic regime. In Indonesia, even an incumbent president's power must be backed by at least a minimal consensus among the military and bureaucratic elite. Even given the substantial power accruing almost automatically to the head of state and the president's natural primacy in declaratory politics, in bureaucratic polity no president can survive if he sides with a major nonelite group that is bent on rapidly redistributing the very real economic and political privileges entailed in elite membership and government employment. The pictures of the bodies of the murdered generals that were telexed to army units throughout Indonesia supplied emotionally compelling proof that the PKI was willing to use violence against elite members and, if necessary, to destroy the officer corps in order to change the direction of Indonesian political development. The pictures were symbolic proof that the PKI was out to change a way of life rather than merely to install another phase of the bureaucratic polity.[3]

The events of 1965/66 constituted a period of transition in which one ruling circle of the polity was replaced by another. The struggle among the supporters of President Sukarno and the army and the students was a very real one in which elements normally circumscribed from political participation were brought in by contending sides. However, this brief upsurge of mass participation was tempered by two facts. First, the issue of who rules was ultimately decided by the ability of officers with direct command of troops to surround the palace on March 11, 1966. Second, student movements are elite movements, and at least on the anti-Sukarnoist side the students were stage-managed by elite members. The ephemeral nature of the student mobilization into politics and its dependence on the older generation for leadership and financial resources were evidenced by the rapidity with which the movement collapsed in 1968/69 once the "elders" withdrew their behind-the-scenes support from the once-mighty KAMI (Indonesian Student Action Alliance).

Obviously, the rampage of killings that descended on Central Java, East Java, and Bali was not carried out directly by segments of the Jakarta elite (see Sloan 1971; Mortimer 1974; Hughes 1967: 119-96). The elite proceeded indirectly by mobilizing the most effective existing network for violence, the rural religious teachers (*kiyayi*) in Central and East Java. Within traditional Islamic doctrine, the *jihad* or holy war has an accepted place, and this traditional symbolism in the past has been used with telling effectiveness to rouse the traditional peasant masses to political violence. However, the peasantry did not move without direction from the elite. If the killings were a religiously motivated mass contagion or an anomic explosion of protest against the privations of Guided Democracy, one would have predicted that the ferocity of the jihad would have been felt most heavily in West Java, the fervently Islamic birthplace of the Dar'ul Islam, but anti-Communist killings were virtually absent from West Java in 1965/66 in spite of the fact that the PKI had a very substantial following in the province. The absence of the killings is explained by the refusal of the

---

3. The coup behavior of the Communist party stands in marked contrast to the other rebellions and attempted coups of the period. If one discounts the assassination attempts directed against the president and analyzes the behavior of the Lubis plotters in 1956 or of the PRRI rebellion in Sumatra in 1958, one can see that intra-elite violence was largely absent. The plotters were imprisoned or placed under varying forms of house arrest, but they all lived, and in some cases informally rejoined the struggle for power. No event in postwar elite politics paralleled the murder of the six generals. (On coup behavior and the ways in which the PKI transgressed the "rules of the game" of Indonesian elite politics, see Chapter 3 by Sundhaussen; McVey 1971: 166, 175; Willner 1967: 516-17.)

army high command in West Java to sanction such activities in the months immediately following the coup. Until his removal, Major General Ibrahim Adjie, commander of the Siliwangi division, kept West Java peaceful. In the days immediately following the coup, thousands of PKI members voluntarily turned themselves in to the authorities in West Java, and after renouncing their PKI links and stating that they had been misled they were generally allowed to return to their villages. Prominent leaders were imprisoned, and several village grudges were settled under the banner of anticommunism, but the mass following of the Communist Party in West Java was allowed to divest itself of its PKI affiliation in the absence of violence on the part of either the authorities or fellow villagers.[4]

Although the coup and subsequent events sharply defined the limits of presidential power, other constraints on presidential freedom of action always had been present. Most of these were imposed by the army's resistance to particular policy initiatives (Feith 1963). For example, Sukarno's initial *konsepsi* of Guided Democracy included PKI participation in the cabinet. However, the army successfully resisted this development throughout Guided Democracy. Furthermore, Sukarno's power was limited also by the substantial autonomy of regional army commands, and in many instances he was allowed to reign but not to rule, being forced to negotiate with rather than command his own subordinates (Willner 1970). Similarly, the power of the army to maneuver during this period of basically bipolar politics was limited by Sukarno and his allies in the PKI and other parties.

The major evolution of the Indonesian bureaucratic polity with the passing of Sukarno has been a steadily increasing concentration of power. Under Sukarno the center had little ability to change the daily lives of the citizenry, and, in addition, this small amount of power was dispersed among the president, the army, and the officials, major and minor, who could ignore the orders of the central authorities. With the advent of the New Order the limited power flowing in the system has been concentrated in a few hands surrounding the president in Jakarta. The major change is *not* that the total amount of power has vastly increased; on the contrary, central government programs requiring wide participation by the peasantry, such as miracle rice and family planning, have failed to reach their objectives.[5] The most fundamental limit on the power of the president is that common to all bureaucratic polities: Inability or unwillingness to organize and mobilize the masses into politics on a regular basis means that bureaucratic polities find it difficult, if not impossible, to mobilize the general population to make sacrifices for particular national programs. Although the

4. This information comes from the field observations of Karl D. Jackson in the villages of West Java in 1968/69.
5. Agricultural development programs such as BIMAS and BUUD usually have failed to reach their goals. On these programs and their shortcomings, see Chapter 4, "Bureaucracy in Political Context: Weakness in Strength," by Donald K. Emmerson; Chapter 5, "Indonesia's New Economic Policy and Its Sociopolitical Implications," by Bruce Glassburner; and Chapter 12, "Bureaucratic Linkages and Policy-Making: BIMAS Revisited," by Gary E. Hansen. On family planning, see Hanna (1971) and Tan (1971).

isolation of the bureaucratic polity from society enables it to remain in power, the same isolation prevents it from achieving goals which require substantial voluntary participation from the populace as a whole. Unlike single party mobilization systems or multiparty mass democracies, bureaucratic polities find it difficult to expand power because bringing new groups into politics on a regular basis would ential sharing the benefits of government beyond a restricted official class.

This is not to say that bureaucratic polities are entirely devoid of mobilization. For certain tasks such as launching a demonstration, getting out the vote, or killing Communists, the Indonesian bureaucratic polity has proved itself an efficient mobilizer. The important distinction, however, is between short-term mobilization from above and long-term movements having their roots in organized, enduring social, economic, and religious cleavages in the society. Short-term mobilization from above occurred in Central and East Java in 1965/66 when the army passed the word to a selected number of village and religious leaders that the time had come to settle the score with the Communist party. In 1971, the bureaucracy and the army were mobilized to secure a pro-government vote, and the government party, GOLKAR, won an unprecedented 62.8 percent of the vote. However in both cases the mobilization was short-lived and initiated from the top. Furthermore, the creation of GOLKAR did not result in a new political force, independently generating demands and participating in government decision-making at the highest levels. GOLKAR, like political parties in most bureaucratic polities, has been used "to occupy political space" (Schmitter 1974) rather than to foster frequent and regular mass mobilization or participation (Linz 1975: 285).

The cleavage between orthodox and nominal Muslims, which cuts across Indonesian society, further limits the actions that may be taken by the official class. This cleavage between *santri* and *abangan* has not, however, precluded meaningful cooperation and alliances in daily politics within the elite. For example, the NU (Nahdatul Ulama) during Guided Democracy repeatedly supported Sukarno in de facto cooperation with the PNI and PKI (see Chapter 7 in this book and Willner 1967). However, when government acts are perceived as threatening the vital interests of the orthodox Islamic community, substantial opposition will arise. In such instances, the official class is usually split, and either no decision is reached or the offending action is modified or withdrawn. However, it should be emphasized that such events are rare. During the course of the New Order, orthodox Muslim party leaders have been rather systematically excluded from real power, yet the full ire of the *ummat Islam* (the community of Islam) was roused only in regard to the government's marriage bill in 1973 (see Chapter 4 in this book). Other instances have also involved the applicability of the Islamic law and attachment to the concept of an Islamic state (see Chapter 7 in this book and Boland 1971).

Finally, the international arena constrains the activities of the official class ruling a bureaucratic polity. To the extent that outside aid and private capital are perceived as necessary to meet regime ends, domestic political activities will be tempered to meet the economic and political preconceptions of potential donors and investors. Though the Indonesian foreign-policy-making elite views the outside world as threatening and potentially hostile, the necessity of outside aid, under Sukarno and Suharto alike, has affected substantial policy decisions. The most obvious example of foreign influence is supplied by the conditions imposed on Indonesia by the IMF and the Western donors in return for the resumption of large-scale aid after the fall of Sukarno (see Crouch 1976; Rudner 1976). These included not only domestic economic austerity but also the abandonment of a major Indonesian foreign policy initiative, the Crush Malaysia campaign (Weinstein 1972). Although the vast majority of the Indonesian population may not have significant influence over government decision-making, donor organizations have a clear, albeit limited impact. An axiom of bureaucratic polity is that the greater the reluctance or inability to mobilize outside groups into the regular political and economic decision-making process, the greater the dependence on foreign resources for the inputs necessary to initiate economic change.

Because bureaucratic polities stress technical and administrative solutions while de-emphasizing the need for participation and mass mobilization, they usually lack inspiring ideologies and hence are peculiarly vulnerable to international criticism. Even if they achieve their economic development goals, said achievements often are lost in a welter of criticism regarding denial of freedom in their societies. To the leaders of bureaucratic polities this criticism contrasts markedly with the willingness of foreign intellectuals to excuse the absence of civil liberties in one-party mobilization regimes whose drive for industrialization is paired with an attractive, usually revolutionary ideology. This inherent double standard makes bureaucratic polities doubly sensitive to their image problems abroad (see Linz 1975: 264-74).

CONCENTRATION OF POWER

With time, bureaucratic polities tend to concentrate power in fewer hands (Riggs 1966). The total amount of power available in bureaucratic polity is limited because of the inability or unwillingness of the bulk of society to participate in national decisions. The total amount of power available to all elite competitors is perceived as fixed or stagnant, and therefore personal power can be increased only at the expense of other power-holders. The competition for power and access to lucrative posts is largely perceived as a zero-sum game in which the powerful triumph not by mobilizing new classes or groups into politics but by eliminating individuals or groups from the ruling circle. In systems dominated by mass parties, leaders maximize their power by gaining new adherents, whereas in a bureaucratic polity the power of individual leaders is increased by dividing the sum total of power available within the bureaucratic sphere among a diminishing number of leaders. This process of power concentration may continue until the ruling circle becomes so small that it is easily toppled by another circle in a bloodless coup.

The political history of the New Order has been characterized by the decline of political competition and by the elimination of groups from the ruling circle that originally gained power in 1966 (see Weinstein 1976). President Suharto came to power at the behest of a diverse coalition of supporters within the elite. His supporters included the army radicals who sought a rapid break with Sukarno as well as with the old party system; the army centrists who sought the same general goals but at a more moderate pace; the student leaders who wanted early elections, investigation of corruption, and limitation of the military's political power; political party leaders who desired a favorable election law and early elections; leading bureaucrats and technocrats, including the most Westernized intellectuals, who sought rapid economic growth and development; and the Muslims who hoped to return to the councils of power, from which Sukarno had banished them. Of these groups, only the army centrists and a limited number of the bureaucrats and technocrats have maintained or increased their influence over national decision-making under the New Order (see Feith 1968; Hindley 1970).

In the seemingly inexorable process of concentrating power, those who had demonstrated to bring down the old regime, the student action fronts (KAMI-KAPPI), and those most responsible for dismembering the PKI in the countryside, the Muslim politicians, were the first to fall by the wayside under the New Order.[6] By mid-1969, if not earlier, KAMI was no longer a credible political force. In turn, the Muslim political party leaders were rapidly excluded from national decision-making as well as from any reasonable opportunity to increase their power via the ballot box. The Masyumi was not legalized, and its most prestigious national leaders were prohibited from serving in the vanguard of its replacement, the PMI, which was created with the government's permission in 1968. Prior to the national elections of 1971 the leaderships of both the NU and the PMI were packed with government-anointed leaders, thus insuring continued cooperation with the government in the event that the Islamic parties did well in the upcoming elections. After the lackluster performance of the ummat Islam in the 1971 elections, the Islamic parties were required by government order to regroup, forming the Development Unity party (PPP). Further, the Department of Religious Affairs, the largest government department which for eighteen years had been controlled by the NU, was given to a nonparty man and substantially reduced in size. At a single blow this demolished the NU's patronage network, which had extended from Jakarta down to the village level. Finally, in 1973 the first draft of the government's new marriage law threatened to restrict sharply the jurisdiction of the Islamic courts (see Chapter 7 and Chapter 4 in this volume).

With the approach of the 1971 elections non-Islamic opposition parties

6. While power over national decisions concentrates as regimes increase in age, this does not preclude decentralization of planning and implementation within the bureaucracy. Similarly, concentration of decision-making power at the national level does not preclude cooptation of increasing numbers of individuals into government jobs, thus dispensing the fruits of status without yielding the substance of power.

were also "retooled" (to use Sukarno's phrase), that is, leaders acceptable to Suharto were installed at party conventions in response to heavy pressure emanating from the president and his advisors. As a result, the 1971 election was contested by party leaders publicly pledging full support to President Suharto and his New Order. In the election the PNI, which had been the largest party in 1955, lost its mass following and the core of its bureaucratic constituency passed to GOLKAR (the coalition of pro-government organizations created to carry the president's banner in the election). With the PKI prohibited from participating, the PMI receiving only 5.3 percent, and the PNI being reduced to 6.9 percent of the vote, GOLKAR won a victory of historic proportions by gaining 62.8 percent of the total vote. Only the NU maintained its support at the 1955 level by capturing 18.7 percent of the vote. When the 236 GOLKAR seats were supplemented by the 100 seats that Suharto was legally allowed to nominate, the government possessed a nearly insurmountable 73 percent majority in parliament (see Chapters 6, 4, and 3 in this book). The size of the government majority effectively detracted from Parliament's importance because the result of any debate was normally a foregone conclusion. As is usually the case in bureaucratic polity, Parliament is not the center of the struggle for power but exists to give legitimacy to decisions already determined in the highest echelons of the ruling circle.

Two additional government actions have further diminished the role of individual party leaders. First, the non-Islamic parties were required to combine into a single party, the Indonesian Democratic party. Second, government regulations formally prohibited all political activity in the villages between elections, thus severing whatever tenuous links existed between the urban political party leaders and their rural followers.

The army radicals who had been so instrumental in bringing Suharto to power were also slowly pushed aside. Generals prone to devising plans for restructuring the political system rapidly found their way into either retirement or the diplomatic corps. Thus, generals Dharsono, Kemal Idris, Sutopo Yuwono, Sarwo Edhie, and Sumitro were replaced. Likewise, General Nasution, having led the military through the difficult days of the 1950s and early 1960s, was slowly shorn of his political power.

Finally, at the conclusion of the anti-Tanaka riots of January 1974, the nontechnocratic civilian modernizers, such as Soedjatmoko, the former ambassador to the United States, found themselves out of power. This group, consisting mainly of adherents of the old PSI party, was driven from power by the accusation that it instigated the riots that had embarrassed the government.

DISTINGUISHING BUREAUCRATIC POLITY
FROM MILITARY RULE

Bureaucratic polity is not synonymous with military rule even though military officers may be the most decisive power-holders in a particular regime. In Indonesia the army is the critical institution supplying unity and stability to the national executive; however, the basic style and goals of the government are bureaucratic and technocratic rather than military. The ideas of the civilian technocrats have probably had more impact on policy in Indonesia than in almost any other country in the Third World. The technocrats' views have been decisive in setting an economic course emphasizing stabilization, balanced budgets, restoration of the market system, agricultural development, and an open door to foreign capital (see Chapter 5 in this book).

Although power has been concentrated in President Suharto's immediate entourage and the Indonesian bureaucracy increasingly has been "backboned" with military officers, the regime continues to reflect policy priorities not typically associated with military dictatorships. The president is a former general, but policies, if anything, are less favorable to the military establishment's institutional interests than were the policies of Guided Democracy. The New Order has sought broad-gauged economic modernization, attempted to apply the green revolution to Indonesia's food problems, and adopted the quite unmilitary habit of drastically reducing the size of the Indonesian military establishment. This last policy has resulted in substantial budget reductions and a manpower reduction from nearly 600,000 in 1967 to 420,000 in 1974. By 1979 another 70,000 men are to be cut from the military payroll (see Chapter 4 in this book). Also, through the reorganization of the armed services, more frequent rotation of regional commands, and the early retirement of political officers, the present government of Indonesia has become the master rather than the servant of the military establishment (see Chapter 3). Finally, the term *military rule* can connote regimes characterized by high rather than low mobilization and participation, thus implying a type of military populism wholly foreign to the Indonesian bureaucratic polity.

Bureaucratic polities rarely maximize economic rationality, organizational efficiency, and economic development. Although many of the ends associated with economic modernization may be pursued by a particular ruling circle, there is nothing in the political character of bureaucratic polity that requires this outcome. Guided Democracy proved beyond doubt that a bureaucratic polity could cast caution to the wind while pursuing inefficient, economically ruinous, and seemingly irrational policies. Although at present the symbol-wielders have been displaced by more pragmatic modernizers, the political system remains one in which a given ruling circle is accountable to fewer than 1,000 out of 130 million citizens, and hence, so long as the ruling circle satisfies the personal goals of this Jakarta-centric elite, it will be allowed to endure. The president will continue to be deferred to even if his policies seem economically irrational for the nation as a whole. The primacy of foreign policy over economic priorities that characterized the Sukarno era is a case in point. Although the seizure of all Dutch enterprises during the campaign to liberate West Irian and the massive weapons expenditures entailed by the Crush Malaysia campaign had predictably catastrophic effects on the economy as a whole, the president's policies were followed because important groups within the ruling circle, particularly the army, thereby increased their organizational share of the wealth and influence available to the ruling circle.

COMPETITION FOR POWER WITHIN THE RULING CIRCLE

Under the Old and New Order, power has been garnered in personal competition for the legitimation of programs and symbols by the president. Under the New Order, the competition is fought between circles of high-ranking bureaucrats and military officers. Each circle is held together by an elaborate system of personal ties and mutual obligations (see Chapter 12 in this volume and Anderson 1972a, Fagg 1958, Feith 1962). The personal ties are those of kinship and family as well as those of long-standing friendship, often extending back to some climactic personal event such as common participation in the Revolution. Because kinship relationships are so common among the Indonesian elite, such ties alone are not sufficient basis for inclusion in a circle. Likewise other primordial attachments such as religious *aliran* are not a sufficient basis on which to predict the fluctuating alliance pattern. It was particularly evident under the Old Order that the pattern of alliance linked adherents of contrasting religious beliefs. Although aliran is an important source of group solidarity, it alone cannot explain the quiltwork of alliances underpinning Jakarta elite politics. Similarly, although ideological commitments play a part in circle composition, their influence is relatively weak, as Left-Right distinctions tend to be submerged in the pursuit of power. Patron-client bonds are frequently the vital connecting link in coalitions spreading across aliran, ethnic group, and family demarcations.

The leader of the circle of clients, even at the elite level, is expected to perform the traditional functions of the patron, that is, to care for the material and status needs of the clients as well as to act as an advisor on ideological, personal, religious, and mystical matters (see Chapter 7, this volume). Unlike similar relations at the nonelite level, patrons in elite politics are more specialized in function and more materialistic and opportunistic in orientation. Patrons cultivate new clients, and clients having multiple patrons frequently switch their major allegiances as the political winds change. In addition, these informal groups create cliques within the same ministry as well as cutting across organizational boundary lines. The truly powerful patron is one who has the capacity to concentrate within his circle clients of varying intellectual, social, official, and financial resources, thus making his person the vital connecting link in the exchange pattern animating the circle.

The rewards sought by competing circles are multifaceted, involving organizational goals directly related to particular policy ends and likewise related to the preservation of the power and welfare of the circle leader and his followers. Individual competitors for power are simultaneously embedded in both formal organizational structures and informal personal alliances. Each of the formal organizations has a set of organizational objectives or service goals usually specified by laws or administrative regulations. In addition, there are nonservice goals, namely, maintaining the prestige, internal coherence, and wealth of the groups making up the organization. As the nonservice objectives of the individuals comprising the organization may be fulfilled by patron-client groupings extending across organizational boundaries, service and nonservice goals often push the same individual in different directions. In any organizational context a mix of service and nonservice goals animate decisions, but what is distinctive about bureaucratic polity is that nonservice goals tend to predominate when there is conflict over limited resources.

Powerful external political forces do not exist to control the activities of the elite, and hence controls over the mixture of service and nonservice goals must spring from within the elite itself. As a result, the nonservice goals of individuals and groups tend to prosper at the expense of organization objectives. The two most noted Indonesian examples of this phenomenon are provided by the near bankruptcy of PERTAMINA, the national oil company (see chapters 3 and 4), and the inability of BULOG, the rice stabilization agency, either to maintain price stability or substantially boost peasant income (see Chapter 5 in this volume; also Crouch 1976 and Rudner 1976). In both cases the directors of the agencies and the long chains of clients extending downward from the directors' closest confidants have prospered while the organizational objectives have faltered.

The predominance of nonservice goals does not necessarily preclude over-all organizational effectiveness. The critical question is how severely the balance is tipped in favor of nonservice goals. Reduction in the size of the Indonesian military establishment and the financial problems of PERTAMINA serve as illustrations of reasonable and excessive pursuit of nonservice goals.

An example of policy objectives being achieved in spite of the prominence of nonservice goals is the reduction of the size of the military establishment. The combination of the post-1965 purge of the bureaucracy, the subsequent infusion of military leaders into civilian posts, and the increasing health of the economy as a whole has meant that the size of the military establishment could be substantially reduced without disturbing the sense of self-worth and the standard of living of the officer corps. In contrast, in almost all organizations at the close of Guided Democracy there were no slack resources whatever, and the satisfaction of personal or group objectives precluded the accomplishment of almost all organizational ends. The vital point here is that bureaucratic polities are capable of substantial effectiveness, especially to the degree that particular policies do not require the mobilization of wide segments of the population. The nonpartici-patory nature of bureaucratic polity does not rule out a substantial rate of economic growth, especially when much of this growth can be undertaken directly by the official class, for example, increasing revenues, raising bureau-cratic efficiency, reinvigorating foreign investment, or revitalizing transportation networks. This is especially true to the extent that the satisfaction of both service and nonservice goals can increase simultaneously because of the existence of slack resources.

The financial crash of PERTAMINA in 1975 illustrates the failure of an organization in which the satisfaction of nonservice goals excessively out-distanced the fulfillment of normal business operations. Under its flamboyant director, General Ibnu Sutowo, PERTAMINA undoubtedly "got things done."

International contracts were well negotiated, a massive oil operation was built, and nonpetroleum projects (from hospital and hotel construction to a steel mill and fertilizer factories) were started, and in some cases completed. PERTAMINA seemed well on its way to becoming Indonesia's first conglomerate. However, most foreign observers who tagged PERTAMINA as Indonesia's best business organization mistook effectiveness (the ability to accomplish organizational ends) for efficiency (the ability to reach these goals with reasonable financial costs). The record of PERTAMINA, from its heyday in the late 1960s through the crash of 1975, illustrates that when resources are plentiful enough to satisfy both nonservice goals and normal business operations, organizational objectives can be achieved rapidly and even dramatically by an organization in which nonservice goals predominate. However what Western leaders and many Indonesians failed to appreciate was that effectiveness is not efficiency, and in the 1970s the costs of satisfying nonservice goals simply became too high even for PERTAMINA to absorb. Cost overruns, the acceptance of excessively high bids from subcontractors, and the pursuit of objectives almost without regard to cost, combined with a tightening international money market, lead to the collapse of PERTAMINA and the necessity for the government of Indonesia to assume responsibility for perhaps as much as $10 billion in outstanding obligations (see Hanna 1971; McDonald 1976; Jenkins 1976; Arndt 1975; Coggin 1975).

In judging the performance of an organization within the context of bureaucratic polity, the important question is not whether corruption exists; corruption will always exist when forces capable of restraining a particular ruling circle are weak or absent. However, the existence of corruption need not preclude organizational effectiveness; in fact, a limited amount of corruption may be requisite to substantial achievements within the Indonesian bureaucratic polity. The problem for PERTAMINA and for the New Order in general is not whether the *absolute* amount of corruption is increasing, but whether corruption as a *proportion* of total resources is expanding. If corruption as a proportion of total resources is expanding rapidly, organizational goals will falter, and progress will come to a grinding halt. PERTAMINA not withstanding, it is my judgment that while the *absolute* amount of corruption is undoubtedly increasing in Indonesia, as a proportion of total resources it is not as high as under the Old Order. Corruption is increasing, but because of the existence of slack resources, organizational achievements are multiplying at an even faster rate, and hence the state is progressing albeit at a less than optimal rate (see chapters 3, 5, and 12 in this volume and Smith 1971, Hanna 1971).

Under the New Order the resuscitation of the export sector and the influx of foreign capital along with the control of rampant inflation have supplied the slack that has allowed less than optimally efficient organizations to perform effectively. While the Suharto regime has repeatedly been criticized for pursuing "growth at the expense of development," within the logic of bureaucratic polity the strategy adopted maximizes effectiveness by concentrating slack resources and insures continued elite support. The strategy adopted is well matched with the limited capacity and the political requirements of a bureaucratic polity.

The general ideological bearing, view of economic development, and degree of political astuteness of the president and his immediate advisors are vital, because the president is the final arbiter in the Indonesian bureaucratic polity at the present time. It is Suharto who decides who gets what share in return for supporting the president and his programs. As long as resources are supplied to meet the nonservice goals of the active political elite, the president's inclinations determine broad policy outlines, even though he may yield on specific points. The president's policy line will be followed regardless of whether it intones "To hell with your aid" or cancels confrontation with Malaysia to obtain foreign aid. More than in most political systems, the personal beliefs of the chief executive leave their stamp on policy outcomes both large and small.

However, Indonesian bureaucratic polity is not a personalistic or sultanistic regime. The power of the president is neither unlimited nor arbitrary, and it is not based solely on charismatic authority. Suharto is as likely to be obeyed as his more magnetic predecessor. Furthermore, although wide decision-making authority is given to the president in the Indonesian bureaucratic polity, he is in the long run accountable to the bureaucratic and military elite. Finally, in compelling compliance from subordinates in the regime and the country, the leaders of a bureaucratic polity do not base their claim on traditional legitimacy but on legal authority derived from the March 11, 1966 grant of emergency power to General Suharto, the election of Suharto as president in 1967, and the 1971 national elections. Although power is concentrated in the hands of the president, it utilizes constitutional channels and is limited ultimately by the values and interests of the bureaucratic and military elite.

OVERTURNING A RULING CIRCLE

A major drawback of the type of analysis we have been engaging in here is that it tends to be static in its predictions, forecasting "what is" rather than specifying the conditions under which major changes will take place. There are two different kinds of change that must concern us: (1) the replacement of one ruling circle by another, and (2) the replacement of bureaucratic polity by another form of government. The first of these results in a turnover of personnel holding the highest offices but preserves the basic form of the polity, whereas the second replaces the office-holders and restructures the entire system of participation.

During the hegemony of a bureaucratic polity many changes transpire, leaders die, a counterelite may replace the ruling circle, the ruling circle may concentrate power by expelling members, and policies may change radically either with or without a change in the personnel carrying them out.

The alliance system binding together the disparate parts of the ruling circle of a bureaucratic polity is largely uninstitutionalized, that is, it perishes simultaneously with its chief leaders. Power is derived from the indispensability of particular persons as links capable of committing whole groups to policies and programs. The most indispensable of all these links is the presidential one, and the death of the president produces a profound crisis that may occasion a complete realignment of forces within the bureaucratic polity. Even rumors of the impending demise of a president can ignite a bitter struggle between rival factions. In Indonesia in the summer of 1965, rumors of the declining health of President Sukarno led the PKI leadership to initiate contingency planning which eventually brought forth the fateful events of September 30 (Hindley 1970: 34). Similarly, under the present ruling circle, any decline in the health of the president or indication that he might retire to private life would set in motion a struggle for power in the highest strata of the present ruling circle as well as among potential counterelites.

International events also can affect the composition of the ruling circle of any bureaucratic elite. For example, in Thailand the office of the prime minister repeatedly changed hands at the close of the Second World War to adjust the Thai position to the geopolitical winds blowing at the time (Riggs 1966: 231-36). Indonesia's position as an archipelago, however, isolates the Indonesian bureaucratic polity from this variety of direct military pressure, and her tradition of neutrality in foreign policy insures that except in the case of a fundamental international realignment or massive foreign policy debacle, international events probably will not bring about the demise of an entire ruling circle. International considerations, nonetheless, affect the presence or absence of particular groups within the ruling circle. For example, the economic respectability conferred on the present circle's policies by the presence in the cabinet of the Western-trained economists known as the "Berkeley Mafia" is a major reason why these individuals have not been eliminated from power during the course of the New Order.

In addition to death and international events, the most likely source of the replacement of one ruling circle by another is elite competition. Pressures always exist that favor change, and these pressures usually emanate from segments of the elite that are cut off from sharing in the perquisites of power and office. With the concentration of power during the New Order, for instance, the party elites, the Islamic leaders, the army radicals, and the civilian radicals continue to be overtly and covertly critical of the personnel and policies of the government. Likewise, students and intellectuals who have not been able to find billets in the bureaucracy or officer corps commensurate with their educational attainments are also the natural enemies of the regime. An axiom of bureaucratic polity is that members of the university community not directly tied to the ruling circle are likely to oppose the ruling circle if it is either unwilling to produce (or incapable of producing) sufficient positions for them in the civil service and officer corps.

Long-term successful management of a bureaucratic polity requires balancing the need for economic expansion with the necessity of preventing rapid change. An economic growth rate which is slow but steady supplies the ideal climate for the maintenance of a state ruled by and for its official class. Slow but steady growth allows the ruling circle to expand the positions available within the bureaucracy and officer corps, thus coopting potential opponents without restricting its own access to resources. Further, gradual expansion provides opportunities in the private sector for those eliminated from the ruling circle, giving potential opponents a stake in the regime and in the system.

In contrast, rapid change creates instability in a bureaucratic polity. To the extent that change takes place rapidly, the bureaucratic polity will have difficulty in controlling the expansion of education and in providing suitable official positions for the products of the educational system. Furthermore, the concomitant rapid urbanization, regardless of whether it results in growth of the primate city or in the creation of rival centers, will make the twin strategies of coercion and cooptation more difficult. Rapid economic and social change is likely to increase pressure for political change, but takeover by a competing elite circle is more likely than fundamental reform or revolution at least until a substantial amount of industrialization has transpired. The growth of pressure for an elite turnover is intensified when rapid growth brings forth alternative nongovernmental circles of patrons who are not entirely dependent on government largesse as their prime source of wealth. An emerging independent business class can provide the financial assistance necessary for maintaining the counterelite as well as for provisioning the "spontaneous" student demonstrations presaging the overthrow of a ruling circle.

However, engineering a successful attempt to overturn the ruling circle requires more than the students, displaced elite members, and backers in the business community. To be successful, elements of the officer corps having direct operational command of troops in or near the capital city must be included in the plot. An axiom of bureaucratic polity is that a ruling circle becomes vulnerable to a coup only in the event that the process of concentration alienates substantial elements of the officer corps. In the Indonesian context, for example, Sukarno became vulnerable to displacement only when the acts of the PKI and his own actions during and after the abortive coup alienated key troop commanders in Jakarta and Bandung. In contrast, although General Sumitro in 1974 enjoyed wide support in several sectors, he could be summarily dismissed by President Suharto because those in operational command of troops generally were not as alienated from the regime in 1974 as their forebears had been in 1965.

TRANSFORMING A BUREAUCRATIC POLITY

Empirical research in societies as disparate as Argentina, Bangladesh, Chile, Nigeria, Israel, and India indicates that modern education, involvement in modern organizations (especially factories), and exposure to mass media all lead to the growth of personal and political efficacy which result in an increasing tendency for individuals to seek involvement in political life (Lerner 1958; Inkeles 1969; Inkeles and Smith 1974). At present, Indonesian society lacks all the social preconditions that would predict expanding pressure for mass political participation. The vast majority of the population is very poor by any standard, with per capita gross national product in 1970 equaling $70-80 (see Sievers

1974: 299-318, 362, 366; Hanna 1974). On most indices of economic well-being Indonesia ranks poorly in comparison to other, relatively prosperous, nations of Southeast Asia such as Singapore, Malaysia, the Philippines, and Thailand. Most of the labor force (62 percent in 1971) is engaged in agriculture, while slightly less than 10 percent is employed in industry. Furthermore, agriculture (especially on Java) is to a large extent noncommercial, conducted on very small plots of land and fueled by labor exchange rather than by wage labor. At the village level, education beyond a minimal three years in the Sekolah Desa is still fairly rare. Even in the relatively well-off province of West Java, official statistics peg the rural illiteracy rate at 42 percent, while functional illiteracy may run as high as 70 percent of the rural population (Biro Pusat Statistik 1972: 16-17). Finally, exposure to newspapers, radio, and television outside the major metropolitan areas is still very limited (see chapters 8 and 9, this volume, and Jackson and Moeliono 1972).

Under the New Order substantial economic growth is taking place, with GNP expanding 7 percent per annum. Per capita food consumption figures, the growth of rural trade and manufacturing, and increasing structural differentiation in the society all indicate that a portion of the increased wealth is, indeed, trickling down from the narrow bureaucratic elite to other members of the upper half of Indonesian society (see Chapter 5 in this book and King 1974, Montgomery 1975). However, even if the current growth rates were maintained for the next twenty-five years, per capita income would only reach the level currently found in countries such as Egypt, the Philippines, and Thailand (Sievers 1974: 309-18, 386-87). Hence, on the basis of economic and social indices alone one would certainly not predict a rising groundswell of popular demand for political participation. Although riots and minor rebellions are to be expected under any ruling circle, the social and economic conditions are not conducive to the rapid emergence of grassroots movements capable of both thrusting forward and protecting their leaders from the twin dangers of coercion and cooptation by the ruling circle of the bureaucratic polity (see Chapter 12).

Of course, more is involved in the rise or fall of an authoritarian system of government than merely social and economic preconditions (see Linz 1975: 292-301). Although expansion of education, mass media exposure, involvement in modern organizations, and general social mobilization (Deutsch 1961) produce individual attitude changes favoring involvement in politics, the existence of these attitudes is neither a necessary nor a sufficient condition for the appearance of participatory behavior for the system as a whole (Huntington and Nelson 1976). Attitudes are transformed into political behavior only through the organizations and institutions created by elite choices. Institutions favoring democratic participation can be created well in advance of the social and economic preconditions for mass political participation. The Soviet, Chinese, and North Vietnamese experiences indicate that disciplined elites can create mobilization regimes capable of fostering and tightly controlling political participation without waiting for the effects of the industrialization process (see Berman 1974). Finally, present day Brazil and Franco's Spain show that basically nonparticipatory systems can be maintained in the face of individual de-mands for participation arising with industrialization. Once firmly established, authoritarian regimes can prove adept at controlling and channeling pressures for participation generated by on-going social change. Elite and counterelite choices are critical in determining whether continued socioeconomic change leads to (a) development of a competitive democratic system based on mass political parties and a participant citizenry, (b) movement toward a single-party, ideologi-cally based mobilization regime, or (c) continuation of a bureaucratic polity.

It is clear from the political history of Indonesia since independence and from the elements of structure and culture reviewed in the next chapter that the most likely outcome over the next several decades is the maintenance of bureaucratic polity. Although policy directions may be altered, political partici-pation and power probably will continue to be monopolized by the highest levels of the military and bureaucratic elites. If transformation to a more participatory system of either the democratic or single party variety occurs, it will be imposed from above or devolve from the international arena. A list of the circumstances that might lead to the premature destruction of a bureaucratic polity are (1) a massive foreign policy disaster discrediting the military; (2) a sustained rural insurrection threatening the capital city and thereby discrediting the military; (3) an unraveling of power at the center, similar to 1965, in which power could be seized by a reformist or revolutionary subelite if the group itself possessed significant, independent military power and faced a divided national military establishment; and (4) the emergence of a leader of the ruling circle personally committed to expanding participation from above.

In the present Indonesian context, none of the circumstances that might lead to an early end of bureaucratic polity is probable. Given the relatively unadventurous nature of Indonesian foreign policy under the New Order, it is unlikely that the Indonesian military will suffer the kind of humiliation that befell the Greek junta as a result of the Cyprus crisis of 1974. Given the absence of both commercialized agriculture and large land holdings, and the continued strength of traditional authority relationships in village life, the most probable type of insurrection on Java is an orthodox Islamic one which would have a low probability of success (see Jackson and Moeliono 1973: 12-57; Mortimer 1974). In light of the 1965/66 eradication of forces desiring radical change in the rural social system, the likelihood of a significant leftist, rural insurrection would seem low, at least for the next decade.

An unraveling of power similar to the near collapse of the state in 1965 is improbable, given the present trends. The present government is much too cautious and effective for this outcome to become very likely, although repeated student riots or long dry seasons resulting in a series of rice shortages could conceivably lead to serious challenges to the regime.

Of the four circumstances that could put an early end to bureaucratic polity in Indonesia, the last is the most probable (or should we say, least improbable). On the death or retirement of President Suharto, the possibility exists that a reformer or revolutionary will emerge as circle leader and will use his power to foster the growth of mass participation of either the revolutionary or democratic variety. Although this scenario is the most likely of the four, it remains distinctly improbable. The odds favor Suharto being succeeded by a military leader reflecting the values and interests of the present ruling circle. It is doubtful that the next leader of the bureaucratic polity will be any more inclined than Suharto to share power across a wider social spectrum.

2 The Political Implications of Structure and Culture in Indonesia

KARL D. JACKSON

NOW THAT I HAVE sketched the most salient features of bureaucratic polity and their relevance to Indonesian politics, the structural and cultural variables explaining the durability of bureaucratic polity in Indonesia must be identified. The structural considerations include the social and physical factors that have shaped the Indonesian polity, such as the geographic and economic character of the country, the sociological structure of its society, the institutional basis of the mass media of communication, and other objective elements which have inhibited political participation. The cultural variables include the traditional Javanese concepts of self, ideal social behavior, patronship, and power that continue to influence modern Indonesian politics.

With more than 3,000 islands scattered along a 3,200-mile arc extending from the tip of Sumatra southeastward to Irian Jaya, Indonesia has perhaps the most awesome physical impediments to national integration of any state in the Third World today. The geographically dispersed quality of the archipelago is only partially ameliorated by the concentration of two-thirds of the population on the island of Java. Mountains and coastal swamps segment the major islands internally and large bodies of water such as the Java Sea prevent direct contact among the peoples of the major islands.

Even in an age of modern technology, communication with the hinterlands in Indonesia is difficult by any standard, and the lack of modern infrastructure limits the capacity of both government and populace to affect each other. Indonesia lacks the hypothesized prerequisites for national integration (Deutsch 1953; Jacob and Toscano 1964). Railway service is limited to the islands of Java and Sumatra. The amount of track in service has declined absolutely since 1939, which means that the per capita reach of the railroads has been cut in half since then. During the past decade the decline in passengers and freight carried by the railroads has been partially balanced by an expansion in truck, car, and motorcycle transportation.[1] However, the upsurge in the number of cars and motorcycles has not greatly increased national integration because there are few

1. From 1939 to 1972, on a per capita basis the number of freight kilometers declined approximately 40 percent. After independence per capita passenger kilometers did rise substantially but began declining in the mid-1960s. By 1972 passenger kilometers traveled by train barely exceeded the 1939 level on a per capita basis.

hard-surfaced roads on which to drive (see Biro Pusat Statistik 1957: 153, 1968: 285, 1974: 293, 295).[2] Although the total number of roadways maintained by the central and provincial governments has risen by 30 percent since 1939, the population has grown by 72 percent. In 1939 the central and provincial govern- ments maintained 0.39 kilometers of road surface per 1,000 inhabitants, whereas in 1971 there were only 0.29 kilometers. The fact that Indonesia in 1971 had only 6,637 kilometers of railroad and 15,489 kilometers of asphalted road indicates how physically isolated most of the country is. Java is the most densely populated island in the world, yet access to most villages more than a few miles from the main roads is only by high-wheeled truck, motorcycle, or horsedrawn transportation. The majority of villagers rarely have contact with even the district towns. Because there are few all-weather roads the central government cannot readily affect village life and, conversely, villagers can demand little of the national government (see Biro Pusat Statistik 1968: 282, 1974: 289; Jackson and Moeliono 1972).

In contrast to the declining reach of roads and railways, interisland transportation has increased substantially since the advent of the New Order. Air travel has mushroomed, with domestic air passengers trebling since 1967, but air travel is limited almost exclusively to the highest level of the elite (Biro Pusat Statistik 1974: 360; United Nations 1975: 491-92). Moreover, the number of air passengers is still low relative to most Southeast Asian nations.[3] Interisland seaborne trade is of greater importance because more individuals and goods are carried by sea than by civil aviation. Interisland trade has increased substantially since World War II in spite of disruption from the nationalization of the Dutch shipping line (the KPM) in 1957, the civil war in the Outer Islands from 1958 to 1961, and the general decline in the economy in the last years of Sukarno. The average yearly interisland freight was 14,865,000 gross tons for the period 1969-1971, an increase of 165 percent over the annual average for 1956-1957 (Biro Pusat Statistik 1968: 248-57, 1974: 282). However, these developments in interisland transportation probably have had minimal effect on national integra- tion because the total remains small relative to the size of the Indonesian population.

Other forms of modern communications are more undeveloped than interisland transportation. Although radio has made it possible for the presi- dent's voice to be heard simultaneously throughout Indonesia, it may take six months or more by sea-mail for the written text of the same speech to reach such a place as Menado in North Sulawesi. Although radio is the only mass medium covering all of Indonesia, its effectiveness is limited because the vast

2. In passenger cars per 1,000 inhabitants Indonesia lags far behind most other nations in Southeast Asia. In 1972 Indonesia had 2.3 passenger cars per 1,000 inhabitants whereas Thailand had 6.6, the Philippines 7.5, Malaysia 30.2, and Singa- pore 81.4. Only Burma had fewer passenger cars than Indonesia on a per capita basis. The same general rankings are found for commercial vehicles (United Nations 1975: 439).

3. In 1972 Thailand had fewer domestic air passengers per 1,000 persons than Indonesia, but Malaysia and the Phillippines each had at least five times as many passengers per capita on domestic flights (United Nations 1975: 491-92).

majority of Indonesians do not own radios. Indeed, Indonesia ranks near the bottom of all countries in number of radios per capita. Although estimates vary substantially, it is doubtful that the total number of radios in Indonesia exceeded 3.2 million in 1971, giving the country approximately 25 radios per 1,000 inhabitants, as compared to 41 for Malaysia in 1968, 45 for the Philippines in 1968, 79 for Thailand in 1971, 120 for the Republic of Vietnam in 1970, and 150 for Singapore in 1971 (United Nations 1974: 817).[4] Radio, at least theoretically, represents the best way to contact Indonesian villagers, yet the number of receivers is still so small that the majority of Indonesian citizens do not regularly listen to the radio.

Television viewing is limited both geographically and socially. Until recently Indonesian broadcasting was limited almost entirely to the island of Java (see Chapter 8). Only the very rich can afford television sets, and the cities of Jakarta and Bandung account for 75 percent of all receivers in the country. Comparatively, in 1971, Indonesia had only 0.8 television sets for every 1,000 persons, in contrast to Thailand with 7, the Philippines with 11, the Republic of Vietnam with 25, and Singapore with 82 (United Nations 1974: 817).

Newspapers are a city phenomenon, reaching at best between 5 percent and 10 percent of the total Indonesian population. Only urban adults who can afford to purchase nonessential goods are regular newspaper readers (see Chapter 8). Even on Java, newspapers do not reach villagers. According to the few available surveys, the majority of villagers have never read a newspaper. Total newsprint consumed by Indonesia in 1971 was among the lowest in the world, 0.2 kilograms per inhabitant, which is slightly less than India and lags substantially behind such countries as the Republic of Vietnam with 1.1, Thailand with 1.6, the Philippines with 1.8, Malaysia with 3.1, and Singapore with 14.4 (United Nations 1974: 519).

Not only do the print media fail to integrate the urban with the rural sectors of society but, as Makarim has shown, within the capital city most newspapers, *Indonesia Raya, Pedoman,* and *Harian Kami,* appeal to different tion, and social class. In essence, mass media in Indonesia are elite institutions, and most newspapers lack a mass public (see Chapter 9). The very influential newspapers, *Indonesia Raya, Pedoman,* and *Harian Kami* appeal to different elements in the limited intellectual audience, and among them they have a combined circulation of less than 35,000 copies. *Berita Yuda* and *Angkatan Bersenjata* are read by the military. Together they print approximately 20,000 copies daily, of which perhaps 8,000 are distributed free of charge. *Abadi* has a very small circulation even by Jakarta standards and is read primarily by the Islamic modernists. *Merdeka* (circulation 40,000) is read by very nationalistic and religiously syncretic elements. There are only two mass circulation newspapers, *Kompas* (circulation 200,000) which originated in the Catholic and

4. It is difficult to estimate the number of radio sets in Indonesia with certainty. For instance, the estimate for radio receivers used by the United Nations *Statistical Yearbook, 1973,* is 10 million radios higher than the highest figure printed in Biro Pusat Statistik 1974. Therefore, we have used the estimate derived by Astrid Susanto in Chapter 8 of this volume.

Protestant communities and *Pos Kota* (circulation 100,000) which is the closest thing to a lower class tabloid. *Kompas* and *Sinar Harapan* (circulation 70,000) are the only newspapers that cut across many communities, thereby reaching a diverse readership.[5]

Limited newspaper readership and the tendency to use the "mass" media for elite communication reflect the lack of a large public demanding participation in national politics. The Jakarta press usually mirrors rather than criticizes the government. The overturn of a ruling circle results in a rapid transformation of the personnel and ideological content of the press. Even when overt censorship is absent editorial criticism is carefully constrained within the overall ideological guidelines transmitted via interpersonal communication networks from the ruling circle to important editors (see Chapter 9). Although the press in relatively uncontrolled periods, for example, 1966-1969, can provide useful criticism of government programs, such reports are usually extremely circumspect and often indirect enough to make it almost impossible for a mass readership to comprehend the subtleties being used. When the crescendo of criticism rises in the press, as it did in late 1973, this usually signifies a substantial struggle for power within the ruling circle rather than the aggregation of demands from wider segments of the public outside of the Jakarta elite. As in the case of most institutions in a bureaucratic polity, the press reflects the elite rather than the articulation of the demands of the fragmented and usually unmobilized masses.

Finally, telephone and postal services are not heavily utilized and have limited capacities. Although the number of telephones has risen by 152 percent between 1966 and 1972, there are still only two telephones for every 1,000 inhabitants, and these maintain contact within and between cities and not between cities and the villages where more than 80 percent of the population resides (Biro Pusat Statistik 1974: 336). In spite of the rapid increases of the last several years, Indonesia still lags substantially behind such countries as India, Thailand, the Philippines, Malaysia, and Singapore in the development of telephone infrastructure.[6] Finally, Indonesians exchange letters through the official postal service less frequently than almost any other country in Asia, and the number of pieces of mail handled actually fell by 17 percent between 1961 and 1972 (Biro Pusat Statistik 1968: 314-15, 1974: 334-35).[7]

5. Circulation figures for Indonesian newspapers are unreliable. The above figures were gathered from informal sources and hence are probably lower than the figures customarily released by the newspapers themselves. Further, it should be noted that *Indonesia Raya, Pedoman, Harian Kami,* and *Abadi* were closed by government order following the riots of January 1974. *Abadi* has since reopened under a new board of editors.

6. In 1972 there were 2 telephones per 1,000 inhabitants in the Republic of Vietnam, 3 in India, 6 in Thailand, 10 in the Philippines, 19 in Malaysia, and 101 in Singapore (United Nations 1975: 535).

7. In 1972 Indonesian domestic mail (including military and government mail) amounted to only 1.4 pieces per capita as compared with 2.7 for Burma, 3.0 for Thailand, 11.2 for India, 17.6 for the Philippines, 23.4 for West Malaysia, and 40 for Singapore (United Nations 1975: 524-25).

It is clear that Indonesia at present lacks the infrastructure found in most functioning participatory democracies and single-party mobilization systems. All of the weaknesses in communication and transportation which we have detailed isolate the Jakarta elite from its far-flung citizenry. The weakness of these links helps the bureaucratic polity to remain in power but limits the capacity of any ruling circle to effect changes that require sustained, nationwide participation.

Ethnic, Linguistic, and Religious Impediments to Participation

Historically, physical obstacles to national integration produced a plethora of linguistic and cultural groupings that grew up in separate corners of the archipelago and in different sections of the same island. Indonesian society is fragmented by more than 300 different ethnic groups and 250 distinct languages. The cultural communities of Indonesia can be divided into four major categories: the multi-ethnic cosmopolitans of the major cities, who are the cultural models for modern Indonesia; the commercially oriented, strongly Islamic coastal people in Sumatra, Kalimantan, and Sulawesi, who share a common linguistic and cultural heritage derived from centuries of interisland trade; the populous Islamic, syncretic, and Hindu cultures of Java and Bali that are based on wet rice farming on the densely populated lowlands and plateaus; and the isolated interior peoples of the Outer Islands who live by slash-and-burn agriculture and have been least influenced by the Hindu-Buddhist, Islamic, and Western cultural waves that have engulfed Indonesia successively during the past 1,500 years (see H. Geertz 1963: 24-96; Fisher 1964).

Structurally, Indonesia is further divided by linguistic differences. The Indonesian national language, derived from coastal Malay, is taught in the schools and spoken throughout urban Indonesia. However, at the village level the understanding of Indonesian is often minimal, and effective communication depends on the more familiar regional languages. Many individuals in both town and country operate equally well in both Indonesian and in the local language; but often, even in the offices of the national bureaucracy, the preferred language, especially for sensitive communication, is the mother tongue of the particular region.

The Indonesian Chinese

The single most obvious racial division existing in Indonesia is between Indonesians and the Indonesian Chinese. The approximately 3 million Indonesian Chinese are the backbone of commerce and are often feared and despised by Indonesians who have been exposed to them in the urban context. Anti-Chinese prejudice has not been softened by the fact that most Indonesian Chinese are more Indonesian than Chinese in language, life style, and appearance. The majority of Chinese on Java have been there for generations, have adopted the Indonesian national identity, and many speak only Indonesian languages (see Skinner 1973). The actions of colonial and, to a lesser extent, the postcolonial regimes have been largely responsible for impeding the assimilation of the Chinese into Indonesian society.

Under both Sukarno and Suharto the government has responded to Chinese dominance in business with restrictive legislation and special privileges for Indonesian businessmen (known as *pribumi*) (see Chapter 5 in this volume). However, the New Order has brought several changes that have eased pressures in the economic sphere while simultaneously increasing pressures for cultural assimilation (see Suryadinata 1976). In the search for development capital, the government has sought to encourage foreign and "domestic foreign capital," particularly in the industrial sector. As a result the Chinese as a group have become more conspicuous than ever in big business. At least until the promulgation of new regulations after the 1974 riots, the vast majority of joint ventures concluded by Japanese and other foreign business corporations had ethnic Chinese as their Indonesian partners. Also, it is public knowledge that prominent members of the ruling circle have had very extensive and profitable relationships with Chinese businessmen who act as their agents and benefit disproportionately from favorable government action (see Crouch 1976). In contrast to these economic policies that have tended to reemphasize the unique and enviable position of the Chinese entrepreneur, the government has instituted policies facilitating eventual Chinese passage into the Indonesian community. Thus, the Chinese language schools have been nationalized, the naturalization process has been eased, and the Chinese have been pressured to adopt Indonesian surnames.

In spite of its economic strength the Indonesian Chinese community is politically vulnerable. Although the community is adept at buying protection, the large social disturbances of recent years (the anti-PKI slaughter, the 1973 riot in Bandung, and the January 1974 riots in Jakarta) have had unmistakable anti-Chinese overtones. The Chinese business community contributes to the maintenance of bureaucratic polity by unofficially augmenting the incomes of the highest levels of the bureaucracy and military. The bureaucratic polity can extract unofficial taxation from the Chinese business community, confident that "squeezing" the Chinese, even if exposed, will not discredit an official with the Indonesian public. Because any Indonesian government can court instant popularity by enforcing anti-Chinese regulations, the economically influential Indonesian Chinese community remains very much the servant rather than the master of the Indonesian bureaucratic polity.

Indonesian Islam

As 90 percent of Indonesians are Muslims, it might be assumed that religion would be a uniting force capable of bridging other divisions in the society. Yet in Indonesia even religion divides, for differences between the modern and traditional orthodox Muslims, on the one hand, and the syncretists (or nominal Muslims), on the other, provide one of the deepest, most enduring cultural (and in some instances political) cleavages in the country. In addition, divisions of organization and religious belief within the orthodox Islamic community are also a permanent part of Indonesian social life. The inability to find a common set of symbols, rituals, beliefs, and organizational structures to unite the entire Indonesian Islamic community has been at the root of Islam's failure to emerge as a dominant political force in independent Indonesia (see Chapter 7 in this volume and C. Geertz 1960, Jay 1963, Hindley 1966, Boland 1971, Jackson 1971: 301-438).

Ever since the work of Geertz and Jay in the 1950s, the religious differences found in Java have become a fundamental analytic device utilized by political scientists to explain political cleavages at the elite level, aspects of mass electoral behavior, and the general process of political affiliation. The four "'currents' of fundamental allegiance" (McVey 1969: 12) dividing Java are modern orthodox Islam, traditional orthodox Islam, *priyayi* beliefs, and syncretism. The modern orthodox Muslims take their inspiration from the movement to adapt Islam to the modern world by reforming and purging it of the heterodox accretions attached over the centuries to the original body of Islamic beliefs. The traditional orthodox Muslims adhere strongly to the very accretions that the modernists are attempting to expunge from Islamic practice. Both modern and traditional orthodox Muslims are referred to as *santri,* connoting a devoutness acquired through studying under a distinguished religious teacher in one of the many rural religious boarding schools (*pesantren*). Priyayi beliefs, descending from pre-Islamic court culture, stress Hindu-Buddhist mysticism, highly developed dance, drama, and the refined etiquette that remains the model for elite behavior. The syncretist (*abangan*) religious variant is highly eclectic, emphasizing especially animism but including elements of Hindu-Buddhist and Islamic rituals and beliefs.

According to Geertz each constellation of religious beliefs is associated with a particular set of social, economic, and political structures. The Islamic modernists affiliate with the Muhammadiyah, the old Masyumi, and the PMI, whereas traditional Muslims attach themselves to the Nahdatul Ulama. According to the hypothesis, both of these groups of santri, like Weber's Protestants, tend to be in the forefront of individual economic activity. Those holding priyayi beliefs are prominent in the bureaucracy and in Western intellectual circles, forming the backbone of the PNI, PSI, and to a lesser extent GOLKAR. Syncretists dominate Javanese village culture and find political expression through the PNI, the PKI, and more recently GOLKAR.

Looking back over two decades, the influence of religious beliefs on political party affiliation now seems more indirect, one among several important variables influencing political behavior in different ways at various levels of the polity. The postwar struggle for power in Jakarta has been dominated by the political symbols of religious differences from the early struggle over the preamble of the Constitution of 1945 to the controversy surrounding the marriage law in 1973. However, regardless of the strength of communal antipathies at the mass level, political party leaders have forged political alliances with the ruling circle, even when these alliances were in clear contradiction of religious imperatives. As Samson indicates in Chapter 7, religious beliefs are not a sufficient explanation of political behavior. The traditional Nahdatul Ulama have been most willing to cooperate with secular nationalists such as President Sukarno, the PNI, and most aspects of the New Order; in contrast, the adherents of the

PMI and the banned Masyumi, for all their rationalism and pragmatism in confronting modernity, have been less accommodating to secular and syncretist political forces. Although religious organizations vary, like other organizations in the bureaucratic polity they follow the axiom that when ultimate policy ends conflict with the interests of the groups comprising the organization, the former give way to the latter.

Shifting the analysis now from national leaders to villagers, there is no doubt that Islam influences voting patterns in national elections. It is important, however, to distinguish between the influence of Islamic beliefs per se and the impact of Islamic leadership structures. From a comparison of the 1955 and 1971 election results it is apparent that religious beliefs account for only a part, perhaps a relatively small part, of the variance in voting behavior. The percentage of the total vote garnered by the Islamic parties fell from 44 percent in 1955 to 27 percent in 1971.[8] Unless one accepts the farfetched hypothesis that the number of orthodox Muslims decreased rapidly over the seventeen-year period, it is difficult to escape the conclusion that religious beliefs and voting choices are not perfectly correlated. In both elections there were orthodox villages that voted for the Islamic parties, but there were also strongly orthodox villages that did not vote for religious parties. Moreover, during the postwar era, there are single villages that have moved back and forth across the political spectrum during and between elections in spite of the assumed stability of religious beliefs. It is difficult to believe that religious beliefs alone account for political choice in a village which has gone from Masyumi to NU (both religious parties) to PNI and PKI (both secular parties) and back to NU and finally to GOLKAR in 1971.

Although there are few systematic studies of the relationship between religious values and Indonesian political behavior, the substantial electoral turnover in 1971 suggests that variables other than religious beliefs must be considered.[9] The single most important of these is the influence of local leadership structures (see Soedjatmoko 1956: 131; Koentjaraningrat 1967: 279; Willner 1967: 515; Jackson and Moeliono 1973: 42-51). The village world is character-

---

8. This decrease cannot be explained by changes in turnout and registration qualifications. In 1955 87.7 percent of registered voters cast a valid vote, and in 1971 this figure reached 94 percent. Also, the total votes cast for all political parties was slightly greater than in 1955 on a per capita basis. This is why the absolute number of votes cast for the Islamic parties fell by only 11 percent (compared to 1955), while the Islamic percentage of the total vote fell off by 17 percent (see Hindley 1972: 58).

9. Even though twenty years have passed since Geertz and Jay did the field work generating the original hypotheses, to my knowledge not a single study has been carried out which adequately and independently measures religious values and voting behavior and alternative explanatory variables. Election studies in Indonesia have not measured both voting and values at the individual level. Instead, most election analyses have utilized aggregate data on voting behavior while guessing at religious views, even when "explaining" election outcomes as a function of religious values. Religious beliefs are imputed from voting behavior, and in circular fashion religious beliefs are then used to "explain" voting patterns. Until new data are generated by more sophisticated research, statements about causal connections between religious values and political behavior can be considered only as fascinating but empirically unsubstantiated hypotheses.

ized by imperfect political information and generally low individual political efficacy, particulary with regard to national issues. Hence, village leaders have a relatively free hand in influencing how common villagers vote, and in many instances this has more to do with the secular interests of the village than with the religious dimensions of GOLKAR or some other national political party. In turn, village leaders themselves are dependent on limited sources of political information, the most important of which are usually personal sources. Because findings capable of settling the question are unavailable, we cannot be certain what relative weight should be given to religious beliefs and local leadership as variables. However, the decline in the Islamic vote and the collapse of the PNI suggest that a great deal of attention should be given to the ability of local leaders to change the political window-dressing offered by their villages to the outside world.

The 1971 election illustrated how comparatively easy it has been for a ruling circle to produce a favorable electoral outcome, even without using totalitarian methods. Religious parties were allowed to stand for election, and conceivably they could have done quite well if the entire Islamic community had remained faithful to the political cause of Islam. However, the 1971 results indicated that Islam is not a particularly effective antigovernment force so long as an assertive president commands a relatively united and loyal army and bureaucracy. The tradition of deference to the ruler in Jakarta is strong among the less-educated common people. Unless there are visible signs of dissolution at the center and unless traditional village leaders take an explicitly antigovernment stand, villagers naturally tend to favor the government. Voting "for Suharto" is both safe and psychologically satisfying in villages which for a millenium or more have dealt successfully with central governments by appearing to acquiesce while preserving village autonomy over local, and hence more vital, aspects of life.

Coercion or the threat of coercion are important in direct proportion to the apathy of those being coerced. Peasants generally are aware of the government's ability to take short-term revenge on those daring to oppose "on a matter of principle." The 1965-1966 anti-PKI slaughter provides an ever-present example of the government's short-term capacity for exerting force. However, peasants are equally aware that the government does not possess the instruments of control that would allow it to reach constantly into each and every hamlet in the country. The role of physical coercion can be understood only against the backdrop of 1965-1966 and in the context of low individual commitment to affecting the "goings on" in Jakarta. The past pogrom, low political efficacy, and inconsistent governmental penetration are parallel reasons why a little coercion goes such a long way at election time in Javanese politics (see Ward 1974).

Although coercion is not unrelated to Indonesian politics its importance is often overestimated. Bureaucratic polities are not totalitarian police states relying disproportionately on repression, fear, and naked force. Bureaucratic polities usually do not possess the organizational apparatus required for continual systematic terror, and the mobilizing effects of constant mass coercion contradict the nonparticipant nature of bureaucratic polity. Widespread, systematic use of government violence would require an organization and ideology penetrating the periphery of society, and this organization by its very existence might rival the national elite's hegemony in national decision-making. Finally, the complexity of administrative procedures, corruption, and paternalism characterizing bureaucratic polities dampen the repressiveness of any particular regime.

For all these reasons, cooptation rather than coercion is the prime weapon utilized by bureaucratic polities to insulate themselves from the effects of mass political participation. The leaders of potential rival circles are coopted into the ruling circle with offers of prestige, wealth, and limited power (Linz 1975: 265-66). In Indonesia, groups gain power only when their leaders are coopted into the ruling circle by the circle leader, and selection by the president is more important in creating power than a mass following. Cooptation leaves potential mass movements largely leaderless and repeatedly has been used with telling effect on student leaders, the press, the bureaucratic constituency of the PNI, and the PMI. Mass movements, to use Hindley's phrase, are "domesticated" by having their leaders coopted into the ruling circle (Hindley 1962).

Urbanization and the City of Jakarta

Another basic structural characteristic of Indonesian society is the divide between urban and rural people. According to the 1971 census, 83 percent of all Indonesians live in villages, and there are only twenty-seven cities with more than 100,000 inhabitants. The overwhelmingly rural character of Indonesian society is, however, changing as urban growth takes place. In recent years the urban population has grown at an annual rate of 4.5 percent, and for at least the next ten years the urban population is expected to increase at approximately the same pace, exceeding the high growth rate projected for the population as a whole (see United Nations 1970).

The reason many Indonesians are moving to the cities is that most things in life worth having are located there, and especially in the capital city of Jakarta. Although foreign observers of the quiet and beautiful pace of village life may assume that a move to the noise and filth of the cities can be an act only of last resort, those making such a move generally perceive that they are improving their standard of living. The rich, the famous, and the powerful live in the city, usually the capital city. Sharing proximity with them means sharing, though perhaps only vicariously, a degree of their power and good fortune. Villages are seldom visited by government officials, and the centers of bureaucratic activity are the cities. Social services other than primary schooling are almost never available in the villages, for doctors, nurses, hospitals, mail service, electricity, telephones, high schools, universities, and the government department offices are all located in the towns and cities. The immigrants are drawn less by some irresistible, irrational lure of the excitement of city life than by jobs, educational opportunities, better nutrition, longer life expectancy, and a higher probability that they will be able to watch their children grow up rather than bury them before the age of five.

City life even for the poor is less controlled and more egalitarian than life in the villages. There are more opportunities for social mobility than in village Java, where the scarcity of land makes social mobility a zero-sum proposition. City life is less stable, allowing greater scope for individual initiative. Loyalty patterns take on a more materialistic direction, with the traditional lifelong relationship of the village elder to his followers being replaced by a patron-client linkage which is more limited in time and more reciprocal in character (see Chapter 12, this volume).

Jakarta is the chief city, with a population exceeding 4.5 million in 1971, compared to the second largest city, Surabaya, with 1.5 million. For the past thirty years (1941-1971) the population of the capital city has been expanding at an average of 8 percent per annum, and currently the city constitutes 4 percent of the total population of Indonesia (Kantor Statistik D.C.I. Jakarta 1973: 11). Although Surabaya is Indonesia's industrial center, Jakarta is the chief administrative and commercial metropolis. It is the magnet around which cluster all significant political actors. Control of Jakarta is equivalent to control of the Indonesian state apparatus because the most important bureaucratic, military, and political personages reside there. It is the headquarters from which orders flow to the country's more than 2 million civil and military employees (see Chapter 4).

The extent to which the Indonesian elite clusters in Jakarta is illumined by a few social statistics. The 4 percent of the national population residing in Jakarta contains 27 percent of all university graduates and 16 percent of the total number of high school graduates (Biro Pusat Statistik 1975: 81). Thirty-five percent of all private automobiles are registered there, and the citizens of Jakarta possess 55 percent of all the television sets, 10 to 15 percent of the radio receivers and most of the newspapers in Indonesia (Biro Pusat Statistik 1974: 292-93, 342-43; Kantor Statistik D.C.I. Jakarta 1973: 49, 86, 99-100). Finally the Istana Negara or National Palace, the residency of the president, is located in Jakarta, and virtually all important decisions in the military and bureaucracy pass through the circle immediately surrounding the president or to the president himself. So much of the national elite is concentrated in the capital city that Jakarta, rather than the enormous population of the country as a whole, serves as the prime arena of political life.

Given the structural characteristics of Indonesian society, it is highly probable that the bureaucratic polity will endure as the predominant form of government and that Jakarta will continue to be the magnetic political and social center. Because the Indonesian Chinese are politically weak but economically successful they supply the ruling circle with a ready source of informal taxation. Although deep ethnic, social, and religious divisions exist within the society, the underdeveloped nature of communication infrastructure and the internal fragmentation evident within each primordial grouping largely preclude regular mobilization of these groups into politics at the national level. Unmobilized primordial groupings, fragmented communication infrastructure, and steady economic expansion all lead to the prognostication that although ruling circles may change, bureaucratic polity as a system will probably endure until either the social parameters have been substantially altered or until a peculiar set of political circumstances brings about a premature end to this system of government.

THE CULTURAL BACKGROUND OF INDONESIAN BUREAUCRATIC POLITY

The traditions of Javanese culture continue to influence present-day Indonesian political culture, and the concepts of power and social organization prevalent on Java are peculiarly well-fitted to the presidential variety of bureaucratic polity. In turning to culture, we are moving toward the subjective realm and away from the objective characteristics of the society. We will concentrate on the expressive symbols, values, and typical modes of social behavior that shape and control the expression of power. Hence, the remainder of this chapter will deal with motivations and with understanding the social and psychological precursors of Indonesian political behavior.

Leader-Follower Relationships

Social life on the island of Java is dominated by a system of relatively autonomous, highly personal groupings, bound together by a diffuse sense of personal reciprocity found between patron and client. Each group or circle is composed of a set of dyadic, face-to-face, unequal but reciprocal obligations between individual leaders and followers. The circles tend to be socially heterogeneous in that "haves" and "have nots," educated and illiterate, and even individuals from diverse ethnic and religious backgrounds can be bound together in a vertical chain of patron-client linkages. In the traditional village context the circle leader is expected to serve as provider, protector, educator, and source of values of all those who have established a dependency relationship with him. In turn, the follower is expected to reciprocate by volunteering his labor, his vote, and in some cases even his life, although these obligations are seldom explicit either when incurred or called due.

These personalistic structures are found in the presidential palace as well as in the villages. Some of the circles are quite large, connecting different ethnic groups, organizations, and religious variants, whereas others confine themselves to the formal boundary lines of organizations or primordial associations. Most circles are limited in geographic scope, and integration occurs only to the extent that circle leaders are in turn subordinate members of still more important circles presided over by a man of regional or national significance.

If one wishes to visualize Indonesian social life, it is inappropriate to think in terms of the pyramidal model so commonly used in describing many Third

World societies. Instead, one must think of an extremely complex molecule in which the different atoms have their separate nuclei and their circling electrons, but the bonds between the atoms can often be very weak and, indeed, many atoms have no bonds between them at all. In this way Indonesian social life is composed of a multitude of groupings, each with its own elite and mass elements bound together by an elaborate set of personal relations, but only tenuously connected to surrounding social groupings.

The incomplete and fragmented nature of the chains of social communication accounts for one mobilization paradox of bureaucratic polity. The chains just described can be mobilized selectively to carry out specific, short-term tasks, for example, political violence against a particular group; however, long-term mass mobilization along ideological lines is nearly impossible because most networks remain unconnected to one another and the larger ones tend to be socially heterogeneous, thus precluding attempts to mobilize through a straightforward appeal to class, ethnic, or religious differences.

Bapakism (literally, fatherism) is a term frequently used by Indonesians to describe this complex system of social relations. The *bapak* (father) is the leader of a circle of clients and is expected to care for the material, spiritual, and emotional needs of each of his followers who are called *anak buah* (children). In return the anak buah are expected to be at the bapak's beck and call to pay deference, make contributions, participate in family ceremonies, join or leave political parties, and in some cases even defend the patron's life. These diffuse, personal, face-to-face, enduring, noncontractual relationships are the primary social cement integrating Indonesian organizations to the limited degree that they are integrated at all. Only when a bureaucrat is a bapak can the official be sure that his orders will be carried out. Only if a town notable has had an enduring, respect-filled relationship with a village leader can the town notable's political party expect to do well in the village (see Chapter 12).

Substantial inequalities of income and opportunity exist throughout Indonesia, but except for brief periods such as during the Indonesian revolution these have not been translated into widespread political alienation because of the prevailing notion that society should be hierarchical and that all men and women are inherently unequal at birth, in the marketplace, before the law, and especially in the halls of government. The near-palatial life style of some of the Jakarta elite has not inspired class consciousness among the masses. With few exceptions, the downtrodden have not risen to strike down the oligarchical establishment; on the contrary, most groups aim at insinuating their own leaders into the hierarchy rather than destroying the system of manifestly unequal rewards.

More specifically, in Indonesia every man is perceived as having his station and its duties. Social justice is interpreted as carrying out the responsibilities of *justly unequal* roles. Because of God-given high status and wealth the patron must lead, educate, and care for the material and spiritual needs of a large group of clients. Great satisfaction and psychological security are derived from the act of giving deference and respect to persons of higher rank in the social hierarchy and from receiving deference from those below. Within the system, social injustice and corruption are felt only if a patron fails to redistribute his bounty among his clients or if the patron in adapting to market pressures abandons the diffuse responsibilities of a bapak toward his anak buah.

The rising generation of university students constitutes a partial exception to these generalizations. They are the group most likely to label the relationships between bapak and anak buah as feudal and corrupt. It is as yet uncertain whether the vehemence of student criticism stems from their being partially excluded from the system because they are unable to obtain bureaucratic positions consonant with their educated status or whether it is derived from a thorough rejection of the system of their elders. Anticorruption campaigns often are attempts by political "outs" to oust the "ins" rather than to change the system of selective distribution of the benefits of government.

Unequal distribution of the fruits of economic growth is not necessarily perceived as unjust. So long as some benefits are distributed to subordinate oligarchs for subsequent redistribution downward through their independent networks of followers, the system will not be weakened by inequality. The greatest peril to any regime is not what Westerners call corruption but the possibility that, as the elite expands with economic growth, corruption may not become sufficiently widespread. To the extent that power has been concentrated in fewer hands during the last five years, there is an increasing concentration of the benefits of bapakism, and this has produced pressures (although by no means overwhelming ones) to expand the ruling circle to include members representing deprived segments of the social elite.

Need Dependence, Concept of Self, and Ideal Interpersonal Behavior

A need for dependence (as expressed in bapakism), a desire to keep separate internal feelings and overt social actions, and a drive to achieve the most refined, smooth, and civilized (*halus*) manners are among the primary forces motivating Indonesian social and political life.

Although the person of the bapak is the locus of wealth, information, religious wisdom, and political values for the anak buah, more importantly he is also a wellspring of respect, solicitude, affection, and status in a culture in which abiding friendship may be a rarity and one's status is always tentative. Jay has noted that bonds between peers that transcend time and immediate interests are even rarer in Java than in supposedly cold and impersonal industrial societies (see Jay 1969: 201-06). The concern for embedding oneself in secure bapak-anak buah dependency relations may flow at least in part from the absence of other enduring affect-laden, dependable relationships in the culture.

Child-rearing practices among the Sundanese and Javanese may reinforce the need for establishing dependency relationships (see H. Geertz 1961: 105-22; Jay 1969: 99-104; van der Kroef 1958: 37-42). Every whim and cry of the young child is immediately satisfied, and he is constantly held and caressed by his parents. However, after the age of five the unlimited gratification and warmth of the parent-child relationship give way to an austere, impersonal coolness where open displays of affection are dramatically reduced, and the father-son relationship even in adulthood remains distant and respectful rather than reciprocally warm and affectionate. In addition, the virtually discipline-free atmosphere of early childhood is replaced by a sharp demand for self-control of all emotions. The high valuation placed on creating a warm, enduring dependency relationship with a bapak becomes comprehensible in light of the ephemeral nature of most relations between equals and the transient nature of the warm and open father-son relationship of early childhood.

Social status rather than wealth is the major social objective on Java. The entrepreneur who accumulates and saves without showering his bounty upon his neighbors is derogated. Status is defined not by wealth but by having a large retinue of dependents. The more a person gives and redistributes his wealth and knowledge, the larger will be his circle of clients acknowledging him as bapak, and hence the more elevated will be his social standing thoughout the community. The exchange of gifts and wealth for loyalty and obligation is the process by which material wealth is transformed into status and respect. Likewise, initiating the ignorant into the world of knowledge, be it secular or sacred, in the university or the village, is an act for which the dependent will always owe respect and give status to his teacher.

Gifts are bestowed on many occasions and, along with the use of respect terms in Javanese and Sundanese, they provide a means for stratifying new relationships and for extinguishing status ambiguity. What Westerners often mistake for corruption is a culturally legitimate way of initiating a dependency relationship. For instance, on meeting a village headman for the first time it is not improper to bring a gift, and the presentation is not perceived as bribery. But in accepting the gift the official is obliged to reciprocate in some manner. To give a gift is to initiate a potential dependency relationship; if the recipient does not give some token, and preferably more valuable, gift in return, it is an implicit admission of the recipient's subordinate position. What is important is not the nature and magnitude of the gift, but the act of giving. Bapak and anak buah constantly bestow minor gifts upon each other, these gifts being emblems of the relationship providing proof that it, at least, remains stable in the otherwise unpredictable social world.

Within the Javanese and Sundanese social worlds the individualist who "goes solo" is considered to be a maverick and a fool because most desirable goods in life such as government jobs, scholarships, rank in the army, and the opportunity to travel abroad come to the individual only as a result of his bapak's access to these social goods and the bapak's willingness to favor him disproportionately in redistributing these goods.

Political relationships at the elite level in Java are always fragile and unstable. Military coups and political cabals almost always fail because key individuals do not carry out their agreed-on assignments. Failure is the norm for conspiratorial behavior at least in part because Javanese culture values indirectness, subtlety, and the repression of open emotion, and derogates any overt expression of disagreement with the plans of a superior. There is a tendency to say yes, when one actually has no intention of fulfilling a request. What the outsider bemoans as lack of sincerity is less important to the Javanese than concealing all overt signs of dissonant feelings for as long as possible. In this culture individuals are preoccupied with controlling and flattening out the inner world (*batin*) of their emotions and segregating it from the outer world (*lair*) of their actions. The goal with respect to the inner self is to control all feelings and ensure that one's passions are kept at a constant, reserved pitch, never becoming direct, open, and apparent from one's outward activities. Emphasis is placed on veiling one's motives in ritualized etiquette and perfect manners. Political commitments are especially indecipherable among the Javanese who, in Geertz's words, have "a bifurcated conception of the self, half ungestured feeling and half unfelt gesture" (C. Geertz 1975: 49).

With respect to both the inner and outer worlds, the goal is that of a proper ordering of certain values, all of which are related to the Javanese concept of halus (pure, refined, smooth, subtle, and civilized). The sophisticated Javanese assumes that the words of public figures are often only a mask concealing other goals and intentions. Ritual and reality intermingle, to the consternation of foreign observers operating on the mistaken assumption that the Javanese makes a dichotomous distinction between his real and concealed intentions. Instead, as Anderson has pointed out, the halus political gamesman is admired for his sudden transformations of position and the rapidity with which he outflanks his opponents by altering his symbols and ideology (Anderson 1966: 115). Much of the activity of political leaders under both the New and the Old Order has concerned the creation and propagation of new political symbols. To outsiders the symbols often seem to contradict themselves internally, such as Sukarno's NASAKOM formulation which envisioned a working ideology combining the insights of nationalism, religion, and communism. Yet the nation for a time adopted NASAKOM wholeheartedly and ignored the obvious incompatibility of Islam and communism.

This was possible because the acceptance of internally contradictory symbolism is difficult only if accepting the symbols implies present or future behavior. However, in Indonesia adopting a symbol need imply little about action. Within the traditional village religious school, the *pesantren,* the good student is the one who can recite perfectly the Arabic incantation, the words of which he does not in the least understand. The whole point of incantation in the *pesantren* and symbol-wielding in politics is to signify that one is powerful by manifesting personal control over the seemingly incomprehensible and, therefore, magical (Anderson 1966: 92). Facility in symbol manipulation is evidence of esoteric knowledge which in turn is a traditional sign that a man has great power. Finally, the preoccupation with symbol-wielding becomes comprehensible if we also assume that much of politics is ritualized drama masking the distribution of rewards to particular retainers rather than a means of attaining concrete ends for broadly defined sections of the citizenry.

The desire to appear halus has several important social corollaries. Because the cultural model emulates indirectness, frankness and aggressive activism are usually counterproductive and unrewarding. Power is seen as being an innate quality; one either has it or one does not (Anderson 1972a). The person who is seen expending boundless energy in pursuit of particular goals is perceived as dispersing and losing power rather than gaining it. The powerful figure cultivates the illusion, if not the reality, of never having to exert himself strenuously to accomplish his ends. The truly powerful figure is seen as the person whose slightest directions are obeyed automatically by his followers.

The Indonesian distrust of action and admiration for passivity produces interesting priorities in organizations and institutions which in other cultures are presumed to be dedicated to action. As designing plans is relatively passive while implementation requires action, attention and high status go with the former rather than the latter. Progress in bureaucracies is often impressive until the moment when implementation is required.

Indonesian indirectness and the desire to avoid personal friction may force policy-makers to function without self-correcting feedback for their policy initiatives. Deference to superiors and the desire to avoid interpersonal conflict lead to a largely downward, one-way flow of communications. For instance, under the first five-year plan, REPELITA I, programs mobilizing the peasantry for rice production and birth control followed a boom-bust cycle. The public's expectations were raised to unrealistic heights, only to be dashed when performance fell far short of plan objectives. In part these failures can be attributed to the absence of feedback mechanisms allowing policies to be adjusted to local realities.

Major programs are initiated in Jakarta with little or no lower level consultation. National goals are set often without regard for available resources, and a plan achieves a symbolic life of its own, independent of the activities required to make it a reality. Next there is a rush to endorse the plan. Official and nonofficial groups seem to compete with one another to affiliate most fervently with the plan as a symbol while assiduously avoiding any definite commitment to action.

The tasks implied by the plan are subdivided down to the village level, with each unit being assigned its responsibility often without regard for whether the goals or procedures are suited to existing physical conditions or peasant attitudes. Rather than being crude by acknowledging peasant resistance or that the plan is simply unworkable, local leaders promptly acquiesce. When the government official is safely sequestered in his faraway office, the villagers carry out the symbolic elements of the plan along with those aspects which meet actual village needs. In the meantime officials throughout the hierarchy assure their superiors that all plan targets will be reached, and the predictable short-comings burst upon the public with little or no warning. Often the extent of the failure is made clear only by suddenly soaring urban rice prices. Negative feedback usually comes too late, and the failures are so catastrophic that the entire policy has to be suspended (see Chapter 11). But self-correcting feedback structures are not added to the system as a result of the policy debacle, and the whole process begins anew with fresh programs and a new set of symbols.

Predisposition to Violence

No description of Indonesian culture should neglect the marked proclivity for violence manifest throughout the postwar era. This predisposition to violence found outlet in the substantial number of civil disturbances, most notably the rebellions following the grant of sovereignty from the Netherlands, the movements aimed at creating an Islamic state during the period 1948-1962, the PRRI civil war between 1958 and 1961, and the brief but extremely violent campaign against the Communist party in 1965/66 (see Feith and Lev 1963: 32-46). Because of these instances of large-scale, political violence Indonesia ranks among the most violent countries in the world (see Taylor and Hudson 1972: 102-23, 172).

In addition, unorganized violence is readily apparent in village and city life. Although the priyayi ideal may demand repression of all interpersonal aggression, in reality emotions do break through and complete self-control, indirectness, and passivity frequently give way to bloodshed. Violence is rare at the elite level, but it is a fact of life in the city *kampungs* and the villages. In the city, captured house thieves often are released in the custody of neighborhood officials so that they can be returned to the scene of the crime for "justice" at the hands of their victims. In villages, disputes often lead to violence although incidents rarely reach the public press. Long-simmering resentment may be released during periods when central government control falters, allowing non-political scores to be settled. Thus, many of the untold deaths in 1965/66 probably had more to do with village feuds than with PKI politics.

The predisposition toward violence is admitted even in structured interviews. In a sample survey conducted in 1968/69 in West Java, nearly two-thirds of the respondents volunteered a willingness to kill if their religion were insulted, and this was equally true for the orthodox Muslims and the syncretists in the sample.[10] Justice toward individuals not protected by personal connections to a village community may be swift and complete, and outsiders caught committing robbery often are summarily lynched (see Jay 1969: 293, 364). Many supposedly binding social norms disappear in confrontations with individuals having no personal relationship to the community.

The Traditional Concept of Power[11]

In Java power is conceived as independent of the ability to enact change in the larger society, and being perceived as powerful need have little to do with

10. This datum is from the survey research project conducted by Karl D. Jackson and Johannes Moeliono in villages between Bandung and Garut in West Java (see Jackson 1971).

11. Many of the observations in this section are dependent, directly or indirectly, on Benedict Anderson's essay, "The Idea of Power in Javanese Culture" (Anderson 1972a: 1-69). (See also Willner 1970, Fagg 1958).

exercising power on a regular basis. To be powerful, it is *not* necessary to hold formal decision-making authority or to be perceived as an active energetic force critical to daily decision-making activity. According to tradition, whenever the opportunity exists, power should be husbanded rather than used, concentrated rather than exercised. Power is a matter of status rather than action, of being a natural object of deference rather than a person actively seeking out, ordering, and energizing subordinates in the pursuit of concrete organizational goals. As we have seen, excessive activity and exertion are scorned in Javanese culture, and traditionally the truly powerful man is the one who sits motionless while his enemies energetically posture and exercise their power, giving evidence that they are so weak that they are forced to make the first move, dissipating their power rather than concentrating it (see Willner 1967).

Traditional imagery concerning power emphasizes the means by which power is concentrated. Traditionally power was obtained through fasting, meditation, and withdrawal from normal pursuits to commune with the supernatural and concentrate the essence of esoteric knowledge. Rural rebellions against the colonial regime abound with instances of natural leaders withdrawing to the mountain top to fast, pray, and meditate before raising a rebellion. Likewise, consultation with seers before making a political decision is important because this buttresses a leader's claim to authority with supernatural legitimacy (see Lubis 1969: 176-86; Hanna 1967 and 1967*a*).

Rituals, ceremonies, and political rallies can be used to advertise the fact that a particular political leader is the locus of real power. The de facto (and perhaps de jure) leader of a village will be seen conspicuously altering the seating arrangements for leaders as they arrive at a village rally. By ordering the hierarchy of status, he gives evidence to all that he is more powerful than any and all. Regardless of the formal purpose of the meeting, the paramount leader has demonstrated his status and thereby reinforced his position. Similarly, President Sukarno's ability to convene in front of his podium, on the same public platform, Communist and traditional Islamic leaders gave visual demonstration of his great personal power. His ability to combine political opposites (in symbols such as NASAKOM and in public rallies) reinforced his position by publicly testifying to the subordination of all party leaders and ideologies to the personality of the president (see Anderson 1972*a*).

The purpose of such rituals is designating oneself as the center to whom all others naturally will turn for advice and direction. Once a man is publicly perceived as a natural leader, other actors (sometimes even opponents) can be absorbed into his designs. Once designated as a person to whom other important individuals turn for advice and leadership, the quality of obedience is assured and leadership is no longer entirely dependent on whether intended outcomes are achieved. Power is not necessarily utilitarian; people with power simply "have it" and need not "use it" in order to preserve the fealty of their followership.

The relationship of wealth to power on Java contradicts many Western and particularly American expectations. In Java, political power leads naturally to wealth, rather than the reverse. As noted, wealthy Indonesian Chinese do not have significant political power, and the Indonesian entrepreneurial class is dependent on government rather than dominating its decisions. Major Indonesian officials, their families, and their clients prosper handsomely from association with governments, but they strive to avoid being perceived as conspicuously using their government positions to enhance their personal wealth. Further, the more personal the material indulgence, the more negative the stigma. Personal indulgence is evidence that power is being diffused rather than concentrated. Using state resources to improve the living standards of subordinates is a legitimate function of the bapak, whereas personally utilizing all that one appropriates rather than redistributing it is corrupt and unjust even by the most traditional standards. The preferred style of maneuver is one in which wealth appears to flow spontaneously to the power-holder as part of the natural scheme of things. The line between acceptable material benefits and improper gain is not a matter of the amounts involved, but a matter of the political legitimacy of the central figure and the extent of redistribution. As long as the power position of the central figure is believed secure, there is an acceptance of the propriety of his ever-increasing grandeur. Sukarno's luxuries were accepted while his power was unquestioned, but many of the political actors who had shared in his profligacy were quick to charge him with personal corruption when his political star had begun to wan. When doubts about legitimacy arise, the immediate suspicion is always that the powerful have been personally corrupt.

According to the traditional Javanese concept of power, the total amount of power available is fixed and static. This supplies a traditional foundation for the present-day notion that the power of a political figure can be increased only by dispossessing other actors. In addition, the concept that the available quantum of power remains static partially explains the ruling elite's reluctance to mobilize the electorate through either a single-party or multiparty system. Power descends from the macrocosmos onto the ruler, and it cannot be expanded through mass participation. Portions of the total amount of power are granted by the ruler to other political actors in return for deference and loyalty. The concept of increasing power by expanding participation is foreign to the traditional concept of power.

In sum, power in Indonesia traditionally has been more personal than public, more symbolic than utilitarian, more reserved than purposeful, and above all more a matter of status and prestige than of programs and activity. Traditional concepts do not dictate all political behavior in modern Indonesian politics, but they continue to have substantial impact, even in the highest councils of government. As the technocrats themselves recognize, at least a portion of the difficulty in implementing modernizing schemes on Java can be ascribed to the continued attraction of these traditional concepts of power within the bureaucracy and the society as a whole.

PART II: Institutions

3 The Military: Structure, Procedures, and Effects on Indonesian Society

ULF SUNDHAUSSEN

THIS CHAPTER EXAMINES the position of the military in present-day Indonesia. In the first section an attempt is made to explain how the military rose to the position of power it holds at the moment and to what extent it controls state and society. In the second part its internal organization is analyzed, particularly in regard to the question of who controls what power. This theme continues into the third section, with special focus on the degree of intramilitary cohesiveness, the position of the president, and the way decisions are made within the military. The concluding part explores the chances for political change in Indonesia.

RELATIONS BETWEEN THE ARMED FORCES AND THE STATE

Probably the most striking feature of civil-military relations in Indonesia is that it took so long, more than twenty years, for the military to seize political control. For most of that period the Indonesian political scene offered the kind of setting that tempts a reasonably politically minded army to take over. The civilian leadership was bitterly divided and failed to provide strong leadership for the young republic. Moreover, civilian governments came, justly or unjustly, to be seen as selfish, ineffective, lacking responsibility and maturity, and riddled with corruption.

The relationship between civilian elites and the military was further complicated by the attempts of politicians to gain political control over the army by indoctrinating the officer corps in a particular party ideology or exploiting for their own ends any disagreement that existed in the military. For instance, the Socialist Sjahrir administration, formed in November 1945, was seemingly convinced of the necessity to "put the officers in their place" and to indoctrinate them in the government's brand of socialism. It tried to impose a Red Army-type structure of political commissars on the regular republican army,

This essay is largely based on interviews with officers, conducted between February 1967 and January 1969, in January/February 1973, and in January/February 1974. I am deeply indebted to professors Herbert Feith and Rex Mortimer for their critical comments. All conclusions are, of course, my responsibility.

implicitly labeled its Dutch-trained officers colonial mercenaries, and described the Japanese-trained officers as "having sold their souls to the Japanese." But the officers rejected any ideological commitment that went beyond their sense of nationalism and a general anticolonialism, and deeply resented being called "Japanese-type fascists and militarists" (see Nasution 1963: 262-70, 124-27). Retrospectively, the defense policy of the Sjahrir administration can be summarized as having forced the officer corps into politics to preserve their ideological autonomy, and as having laid the foundation for the mutual distrust and antagonism between civilian and military elites which have characterized Indonesian politics ever since.

Another example of ill-conceived policies of civilian politicians toward the military occurred in 1952 when President Sukarno and the parliamentary opposition made use of disgruntled officers to interfere with the ongoing process of turning the wartime guerrilla army into a professional, nonpolitical military, a policy designed to indirectly discredit the "administrator"-type cabinet of Prime Minister Wilopo.[1] In the ensuing series of political and military moves and countermoves President Sukarno did not hesitate to instigate mutinies and revolts in various army divisions against the cabinet and the then army leader Colonel A. H. Nasution, even after it had become abundantly clear the president's side had clearly won the battle. These tactics by the anti-Wilopo forces not only undermined the authority and the legitimacy of the cabinet, they also eliminated all hopes of transforming the Indonesian army (TNI) into a professional, nonpolitical arm of the government.

But these politicians were not allowed much time to exploit fully the disagreements in the army. In early 1955 senior officers of both main factions, those who had supported and those who had opposed the policies of the headquarters in 1952, assembled in Jogjakarta to heal the rifts in the army. They resolved to prevent the politicians from exploiting their differences any further and committed themselves to observing professional standards on such issues as promotions and appointments.

These resolutions were put to the test by the cabinet of Prime Minister Ali Sastroamidjojo the same year, when the government appointed Bambang Utojo as new army commander. The officer corps unanimously rejected the appointment on the grounds that he was much too junior for this position and that his appointment was clearly political. The cabinet was forced to resign and Nasution, sacked in 1952, was reappointed as army commander. In a way the Jogjakarta conference constituted a watershed in the relationship between political leaders and the military. Hitherto, one could argue that the politicians harassed military leaders and interfered with what the officers regarded to be the military domain. From 1955 onward the military became increasingly assertive in the civilian sphere.

1. For the distinction between "administrators" and "solidarity-makers" in Indonesian politics of the 1950s, see Feith 1962: 24. The civil-military relationship in 1952 is described in Feith 1962: 246-73, and Sundhaussen 1971: 206-40.

Most of Nasution's energies after his reappointment as army commander initially were directed toward establishing himself as a real commander and not just the *primus inter pares* army commanders had tended to be. This task was made more difficult by rebellions of anti-Communist, anti-Sukarno officers in West Java, Sumatra, and Sulawesi who, moreover, were threatened in their entrenched positions of power by Nasution's reform programs aimed at, among other things, liquidating warlordism and enforcing the recognition of the army headquarters as the chief, if not the only, decision-making body in the army. In swiftly crushing the rebellions Nasution became the undisputed leader of the army (Sundhaussen 1971*a*: 196-99).

At the same time Nasution took the army gradually into politics. When the second Ali Sastroamidjojo cabinet collapsed in March 1957 and no majority could be found in parliament to form another government coalition, Nasution proposed a martial law administration. In the absence of any viable alternative, President Sukarno declared martial law and appointed a caretaker government responsible primarily to the president. Although the Jakarta scene was clearly dominated by Sukarno, army officers became martial law administrators in the provinces. When, in the framework of the West Irian campaign, Dutch property was nationalized in late 1957 military men also came to take charge of economic enterprises.

Was the army then, as many argued, set on a course where it would gradually take over the government, or seize it in a coup d'état, as happened increasingly during the late 1950s in the new states of Asia and Africa? Nasution, a Dutch-trained officer who held high respect for the principles of legality and who, moreover, was well aware of the stature President Sukarno enjoyed among many of his officers, categorically ruled this out, and in what has become known as his "Middle-Way" speech defined the political role of the army by stating, "We do not and we will not copy the situation as it exists in several Latin American states, where the army acts as a direct political force; nor will we emulate the Western European model, where armies are the dead tool [of the government] ..." [*Pos Indonesia,* November 13, 1958]. He argued that the army, having fought for the independence of the nation even after the government had given itself up to the Dtuch in 1948, had the right to participate in the decision-making processes determining the destiny of the country. The army should not be seen as trying to dominate the country, but as a social-political group entitled to play a role as one of the forces determining and executing national policies.

President Sukarno implicitly agreed with this role definition for the army, and when the system of Western parliamentary democracy officially was buried in 1959 and replaced by Sukarno's Guided Democracy the military, like a political party, gained representation in the cabinet, the Parliament, the People's Deliberative Congress (MPRS), and the civil service. Guided Democracy came to be seen as a political system in which President Sukarno was the dominant figure, with the army as the major "junior partner" in the government and the Communist party (PKI) dwarfing all other political parties in terms of influence and membership and increasingly threatening the power of the military (see Feith 1963, Mortimer 1974).

This system of triangular politics, unstable as it had been from its inception, broke down completely on October 1, 1965, when a group of middle-ranking army officers in contact with the PKI and led by one Lieutenant Colonel Untung, with the assistance of air force personnel and Communist youth groups, kidnapped and killed the then army commander, General A. Yani, and five of his closest associates. (Nasution, then chief-of-staff of the armed forces and minister of defense, narrowly escaped the same fate.) Simultaneously, dissident elements in Central Java rose in support of the Untung "coup."

The acting army commander and commander of the Army Strategic Reserve Command (KOSTRAD), Major General Suharto, acted swiftly to crush the Untung movement in both Jakarta and Central Java. However, for Suharto and the officers around him, as well as for the anti-Communist politicians who rallied to his standard, there was no doubt that, given the viciousness of the murders of the generals which introduced a new level of violence into Indonesian politics, the Untung "coup" must have been masterminded by the PKI. There has been a wealth of contradictory studies on whether, or to what extent, the PKI was indeed involved in the Untung "coup." For the purpose of this essay it suffices to note that the army leadership, the main political actor in the period following the Untung "coup," was convinced that the real culprits of the events of October 1 were primarily to be found in the PKI leadership. In the following six months the PKI was physically wiped out. Hundreds of thousands of Communists died at the hands of their nationalist or Islamic fellow villagers, who were often supported or encouraged by local army commanders.

When President Sukarno attempted to shield the PKI, he found himself confronted by increasingly hostile student masses which, protected and incited by anti-Sukarno radicals in the army, staged prolonged and violent demonstrations. Sukarno finally was forced to give General Suharto far-reaching powers "to restore order and guarantee the safety of the president." And when Sukarno refused to review his internal and external policies, which had brought Indonesia as close to bankruptcy as an independent state can get, the People's Deliberative Congress, constitutionally the highest policy-making body, now purged of Communists and Sukarnoists and chaired by General Nasution, instructed General Suharto to form a new cabinet (Department of Information 1966: Decisions 13 and 23). As Sukarno remained uncooperative in establishing the "New Order" without the PKI and with pragmatic economic policies, the MPRS elected an apparently reluctant General Suharto as acting president in March 1967 and as full president in the following year.

The New Order of General Suharto is a far cry from Nasution's "Middle-Way" concept of 1958.[2] Initially Suharto and his associates assured the nation

---

2. Nasution himself drifted gradually into political oblivion. Sukarno replaced him in February 1966 as minister of defense with General Suharto. For some years thereafter he chaired the MPRS. He is now retired.

that Indonesia was not "drifting into militarism" and pointed out that the New Order was an alliance among the military, the students, the technocrats, and those party politicians who wanted to work for a new political order in Indonesia (see *Kompas,* July 3, 1969). But this "alliance," if it ever existed in any true sense, soon collapsed, rendering the "junior partners" completely powerless save for the limited objectives the students could attain by street politics.

The 1971 national elections, the second ever held in Indonesia, made abundantly clear that the military was the real and only center of power (see Nishihara 1972, Ward 1974). In these elections, in which local army commanders and civil servants often put massive pressure on the electorate, 236 out of 360 seats were won by the army-controlled Functional Groups (GOLKAR), a conglomeration of professional associations, interest groups, trade unions, youth, veterans' and women's groups, which had been built up as the government party. Moreover, another 100 seats were filled by appointment of the president, who gave 25 seats to GOLKAR activists and 75 to military representatives. Thus the government came to control 336, or 73 percent, of the 460 seats in parliament. The nine political parties which existed before the elections could together capture only 124 seats. This dismal result can be explained only in part by the army's intimidation of the masses. Although the Islamic Nahdatul Ulama launched a fierce campaign of its own and managed to maintain its following, the electioneering of the other parties lacked drive and power of conviction. To add insult to injury, after the election the government pressed the parties to reduce their numbers and unite into two larger parties, arguing that divided they could hardly form effective parliamentary factions. The parties complied, with the former Nationalists and the Christian parties forming the Indonesian Democratic party, and the four Muslim parties uniting in the Development Unity party (see *Indonesia Magazine* 1972: 4-8). But more had to be done to save the parties from total oblivion. The Political Stabilization and National Security Council, formed after the January 1974 riots and chaired by Suharto, decided on a monthly government subsidy of Rp. 2.5 million to each of the two new parties and to GOLKAR, and promised Rp. 30 million for each party congress to be held (see *Kompas,* March 16, 1974). On the other hand, a party bill put before Parliament in January 1975 stipulated that the president could "freeze" the leadership of any of the three parties and insist on the forming of a new party executive (see *Kompas,* January 15, 1975).

Disregarding the apparent dependence of the parties on the government, army leaders studiously deny that the military is running the nation, or that the present Indonesian regime is a military dictatorship. They insist that the post-Sukarno system of government is strictly based on the "revolutionary" Constitution of 1945, which stipulates a democratic form of government. Admittedly, the Indonesian brand of democracy is not, like in Western liberal democracies, based on the principle of *separation* of powers but in accordance with the 1945 constitution "stresses the *distribution of powers*" (my italics) and rejects any system of checks and balances as typically Western and unworkable in Indonesia (see Sunandar Priyosudarmo 1973: 6, the most recent and most comprehensive account of the government's view on the present system of government; the author, a major general, wrote the document in his capacity as secretary general of the Ministry of the Interior). This interpretation of the constitution both frees the government of the restraints. through which parliaments and the judiciary in Western societies attempt to control the executive and at the same time provides, in practice, for heavy government intervention in the legislative and judicial fields. But the lack of clearly defined power relations in the New Order's "Pancasila democracy" is pronounced to be not merely a façade behind which the government makes all the decisions. The process of decision-making is nationally based on *mufakat* (unanimous consent of all), reached by way of *musyawarah* (extensive deliberation) (see Sajidiman Surjohadiprodjo 1971: 80; Sundhaussen 1973). In theory, therefore, everyone has a say in the decisions affecting the nation.

There are, indeed, instances where the government may be seen as having bowed to the will of opposition forces. One example is the 1968 debate on the election laws, although in that case the political parties' representation in parliament still outnumbered the military delegates and their GOLKAR allies. But in autumn 1973, when the government controlled an overwhelming majority in parliament. Suharto gave in to pressures by the Development Unity party (the alliance of all Muslim parties) on the explosive issue of a new marriage law. Furthermore, it seems that the government has turned its attention to the problem of reviewing its "development strategy" after the latent criticism of the government's social and foreign investment policies erupted in January 1974 in two days of violent rioting in Jakarta.

But these three cases are exceptions rather than the rule. Descriptions of New Order politics abound with accounts of the government and the army "using steam-roller techniques" to intimidate other political forces. So, for instance, the government has intervened in party congresses and manipulated the election of party leaders. The government has interfered with the internal affairs of trade unions and such organizations as the Journalists' Association. In what it calls the concept of "monoloyalty," it has forced civil servants to join and vote for the government-controlled GOLKAR or to get out of the service. And it has barred political parties from operating and maintaining branches at the sub-district and village levels. The president's special advisor for political affairs, Major General Ali Moertopo, argues that "in this way people in the villages will not necessarily spend their valuable time and energy being involved in the political struggles of parties and groups, but will be occupied wholly with development efforts" (Moertopo 1973: 86).

The weakness of the political parties almost matches that of the parliament. First of all, parliament is fully controlled by the government through the military and GOLKAR factions. In addition, the few supervisory functions formally left to parliament often are abused and circumvented by those in the center of power. For example, parliamentary committees theoretically have the power to ask ministers to report on their respective portfolios in a *rapat kerja* (working session). Although some ministers comply, others do not. The minister of the interior, Lieutenant General Amir Machmud, is reportedly notorious for having to travel urgently somewhere whenever he is invited to appear before a parliamentary committee.

Similarly, the judiciary is hardly able to fulfill its formal functions. Although the minister of justice is a civilian, the attorney general is an army general. And it is the latter who decides whether someone should be prosecuted or held without trial, provided, of course, the security agency of the Ministry of Defense and Security (KOPKAMTIB) has not already taken an interest in a case that may fall within the sphere of national security. As a rule, all political "crimes" are regarded as endangering national security, and if such cases are tried officially at all they may well be handled by a military tribunal rather than a civilian court.

The military is particularly well entrenched in the executive branch of the government and the central administration. The cabinet is led by General Suharto, who can employ or dismiss his ministers at will. Although the number of military men in the cabinet has steadily declined since the late 1960s, some of the key ministries, like defense and security, interior, industry, education, and the all-important state secretariat, continue to be held by army generals. Almost all positions of secretary general, the top administrative post in each ministry, are filled by generals. In important ministries the new position of inspector general has been created, and is occupied mainly by generals. Furthermore, many directors general are military men. Thus civilian ministers, mainly drawn from the ranks of the so-called "technocrats," are unable to make even relatively minor decisions without involving the military officers in their respective departments.

Moreover, the military increasingly has usurped the top strata of the diplomatic and consular corps. The initial justification was that the embassies in the vicinity of Indonesia should be headed by generals, for strategic and security aspects determined Indonesia's foreign policy in Southeast Asia. In fact, Indonesia's policy of regional cooperation and the formation of the Association of Southeast Asian Nations (ASEAN) was based on the army's perception of Indonesia's political and strategic needs in the region (see Polomka 1973 and 1974). At least until very recently General Ali Moertopo was seen to be continuing to meddle in Indonesia's foreign policy, to the great annoyance of the Department of Foreign Affairs. However, an ever-increasing number of generals, mostly men who had helped bring about the New Order but whom the government now wants to be rid of, have been given ambassadorships as far afield as Europe and America.

Furthermore, military men run government agencies such as BULOGNAS, the National Logistics Board responsible primarily for the provision and distribution of rice, and ANTARA, the national news agency.

On the legislative side, seventy-five officers sit in the central parliament, one of them as a deputy speaker. In the People's Deliberative Congress military representation is even stronger. As long as the congress had to be utilized in the toppling of the late President Sukarno and in changing basic policies, a general, A. H. Nasution, presided over it.

The military is entrenched and represented at the provincial level as well as at the political center. Military men sit in both the provincial and district parliaments, and often provide the speakers. Moreover, the positions of provincial governor and district officer, both semi-elective positions, often are held by military men. In 1974, some 80 percent of all provincial governors were generals, and the percentage of lieutenant colonels serving as district officers was believed to be not much lower. The procedure of appointing governors certainly provides the government with ample opportunity to assure that no "undesirable" elements gain important executive positions. The president chooses the governor from a list of three candidates submitted by the provincial parliament (DPRD), and if he does not approve of any of the candidates, he may ask the DPRD to provide him with another list of candidates. The district officers and mayors of cities are selected similarly by the minister of the interior from a list of candidates provided by the district and city assemblies. Although the government thus has the means to secure the appointment of military men, it should be borne in mind also that many provincial and district assemblies clearly favored the appointments of generals and colonels, even before the 1971 elections, when political parties still had an important say in these assemblies. This has to do with the reluctance of party politicians to back a candidate from a rival party; they would rather vote for someone who is considered "neutral" in party politics. Also, army officers often were seen as being in a better position when dealing with the central government, using the "old boys network" to secure favors for their region from their military friends in the government, or getting military civic action programs going in their respective areas. This sort of reasoning, often but not always combined with a degree of pressure, also occurs in the elections of village heads, which frequently are won by local army sergeants or policemen.

From 1957 onward the army had a fairly high degree of control in the provinces. This was further strengthened by Sukarno's creation of so-called Regional Executive Authorities (PEPELDA), which were usually headed by the army area commander (*panglima*). But with the increasing infiltration of the regional civil service by the military, the government could afford in 1967 to dissolve the PEPELDA and replace it with another regional authority, the Musjawarah Pimpinan Daerah (MUSPIDA), with the governor as chairman (see *Instruksi* 1967). By doing so the Suharto government appeared to "civilianize" regional government but in fact transferred power only from the active army commanders to other generals acting as provincial governors, thus retaining its firm grip over the provinces.

Military men are not active only in the political, administrative, and diplomatic fields; they also play a prominent role in the country's economy. Since 1957, and particularly since Dutch enterprises were nationalized in 1958, officers have been appointed to posts in state enterprises such as estates, hotels, transport enterprises, and trading companies. Military men were primarily appointed to supervisory and personnel management jobs, whereas economic management was more often delegated to civilians with a higher degree of expertise than army officers could offer (see Mackie 1961: 344). The most celebrated — and most criticized — case of military men assigned to economic jobs, and for some considerable time also the greatest success story, was the handing over of some defunct oil wells in North Sumatra in October 1957 to the then Colonel Dr. med. Ibnu Sutowo and a group of army officers who developed the wells into PERTAMINA, Indonesia's national oil company (see Bartlett 1972). PERTAMINA both produces oil and controls all oil contracts with foreign companies, and has branched out into a large variety of other economic activities.

The criticisms leveled against Ibnu Sutowo were manifold. First, PER-TAMINA was seen as a state within the state, a national company so independent it defied all attempts by the state to control its policies and finances. The latter charge must be accepted as true, but one also has to bear in mind that Ibnu Sutowo was placed in this job by Nasution to supply the army with extra funds, since the allocation for defense in the national budgets had never been large enough to sustain the army's bare existence, let alone finance large-scale operations of any kind. The coming to power of Suharto initially brought no relief to the official budget of the army (in 1967 the Suharto government cut the defense expenditure proposed by the Ministry of Defense by 60 percent, allocating only 28 percent of the national budget to defense and security; see *Jakarta Times,* September 6, 1967) and Ibnu Sutowo was obliged to continue contributing significantly to the extrabudgetary funding of the army. Thus given the special character of his assignment, one could hardly expect Ibnu Sutowo to open his books to public scrutiny. But not even Suharto seems to have had a clear picture of PERTAMINA's financial position and reportedly for some time had to ask the oil magnate for money whenever he wished to undertake projects not budgeted for in advance in the state budget.

Ibnu Sutowo financed singlehandedly a large variety of undertakings, often for political and personal reasons of his own, like sponsoring a students' conference to ward off their criticism of him, or building a new hall in the Army Staff and Command School to forestall disaffection among his colleagues in the army. He looked after the employees of PERTAMINA — too well, according to his critics — paying high salaries, bonuses, and expenses. How, he argued, "can we tell people about the benefits of education if we educate them and then pay them only enough for rice and shelter?" (Bartlett 1972: 13). He built houses and new office blocks and justified the considerable expense by saying that "we must maintain some level of affluence that will make our role credible" in the eyes of international oil companies with which he was locked in bargaining. Presumably on the strength of this argument he purchased the only Rolls Royce in Indonesia for his company. He was also seen as personally corrupt and furnished evidence for this allegation by his rather extravagant life style.

One allegation that was not made against him until fairly recently was that of inefficiency. Even after PERTAMINA experienced serious financial difficulties in early 1975, due to its overexpansion into other economic activities which could be financed only by expensive short-term loans in a tightening international money market, he was not sacked immediately although a considerable number of military and civilian leaders were after his blood (see *Kompas,* March 26, 1975; *Tempo,* April 5, 1975; Arndt 1975: 3-8). But when he, well beyond the normal retirement age, was finally "honorably discharged" in March 1976 and replaced by an army general specializing in finance and budgeting, government leaders assumed a share of the responsibility for PERTAMINA's financial near-collapse; after all, PERTAMINA's overcommitment in other economic fields was not solely an expression of Ibnu Sutowo's empire-building but at least partly also the result of the government off-loading responsibility for often unviable development projects onto PERTAMINA.

Few officers running state enterprises match Ibnu's efficiency and expertise. With most lacking technical skills or having the wrong skills for their assignments their performance can be dismal, especially if the dimension of corruption is added to it. But it should be pointed out that highly inefficient and corrupt officers often enough are replaced, especially when other officers and technocrats with appropriate skills become available.

Accusations of inefficiency and corruption also are directed against many officers in political, administrative, and diplomatic posts. Particularly in some Outer Islands provinces, military commanders and military governors are sometimes engaged in illegal barter trade across the national border, either directly or through officers acting as middlemen. More often Chinese businessmen are used to cover up the unofficial economic activities of officers in both military and civilian posts.

Those who criticize the inefficiency and corruption among military men are basically either Western-educated intellectuals and journalists, or people who temporarily are denied a share of the cake, like students or party politicians. But corruption is not something that infected Indonesia when the military moved into the administration and the national economy, though its volume has increased now that there is more to share. Corruption, as we understand it in the West, was introduced to Indonesia by the Dutch East Indies Company, which largely left its employees to fend for themselves. Corruption is also part of the "feudalist and traditional, primitive culture" of Southern Asia, as an Indonesian scholar asserts, and affects whoever is in power, whether they are military or civilian rulers (Soedarso 1969: 88).

However, to be content with the notion that corruption is just a cherished tradition among the Indonesian upper classes would mean neglecting several important aspects. First of all, my own observation is that by no means all officers are enriching themselves. A large number of generals and colonels, probably a majority, are not personally corrupt and have remained almost as unsullied and as poor as they were when they joined the army almost thirty years ago. Furthermore, the wage structure in Indonesia is such that until recently a man employed by the state could live only for one week on his monthly salary (this is gradually changing for the better) (see *Bulletin of Indonesian Economic Studies,* March 1975: 14). So people have to find money somehow to support their families, and although moonlighting is not an option for everyone, an office may provide the opportunity to obtain money illegally. Moreover, in the feudalist value system of the Javanese *priyayi* a man in charge of others, be he the head of a government office or the commander of a battalion, is obliged to support his men. Thus, funds obtained through corruption are used mainly to guarantee the livelihood of one's subordinates. Finally, there are cases in which officers are placed in a civilian position for the express purpose of raising funds for the army. For these reasons the government or the army command can do hardly anything about corruption.

There have been laws passed against corruption, at least as early as 1960, and every so often the government conducts special investigations in response to pressures from those circles who have little opportunity to partake in corrupt practices and/or who cannot be bought off. But these are bound to remain nominal efforts so long as the government cannot pay wages that will provide a decent living for state employees. When in the early 1960s General Nasution made a real effort to wipe out corruption by launching his Operasi Budhi, the Sukarno government had to frustrate his efforts partly because his self-righteous attitude did not take into account the financial condition of state employees.

The allegations of inefficiency equally need qualification. There have been enough instances of dismal failures, but although some officers did ruin state enterprises, civilian entrepreneurs lost their own businesses as well, partly because of a general lack of expertise in Indonesia and partly because of the effect of government policies. During Sukarno's regime state enterprises, whether run by military or civilian managers, collapsed because they were plundered recklessly by the government with no provision allowed for reinvestment and maintenance. In the New Order, indigenous enterprises, regardless of whether they are run by military men or civilians, suffer equally from the onslaught of foreign enterpreneurs and cheap imports. Thus, officers assigned to civilian tasks often fail not so much because of personal shortcomings but because of circumstances that are often beyond their control.

Officers assigned to civilian tasks often know clearly their own limitations and the difficulties of their jobs, but few would state this as publicly and as bluntly as Major General Solihin, who confessed "to be ill at ease" in his new job as governor of West Java (*Angkatan Bersenjata,* January 12, 1970). Army leaders also are well aware of the shortcomings of the system of putting military men in civilian positions. While Nasution has argued that the performance of officers could be improved by providing clearer guidelines and stricter supervision (Nasution 1971: 106-18), others would only partly agree with this assessment and blame shortcomings also on bad personnel decisions (Isman 1967: 7). But, however different the explanations of the failures of officers in civilian assignments are, few in the army would disclaim that the whole system, variously described as Civic Mission, Dwi-Fungsi, Dwidharma, Karyawan, or Kekarjaan, has its merits and should be maintained for some time to come.

Apart from the fact that additional funds are raised for the army by officers in civilian positions, and that the Civic Mission scheme provided jobs for the many surplus senior officers who otherwise would have to be retired on a very small pension, the argument runs that the whole nation is benefiting from this system. Military men often may not have the appropriate skills needed for their civilian jobs, but they see themselves as having more to offer than civilians who may not have much expertise either and, moreover, lack the officers' "men management" skills, their discipline, and their willingness to take initiative. And indeed, there would hardly be an entrepreneur in Indonesia more enterprising than General Ibnu Sutowo. With regard to the regional civil service, officers point out that formerly a minister of the interior had little control over a governor coming from a different party, and the governor in turn had next to no means to enforce his decisions on district officers belonging to a different party. But with officers penetrating the regional civil service, the dimensions of military discipline and hierarchy are added to the civilian hierarchy structure: the minister, a lieutenant general, gives orders to the governors, usually major generals, who direct lieutenant colonels serving as district officers. So the central government can be sure its instructions are obeyed.

Thus, one may conclude, the military is now firmly in control of every sector of public life in Indonesia, leaving little or no room for maneuver by any other political force, and permitting public criticism only to the extent that it does not really challenge the foundations of the regime (at least until the riots of January 1974, Indonesia had an extremely free and lively press, though).[3] The military will justify this situation by arguing that the political parties, with the exception of the now-defunct Communist party, have shown little initiative and have produced no constructive political or economic proposal since they rendered parliament ineffective in 1957 through their "endless bickering" and their inability to form a government majority in the house. As the officers see it — and they are the only political force that counts in present-day Indonesia — the country is in dire need of economic reconstruction and development, for Indonesia is the country with one of the lowest per capita incomes in the whole of Southeast Asia and with huge problems of unemployment and land shortage on Java. The country will have to apply itself single-mindedly to the task of solving its economic problems and for the time being cannot afford to have "divisive party politics" getting in the way of these efforts. Therefore the country simply has no other choice but to follow the leadership of the military in the quest for progress and development.[4]

3. It was possible to demand publicly the dissolution of parliament and new elections free from government intervention and manipulation, an end to the military's Civic Mission, the disbanding of KOPKAMTIB, and the purging of the state apparatus of "thieves of state funds." See *Abadi*, January 9, 1974. However, after the riots *Abadi* was one of the newspapers banned by the government.
4. It is debatable whether the development strategies employed by the Suharto regime are, indeed, the most suitable ones for Indonesia, and criticism of these strategies has mounted both inside and outside Indonesia. For a highly critical evaluation of Suharto's development policy, see Mortimer 1973.

THE INTERNAL ORGANIZATION OF THE
INDONESIAN ARMED FORCES

At present the Indonesian Armed Forces (Angkatan Bersenjata Republik Indonesia, or ABRI) consist of the military (*Angkatan Perang*, or APRI) and the national police (POLRI), both directed by the Department of Defense and Security (Departemen Pertahanan-Keamanan or HANKAM).[5] This was not always the case. Civilian leaders tried for a long time not only to keep the police apart from the military but also to prevent the establishment of an effective unified command for the army, the navy, and the air force in order to be able to play off one service against the other. When a joint armed forces staff was created in June 1962 little power was given to it and the possible unifying impact was counterbalanced by elevating all service chiefs-of-staff to commanders and cabinet ministers.

When Suharto came to power serious efforts were made to achieve a higher degree of unity in the armed forces. Announcing the merger of the cadet schools of all four services into one Akademi Angkatan Bersenjata Republik Indonesia in December 1966, Suharto stressed the absolute need for integration of the armed forces (Radio Republik Indonesia, October 5, 1966). In the following year the ministries of the army, the navy, the air force, and the police were abolished and service commanders stripped of their cabinet status (see Jakarta *Times,* September 6, 1967).

One has to assume that the assault on the relatively great independence of the services met with some resistance inside these services, as two years passed before further moves toward the integration of ABRI were made. Finally, in October 1969 a number of sweeping changes were introduced (see Keputusan Presiden Republik Indonesia, no. 79/1969, 1970; *Kompas* October 7, 1969; *Indonesia Magazine* 1969; *Sinar Harapan,* November 10, 1969). First, all service commanders were further downgraded to chiefs-of-staff, which was not only a loss of status but also signified a reduction of power and functions. Second, all operational responsibilities were taken from them and delegated to HANKAM, as a result of which, for all practical purposes, they lost control over their respective combat troops. Third, the service headquarters lost all their political functions, and the sections involved in politics were eliminated. Before these changes were introduced, the army's intelligence section (*seksi* I) and the so-called "territorial section" (seksi V), formally responsible for liaison with the population, had been the prime agents of New Order policies throughout Indonesia. In the 1969 reorganization seksi V was abolished, and the intelligence section politically emasculated. The "Karyawan section" (seksi VI), which selected officers for assignment to civilian positions and supervised them, was dissolved along with the rather mysterious seksi VII, which raised

---

5. Until recently the Civil Defense Organization (HANSIP) was also under the direction of HANKAM but is now organizationally the responsibility of the minister of the interior.

extra-budgetary funds. What was left with the headquarters of each service was the responsibility for combat intelligence, recruitment and training, personnel management, and planning. Thus, in effect, former service commands had been reduced to purely administrative units, with no power base of their own and unable to dictate national or defense policies.

All political functions, all policy decision-making in the defense and security field, and the ultimate control over combat troops were vested in HANKAM headed by General Suharto himself in the double function of minister of defense and security and commander of the armed forces (he resigned in 1973 from both these posts). The staff of the ministry (Staf HANKAM) consists almost exclusively of officers of the four services. Army officers are predominant, though, for the army is not only by far the largest and politically most powerful of the military branches but also has the largest number of officers available. But Suharto has been careful not to antagonize the navy and the air force unduly by relying too heavily on his army comrades in staffing HANKAM and has assigned some of the top positions to admirals and air marshals. The most underrepresented force is the police, which cannot obtain positions within HANKAM that deal primarily with defense aspects and may be recruited only for posts related to security aspects.

In its 1969 setup the Staf HANKAM consisted at its top level of the armed forces commander, his deputy, and his private staff. The assistant for general planning, the inspector general, and the finance inspector reported directly to the commander. At the third level was a general staff, a "departmental staff," and a "staff for nonmilitary affairs." The general staff consisted of the sections for intelligence, operations, personnel, logistics, "territorial," and communications and electronics. The departmental staff, designed as the administrative center for all four services, consisted of sections for manpower, material, finance, education, law, and social order and security development. The staff for nonmilitary affairs consisted of three sections, namely, social and political development, personnel in civilian positions, and civic action. The chief-of-staff of the general staff was selected from the navy, the departmental staff was headed by an air vice-marshal, but the politically most sensitive position of head of the staff for nonmilitary affairs was given to Major General Darjatmo of the army, a trusted follower of Suharto.

Subordinated to HANKAM were the headquarters of the four services, the integrated training installations, and a large variety of military organizations such as the Military Police, the Information Center, the Armed Forces History Center, Military Industries, the Office of the Military Prosecutor General, and so forth. HANKAM's control over the combat units was exercised through the National Strategic Command (mainly responsible for combating external threats), the National Maritime Defense Command, the National Air Defense Command, and six Defense Region Commands (Komando Wilajah Pertahanan or KOWILHAN).

While the new organization of HANKAM and its relationship with the four service headquarters were seen as a means to strengthen Suharto's grip over the navy, the air force, and the police (*Pedoman,* December 12, 1969), the establishment of the KOWILHANs was a significant step in centralizing the lines of command in the army itself.

The Indonesian army initially was not formed by the government or a central military headquarters, but literally sprang up locally in 1945 in response to the threat of Dutch reoccupation of the archipelago. Thus from the outset central authorities had only very limited control over the fighting forces.

The independence of the front-line troops from a central command was reinforced by the military inferiority of the Indonesian forces vis-à-vis the well-armed, well-trained Dutch military machine. It forced the Indonesians to adopt a guerrilla – or "territorial" – strategy in which the Republican forces made up for their inferiority by better knowledge of the terrain and the support of the local population. Part of this "territorial" strategy is, of course, that the same troops operate permanently in a given area and, if necessary, without orders and supplies from the central command. Nasution, the chief architect of the "territorial" defense concept, recognized that guerrilla warfare would remain the primary form of defense until Indonesia could afford economically to build "a modern army," an army with modern, heavy equipment and a higher offensive strike capacity (Nasution 1965: 70). So during the wars of independence units were assigned to defend particular areas, and after national independence was achieved Indonesia was split up into seven "military territories," with seven "divisions" responsible for the defense and internal security of their respective "territories."

Given the military capacity of the Indonesian National Army (TNI), this was strategically a sound concept. Moreover, it also reflected the political realities within the TNI, where "division" commanders increasingly enjoyed the loyalty of their subordinates and were therefore difficult to dislodge from their positions. Furthermore, employing the experiences of the previous guerrilla war, the "territories" were subdivided into district commands (KODIM) and sub-district commands. These commands had no combat troops at their disposal but were designed to maintain liaison with the population to keep the people battle-ready at all times, and provide the administrative backup in case combat troops had to operate in their respective areas.

However, the "territorial" system also led army "divisions" to identify with the grievances of their respective "territories" and fostered the growth of warlordism, which army headquarters was unable to check. The outbreak of regional rebellion, spearheaded by warlords in Sumatra and Sulawesi, in 1958 finally forced a showdown between regional commanders and the army headquarters. Nasution, who was able to crush the rebellion, reduced the power of the "division" commanders (*panglimas*) by a substantial reshuffle and by breaking up the seven "territories" into 17 military area commands (Komando Daerah Militer, KODAM).

But the power of the panglimas remained substantial nevertheless. Admittedly, the *rapat panglima,* regular meetings between the army chief-of-staff and the regional commanders, changed from a situation where the chief-of-staff was hardly more than a *primus inter pares* to briefings in which Nasution could give orders. But the panglimas still demanded a say on the board for the promotion and appointment of high-ranking officers (WANDJAKTI) and retained political importance in the provinces as regional martial law administrators.

The setting-up of so-called interarea commands (KOANDA) for the KODAMs in Sumatra, Kalimantan, and East Indonesia (not Java!) had little impact on the still relatively high degree of political independence of KODAMs in the Outer Islands, for the KOANDAs were given no more than coordinating functions. In fact, at the close of Guided Democracy the panglimas seemed to have become more independent of the army headquarters again, due to their being drawn increasingly into politics by President Sukarno.

When General Suharto came to power, one of his foremost aims was to eliminate the position of political power panglimas still enjoyed. Those panglimas — and other officers as well — who could be seen as sympathizers of either the PKI or Sukarno were relieved of their positions in 1966-1967. But army officers "to the right" of Suharto, with strong anti-Sukarno and Western-liberal inclinations, like Major General Dharsono, panglima of the West Java Siliwangi division, and Major General Kemal Idris, commander of the Strategic Reserve, had to go too. Most high positions in the army, foremost the commands of KODAMs, gradually were filled with officers who were politically reliable and unambitious.

The establishment of the KOWILHANs in 1969 was the final step in emasculating the KODAM commanders. The six KOWILHANs set up in 1969 contained the seventeen KODAMs in the following way:

KOWILHAN I (Sumatra)
  KODAM I/ Iskandar Muda (Atjeh)
  KODAM II/ Bukit Barisan (North Sumatra)
  KODAM III/ 17 Augustus (West Sumatra, Riau)
  KODAM IV/ Sriwidjaja (South Sumatra, Djambi, Lampung, Bengkulu)

KOWILHAN II (Java and Madura)
  KODAM V/ Djaja (Greater Jakarta)
  KODAM VI/ Siliwangi (West Java)
  KODAM VII/ Diponegoro (Central Java, Jogjakarta)
  KODAM VIII/ Brawidjaja (East Java)

KOWILHAN III (Kalimantan)
  KODAM IX/ Mularwarman (East Kalimantan)
  KODAM X/ Lambung Mangkurat (Southeast Kalimantan)
  KODAM XI/ Tambun Bungai (Central Kalimantan)
  KODAM XII/ Tandjung Pura (West Kalimantan)

KOWILHAN IV (Sulawesi)
  KODAM XIII/ Merdeka (North Sulawesi, Central Sulawesi)
  KODAM XIV/ Hasanudin (South Sulawesi, Southeast Sulawesi)

KOWILHAN V (Lesser Sunda Islands)
  KODAM XVI/ Udajana (Bali, West Nusatenggara, East Nusatenggara)

KOWILHAN VI (Maluku, West Irian)
　　KODAM XV/ Pattimura (Moluccas)
　　KODAM XVII/ Tjenderawasih (West Irian)

The KOWILHANs, in contrast to their forerunners the KOANDAs, are operational commands, that is, they are responsible for and direct the movements and activities of all combat troops in their region. A KODAM has become little more than an administrative unit in the territorial structure of the Indonesian army, with responsibilities for the general administration, training, personnel, logistics, and welfare of the combat troops in its area and in charge of the "territorial army" (see *Organisasi dan Prosedur Komando Daerah Militer* 1972). The "territorial army" has increased over the last fourteen years or so in the drive to provide a higher degree of internal security and stability, and to help in discharging the army's responsibilities first as martial law administrators and then as the chief agents of New Order policies. By 1976 the territorial structure of the army consisted of the KODAM itself, reporting directly to HANKAM on territorial affairs, with several military resort commands (KOREMs) below it, district commands (KODIMs) at district level, military rayon commands (KORAMILs) at subdistrict level, and the Bintara Pembina Desa, sergeants representing the army at village level. But the activities of the "territorial army" were also more strictly controlled by HANKAM. Having already lost all formal political power with the dissolution of the PEPELDA in 1967, and with effective control over their combat troops transferred to the center, the panglimas have ceased to be independent sources of power. Warlordism has thus arrived at its final conclusion.

Although the navy and air force in 1969 retained control over some of their combat units through the continuing existence of the Maritime Defense Command and the Air Defense Command, the KOWILHANs were given control over some naval and air force units. Accordingly, the KOWILHANs were staffed jointly by the three services. KOWILHANs I (Sumatra), II (Java and Madura), and IV (Sulawesi) were commanded by army generals, KOWILHAN III (Kalimantan) went to a vice air marshal, and KOWILHANs V (Lesser Sunda Islands) and VI (Maluku/West Irian) were given to admirals.

This was as far as Suharto dared to go in 1969. There was grumbling in the navy and the air force for having lost their independence. But there was some unhappiness in the army too, where sections of the officer corps resented the loss of political power in the regional commands and, given the interservice rivalries inherent in the military the world over, having to serve in some instances under a navy or air force officer.

But the 1969 changes were still short of total integration of the armed forces and their total control by HANKAM. By 1973, and through to 1974, the "final year of the consolidation and integration of the armed forces," according to Minister of Defense and Commander of the Armed Forces General Panggabean, new changes were introduced to tighten the grip of the ABRI commander over the forces and to turn the Indonesian military into an at least organizationally modern force (*Sinar Harapan,* February 8, 1974). In May 1973 the small

KOWILHAN V was abolished and the Lesser Sunda Islands incorporated into KOWILHAN II (Java and Madura). KOWILHAN III also was dissolved and West Kalimantan given to KOWILHAN I (Sumatra), while East and Central and Southeast Kalimantan became part of the KOWILHAN centered on Sulawesi (see Figure 1). The KODAM in Central Kalimantan was dissolved too, and its defense area incorporated into the defense area of the KODAM Lambung Mangkurat with headquarters in Banjarmassin, Southeast Kalimantan. Furthermore, the National Maritime Defense Command was dissolved. At HANKAM level new changes came in February 1974. The inspectorate for finance supervision, held by an air force officer, was abolished. The general staff, commanded by Air Marshal Sudarmono, was transformed into an operational staff and the "departmental staff," over which General Hasnan Habib had assumed command in 1973, was renamed the administrative staff. The new operational staff lost its sections for personnel and logistics to the administrative staff and gained the section for social order and security development from the latter, and the civic action section of the "staff for nonmilitary affairs" merged into its territorial section (see *Merdeka* and *Sinar Harapan,* February 8, 1974).

The overall results of the changes of 1973-1974 were not only a strengthening of control by the minister of defense and security over the military and a more modern and efficient central organization; both the navy and the air force lost out even further to the army, which increased its hold on the Staf HANKAM. The navy was particularly hard hit by the abolition of the Maritime Defense Command.

So far, little mention has been made of the Komando Operasi Pemulihan Keamanan dan Ketertiban (Operations Command for the Restoration of Security and Order, KOPKAMTIB), an organization within the Indonesian defense establishment. Set up in the wake of the Untung "coup," it played a role in eliminating the PKI and its followers both within and outside the state organizations. By 1968 its role had become obscure and its presence as an organization was hardly felt.

But in the view of Suharto this was an organization that could be revived for keeping the country politically under control. It could be used against the remnants of the Communist party and the sympathizers of Untung, as well as against any other political grouping that threatened the regime. All that was required was to classify any political "crime" such as holding demonstrations (banned since the end of 1965) as a threat to the internal security of the country. This, indeed, became the practice under the New Order.

A presidential decree of March 3, 1969, practically reactivated KOPKAMTIB (see *Pedoman,* March 20, 1969). It was headed by the president himself, with the army commander as his deputy. It had a small staff of its own, but the general staff of the army command served also as the KOPKAMTIB general staff. In the changes that occurred later in 1969 General Panggabean, the army commander, became deputy commander of the armed forces and commander of KOPKAMTIB, with Lieutenant General Sumitro as his deputy in KOPKAMTIB. Also, the newly constituted general staff of HANKAM came to

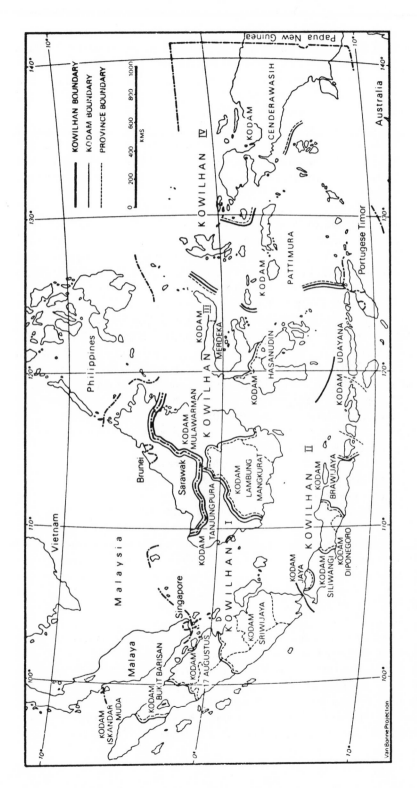

FIG. 1. KOWILHANS and KODAMS, 1973.

function as KOPKAMTIB's general staff as well, with the chiefs of the departmental staff and the staff for nonmilitary affairs serving also in KOPKAMTIB as
second-echelon chiefs-of-staff (*Kepala staf harian*). Thus the KOPKAMTIB
organization was closely interwoven with the organization of HANKAM. Its role
definition was to take care of all internal security aspects in the widest sense and
included the powers of assuming supreme control over combat troops if large-
scale security operations were necessary, and screening all military organizations
including HANKAM for military men involved in unwarranted political activities.
At the regional level the commanders of KOWILHANs and KODAMs were made
agents (*pelaksana chusus,* special executors) of KOPKAMTIB in matters concerning internal security.

Under the energetic leadership of Lieutenant General Sumitro, the deputy
commander and real master of the organization, KOPKAMTIB swiftly assumed
the roles which the army intelligence and army territorial sections had played in
controlling and supervising the country politically. It soon emerged as the most
oppressive and most feared agency of the regime, interfering in the political
activities of every social-political organization and arresting people at will.

The status of KOPKAMTIB as an organization within the jurisdiction of
HANKAM became obscured in early 1973 when General Panggabean relin-
quished his position as KOPKAMTIB commander to Sumitro. In a way the
status of KOPKAMTIB was further enhanced by the promotion of Sumitro to
full general and the appointment of the navy commander, Admiral Sudomo, as
deputy commander of KOPKAMTIB. It seems that Sumitro may have regarded
himself as equal to Panggabean, who had become minister of defense and
security and armed forces commander (with Sumitro as deputy commander), for
he began playing politics in public in a way which was neither endorsed by
President Suharto nor General Panggabean.

After the riots of January 1974, which were at least partly blamed on the
previous political activities of Sumitro (see following paragraphs), he was sacked
from his position as KOPKAMTIB commander and the post was assumed by
Suharto himself, with the daily running of the organization delegated to Sudomo
as chief-of-staff of KOPKAMTIB. With President Suharto as the new commander
(who, it will be remembered, is retired from active military duty), the organizational ambiguity over the status of KOPKAMTIB is further highlighted rather
than resolved.

The   activities of KOPKAMTIB partly overlap with those of two other
agencies which, although they are organizationally not part of HANKAM, need
to be mentioned here. One is the Special Operations Service (Operasi Chusus,
OPSUS) which is directly responsible to the president. It is headed by Major
General Ali Moertopo, who was also a member of the president's private staff
until it was dissolved in early 1974. OPSUS was set up by Suharto during the
West Irian campaign as a special combat intelligence unit under the then
Lieutenant Colonel Moertopo. It was OPSUS and Ali Moertopo who made
contact in 1964 with the Malaysians while the anti-Malaysia "Confrontation"
was still on, and it has since functioned as Suharto's special instrument in

delicate foreign affairs matters. But OPSUS is also an internal intelligence cum political liaison office which conducts political operations such as making sure that a People's Deliberative Congress session goes according to government expectations, or preparing and supervising the "Act of Free Choice" in West Irian in 1969. It is in its internal operations that its activities sometimes overlap — or even clash — with those of KOPKAMTIB. Being only a small outfit, with few full-time staff in the head office but agents in many government bureaus, has somewhat influenced its style of operations, which accents persuasion rather than coercion, the latter characterizing the working of KOPKAMTIB.

The other organization to be mentioned in this context is the State Intelligence Agency (Badan Intelidjens Negara, BINEG, often still referred to under its former acronym BAKIN), also responsible directly to the president. Its leading positions are filled by intelligence personnel from the army, the navy, the air force, the police, and the office of the prosecutor general, and traditionally it is headed by an army general. Until the riots of January 1974 its chief was Lieutenant General Sutopo Yuwono, who was replaced by his predecessor, Lieutenant General Yoga Sugama, apparently because he failed to predict the course and severity of the riots. According to now Major General Yoga Sugama, BINEG or BAKIN is formally responsible for political intelligence outside the defense and security field, (*Sinar Harapan,* December 12, 1969) but as a clearcut delineation of competences is lacking, its activities tend to overlap with those of both OPSUS and KOPKAMTIB. However, BINEG's activities hardly include the mounting of operations; it is usually confined to research and analysis only.

Although the structural organization is sufficiently publicized and discussed, the exact size of the military is a fairly well-guarded secret. During the anti-Malaysia Confrontation the military and the police accounted for over half a million men. The rise to power of General Suharto was seen in some army circles as providing the opportunity to further increase the size of the military, and two secret studies on manpower originating from army headquarters in the middle of 1966 called for a gradual increase in the strength of the army alone to 420,000 men. But Suharto decided that the primary objective of his government was economic rehabilitation and development, and accordingly the defense budget was slashed savagely.

At least since 1969 the strength of the military has gradually dropped. Soldiers who had become too old to be employed in a fighting organization were discharged in increasing numbers. Although the army headquarters announced that 50,000 of its soldiers would be discharged over the following five years, this figure seems to be well below the number that actually were discharged during that period (see *Indonesia Raya,* September 30, 1969). At the same time, the military lacked the finances to train, equip, and pay new soldiers sufficient in numbers to fill the gap created by the mass discharges. By now most units are under strength. For instance, the Siliwangi division of West Java, traditionally the numerically strongest division in Indonesia, dropped from 55,000 men in 1968 to 22,000 in 1974. Reportedly, the entire army has sagged to a strength below

Figure 2
The Organizational Structure of the Department of Defense and Security, 1974

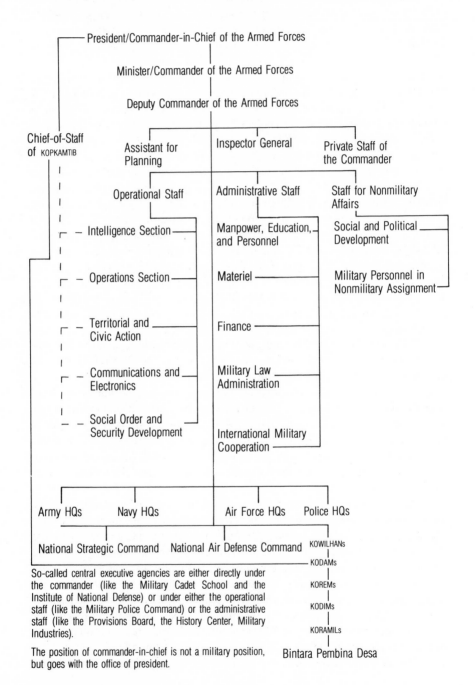

So-called central executive agencies are either directly under the commander (like the Military Cadet School and the Institute of National Defense) or under either the operational staff (like the Military Police Command) or the administrative staff (like the Provisions Board, the History Center, Military Industries).

The position of commander-in-chief is not a military position, but goes with the office of president.

200,000 men, and its strength envisaged for 1978 is 180,000 men (*Kompas*, September 29, 1973); the air force is to be reduced from 33,000 men in 1973 to 20,000 by 1978; and the navy is to make substantial cuts in its manpower too, particularly in the marine corps. The only force apparently not seriously affected by the general personnel reductions in ABRI is the police, which needs to keep up its strength for day-to-day law enforcement tasks.

POWER, INFLUENCE, AND COMMUNICATION
WITHIN THE MILITARY

The question of how the military is run and, ultimately, how the military is able to run the state, is determined by who exercises power within the military (that is, by who has the power to make decisions and is in a position to enforce them); by who has influence (meaning who can influence effectively the opinions of those who make the decisions); and how, formally or informally, the power structure is kept intact (see Sundhaussen 1976). Four problem areas will be discussed in this section to answer these questions. First, I will evaluate the degree of divisiveness and cohesiveness in the armed forces in general and in the army, the most powerful of the four services, in particular. Second, I will analyze the relationships among the president, the commanders of the armed forces and the army, and the troops. Third, I will try to establish how decisions are made and, finally, look at those officers who are able to communicate closely with the president and influence his decisions.

Western political scientists in the few analyses written on the military have tended to concentrate rather singlemindedly on the degree of divisiveness in the army (see Sundhaussen 1972). And there are, indeed, a sufficient number of incidents in the past to support a view that the army has been politically divided. Probably the most serious challenge to military discipline and hierarchy occurred as late as October 1, 1965, when dissident army and air force officers in contact with Communist leaders kidnapped and killed the then army commander, Lieutenant General A. Yani, and five of his closest associates.

Overlooked by these analysts was the almost simultaneous trend toward solidarity, conformity, and cohesiveness within the army (see Sundhaussen 1971*a*). This trend can be explained by a variety of fairly compelling reasons. First of all, none of the rebellions, mutinies, and acts of violence against the central military authorities, with the qualified exception of the mutinies in the aftermath of the October 7, 1952 Affair, succeeded in whatever were their ultimate aims. Rebellious officers were either kicked out of the army or even killed. By the end of 1958 it had become clear to the officers that they must either conform to the principles of military discipline and hierarchy or lose at least their jobs. Moreover, those officers who in their twenties and early thirties had been easily tempted to challenge central authority came to be middle-aged, more cautious men who were less willing to risk their positions for the sake of playing their own politics.

Second, Nasution in his "Middle-Way" speech, gave the army officers a new sense of purpose a new persuasive and attractive ideology that depicted the army as savior of the nation from political turmoil and as agent of national integration and modernization. Furthermore, with the opening up of lucrative civilian assignments for military men, quite a few officers developed economic interests which they could pursue only if they toed the line and stuck as closely to the army headquarters as possible.

But, one could argue, the Untung "coup" did occur despite army officers becoming older and more cautious and despite the army's new ideology and vested interests. Although this is undeniably true, one should also keep in mind that Untung had pitifully little support: it was an action by a very few, very disgruntled officers who had missed out in promotions and in economic perks and who, moreover, had their loyalty to the army superseded by loyalties to the president and probably the Communists. But to conclude, as some observers do, that another Untung-type action of violent dissent may still occur means to overlook a number of important developments which militate against such a possibility. One is that the armed forces, and particularly the army, have been ruthlessly purged of elements who could be identified even vaguely as having leftist and Sukarnoist orientations. This latest and largest purge of the officer corps again made clear that there was no place in the army for officers who want to play their own political games, and it had the effect of further cleansing the army of those who were unwilling to follow the orders and policies of the headquarters. Even the extremists on the opposite side, the dedicated anti-Sukarnoist officers gathering in the All-Java Commanders Conference (on their policies, see Roeder 1969: 244-46), particularly generals Dharsono, Kemal Idris, and Sarwo Edhie, were relieved of positions in which they could force Suharto's hand. Second, with the liquidation of the PKI and the toppling and later death of Sukarno, there is simply no ideological center stronger than the army's ideology around which dissatisfied officers could rally and which could diminish the loyalty of dissident officers to the army effectively. To be sure, there are many officers who are dissatisfied with the Suharto government, or with such aspects of it as corruption in the administration and the economy of the country. But although they are critical of the shortcomings of the present regime, they can see no other force or grouping that could replace Suharto and the army in the running of Indonesia. Third, the economic lot of officers and soldiers, like all state employees, has improved compared with the miserable economic conditions they had to put up with during Guided Democracy. This economic improvement also creates to some extent a sense of loyalty to the regime. And finally, the campaign for ideological cohesiveness in the army and the armed forces has been markedly stepped up since the Untung "coup."

The ideology of the army is based, very roughly, on three sources. The first one consists of policy statements by the late General Sudirman, the ascetic army commander during the Indonesian war of independence who became a legend during his lifetime. When in the turbulent politics of the wartime republic various political parties and groupings tried to draw the army, or sections of it, into their orbit, General Sudirman decided that "the army is the property of the whole people of Indonesia" and therefore could not take sides in the internal power struggles among politicians. But to give his army a bit more ideology than just nationalism and anticolonialism, he prescribed that "the political foundation of the army is the Pancasila and the 1945 constitution." These policy statements were, in a slightly different form, incorporated into the set of army principles drawn up in 1951 (see Army History Center 1967).

The second source of the army's ideology is Nasution who, however, draws heavily on Sudirman in order to legitimize his own views. Throughout Nasution's speeches and writings can be found references to the decisive role the army played in gaining independence for Indonesia. And because the army played such an important role in establishing the Indonesian nation, it must have the right to participate in determining the fate of the nation it helped to create. He also points out that parliamentary democracy collapsed from within, and he uses General Sudirman's political pronouncements to demand and legitimize the return to the 1945 constitution, which could be interpretated as providing the opportunity for a political role for the army. Sudirman's dictum that the army is the property of the whole people Nasution reinterprets to mean that it is not just the property, "the dead tool," of the government. Being responsible to the whole nation, the army must play a political role of its own, based on the interest of the whole population. It should not assume total political control and develop the attitudes of the military in "Latin American banana republics." Rather, it should work within the framework of the 1945 constitution which stipulates parliamentary institutions and the election of presidents.

Nasution's "Middle-Way" concept needed redefinition after the Untung "coup," when the army emerged as the dominant political force in Indonesian politics. An army seminar held in August 1966 in the Army Staff and Command School in Bandung concluded,

> If at first the army had only a limited role in its activities in the civil field, later, for a variety of reasons constituting a national crisis, the army was forced to spread its wings and expand its role. . . . All the people's hopes for well-being are focused on the Armed Forces in general, and the army in particular (as agents of national integration, political stability, and modernization). So for the Armed Forces there is only one alternative: to realize what has been entrusted to them by the people, and to implement the aspirations of the people. For all of these reasons the Armed Forces have an interest in the formation and shaping of a responsible government, a government which is strong, and a government which is progressive [Doktrin Perdjuangan TNI-AD "Tri Ubaya Cakti": 18].

The army fulfilled at least part of this promise by setting up a government which is strong, provides political stability, and turns its attention to the economic problems of the country. This government came into being by strict observation of the letter of the 1945 constitution, that is, Suharto was elected by the People's Deliberative Congress (under the chairmanship of General Nasution the congress was purged of leftists and Sukarnoists, though), which also set down the basic guidelines for the policies of the Suharto government.

An ideological problem arose when officers who had participated in the war of independence and thus established their "historical rights" to take part in politics reached their retirement age and had to be discharged. Officers who were recruited after the "revolution," mainly after 1958 — the so-called Young Generation (Generasi Muda) — and who are replacing the older officers have neither the "historical rights" nor the experience that led the "1945 Genera-tion" to behave as it did. To bridge the gap between the two distinct generations of officers and to secure the continuation of the army's present political role, another conference was held in Bandung in March 1972 in which the Generasi Muda was advised that in order to fulfill the social-political tasks of the army they would have to adopt the values and orientations of the Generasi 1945 (see Army Headquarters 1972: 31).

It has been noted that both Nasution and the 1966 army seminar did not isolate the army from the other services in overall objectives and, in a way, spoke on behalf of the other services as well. However, there has not been much political and ideological cohesiveness between the army and the other three services. Reportedly, in February 1967 the navy and the police even threatened to take military action against Suharto if he dared to put Sukarno before a military tribunal (see Polomka 1971: 91). On the other hand, the same people who had threatened military actions against Suharto assured him a month later of their absolute loyalty (see Statement of the Joint Armed Forces Commanders of March 13, 1967, in *Armed Forces Daily Mail,* March 15, 1967). But since then the sacking of Sukarnoist officers and their replacement by New Order-oriented officers in all services, and the 1967 and 1969 structural changes have brought the navy, police, and air force firmly under Suharto's control. In addition, the contents of a defense doctrine for all services worked out in a seminar in late 1966, which include definitions of ABRI's social and political functions almost analogous to those of the army, seem to have been in the meantime fully accepted by navy, air force, and police officers (see Defense and Security Staff 1967).

Some observers, however, continue to see serious divisions not only among the four services but within the army itself and describe the riots of Janu-ary 15-16, 1974, as the most dangerous threat the Suharto government has ever faced, primarily because army leaders were seen to be involved in it. What happened, briefly, is that General Sumitro responded by the end of 1973 to the growing disenchantment among particularly the students with the government's economic policies by travelling to the major campuses in Java promising "a new social leadership" by April 1, 1974, the beginning of the second five-year development plan. At the same time he appears to have defended the American-trained economists of the National Planning Board (BAPPENAS) who were responsible for the economic policies of the regime, and he seems to have accepted, if not actually encouraged, the notion that the president's private assistants, major generals Sujono Humardhani (economic affairs), R. Suryo (finance), and Ali Moertopo (political affairs), were to be blamed for the shortcomings in the economic policies because of their unwarranted interference and their corruption.

Ali Moertopo basically disapproved of fraternizing too openly with critics of the regime but was willing to take into account the substance of their criticism, and consequently attacked the technical approach of BAPPENAS, which had failed to take into account the social and political implications of their prescribed policies. Moreover, being pushed somewhat onto the defensive he lashed out at Sumitro, implying rather maliciously that the promise of a "new social leadership" was a challenge to Suharto himself. At the end of December Suharto briefly summoned the warring parties and told them that they were no more than his assistants and had to either learn to work together for him or resign. When Sumitro demanded a chance to explain his activities, he was curtly ordered to appear before the press jointly with Ali Moertopo and deny any serious differences of opinions between the two of them. In this press conference Sumitro also made clear that his promise of a "new social leadership" was never intended to be a challenge to the president (see *Harian Kami,* January 3, 1974; *Kompas,* January 3, 1974). However, on January 15 the students took to the streets ostensibly to demonstrate against visiting Japanese Prime Minister Tanaka and Japanese "economic imperialism," but in fact aimed their protest primarily against the economic policies of the Indonesian government and demanded the dismissal of the president's private assistants. When these demonstrations quickly developed into riots in which youths and even schoolchildren from Jakarta's slum areas burned cars, offices, nightclubs, and the Senen shopping center, Sumitro's political fate was sealed, for he was regarded as having at least indirectly encouraged the students to demonstrate in the first place. On January 26 the BAKIN chief, Lieutenant General Sutopo Yuwono, was sacked because he had not predicted the outbreak of violence and was also rumored to be sympathetic to the students, and two days later Suharto relieved Sumitro of his position as commander of KOPKAMTIB and assumed command over it himself. (On March 21, 1974, Sumitro resigned his remaining post as deputy commander of the armed forces and asked for early discharge from military service.) Partly to be seen as responding at least to some extent to the demands of the demonstrators, and partly to prevent Ali Moertopo and the other private assistants from becoming too powerful, Suharto also formally dissolved his private staff.

In regard to army cohesiveness some cracks had been showing, some observers will argue. But at no stage was the army's political function and domination questioned. Suharto's position as leader and president was not challenged at any stage, and "the Sumitro coup," advertised for several years by Western analysts, did not eventuate. There are on the flourishing Jakarta rumor market a great number of "insight stories" dizzying in their variety and contradictions, but there is no evidence at all of plots among army officers or movements of "rebel" troops.[6] At the most one may see in the controversy

6. As troops were under strict orders to use only "minimal force" against the demonstrators (on the first day of the riots they were not even issued live ammunition) and the Jakarta garrison consists of only one infantry brigade (4,000 men), a strategic reserve brigade was mobilized. On direct orders from Panggabean himself, a Raider battalion from the Central Java Diponegoro division and two Raider

between Sumitro and Ali Moertopo the beginning of the struggle of the *diadochi* which, however, came a bit too early. It would be more realistic to see it as a clash of two very strong personalities in which one, Sumitro, was powerful by virtue of his office and the other powerful because he had the unlimited trust of the president, each of them trying to establish himself as the second most powerful man in the country. Moreover, as Sumitro himself believes, this clash may have been carefully manipulated by forces outside the army who saw a political advantage in setting the two generals against each other (see *Kompas,* January 3, 1974).

If any conclusion can be drawn from the circumstances surrounding the January 15-16 riots, it must be that President Suharto is clearly in control of the armed services and can reshuffle and dismiss even top personnel without great difficulties. Before 1967 military leaders had a great deal of independence and constituted power centers of their own, but when Suharto in March 1967 combined the offices of president and commander of the armed forces in his hands and later changed the command structures in the defense establishment, this independence withered away and left him in a position of undisputed power and authority. The fact that he resigned later from both the post of minister of defense and security and as commander of the armed forces did not seem to have affected his authority in the services. And in any case, having taken over the command of KOPKAMTIB once more, he has secured his control over the military even further.

But Suharto is not only in control because he occupies the top position in the military and civil hierarchies (as president he is also supreme commander of the armed forces) and because he controls KOPKAMTIB. Through a careful personnel policy he has surrounded himself with officers who either have no political ambitions, like the minister of defense/commander of the armed forces, General Panggabean, or are totally devoted to him, like Ali Moertopo. Officers with political inclinations which did not coincide with his own views, be they left-oriented or right-wing, were relieved of sensitive and powerful postings. Sumitro and Sutopo Yuwono are only the last victims of this policy. Moreover, Suharto likes to work closely with officers of his own cultural background, which is *abangan* – Central Javanese, and officers he has known personally for a long time, which limits his close entourage to officers from his Central Java Diponegoro division. Although this appeals to the Javanese officers, who traditionally make up for some 70 percent of the total officer corps, he is careful to allot a number of top positions to non-Javanese officers (Panggabean is a Toba Batak from North Sumatra, and the air force chief-of-staff, Saleh Basarah, is a Sundanese from West Java) in order not to alienate the other ethnic groups in the officer corps. He has even been able to convince non-Javanese officers that it

---

battalions from the East Java Brawijaya were flown into Jakarta, and the nearby Army Paracommando Regiment (RPKAD) was rushed to the capital.

It should also be noted that apparently quite a few young soldiers were sympathetic to the student demonstrators, but acts of direct and active support of soldiers in the following riots were confined to a very few, isolated cases.

is his right and furthers his efficiency to surround himself in his daily work with men he knows and who share his values.

Furthermore, Suharto's policies both in the civilian and military fields by and large appeal to the military. The economic policies particularly have to a varying extent benefited all state employees who under Sukarno had a hard time making a living. Also, the policy of integration of the armed forces and centralization of command, although hampering the ambitions of some officers, are seen by most as providing stability and guaranteeing peace within the forces. To the great majority of officers, if not to all of them, the prospect of military coups or violent interservice rivalries are by now objectionable, signifying the collapse of the principles on which a modern army is built, namely, discipline and hierarchy, and endangering the position of power the military enjoys at present.

Also, Suharto's position of power is based on what are seen as his personal virtues and his indispensability. Although there seems to be little doubt in the minds of most officers that his wife and his closest confidants are involved up to their necks in shady dealings and corruption, he himself is seen as clean and pure. The fact that he does not fire men like Sujono Humardhani who, rightly or wrongly, is regarded as the most corrupt officer close to Suharto, is seen by many as a virtue: he is loyal to his friends even if they do wrong. Furthermore, virtually every officer of the 1945 Generation would, at this stage, oppose the return of a civilian government for political parties seem to lack the capacity to hold the nation together, to formulate policies, and to form government majorities in the parliament. No one else within the military is seen to command enough respect and authority to replace Suharto. Neither the retired Nasution nor Panggabean is regarded as eligible for the presidency for they are both Sumatrans, and the presidency is still the domain of the ethnic Javanese who make up about half of the Indonesian population. Sumitro has never built a clientele outside his home province, East Java, and Ali Moertopo has lost touch with his colleagues completely, having been outside the military establishment proper for the last decade. So Suharto's possible unwillingness to stand for yet another term as president, an inclination of which he speaks occasionally in private, is seen by New Order leaders as a major national disaster.

Finally, like Nasution in his day, Suharto has given the military a new sense of purpose by putting it more or less in charge of every aspect of public life in Indonesia. But whereas Nasution developed concepts by himself and then faced the task of selling them to his officers, Suharto, building on Nasution's concepts, institutionalized deliberation among officers at seminars which then produced new doctrines.[7] This practice gave officers a feeling of participation and minimized the effort involved in convincing all sections of the officer corps of the value of those new doctrines. Of course, enlarging the responsibilities of

7. It should be pointed out, however, that Nasution experimented with this type of officers' participation when he delegated the task of formulating some of his less contentious ideas into doctrines to the Army Staff and Command School. For an example, see Pauker 1963.

the military and increasing military penetration into civilian fields also enhanced the prospects for officers to obtain lucrative jobs, which is pleasing particularly to those officers who are facing discharge in the near future.

But officer participation in the deliberations over new doctrines in no way means that Suharto has lost control over the formulation of government and HANKAM policies. Official military doctrines in Indonesia more often than not reflect existing realities rather than direct the way to new developments. Thus, military seminars of the kind that result in new doctrines serve first to legitimize existing circumstances vis-à-vis the officer corps by having officers debate relevant issues and approve them.[8] Of course, such seminars are firmly controlled and directed by officers close to Suharto, and opening addresses by Suharto or Panggabean confine a seminar to the issues they want to see debated. What is finally left to the seminar is to spell out the details.

In discussing decision-making in present-day Indonesia one should distinguish clearly between decisions made in the military field and decisions on general national politics. In regard to the military there has been a development toward the decision-making procedures used in professional, modern armies. As mentioned earlier the regional commanders had by the late 1950s lost their power to participate in formulating official defense policies and the once all-important rapat panglima degenerated into briefings in which the commander gave orders. The WANDJAKTI responsible for promotions and appointments of high-ranking officers also lost its significance as Suharto started to implement his own personal policy regardless and in advance of the recommendations of this board.

Decisions in the field of defense are made by the minister of defense and security/commander of the armed forces in the *rapat pimpinan* (leadership meeting), which gathers about once a month and consists of the minister, the deputy commander of the armed forces, the service chiefs-of-staff, and the chiefs of the three HANKAM staffs. After lengthy deliberations, and after the minister has heard all views, he decides on the course to be taken. There is no voting in the rapat pimpinan.

Planning for the implementation of ministerial decisions is left to the *rapat pembantu pimpinan* (assistant leadership meeting) consisting of the deputy commander of the armed forces, the chiefs of the three HANKAM staffs, the assistant for general planning, and the inspector general. The actual implementation and supervision, as well as detailed planning, are the responsibility of the *rapat paripurna* (complete staff meeting) with the minister in the chair, and including the service chiefs-of-staff, the chiefs of the HANKAM staffs, and all assistants and heads of HANKAM sections.

8. The army seminar in August 1966 was probably an exception in that it went beyond the task of formulating (or reformulating) the "Tri Ubaya Cakti" doctrine by issuing political advice to the government (see Sumbangan Fikiran TNI-AD kepada Kabinet Ampera). It is not entirely clear whether the anti-Sukarno hawks who were prominent in the organization of the seminar meant to influence Suharto, or whether Suharto actually welcomed and ordered this document to demonstrate that the army was fully backing his policies.

Since Suharto resigned as minister/commander of the armed forces, the procedure on sensitive issues has changed slightly. Suharto's successor, General Panggabean, now consults with the president before he announces his decisions in the *rapat pimpinan.*

The rapat pimpinan potentially could be the center of the military's political power. But the HANKAM reorganizations, as well as the centralization of command in HANKAM, were both designed and carried out with the view of denying the military an active role in national policy formulation and confining it to no more than unquestioning support for the government. Suharto dominated the rapat pimpinan long enough to deprive it of an active political role, and his policy of promoting only personally loyal and/or unpolitical officers to top positions is likely to sustain the "nonpolitical" character of the rapat pimpinan for some time. The top brass assembled now in the rapat pimpinan have accepted their limited political role and reportedly have never used this organization to influence national policies and political decisions of the government.

One of the few political problems HANKAM is still involved in is that of assigning military personnel to civilian jobs. This is a highly political problem, partly because the lucrative assignments are desired by many officers without an active military assignment and are therefore difficult to distribute without alienating sections of the officer corps, and partly because public resistance is mounting against the *karyawan* system, particularly from civil servants, diplomats, and prospective state employees (students) whose careers are endangered and promotions frustrated by officers taking all the top jobs. Thus the government and HANKAM face the difficult task of justifying the karyawan scheme vis-à-vis the public and proposing officers who at least will not draw more criticism against the scheme.

The highest body within HANKAM to screen officers for civilian assignments is the *dewan kekaryan pusat* (probably best translated as central civic mission board), consisting of the minister of defense and security, the service chiefs-of-staff, the chief of the HANKAM staff for nonmilitary affairs, Lieutenant General Darjatmo, and the heads of sections of this staff. Here proposals are worked out for appointments on the central government level and submitted to Suharto. The final decision on appointments of officers as cabinet ministers, ambassadors, heads of government agencies or government departments, and provincial governors are, of course, the prerogative of the president.

On a lower level exists the *dewan kekaryan wilajah,* chaired by the commanders of KOWILHANs and attended by the *panglimas* and other high staff officers. This board makes recommendations for the appointment of district officers (*bupatis*), which have to be confirmed by the minister of the interior, and positions of bupati ranking. On the KODAM level a dewan kekaryan daerah, chaired by the panglima, proposes military personnel for civilian positions on subdistrict and village levels.

None of these boards is able to push through a candidate without getting approval from a higher authority. In the case of the dewan kekaryan pusat, as noted, the president makes the final decision. But the recommendations of the dewan kekaryan pusat can be intercepted before they reach the president by the *dewan kekaryan nasional,* which consists of the whole dewan kekaryan pusat plus the vice-president, the Sultan of Jogjakarta, the foreign minister Adam Malik, and various other ministers and high-ranking civilians, and in which the civilian component may put up serious objections.

Officers who are assigned to civilian positions remain members of the armed forces and can be recalled from their positions at any time by the military authorities. Policies regarding the karyawan scheme are decided by the president, and formulated and enforced by Lieutenant General Darjatmo through his staff, and particularly through the Karyawan Management Board (BAPINKAR). The BAPINKAR is the central administrative unit for officers in civilian jobs, which contacts them regularly disseminating information and policies, and collecting the quarterly reports of all military personnel in civilian positions. This system guarantees that officers in civilian assignments do not stray too far from the policies of the government, and if they do so they can be recalled immediately.

The picture drawn here is that of a united military, modern and almost "nonpolitical" in outlook, and a highly centralized authority structure in which one man, President Suharto, holds all power. Such a description of today's military in Indonesia needs to be qualified somewhat, though. First of all, in an organization as large as the Indonesian military there are bound to be different opinions, values, and attitudes. As noted, such differences, indeed, do exist. But differences do not anymore, as in the past, erupt into rebellions, mutinies, and violent action. For reasons outlined already they can be contained and have become manageable for the leaders. Those who want to – or do – criticize the government or HANKAM have to get out of a military that has become as disciplined and hierarchical as Western armies. Officers who even vaguely come to be suspected of not toeing the line are severely penalized.

Second, although Suharto appears to be solidly in control of the military and thus can be seen as having the power to make all the decisions, there are officers who are able to influence Suharto in his capacity as decision-maker, either by virtue of the character of the office they hold, or because they are trusted by the president. These officers offer their opinions and evaluations, or supply information which would otherwise be hard to obtain. As Suharto is known for never rushing into decisions, the opportunity for these officers to influence the president is, indeed, great.

General Panggabean is one of the few officers who always has access to the president. All decisions concerning the military are either proposed by Panggabean or at least made after Suharto has consulted him. Sumitro, when he was still KOPKAMTIB commander, had a near-monopoly on information on all security matters and, like Panggabean, would either propose the measures to be taken or would be at least consulted. The same would be true of Admiral Sudomo, his successor. The list of officers on active military duty who have relatively free access to the president should include General Surono Rekso-dimejo, the deputy commander of the armed forces, who has a close personal relationship with Suharto based on long common service in the Diponegoro division. He is almost certain to become the new armed forces commander when Panggabean retires.

The other officers able to influence the president do not hold assignments within the military proper. These include, first, the members of his private staff. Although this private staff was dissolved in early 1974, its former members are likely to continue enjoying the confidence of the president. Probably most important among them is Major General Ali Moertopo, who advised Suharto on political problems and has carried out many delicate missions for him, both internally and overseas. Ali Moertopo supplies the president with information that is not easily available and, besides drawing his attention to a political problem, may offer to solve it personally as well. Moreover, he is probably the foremost ideologue of the New Order, and his writings and the reactions they evoke often serve as a sounding board for national policies which have not yet been officially decreed (see Moertopo 1973 and 1973a).

Equally, the special bond that exists between Suharto and Major General Sujono Humardhani is unlikely to be terminated by the official dissolution of the private staff. Sujono is not only Suharto's chief economic advisor but, more importantly, is also the spiritual guide of Suharto, who is deeply committed to Javanese mysticism. It is said that there exists a total spiritual union between the two men whereby a prayer by Sujono on behalf of the president fully substitutes for a prayer by Suharto himself. Also Major General Suryo, Suharto's financial advisor, who has kept out of the limelight in the last few years, is likely to continue having the ear of the president.

A rising star in the Indonesian power structure is Major General Sudharmono, who combines in his hands the offices of presidential private secretary, state secretary, secretary of the cabinet, and minister of state/coordinator of all ministers of state. He acts as the go-between between the President and all ministries, coordinates all cabinet activities, and everyone except the men of Suharto's "inner circle" have to go through him if they want to see the president. Suharto is said to rely on him completely for the actual running of the government.

Finally, two more figures have to be included in Suharto's "inner circle." One was, at least until 1975, General Ibnu Sutowo, who had endeared himself to Suharto by financing particular economic and political projects of the regime through his efficiency and tough bargaining with foreign oil concerns and by supplying extrabudgetary funds to the army whenever these were required. For instance, the army operations against PKI strongholds in Central Java in late 1965 reportedly could be carried out only because Ibnu Sutowo made available the required funds. Ibnu had been the target of protracted criticism for corruption, but before the PERTAMINA crisis became fullblown Suharto curtly dismissed all suggestions to sack him, pointing out that he knew of no one who could do Ibnu's job. The president saw in Ibnu an entrepreneur who had proved to Indonesia and the world that Indonesians can be successful business managers, an image now likely to be shattered.

The other name to be mentioned here is Lieutenant General Yoga Sugama, who replaced Sutopo Yuwono as head of BAKIN, the state intelligence organization, an assignment he had held already until 1969. The unusual procedure of appointing an officer to a position he had held five years previously is to be explained by the fact that Suharto wanted someone in this position he could trust completely, and Yoga like no other intelligence officer, with the possible exception of Ali Moertopo, has the full confidence of the president.

It should be noted that the officers of Suharto's "inner circle" have no established military power base of their own. Even the officers on active military duty have no combat troops loyal to them personally, as was the case some years ago. They enjoy their present position of influence only because they have special skills useful to Suharto and, more importantly, because they have the confidence of the president.

No instances are known in which all the confidants of Suharto have combined their efforts to convince the president of a particular policy. Some of them may close ranks occasionally, though, as happened when in December 1973 Ali Moertopo and Sujono Humardhani jointly attacked BAPPENAS and Sumitro. But basically they compete against one another for the ear of the president, and contacts among most of them are irregular at best. Suharto can only gain from the diversity of his "inner circle" and seems to be well aware of this. But when the competition and lack of unity among his advisors becomes disruptive, as in the recent quarrels between Sumitro and Ali Moertopo, he firmly steps in and reminds them of their duty and position.

Thus the nature of the relationship between the president and the men around him is clearly established and does not allow for mis- or reinterpretations. Suharto makes the decisions, and the officers of the "inner circle" are confined to the — often very important — roles of providing and analyzing information, or in some cases carrying out politically delicate presidential decisions.

In summary, it must be concluded that the military, and especially the army, has reached a new peak in terms of cohesiveness, discipline, and hierarchy. Moreover, it has been compelled by Suharto to play a very limited political role. Practically it is confined to fully supporting President Suharto's regime without interfering in the decision-making process. Thus it could be argued that the New Order is a military regime only insofar as the military is the main pillar of power. In terms of authority structure, it is not a polity with a collective military leadership, or *junta,* nor can it be seen as possessing any relatively important centers of power independent of the central authority, forcing the president into a continuous process of bargaining with other officers. Rather the New Order has come to resemble personal regimes such as those of Kemal Ataturk and Nasser, in which army leaders in the role of president use the military for the purpose of policy implementation but successfully deny it a role in policy formulation.

This present relationship between the president and the military is unlikely to change in the next few years, for Suharto controls the personnel policy of

HANKAM and thus will be able to fill the decisive posts in the defense establishment with men he trusts and who are willing to serve him loyally. And as long as Suharto can maintain this relationship between himself and the military command, he will control the military and, through the military, the whole country, for there is no other organized force capable of challenging him. GOLKAR is under tighter army control than ever, having "elected" General Panggabean and other generals to most of its leadership positions. Neither of the two political parties has the strength or determination to seriously attack the president. None of the civilian ministers in the cabinet has a power base of his own, and each owes his position solely to Suharto. Although some ministers have the ear of the president and can influence his decisions to some extent, particularly in the economic field, Suharto is clearly the man who makes the decisions in the cabinet.

PROSPECTS

The present power configuration in Indonesia may well change toward the end of this decade, when officers of the 1945 Generation have retired and the Generasi Muda has taken over the military. What their politics is likely to be is difficult to predict at this stage. But it should be remembered that the differences in the outlook of the Generasi Muda and the Generasi 1945 had the military leadership worried enough to organize the March 1972 seminar, in which the attitudes of the younger officers were to be synchronized with those of the older officers. Although army leaders claim that the seminar bridged whatever differences existed between the two generations of officers and proudly produce the *Dharma Pusaka 45* (see Army Headquarters 1972) as evidence, there remains some doubt as to the extent of this success.

This doubt is based on the fact that the younger officers have completely different training and political experiences. Many of the 1945 generation had little formal qualification to become officers, and only the struggle for Indonesia's independence swept them into positions of authority and command. Their political orientations were highly diverse and only a process of ideological indoctrination with army doctrines, a constant struggle with politicians, recurrent purges of the officer corps, and their acquisition of vested political and economic interests turned them over a period of more than twenty years into the cohesive group they are now. By contrast, the young officers recruited since 1958 lack all these experiences. They were from the beginning given a professional training equal to that of cadets in Western armies which thoroughly qualified them for their profession. Their political education or indoctrination first in the Akademi Militer Nasional (AMN) and since 1966 in the Akademi Angkatan Bersenjata Republik Indonesia (AKABRI) was based on the directions of the headquarters and the official doctrines. They are first professional officers, and the minority among them interested in politics is presumably much smaller and much more unified than the politically engaged minority among the older officers.

Their professionalism is likely to work against interservice rivalries and particularly against interdivisional competition. Much of the earlier unrest in the army may be seen as the result of jealousies and rivalries among the larger army divisions, but this has to be regarded now as a feature of the past. The officers of the Generasi Muda have no particular loyalty to the divisions or KODAMs to which they were allotted but distinguish themselves rather in terms of the year they served in the AMN or the AKABRI and their respective weapons systems. The fact that cadets from all services serve together in the first year in the AKABRI in Magelang is also likely to diminish the chances for renewed outbreaks of interservice clashes.

Although these distinctions between the older and younger generations of officers are in keeping with the overall aims in the planning of Indonesia's military as a modern and unified force, there are also aspects which are highly disturbing to the 1945 Generation. The recruitment of cadets is so selective that there exists the distinct possibility that the new officer corps will become elitist to the extent where it will be completely divorced from society. For instance, the intake for 1974 was only 267 for all four services, from a pool of more than 20,000 candidates (see *Kompas,* January 26, 1974). This could have far-reaching repercussions for the Indonesian defense strategy, which is still based on guerrilla warfare and thus on the active support of the population, and also for the political strategy of "national resilience" which stipulates the cooperation of all sections of society in repulsing ideological subversion and infiltration (see Moertopo 1973: 102).

A strongly elitist attitude in the Generasi Muda may conceivably lead to a continuation of the contempt of the older officers for "the bungling party politicians" or even to a still higher degree of intolerance vis-à-vis "inefficient civilians," thus cementing military rule in Indonesia. On the other hand, there are signs of discontent among the Generasi Muda with the authoritarian politics of the present regime which, however, do not emerge easily into the open because of the strict observance of professional norms by the young officers. For instance, in the recent campaigns of the students against government policies, the sympathies of many young officers seem to have been quite clearly with the students.[9] Apparently, the young officers do have a reasonably close social contact with students and young intellectuals, and there is a feeling of mutual understanding which is partly the byproduct of officially sponsored seminars of young officers and cadets with students and intellectuals. This understanding could equally conceivably lead to at least a reduction of military involvement in politics after the Generasi Muda has taken over HANKAM.

To confound even further any speculation in regard to the politics of the Generasi Muda after 1980, two more considerations have to be taken into account. The limited intake of cadets will lead to an acute shortage of officers

---

9. As a young officer put it to me after the January 1974 riots, "I was genuinely in agreement with the students. But if I had been ordered to shoot at them I would have followed orders."

after the older officers have retired. That may mean there will just not be the military manpower available to penetrate the civil service and the national economy to nearly the extent practiced at present, in which case civilians are bound to reoccupy the top positions currently held by military men.[10] This may well constitute the first step in the military's retreat to the barracks. On the other hand, the military could try to hang on to its present position of power despite having to reduce its manpower commitments in civilian fields.

Second, a retreat from politics by the military will depend on whether civilians organize themselves into effective political groupings capable and willing to assume governmental responsibility. As it stands, civilian political organization is so unimpressive and unconvincing that not even the most liberal officers would consider surrendering political power to present political leaders.

Thus, although the present power structure is likely to be sustained as long as officers of the 1945 generation are in command of the military, politics in Indonesia may change considerably in the 1980s, depending not only on the direction in which the attitudes of the new officer corps will develop but also on the ability of a new generation of civilian leaders to take political initiatives and to convince the military of their administrative capability and political reliability. A process fostering mutual understanding and respect between young officers and young political leaders may already be under way.

10. Generals retire at the latest at the age of fifty-three from active service and enter a preretirement stage of two years in which they still draw full pay, before they are finally pensioned off at the age of fifty-five. However, for officers on civilian assignments the retirement regulations are less strictly observed. These officers presently are grouped into four categories, according to their usefulness. The officers of the greatest usefulness (category A) are likely not to be discharged when they reach retirement age. There is the distinct possibility that A category officers, and probably also veterans, may continue dominating the civil service even after Generasi Muda officers have been promoted into the top HANKAM positions.

4.
The Bureaucracy in Political Context: Weakness in Strength

DONALD K. EMMERSON

WHEN AMANGKURAT I took over the Mataram empire in the mid-seventeenth century its "bureaucracy" was a loosely cohering, lightly controlled, vaguely bounded, functionally almost undifferentiated array of notables appended to and overlapping with the royal family-in-court. In range and depth of impact on the daily lives of the peasants of Java, their impress was weak.

Under Amangkurat's rule, things began to change. Whereas his predecessor had sought to reduce the autonomy of local notables through marriage into the royal family, Amangkurat brought them physically to his court, where he could keep an eye on them, and placed the administration of outlying areas in the hands of *ministrables* whom he frequently replaced in order to forestall any challenge to his authority. Whereas before the king's writ had faded rapidly along the radius from palace to periphery, Amangkurat I set about to deepen and extend his control over the realm and its component parts. He introduced money taxes, made the foreign rice trade a state monopoly, and enforced a stricter, more comprehensive regulation of Javanese life down to the village level (Rouffaer 1931; Schrieke 1955: especially 74-76, 184-185; Moertono 1968).

Compared to Sultan Amangkurat, who ruled in Mataram for thirty years (1646-1677), Suharto's presidency in Indonesia (1968-?) has only just begun, and the sources, scope, and uses of political power then and now are obviously not the same. Nor does history literally repeat itself. But if Amangkurat built Indonesia's strongest precolonial bureaucracy, Suharto has done the same for the postcolonial period to date. (Compare Taufik Abdullah in *Kompas,* April 10, 1976, with C. Geertz) (1956: 48.)

First, Suharto set out to control the gargantuan *size* of government. He cut the number of ministers to a fourth of what it had become in the late days of

My acknowledgments include indispensable research funds by the Ford Foundation, the U.S. Office of Education, and the University of Wisconsin and helpful criticism by Carolyn Emmerson, Herbert Feith, Bruce Glassburner, Ronald Hatley, Karl Jackson, Dwight King, Nico Nordholt, Sartono Kartodirdjo, Norman Uphoff, Peter Weldon, and Judy Williams. Opinions and (no doubt) errors are my own. Accumulated over three and a half of the happiest years of my life spent in their country, my debts to Indonesians are beyond enumeration.

Sukarno's regime. He rid the rolls of thousands of persons associated with the Left in the years before 1966, when the Indonesian Communist party (Partai Komunis Indonesia or PKI) was large and legal. He limited new hiring and promoted early retirement.

Second, Suharto made his administration more *loyal.* Officers were recruited to toughen the bureaucracy with an exoskeleton of military command. Ministries that had been the sinecures of political parties were restaffed with civilians whose lack of an outside base made them more susceptible to central condition. Alternative objects of loyalty – political parties and labor, peasant, and student unions – were banned, amalgamated, or replaced by semiofficial bodies in which membership was automatic, preclusive, or both.

Third, the president made the bureaucracy more *active.* Tax revenue went up, and within it the ratio of direct to indirect levies. So did expenditure, and within it the proportion actually spent on development. To improve their performance, civil servants were given pay boosts, first selectively and then across the board. In successive five-year plans, broad goals were laid down for redefinition operationally as targets to be met at specified places within specified times.

In this chapter, by reviewing these characteristics of the Indonesian bureaucracy – its size, loyalty, and activity – I hope to describe and interpret it. My argument will run as follows: With a strategy of political repression and economic growth, the leaders of Indonesia's New Order have accomplished much. Not the least of their achievements is an accumulation of power unprecendented since Japan tried to mobilize the islands during World War II. The attempted coup and countercoup of 1965-1966 restructured politics more sweepingly than any events since the occupation and revolution of the 1940s. The head of state and founder of the nation, Sukarno, was disgraced, key policies of his regime were reversed, and the huge leftist constituency he cultivated was swept off the political map. Neither Indonesia's civil war in the 1950s nor the introduction of Guided Democracy shortly thereafter had such dramatic effects. It is not surprising that this contrast with the recent past should have been used to validate the ways of the new administration: After Sukarno's bureaucratic morass, where policies were more likely to get lost than take shape, it was easy to conclude that stronger government could only mean better government.

I affirm the distinction, but I question the conclusion. The comparison with Sukarno's admittedly ramshackle regime is a laurel on which its successor can no longer comfortably rest. Nor is optimism based on the past a useful guide to the future. In remaking the bureaucracy from an arena for political conflict into an instrument for economic growth, choices have been made and costs incurred. To put it starkly, in the terms of this book's title, power has been concentrated at the cost of open communication.

Can a bureaucracy be both powerful and open? Beyond what optimal point does an additional increase in the capacity to satisfy needs mean a decrease in sensitivity to them? In a hierarchic political culture where urban elite and rural mass are already far apart, as on Java where two-thirds of all Indonesians live, the optimum may be soon reached and easily passed: The stronger the ruler, the more impervious. In the extreme, as feedback channels are shut down and mass grievances pile up unrecognized at the entrances, violence may take over to flush out the system.

I am not prepared to say this will happen, especially not on a revolutionary scale. More likely is endemic, sporadic turmoil of the kind Huntington (1968) predicts for "praetorian" states. But whatever the future holds, recent changes in the bureaucracy and its political context have posed this issue of power and communication in a way no amount of enthusiasm for strong government can erase.

Concretely, Suharto has made political control a sine qua non of economic growth. And dramatic aggregate growth certainly has been achieved (see Chapter 5 in this volume). But the press has been curbed or banned. Demonstrations and strikes remain illegal. Non-Communist critics of the regime have been arrested and sentenced; others are subject to interrogation. On the Left, the number of political prisoners still runs well into the tens of thousands, and the purges continue. In major cities, riot troops practice quelling mock demonstrators. Villages are sealed off from political activity independent of the regime.[1]

If bureaucratic strength is the capacity to dispense with feedback, it may prove a weakness in disguise. And as the regime in Indonesia pays more attention to the goal of social justice pressed on it by its critics and spelled out for it by the nation's highest legal body in 1973, that weakness is more likely to be exposed to view. A narrowly based government, if it is strong enough, can extract resources and enforce targets of production without bothering about competition or criticism. But that strength could prove a liability when the same regime is asked to repattern the flow of benefits on behalf of poor people who are politically little more than a cast of extras for periodic managed elections. It is in this sense that as economic growth generates new demands for its more equitable distribution, each successive five-year plan may prove more difficult for the bureaucracy to negotiate — precisely because of its enhanced capacity to do without the public it is being exhorted to serve. The paradox of bureaucratic weakness in strength in Indonesia is what this chapter is about.

SIZE: DYNAMICS OF EXPANSION

The Indonesian bureaucracy has grown even faster than the population with which it deals. In Java in the late nineteenth-century less than a tenth of 1

---

1. Estimates of the number of persons still detained because of suspected links with the PKI vary from a low of 30,000 to 55,000 and higher. The first figure is Foreign Minister Adam Malik's (*Surabaya Post,* November 2, 1974); for higher figures, see Budiardjo 1974. (In 1965/66, according to Malik, there were 300,000 political prisoners.) Antiriot exercises have been held in Jakarta, Bandung, Surabaya, Jogjakarta, Medan, Palembang, Ujungpandang, and Jayapura. See *Masa Kini* (Jogjakarta), August 14, 1974; *Bhirawa* (Surabaya), August 28, 1974; and *Sinar Harapan* (Jakarta), October 1, 1974.

percent of the inhabitants ruled over the huge remainder. By 1930 Java's government employees had increased to around 1 percent of its population. By the mid-1960s the percentage had more than doubled for the country as a whole and had risen even more steeply on Java because the central government was — and still is — located there. In the last hundred years the number of public employees in Indonesia has increased, very roughly, around five hundred-fold, compared to a "mere" five- or sixfold increase in the population. (See, in order, de Kat Angelino 1931: 71; Day 1966: 418; Fagg 1958: 201; *Warta Berita,* August 18, 1968 [AB]; *Suara Karya,* January 31, 1974; Nitisastro 1970: 35, 60.)

Historical Overview

The story of juggernaut government in Indonesia is much more than a record of numerical growth. Even in briefest outline, as here, it points to qualitative changes and continuities: how the bureaucracy owes its central place in Indonesian life to biases in its favor shared by Javanese culture and Dutch colonialism, how its expansion reflected a shift in its assigned task from extractive growth to national welfare, and how first the Japanese and then Sukarno, the military, and the parties breached its professional standards and poured their own men across.

Colonial precedent: Extractive growth

The economic interest of the Dutch East India Company was extractive. Its political interest was secondary: to control the local population only insofar as that might accelerate and assure the upward flow of agricultural products, spices at first and later coffee and other crops. In the office of regent or regional head (*bupati*), the company found a lever with which to pry up and skim off this surplus. Regents disinclined to deliver the goods were reminded that their obligation was not unlike the tribute they had been required to furnish the Sultan of Mataram, with the advantage that they would now be compensated, after a fashion. If necessary, reminders gave way to the threat or use of armed force (for example, de Haan 1912: 376-377).

Under monopoly conditions in which underpaid, undersupervised company officials maneuvered and coopted the Javanese nobility, abuses were rife. The view sometimes heard among Indonesian intellectuals today, that corruption in Indonesia is merely a redefinition of behavior traditionally sanctioned by the Javanese, overlooks its foreign (Dutch) and structural (economic) inspiration during this period.[2] The principle of "get what you can while you can" (*mumpungisme*) certainly operated at the time in the minds of men sent out from Europe more as buccaneers and barons than as minions of a sober regime.

The company went bankrupt toward 1800 and its debts were taken over

2. More nuanced is Soedarso 1969. He explains corruption as the product of an indigenous culture — hierarchic, communitarian, and nonmaterialist — frozen in place by colonialism and thus unprepared to handle independence and modernization on any but its own feudal-familial terms.

by the Dutch state. In the ensuing century the goal of political control received higher priority, both to increase extraction and to prevent distractions like the costly war with the insurgent Mataram Prince Diponegoro in 1825-1830. The economic hallmark of the century was the arrangement, first introduced in 1830, whereby peasants were forced to plant and harvest specified export crops, notably sugar, in the island's rich volcanic soils. Again the crucial link tying Javanese farmers to European markets was the regent, who became less a local notable and more an official of a centralized regime.

This "culture" system was replaced with a "liberal" period and ultimately, in the early twentieth century, with an "ethical" policy, each in some was a misnomer and all recapitulating a basically exploitative relationship. The goals of increased extraction and control required a larger, more reliable, and more capable native apparatus beneath the regents – some 1,400 territorial officials (*wedana* and *asisten wedana*) on Java as early as the late nineteenth century. In 1879-1880, three decades after a decision had been reached in principle to train the sons of regents in native administration, three "schools for chiefs" were set up in western, central, and eastern Java; they were later reorganized as administrative training centers open to the sons of commoners too. In 1882 certain obligatory labor services previously rendered to the regent by the local population were abolished, further reducing his autonomy and tying him still more closely to higher, secular, central authority. These and related reforms implemented the earlier intentions of Governor Daendels (1808-1811), a Dutch Amangkurat of sorts who had sought to bureaucratize and centralize the weaker, looser, and more indirect rule of the company.[3]

In 1899 a reformist Dutchman argued for the repayment of Holland's "debt of honor" to her colony by promoting education, irrigation, and emigration from Java to the Outer Islands, albeit within the framework of continued colonial rule and profit (van Deventer 1899). In the twentieth century this third bureaucratic goal—welfare—gained acceptance and justified further increases in personnel. Educational and health establishments were set up and staffed; railroads, roads, and water works employed native officials in construction and maintenance all over the island. In the 1920s, buoyed by economic prosperity, indigenous participation in the civil service expanded sharply, leveling off only with the depression of the 1930s. By 1940 perhaps a quater-million persons were on government payrolls of one sort or another, including military personnel and temporary workers. The number dropped with the departure or internment of Dutch officials in 1942, then rose again as the Japanese reemphasized extraction to feed their Pacific war machine and mobilized Indonesians to that end.[4]

3. The uniqueness of these men should not be exaggerated. Much of what Amangkurat accomplished was made possible by the efforts of his predecessor Sultan Agung (1613-1646), just as Daendels's successor Stamford Raffles (1811-1816) in a brief period of British rule occasioned by the outcome of Napoleonic warfare in Europe also sought to regularize the administration into a vertical hierarchy right down to the village. For the nineteenth century estimates and reforms, see de Kat Angelino 1931: 25-28, 71, 76-79.

4. On educational policy in the late colonial period, see Brugmans 1961, van der Wal 1963, Thomas 1973. On expanding native participation in the civil service, see

National independence: Widening the mandate

When nationalist leaders declared Indonesia's independence in August 1945, they committed the new government to a grand agenda. The constitution they adopted that month, and in effect today, declared employment, education, and a decent life the right of every citizen. The state would care for the poor, look after waifs, and control and use the nation's resources to bring about prosperity. Based on faith in One God, the state would also guarantee freedom of religion (*agama*) or religious belief (*kepercayaan*).[5] To implement these broad designs, the constitutional convention acclaimed Sukarno president, Mohammad Hatta vice-president, and gave them on paper eleven ministries to work with.[6]

At this convention a coalition of Christians and nominal Muslims — for Islam is a majority in Indonesia only in name — thwarted the Muslim leaders' hopes of founding an Islamic state. But once the armed struggle for independence had begun, a united front became imperative. In January 1946 the Muslims won what they had lost the previous August: a twelfth ministry, the Ministry of Religion.[7]

Because of the breadth of Islamic law and the sheer scope of human activity the new department was supposed to regulate, and because Islamic organizations, especially the Muslim Teachers' party (Nahdatual Ulama or NU), controlled it and used it as a place to employ the politically faithful, the Ministry of Religion increased rapidly in size. By 1971 it had become the largest of all the ministries. Fully one-third of all Indonesia's half-million civilian departmental employees worked for it. Education and culture accounted for another third, while fifteen much smaller ministries divided up the remainder (Biro Pusat Statistik 1972*a*: 60-61).

Sukarno's years: "Jobs for the boys"

The growth of the rest of the bureaucracy has been only slightly less hypertrophic. From some quarter-million employees in 1940 (Geertz 1956*a*: 14, n. 118), it swelled tenfold to two and a half million by 1968, the eve of Suharto's first five-year plan (*Warta Berita* August 18, 1968 [AB]). Spurring the expansion was an image of government not only as promoting welfare indirectly through its programs but as a stock of money and status to be shared directly by its incumbents.

After independence had been won and a unitary republic established in 1950, and as political parties organized and competed in national and local

---

Hart 1932: especially 333; Vandenbosch 1941: 168-71. The estimate for 1940 is from Geertz 1956*a*: 149, n. 118. Data on Japanese personnel policies are scarcer, but see Hatta 1971, especially Frederick's introduction.

5. *Undang-undang Dasar 1945,* preamble and parts X-XI and XIII-XIV. *Agama* and *kepercayaan* appear together only once in the constitution, in article 29.

6. The most complete available record of these decisions and the debates surrounding them is Yamin 1959: 453-68. The ministries were home affairs, foreign affairs, defense, justice, finance, economy, health, education and culture, social affairs, communications, and information.

7. Emmerson 1972: part II.B, especially 159-91, recounts the fate of the Islamic state in the August debates; see also the references therein. On the birth of the Ministry of Religion and its subsequent development, see Lev 1972: 43.

elections in the mid-1950s, the idea that government should improve the
people's lot became widespread and unassailable. Hopes were high and government expanded to meet them. Bureaucratic penetration of the economy increased sharply in the late 1950s with the nationalization of Dutch enterprises.
Political and military occupation of the bureaucracy also increased. Victorious
parties settled themselves into "their" ministries – NU in religion, the PNI
(Partai Nasional Indonesia) in home affairs and information – and sought to
enlarge these bases of patronage and power. The armed forces also spread their
presence and raised their budgets through successive campaigns to defeat Islamic
and regionalist rebellions, to recover West Irian from the Dutch, and in confrontation with Malaysia. In parts of the Outer Islands, martial law meant virtual
army rule.

The Communists' stake in government also rose, although aside from a
certain strength in local, especially municipal administration, the PKI was not so
well entrenched as the statist NU and PNI or the military. As these various
groups jockeyed for influence, bureaucratic inflation became an expedient way
of cushioning conflicts among them; so did government spending, which contributed to rampant economic inflation in the 1960s. Sukarno sat in the middle,
feeding these conflicting appetites for position to keep them in some kind of
balance and to reassert his own indispensability in the process.

In 1956 Sutan Sjahrir, prime minister for a time in the revolutionary
republic, wrote that "the administration is overstaffed for its task" and disapproved of the "large amount of state interference in economic affairs, inherited
from the Dutch." By the early 1960s his judgment had grown more severe. He
saw an outright "breakdown in administration," for which

> it's not a bit of use our continuing to blame the Dutch. Before the war
> there were 40,000 civil servants. Now there are more than a million. They
> get in each other's way and slow everything down. But, in effect, they're
> on the President's payroll. You would call his policy one of "jobs for the
> boys."[8]

Sjahrir was not the only ex-official in the mid-1950s to argue that
deflating the bureaucracy would improve its performance. A former finance
minister, doubtless seeing a need to shift budgetary priorities from maintenance
to development, said the rolls could be cut by a third; a former minister of
communications described the surfeit of personnel in the government-owned
railway system, where there were twelve officials per kilometer of track, as a
case of "more meat than brains" (van der Kroef 1956: 129). Sukarno himself
denounced the "strangling bureaucracy" as a confounder of good relations

---

8. The first quote is from Sjahrir 1956: 119; the second is from Stevenson 1963:
45. Sjahrir's figures are too small, especially the first, but also the second: one source
in 1955 gave a figure of 1.8 million, another in 1962 counted 1.2 million. The 1955
source is the U.S. Labor Department's Bureau of Labor Statistics as cited by Fagg
1958: 202 and n. 79; the 1962 figure came out of a census of civil servants run that
year and may itself be an underestimate.

between Jakarta and the provinces (*Antara* news bulletin, New York, April 30, 1957, as cited by Fagg 1958: 202). Yet the rolls continued to lengthen. Budgets were not reallocated away from routine expenses, little was done to raise quality over quantity, and the one experiment in decentralization was abandoned with the outbreak of civil war late in the decade (Legge 1961; Maryanov 1958).

By the late 1950s, foreign firms had been taken over by the state, an enlarged educational system was producing fresh waves of applicants for government jobs, and the effects of party competition were being felt throughout the administration. All these things helped inflate the bureaucracy. In 1959 and 1960 Sukarno dissolved the nation's elected deliberative bodies and replaced them with wholly appointed ones. Departments and agencies proliferated. By the time of the attempted coup on October 1, 1965, there were ninety-three ministers, more than eight times the number laid down by the constitutional convention twenty years before.[9] Sukarno's political economy was geared to short-term expenditure and consumption rather than long-term savings and investment, and it operated without either a strong center capable of making patronage-depriving decisions or a strong antibureaucratic cultural tradition. A proliferation of monuments, speeches, uniforms, and circumvented regulations, Guided Democracy was a prime example of Gunnar Myrdal's "soft" or undisciplined state (Myrdal 1963).

Cultural Explanation, Historical Continuity, and 1965

Facilitating bureaucratic gigantism in Indonesia is the prestige value of a government career in the eyes of many Javanese, whose ethnic group makes up around half of Indonesia's population and more than half of her public employees. Classical Javanese political culture was hierarchic and concentric. Unconditional respect was owed to one's teachers, one's king, and one's parents, while the living core of society was the *negara.* Today the latter term, referring both to the royal palace-capitals that survive from Java's imperial past (among them, the Mangkunegaran in Solo) and to the Indonesian nation-state (*negara Indonesia*), reexpresses an old notion in a new form. In the words of a Javanese psychologist, "the Javanese are still inclined to serve the state" — in the double sense, he might have added, of wanting to become civil servants and readily deferring to those who already are. (On Javanese authority figures, see Selosoemardjan 1965; the quote is from Hardjoprakoso 1969: 1-2, as cited by Smith 1971a: 26.)

Nor is this predilection an irrational quirk. It made practical sense under the Dutch, who made government more powerful, practicing bureaucratic capitalism and subsuming politics under administration, and who made nonbureaucratic careers less attractive, allowing a racially and religiously alien minority (the Chinese) to become the commercial elite.

From this double standpoint of sheer cultural inertia and the structural

9. Ministerial positions actually numbered 104, but eight individuals held 2 such posts and one (Chairul Saleh) held 4. I have used the list in Finch and Lev 1965: App., 6-12 and 13, n. 2.

limitations of a colonized patrimonial polity, it would not be hard to draw a picture of the bureaucracy stressing its persistence through time. It could be said that the precolonial king's servants (*punggawa*), the colonial rulers of the realm (*pangreh praja*), the post colonial tenders of the realm (*pamong praja*), and today's civil servants (*pegawai negeri*) have more in common than not, especially their deferential style, and that they continue to consume resources more than developing them. In much of the literature on Indonesian government, just such a stress on historical continuity and on cultural limits encourages skepticism toward any possibility of change.[10]

The choice between continuity and change is in part the equivalent of an aesthetic choice, say, between yin and yang; one cannot talk of one but in relation to the other. But it is also an empirical matter to the extent that significant change has taken place. I think it has. Compared to what it was during the first two decades of independence, the bureaucracy today is less inflationary in size, less dispersed in its loyalties, and more able to act. For the political context of administration in Indonesia, 1965 was a watershed.

Purging the Old Order: A "Blank Check" against Breakdown

By 1965, not even Sukarno's rhetoric could conceal the social and economic rifts opening in the countryside or the damage to political stability dealt by hyperinflation in the cities. Rumors of coups circulated amid signs that the president was ill and might not be able to continue to manipulate the situation safely. On the night of September 30, ostensibly to forestall a right-wing military takeover, leftist officers with links to the PKI prepared to assassinate a number of anti-Communist generals including the army commander. The next day, after the killings, then Major General Suharto took charge of the army. Within six months he had acquired in writing a broad mandate from Sukarno to restore order and security.

With this "blank check," Suharto destroyed the PKI and made the army the most powerful political force in the country. Meanwhile, offically tolerated if not sponsored anti-Communist reprisals were underway on an unprecedented scale. Between a tenth and a quarter of a million accused leftists died, possibly more, not to mention victims of arrest and ostracism. All these events created three conditions with regard to the bureaucracy that had never before existed at the same time to the same degree: a blanket reason to cut personnel, the coercive capacity to do so, and a crisis atmosphere in which ends could be made to justify means.

With the plotters in disarray, public revulsion over the generals' murder rising, anti-Communist students in the cities denouncing the PKI, and the decimation of the party itself in full swing in the countryside, it became clear that Sukarno's revolutionary troika — nationalism, religion, and communism (NASAKOM) — was coming irreversibly apart. As this realization spread through

10. The stress on continuity is evident, for example, in Willner 1970; Benda 1966, 1965. Among authors who have used cultural explanation to advantage are Benedict Anderson, Bernard Dahm, Clifford Geertz, and Soedjatmoko.

the bureaucracy in 1966, accelerating in March when Suharto used the mandate he had just obtained from Sukarno to dissolve the huge cabinet and arrest leftist ministers, a deadly bandwagon reaction set in. So many civil servants were dismissed or arrested on charges of complicity in the coup group, now called the "G30S/PKI" ("30th of September Movement/PKI"), that the conspiracy could not possibly have kept its plans secret, not if all those accused of knowing about them in advance actually did. It was a time of lists. Not only did the names of targeted leftists circulate, but it became a matter of some pride to surviving officials, especially those with vaguely suspect pre-1965 connections, that their names had cropped up on rosters of intended victims reportedly drawn up by the PKI around the time of the coup.[11]

Whether the assassination lists were real or not, the counterlists of suspected leftists definitely were. Screening boards were formed in each department to sift the political sympathies of its employees. A central investigating team in the Department of Defense and Security coordinated the effort. Official accountings I saw in 1968 showed 23,520 persons mustered out of the bureaucracy under one guise or another in 1965-1967, about 1.5 percent of the million and a half public employees on whom data were gathered. But this figure is incomplete — excluded, among other categories, were the armed forces and state corporations — and probably sharply underestimates the case even among civil servants who were covered.[12] How many thousands were killed or fled before they could be denounced by their colleagues one can only guess.

The figures I did see showed that among departments, agriculture was the hardest hit, which fits a picture of leftist strength in that sector: The largest farmers' organization (Barisan Tani Indonesia) was a PKI affiliate, while in the department itself, left-wing PNI influence was strong. The most affected provinces, measured by the percentage of central government employees laid off in each, were Bali, East Java, Lampung, and West Sumatra, and this too jibes with local political patterns.[13] If the true extent of the dismissals were known,

11. I say "reportedly" because I was never given adequate proof that these latter lists existed. But they were mentioned frequently in my interviews with officials and politicians in 1968-1969. A typical informant had not himself seen the death list carrying his name but had been told of its existence by a friend "who would not lie to me." The way these experiences were related leads me to believe that most of them were shaped in whole or in part by the need to prove distance from a pariah group.

12. The figure was calculated from information scattered through two long reports by the minister of manpower (nos. 3625-013/DSPP/67 and 4496-020/DSPP/67 dated September 30 and November 29, 1967, respectively), which are sources for the next paragraph too. Ironically, three-fourths of these civil servants were fired on the authority of the "Crush Malaysia Command" (Instruksi Kogam no. 9), an Old Order military structure put to a purpose Sukarno never intended it to serve.

13. On the Department of Agriculture, see Hansen 1973: 51-52. In Bali the PKI had been struggling with the PNI before the attempted coup; afterward much blood was shed. In East Java Muslim landowners hunted down the radicals who had been seizing their land. West Sumatra also experienced a sharp Muslim reaction, though with fewer leftists to round up. In Lampung too the PKI had made its presence felt, especially among immigrant Javanese plantation workers.

however, including figures for regional employees, Central Java and North Sumatra as centers of PKI strength probably would also rank high.

An illustration of the way in which political purging and administrative reform were combined at this time is cabinet presidium instruction no. 11 of 1967. Aside from requiring all government agencies to break relations with personnel involved in the "G30S/PKI," instruction 11 provided for compulsory retirement at age fifty-six, automatic firing of employees unaccountably absent for three months or more, reassignment of staff from one agency to another according to workload, and better discipline through observance of office hours. From my admittedly limited observation in 1967-1969, these provisions were implemented, in the order listed, with roughly declining zeal. Not even proved corruption could lead to a legally dishonorable discharge from government service; only declared involvement in the "G30S/PKI" could do that.[14] The political purge became a handy excuse to reduce the bureaucracy's bulk.

Measures against inflationary spending also had an impact on the bureaucracy. Higher- and lower-grade civil servants were paid only half and three-fourths of their salaries, respectively. Emergency imports of American bulgur wheat partly replaced subsidized rice as a payment in kind. In the first seven months of 1967 requests were submitted for the firing of some 20,000 employees in overstaffed and inefficient public corporations that had long run in the red despite (or because of) government subsidies. By late July half of these had been granted (Department of Manpower 1967a: 6), and what was left of organized labor could not object for fear of attracting the fatal "G30S/PKI" label.

Recruitment was curbed through a freeze on new hiring and the requirement that applicants produce an affidavit of noninvolvement in the attempted coup. As public and private agencies scrambled to act more royally than the king, these certificates were inserted as prerequisites into a whole range of transactions. Years later a child entering school might have to produce proof of his innocence in 1965 even though he or she had been only five years old at the time.

That the government could take such drastic steps — and that it still can[15] — represents a significant break with the past. The authoritarian character of Sukarno's regime did not mean it could get away with anything. On the contrary, the diffusion of responsibility and the spread of cliques throughout the bureaucracy made superiors unwilling to discipline subordinates for fear of the consequences. A bureaucratic patron felt obligated to protect his clients; nor could he keep them to standards he was himself violating.

14. This authority was spelled out in decision no. 28/KOPKAM/10/1968 issued by the head of the Command for the Restoration of Security and Order (PANGKOP-KAMTIB), at that time General Panggabean.

15. In 1973, for example, mass dismissals occurred in finance, public works and electricity, and the state railways. See *Harian Kami*, November 12 (editorial) and December 5, 1973.

These pragmatic reasons for inaction were reinforced by the latent nature of power as conceived by many Javanese: that it is most concentrated in that individual who needs to use it the least. In the 1950s, generalizing from a study by Donald Fagg, persons in positions of authority were ambivalent. They had to behave simultaneously as if they had real authority to do what they wished and as if that were a fiction to be protected from the test of reality.

As Fagg has written of the Javanese subdistrict officer or camat:

> The reason for cultivating and gaining some minimal degree of support from even those of his constituents who can do him the least good is that they can do him the most harm. He cannot rest content with a solid bloc of supporters . . . . What he needs, in effect, is a unanimous vote of confidence in his identity and capacity as Pak Camat [literally, Father Subdistrict Head]. One overly strenuous negative ballot may be his undoing. One unanswerable challenge to the structure of his authoritative capacity may topple the whole edifice. What he is endeavouring to do is to maintain a useful fiction.

The transfer of the parental role to the realm of government also supported this arrangement: a successful father should not have to discipline his children (see Fagg 1958: 565-68). One could say of Sukarno that he was a dazzling performer in this art of government "on tiptoe" (as Fagg called it), brought down by a series of reality shocks in 1965-1967 that not even his "useful fiction" could survive.

At issue in this break with the recent past is much more, of course, than the size of the bureaucracy. In the 1950s and early sixties the bureaucracy had not only grown flabby; it had become unresponsive to direction from above (Feith 1962: 313, 366-73; Feith 1964a: 257). To change it from a political arena into an administrative tool, first its loyalty would have to be ensured.

LOYALTY: THE POLITICS OF CONTROL

Children once learned the letters of the Javanese alphabet with the aid of a mnemonic about a king who sends one retainer to fetch the royal dagger but forgets to cancel his standing orders to another to guard the weapon at all costs. When the two officials meet, the one refuses to surrender the dagger while the other will not leave without it. A fight ensues that ends with the two men killing each other, each one faithful to his instructions. Whereas younger, urban, Western-educated Javanese might find here a lesson in the stupidity of blind obedience, to many of their rural elders the story shows instead the nobility of loyalty unto death.

If in precolonial and colonial days reality already fell short of this cultural ideal, in the bureaucratic explosion of the 1950s the two were distant indeed.

Loyalties were dispersed and personal, linking you to whomever you owed your job — he might be a politician, a general, or a businessman — and obliging you to help him in return. Incoming ministers, of whom there were quite a few in this period of cabinet instability, sometimes restaffed their offices several ranks deep with men they could trust, further impeding the growth of loyalties that were long run, institutional, and career centered rather than merely benefactor specific.

An excerpt from an interview with a bureau chief in one of the smaller departments in 1969 illustrates the situation in the late 1950s and early 1960s:

> A became minister in 195-. He and I had been in the same political party, so he brought me in as head of personnel. A rival political party had been making inroads into the ministry, and he wanted to replace them with people from our party. I was given — secretly, of course — the duty of ousting their people from the ministry and bringing our people in. I did this. [Then, he said, in self-defense:] But I always saw that at least the quality of our man wasn't less than the fellow he was to replace. And anyway, in those days everyone was trying to put people from his own group into government offices. . . . Later, when B came in as minister, the first person he fired was me. Even though we'd worked together years earlier. He called me into his office and apologized, but he fired me. He said it was the wish of the masses. I knew which masses he meant [that is, B's party]. So I left. I went back to A [who had meanwhile become a minister without portfolio] and asked for help. He got me a job, but there was nothing to do; they just added my name to a payroll. I would go to the office and sit around, reading the paper or chatting, before going home again. And the next day the same. For two years.[16]

Especially in the later Sukarno years, surface unity in the bureaucracy was obtained by ritual obeisance to imposed slogans; loyalty was ideologically defined and weak. As political acrostics proliferated — DEKON, JAREK, MANIPOL, NASAKOM, NEFOS, RESOPIM, TAVIP, and so on (see Weatherbee 1966) — paying lip service to them became easier and more meaningless. In 1959, presidential regulation no. 2 forbade all top-category civil servants from belonging to political parties, but it was never seriously applied except to members of the Islamic reformist Masyumi and the democratic socialist PSI (Partai Sosialis Indonesia), which were banned the following year. The PNI, NU, and the military continued to penetrate a bureaucracy the loyalties of whose personnel they diversified and divided.

Negative Allegiance to the New Order:
Between Communism and Islam

Suharto's signal achievement is to have forced all these affiliations into a single, exclusive, and mainly negative mold of allegiance to official organizations

16. Interview, Jakarta, February 20, 1969. The excerpt summarizes notes taken immediately afterward. This man was later imprisoned for six months without trial for having harbored someone with PKI connections — a relative — in his house.

under his control, including the armed forces. You were presumed loyal to the extent that you were not suspected of sympathizing with the PKI or the regime that had allowed it to prosper. Suharto did not organize displays of public solidarity in part to draw the sharpest contrast between his style and the emotional extravaganzas in which citizens had proclaimed themselves supporters of Sukarno "without reserve." In its early years, the New Order — its name alone professed change — tried hard to be a negative of the discredited Old.

For a time, religion underscored the difference. So long as its victory was still hypothetical, the New Order needed Muslim support. Conversely, the stronger the generals' grip, the more they felt they could exercise their old suspicions about where organized Islam's loyalties really lay. Because the fate of political and bureaucratic Islam became a case study in the politics of control, it merits special attention here.

Islam ascendant, Islam eclipsed

In 1965-1966, leaders of the banned Masyumi, the opportunistic NU, and the militant Islamic Students' Association (Himpunan Mahasiswa Islam) entertained high hopes. Ideologically as theistic opponents of godless communism and politically as participants in the anti-PKI pogrom, especially in East Java and parts of Sumartra, they looked forward to an anti-leftist regime that would accommodate Islam.

Symbolically, they did well. Religion was given an expanded ceremonial role. Public references to God and to belief in God became more frequent. A decision (no. 27/1966) of the Provisional People's Consultative Assembly (Majelis Permusyawaratan Rakyat Sementara or MPRS) made religious — in practice, mainly Islamic — instruction compulsory in public and private schools from primary through university levels. The closing of the canteen at Parliament during the Muslim fasting month for the first time in memory in 1968 was a small sign of the times.

In this auspicious climate, the Department of Religion, still under NU control, quietly increased its strength. In 1967-1971, when most departments were either holding the line or reducing their personnel, religion increased its complement by an astonishing 60 percent to 162,872 employees, edging out education and culture to become the nation's biggest ministry.[17]

Religion had by far the highest rate of growth of any comparable department during this period — and probably any period from 1958 through 1971. The accretion of personnel in a few other ministries in 1967-1971 followed their absorption of new responsibilities; the Department of Communications, for

17. Education and culture increased over the same period by only 2 percent. From 1958 (26,868) to 1963 (34,832), religion registered "by far the greatest rate of growth [30 percent] among larger departments." Its rate then rose steeply to 192 percent between 1963 and 1967 (101,536). The 1967 and 1971 figures are, respectively, from "Djumlah Pegawai Negeri/ABRI/Sipil ABRI/Pensiunan dan Pegawai Daerah Otonom pada Achir Th. 1967 KBN/DSPP" dated April 24, 1968, and Biro Pusat Statistik 1972a: 60-61. Religion's 1958 and 1963 figures are from Central Bureau of Statistics materials as cited by Lev 1972: 52, n. 40, where the quoted comment also appears.

example, added a directorate general for tourism, incorporating staff already employed elsewhere. But because religion's basic structure and duties remained unchanged, its expansion was less defensible.

In the end these upward trends mattered little. Far from increasing their leverage, both political and bureaucratic Islam in Suharto's Indonesia have been eclipsed. Suharto and the generals on whom he relies were brought up in a Hindu-Javanized milieu that made them more nominal (*abangan*) than practicing (*santri*) Muslims. Nor have they forgotten the threats to national unity they saw coming in the forties and fifties from militant, separatist Islam as well as the PKI, threats they had been called on as army officers to quell in the name of the nation. To forestall disruption from either source, army spokesmen of the regime in the late sixties and early seventies posed a symmetry of dangers from the extreme (PKI) Left and the extreme (Islamic) Right.

The regime first moved decisively against Islam's old party base, refusing to rehabilitate Masyumi and interfering in attempts to form a successor organization. After defeating them in the July 1971 elections, the government herded the Islamic parties into a single enclosure. Not even permitted to call itself Muslim, this new assemblage — the Development Unity party (Partai Persatuan Pembangunan or PPP) — held merely a fifth of the seats in Parliament. (On these events, see Samson 1968, 1971-1972, and 1973, as well as chapters 6 and 7 in this volume.) Because the goal in this first phase was to suppress or domesticate Muslim leaders and organizations that might revive the issue of an Islamic state, the accommodationist NU emerged relatively unscathed, notwithstanding official interference in its December 1971 congress.

But the abangan generals soon moved directly against Islam's bureaucratic base as well. In September 1971 an eighteen-year tradition of uninterrupted NU influence in the Department of Religion was suddenly broken with the appointment of a "religious technocrat" as minister, Professor H. A. Mukti Ali, a man unaffiliated with any political party (*Tempo,* October 2, 1971; Lev 1972: 259-61). Although he was not expected to preside over the actual dissolution of Islam's bureaucratic empire, he was expected to shape it up (the Indonesian word *penertiban* describes almost any steps to "take care" of a situation) by bringing it more firmly under the control of Suharto's governing alliance of officers and experts.

One of the first things the new minister did was to rein in the beast. In the first three months of 1972, if one can believe the figures, the department actually shrank by 5 percent to return to second place in size beneath education and culture. This may represent the first instance of a reduction in personnel in the history of the Department of Religion. A year later, the department's development budget was cut by one-third, from 1.2 million Rupiahs in 1972/73 to 800 million in 1973/74. In 1973/74, for example, state subsidies to private religious institutions were eliminated. A Muslim newspaper in Jakarta reported rumors, unfounded as it turned out, that the department would be dissolved.[18]

18. Religion employed 154,432 persons as of March 31, 1972. The figure appears in a listing for other departments as of December 31, 1972, along with a note that

Further defeats

In 1973 three focal points of change affecting bureaucratic Islam were religious symbolism, religious education, and religious justice. In March the People's Consultative Assembly (Majelis Permusyawaratan Rakyat or MPR), incorporating the new Parliament formed from the 1971 elections, laid down a set of guidelines for state policy (Garis-garis Besar Haluan Negara or GBHN) as a mandate for Suharto to execute until his current term as president expires in 1978. The GBHN was a triple defeat for Islam. Whereas at its previous meeting in March 1968 the provisional assembly (MPRS) had been deadlocked over religious questions, no such stalemate blocked the work of the 1973 MPR: Muslim spokesman in the latter body were fewer and weaker, the secular-abangan regime stronger, and the atmosphere less favorable.

First, symbolically, the MPR undercut Islam's position by describing the Indonesian people as "embracing and upholding a variety of religions and beliefs about God the One" and by referring repeatedly to "religion [agama] and belief [kepercayaan]" as if the two had equal status. Whereas the more precise term *agama* meant a world religion with an organization, a holy book, and certain behavioral rules, the addition of kepercayaan legitimated a whole heterodoxy of notions of the Almighty, including abangan mystical beliefs that are anathema to santri Muslims. By repeating and even capitalizing both words, the GBHN formula went much further than the constitution in seeming to legitimize any nonpolytheistic belief in God. The Muslim PPP resisted the phrase in the corridors, but had to give in.[19]

Second, the 1973 MPR stressed religious freedom and interfaith coopera-tion, rather than prescribing religion as a foundation of development as the 1966 MPRS had done. Over these issues in 1973 Muslim leaders found themselves pitted against the government's military-civilian alliance of functional groups, GOLKAR (for Golongan Karya). Between a GOLKAR plan to abolish the teaching of religion in the schools and the Muslim hope on the contrary to reaffirm the 1966 MPRS declaration of religious instruction as basic to their curriculum, the MPR in 1973 tilted toward GOLKAR. Although falling short of

---

because of the continuing "penertiban" in religion no more recent assessment of its size was available (Manihuruk 1973: 16-18). The only other decline recorded for 1971/72, in the tiny Department of Trade, was so slight (1 percent or forty-four persons) that it could reflect a mere error of enumeration. The 1971 figures for comparison are from Biro Pusat Statistik 1972*a*: 60-61. On budget cuts, the rumors, and criticism generally, see respectively *Abadi,* January 4 and 22, 1973, and Soleiman 1972.

19. *Ketetapan MPR No. IV/MPR/1973 tentang Garis-garis Besar Haluan Negara* [henceforth GBHN], chap. II.*E*.1.*b* and passim; *Tempo,* March 31, 1973. Addressing the MPR ten days before the assembly adopted the GBHN, Suharto remarked that Indonesians "follow differing religions and beliefs." (The speech, delivered on March 12, 1973, was reprinted in full in *Suara Karya* as "Pidato pertanggungan jawab . . ." not long afterward.) To give kepercayaan a national organizational base, a conference of mainly abangan mystical groups (Musyawarah Nasional Kepercayaan) was convened in December 1970 and a second was held four years later with moral and material support from the president (*Sinar Harapan,* May 16, 1974; *Indonesian Current Affairs Translation Service Bulletin* [1974], p. 862). Also see C. Geertz 1972.

abolition, the GBHN no longer actually required religious instruction even in government schools.[20] Also against the wishes of Muslim politicians, the MPR revoked decision no. 27/1966, which had lent symbolic importance to the role of religion and to Islam as the religion of the majority.

Third, and virtually unnoticed at the time, the GBHN provided for the unification of law "in certain sectors." One of those sectors turned out to be marriage and divorce, previously a matter regulated separately in the Muslim case by the Department of Religion through a panoply of courts applying Islamic law. For later that year the government submitted to Parliament a uniform, national marriage and divorce bill that provided no role whatever for religious courts, instead laying down terms in part contrary to Islamic law and enforceable entirely by the secular judiciary. If enacted, the draft law would have virtually deprived the directorate of (Islamic) religious justice, one of the largest in the Department of Religion, of its reason for being.

So vocal and pained was the outcry from Muslim leaders this time that the army eventually abandoned the secular intellectuals and Christians in GOLKAR and worked out a compromise bill far less devastating to Islam and the Department of Religion. But even in this bill, now law, religion is once again qualified with the escape phrase "and belief" and every ruling by a religous court will have to be "strengthened" by the secular judiciary.[21]

This bill was adopted by Parliament in December 1973 and signed into law by the president early in January 1974. But the necessary clarifying decree was not issued until April 1975 and the law did not actually come into effect until the following October. This lag of nearly two years between approval and activation, normal delay aside, shows how reluctant the government was to resolve the law's ambiguities. For if favoring Islam might enable it to refurbish its bastion in the Department of Religion, undercutting it could trigger protests and demonstrations like those that had greeted the original draft bill. In the end, the regime followed a strategy of "something for everyone" — including secular civilians in GOLKAR (especially women's organizations opposed to polygamy and easy divorce), abangan generals eager to sanction Hindu-Javanese "belief" as a legal alternative to Islamic "religion," Muslim leaders resentful of any secular usurpation of the roles of Islamic courts, and non-Muslims anxious for guarantees that they could continue to marry and divorce beyond the jurisdiction of those courts.

In general, Muslim loyalties to the regime have been less sought after then

20. GBHN, chap. IV.D.b; *Tempo,* March 31, 1973. The Department of Religion will feel most deeply any future reduction in religious instruction. About 70 percent of its budget is spent on Islamic education (Lev 1972: 261), much of this presumably for teachers' salaries. By the department's own admission, only about half of these teachers are active, and they are concentrated on Java out of proportion even to that island's population (*Merdeka,* January 28, 1974).

21. The draft bill was reprinted in *Sinar Harapan,* September 3-6, 1973; among published editions of the actual law is Saleh 1974: 85-116; the quotes are from articles 2(1) and 63(2). For details of the marriage bill controversy, see Emmerson 1976: 228-46.

engineered. Leaders have been cultivated and parachuted into power in Muslim organizations, leaders who were willing publicly to renounce the idea of an Islamic state and to speak instead of enlarging Islam's contribution to social and economic development. In 1974, after banning the sole surviving Muslim daily in Jakarta, the regime brought out an "Islamic" replacement among whose editors figures a man whom the abangan generals around Suharto had maneuvered into office in the PSII (Partai Sarekat Islam Indonesia) the previous year. Meanwhile yet another purge of suspected leftists quietly shook the universities and corporations.[22]

In short, bureaucratic transformation in Indonesia has meant the cutting of links and the clearing of space around the regime. That at the last minute the army compromised on the marriage bill shows it has not isolated itself completely. But that it did so only after the Muslims threatened counterforce shows how coercion in the name of stability can be self-undermining.

"Departyization"

One by one, student, youth, labor, and peasant organizations have been detached from the mother parties that used to feed them and have been allowed to break up for lack of funds or to reattach themselves to GOLKAR as the sole legitimate grouping of nonparty "functional" (categoric) associations. By the time of the election, some two hundred organizations were sheltered under GOLKAR's banyan tree symbol. In 1972 alongside the Islamic PPP, the Christian and nationalist parties announced plans to fuse into an Indonesian Democratic party (Partai Demokrasi Indonesia or PDI); by 1973 the MPR could declare that only three groups would compete in the next general elections, to be held in 1977: the PPP, the PDI, and GOLKAR.

As the parties were manipulated, defeated, and combined, steps were also taken to insulate the bureaucracy from their influence. At first, in 1966, Sukarno's presidential regulation no. 2/1959 outlawing party membership for senior civil servants was reactivated. But by mid-1967 only a bit more than a tenth of the roughly 30,500 employees affected had reported the status of their party affiliations (Department of Manpower 1967). In the end the regulation was not actively enforced. New Order leaders may not have felt strong enough to apply it; Sukarno was president until March 1967 and Suharto did not acquire the title for another year. The generals also may have been embarrassed to revive a measure of an Old Order against which they were then trying hard to establish their identity.

"Departyization" moved into high gear as the 1971 elections approached.

22. By 1974-1975, the operative charge was no longer "involvement" but "an indication of involvement." Any sign of any association with a PKI-sympathizing organization was prima facie grounds for screening an employee. In east Java, firms were given long lists of workers to fire and deadlines by which they had to fire them. University teaching staffs were also affected. According to a rare press report on the subject in *Masa Kini*, July 22, 1974, a spinning mill in Cilacap in Central Java had until March 1975 to get rid of more than five hundred employees.

As a legitimizing device, the elections that Sukarno had postponed indefinitely would be held, but for control reasons their outcome would have to be assured: a victory for GOLKAR over the parties. That job fell in large part to two generals, Minister of Home Affairs Amir Machmud and presidential advisor Ali Moertopo; while the latter spearheaded GOLKAR's election campaign, the former worked to transform the territorial administration, from governors down to village chiefs, into GOLKAR's single greatest electoral asset.

It would be misleading to call the effort to ensure loyalty to the government "depoliticizing." Not only have attitudes toward administrative reform been politicized, as already noted, but also attitudes toward more mundane things like crime, urban poverty, and accidents in public installations. Throughout the New Order the PKI has been blamed for stealing telephone wire, its agents have been discovered "masquerading as vagrants," and the occasional train wreck or port fire quickly has been called sabotage by officials trying to avoid blame for their own negligence.[23] Likewise, dismantling Islam's party base has made religious questions politically even more sensitive than they were before. Although it is no less ugly a term than "depoliticization," "departyization" is preferable because it is more precise.

The regime has not only tried to deny the parties access to the bureaucracy. Bureaucratic loyalties also have been organized from within. Under a first strategy, armed forces personnel have been introduced to "backbone" a flaccid administration with an exclusive chain of command downward from, and loyal upward to, General Suharto. Under a second, blanket organizations have been created and imposed on employees to secure their undivided allegiance (*monoloyalitas*). Of these two approaches, the first has worked better than the second.

Backboning the Bureaucracy: Officers in Office

Militarizing a bureaucracy by placing officers in its key positions can have contrary effects. Among crucial determining conditions, other things being equal, are the authority of the military, its internal cohesion, and the way its men are inserted into civilian jobs. If the military lacks power and prestige, if it is internally divided, and if its officers are given important posts in peripheral areas beyond constraint by the center, warlordism is a likely result. Militarization of this kind far from consolidating a bureaucracy can tear it apart. But if the army is powerful, prestigious, and united, and if its takeover begins at the top and in the center and then moves carefully down and out, militarization can in principle strengthen a bureaucracy. Compared to the late 1950s, when the army's penetration of the political economy of the Outer Islands exacerbated

---

23. Illustrations are plentiful in the Indonesian press from 1966 onward. Such thefts are more likely the work of ordinary people with economic motives who sell the wire or use it to fashion crude utensils. As for the notion that vagrants are subversives in disguise, a hunted man would seem least likely to walk about as the sort of person most likely to attract police attention — unless, of course, his destitution were involuntary.

strains within it and facilitated a civil war implicating colonels and lieutenant colonels on Sumatra and Sulawesi, army participation in government in the late 1960s and early 1970s more closely approximated these three conditions of success. A fourth condition, of course, is the competence of officers to perform civilian jobs.

Militarization as the placing of officers in government jobs can be represented by a set of curves showing changes in the military's share of such posts at different administrative levels. Along the topmost curve, at the level of the presidency, militarization has been complete: a general (Suharto) has replaced a civilian (Sukarno). Curiously, however, whereas Sukarno enjoyed wearing his honorary military titles and medal-bedecked uniforms, Suharto avoids displaying his own. This irony of symbolic compensation versus camouflage applies, I think, to the two regimes as well — that is, the curves that can be drawn for the lower reaches of government suggest that Suharto has lowered, so far as its visibility is concerned, an increasingly powerful military profile.

The militarization of cabinets is the easiest to chart, for they are highly visible and their members' names and affiliations are readily available. Here the irony of style against substance is strikingly reproduced. The percentage of heads of departments who were officers remained zero from 1945 until 1957, increased to 11 percent in 1957-1958, more than tripled to 37 percent in the first presidential cabinet inaugurated in 1959 under Guided Democracy, and reached an Old Order peak of 41 percent the following year. The figure declined somewhat in 1962-1963 but returned to the 40-41 percent level in 1964-1965. In 1967 Suharto became acting president, but in October of that year the proportion of officer-ministers rose only slightly to 43 percent. In succeeding cabinets the figure declined steeply to 33 percent in June 1968, 22 percent in September 1971, and 18 percent in the second development cabinet introduced in March 1973, returning to 24 percent by 1975.[24]

As officers declined proportionally at the cabinet level, civilian technocrats replaced them. Over the period 1967-1973, while officer strength fell among department heads, civilians with academic degrees increased their share from 38 to 77 percent, and among the latter most could be classified as technocrats in that they also had no party ties.[25] By the second development cabinet, of all twenty-two ministers with or without a department, only one (Adam Malik) was neither a general nor held a higher degree.[26]

24. I have defined "heads of departments" as ministers who held portfolios and whose roles were not merely to coordinate the work of subordinates or advise superiors. The figures through 1965 were calculated from the lists in Finch and Lev 1965; the lists used in reaching the New Order figures were, in order, Secretariat of the Ampera Cabinet 1967; Badan Penerbit Almanak Jakarta 1972: 8-10, 17-18; Badan Penerbit Almanak Jakarta 1973: 25-26; Indonesian Consulate General in Hong Kong 1975: 174-76.

25. A third category, nondegree-holding civilians, declined from 20 percent to 6 percent. Percentages figured using the full cabinet as 100, including nondepartmental ministers, are insignificantly different.

26. The 17 technocrats shared 24 academic titles among them: 8 professorships, 8 doctorates, 4 engineering degrees, 3 law degrees, and 1 terminal master of arts. Over

From the figures for Sukarno's and Suharto's cabinets alone, the logic of the Indonesian armed forces' participation in government would appear perverse: militarization by a civilian, civilianization by a general. The appearance is misleading, however. The military's acquisition of economic and political prominence in the Old Order flowed from events – the nationalization of Dutch enterprise, the civil war, and the campaigns for West Irian and against Malaysia, for example – over which Sukarno exercised only partial control. He did not set about to make the military into an important political force, but he recognized that fact as it happened by incorporating officers into his cabinets. Cooptation rather than exclusion also matched his inclusionary style (Dahm 1969).

As for Suharto, far from civilianizing government, he deepened and expanded the officer-bureaucrat category. Although the proportion of officers at the most public level – the cabinet – has declined, the percentage in important lesser posts – secretaries general, directors general, inspectors general, and the like – appears to have increased or remained high. At these less visible but still crucial levels, a substantial military presence would appear to have strengthened the capacity of the government to implement policy, by toughening the chain of command and by enabling officers to play watchdog roles "underseeing" civilian ministers.[27]

As at the cabinet level, the infusion of officers into regional administration

---

half these men were trained in economics (7), law (3), or both (1), the rest in engineering (2), agriculture, medicine, public administration, and Islamic studies (1 apiece). Of all 22 ministers, over two-fifths (9) studied at one time or another in the United States, a majority of these (5) in economics at the University of California, Berkeley. On the technocrats' backgrounds, outlooks, and roles in Indonesian policymaking, see MacDougall 1975. For an influential if crudely conspiratorial view of these men as brainwashed pawns of the CIA and the Ford Foundation, see Ransom 1973, 1970. By 1975, 3 of the 6 generals in the cabinet, including those without departments, themselves had advanced degrees (Indonesian Consulate General in Hong Kong 1975: 174-76).

27. I reached these conclusions by comparing two personnel lists: Secretariat of the Ampera Cabinet 1967 and Badan Penerbit Almanak Jakarta 1973. Unfortunately, military ranks were omitted from the 1973 directory. The comparison therefore had to be made with the help of persons familiar with the individuals themselves. I did this in several interviews in Jakarta in March and early April 1974. Asked whether the military's subcabinet presence had increased or decreased in recent years, each informant testified to an increase. Informants were selected for their knowledge of the leadership of more than just a few departments. Because of the sensitivity of the question and the number of names on these lists (685 on the first, 739 on the second), I have not tried to compile complete statistics for both periods. For the first period (1967), however, the percentages of officer-officials at the five levels immediately beneath the presidency were, in order, 43 (ministers), 55 (secretaries general), 43 (directors general and inspectors general), 17 (directors and inspectors), and 12 (bureau chiefs). In other words, officers were most concentrated (forming an absolute majority) at the one level (secretaries general) where incumbents were relatively more powerful and less visible – optimal conditions for the quiet but effective and long-term penetration of a bureaucracy. The fact that inspectors general and inspectors were two to three times more likely to be military men than directors general and directors, respectively, suggests the same trade-off between power and invisibility, for inspectors general and inspectors are supposed to exercise internal, including financial, control. For some public perceptions of decision-making among directors general, see Emmerson 1973.

antedates the New Order; in the early 1960s several governors were army men (Jaspan 1967: 14). By 1965 the percentage of governors who were officers had risen to 48, by 1968 to 68 (Crouch 1972: 213), and by the 1970s only a small fraction of those filling the position were civilians. In the words of a contemporary private joke, "Under colonialism, we had a governor-general; now that we're independent, we have general-governors."

Available data, though not always comparable, suggest that the armed forces' penetration of subgubernatorial positions also has increased. Between 1965 and 1968 in a sample of nine provinces (West, Central, and East Java; Jogjakarta; North and South Sumatra; Lampung; South Sulawesi; and West Kalimantan) the percentage of district heads (bupatis) and mayors who were members of the armed forces nearly tripled, from 21 to 59 (Crouch 1975: 525). Among all 271 bupatis and mayors in the country in 1969, 54 percent were officers (Crouch 1975: 526). A year later, 59 percent of all the bupatis in Central Java, South Sulawesi, and West Sumatra were military men (Smith 1971a: 126). In the early 1970s in East Java the military's share of district headships rose from 72 to 84 percent – comparing lists prepared by the Statistical Bureau of East Java (Kantor Sensus dan Statistik Propinsi Jawa Timur 1972: 5-6) for 1971 and by the American consulate in Surabaya for 1973. If an overall trend can be inferred from these data, it runs steadily upward.

Within the officer-bureaucrat category at these various levels, the army's preeminence has been established. Whereas in 1967-1968 the navy, air force, and police were represented with one minister apiece, compared to the army's six, in 1973 all three military ministers were army generals whose loyalty Suharto had rewarded and whom he felt he could trust (Secretariat of the Ampera Cabinet 1967; Badan Penerbit Almanak Jakarta 1973: 25-26). Of the eleven military secretaries general in 1967, ten – 91 percent – were army generals (Secretariat of the Ampera Cabinet 1967). Of 47 military bupatis in Central Java, South Sulawesi, and West Sumatra in 1970, 93 percent were in the army (Smith 1971a: 126); of 24 in East Java in 1971, 83 percent were (Kantor Sensus dan Statistik Propinsi Jawa Timur 1972: 5-6). Most of the army men in district headships were lieutenant colonels.

At the outermost rings of administration, in the subdistricts and villages, militarization takes a slightly different form. Although there has been talk of increasing its autonomy, the subdistrict (kecamatan) remains basically a transmitter, receiving directives from the district (kabupaten) and impressing them, in turn, upon the village (desa). The army maintains its own hierarchy down to and including the villages. Except for patently insecure areas, the office of subdistrict head (camat) generally has been left to civilians. Instead of risking its overextension by replacing these with its own men, the army in 1974 began to give military training to some of the better educated camats (Sinar Harapan, May 20, 1974). Future graduates of this program would receive officer status in the army reserve. The goal of this kind of socialization is apparently to strengthen local administration against any future emergency and to make the camats – who in 1970 numbered 3,060 in the country and 1,520 on Java alone (Biro Pusat

Statistik 1972*a*: 15) — more loyal and responsive to their military superiors in civilian government.

Finally, the armed forces themselves have been reorganized to limit their size, ensure their unity, and establish army control over the whole. Knowing that just as bureaucratic expansion weakened civilian government, expansion of the military would also undermine its unity and control, Suharto has cut back the armed forces from nearly 600,000 men in 1967 to about 420,000 in 1974, and apparently intends to reduce the number still further to around 350,000 by 1979. By rotating regional commanders fairly frequently, he has inhibited the growth of local constituencies; the price of outspoken independence, several generals have discovered, is an ambassadorship.[28]

The competence of officer versus civilian bureaucrats is harder to assess. But military men in government do appear to be a force for change: by social origin, by style, and by institutional identification. In 1968-1969 in a small random sample of the bureaucratic elite (Emmerson 1976), the officers' backgrounds tended to differ from those of their civilian colleagues. The fathers of the military men, for example, were more likely in colonial times to have worked in the private sector than the fathers of civilian administrators, who more often were carrying on a tradition of family public service. By social origin, the officers represented a break in the already mentioned historical chain from pangreh praja to pamong praja to pegawai negeri.

Officer bureaucrats in 1968-1969 were also markedly action-oriented and identified much more strongly with the armed forces than with civilian government. Several had difficulty transferring command styles of leadership that had worked well in military life into the far more amorphous bureaucratic milieu in which they now found themselves. In the army, one of them complained, you gave an order and it was carried out, whereas in the bureaucracy it might just sink down one or two levels and then stop, with nothing done. Another also stressed the need for things to get done; even makework was preferable to idleness among subordinates. Other research done about the same time found that compared to their civilian counterparts, army bupatis appeared more interested in productivity and performance, less obliged to distribute patronage to political or family connections, and more inclined to tour their subdistricts to keep abreast of local conditions (Smith 1971*a*: 128, 138, 242).

My subsequent though less systematic interviews with civilian and military officials in Jakarta and in East Java in 1974-1975 have strengthened these

---

28. The State Treasury and the Department of Defense and Security gave the 1967 figure in their "Klasifikasi Tenaga Kerdja Pemerintah." The estimate for 1974 and the projection for 1979 were obtained from an American military source. According to this latter information, which appears reliable, Indonesian military leaders plan further reductions to around 275,000 by 1989, although that only indicates current intent, not future performance. All these figures include the police. On plans for reducing the armed forces, also see the Jakarta Newspapers *Harian Kami* and *Indonesia Raya* (April 9, 1973) and *Kompas* (July 2 and September 12, 1973), and Chapter 3 in this book, where details of armed forces reorganization also can be found.

impressions. Because they identify so much more strongly with the armed forces, and because the military leads the New Order, officers in office tend to preserve and apply the no-nonsense leadership to which they have become accustomed. Whatever this may mean about the quality of work, work is at least demanded. Because of their higher, prior allegiance, officer-administrators appear less reluctant than civilians to discipline their subordinates. In short, they are not walking "on tiptoe" to maintain a "useful fiction." They are instead moving the bureaucracy toward a pattern of administration that, wiser or not, is more decisive.

In sum, the army's coercive monopoly, its political preeminence, its chain of command and obedience, its career attraction, and the strong identification of its members have made it, relatively speaking, a heavy organization in a soft state. By militarizing the bureaucratic hierarchy, Suharto has been able to make it more of an instrument, less of an arena.

Organizing Officials: Toward "Monoloyalty"

Alongside the selection of military men for public office, bureaucratic loyalties have been organized through a second strategy: conscription. Using his Department of Home Affairs — charged with the "guidance" of domestic politics in Indonesia (*Kompas*, April 29, 1974) — Minister (and General) Amir Machmud has built on a base of previously existing pamong praja associations a structure that incorporates, in theory, all of the nation's civil servants.

The idea of insulating government from politics is not new. It has found support in a succession of pamong praja-centered bodies running back into Dutch times. The three latest chains in that succession — the Serikat Karyawan Dalam Negeri (SKDN), KOKARMINDAGRI, and KORPRI, all centered in home affairs — bear discussion not only because they show growing formal control, but because they rest on an historic consensus between civilian experts and army officers that lies at the heart of the New Order: antipathy to party politics.

In the Ministry of Home Affairs in the last three years of Guided Democracy, the SKDN fought to keep party politics out of territorial administration. The parties and their mass organizations, one SKDN leader told me in 1969, were the natural enemies of good government:

> Whereas they stress social control from the bottom up, we in the pamong praja feel too much of this sort of thing can cause anarchy, especially in a society like ours where people are not yet ready to exercise social control responsibly — for lack of education, among other things. In our situation in Indonesia, an expert professional administrative force is still essential.

Young, civilian, and Western educated, he could have been justifying the whole New Order.

Like other professionals in home affairs, he blamed the politicization and weakening of public administration in Indonesia on the elected Parliament that had voted law no. 1 of 1957 empowering each provincial or district legislature directly to elect a head of government for its region. By politicizing the office of

regional head, argued the SKDN, the 1957 law had encouraged the separatist
ambitions and political quarreling that pushed the country into civil war the
following year. The SKDN wanted all positions of executive responsibility in the
regions filled by appointment from a disinterested center. If the parties controlled these positions schools would not be built where the need lay but where
the strongest party's supporters lived; expertise and rational planning would be
sacrificed to political greed. Or so my informant argued (in interviews in Jakarta
on January 15 and 29 and February 19, 1969).

In December 1966, with the PKI in shambles, antiparty sentiment spreading, and the army's star rising, pamong praja leaders met and grouped all home
affairs-related personnel in a home government functional staff corps (Korps
Karyawan Pemerintahan Dalam Negeri or KOKARMINDAGRI). According to its
founders (Wajong 1967: 186-226), because the parties served their own interests
more than the national interest they had more distorted than expressed the
popular will, yet they had grown so strong that the ruling authority had been
forced to compromise with them to avoid tension, and because of this government had lost respect and grown unstable. Elected party representatives therefore should be limited to only half the seats in the nation's legislative bodies,
national and regional; representatives of functional groups (*golongan karya*),
including KOKARMINDAGRI and the armed forces, should be appointed to fill
the remaining half.

Regional heads too should be appointed, not elected. Expert career professionals (by implication, the pamong praja and the armed forces) should be
given an expanded role in government. They would promote development by
increasing revenue collection and by using the state budget to rehabilitate the
economy and make it more productive. They would guard the population
against power plays by partisan groups. A banyan tree under whose branches the
people could find shelter symbolized government's protective role, while sheafs
of rice and cotton flanking the tree signified its mission to ensure adequate food
and clothing for the population – just as they would on GOLKAR's standard in
the 1971 elections. What is interesting is not only that KOKARMINDAGRI's
ideas became a program for control and development in the New Order, but that
they were spelled out only weeks after the attempted coup. Departyization was
an already available position lacking only the power to realize it.

The 1971 elections further concentrated that power. As they approached,
the pressure to join KOKARMINDAGRI increased. Even village heads were
urged to sign up, although they were in principle neither appointed nor paid by
the government. By December 1970 KOKARMINDAGRI claimed 800,000
members in administration throughout the country; by the following April
GOLKAR had formally committed itself to building "a government structure
that knows only a single loyalty." To that end, according to presidential
regulation no. 6/1970 as interpreted by Minister Machmud, civil servants in all
departments were denied the right to engage in political activity (read party
activity) and were required to show "monoloyalty" to the government (read

GOLKAR). Although the regulation originally had been aimed only at home affairs employees, President Suharto personally approved this broader interpretation and its enforcement. (See Indonesian Student Press League 1972: 75-77, 104; also Liddle 1973.) In 1971 some 600 civil servants who refused to affiliate with GOLKAR were simply fired (*Tempo*, May 24, 1974).

KOKARMINDAGRI's success in rolling out a winning vote for GOLKAR could be seen in the fact that the party suffering the greatest defeat had been the electorally strongest party in 1955 and had enjoyed the greatest bureaucratic base under Sukarno: the PNI. Civil servants apparently shunned the PNI en masse for the safety of the banyan tree. Comparing the 1955 and 1971 elections, despite a 45 percent increase in the voting electorate (all ballots cast), the PNI lost a staggering 4.6 million votes. Proportionally, the loss amounted to 55 percent of the PNI's 1955 poll; among seven other parties that contested both elections, only the tiny Murba party did worse. The Muslim vote in the two elections, on the other hand, decreased by only 1.6 million or 10 percent; NU in particular held its own.[29] This difference in the damage done by GOLKAR, which garnered 63 percent of all the votes cast in 1971, is attributable to the secular-bureaucratic base and thrust of GOLKAR's campaign. Whereas NU had religious roots outside of government, the PNI did not; NU's bastion in the Department of Religion also had not yet been dismantled. (Figures calculated from Alfian 1971a: 9, citing van Marle 1956: 258, and from Lembaga Pemilihan Umum 1971.)

If the SKDN had been limited to home affairs employees, and if KOKARMINDAGRI had spread a much wider net, in November after the election a new organization was created by presidential decision to encompass all civilian public employees in the country, at every level, from national to village government, and in every kind of agency, from public schools to state corporations. This Corps of Civil Servants of the Indonesian Republic (Korps Pegawai Republik Indonesia or KORPRI) was meant to be the sole organization in their lives outside the office.

KORPRI's structure could hardly be more top-down. Its executive council comprises the minister of home affairs as chairman and as members all the departmental secretaries general and the state secretary; as the chairman, the state secretary, and nearly all the secretaries general are generals, army control is guaranteed. The governor is automatically KORPRI chairman in his province, the bupati in his district, and so on, and KORPRI leadership at each level must be approved by the leadership one level higher. Of KORPRI's five objectives, only the last one mentions the welfare of the civil servant and his or her family; the others stress patriotism, discipline, and devotion to duty (see the presidential decision no. 82/1971 creating KORPRI). The second five-year Plan (vol. 3, pp. 30-34) specifies KORPRI's task as regulating the political life of Indonesia's civil

---

29. "Muslim vote" is defined as Masyumi, NU, PSH, and Perti in 1955 and the last three plus the Partai Muslimin Indonesia in 1971.

servants. It seems fair to conclude that KORPRI is more an instrument of control than a manifestation of sincere loyalty to government institutions and
incumbents.

As for GOLKAR, it too is strictly a top-down affair. The following public
outburst by its chairman, Major General Amir Moertono, is an extreme illustration of coercive thinking among its army leaders. He apparently had been
angered by certain unnamed intellectual critics who had disparaged GOLKAR
and had belittled him as "a kid still wet behind the ears" (*anak kemarin sore*,
implying he had neither experience nor popular support).

Now that GOLKAR had won the 1971 election, Moertono told his
audience, its opponents would be fenced off and immobilized:

> Where can they run to? It's as if we were hunting deer, and fenced in the
> whole field. The deer wants to run north? It'll be shot. To the south? It'll
> be shot. To the west? It'll be shot there too. They have no choice but to
> follow us, that is, to save themselves; we'll keep them as pets. Otherwise,
> they'll be butchered. We've fixed all our strategies. We're on the Tokaido
> Line [Japan's express railway]. The others are still on the cane-car line [a
> reference to the narrow-gauge flatcars used by sugar factories on Java].

Moertono admitted that he "was not elected, but dropped by the president"
into the GOLKAR chairmanship. The main thing, he told his audience, was to
ignore the "anti-GOLKAR monkeys." He also urged his audience to "think
rationally. Don't think like peasants."[30]

Such extreme views are not universal, nor has GOLKAR in practice been
so efficiently repressive. But even discounting the rhetoric, GOLKAR and its
component KORPRI are clearly meant to control and cultivate an utterly
reliable civilian apparatus. In an interview with KORPRI Secretary General (and
Brigadier General) A. E. Manihuruk in Jakarta on April 6, 1974, I was struck by
his use of military command analogies to describe his ideas of sound administration – specifically, the planning and execution of the invasion of Normandy in
1944. I asked him whether such parallels were realistic in view of the fact that an
armed force is normally so much more cohesive than a civilian bureaucracy.
That, he replied, is precisely KORPRI's role: to imbue the civil service with the
kind of internal discipline, loyalty, and esprit de corps the armed forces enjoy.

But KORPRI has yet to prove itself. It is still largely coercive: in 1974 the
military bupati of Pasuruan in East Java, KORPRI chairman in his district by
virtue of his position, assembled the organization's members and warned them
he would not hesitate to fire any among them who had voted for one of the two
political parties (instead of GOLKAR) in the last election – if they dared do the
same thing in the next (*Djawa Pos*, February 4, 1974). And coercion is resented:
in the city of Malang in the same province, a civilian KORPRI member did not

---

30. Moertono was speaking to a congress of a GOLKAR member organization in
Sarangan, East Java. My source is the armed forces newspaper *Angkatan Bersenjata*,
June 6, 1972. Nono Anwar Makarim has interpreted the meaning of the speech in
"Indonesia's Next Nationalism," a mimeographed paper written in October 1972
(and later published in *Pacific Community*), pp. 1-2.

conceal his distaste for the forced organization of employees by their employer (interview, May 20, 1974). In towns and villages, KORPRI's presence appears as one more signboard among those already lining the street in front of the village head or camat's office. At that level, it is just another face of official power.

To summarize, the New Order has broken with the Sukarnoist past in its attempts to ensure the undivided allegiance of its employees: the systematic application of departyization, militarization, and monoloyalitas are an original achievement of the regime. Under departyization, it has destroyed objects of competing allegiance or rendered them politically impotent. Sukarno banned Masyumi and the PSI, but he did not try to liquidate their members, Sukarno also tried to regroup the parties and to balance them with functional groups — his plans for a national council and a national front are examples — but he was unable to supersede them altogether.

Under militarization, the new government has backboned its administration with army officers. Under Sukarno, the military also moved into government, but merely as one among many contending groups. Then army penetration of a civilian-led government meant a further dispersal of power, whereas now officer officials under an officer president have accomplished the opposite by making the bureaucracy more answerable to commands from a single center.

Lastly, under monoloyalitas, the scaffolding for the GOLKAR's "government structure that knows only a single loyalty" has been set up. For all Sukarno's revolutionary rhetoric, he really raised only symbolic superstructures to which lip service could be paid while older, more meaningful ties were retained. In this light, his rhetorically radical regime appears far more conservative than Suharto's. Although Sukarno spoke often of "retooling" government to guarantee loyalty, it was left to Suharto to concentrate the power to do the job.

Of these three methods of the New Order, the third has been the least successful. Whereas the army commands strong positive loyalty among its officers, who have volunteered and been selected, KORPRI still only preempts the alternatives for those it automatically enrolls. Indeed the two reflect contrary strategies of organization: While the army is being compressed into a more solid force, KORPRI remains a category more than a corps.

But there are other reasons for identifying with the government for which one works: wage incentives, for example, and the satisfactions of a job well done. They involve neither the curbing of bureaucratic expansion nor the imposition of formal control. They touch instead the analytically much more elusive dimension of bureaucratic activity or performance: the uses to which the tool is being put.

ACTIVITY: THE COSTS OF GROWTH

Activity is a product of ends and means. On the former score, the government's public goals today are vast. From the rehabilitative priority of the early New Order, the government went on to promote economic growth, and in the 1973 GBHN it heavily emphasized distributive justice as well. Even the following incomplete summary of the tasks of government as specified by the GBHN will show just how encompassing and demanding the scope of formal bureaucratic responsibility has become.

According to this document, the government should promote a more equal distribution of the benefits of growth across income groups and regions by taxing wealth, providing credit, promoting cooperatives, making low-cost housing and health care widely available, and by strengthening the position of the economically weak (indigenous) majority as against the economically strong (Chinese) minority. It should speed the expansion of employment opportunity through increased vocational training, more labor-intensive technology, and improved industrial infrastructure to attract investment. It should regulate demographic growth through family planning on Java and Bali and by redistributing people away from these islands. It should improve and expand educational opportunity, protect the natural environment, support traditional culture, guarantee women's rights, encourage a healthy press, destroy subversion, and work for the stability of Southeast Asia. And in order to do all these things it should simultaneously fashion itself into a strong, authoritative, effective, efficient, honest, loyal, obedient, dedicated, and expert instrument of development.

Words are cheap. But if its emphasis on government as an instrument of distributive justice is to be taken seriously, the second five-year plan (1974-1979) places a considerably greater strain on the bureaucracy than the first (1969-1974).

Revenue and Expenditure: Taking More, Doing More

From the first through the last year of the initial five-year plan (fiscal 1969/70 through 1973/74), Indonesia's budget more than tripled in size. Budget increases in this period averaged 63 percent annually, well ahead of the inflation rate.[31] On the revenue side, the ratio of domestic to foreign financing was raised from 2.6:1 to 4.7:1. The ratio of direct to indirect taxes was doubled and its direction reversed, from 0.6:1 to 1.2:1. And although the oil boom was largely responsible for both contrasts — the budget classifies oil corporation taxes as domestic and direct — even excluding oil receipts, direct tax revenue rose faster (272 percent over this four-year period) than indirect revenue (214 percent). Other direct tax revenues, including nonoil corporate and personal income levies, registered increases of between 183 and 271 percent, while in the period

31. In fiscal 1973/74 Indonesia more than tripled the price of her crude oil for export, which allowed an increase in the realized 1973/74 budget by more than a fourth. Press reports of the supplement (for example, *Indonesian Daily News,* May 27, 1974) did not break it down, so I have ignored it. But it means that some of the figures in this and succeeding paragraphs underestimate the growth that has actually occurred. For example, including the supplement, over the first five-year plan the budget actually more than quadrupled in size for an average annual increase of 86 percent. Finally, even the budget as revised upward does not cover certain large receipts and expenditures — involving notably the state oil company and the armed forces. On the oil price rises, see Antara's English-language news bulletin for March 31, 1974 (*AB*).

1969-1973 inclusive, land tax (Ipeda) receipts increased by 149 percent. Early in the first five-year plan the base salaries of officials in the Finance Department, where tax-gathering responsibility rests, were increased ninefold in an attempt to boost revenues and decrease their leakage once collected.[32] This effort to extract more domestic resources stands in contrast to the situation in the late 1950s and the inflationary early 1960s, when revenues declined relative to payrolls.[33]

Direct taxes generally are harder to gather than export, import, and excise taxes because they are not geared to a specific transaction and because they involve many more collection points;[34] rates of their collection are thus rough indicators of (extractive) bureaucratic performance. However, direct taxes are not necessarily less regressive than indirect ones. In an agrarian economy where import and sales taxes are levied mainly on products bought by better-off consumers, the reverse may hold. Rising Ipeda receipts testify to the bureaucracy's systematic penetration of the populace — land taxes were collected from 21.2 million Indonesians in 1971 — but their effect may run contrary to the GBHN's stress on distributive equity by worsening an already skewed income distribution. All landowners must pay the tax, even those with miniscule plots sufficient for only the barest subsistence. (*Average* holdings per taxpayer on Java in 1971 were between four- and six-tenths of one hectare.)

The land tax must be paid in money and it tends to be collected on Java at harvest time when the farmer can be expected to have rice on hand, yet this is the time when his conversion rate (the price of rice) is most disadvantageous (lowest). The poorest areas on Java tend to be those where collection rates are highest, which suggests the role of coercion and fear. Lastly, those who pay the

32. Wages have been used also as a lever to lift productivity elsewhere in the bureaucracy. During the first five-year plan civil servants enjoyed a succession of salary increases; at the outset of the second plan in April 1974, base salaries were doubled and in some cases quadrupled. An inflation rate of around 25 percent annually after 1972 mitigated the boon, however. Wage policy also has been used as a disincentive. A salary supplement geared to the number of children of a civil servant has been limited to three. The actual effect, if any, of these reforms on job performance and family size remains, to my knowledge, unresearched.

33. Basic statistical evidence for this paragraph can be found for 1969-1970 in Biro Pusat Statistik 1972a: 286-87, and for 1973-1974 in *Kompas* May 4, 1974. Because land tax revenues were not included in the national budget until fiscal 1972/73, Ipeda directorate figures for calendar 1969 and 1973 were taken from Booth 1974: 61. The last sentence relies on Smith 1971a: 173 and Biro Pusat Statistik 1968: 330, 334. Government statistics are subject to intentional and unintentional misreporting; budget-making in Indonesia even today is partly a political numbers game. Insofar as the present regime's legitimacy rests on development, for example, officials would appear to have an interest in impressively high figures on development expenditures. Nevertheless, however grossly, the available figures do reflect a real trend toward increased bureaucratic extraction and disbursement.

34. With few exceptions, Indonesian sales taxes are not collected from retailers; to do that would mean policing millions of transactions daily, an impossible task even for this regime. Instead, the tax falls at the point of greatest value-concentration, in the factory, as the items are processed through it; typically the tax official will have an office in the factory complex where he need check only the firm's records of production and collect his levy in bulk.

tax do not necessarily benefit from it, a substantial portion apparently is siphoned off in administrative fees of one kind or another or reinvested in bureaucratic capacity (office buildings and official vehicles), rather than being channeled directly into socioeconomic betterment or being used to improve the quality of administrative personnel. One reason the latter priorities are possible is that taxpayers lack the organizational voice to demand a greater return.[35]

These qualifications suggest that although domestic resource extraction, even excluding oil, has increased under the New Order, the burden has fallen disproportionally on the shoulders of those who are less able to pay and also less able to avoid paying. If it can be assumed that those who own land in the cities are on the whole more able to pay and avoid paying than those who own rural land, then official statistics too suggest that the more vulnerable are being pressed harder: If taxes collected as a percentage of taxes targeted is an indicator of extractive pressure – bureaucratic "capillary action" – then such pressure has been greater on rural than on urban landowners. In the rural case in 1969-1973, tax collection rose from 68 to 106 percent of the corresponding annual target; by 1973 in fact more tax was being sucked up than planned – if one can believe the figures. (Nor were targets ever reduced; on the contrary, for rural land they increased 1.6 times during this period, and in the urban case, starting from a much lower initial goal, even more.) In contrast, receipts as a percentage of the annual target for urban land in these years rose from 58 to 86, a respectable increase but one that actually allowed the inequality between greater rural and lesser urban tax pressure to double – from 10 to 20 percent (based on data in Booth 1974: 61). On the other hand, annual increases in 1969-1973 in the amounts obtained from urban landowners as well as in the rate of extraction compares favorably with the record of the Old Order in 1960-1965, when urban land tax realizations slid to zero despite massive inflation (Biro Pusat Statistik 1968: 331).

On the distributive side of government, relatively large expenditures have been the norm in independent Indonesia; from 1950 through 1965 only once (in 1951) did receipts exceed disbursements. Not until the last years of Sukarno's Guided Democracy, however, did the art of the unbalanced budget reach truly grotesque proportions: whereas budget deficits increased on the average by 35 percent each year in 1950-1955 and by only slightly more (38 percent) annually in 1955-1960, the bureaucracy's rate of descent into the red more than quintupled under Guided Democrary (1960-1965) to an annual average of 200 percent (Biro Pusat Statistik 1968: 327). What is more, the great bulk of official outlays – some 70 percent according to Smith (1971a: 173) – did not promote development directly but was spent instead on food and wages for civil servants, that is, on the bureaucracy's own self-perpetuation.

Aside from balancing its budgets (until the PERTAMINA crisis – see

35. This assessment of Ipeda is based on Booth 1974 and on conversations with Indonesians involved in agricultural policy in Jakarta and Malang in March-May 1974. About 70 percent of Ipeda receipts come from individual rural landholders rather than from holders of urban, estate, forest, or mining land.

following paragraphs), the New Order has managed to spend more, and to increase spending faster, on development than on salaries (see Biro Pusat Statistik 1972*a*: 286-87; *Kompas*, May 4, 1974). Nor have the effects of this activist policy been limited to the large cities. In the single fiscal year 1974/75, the first of the second five-year plan, total planned central government subsidies to build or improve provincial, district, and village roads, schools, irrigation works, and so on (as calculated from Hady 1974: 70) exceeded by 77 percent the level of the previous fiscal year, a rate of expansion well ahead of inflation and higher than the 63 percent average annual boost in total public spending registered during the first five-year plan. Still further increases in subsidies for regional development were scheduled for 1975-1976.

Examples of Weakness in Strength: Oil, Sugar, and Population Control

Undeniably, Suharto's Indonesia has an activist bureaucracy. The quality of its actions, however, is much harder to assess. One cannot logically infer an improved performance from data that prove increased activity; busy governments are not necessarily more beneficent than idle ones and aggregate statistics are by definition acontextual, whereas performance implies success in relation to specific goals, sites, resources, behavior, and so on. Limited space prevents more than a brief review of three important cases — oil, sugar, and population control — that illustrate the theme of weakness in strength. The goals used are those expressed by the regime itself: to promote economic growth while redistributing its benefits more equitably. My point is not to locate the New Order on a scale from success to failure but to identify relationships between what the government is, what it does, and what it says it does.

Oil

Indonesia's economy under the New Order has attained a yearly growth rate of around 7 percent, to cite Bruce Glassburner in this book. The single most important ingredient in that achievement is petroleum, over whose exploitation the state oil enterprise, PERTAMINA, has exercised direct and general responsibility. What appears to be an obvious success story bears a closer look, however, in relation not only to economic growth (the extraction of oil and its sale at a high price to increase national income) but also social justice (the beneficial and equitable spending of that increment in income), for to accomplish the first task is by no means necessarily to achieve the second.

As for growth, the sheer volume of petroleum taken from beneath the soil did increase by more than 60 percent in 1970-1974, although the flow slackened in 1975. A rising world price both stimulated this expansion in the scale of extraction and greatly magnified the financial consequences for Indonesia: From fiscal 1969/70 through fiscal 1974/75 receipts from the export and domestic sale of oil grew by nearly 1,400 percent and enabled a doubling of the relative contribution of oil to state budgets (from 27 to 55 percent) that were themselves expanding rapidly (calculated from data in Adin 1976: 4-5). The impressiveness of these figures is reduced if the "slippage" between what oil earned for

PERTAMINA and what PERTAMINA earned for the state is considered — a loss of well over $30 million in unpaid assessments dating back to the 1950s according to one incomplete accounting by the civilian chairman of the Supreme Advisory Council (Wilopo 1976: 55) — but even then, clearly, oil has made a mammoth contribution to the nation's aggregate economic growth.

The word "windfall", often used to describe Indonesia's profits from petroleum, implies that they resulted from international events beyond the control of the man who headed the state oil enterprise from its formation in 1957 until March 1976, Lieutenant General Ibnu Sutowo. Certainly the industrial world's dependence on oil and the existence and solidarity of the Organization of Petroleum-Exporting Countries (OPEC) were crucial preconditions of success. Much of what PERTAMINA achieved was due not to its managers' skill but to the simple fact that they found themselves sitting on a suddenly more valuable — 400 percent more in the single year 1974 (Wilopo 1976: 55) — pool of black gold. Just how much of that achievement can be explained in this way is harder to say.

General Sutowo's thinking was as expansionary as the value of the unique resource he was supposed to exploit. His plans for PERTAMINA and its role were grandiose: to remake the future and face of Indonesia. He believed that because most of his countrymen could not imagine the vistas he saw, they could not be expected to understand the need for great changes to realize these; thus he tried to use public relations to educate people to accept what PERTAMINA was doing on their ultimate behalf. He objected to foreigners' characterizing Indonesia as poor — he did not want his country pitied or patronized — and in private he ridiculed the beggar's role of the civilian technocrats who journeyed, hat in hand, to Western capitals asking for aid; no foreign donor, rather her own wealth in oil, would realize Indonesia's potential. Because of his power he could get things done, an ability that enhanced his appeal to American businessmen, some of whom liked to say that what Indonesia needed in order to modernize was a hundred more Sutowos — or words to similar effect.[36] In my own view, however, the value-concentrating nature of oil as a resource shaped the general's power-concentrating kind of leadership more than his kind of leadership helped to build up the value of oil as a resource.

Perhaps the earlier stages of an oil industry call for the risk-taking, big-thinking buccaneer, someone who can speed exploration and extraction by circumventing a sluggish regular bureaucracy. But the lack of accountability such a leadership style implies served Indonesia poorly. Just as Sutowo avoided external accountability (see, for example, Tobing 1976: 51), his apparent faith in the inexhaustibility of the resource he managed seems to have encouraged him to ignore internal controls too: thinking big meant spending big; costs and cost overruns might pile up, but the value of oil was still greater and would enlarge

---

36. Unless specified otherwise, sources for this and the next two paragraphs are Sutowo 1974, including my notes on his oral remarks, and conversations in New York and Jakarta over the years.

still faster. PERTAMINA began to look less like a profit-making operation and more like an institution for national development (of a kind), as Sutowo himself described the company. In his eyes, the book-balancers in the Department of Finance were small-minded men; the point was to act, to spend. And spend he did, on motels, restaurants, golf courses, monuments, a convention hall, a steel mill, an airline ... to say nothing of the "extrabudgetary" payments made to highly placed persons for "nonroutine" purposes. This activity catered mainly to middle- or upper-class tastes, however. The munificence of his life-style, Rolls-Royce included, matched the breadth of his horizons, but the latter did not encompass redistributive social justice, which to him smacked of merely shared poverty (see Sutowo 1976).

In the end, the general turned out to be a Texan in Appalachia; his resources proved finite after all. To keep his projects afloat, he borrowed more heavily and on shorter terms from abroad. For a time the mystique of the black pool, augmented by his own reputation, sufficed to quiet his creditors, but their patience wore thin, and he could not pay. In 1976 no one really knew, least of all Sutowo himself, how large his debts were; the figure of 10 billion dollars (mentioned, for example, by A. B. Nasution 1976: 58) appeared to be a conservative guess. As of 1975, according to the civilian minister of mines who had struggled behind the scenes to restrain Sutowo's financial irresponsibility PERTAMINA could not even show a profit. The following year the general was fired by a still higher general, President Suharto, (Mohammad Sadli, cited in *Tempo*, May 22, 1976).

The PERTAMINA fiasco cannot be dismissed as a mere matter of "cash-flow irregularities" or "temporarily insufficient liquidity." Real deprivations were inflicted on large numbers of Indonesians by Sutowo's uncontrolled, capital-intensive, luxury-centered activism. The company's reckless domestic spending doubtless contributed to the trebling of the pace of inflation from 9-10 percent in 1971 and 1972 to 34 percent in 1973 and 1974, although the rate slowed to 17 percent in 1975 (based on the consumer price index for Jakarta). Peasants rendered landless by PERTAMINA's building projects – "beachheads," Sutowo liked to call then – were sometimes not paid at all or sold out at low prices to speculators who had advance knowledge of the company's plans (see, respectively, *Kompas*, March 12, 1976, and Marzali 1976); the latter event shows how power, through privileged access to information, can enhance itself. Critics also could measure the sheer waste of a precious resource – the empty high-priced luxury accommodations, the mechanized estates where rice would end up costing more than it was worth to grow, the fantasy of a floating fertilizer plant, and everywhere high overheads and overruns (see, for example, *Kompas*, April 8, 1976) – by the value of more productive opportunities foregone, as funds were diverted to bail the company out of its debts. On the expenditure side, by the criterion of beneficial development, PERTAMINA performed disastrously.

The political economy of oil in Indonesia is a case of weakness in strength. Sutowo concentrated so much power in his person, made enough timely payments to enough important people, and managed to avoid accountability for so long that he could make large mistakes with impunity. Inside government, the "exclusive centralization" (A. B. Nasution 1976: 57) of responsibility for petroleum inhibited the transmission of information about PERTAMINA's performance to, and the flow of corrective feedback from, the Departments of Mines and Finance, the Central Bank, the National Planning Agency, Parliament, and other institutions. Outside, the press dared not expose the scandal until the government itself had done so; the company's power was a loud noise drowning out communication. That Suharto could in the end simply fire a general whose position seemed impregnable can be interpreted to mean that the New Order is a hard state able to discipline its own, but that Sutowo could get away with so much for so long suggests the opposite.

Sutowo's notion of development focused on physical plant, technology, infrastructure – *bangun*, the root of the Indonesian word *pembangunan* or development, meaning "to build" in a material sense. But bangun also means "to wake up" or, figuratively, to enable millions of individuals to improve their lives through heightened awareness. The latter task is not merely to concentrate value for growth, but to enable people to share in its benefits, and thus to ensure development of a broad popular base. Compared to its success in generating aggregate growth, by this far more demanding second standard, the bureaucracy has not done so well.

The regime's own statistics support this judgment: They suggest that annual economic growth exceeded annual population growth by around 4.5 to 5 percent during the first five-year plan (1969-1974), but they also indicate that farmer incomes rose only about 7 percent over this entire period, and that some 65 percent of Indonesian households practice farming (*Surabaya Post*, April 24 and November 8, 1974, quoting the minister of agriculture). By inference, the incomes of a nonfarming minority of the population, notably the urban middle class, must have risen much faster than those of the agrarian majority. Survey and census data also show increasing inequality of incomes within Java's large cities and between Jakarta and the rest of the island (*Kompas*, February 16, 1976; Esmara 1975; King and Weldon 1975; Hanna 1974).

What of the distribution of value within rural areas and its relationship to public policy? In search of an answer, I will look at local administration in East Java as it has affected the distribution of benefits from one primary foodstuff, sugar. (In this volume, chapters 5 and 11 deal at length with rice.) East Java exemplifies both the backboned bureaucracy and dynamic growth; officers may well hold more of its offices than elsewhere on Java, and in 1974 it was named the best performing of any province in Indonesia during the first five-year plan (*Angkatan Bersenjata*, August 22, 1974). If development with a firm hand works, it should be working here. At the same time, some of Indonesia's worst poverty is in East Java, so the question of equality is starkly posed. Following the case study of sugar, I will briefly review two additional policy areas where redistribution and behavior change rather than mere material increase define success: family planning and transmigration.

Sugar

Sugar in Indonesia is grown three different ways: by the sugar company on its own land or on land rented from farmers, or by the farmers themselves on their own land. East Java alone accounts for about three-fifths of national production.

Demographic pressure has reduced the use of the first method in East Java, but in 1974 the Jatiroto sugar factory in Lumajang district still owned about 6,000 hectares of arable land on which it planted, tended, and harvested cane. Labor for these tasks was drawn in part from a permanently available pool living on this property in company houses in company settlements under company government. The gap in living standards between land-owning farmers in the villages and these agricultural laborers was striking. Estimates of the average daily rate for cutting cane in Jatiroto in 1974 ran from 75 to 300 Rupiahs (roughly 20 to 70 cents) — depending, respectively, on whether my informant was a government or a company official.[37]

Because the company owned their homes and land, the workers were disinclined to make improvements. Their physical settlements as close to the cane as possible (which saved time moving them to and fro) and their lack of transport cut them off from village communities of which they were legally a part. Being on constant call to work in the fields, they might have been unable or too tired to attend village meetings even if the company had encouraged them to do so, which it did not. The fact that company foremen and settlement heads were either the same people or in close cooperation opened the workers to easy abuse. In one settlement, an independent-minded employee with an above-average education and growing popularity was unilaterally "retired" by the company and eventually reduced to accepting charity in food and clothing; in the end, he left to seek work elsewhere.

The distribution of access to government services was also highly skewed. In the company settlements, village development programs were rarely felt, although the company did allow workers to ride its cane cars over its railway to its hospital to receive birth control information and devices. The government's family welfare program was allowed to instruct the women in cleanliness and cooking, but the program chairwoman in each settlement was the wife of the local labor boss, so this activity too stayed under company control. In one informant's words, the sugar factory was a "state within the state" — a PERTAMINA in miniature.

Whereas villagers in Jatiroto were better off than workers, economically

---

37. The field work on which this and the following paragraphs are largely based was done in August 1974. The estimate of East Java's contribution to sugar production is by its governor, cited in *Sinar Harapan,* November 11, 1974. Workers are paid by the amount of cane cut; a wage based on time instead of output, one factory official told me, would make them lazy. Daily rates on coffee, rubber, tea, cocoa, and tobacco plantations in East Java have been knowledgeably estimated as averaging Rp. 150, with a low of only Rp. 35 or about 8 cents (*Kompas,* August 8, 1974); these low wages are maintained despite rising output and higher profits.

and politically, at the top this difference was reversed: the power of the subdistrict officer was dwarfed by that of the factory head. While the managers' homes sprouted television aerials, the camat worried about ways to change the roofing material on the houses of poor people in his district, especially in the settlements, from sugar-cane leaves to clay tiles. Because Indonesian subdistricts are purely administrative units, without the power to tax on their own behalf, it is easy for a large firm that happens to be located in one of them to supplement the salaries of a few subdistrict officials, build the odd hospital, mosque, or school, and leave it at that. Public relations to legitimate an unequal power relationship replace communication and coordination for development – one thinks again of PERTAMINA.

In Jatiroto, as in other sugar areas in 1974, farmers were required to rent their land periodically to the factory for its use during one full sugar cycle of about sixteen months from planting to harvest. The amount of the rent was determined in Jakarta. Although the head of the company in Jatiroto assured me that the farmer did not lose on this transaction, in fact the farmer paid an opportunity cost of at least 50 percent of what he could have made had he kept his land and planted it, say, in rice. Inflation only worsened the farmer's disadvantage, for the rate was fixed whereas the price of the foregone rice was not.

In effect, rice was being sacrificed to sugar, and income was being shifted away from the farmers to Jakarta. (Sugar mills normally sell their output to central government banking and marketing institutions at predetermined prices, and even greater profits apparently accrue at this latter stage than at the point of production.) With world sugar prices high, Indonesian per capita consumption rising, and the domestic supply still insufficient to meet internal demand, the government ordered massive increases in production. Some mills, including the one in Jatiroto, were told to double their output within a few years. Company managers in turn transmitted the pressure of these targets to the rice farmers in two ways: by trying to shorten the interval between the times when a given piece of land was scheduled for company use and by increasing the area in which this system of obligatory periodic rental operated.

Because it was in practice mandatory, the system implicated local government. The village chief guaranteed that the land would be turned over when the time came. Elected by the villagers, he had to try to explain to them why they should do something so obviously against their interests. Sometimes they were told that rental was a patriotic act that would promote development, that sugar was a vital commodity, that dependence on foreign imports had to be reduced, and that in any case the state was constitutionally in charge of all the land in the country.[38] One village chief told me of a poor man with only a tenth of a hectare who begged not to have to turn over his sole means of subsistence, and of having had to apply the law even to him.

38. This rendition of article 33.3 in the constitution omitted the rest of the sentence to the effect that the land should be used to make the people as prosperous as possible.

In 1973 a better-off Muslim landowner in a village in Jatiroto refused to turn over his property when his turn came. When the land was taken anyway, he sued in court, lost, appealed to a higher court, and lost again. As of August 1974 he still had not been paid for the use of his land, even though the cane grown on it had already been milled into crystals at the factory and sold.

Also in 1973, a number of farmers refused to sign rental agreements. They were thrown in jail, where they still refused. One of them, knowing that a previous association with a leftist organization made him especially vulnerable, decided to break ranks and curry official favor by signing the contract. Instead the local army commander made him an example of "PKI infiltration" and struck him in the face in front of the remaining prisoners to show what continued refusal would bring. The man's jaw and the back of the farmers' resistance were simultaneously broken (*Tempo,* August 11 and November 10, 1973). The commander retired from active duty not long afterward.

The forced rental system illustrates the costs in equity of iron-handed growth. Fear of the PKI label makes civil servants reluctant to defend the peasantry, even though many privately sympathize. Farmers are afraid for the same reason, and they lack an organization to express their grievances. Local officials with full knowledge of the inequities around them do sometimes seek redress at higher levels, where power is concentrated and information less adequate, but they are inhibited from doing so to the extent that subordinates are expected above all to meet the targets of production set by superiors and not ask questions. Outsiders and higher-ups do sometimes visit the villages to acquire the knowledge to match their power to recommend or initiate change, but these delegations often operate under severe constraints of time and access.

Complete pessimism is unwarranted. Upward communication does occur. In response to it in 1974, the central government raised the base rental to Rp. 140,000 per hectare from an even lower previous rate at which the farmer's opportunity cost in rice may have exceeded 75 percent (*Tempo,* November 10, 1973). Early the same year a Surabaya newspaper reported without comment the wishes of farmers in Sidoarjo subdistrict to move from fixed rentals to a share of the crop (*Djawa Pos,* February 2, 1974). Late in the year a court in Pasuruan to the southeast appeared likely to convict a village head for renting farmers' land to the local sugar factory without having obtained their signatures first, and for helping himself to a part of the rental money, although the possibility that factory employees encouraged these acts was not raised (*Bhirawa,* November 4 and 12, 1974). At about the same time, a committee of the East Java regional legislature issued a draft memorandum implying that even under the higher rents the farmers' opportunity costs exceeded 50 percent and suggesting that each farmer receive one-fourth of the crystalline sugar milled by the factory from cane grown on his land (*Bhirawa,* November 5, 1974). The latter reform, championed by a police officer in GOLKAR, would certainly raise farmer incomes and make them less vulnerable to inflation. By early 1975, despite sugar company opposition, it appeared likely that shared production between factory and farmer would eventually replace fixed rents, although the crucial question of the size of the shares remained unanswered (interview, Surabaya, February 26, 1975).

The third method, whereby the farmer grows cane on his own, delivers it to the factory to mill, and receives 50 percent of the resulting crystals, also favors the company, which thus avoids cultivation, harvest, and transport costs entirely. In 1974 sugar managers in East Java preferred this system, under which "sugar-minded" farmers voluntarily would grow cane for the company. But the yield in crystals from farmer-grown cane is generally less than what the company could achieve itself. To remedy this, a packaged agricultural extension program is envisaged along the lines of BIMAS for rice. One hopes the difficulties described by Hansen (in Chapter 11) in that case will not be repeated in this one.

Family Planning and Transmigration

In fiscal 1973/74, an estimated 1.4 million Indonesians on overpopulated Java and Bali accepted contraceptive devices for the first time, an increase of 661 percent over the figure for 1970/71; previous acceptors visited family planning clinics an estimated 8.4 million times, mainly to replenish their pills or have their IUDs checked. East Java is the country's largest and one of its most densely populated provinces, so the central government had set for it the highest goal of any of the six participating regions: half a million new acceptors by the end of the fiscal year. But the energetic civilian governor, as if to prove his administration could outperform its competitors, raised East Java's target by another hundred thousand. In the end, even that was exceeded: East Java contributed nearly 650,000 or almost half the grand total of new acceptors that year, and won high praise from the national head of the program (*Surabaya Post*, April 4 and October 22, 1974; Tan 1971: 6).

These figures are impressive. But what do they mean? They may be inaccurate even in their own terms. Money incentives to accept the new devices opened opportunities for local officials to pocket funds and falsify acceptance records. In 1973/74 the only local government in East Java that did not surpass its target was the city of Surabaya. This may indicate a poor performance, but it could mean the opposite, that in the provincial capital records were kept more accurately than in rural areas. Similarly in the early 1970s, of the six provinces enrolled in the program only Greater Jakarta failed to exceed its quota, whereas its record-keeping procedures appeared relatively advanced (Tan 1971: 7).

Certainly the pressure of targets can become a reason either to inflate acceptance figures or to concentrate on inserting the new technology rather than reorienting outlooks and behavior from within the recipient's own frame of reference. The findings of one researcher in a village in the Special Region of Jogjakarta suggest that children in rural Java, far from being an economic drag on their parents, may yield significant economic benefits in productive labor even in the present situation of crowded communities and limited opportunities (B. White 1973). If this is true, then for family planning to succeed in the long run parents must be encouraged to sacrifice a part of their current self-interest for the future interests of their children. Cast in this frame, birth control is not a technical but an economic and psychological problem.

The advantage of contraceptive technology in the hands of a strong state is that it can be forced on people without having to remotivate them, and its receipt offers a neat measure of success. Long-standing attitudes expressed in sayings that correlate children with good fortune may be harder to revise, especially if they are in the short run rational. Even if officials do try to change attitudes – and many undoubtedly do – the results are qualitative and thus harder to use as a criterion of bureaucratic performance compared to the number of devices dispensed.

Each acceptor receives a card proving participation in the program, and these cards are passports to various opportunities. In one subdistrict of East Java's Ponorogo district, for example, without this card one could not plant rice on land belonging to the state forestry company (*Bhirawa,* July 29, 1974). Although such linkages make acceptance a more rational act of immediate self-interest, they dilute its intended meaning. The sincerity of acceptance under these terms is questionable. Under the pressure of targets, many Javanese women have doubtless accepted pills to obtain the card and then simply discarded them or used them but not bothered to replenish them; many condoms have no doubt been received the same way by Javanese men. In some areas, authorities have responded to these evasions by specifying IUDs, which once inserted are not easily removed, but the pill is still by far the most commonly received device – 63 percent of all acceptances nationally in 1973/74 and even higher (66 percent) in the model province of East Java (*Surabaya Post,* April 24 and 30, 1974).

Another official response to overpopulation on Java and Bali, transmigration, is open to the same criticism. Performance is measured logistically by families moved instead of developmentally by their success in adapting to and improving their new environs on one of the outer islands. As with birth control acceptors, drop-outs among transmigrants are statistically invisible. As participants in the program are processed through various stages on Java, they may be taken advantage of by corrupt officials. Promises made before the trip do not always match realities afterward. In the Outer Islands some migrants found that markets for their agricultural products did not yet exist or were inaccessible. In other cases, postarrival services were inadequate or absent, often for lack of coordination between transmigration officials and their counterparts in other departments.[39]

These difficulties are not insuperable, and there are signs the regime is trying to overcome them. In 1974, for example, the president ordered transmigration coordinating boards formed on recipient Outer Islands. But straightening skewed distributions of people or wealth into line with the GBHN will prove far more elusive than the value-accumulating goals of the first five-year plan.

39. All these and other criticisms can be culled from the press coverage of transmigrants' experiences; *Kompas* alone published three series of articles on the subject in mid-May and mid-October 1974 and again in late January 1975.

Summary: Penetration for Growth

Real growth has taken place. Per capita income has risen, though no one knows by how much. Roads have been improved. Hotels and factories have been built. Savings deposits have accumulated. There is little question that upper-middle economic strata are better off today than they were in the inflationary chaos of the late Sukarno years. But the lofty redistributive goals of the GBHN are a long way away. Essentially what has happened is that government has enhanced its capacity to penetrate society but has not yet used that capacity successfully to redistribute the benefits of growth or to create conditions in which large numbers of people will autonomously behave more in some public interest. To increase food production in socially more equitable ways and to limit and redistribute a large population requires knowledge of and sensitivity toward the discrete circumstances of millions of landless laborers, smallholders, parents, and parents-to-be. Were the bureaucracy as responsive as it is strong, such goals would be more easily achieved.

The bureaucracy today is significantly different from what it was in the 1950s and 1960s. It is less a milieu, more a machine. Its inflationary expansion has been checked. Its vertical loyalties have been tightened. It has been running at higher and higher levels of activity. Oil and timber as sources of dramatically rising wealth, the army and the computer as symbols of drastically enhanced control, repression and intimidation as strategies of departyization – all these things have concentrated power. Insofar as Indonesia is no longer a soft state, will its new hardness be used to better the lot of large numbers of poor and powerless people or to keep them quiet, obedient, and finally unrewarded?

POWER AND COMMUNICATION: CONCENTRATION AND CLOSURE

Improved communication between the authorities and the population can facilitate or correct official policy; public relations are important to the first purpose, social criticism to the second. For PERTAMINA, as already noted, General Sutowo stressed public relations. For Indonesia, General Suharto also understands communication in a mainly facilitative sense: '

> Communication is necessary because the people need to know and understand in which direction they're being led. . . . If the people know that the direction being pointed out to them is for their own benefit, if they feel that the steps being taken are also in their own interest, if they are convinced that the people are being led to a better life, then definitely they'll accept government policies that have been laid down and execute them with full awareness and enthusiasm [Suharto 1974].

On January 11, 1974, four days after the president gave this interpretation, a delegation of student leaders read their own view aloud to him. These were their first two points:

> 1. Governmental affairs should be conducted with a leadership that is more open, that enlarges the distribution of authority both horizontally and vertically to avoid centralization.

2. Institutions for channeling public opinion must be strong and function well, and to guarantee maximum popular participation [and] the effectiveness of development, government should consist of both professionals and people who enjoy social support.[40]

Whereas Suharto looked at the population and saw a need for psychologically sincere compliance with elite-determined policies, the students looked at the elite itself and saw a need for shared authority and institutionalized public criticism. Massive demonstrations in Jakarta four days later showed the distance between these two perceptions.

Perceptions aside, the reality of bureaucratic power and communication in Indonesia is, in essence, that the sources of decision-making power and the senders of attention-getting messages tend to be located in one and the same place: the bureaucracy's upper and central reaches.

Top-down Authority

The top-down organization of KORPRI and GOLKAR already have been discussed. Within the bureaucracy itself vertical linkages also run mainly down and out, plugging higher, central policy-makers into lower, local implementing nets rather than encouraging the latter to become more downwardly responsive to local publics and clienteles or more upwardly critical on their behalf. Under the draft bill on regional government submitted by the central government to Parliament in May 1974, regional heads would no longer be appointed from a list of candidates put forward by the regional legislature. Whereas before, in theory at least, partly elected representative bodies structured a choice by higher officials, by the terms of this bill those higher officials would in effect be structuring a choice by even higher officials (Dewan Perwakilan Rakyat 1974).

Before becoming law no. 5/1974 in July, the bill did undergo some changes that showed the minister of home affairs could not expect Parliament to repeat his views verbatim. But the amendments did not alter the law's top-down thrust: for example, although nominations for governor are to be agreed on jointly by the minister of home affairs and provincial legislative leaders, the minister alone is empowered to decide what constitutes agreement (Tambunan 1974: 89). This is vertical government with a vengeance.

Aside from a legal structure that concentrates authority in principle, authority is rarely delegated in practice. Among 551 regional officials from governor's staffs to camats in three provinces interviewed by Theodore Smith in 1969-1970, 44 percent said their superiors "never" (35.4) or "seldom" (8.1) delegated nonroutine decisions to them, compared to only 28 percent who answered "sometimes" (19.6) or "often" (8.0), and 29 percent who did not answer at all.[41]

40. The declaration was adopted by student council leaders from fifteen higher educational institutions in Jakarta at a meeting held in Cibogo, West Java, on December 30, 1973. The text as translated here was published in *Abadi,* January 14, 1974.
41. Recalculated from data in Smith 1971*a*: 186. The provinces are Central Java, West Sumatra, and South Sulawesi. Nearly two-thirds of the "no answers" came from

Although counterpart data for central officials are lacking, the senior civil servant in Jakarta who struggles with a heavy burden of responsibilities while subordinates read newspapers in an adjoining room still can be found. It is ironic that the man who should know the most about delegating administrative responsibility, the minister for perfecting the state apparatus, Sumarlin, should have tried to impress reporters with his accessibility by saying, "Anyone can phone me. Just ring me up. Here's my number: 49322. I'll answer the phone myself" (*Tempo,* April 14, 1973). Asked to comment on criticisms that he ran PERTAMINA as a "one-man show," General Sutowo denied the charge but showed that he was not the sort who liked to delegate authority "In the early days, things were different," he mused. "Then I knew the details of each machine down to its screws." But "now, with PERTAMINA as big as it is, I can't possibly stay on top of every problem. *I wish I could*" (*Tempo,* January 18, 1975).[42]

Why is authority so rarely delegated? First, the gap in talent and training between a superordinate and his subordinates may be too great to allow much faith that the latter will accomplish a delegated task. Anyone who has dealt with senior officials in Indonesia probably has met at least several whose administrative assistants and secretarial staff were barely competent. As experts in specialized fields, civilian technocrats may find it especially difficult to delegate decisions on topics close to their professional self-esteem. But these reasons for nondelegation only confirm themselves by denying subordinates the chance to become more skilled and experienced; Smith (1971*a*: 187-88) calls this the "authority trap."[43]

Second, the Javanese concept of power (*kasekten*) has charismatic overtones that make it indivisible, something that adheres to one person rather than being a function of particular relationships between people (Anderson 1972*a*). Authority also tends to be seen in extremely personal terms; the equivalent Indonesian root words *wibawa* and *kuasa* imply, respectively, an almost French sense of someone's palpably authoritative *presence* and a sense of firmly grasping authority in one's own hand, of being indisputably in charge.

A vignette and a survey will illustrate how power is linked to personality in the bureaucracy. When Minister Machmud began his term of office in January 1969, he had the following statement, here reproduced in toto, put up on a display board just inside the main entrance to the ministry:

Know me . . .
The expert (can) read people from their physical appearance.

---

camats, and given the relative lack of autonomy at the subdistrict level it is likely that these missing answers could they be known would be mostly "never" or "seldom." A similar guess is made by Smith 1971*a*: 185, 201 (n. 16).

42. A GOLKAR leader once replied to criticism that his organization was unapproachable by giving out his home address and telephone number (*Pedoman,* October 10, 1973).

43. According to Shaplen (1974: 57), "the gap between top-level experts and low-level bureaucrats is growing rather than narrowing as economic development becomes more complex."

Read me, my eyes, my ears . . .
My hobby is work.
I don't like to keep things in my heart (my heart must stay clean).
What goes into my heart I must bring out.
What is good I call good, what is bad I call bad.

Major General Amir Machmud
Minister of Home Affairs

At about the same time, in answer to an unfinished sentence beginning "A leader must . . . ," some 250 middle-level civil servants consistently favored predicates of being that described a desired personality over predicates of doing to indicate a desired performance.[44] Insofar as Indonesians identify the exercise of authority with a leader rather than a task, they would no more expect him to delegate authority than to make someone a gift of his eyes and ears, to use the minister's image.

Third, a political atmosphere in which security and stability are all-important discourages independence. To the recipient, delegated authority may be unwelcome. If its exercise involves a risk of controversy, he may gladly relinquish it upward for safety's sake. Subordinates know that responsibility can fix blame in a crisis. After the student demonstrations of late 1973 and early 1974 in Jakarta, a newly appointed minister of education and culture, Lieutenant General Syarif Thayeb, banned political activity on the nation's university campuses and charged the rectors with full responsibility for anything that might happen in their institutions. As a result, authority in university administration, especially for student affairs, flooded up to the rector, who now had to concern himself with even the details of "rag week" and the hazing of freshmen – for on those occasions in the past students had staged parades satirizing the government.

Fourth, when demands are made on subordinates they may generate an emergency atmosphere inimical to the institutionalized sharing of authority. Senior officials often demand that data be gathered, reports be written, or meetings be prepared on very short notice. A minicrisis is created in which subordinates focus exclusive attention on the new task; the more conscientious among them may work flat out to achieve it in time. Satisfaction afterward derives from the fact of having met the boss's demands and perhaps having drawn overtime pay or an honorarium in the process. The minicrisis also repersonalizes the authority of the senior official, for he has placed himself at the center of it, risking his reputation before his own superiors. Meanwhile other tasks are postponed and long-run planning is inhibited.

Even the spatial distribution of civil service ranks engenders top-down government. In 1971, comparing the centrally paid staffs of the seventeen departments, there was an almost perfect positive correlation between the ratio

44. These were convenience samples surveyed during in-service training courses in Jakarta and Bandung.

of senior to junior personnel and the ratio of those working in Jakarta to those in the regions (based on Biro Pusat Statistik 1972*a*: 60-61 and Manihuruk 1973: 97). The more centralized the department, the higher ranking its employees. The same disparity in rank occurred even more strikingly between centrally and locally paid civil servants. There were only 82 central employees in the lowest wage category (I) for every one in the highest (IV), whereas in the regional service bottom-grade workers outnumbered those in the top category by a margin of 1,792 to 1 (based on Biro Pusat Statistik 1972*a*: 60-61 and Manihuruk 1973: 26). Insofar as rank rewarded experience and skill and bestowed authority, departments and persons most likely to be in direct contact with the mass of the population were the least recognized, and this in a country where around 96 percent of the people live outside the capital. Small wonder that regional service is unpopular. Central government employees who spend their professional lives working in a regional administration are not considered its employees but are merely seconded to it while they continue to be paid out of central treasury funds, an anomaly that dates back to the pamong praja's pride in association with the "magic center."[45]

Wage ranks are imperfect indicators of performance, but it does appear true that an excessive concentration of talent and responsibility in the center has bled the provinces of brains and authority.[46] One consequence is the common practice of letting even minor administrative decisions at the provincial level and below pile up until someone can carry the lot to Jakarta to be taken care of face-to-face in a busy week of office-hopping, a traffic pattern encouraged by central officials who rarely venture from Jakarta except on ceremonial occasions (see Mitchell 1970; Smith 1971*a*: 12, 176, 216-18, 234 [n. 17]). Given the correlation between rank and centrality, unless there is a structural shift in career incentives in favor of regional service, attempts currently underway to increase the ratio of senior to junior personnel as a means of improving the quality of administration may make the circulation of talent and power even more centripetal than it already is.[47]

45. The correlation (Pearson's *r*) between departmental ratios of those in senior to junior grades — (IV+III):(II+I) — and of those in Jakarta to those in the provinces was 0.9. When I accompanied an official of the Department of Home Affairs on a visit to its training academy (APDN) in Padang, West Sumatra, on September 16, 1974, the question uppermost in the minds of the students was how they could avoid the regional service, which would mean working only within West Sumatra, and enter the central service, which would allow their assignment anywhere in the country including the national capital. On the "magic center," see Heine-Geldern 1956.

46. In the 1960s the Civil Servants' Wage Regulation (Peraturan Gadji Pegawai Negeri) was usually referred to by its initials PGPN, which were only half jokingly reinterpreted as "Smart or Stupid, Your Fate's the Same" ("Pinter Goblok Pada Nasibe"). Smith (1971*a*: 217) found about 30 percent of a sample of fifty-four regional economic planners believing that "connections" (family, political, and other) were the most important factor in determining promotions in their province, whereas 20 percent each named "experience/years of service," "education and training," and "ability (efficient/effective work)." Percentages have been recalculated.

47. In his March 1973 speech (see fn. 19), Suharto pointed to an absolute decline in 1969-1972 in the number of civil servants in the lowest wage category (I) and an increase in the number of those in the highest (IV) as evidence the government was trying to improve the quality of its employees.

The concentration of authority at one level exacerbates another problem: a lack of coordination among officials at lower levels. In the regions, central government employees — paid from Jakarta and promoted by and accountable to separate national agencies that are based there — have little incentive to mesh their activities or to consult with the regional head and his staff. A bupati in West Java in 1974 told me he had trouble finding out what all those central employees were doing in his district, let alone coordinating their activity. At about the same time the governor of East Java remarked that his two greatest enemies were the Solo River (which floods) and poor coordination among these "vertical agencies" (*instansi vertikal*) in his province. In East Java, the lack of joint planning between the Department of Public Works and Electric Power and the Department of Agriculture reduced the potential benefit of the huge hydroelectric dam built at Karangkates, to cite one example (conversations, Surabaya, March 1974).

Some vertical agencies will defeat attempts to coordinate authority at lower levels for fear of being bypassed: home affairs' unwillingness to let provincial and district development planning boards play a coordinating role and its desire instead to make them advisory staffs to the regional head is one example. Another is the successful resistance of the agricultural banking system (Bank Rakyat Indonesia) and of home affairs' village development service (Pembangunan Masyarakat Desa) to a proposed subdistrict-level rural credit program that would have gone around them (conversations, Jakarta, January-February 1974; also see Smith 1971a: 182). Problems of coordination in the performance areas spotlighted earlier have arisen on oil policy between PERTAMINA on the one hand and mines and finance on the other, among trade, finance, and agriculture on sugar policy, and between transmigration and cooperatives on the one hand and agriculture, health, and education and culture on the other in the preparation of resettlement sites and the provision of welfare facilities to transmigrants.

One-way Communication

Nondelegation of authority and poor coordination are intrabureaucratic problems. What of the interface between officials and the public they are supposed to serve? A survey of rural respondents in Java, Sumatra, and Sulawesi in 1973 suggests that concentrated power and modern technology are reinforcing the one-way nature of communication between government and society in Indonesia (Team Penelitian 1973).[48]

In 1973, villagers were asked their major sources of information about two

48. Within each of five areas — Greater Jakarta, West Java, Lampung, South Sulawesi, and Central Java including the Special Region of Jogjakarta — a sample of nine villages was stratified to comprise three villages relatively open to outside communication (for example, near a city), three relatively closed (isolated), and three in an intermediate position. The survey was conducted rapidly and apparently without a pretest — the Lampung report is especially weak — but the patterns it yields are consistent and the raw data fascinating. I used the latter to develop percentages, which are not footnoted because they synthesize evidence culled from pages and foldouts scattered throughout the study. Also see Chapter 8 in this book.

government programs, agricultural intensification and family planning, and
their answers were then distinguished by type of communication. On the average
in each of the four areas for which comparable data are available (Central Java
including Jogjakarta, Greater Jakarta, Lampung, and South Sulawesi), 50 percent of the approximately eight hundred persons answering the question cited
mainly one-way communication from a formal authority figure (local officials
and especially village heads), 41 percent named a strictly one-way communication through a nonhuman channel (primarily radio but also the press and
occasionally film), and only 6 percent referred to two-way informal communication with peers (mainly with friends and neighbors but also in foodstalls and at
the market). Communication also appeared mainly ex post facto; in West Java
on the average nearly twice as many respondents said they were not consulted
before development projects were undertaken in their own village as said they
were. By this evidence, the flow of information and advice runs primarily down
and out from formal authorities through one-way media to target populations.

The formality of the process of communicating about development
appears to correlate negatively with the success of the advertised program. In
1973, compared to government officials, local influentials such as elders and
religious figures were virtually uninvolved in this process, despite their considerable prestige. Formal authorities tended to communicate formally, most often
(except in Jakarta) by assembling the people and making a speech. Yet many
villagers preferred face-to-face contact in the villagers' homes as a more enjoy-
able format in which they also understood better what the official was trying to
say, perhaps in part because at home they could more easily ask questions.[49]

Evidence from the 1973 survey and Smith's research in 1970 also suggests
that face-to-face formats yield better results. In 1973 in Central Java and
Jogjakarta (and in all other regions from which comparable data were obtained)
strictly one-way communication through nonhuman media (radio, print, film)
was a more important source of information about family planning than about
improved agriculture. Correspondingly in 1970, 72 percent of the family planning programs in a sample of 69 villages in Central Java were said by the village
chiefs to be running poorly, whereas 79 percent of the heads of 298 villages in
three provinces where agricultural extension efforts were underway, including
Central Java, thought these programs were working well.[50] Because it is labor
intensive, face-to-face communication also better meets Java's need for jobs.

In West Java, the 1973 survey revealed, village meetings where ostensibly
people could voice their views and take part in decisions had turned into briefing
sessions held by the village head for his assistants. If they took them anywhere,

49. These findings underline the advice of Jackson and Moeliono (1972) that the
way to reach rural communities is not through formal mass media but through
informal tranditional networks of influence and obligation. Also see Hofsteede 1971
and Chapter 12 in this book. Whether such media would distort the "modernizing"
message or not is another matter.

50. Recalculated from Smith 1971*a*: 105. Rice intensification (Bimas) in the
three provinces (Central Java, West Sumatra, and South Sulawesi) won a 68 percent
favorable rating.

respondents preferred to take their problems directly to the village head – the single most important source of information about development (Universitas Padjadjaran 1973) – which suggests that overconcentration and nondelegation of authority also are problems at the village level. In South Sulawesi village meetings appeared formal and coercive in part because they were held mainly in government buildings during working hours. Farmers sometimes felt they could not leave their fields to attend, and from the physical presence of those who did, concluded the authors of the report, one could not infer psychological participation.

As for the voicing of grievances to officials, according to the survey, this kind of reverse communication is uncommon and sometimes unfruitful. In Central Java and Jogjakarta, among villagers who experienced some loss after following official advice (for example, illness after using birth control or a poor harvest after joining a rice intensification program), only 36 percent reported their loss to the authorities. And among these, only half felt their complaint had received serious consideration; the rest said the person to whom they had spoken had either ignored it, had said he would pass the matter up to a superior official, or had made a pro forma promise that something would be done. This 50-50 split was at least slightly better than the 45-55 breakdown on the same item in South Sulawesi.

The survey also contains fragmentary evidence that in the poorest areas development messages are most monopolized by officials and public recipients are most passive. Within the Central Java-Jogjakarta sample, 93 percent of the respondents in the depressed region of Gunung Kidul named officials as their main source of information on agricultural intensification and family planning compared to only 43 percent among respondents in the other two, better-off districts (Klaten and Bantul) combined. In Gunung Kidul 75 percent did nothing about a loss they experienced from trying to apply official advice compared to only 56 percent in the two more advantaged districts. And among those who did report the matter to an official, the lowest percentage receiving serious attention (43 percent) was in Gunung Kidul, whereas in Klaten, a model district, the figure was 80 percent. Combined with the previous evidence that land tax collection rates are higher in less well-off areas, these data point to a viciously circular relationship on Java linking poverty to passive dependence to extractive, indifferent government and back to poverty again.

In the years preceding the demonstrations in Jakarta in January 1974, student leaders repeatedly criticized the lack of effective feedback from ruled to ruler. Just two months earlier General Sumitro, then head of the feared Command for the Restoration of Security and Order (KOPKAMTIB), appeared to support a "new pattern of leadership" for the country in which officials at all levels would engage in "two-way communication" with the people (*Berita Yudha,* November 15, 1973). "You need no longer be afraid," Sumitro said publicly, "if you have a different opinion" (*Kompas,* November 19, 1973). Taking him at his word, one young critic of the regime, Imam Waluyo, announced the forthcoming birth of a new political party, an Indonesian Freedom

Movement (Gerakan Kebebasan Indonesia or GKI). GOLKAR he described as a rootless body formed from above to serve the interests of people in power. Directly criticizing Suharto, he came out flatly for civilian rule (*Abadi*, December 24, 1973).[51]

But the GKI was never launched. Waluyo was arrested in January along with other critics of the regime. (He was held without trial for a year, then released.) A number of newspapers were forced to shut down. Sumitro resigned his army commission in March 1974. In December, the first in a series of trials of student leaders and intellectuals implicated in the January disturbances ended in a six-year sentence for the defendant.

In sum, top-down authority and one-way communication characterize the Indonesian bureaucracy both internally and in relation to the society it administers. Unresponsiveness to social problems, among them long-standing inequities in distribution and in the concrete circumstances of millions of individual villagers, is a necessary cost of this kind of political and administrative closure.

Administrative Reform

Credit, where due, must be given. Sincere efforts are being made or planned to bring about increased administrative efficiency. Procedures for allocating and committing funds have been regularized. Although corruption and conspicuous consumption by senior officials remain very serious problems, some measures have been taken against them. Wages have been raised to boost performance and reduce temptation. Overall, the bureaucratic system is being simplified, its routines made more uniform. In 1974, for example, a comprehensive civil service law was enacted to integrate or replace some 172 separate statutes; among them, several dated from Dutch times (Manihuruk 1973: 101-20).

To improve bureaucratic communication, these things were done or planned in 1974: the first computerized census of all public employees was completed; its results were expected to fill many gaps in information about who, where, and how many they were. The Department of Defense and Security began to computerize its administration. So did the government of Greater Jakarta. Plans were underway to knit the archipelago together under a domestic satellite serving fifty telecommunication stations in twenty provinces; defense and security and PERTAMINA already had reserved their channels. To speed the flow of accurate information, the base pay of government researchers was quadrupled. Officials were urged to describe conditions truthfully instead of stressing the good side to please superiors. Whereas before a civil servant's pension had to be determined manually by solving a complex equation, in 1974

---

51. Waluyo had been active in student demonstrations against Mrs. Suharto's tourism project two years before. On the latter events and on youth-regime conflict generally, see Emmerson 1973*a*. For more on "two-way communication," see *Merdeka*, February 16, 1974, citing the minister of information; Soendoro 1974; President Suharto's Independence address in August 1973; and *Sinar Harapan*, August 4, 1972, quoting the secretary general of the Department of Religion.

it could be done in seconds. Professors in state universities were more likely to get their grades in on time lest their negligence show up as an embarrassing blank on the printout at the semester's end.[52]

The secretary general of KORPRI, Brigadier General A. E. Manihuruk, who in the mid 1970s also headed the State Employees Administration Agency (BKAN), spearheaded many of these reforms. He wanted to reward performance. Pay was (and still is) determined by wage grade, but people in the same grade might be doing very different things. One man might be working in an office where it mattered little whether he showed up on time or not; another in the same grade might be guiding pilots to runways from an airport tower. Because the latter's task required greater concentration, asked Manihuruk rhetorically, should the air traffic controller not work less and, because it was more vital, be paid more? To bring pay and promotion closer to performance, Manihuruk wanted each employee to be rated by his immediate superior. The tendency had been to pass this responsibility up the line; an official might evaluate forty persons beneath him without knowing their daily work well enough to judge its quality.

Although this last reform, if enacted, would have delegated the authority to evaluate personnel, Manihuruk did not see personalized or undelegated authority as a general problem. When I finally raised the subject in my interview with him (Jakarta, April 6, 1974), he agreed that technical jurisdiction (*wewenang*) could be delegated, but not responsibility (*tanggungjawab*). And he stressed that an official must always consider himself personally responsible for any mistakes his subordinates may make. Admirably heroic in an individual leader, this stance can help keep an institution locked in Smith's "authority trap," especially if the gap in skills between leaders and lesser personnel is great.

Nor will enhanced efficiency significantly improve the capacity of the civil service to serve the public so long as the concentration of power and information makes government so invulnerable to feedback; to argue otherwise is, again, to confuse a technical with a structural problem, or so it seems to me. On the contrary, such streamlining may render the bureaucracy even less subject to deflection by the social atmosphere in which it moves — ironic confirmation of the GOLKAR chairman's metaphor of the Tokaido Line.

CONCLUSION

Along this chapter's three main variables — size, activity, and loyalty — the Indonesian bureaucracy is being rationalized, energized, and coerced all at once. I want now to speculate about where each of these trends may lead.

52. This paragraph draws on interviews in Jakarta on April 1 and 6, 1974, and in Bandung on January 28, 1975. Suharto exhorted civil servants to be frank in his 1973 address to the MPR cited earlier. Since then many others have voiced the same sentiment, as in this headline from the *Indonesian Daily News* of May 27, 1974: "Tell the Truth [Says] Maluku Governor: No Yesmen Needed."

Rationalization

As the metaphor implies, a streamlined bureaucracy will penetrate farther and faster, and in the world's largest archipelagic nation, that will be no mean feat. As modern technology expands the area of its effective presence, the bureaucracy may become an even more important symbol of national identity than it already is (see Bachtiar 1972: 18-27). Lastly and most problematic, if rationalization improves official responsiveness to local needs, the "filling" of political independence with economic growth *and* social justice could also proceed.

However, penetration and responsiveness are not the same thing. As I suggested at the end of the previous section, rationalization may actually reduce incentives for officials to sensitize themselves to local situations. Hints of this less attractive outcome lie in the way new technology is being used. Computers are expanding the amount of data processed by the bureaucracy, but access to that information is being concentrated in a few expert hands. The circulation of newly gathered "sensitive" statistics is already being restricted. Advanced communication systems will not automatically encourage local feedback. That will depend on who mans the channels. It is entirely possible for a stationary satellite to relay elite messages overhead while in a city on the ground — as in Malang where I wrote these lines — half a million people live without a hometown newspaper.

In East Java, deeply penetrated as it is, no newspapers at all are published where 95 percent of the people live, namely, outside the capital city of Surabaya. Requiring a level of investment and an economy of scale most readily assured in commercial and administrative centers, the new technology is doubly "capital" intensive.

Advanced technology also may be used to reinforce the already mostly one-way nature of communication across the gap between the government and populace. By 1977, partly to guarantee the election scheduled then, Indonesia's domestic satellite is expected to be transmitting messages to the population through a television set placed in every village in the country (*Surabaya Post,* January 30, 1975) — although the timing appears unrealistic. Regional programming is also planned, but because conditions for creative use of the new media are least available to villagers, they are far more likely to receive than generate information. If the sets are placed in front of the homes and offices of village chiefs — following the practice of installing a public set in the camat's compound in some subdistricts on Java — the near-monopoly of official wielders of information in the poorest, most passive areas will increase.

Lastly, empowering bureaucrats with the new technology could encourage them to raise the scale of their plans prematurely and to trade detailed knowledge of local conditions for the false security of across-the-board policy assumptions. The government already can pick up a successful pilot project and rapidly inflate it to national proportions, ignoring the role of particular circumstances in the original achievement. Illustrations include rice intensification, when a local success in Krawang, West Java, was escalated into the national BIMAS program, and village cooperatives, when BUUDs that had worked in the Jogjakarta region were multiplied by fiat all over the island; Hansen recounts the costs in Chapter 11 of this book.

Activation

A bureau chief in Jakarta once said to me about the people working under him: "The funny thing is there are too many of them to do what they're doing now, but there mightn't be enough of them if they were doing all the things they should be doing. If only there were money!" (interview, February 20, 1969).

Now there is money. The oil boom has fueled the machine. The results of this stepped-up activity can be seen throughout Indonesia, especially in new and improved physical infrastructure: upgraded roads, market facilities, irrigation works, and school rooms. These are tangible benefits. They may not be enough, but they are much better than nothing.

The intangible impact of the new levels of activity on the government and people is less clear. Some foreign advisors in Jakarta worry that regional governments will fast become overextended — following PERTAMINA'S example — beyond their administrative capacity to use their new spending power wisely and that hugh sums will therefore be siphoned off in corruption. The occasional collapse of a newly built schoolhouse because of inferior materials and poor workmanship echoes the point. Others worry about possible dependency effects of heavy subsidization: In 1972/73, according to Department of Finance statistics, 86 percent of an average routine provincial budget came from the central government. A study of the effect of central subsidies on eight villages in Jepara district in Central Java concluded that only two used the money productively and that in general the money reinforced passivity and a sense of dependence on higher authority (Ihalauw 1972: 14, 24).

However, in another study Tinker and Walker reached the opposite conclusion, that the availability of funds

> has had a profound effect psychologically: local government has altered from a holding operation to an agent of change. Hard data is being collected, projections of growth and studies of projects are being made. Like anywhere else, mistakes are being made. Some studies are trivial, some data is falsified, some money is misused. What is important is that something is happening in the local areas with local input [Tinker and Walker 1973: 1, 119].

My own views of the consequences of increased funding and local activity lie somewhere between these assessments. Overall spending priorities still are determined at the center, and corruption sometimes reduces the sums that actually arrive in subdistrict and village offices. But the activation of the regional bureaucracy has meant a devolution of administrative authority. When budgets were absorbed in merely keeping routines and incumbents alive, agendas for practical action had no meaning. Poverty could support only slogans. Now that local government is financially more able, and expected, to do more and more things, priorities arise and compete. Subsidies require some kind of action by local officials. But the population need not be involved in setting priorities at all.

Tinker and Walker called this "executive decentralization," and the term is apt. In no sense is political power being shared. Instead local officials face greater pressure and more opportunities, both handed down by superiors, to implement development projects. Jatiroto subdistrict illustrates the negative and the positive outcomes that can result: In Banyuputih Kidul, the village head pocketed funds meant to build a school; eventually he was removed from office. In Kedungrejo, the village head consulted with community leaders before drawing up an agenda in which projects directly benefiting the most people, notably improved irrigation, received first priority. (Nationally the importance given to irrigation in the 1975/76 budget is encouraging for the same reason.)

The implications of this activity for administrative reform appear mixed. Tinker and Walker (1973: 1, 119) feel that "because there is some leeway available to local officials, coordination functions have been strengthened." My own view is that activating a host of agencies down to the village level, each guarding its separate chain of command and supply, probably has worsened intrabureaucratic coordination. Project-mindedness and large sums have fostered a piecemeal approach to rural development. If resource scarcity encourages the pooling of limited means, increased funding means a system can "afford" more duplication, overlapping, and contradiction. Illustrations have already been given. It is unclear that incoming evidence of this waste will trigger meaningful reform. Officials who head rival agencies are unlikely to coordinate their activities from the top down, whereas the villages utterly lack power to coordinate from the bottom all the separate bureaus that are impinging upon their lives in development's name.

But if it exacerbates the problem of coordination, activating the bureaucracy at lower levels should encou·· the de facto delegation of authority. This effect can already be seen operati·, ·etween government in one spatial unit and government in its subunits. For example, a host of national, regional, and local competitions have been organized pitting district against district, subdistrict against subdistrict, and village against village to determine which ones have turned in superior performances on some dimension of development. Although success criteria are not always clear and political considerations play a role, the winners usually have been those *least* passive or dependent on government at the next highest level, that is, those who made the most out of local resources. Rewarding local performance means acknowledging local responsibility.

That in a more active government superiors will be more inclined to delegate authority to subordinates within the same level or the same agency is much less likely. The logic of Smith's "authority trap" could become even more compelling: superiors could feel that increased budgets require increased control. As the stakes of failure or success enlarge, officials may become even more reluctant to share decisions.

Illustrating both of these effects is Trenggalek, which in 1974 won the title of best performing district in East Java during the first five-year plan. Army

Colonel Soetran, Trenggalek's dynamic bupati, mobilized the only resource his very poor district had in abundance: manpower. Local, compulsory labor planted new crops, reforested hillsides, and built roads and bridges. Without Soetran and his self-styled "commando" approach to development, these things would not have happened. He ran his government as an extension of himself, and he got results. By assuming full personal responsibility he accomplished its de facto delegation downward from provincial and national levels of administration. But he also gathered it from subordinates into his own iron hand. (On Trenggalek, see Wiryomartono n.d.; *Surabaya Post,* August 20-22, 1974; *Kompas,* October 18, 1974.) The lesson will not be lost on future contenders for the crown of regional development, especially in resource-poor places that higher-ups are less likely to want to run themselves and where the population is least able to.

Coercion

Manihuruk's "Normandy" approach, Sutowo's "beachhead" management, and Soetran's "commando" style highlight another key aspect of Indonesia's bureaucracy: the use of coercion, not as a last resort but a starting point. On this score, too, diametrically opposed conclusions have been reached.

In 1951 in the disorderly aftermath of the revolution, a German economist visited Indonesia and came away with strong impressions. "Parliaments," he admonished, with the Indonesian one in mind, "are not places for rhetorical training, but for legislators who are aware of their responsibility." The bureaucracy he found overcrowded and underemployed; responsibility there was "cut into little bits" that fluttered back and forth between time-wasting officials. Instead of a few people executing a commissioned task, "there are committees who decide everything." To achieve "industriousness, discipline, and order," the people would have to grant the government *"power"*; it would have to be able to act "with the will, power, strength, and authority to punish and liquidate with force every rebellion against public order" (Schacht 1952).

Using similar assumptions twenty-two years later, a Western journalist praised the government as having "come to rest in the stable political centre between the unhappy irrelevancies of the early experiment with Western-style forms . . . and the excesses of the Sukarnoist period." He found the New Order "democratic in its authoritarianism – because, after all the tiring turmoil, firm government going somewhere is what the mass of Indonesians, as distinct from some intellectuals perhaps, definitely want." Indeed "Suharto has already succeeded in turning Indonesia right around" and may even have set Indonesians "in a framework of Japanese-like productive unity . . . and thrust" (Stockwin 1973). Again, the Tokaido Line.

Compare these views with this one by an Australian scholar:

> Power is highly centralized, organised explicitly along hierarchical lines, and pervaded by the mystique of a "modernising" program unsullied by the "disruptive" and "divisive" effects of democratic participation in political life. Rights, responsibility, authority reside in the Jakarta elite, filter down through the military and administrative machine, and proceed

from the assumption that the modern enclave is the sole source of dynamism and innovation. The vast majority of Indonesians — the peasants — are looked upon as *bodoh* (stupid) and incurably backward, objects to be bullied, cajoled and, where necessary, appeased by relief measures [Mortimer 1973*a*: 60].

On Java, which is where the most serious problems lie, prospects for democracy are dim. That is something Westerners may lament, but in a hierarchy of human needs freedom seldom comes first. The realistic question in my mind is therefore not democratic participation but official effectiveness. The two are not, however, mutually exclusive. On the contrary, the one can encourage the other by making government more responsive to the priority needs of the population. This may become especially urgent as economic growth multiplies those needs. Soetran's command performance may rest on Trenggalek's relative poverty; inflicted development may erode the condition of its own success. In this sense the regime may be caught in an increasingly deadly trade-off between more power and less communication.

Java may already be undergoing a kind of social transformation by default: a still nebulous and scattered but emerging sum total of unforeseen side effects generated in the heat of a slow fission between a swollen population and advanced technology. Far from reducing the heat, political repression is a third pressure producing it. The irony is that coercion deprives the bureaucracy of something that its rationalization and activation make essential: sensitivity to the needs and circumstances of the public it is now technically more capable of serving.

The future will be shaped in large part by the bureaucracy's ability to straddle the contradictions between its own policies. Because coercion is a wasteful way to increase production among millions of small holders on Java, it undermines economic goals of efficiency and growth. Because repression destroys feedback, it undermines the effort to improve bureaucratic performance. Because budgets bestow power, the decentralization of expenditure undermines the centralization of policy decisions. Insofar as economic growth and the use of advanced technology strengthen the already strong, they facilitate wastage, reduce accountability, and promote social injustice. Because economics and politics are linked through processes of social change not wholly subject to control, by keeping the economy open and active the regime defeats its own efforts to keep the polity closed.

It is in these senses that the bureaucracy's newfound strength is weakness. Conversely, by increasing its vulnerability to the needs of powerless people it could acquire strength. "Tiptoe government" did not act, but hobnail boots are not the answer. My guess is that more and more Indonesians would not hesitate to exchange a government that is firm for one that is just.

5 Indonesia's New Economic Policy and Its Sociopolitical Implications

BRUCE GLASSBURNER

IN THE DECADE since the attempted coup d'état of 1965 the Indonesian government has succeeded in eliminating hyperinflation, has stabilized the value of the rupiah in the market for foreign exchange, has transformed a high rate of capital flight into a substantial private capital inflow, has changed a foreign exchange reserve deficit into a positive balance on the order of $1.3 billion, has maintained rice prices at levels at or below those on world markets, and has generated an overall rate of economic growth in the neighborhood of 7 percent per annum in real terms. Yet the pattern of economic policy remains a prime target of critics of the regime, on grounds that these gains are too narrowly shared, too much reliance is being placed on the market, unemployment has not decreased, and nonindigenous and foreign interests have become too powerful in the process. This study will examine the record of this policy and discuss the issues of this criticism with reference to both their economic and noneconomic aspects.

It is the author's contention that this record is deserving of much of the praise it has received for its remarkable successes, but at the same time that it has many shortcomings. It should be recognized by supporters and detractors alike that detailed and reliable microeconomic data are extremely hard to come by in Indonesia, so that there is much that is simply not known about many aspects of the performance of the economy; hence, distributional performance evaluations to date have been based to a large extent on casual impressions of conspicuous consumption and are frequently (and inevitably) influenced by preconceptions and ideology. It is also important to realize that the time available to the New Order economists to deal with the huge backlog of problems stored up by predecessor regimes has been very short. One decade is indeed a short time in which to attempt to rehabilitate an economy which had been deteriorating since the early years of the Great Depression — a stretch of thirty-five years.

THE PATTERN OF ECONOMIC POLICY, 1966-1975

Stabilization

In 1966 President Suharto's original team of five economic advisors (Professors Widjojo Nitisastro, Mohammad Sadli, Ali Wardhana, Emil Salim, and Subroto) conceived of their task as one that had to be undertaken in overlapping stages of stabilization, rehabilitation, and development. It was their hope that price inflation and the deterioration of the rupiah on international markets could be brought to acceptable levels in two or three years. In September 1966 the Jakarta cost-of-living index had risen 986 percent above that of September 1965, and the rupiah was deteriorating against the U.S. dollar in the (illegal) free market at a comparable pace (Bank of Indonesia, October 1973). By 1969 the rate of rise of the Jakarta price index had slowed to 18 percent, the free market rate against the dollar had been stabilized at the official rate of 378:1, and the rupiah was freely convertible. Since 1969 the price index has risen at an average annual rate of 19 percent, while the exchange rate against the dollar has been devalued only once (in August 1971), by 10 percent.[1] Inflation remains a problem, but its order of magnitude has been brought to levels comparable to those being experienced by other Asian nations.[2] On the other hand, the rupiah's international strength has remained unshaken since the August 1971 devaluation, and there have been occasional rumors that its value against the U.S. dollar might be increased.

This remarkable achievement in public and international finance was accomplished by intelligent but orthodox means. The huge deficit in the government's budget was dramatically reduced in 1967 and was replaced by balance or a surplus in every year since that date (see Table 1). "Balance," in this context, has a meaning quite different from that normally attached to public finance in advanced countries, for it was accompanied by a substantial excess of expenditures over government tax revenues. In 1967, for example, tax revenues were 67 percent of government expenditures, while 28 percent of expenditures were covered by the proceeds of sale of foreign exchange provided by foreign aid. The 3 percent deficit remaining was financed by credits from the Bank of Indonesia. By contrast, the deficit in 1965 had been 64 percent of total expenditures and in 1966, 55 percent.

Similarly, the convertibility and market strength of the rupiah was attributable to a great deal of external assistance, combined with rapid expansion of export earnings. Thus, essential imports did not have to be curtailed, but grew at a rapid rate as well. As Table 2 shows, exports (including oil) increased by 718

1. Because the rupiah is pegged to the dollar, however, subsequent dollar devaluations (in late 1971 and in early 1973) have meant implicit devaluations against nondollar currencies. By the same token, the dollar's strengthening in the last half of 1973 meant a rupiah upvaluation.

2. The 1973/74 rate of inflation (March 1973-April 1974) jumped to the 60 percent range, fed by the huge inflation in international commodity prices as well as by rapid expansion of bank credits. Following a new stabilization policy package of April 1974, however, the rate dropped sharply. Between April and November 1974, the annual rate was a mere 3.5 percent.

TABLE 1

Receipts and Expenditures of the Indonesian Central Government, 1966–1974

(in millions of rupiahs)

	1966	1967	1968	1969/70	1970/71	1971/72	1972/73	1973/74	1974/75[a]	1975/76[a]
Government receipts	13,142	84,900	185,283	334,762	465,137	563,548	748,408	1,171,681	1,577,300	2,734,700
Tax receipts	12,321	58,912	144,998	240,537	331,493	400,527	555,999	917,923	1,333,800	2,439,100
Nontax receipts	821	1,299	4,748	3,167	13,113	27,494	34,609	49,764	29,600	57,000
Foreign loans and credits	—	24,689	35,537	91,058	120,531	135,527	157,800	203,994	213,900	238,600
Government expenditures	29,433	87,555	185,283	334,671	457,929	544,995	736,324	1,164,258	1,577,300	2,734,700
Routine	25,695	70,023	149,746	216,544	288,177	349,095	438,100	713,302	961,600	1,466,300
Development	3,738	17,532	35,537	118,127	169,752	195,900	298,224	450,956	615,700	1,268,400
Surplus (+) or deficit (-)	-16,291	-2,655	—	+91	+7,208	+18,553	+12,084	+7,423	—	—
Foreign loans and credits as percentage of expenditures	—	28	19	27	26	25	21	18	14	9

SOURCES: Bank of Indonesia, October 1973, October 1974, and *Kompas*, January 7, 1975.

a. Budgeted.

TABLE 2

Balance of Payments 1966-1975/76

($ million)

	1966[a]	1971/72	1972/73	1973/74	1974/75[c]	1975/76[c]
Exports, f.o.b.						
Nonoil	424	784	974	1905	1947	1928
Oil (net)[b]	150	204	399	641	2748	3069
Total (net)	574	988	1373	2546	4695	4997
Imports, nonoil, f.o.b.	-550	-1116	-1492	-2613	-4101	-4972
Services, nonoil, net	-272	-320	-438	-689	-1049	-1348
Debt service	--	-78	-66	-81	-90	-89
Balance on current a/c	-248	-526	-623	-837	-545	-1412
Capital inflow						
Official	253	400	481	643	672	625
SDR[d]	--	30	--	--	--	--
Private (net)	18	190	480	549	776	890
Monetary movements	12	-100	-425	-360	-829	-103
Errors and Omissions	-35	+6	+87	+5	-74	--

SOURCE: The 1966 data are from Bank of Indonesia, October 1973. All other data from Indonesian Government Department of Trade.

a. Calendar year. All other years are Indonesian fiscal years — April 1 through March 31.
b. Oil exports net of imports by oil companies.
c. Estimated.
d. Holdings of "Special Drawing Rights" with the International Monetary Fund.

percent between 1966 and 1974/75 — a compound annual rate of growth of 30 percent. Oil exports carried heavy and increasing weight, but it is noteworthy that nonoil exports also grew by 21 percent per annum. (These data are in current dollar terms. About 40 percent of this change is in price increases.) Imports, on the other hand, grew at a compound rate of nearly 29 percent per annum, and net purchases of services also grew rapidly. For that reason it was not until 1972 that foreign exchange reserves began to accumulate, despite the strong export growth performance.

In fiscal year 1974/75 Indonesia was still running an estimated deficit on goods and services of $545 million, balanced by a large surplus in capital account, and this situation was expected to continue well into the second plan period (1974/75-1978/79). Official capital inflows played a major role in this situation, averaging $389 million per annum from 1966 through 1974/75. Private capital inflows in the mid-1970s rose to even higher levels.

Thus, the ingredients of stabilization policy were threefold. First, there was a substantial reduction in the rate of increase in the money supply and in the deficit in the government's budget. Second, tax revenues were increased at a very rapid rate — primarily through improvement in collection rates rather than in rate increases. As Table 1 indicates, tax receipts in 1973/74 were five times those of 1966 in real terms — an average per annum real increase of 22 percent. Third, government revenues were greatly increased by counterpart funds from commodity aid and by the availability of "program aid" foreign exchange which could be sold on the Jakarta bourse. The last factor, incidentally, not only provided a substantial source of rupiah financing but also served to strengthen the rupiah against the currencies of the donor nations — most notably the U.S. dollar and the Japanese yen.

There were several important concomitants of the stabilization policy. First, the government's command over real sources was rapidly restored, after having been allowed in the Sukarno years to dwindle to about 6 or 7 percent of a low and stagnant gross national product. By fiscal year 1973/74 that proportion had risen to 24 percent of a much larger and rapidly growing GNP. Second, the banking system was subtantially reorganized and put more nearly on a self-sustaining basis. Interest rates charged to borrowers and offered to depositors were radically altered to levels which approximated the scarcity value of capital. Third, exporters were offered increasingly attractive legal rewards in the form of exchange rates which were rapidly altered in the direction of true market values; and importers were given access to foreign exchange on an open market. Both exports and imports responded to these incentives and rose at very rapid rates, as Indonesia moved from an essentially autarchical system to an increasingly open system.[3]

3. The "Guided Economy" of President Sukarno was never as autarchical as the legal structure would indicate because of the large amount of illegal trade which took place. Thus, growth rates in official data on trade show more rapid rates of increase than is justified by actual trade flows (see Simkin 1970; L. White 1970).

Restoration of the Market System

The "Guided Economy" of President Sukarno was characterized by a maze of controls on economic activity. The economists of the new regime took it upon themselves to scale down this maze as rapidly as economic orderliness, political resistance, and their own predilections for controls would allow. The task was (and remains) formidable, although much of the control apparatus is still illusory, being largely ignored or subverted by corruption. Greatest success has been with the thicket of rules which surrounded the foreign exchange regime in 1966. The system inherited by the "New Order" (rendered *Orde Baru* in Indonesian) involved differing disequilibrium exchange arrangements for each of many categories of importers and exporters. The procedures adopted to accomplish foreign exchange liberalization are well documented elsewhere — and will not be repeated in any detail here (Glassburner 1970; L. White 1972). Suffice it to·say that by 1970 the multiplicity of exchange rates had been largely eliminated, and the rupiah's overvaluation had been replaced by a general exchange rate that was in the neighborhood of market equilibrium and freely convertible. The importance of this reform for a successful international trade policy can hardly be exaggerated.

Broadly similar attempts to rationalize were undertaken, but with much less complete success, in the banking system, the state enterprises, and the agricultural sector. The intention of the president's economic advisors was clearly to allow the market to work to a far greater extent than in the past, with prices reflecting scarcities much more closely than previously.

It would be easy to exaggerate the extent to which this movement toward freedom in the market place has progressed. To characterize *New Order* — economic policy as "laissez-faire" policy (as has been done occasionally — see Palmer 1972: 149) is to exaggerate greatly. There is no important area of the Indonesian economy that does not remain subject to government intervention. Even in the case of the foreign exchange regime, stability in the exchange rate is maintained by government intervention as a buyer or seller, as the occasion demands. Prices of the services of public utilities (and various other public corporations) remain administered, and on that account move in discrete jumps, thereby inducing a greater public reaction when changes occur than would be the case if they were truly responsive to changes in market conditions from day to day. Furthermore, because prices charged by publicly owned firms are usually raised only when heavy losses require it, these firms continue to drain resources from the budget that might otherwise go into public investment. Ostensibly, state enterprises have been ordered to stand or fall on their ability to meet the market test, but in fact few have effectively made the transition. This is even true of several state banks, whose lending policies have been guided as much by noneconomic as by economic considerations.

The *New Order* policy has been to encourage the revival and growth of the private enterprise sector and, indeed, a vigorous response is clearly in evidence. However, the government has not as yet made any serious attempt to "desocialize" the state enterprises nor many of the agencies of economic intervention created during the Sukarno years. Thus, despite considerable growth of the private economy, the public sector continues to play an important role in directly productive activities as well as in regulation of the economy.

Agricultural Policy

Indonesia's REPELITA, or first five-year plan, for 1969/70 through 1973/74 states the following: "In implementation of . . . development, emphasis is to be centered on agriculture. Thus, the chosen field of battle is the agricultural field. Here the central target is located, effort is to be centralized, and (favorable) results are anticipated" (REPELITA 1969: 15; my translation).

Overwhelmingly, the concern for the agricultural sector has been centered on rice. President Suharto himself has made it clear that self-sufficiency in rice is essential and that reasonably low and stable prices for rice are a commitment of his regime. The REPELITA, accordingly, set targets with self-sufficiency by the end of the five-year-plan period as the essential guidepost. The targets are given in Table 3. These targets were set at a time when enthusiasm for the Green Revolution was high everywhere, but even so their ambition was enough to be perplexing to the agricultural economists in the country. Great hope was placed on the ability of the Indonesian farmer to extend cultivation by rehabilitating the irrigation system and by expansion to unused lands on the outer islands; in addition, he was expected to raise his productivity per hectare by nearly 5 percent per annum. Neither the areal nor the productivity target was likely to be fulfilled in light of the circumstances in Indonesian agriculture at the time of the publication of the plan, and neither was fulfilled. The growth increment was half of that planned for the five-year period (see Table 4). Because of statistical

TABLE 3

Targets in Rice Cultivation for the First Five-Year Plan

Fiscal year	Area to be cultivated (million hectares)	Production (million tons)	Production per hectare (tons)
1969/70	7.60	10.52	1.38
1970/71	7.96	11.43	1.43
1971/72	8.32	12.52	1.51
1972/73	8.76	13.81	1.58
1973/74	9.30	15.42	1.66
Overall increase (%)	22.3	46.6	20.3
Per annum increase (%) (compounded average)	5.1	9.9	4.7

SOURCE: REPELITA, 1969: 158.

TABLE 4
Rice Production in Indonesia, 1968-1973,
Revised Data (calendar year—million tons)

Year	Million tons
1968	11.67
1969	12.25
1970	13.14
1971	13.72
1972	13.30
1973	14.7
Overall increase (%)	26.0
Per annum increase (%) (compounded average)	4.7

SOURCE: 1968-1972, *Nota Keuangan,* 1974/75. 1973, President's State Message, 1974.

revisions, however, the estimate of total rice production for calendar year 1973 (14.7 million tons) is only 5 percent below the 1973/74 target. Recent upward revision of production figures for the period 1968-1972 means that even full achievement of the REPELITA target level would imply much less *growth* than was originally planned. Assessing success and failure in rice production is made complex by the fact that the data are poor (though improving) and are continuously being revised.

It seems fairly clear, however, that the overoptimism of the authors of the agriculture section of REPELITA has not been rewarded. To some extent bad weather is to blame. Until 1972, when drought damaged the crop seriously, production had maintained a reported growth rate of 5.4 percent — well below the REPELITA's 9.9 percent target, but highly respectable by world agricultural growth standards. Nevertheless, weather is the most important variable in agriculture, particularly in countries using traditional peasant technologies, and it is unfortunate that agricultural planners so consistently plan as though normal crop conditions can be expected year in and year out. The upshot of this overoptimism is the creation of overoptimistic expectations on the part of the public in general, and the concomitant political unrest created by their lack of fulfillment. It is encouraging, in this regard, to see that rice production goals for the second plan were scaled down to 4.7 percent increase per annum.

Unrest in the urban areas is closely related to rice policy in Indonesia and frequently is expressed in direct response to rice price increases. It is not surprising, therefore, that serious protests against government economic policy should follow on the heels of a two-year rice price increase (1971-1973) of more than 100 percent (see Table 5). Rice "availability" (government procurement

TABLE 5

Prices of Medium-Quality Rice in Selected Indonesian Cities, 1968-1974
(average prices in rupiah per kilogram, at the
end of the month indicated)

Date	Jakarta	Surabaya	Medan	Ujung Pandang	Annual imports (thousands of tons)	
					Year	Amount
December 1968	41.25	––	44.35	25.4	1968	625
December 1969	49.67	44.5	41.3	40.3	1969	604
December 1970	46.40	41.0	50.0	43.0	1970	951
December 1971	45.30	44.5	45.4	40.0	1971	494
December 1972	78.10	73.8	63.0	60.0	1972	737
December 1973	100.00	75.0	115.0	75.0	1973	1308
December 1974	105.0	90.0	106.0	100.0	1974/5	1516[b]
Overall increase (%)	155	102.0[a]	139.0	294.0		143
Annual increase (%) (average compounded)	17	15	16	26		16

SOURCE: Bank of Indonesia, July 13, 1972, December 13, 1973, and December 19, 1974.

a. 1969-1974.
b. Estimate for fiscal year 1974/75 by U.S. agricultural attaché.

plus imports), according to official data, ran well ahead of the growth of population in the 1968-1973 period (4.4 percent per annum versus 2.2 percent population growth rate). Over the period 1966-1973, total availability increased by 7.5 percent per annum (Bank of Indonesia, October 1973: 185). But growth of per capita availability was insufficient to satisfy growing demand, fostered by a high rate of growth of per capita income (in excess of 4 percent per annum, but presumably substantially higher than that in the cities and lower in rural areas). Rising demand is a function of both population increase and increased consumption per capita – the latter being induced by rising incomes per capita. Demand for rice in the nation rises about 5.5 percent per annum, whereas total production rose from 1968 to 1974 at nine-tenths of a percentage point below that figure, on the average. Thus, despite increases in per capita production, imports would have had to be increased at a rapid rate (16 percent per annum, 1968-1974) in order to maintain stable rice prices, even in the absence of other inflationary factors. Government rice imports in 1973 were at a record level of 1.3 million tons, but prices still rose dramatically, as I have noted. The explanation of this phenomenon is to be sought in general inflationary factors – a rapid rise in the money supply and the dramatic push of external prices. Rice prices on international markets, incidentally, rose much more rapidly than Indonesia's domestic prices. In 1970 the low-grade rice which Indonesia normally purchases from Thailand was obtainable in Asian markets for as little as $90 per ton (which translates into a price of Rp. 37 per kilogram). By the end of 1973 Indonesia was making some contracts at prices in the $450-per-ton range (Rp. 187 per kilogram).[4] In 1974, rice prices were stabilized still more, despite a substantial rate of inflation – again, through a substantial expansion of imports.

The BIMAS program

Not all aspects of agricultural policy of the Sukarno regime were negative. As early as 1963/64 students from the Agricultural Institute in Bogor were involved in "Mass Guidance" (Bimbingan Massal, or BIMAS) in the use of improved seeds and cultivation techniques. The results, although necessarily localized (largely in West Java), were encouraging. It became the policy of the New Order to extend and expand this program, and to emphasize, in the first instance, the use of the dwarf rice which had been developed at the International Rice Research Institute in the Philippines. In later stages comparable attention was to be given to other staple crops and to poultry raising. There seems to be little question that the BIMAS program has contributed to increased production, even though there have been shortfalls relative to plan targets. Padi (unthreshed rice) production growth rates in the last half of the decade were considerably better than they had been in the first half (12 percent increase, 1961-1966,

4. These translations of dollar prices into rupiah prices do not take handling costs into account (they are f.o.b. prices). Indonesian prices were comparable to external prices in 1970, but have been depressed below world prices in the last two or three years. Understandably, some concern has been expressed that outward rice smuggling might be taking place.

versus 30 percent, 1966-1971). However, in the eagerness of both the central and local agencies of government to push the new techniques and seeds, many mistakes were made and much in resources was wasted.

The central problem was that the informed and involved students who launched BIMAS were only a few, whereas the need for extension personnel for an expanded program was huge. The expansion of the program thus diluted it badly, yielding rapidly diminishing marginal returns to additional inputs of effort and finance. Eagerness to produce results led, in 1968/69, to introduction of the so-called BIMAS Gotong Royong (self-help mass guidance) — most inappropriately named, inasmuch as a central feature of it was the use of large European supplier firms to provide fertilizer, pesticides, and technical advice. Large blocks of rice acreage were designated for complete coverage. Farmers were advanced supplies of fertilizers and pesticides and were committed to pay for these inputs by delivering one-sixth of their crop to the government. Officials were so optimistic that little attention was given to the economic validity of this procedure. Coupled, as the program was, with a rice procurement and price stabilization policy which kept padi prices low, returns to participating farmers often were negative. Their reluctance in the face of a losing proposition typically was taken to be peasant conservatism, and heavy pressure was brought to bear on the farmers to comply. Understandably, the peasants evaded and avoided to a large extent, and repayments for the advances of inputs were abysmally bad (see Hansen 1971 and Chapter 11 in this volume). A prominent government official stated, in public, that the cost of the rice obtained by the government from some of the BIMAS Gotong Royong areas cost more, in total, than it would have to import the same amount, by a considerable margin.

The reaction to the entire BIMAS Gotong Royong experience was sufficiently negative to induce President Suharto to make incognito visits to the rice fields of Java in April 1970. The following month the president decided to abandon the effort as a failure. Demonstrating remarkable flexibility, the government introduced a new program ("perfected BIMAS"), which put much more emphasis on price incentives and farmers' individual choice (Mears 1970). Crops were excellent in 1971 and 1972, but drought in the 1972/73 crop year reduced production about 3 percent below the level of the preceding year, which in the face of rapidly rising demand created a crisis. Thus, although it would be wrong to say that the Green Revolution has failed in Indonesia, it has certainly fallen short of expectations. Perhaps it still awaits an adequate trial under reasonably favorable conditions.

Rice price policy

As mentioned earlier, rice price stabilization has been a matter of primary concern to the Suharto regime. This is essentially a consumer-oriented policy in its origins, with far more thought being given to the damping of rice price rises than to the problems of the rice producer. The agency bearing the responsibility for implementation of this policy is BULOG, an acronym for Logistics Board. It is BULOG's task to purchase rice in the harvest season in order to acquire a buffer stock, which can then be released in the interharvest period to prevent seasonal price fluctuations. If domestic purchases fail to build an adequate buffer, BULOG is authorized to purchase rice abroad. BULOG also distributes rice to millions of government servants, whose wages are paid partially in kind. The board thus handles between 1.5 and 2.0 million tons of rice annually.

BULOG's handling of this responsibility has left a great deal to be desired. The board has consistently operated with a lag, being forced into action by circumstances, as opposed to anticipating needs and building stocks well in advance. The result, until very recently, has been that despite improvement over earlier years prices were not stabilized over the seasonal cycle, and heavy reliance has had to be put on imports acquired in the face of rising prices in the months preceding the wet season harvest.[5] Delays in domestic purchases have allowed prices to fall to levels which were disastrous for rice farmers at wet season harvest time (as in 1969), only to be followed by the fall-winter crisis as private stocks of rice began to run short.

In some degree BULOG's failure to act effectively in domestic markets in the past can be attributed to the relative ease with which U.S. surplus rice and wheat could be obtained under Public Law 480. (Japanese rice has also been imported under similar arrangements.) These supplies were not only easy to obtain, but the economic terms on which they could be obtained, and the revenues which their sale in domestic markets provided, made reliance on that source very tempting. However, acquisition of P.L. 480 supplies in time to meet the challenge of the fall-winter crisis became increasingly difficult as the U.S. stockpiles of surplus grain were used up, and by the time of the 1973 world commodity stringency, it became necessary for approximately $600 million to be expended for commerical imports of rice. BULOG is not to be blamed for the drought of 1972/73, of course, but failure to anticipate, both by domestic acquisition and early ordering abroad, has meant that far more foreign exchange had to be spent than would have been necessary with proper manipulation of the stockpile.[6]

The Indonesian farmer has been hampered doubly by the failure of rice price policy. Prices generally have been kept low by world standards, thus offering the Indonesian farmer less in the way of price incentive than he would have had if the market had been allowed to respond freely to world market conditions. At the same time, he has had to cope with wide seasonal fluctuations in prices, which create uncertainty and add to his dependence on money-lenders in the slack season. In some degree price stability and high price levels are

5. There has been considerable improvement over the pre-1966 situation. Source: unpublished planning commission study, 1971. In 1974, the seasonal pattern was *entirely* eliminated — an overreaction which may do serious damage to private rice traders who, in the past, have performed an important storage and time distribution function.

6. Inevitably, in the corrupt environment of Indonesian government, it is alleged that BULOG's "failures" to stabilize rice prices were really successful manipulations which affect opportunities for self-enrichment on the part of BULOG officials. This is certainly a plausible hypothesis, although ineptitude surely has played an important role.

substitutes when regarded from the point of view of incentive effects. It is conceivable, at least, that maintenance of rice prices below world market prices would be consistent with incentives adequate to induce substantial increases in production, provided those prices were fairly predictable from season to season. The Indonesian farmer, in making his planting and cultivating decisions, has to cope not only with the weather and the normal uncertainties of the market but also with the uncertainties of BULOG policy.

Concern about this situation often is expressed at the highest levels in Jakarta. An attempt has been made to design a policy which simultaneously will deal with the need to provide farmers with adequate incentives and will prevent market prices to consumers from rising above politically acceptable levels. A "farmer's formula" (*rumus tani*) has been devised which purports to establish the minimal necessary relationship between rice and fertilizer prices that will allow the farmer to use BIMAS inputs. And also buffer stock stabilization schemes have been worked out in detail for BULOG's utilization. The main impact of the "farmer's formula" has been felt in the subsidization of fertilizer prices. Resistance within the regime to allowing rice prices to rise to a level that will make heavy fertilizer use profitable has forced them to the alternative of selling fertilizer domestically at prices that are also well below world market prices. This policy, like the low rice price policy, is also expensive in terms of foreign exchange. It is argued, however, that on balance the fertilizer price policy is foreign exchange saving, because, in its absence, rice imports would have to be still greater than they are, as fertilizer use expands yields by more than enough to compensate.

Agricultural policy in general

As the preceding discussion indicates, agricultural policy is overwhelmingly concerned with rice production and rice price manipulation – to the virtual neglect of all other aspects. It is not surprising, then, to find that production of other crops has not shown rapid growth. Table 6 shows that a part of the gain made in rice production has come at the expense of other foods. In general only coffee among the crops of small farmers has done well in the period since 1966. Estate crops, on the other hand, generally have progressed tolerably well. Rehabilitation of many plantations, both government and private, has progressed well if not spectacularly (Harvard Development Advisory Service 1972; this report points out that although rehabilitation in copra and sugar planting has been generally unsuccessful, the greatest success appears to be in palm oil production). In sum, agricultural policy since the coup attempt of 1965 has been a very modest success to date. Achievements in the nonagricultural sector have been much more impressive.

The Kabupaten Program

In 1970 President Suharto issued a presidential instruction establishing a program of central government subsidy to the *kabupatens* (roughly the equivalent of counties) of Rp. 50 per capita for the purpose of undertaking local, labor-intensive public works. The objectives were to utilize underemployed local

TABLE 6
Production Growth Rates of Selected Agricultural
Commodities, 1966-1972
(percent)

	Overall	Compound average
Food crops		
Maize	-38.0	-5.5
Cassava	-30.0	-4.4
Sweet potatoes	-52.0	-7.2
Peanuts	1.9	0.3
Soybeans	15.0	2.3
Smallholder crops		
Coffee	100.8	12.3
Tobacco	-24.2	-3.7
Copra	2.1	0.3
Tea	-48.9	-6.8
Rubber	22.6	3.4
Estate crops		
Sugar	44.4	6.3
Rubber	18.2	2.8
Tea	17.4	2.7
Palm oil	58.5	7.9
Coffee	59.7	8.1

SOURCES: Bank of Indonesia October 1973: 184; *Bulletin of Indonesian Economic Studies* 1973, 9(3): 9, table 1.

labor to rehabilitate infrastructural capital and to create new infrastructural capital where desirable. An important by-product was to be greatly increased participation in the implementation of the development effort at the local level. This was seen as a filling in of the gap between the public works programs of the provincial governments and the *desa* (village) program initiated in 1969.

The hypothesis was that there were high payoff projects readily apparent in each locality and that local governments had the necessary planning and executive expertise to carry them off if they could be provided with finances. The funds were not made available *carte blanche*, but rather on receipt in Jakarta of an approved program proposal. Approval was to be made by the provincial office of the Department of Public Works, with a check in Jakarta only for budgetary consistency. A deliberate attempt was made to keep the planning and reporting system as simple as possible and to see to it that higher level reactions to proposals were minimally time-consuming. At the same time, heaviest emphasis was given to projects that were particularly labor intensive and which utilized local materials as much as possible. The hope was that there would be a substantial local "multiplier" effect.

The program is predominantly rural, but *kotamadya* (municipal areas) also have been included. Top priority has been given to work on roads, bridges, and irrigation works. In 1972/73, 79 percent of all projects were in those three categories (33, 29, and 17 percent respectively) (de Wit 1973). In fiscal year 1972/73, there were 2,828 projects reported as being under way. They were reported to have provided direct employment for 436,120 "100-man-day units." These units were seen as the amount of employment required to utilize effectively a seasonally unemployed person. The projects are small, measured financially. In the first three years of operation, 79 percent of the projects were financed at a level of Rp. 5 million or less ($12,048 at the official rate of exchange), and only 11 percent cost more than Rp. 10 million ($24,096) (de Wit 1973).

The officials involved in the implementation of the kabupaten program are convinced that it has been successful on all counts, although it is conceded that it is still very modest in terms of its aggregate employment effects, given the fact that approximately 1.25 million new entrants to the labor force emerge annually. Still, no one anticipates that such a program can meet the challenge of labor absorption without supplementation. It is felt that, aside from employment effects, these are valuable activities, because of the high payoff in external economies derived from roads, bridges, and water control projects in other countries with roughly similar works programs – most notably East Pakistan before partition and South Korea (J. Thomas 1968). There can be little doubt that some funds have been channeled into private pockets, but it is felt generally that most have been properly spent, partly because of a system of public reporting of activities and general public knowledge of the financial scope of the projects. Whether these hopes can be substantiated is problematical, but at least one observer is on record in support of this view (de Wit 1973; the author has received assurances from another official observer as well).

At any event, the government is moving ahead with enthusiasm in its attempt to expand the kabupaten program as rapidly as absorptive capacity will allow. According to the president's 1975 budget speech, the central government subsidy was increased by stages to Rp. 100, Rp. 150, and recently to Rp. 400 per capita (*Kompas,* January 7, 1975). It is at least conceivable that such a rapid increase will do more harm than good. If local planning capabilities are over-taxed in coming up with legitimate projects so as to qualify for the full amount of the subsidy, there will be strong temptation to falsify planning documents in order to do so. This huge increase may be something of an overreaction on the part of government to the pressures being applied to the regime to demonstrate more conclusively its interest in meeting the problems of interregional distribution and labor saturation.

Policy toward Private Investment

The Indonesian government has used a variety of inducements to private investors, including special concessions on taxes, guarantees of compensation in the event of nationalization, guarantees of rights to repatriate profits of foreign-owned firms, high tariff protection, and concessionary credit schemes. The results have been spectacular in both foreign and domestic investment, but there is resentment because of the rapid inflow of foreign capital which has ensued, and the relatively small role played in the entire investment picture by the indigenous Indonesian entrepreneurs. It is widely felt that greater concessions are required in order to bring about a balanced picture, with special consideration given to the *asli* (non-Chinese) domestic entrepreneur.

The legislation that has been given the greatest attention in this context is the foreign investment law, which was promulgated in April 1967 and which was subsequently modified in various ways. It provided for the guarantees against confiscation and for repatriation of profits already mentioned, and also established a company-tax holiday of three years' duration (later lengthened to five years). Foreign firms were (until the early 1970s) also given a wide berth in the use of foreign personnel, being required to use local personnel only when their training and capability was suitable. Subsequently, regulations on use of domestic personnel were tightened, and pressure was applied to train and use Indonesians as much as possible.

The results of this policy have been impressive, in spite of serious problems of organization for the processing of investment proposals and the disorderly state of law pertaining to business (Clapham 1970; Sadli 1970). Gross domestic capital formation jumped from an extremely low proportion of gross national product in 1966 of 4.5 percent to 21.5 percent in 1973, and is rising rapidly year by year (Government of Indonesia 1975). Approvals of both foreign and domestic investment proposals have accumulated rapidly, with foreign investment approvals reaching a cumulative total of $2.03 billion for the period 1968-1972 and domestic approvals reaching a level of $1.7 billion, according to the Foreign Investment Board. The legal and organizational problems alluded to here are indicated in the fact that investment put in place during the same time period (1968-1972) was only 55 percent of approvals (Foreign Investment Board). (To some extent, of course, this is a matter of time lag and rapid growth of approvals.)

As the preceding figures indicate, foreign investment to date has exceeded domestic. But here again, one is observing a problem of time lag. The government initiated its program of inducing foreign investment earlier, and foreign firms responded earlier. The domestic investment law was not promulgated until 1969, and the investment board, until that time, was involved exclusively in approval of foreign proposals. However, domestic approvals surpassed foreign approvals in 1970 and have remained ahead since that time. Domestic *implementation* did not surpass implementation of foreign investments in manufacturing until 1972. There is every reason for the latter flow to continue to rise at a rate greater than that of private foreign investment, more or less indefinitely.

In sum, government policy toward private investment has been an open one, eagerly encouraging both foreign and domestic entrepreneurs to take advantage of the opportunities created by a relatively open economic system with the added incentives of tax remission and high protection. As a result, the industrial sector is rapidly becoming large enough to have major impact on the overall growth rate and on employment. Manufacturing produced 8.9 percent of total output in 1973, and the entire nonagricultural sector produced 57 percent — versus 48 percent in 1966.

SOCIOPOLITICAL DIMENSIONS OF THE "NEW POLICY"

Distributional Considerations

Perhaps the most common charge against the Suharto regime is, that despite the considerable success of its economic policies in general, the benefits of growth are being too narrowly shared. A veritable chorus of criticism has been raised recently with this as the dominant theme (Shaplen 1974; Schanberg 1974; Starner 1974; Dorodjatun 1971: 46; Mortimer 1973). There are several aspects of this problem, namely, the structure of the tax system and its implementation; the geographic distribution of the development effort; the problem of labor absorption; and the problem of conspicuous consumption.

Taxation and expenditure by government

Indonesia's basic tax structure, like that of most countries of the world, is regressive. The bulk of tax revenues are derived from levies on basic goods, either when they are sold domestically or when they are imported. The breakdown of tax receipts for fiscal years 1972/73 and 1973/74 and that budgeted for 1974/75 and 1975/76 is given in Table 7. Direct taxes (other than those on foreign oil companies) constitute less than one-fifth of total tax revenues, whereas indirect taxes, which are predominantly regressive, constitute a much larger proportion. It is notable, however, that these proportions are declining and converging. A further mitigating factor, and one that will become overwhelming in the next few years, is the already large and extremely rapidly growing importance of revenues from oil. Indonesian taxpayers currently finance barely half of their total budget with taxes on local expenditures, incomes, and enterprises, and that proportion is falling. The remainder comes from three essentially external sources: taxes on foreign oil companies, which in 1973/74 provided nearly 30 percent of all (tax and nontax) government revenues; profits from the sale of oil products by the national oil company (PERTAMINA); and proceeds from foreign loans and credits. Together these three sources provided precisely 50 percent of all revenues in fiscal year 1973/74 (Bank of Indonesia, October 1974: 76-77). Thus, although the government's command over real

TABLE 7
Tax Receipts of the Indonesian Government, 1973/74, 1974/75, 1975/76
(million rupiahs)

Tax source	1973/74 (realized)		1974/75 (budget)		1975/76 (budget)	
	Amount	% of grand total	Amount	% of grand total	Amount	% of grand total
Income tax	34,393	3.7	49,300	3.7	52,400	2.1
Corporation tax	44,223	4.8	60,000	4.5	125,600	5.1
Withholding tax	56,745	6.2	70,100	5.2	104,800	4.3
Ipeda[a]	19,501	2.1	24,200	1.8	31,700	1.3
Other direct taxes	5,500	0.6	9,900	0.7	13,000	0.6
Subtotal: Direct "internal" taxes	160.362	17.4	213,700	16.0	327,500	13.4
Domestic sales tax	54,621	5.9	65,800	4.9	109,900	4.5
Sales taxes on imports	50,725	5.5	65,300	4.9	88,500	3.6
Excises	61,674	6.7	67,800	5.1	90,200	3.7
Import duties	128,172	14.0	167,300	12.5	221,400	9.1
Export taxes	68,623	7.4	65,200	4.9	71,700	2.9
Other indirect taxes	49,134	5.3	35,000	2.6	-10,100[b]	-0.4
Subtotal: Indirect taxes	412,949	45.0	466,400	34.9	571,600	23.4

TABLE 7

Tax Receipts of the Indonesian Government, 1973/74, 1974/75, 1975/76
(million rupiahs) (Continued)

Tax source	1973/74 (realized)		1974/75 (budget)		1975/76 (budget)	
	Amount	% of grand total	Amount	% of grand total	Amount	% of grand total
Foreign oil company tax	344,612	37.5	653,700	49.0	1,540,000	63.1
Grand total, tax	917,923	100.0	1,333,800	100.0	2,439,100	100.0

SOURCE: Bank of Indonesia, October 1974: 76-77. The original source includes the foreign oil company tax among direct taxes. Totals may not add due to rounding.

a. Land tax.
b. Includes domestic oil company losses.

resources constitutes nearly 25 percent of gross domestic product, taxes net of foreign oil company taxes constitute only about 12.5 percent, and therefore the regressive impact to the basic tax system is much less serious than it would be if these nontax and foreign-based tax sources were not available.[7]

This relatively light reliance on the domestic tax base suggests that the pattern of government expenditure may have as much (or more) significance in determining distribution as revenues. Table 8 gives this pattern for the last two fiscal years and for the 1975/76 budget. The large proportions accounted for by personnel expenditures and subventions to the regional and local governments (comprising 44 percent of total expenditures in the 1974/75 budget) suggest that the income flows generated by government expenditure should be widely spread, although, of course, it is possible that maldistribution of perquisites and false multiple appointments create increasing inequality. Not much can be said about the other categories of expenditures without more detailed evidence concerning its distribution than is available. Broadly speaking, however, it does not appear that the fiscal system, for all its shortcomings, is the most serious source of inequity. It seems more likely that income concentration, if it is actually increasing, is the result of activities in the private sector. Of course the fiscal system is involved in this problem indirectly, because the pattern of incentives which has been provided to the private sector in the development effort is predominantly associated with taxation. Company tax exemptions and exemption from duties on capital and raw material imports generally are available only to established business enterprises, or new enterprises connected with the relatively wealthy. As the development process proceeds, this should become less true; but in the early stages of rapid growth, it is all but inevitable that the main advantages will lie with those who already have capital and skills. Tax incentive policies are designed to mobilize those resources.

Geographic distribution

It is generally agreed that Jakarta and West Java have benefited from development considerably more than other regions of Indonesia and that urban areas have benefited more than rural areas. This seems highly plausible, although there are no reliable income data by regions which could be used to test this proposition, either as to general direction of geographical distributional pattern or as to orders of magnitude. This is true despite a sustained effort to develop regional income estimates over the last several years (see Arndt 1973). There are really two aspects to be considered in connection with geographic distribution, namely, the regional aspect and the urban-rural aspect. Per capita incomes in the outlying regions are generally higher than those on Java. Hence, to the extent that developmental resources are more heavily utilized on Java than elsewhere, the interregional distributional pattern should be somewhat improved.

7. It is interesting to note that, in Sukarno's grand eight-year plan for 1960-1968, extraordinary revenues were counted on to make the ambitious investment program possible without huge increases in taxes. The New Order, thanks mainly to oil, is realizing that goal to a far greater extent.

The same cannot be said for urban-rural distribution, however, as urban per capita incomes are substantially above those of rural areas. Both governmental and private investment expenditures are heavily concentrated in the cities, with Jakarta being the most favored, and probably other major Javanese cities (Bandung and Surabaya) following most closely. Industrial investment as well as infrastructural investment are concentrated in these metropolitan areas, and income growth rates are probably higher there than elsewhere in the country. This has given rise to strong protests from regional governments, and the central government has tended to respond by developing urban-based projects for such cities as Padang and Ujung Pandang. Although these projects may or may not be economically justified, it seems likely that the effect of this sort of reaction is regressive with reference to the overall pattern of distribution. The heart of the distribution problem in Indonesia is the lagging rural sector on Java, and the oversupply of unskilled labor, most of which is concentrated there. Hence the real challenge for the future is, to borrow Arthur Mosher's phrase, "getting agriculture moving" (Mosher 1966).

Labor absorption

Success in the agricultural sector is not just a matter of improving supplies of food and export crops, although those objectives are clearly of high importance. Economic vitality in the rural areas is essential to the problem of absorption of Indonesia's immense surplus of unskilled labor. Rapid growth in the cities which rapidly outpaces that of rural areas will lead to accelerated rural-urban migration and to growing pools of overt and disguised unemployed in the cities. This is socially undesirable, in itself, but it is also too dangerous politically for any regime to contemplate with equanimity.

Unfortunately, the magnitude of this problem in Indonesia is already staggering. Because of the youth of Indonesia's population (54 percent under the age of twenty), the labor force is growing even faster than the total population. Nathaniel Iskandar estimates that the labor force growth rate is between 2.6 and 2.75 percent per annum (whereas the total population growth rate is between 2.4 and 2.5 percent) (Iskandar 1972). Furthermore, it can be expected that the labor force growth rate will accelerate gradually between now and the end of the century; hence, the annual increment will rise both absolutely and relatively. That increment is already unmanageable, being on the order of 1.25 million persons per annum. It is literally impossible at this stage of development for the urban sector to absorb that increment — either to domicile them or to employ them. Only 17 percent of Indonesia's population, or about 21 million people, are now in the urban sector (McNicoll and Mamas 1973: 28). It would require a growth rate of urban employment of nearly 12 percent per annum to accommodate the entire increment. Furthermore, there is already an unemployment problem of serious magnitude in Indonesia's cities. It follows that the strategy required is one which will keep rural-urban migration down to a level that can be accommodated by a feasible maximum rate of growth of urban employment opportunities.

TABLE 8

Expenditures by the Indonesian Government, 1972/73 and 1973/74

(millions rupiahs)

	1973/74 (realized)		1974/75 (budget)		1975/76 (budget)	
	Amount	% of grand total[a]	Amount	% of grand total[a]	Amount	% of grand total
Personnel	268,862	23.1	405,100	25.7	602,400	22.0
Materials	110,140	9.4	174,700	11.1	267,200	9.8
Subsidies to regions	108,600	9.3	168,400	10.6	279,500	10.2
Debt repayment	70,700	6.1	82,100	5.2	74,200	2.7
Other routine	155,000	13.3	131,300	8.3	243,200	8.9
Subtotal: Routine budget	713,302	61.3	961,600	61.0	1,466,300	53.6

TABLE 8 (Continued)
Expenditures by the Indonesian Government, 1972/73 and 1973/74
(millions rupiahs)

	1973/74 (realized)		1974/75 (budget)		1975/76 (budget)	
	Amount	% of grand total[a]	Amount	% of grand total[a]	Amount	% of grand total
Developmental Expenditures:						
Via departments and institutions	210,255	18.0	260,275	16.5	}	
Via armed forces	7,225	0.6	18,000	1.1	1,050,000	38.4
Regional and local	68,501	5.9	124,750	7.9		
Other	50,850	4.4	87,877	5.6		
Project aid	114,125	9.8	124,800	7.9	218,400	8.0
Subtotal: Development budget	450,956	38.7	615,700[b]	39.0	1,268,400	46.4
Grand total	1,164,258	100.0	1,577,300	100.0	2,734,700	100.0

SOURCE: Bank of Indonesia, October 1974: 78-79.

a. Percentage totals and subtotals may be slightly in error due to rounding.
b. Unexplained discrepancy of Rp. 2 million in official total.

Fortunately, the growth rate of population in Indonesia's cities has not yet reached the high urban growth rates experienced in many other labor-saturated societies. Table 9 gives 1961-1971 growth rates for several major cities. Even so, urban unemployment and underemployment are already a destabilizing social and political fact, and it seems reasonable to expect urban migration to accelerate substantially in the years ahead, even if a much more successful policy of rural development can be launched in the near future. Such a policy calls for expansion of employment in rural industry and trade, for further labor intensification of agriculture, and for very labor-intensive rural public works projects. As noted here, efforts already have been made, in the period of REPELITA I, to promote new labor-using techniques in agriculture and to utilize the labor surplus in public works programs. However, no policy of significance has yet promoted rural-based industry and trade.

The experience to date indicates how difficult it is to bring about changes in agricultural techniques which absorb additional labor. This is because Indonesia already has undergone centuries of "agricultural involution"; hence, techniques are already *very* labor intensive (see Geertz 1963). To be sure, success with the new rice strains requires more attention to water control, pesticide application, and weeding, but harvesting and hulling have become less labor intensive in many areas. The *tebasan* system of cultivation, in which small groups of men are contracted to harvest fields with sickles, has begun to replace the masses of people cutting rice stalk by stalk with the small *ani-ani* (hand-knife). Similarly, the introduction of the simple hand-operated rice huller is displacing teams of rice pounders (Collier et al. 1973, 1973a). These examples illustrate the painful choice problem presented to innovators in labor surplus areas, namely, that of high productivity per head versus employment. If productivity per head is sacrificed to employment considerations, the result will be "shared poverty." But increased productivity per employed worker brought about by substitution of capital is a mixed blessing, unless productive employment can be found for labor displaced by the new equipment and techniques.

To date the only labor-saturated country which appears to have found a solution to this problem is China, where urban population growth has been restrained to rates which can be absorbed in the urban sector. In order to accomplish this, however, it has been necessary to collectivize agriculture and to involve all available manpower in agriculture, rural industry and trade, and public works through a combination of coercion and intense ideological campaigning. Although impressive, these means seem to be well outside the range of either cultural or political possibility in Indonesia, at least for the foreseeable future. In the absence of such mobilization techniques, the regime will have to rely primarily on market incentives combined with publicly financed works programs. As I shall discuss here, the regime has ambitious plans for meeting the labor absorption problem, and they have made a public commitment to meet the challenge.

The subject of labor absorption should not be left without noting that Indonesia is not getting as much labor absorption out of her capital investment

TABLE 9
City Growth in Indonesia, 1961-1971

City	Island	Population in 1971	Average annual growth rate 1961-1971 (percent)
Jakarta	Java	4,576,009	4.6
Surabaya	Java	1,332,249	2.8
Bandung	Java	1,201,730	2.1
Medan	Sumatra	635,562	2.9
Palembang	Sumatra	582,961	2.1
Ujung Pandang	Sulawesi	434,766	2.7
Banjarmasin	Kalimantan	281,673	2.8

SOURCE: G. McNicoll and S. Mamas 1973: table A-7.

in the *industrial* sector as she should, primarily because of policies that favor capital intensification, but also because of the lack of competition in many areas of the small domestic market. This is a typical problem of low-income countries which are trying to induce new investment through the use of tax and license incentives. These incentives usually are linked directly to the amount of capital invested, and no special benefit attaches directly to the level of employment involved with that capital. Tariff concessions, for example, always are made with reference to the volume of a physical commodity (capital goods or raw materials) imported. Capital concessions are made to investors in the form of concessionary interest rates or loan guarantees, both of which lower capital costs relative to labor costs, and induce capital-intensive techniques of production. The program of building industrial parks is an outright capital subsidy. Adam Smith was correct in asserting that capital accumulation is necessary in order to set labor in motion, but he neglected to take substitution effects into consideration.

The Indonesian government should give serious attention to a search for measures to counter these incentives to substitute capital for labor. Tax credits proportional to wage bills might be considered, for example, or even outright employment subsidies. Less protection for import substitution industries and greater "export protection" also will help. Import substitution industries tend, by their very nature, to be more capital intensive than those that conform to the nation's comparative advantage. A generally lower tariff structure combined with an exchange rate which undervalues the domestic currency somewhat could make the industrial growth path significantly more labor-using. Such a strategy also would have the advantage of increasing competition. There is some evidence that entrepreneurs will favor capital-intensive techniques if they are earning enough in monopoly rents to be able to indulge themselves in more "modern" techniques. This typically means machinery designed for factories in nations that have labor shortages (Wells 1973).

Conspicuous consumption

Conspicuous consumption is important primarily because of its symbolic effect, although it also may bring about a reduced rate of increase of saving and a waste of resources. Conspicuous consumption is symptomatic of the emergence of a substantial class of *nouveaux riches,* which, in the face of rising urban unemployment, is extremely offensive to those in the community sensitive to issues of social justice. It is, indeed, objectionable to see large areas of luxury housing being developed while Jakarta's slums fester and the city's *kampong* development program makes only small inroads into the problem. It is painful to see Jakarta's inadequate street system clogged with new automobiles (assembled in Indonesia at very high resource cost), while people's transportation – the *becak* – is banned from those streets. These examples of misplaced priorities in the use of resources have been discussed at great length in print both inside and outside the country. Clearly, it is in the political interest of the regime to curb these excesses.

To some extent, luxury consumption can be met with sumptuary taxation and prohibitions. Indeed, the regime is already practicing these measures, although it is hampered by administrative inefficiency and corruption in implementation of its regulations. Customs duties on luxury imports are as high as any in the world, but they are manifestly not being enforced with any consistency. Sample comparisons of foreign and domestic prices in 1969 and 1972 showed that commodities with import tax rates of 40 percent or more were sold domestically at prices below landed cost plus import taxes in 70 percent of the cases in both years (Glassburner 1973: 104). The problem of control here is a compound one of a tariff structure that is all but impossible to enforce along with a customs service that is both inefficient and corrupt. Efforts to reform the service thus far have been frustrated by the essential impossibility of the task they have been asked to perform. Although the case of the customs service is a particularly severe example, it is indicative of the complexity of the entire set of problems associated with distribution and conspicuous consumption, namely, that it is a compound of intractable problems, involving demographic factors, organizational problems, and corruption.

As significant as conspicuous consumption is, it is doubtful that the resource costs are of great importance. It is typical to observe that Indonesia has such extreme basic needs that luxury consumption cannot be afforded, but in fact Indonesia's main growth constraints at this juncture are organizational and entrepreneurial rather than material. Admittedly, insofar as organizational and entrepreneurial resources are wasted on building of luxury housing and running gambling dens, there clearly is an opportunity cost involved, and it is certainly in the interest of the regime and the nation to redirect those resources. One problem in this connection is that more productive alternative investment opportunities in the private sector are not as readily available as they should be. There is not yet a well-developed capital market in Indonesia, and low-cost housing is much more risky than luxury housing. High rates of return on investment in luxury housing are virtually assured. What appears to be called for is imposition of heavier taxation on real property of high value and subsidization of house-buyers of limited means. Such advice is clearly much easier to give than it is to take. The regime is beset with a myriad of complex problems, and it is doubtful that urban housing has yet moved to the top of the priority list.

Corruption

As has been indicated here, the problems of maldistribution and conspicuous consumption are closely tied up with corruption of various types. Unfortunately, corruption has deep historical roots in Indonesia (Smith 1971), and these have been more deeply implanted by the policies of governments of Indonesia over the last quarter-century. Corruption is inevitable whenever government regulations are imposed which are extremely at variance with market realities. As has been noted, the *New Order* has moved only partially and gradually in the direction of dependence on the market. Consequently, incentives for corruption remain strong. This is clearly the heart of the problem as far as the tariff system is concerned (discussed here in the section on labor absorption). Despite a series of tariff revisions in the last several years, the system remains unenforceable, but opposition to further downward revision of the tariff schedules is strong and is based on the conviction that lower tariffs mean more imports, which in turn would mean more luxury consumption and more competition for local entrepreneurs. However, it is likely that lower nominal tariffs, combined with a greater effort at enforcement, would mean no greater (and perhaps smaller) rate of increase of imports, more tariff revenue for the Indonesian government, and less corruption in the customs service.

The same may be said of other types of tax collection, most notably income tax collection. It is too much to ask of the tax service that they collect any large proportion of that which is due under the personal income tax, both because the marginal rates are high at low levels of income, and because personal income taxation requires voluntary reporting. A mildly progressive schedule with modest rates, combined with rather high exemptions undoubtedly would yield a great deal more revenue and reduce corruption of tax collectors and taxpayers significantly. An example worth citing in this connection is that of the Hong Kong personal income tax, which has a maximum average rate of 15 percent.[8]

Solution to the problem of corruption in connection with foreign investment is probably most likely to be found in the improvement of the regulations and laws surrounding approval and administration. Fees are paid to influence-peddlers primarily because of delays and confusions connected with the procedures of the investment board and compliance with the investment law. To some extent, of course, these are legitimate advisory fees, and they are high because the services rendered are of high value; but there is also a considerable amount of *uang semir* (money lubrication) involved. This problem undoubtedly will persist

8. Hong Kong also has evasion problems, as do all countries using income taxation, but collections are very good by the standards of almost any nation. Indonesia's minimum rate, on taxable incomes of Rp. 4,500 per month ($10.84), is ostensibly 10 percent. The maximum marginal rate is 50 percent. Personal exemptions are Rp. 108,000 ($260).

as long as the backlog of applications is extremely long, because waiting costs are of great importance to investors. It will take strong measures, under present circumstances, to deter government officials from accepting bribes.

Petty corruption is rife in the bureaucracy primarily because the scale of government salaries is so poor that officials are forced either to moonlight, at least partly on government time, or to charge extraordinary fees for services rendered to users of government services, or both. Successive large increases in salaries have not eliminated this incentive, although they probably have reduced the pressure considerably.

The economic costs of corruption are greatly exaggerated by critics of government. The charging of fees (bribes) for the performance of government services when the government fiscal system is performing poorly is probably an economically efficient solution. When government cannot finance itself effectively and cannot pay its employees according to their social value, it is all but inevitable that some other financing (and pricing) system will be substituted for it. It is also quite likely that the allocation of government services will be more nearly consistent with social priorities if prices are charged for them than if they are not. Social losses do emerge, however, when the services are restricted in order to extract monopoly rents. This is a danger in the case of such services as the issue of permits, for which there is no competitive equivalent provided elsewhere in government or in the private sector.

Capital accumulated by misappropriating government funds may provide a source of investment in the private sector. It is perhaps unlikely, but at least conceivable, that such diversions would lead to an allocation superior to that specified by government initially. At all events, such rechannelings do not constitute deadweight social loss, even if the misappropriated funds are entirely consumed.

As Smith has pointed out, the greatest cost is to be measured not in economic terms but in political and social terms. A regime cannot bear indefinitely the political burden of being considered corrupt, and there is evidence that these costs are becoming very high for the Suharto regime. There is also a more general cost: "Corruption may tend to destroy some of a new nations' greatest potential assets, the enthusiasm, idealism, and sympathy of its youth and students. In the event that the idealism and enthusiasm of the younger generation turns to cynicism, not only political stability but long-run economic development efforts are bound to be affected (Smith 1971: 36). It should be added that conscientious and idealistic government servants already established in government find it hard to maintain their dedication in the presence of blatant corruption, and of strong incentives to follow suit.

The Chinese and the Pribumi

As is generally well known, Indonesia has a small Chinese minority (approximately 2.5 percent of the population) which has economic power all out of proportion to its numbers. Their position in "middle trade" was overtly fostered by the Dutch colonial regime, and this position of power was inadvertently strengthened by the Sukarno regime in the late 1950s when foreign entrepreneurs were expelled and Indonesia sought to develop in an autarchical pattern. Indigenous Indonesians historically have been confined largely to minor trade and agriculture, and have found themselves, upon independence, ill-equipped to compete with the Chinese. The indigenous businessmen, usually referred to as the Pribumi, *asli,* or "economically weak," have sought government support especially for themselves, with some measure of success, ever since independence was first achieved in 1949. The Chinese entrepreneurs, however, are a resource, and a very valuable one, precisely because (with many notable individual exceptions) the Pribumi lack the skills, capital, and social orientation to compete effectively in business. Entrepreneurship being in short supply, the Suharto regime has been reluctant to curb the activities of the Chinese rigorously. Not surprisingly, the Pribumi have raised their voices in vigorous protest.

One complication the government must cope with in connection with this problem is that roughly two-thirds of these Chinese are Indonesian citizens. Any activity which discriminates between the Pribumi and the Chinese therefore raises questions of the validity of citizenship. Nevertheless, such discrimination is practiced, and quite openly. The typical discrimination is to make it very difficult for a Chinese businessman to get government permission to invest, where permission is required, or to get preferential credits for investment. The Chinese have responded to this by hiring Pribumi businessmen to act for them, or by establishing other types of symbiotic relationships (called *Cukong* relationships) with people of influence.

The regime has responded to this challenge by attempting to provide positive inducements for the Pribumi, without putting insurmountable road-blocks in the way of the Chinese. The most recent moves have been to establish two new lending, investment advisory, and insurance institutions especially for "small businesses." (These are P. T. Bahana and P. T. Askarindo.) Very probably the time-honored pattern of discrimination against the Chinese will be adopted in the activities of these institutions, and just as likely the Chinese will find means to turn them to their advantage, in the process sharing some part of their advantage with the Pribumi. At the same time, there are many bona fide entrepreneurs among the Pribumi community, and these leaders will find means of using these new concessions to their direct advantage. In the long run, however, it would appear that the solution (if any *can* be found) will be found in expansion of the arena of business activity, that is, through economic growth. The Chinese undoubtedly will continue to occupy a position of inordinate strength indefinitely, but their relative position will be diluted as the scope for new enterprise expands.[9]

The Pribumi are not to be ignored politically. Hostility to the Chinese is all but universal in the Indonesian body politic, including the military and civilian

9. Return of foreign investors in large numbers already has diluted the *relative* position of the Chinese, but simultaneously it has diluted the relative position of the Pribumi. Recently Japanese enterprise has become as much a target of jealousy and criticism as the Chinese.

elite in government. The Chinese are adept at buying protection, but the Pribumi have the deep sympathy of both the rulers and the ruled. The regime undoubtedly will feel compelled to continue to respond to that sympathy with more overt acts of discrimination in favor of the Pribumi.

Economic Ideology

An astonishing feature of the Suharto regime is the presence in the cabinet of seven economists, six of whom have graduate degrees from American universities, and the seventh of whom has a doctorate from a Dutch university. The six, sometimes referred to as "the Berkeley Mafia" or, more often, "the technocrats," are felt by their critics to be doctrinaire "capitalist-roaders." They are thought to have an irrational passion for economic rationalization and for dependence on the market to provide the incentives for development. If there are noneconomic social costs to growth in this pattern, these, they are thought to believe, are someone else's responsibility.[10]

This is a caricature. Although it is true that six of the seven have American training, it is by no means true that they are indifferent to political and social considerations in policy-making, and they certainly cannot be accused of radical anti-interventionism (see Widjojo 1965; Salim 1965). It was inevitable that they would seek to move basic price relationships toward the neighborhood of market equilibrium in the aftermath of the radical irrationalities of the Sukarno regime, but it is also true that in every policy area, government intervention, under the guidance of the cabinet economists, has remained a central feature (see discussion here under "Restoration of the market system").

The Technocrats and the Military

The economists in the cabinet have a long-standing relationship with the military elite, dating from the early 1960s when the military leaders sought the assistance of the university economists in the training of officers at the military academy in Bandung (SESKOAD). Military involvement in the economy has been extensive since the Dutch firms were expelled in the campaign to free West Irian (now Irian Jaya) in 1958. Most of the firms taken over at that time were placed under military management. The officers' need for the assistance of professional economists and administrators became manifest shortly thereafter, and they thereupon called on the dean of the Faculty of Economics of the University of Indonesia, Professor Widjojo, to mobilize his colleagues to give assistance. Subsequently, following the attempted coup d'état of 1965, the economists were called on again, this time to assist more directly in reordering the economic system. Since that time, their position appears outwardly to have

---

10. See, for example, Dorodjatun 1971. Dorodjatun excuses the technocrats on grounds that they have been used as "scout troops" who have successfully drawn the fire of critics and thus identified salient points on the sociopolitical battlefield — but leaves the responsibility for meeting these challenges to the experts in the other social sciences.

persistently strengthened. In each cabinet revision, their numbers have been increased, and the number of military personnel in the cabinet has been reduced.

Nevertheless, the position of the economists is not one of great political strength. They are very dependent on their relationship with President Suharto and Vice-President Sultan Hamengku Buwono IX. When economic policy comes under attack, their staying power is entirely derivative of the power of the military regime. To some extent, of course, they have the strength of their near-monopoly position on economic expertise. However, as is evident from examining the makeup of governments elsewhere, most heads of state consider economists dispensable, and they typically rely on bankers, lawyers, and even military men to make decision on economic policy.

In the early months of 1974, and to a lesser extent since that time, rumors persisted that a cabinet reordering would be forthcoming, and that the prominent economist-ministers would be partially, if not entirely, replaced. However, 1974 passed and even Professor Ali Wardhana, minister of finance, retained his position. Publicly, the target of criticism of economic policy is usually Professor Widjojo Nitisastro, the acknowledged head of the team of economists. However, it is Professor Ali who operates at the cutting edge of fiscal, banking, and tariff policy, and it is he who becomes directly involved with the powerful inner circle of business and government people who are the vested interests that must be dealt with. Professor Ali's dismissal has been repeatedly forecast with assurance by "the knowledgeable" in Jakarta.[11]

REPELITA II

April 1, 1974, marked the date of the beginning of the second five-year plan period. It had been hoped, in the planning commission, that expert resources would be marshaled systematically to pull together a sophisticated planning document, based on research in depth and the combined thinking of a large number of economic experts. But even the plans of planners' plans go awry. The rice crisis and the inflationary problems of 1972/73 kept the attention of Minister of Planning Widjojo and his major subordinates well into the year, with the result that President Suharto was able to discuss the second plan in only the broadest outlines in his Independence Day speech of August 17, 1973, and only a hurriedly assembled plan was promulgated. The plan document was presented to the Indonesian Parliament in March 1974 and published for only very limited circulation (Department of Information 1974). Because of the haste with which it was prepared, and because of the radical impact of changing oil prices, the plan was obsolete on the day of its promulgation. The plan is thus of interest almost exclusively as a statement of qualitative objectives. Revisions of quantitative objectives are being undertaken in virtually all departments of government, but there appears to be no likelihood of a comprehensive rewriting

11. See addendum at the conclusion of this chapter.

in the foreseeable future. To attempt such a revision would require a dramatic shift in planning conception, as the key parameters have become those of absorptive capacity.

It is clear, however, from what has been published that the regime hopes to respond effectively to the challenges described in the preceding pages. Broadly, the second plan is to follow the strategy of the first, with first priority being given to the agricultural sector, but with increased emphasis on regional development, social services, and employment. The plan contains an indicative schedule designed to absorb the entire increment to the labor force over the coming five-year period. This scheme would rely on the nonagricultural sector to absorb 78 percent of the labor increment, with 22 percent to be absorbed by industry, trade, and the services sector (Department of Information 1974: Table 6-2). This is not altogether infeasible, but it will take an expanded effort by comparison with the first plan. Of course, Indonesia's resources have greatly expanded since the eruption of oil prices, so one can expect a more vigorous effort on the part of the government. On the other hand, the nation has serious absorptive capacity problems, as the preceding discussion has emphasized.

Aside from the ambitious labor-absorption program, the plan calls for an average growth rate of gross domestic product of 7.5 percent, with sectoral growth rates as indicated in Table 10. These macroeconomic targets are generally considered to be too modest in light of the oil bonanza, which has outstripped all expectations. Oil exports in fiscal 1974/75 were running at an estimated annual rate of $4.75 billion, net of related imports (April-September 1974), whereas the target figure for the *end* year of the plan period, 1978/79, was set at $3.6 billion, including projected exports of liquified natural gas (Department of Information 1974: Table 9-5, 285; *Laporan Mingguan* December 19, 1974).

However, it would be foolhardy to project this overachievement to the economy generally. Nonoil exports were running slightly below the plan's 1974/75 target, and there were persistent complaints of economic slowdown. These contrasts emphasize the increasingly evident problems of sectoral imbalance in the Indonesian economy. These problems are not analyzed with any degree of sophistication in the plan — as they would have to be if the plan were to be taken seriously as a guide to policy of any specificity.

Finally, the draft contains a statement of five broad goals. They are the following:

1. Adequate supply of food and clothing of better quality and within the people's purchasing power.
2. Adequate household supplies and facilities.
3. Better and more extensive infrastructure.
4. Higher and more evenly distributed social welfare.
5. Greater employment opportunities (Department of Information 1974: 45).

There seems little doubt but that a serious effort will be made to accomplish more in the distributional and employment areas. Corruption, although

TABLE 10

Planned Sectoral Production Growth Rates

for the Second Five-Year Plan

Sector	Average annual growth rate
Agriculture	4.6
Mining	10.1
Industry	13.0
Construction	9.2
Transportation and communications	10.0
Other	7.7
Gross domestic product	7.5

SOURCE: Department of Information 1974: Table 6.1.

unmentioned in the plan, is also in the forefront of the planners' thinking. One can only hope that these policies succeed. If the regime fails in these areas, it will surely not survive the next five years without further, and probably more serious, political disturbances.[12] They have made remarkable progress in a short period of time, but severe political disturbances could lead to major economic setbacks, which the nation, poor as it is, cannot afford.

ADDENDUM

This article was completed prior to the denouement of the failure of the Indonesian national oil company, PERTAMINA, to meet scheduled short-term debts in 1975. By the end of the 1975 calendar year, it had been revealed that total short-term debts in the amount of $1.5 billion had been accumulated by the enterprise and that total indebtedness, short and long term, totalled in excess of $10 billion. Under the leadership of professors Widjojo and Sadli, the government moved quickly and successfully to marshall resources to prevent default. The president-director, Lieutenant-General Ibnu Sutowo, was "dismissed with honor" on March 3, 1976, and replaced by Major General Piet Haryono, who was formerly director of the budget, Department of Finance.

These events have important implications, although none requires fundamental alteration of the conclusions offered in this chapter. The relevant implications follow:

1. The political position of the technocrats in the cabinet has been strengthened because of the fall from grace of General Ibnu, who was without

12. This is not to say that progress measured by these criteria will be sufficient to guarantee political stability. On such matters this author, as an economist, must necessarily defer to his colleagues in political science, who are the authors of most of the essays in this volume.

question the most powerful of the military-economic leaders prior to the emergence of the PERTAMINA financial crisis. The issue of accountability on the part of state enterprises and agencies has come to the forefront — an issue on which the civilian economists have been doing battle, with only marginal success, for the past nine years.

2. Indonesia's public sector international indebtedness has been revealed to be much heavier than was generally thought to be the case. Whereas debt service obligations had fallen to approximately 3 percent of foreign exchange earnings in fiscal year 1974/75, in the wake of the OPEC price boom, a World Bank source now indicates that the debt service to export earnings ratio may mount to as much as 19 percent by 1979. This proportion may not be beyond the level with which the government can cope, but it is well beyond the rather arbitrarily chosen norm of 10 percent.

3. Published data do not yet indicate that development expenditures have been adversely affected by the PERTAMINA crisis, and there is no obvious reason why they must be affected in the period of the second five-year plan. However, sustaining the development effort will depend more than ever on capital inflows, which implies continued, and even expanded, dependence on foreign governmental and private lenders, at increasingly hard terms. Inasmuch as "excessive" dependence had already become a serious political issue, this solution to the problems created by General Ibnu's cavalier performance as president-director of PERTAMINA must be a cause of increasing concern.

4. Public confidence in the general competence of the regime to manage economic affairs has been further shaken. Given that the regime had struggled to establish an image of pragmatism and effectiveness, it is a serious blow for it to be revealed that General Ibnu, the president's comrade-in-arms and close personal friend, managed his enterprise irresponsibly. It seems unlikely that this loss of prestige can be counterbalanced by the emerging prominence of the civilian economists.

For detailed treatment of the story of PERTAMINA's near disaster, see Chapter 4 in this volume, and for support of the preceding conclusions see Glassburner 1976.

6 Participation and the Political Parties

R. WILLIAM LIDDLE

POLITICAL PARTIES once dominated the governmental process in Indonesia. Today, as for a good many years now, they no longer do so, having given pride of place to the military. In their heyday, the parties saw themselves and were seen by many observers as representative of important groups in Indonesian society, groups with distinctive perspectives on political and social life and distinctive demands to make on government. In their decline, the parties' claims to speak individually for large social groupings and collectively for the people as a whole have been under fire from two directions. First, it has been argued by many domestic nonparty political figures and intellectuals and by many foreign observers as well that Indonesia in the 1970s has turned a corner, away from the party-produced conflicts and upheavals of the 1950s and 1960s and toward a more prosperous and internally peaceful future under military and technocratic leadership. Old cleavages, in this view, are being reshaped into a new consensus on development. Second, it has been argued that even at the height of their power and influence the parties were not in fact representative of the society. The old cleavages, in this view, were confined substantially to a small elite group and infected the populace at large only when manipulated by that group, so that a leadership free of division means a reunified people as well.

I disagree with both of these appraisals. In my judgment, the cleavages in Indonesian society which underlay the party system in the early years of independence were real — that is to say, the general ideological positions and specific demands of party leaders reflected with some fidelity the general conceptions of society and politics and the specific aspirations of substantial popular constituencies. Much more imperfectly (as the parties have been subject to considerable outside manipulation for so long) they continue to do so today. This essay is an attempt to establish these propositions, and to suggest what they imply for Indonesia's political future. The evidence that I shall present is my reading of the record of party actions, patterns of interaction among parties, and patterns of interaction between parties and government during the past quarter-century.

I would like to thank Herbert Feith and Karl Jackson for their comments.

PARTIES UNDER THREE REGIMES

In surveying the history of political parties in independent Indonesia, one is struck by elements of both continuity and change. Continuity is apparent in the fact that from the early 1950s until at least 1971 four large parties and a few smaller ones defined, for most participants and observers and despite the shifting fortunes of individual party organizations, the basic structural dimensions of popular politics in Indonesia. The four large parties are the Indonesian Nationalist party (PNI), the party most closely associated with the late President Sukarno until the last years of his political career; the Indonesian Communist party (PKI), illegal since 1965, when hundreds of thousands of its leaders and members were killed following the murder of six army generals; and the two Muslim parties Nahdatul Ulama and Masyumi, the latter banned in 1960 and succeeded in 1970 by the Indonesian Muslim party (Parmusi). Among the smaller parties, Parkindo (Indonesian Christian [Protestant] party) and Partai Katolik (Catholic party) have often featured in national political developments, as has – despite its banning in 1960 – the Indonesian Socialist party (PSI). The substance of this continuity, what it was precisely that continued and why it did so, will be examined in the following section.

Change is also apparent in the partisan vicissitudes briefly outlined here. It is indeed not possible to speak during this period of an Indonesian party system, if by system one means a persisting, uniform pattern of interaction among the leaders and members of a constant set of party organizations. Nor is there a single pattern in the relationship of parties (taken individually or collectively) to the political process. Rather, the period must be seen as a succession of party systems, or better (because of the involvement of nonparty actors and the changing relationship of the parties to power) of participation systems, in which movement is a constant and no pattern can maintain itself for long.

Postindependence Indonesian political history is usually divided into three periods or regimes: parliamentary democracy or cabinet dominance, from the transfer of sovereignty at the end of 1949 until the irreversible loss of parliamentary authority by 1957; guided democracy or presidential dominance, from the presidentially decreed return to the Constitution of 1945 in July 1959 to the assassination of the generals and the destruction of the Communist party in 1965; and the army dominated New Order of President Suharto, from 1965 to the present. This categorization of periods is neither original with me nor undisputed among specialists. My purpose in presenting it is to lay out as concisely and as accurately as possible the main lines of the history of popular participation in Indonesian politics during the past twenty-five years. As my focus is on the political parties, it is useful further to subdivide these periods, on the basis of changes in interparty relationships, intraparty activities, and the position of parties in the political system as a whole, into seven separate participation systems and transitions between systems.

Parliamentary Democracy

The major characteristics of the first participation system, which lasted from the end of 1949 until mid-1953, were the centrality of Parliament in the political process, the weakness of organizational links between the national party leaders and parliamentary delegations on the one hand and the masses they claimed to represent on the other, and the dominance of conservative factions within each of the major parliamentary parties (see Feith 1962, 1958, 1957). Parliamentary government was the choice of the national leadership that had emerged victorious in 1949 over both the Dutch and its own domestic competitors. The first Parliament was a very mixed assemblage, containing representatives of states created by the Dutch during the independence struggle, members of the revolutionary Central National Committee, and members appointed by President Sukarno on the basis of estimated party strengths. In 1952, in a 222-member Parliament, there were 48 Masyumi, 36 PNI, 16 PKI, and 15 PSI representatives. When Nahdatul Ulama, originally an educational and social organization, broke with Masyumi later in the year, the latter's representation was reduced by eight (Feith 1958: 32).

Organizationally, the Muslim parties had the best initial links with the village population. Masyumi was a federation of Islamic organizations, the most prominent of which was Muhammadiyah, a modernist social and educational organization founded in Jogjakarta in 1912, while NU was adding a political aspect to an organization that had existed since 1926. But Masyumi had the problem of large size and diffused power (it was labeled "an elephant with beri-beri"), NU's mass base was largely in East Java, and neither organization had much actual political experience. The Indonesian Communist party, following its near-destruction at Madiun in September 1948, had pulled itself together and begun to build a mass base in organized labor, but it was not yet a major force. PNI had the considerable advantages of being generally regarded as the premier party of Indonesian nationalism and as the party closest to the president (Sukarno had led the prewar PNI, but joined no party after the declaration of independence). It was also well represented in the Ministries of Information and Home Affairs, which controlled the territorial civil service or *pamong praja,* but at least at the beginning of this period it had virtually no village-level organization. The intellectual leaders of the Indonesian Socialist party, who saw disadvantages as well as advantages in trying to create a mass base, relied heavily for their political influence on the quality of their technical and administrative expertise and on their general braintrusting.

The conservatism of dominant party factions was both a pillar of the participation system, as the conservative leaders were the most committed to parliamentary government and also shared many policy goals, and a source of its downfall. To a considerable extent the conservatives owed their prominence to the circumstances of the last years of the independence struggle, when diplomatic expertise, international experience, and political and economic views acceptable to the West were useful commodities, and when domestically the radical wing of the nationalist movement was at its weakest. Once in power, however, they came under heavy fire for their economic policies (too partial to Dutch and Chinese capital, not enough concern for indigenous entrepreneurs), their unwillingness to take a strong stand on the question of Dutch New Guinea (now Irian Jaya), which continued to be held by the Dutch after the transfer of sovereignty over the rest of the archipelago, the generally pro-Western stance of their foreign policies, and their policy of rationalization of the armed forces (in opposition to those who favored a "people's army" trained for guerrilla warfare).

The second participation system, 1953-1956, was marked by serious partisan conflict, extensive party penetration of the villages, and the declining legitimacy of parliamentary government. The central event shaping the period was the passage of an election law in April 1953, which in turn had as its immediate cause the atmosphere of parliamentary and political instability resulting from the army attempt to pressure President Sukarno to dissolve Parliament known as the October 17 (1952) Affair. Dissatisfaction with the unrepresentativeness of the temporary Parliament, believed by many to be the source of such political ills as cabinet instability, slowness of decision-making and avoidance of important issues, had existed almost since the inauguration of Parliament. Until the October 17 Affair, however, it had been balanced by the awareness of many members that they would not likely return to an elected parliament, and more importantly by the fears of some party leaders that the distribution of power among the parties might be changed significantly by an election.

The most widely predicted − and most feared − change in the distribution of power was an increase in the strength of Islamic parties, particularly Masyumi, which raised the specter of a state based on Islamic law and governed by religious zealots. An exchange in January 1953 between President Sukarno, who called for a national rather than an Islamic state, and Isa Anshary, a fiery Masyumi leader from West Java, who charged the president with denying Muslims their democratic rights, set the tone for the election campaign to follow (Feith 1958: 159-63; Compton 1955). Masyumi and PNI (the latter now controlled by more radically nationalist leaders), which had collaborated in two previous cabinets, became the major opposing poles in the campaign, intensifying and making explicit a pattern of division which was to continue through the subsequent periods and into the present. Allied with Masyumi were PSI and the two Christian parties, which stressed similarities in social and economic policy and discounted the importance of Islamic ideology to Masyumi leaders. Allied with PNI was PKI, seeking protection and nationalist legitimacy, and NU, which expected to control the Ministry of Religion in a PNI government.

The approach of elections, ultimately held in September 1955, also broadened the arena of political contestation. Parliamentary maneuvers and seeking the support of such extraparliamentary forces as the military and even President Sukarno became of secondary importance to the creation of as large a mass base as possible. The consequences of this effort were a considerable fleshing out of party organizational skeletons almost everywhere in the country and, in the voting results, a specification of actual party strength (and equally important, its geographical spread) to replace the guessing game of earlier years. But in parliamentary terms the election was a standoff (Feith 1957: 58-59). PNI and Masyumi each obtained 57 seats in the new Parliament (with 22.3 percent and 20.9 percent of the vote respectively), while NU received 45 seats (18.4 percent) and PKI 39 seats (16.4 percent). PNI, NU, and PKI were shown to be primarily parties of East and Central Java, the homeland of the ethnic Javanese, although each had important areas of strength elsewhere as well, and Masyumi emerged very strong in nearly every province *except* East and Central Java. As expected, Parkindo (2.6 percent, 8 seats) and Partai Katolik (2.0 percent, 6 seats) did well in their respective religious communities, but somewhat surprisingly the Socialist party (2.0 percent, 5 seats) turned out also to be both small and localized, with 60 percent of its vote from West Java and Bali. Although an additional 21 parties and other associations of voters won seats in the 257-member Parliament, none was a serious competitor on the national level of the big four.

After the elections, parliamentary authority declined rapidly. Only a small segment of the political elite had ever been deeply committed to the system, and most of these leaders were now either out of favor in their own parties or out of power in the Parliament, or both. Elections had been seen as a panacea, but no single party had demonstrated that it held the loyalty of the people, and it was soon clear that parliamentary political maneuvering would continue as before. Even if a majority party or a stable and purposeful coalition cabinet had existed, it is doubtful that the ultimate outcome would have been much affected, for several powerful extraparliamentary forces were no longer willing to let the conflicts among them be settled within the parliamentary arena.

Guided Democracy

The third period, 1957-1959, is one of transition from parliamentary to Guided Democracy (see Lev 1966). It is marked by conflict between the regions and the center, by the general decline of most parties and the removal from the political arena of Masyumi and PSI, by the rise of PKI, and by the working out of a new pattern of division of authority and spheres of influence between the two power centers which replaced the institution of Parliament — President Sukarno and the army.

Regional dissatisfaction was not a new phenomenon in Indonesian politics, but it was slow in finding effective channels for its expression. In their final attempt to maintain a measure of control in Indonesia, the Dutch from 1946 to 1949 established fifteen states and special territories outside the areas controlled by the revolutionary Republic of Indonesia (see Kahin 1952: chaps. 12, 14). The transfer of sovereignty at the end of 1949 was made to a federal Republic of the United States of Indonesia (RUSI) comprised of these fifteen states plus the Republic of Indonesia. Led for the most part by traditional rulers who were willing collaborators of the Dutch both before World War II and during the Revolution, the federal states were politically out of step with the much larger (in population) and more dynamic Republic of Indonesia, and were easily dismantled and incorporated into a unitary republic within nine months of the transfer of sovereignty. This brief experience with federalism left a bad taste in the mouths of Republican leaders, who henceforth equated regional feelings, loyalties, and demands, even when expressed by bona fide Republicans in the regions, with separatism.

From the regional point of view there was much to be dissatisfied with throughout the parliamentary period. Jakarta was far away, caught up in the narrow parliamentary maneuvering described here, and unwilling to devolve much fiscal or decision-making power on the regions. Civil servants from Java held many high positions on other islands. Government economic policies both directly and indirectly (through inflation) tended to subsidize the importers of Java at the expense of the exporters of the outer islands, particularly Sumatra and Sulawesi. Increasingly during the 1950s these complaints were taken up by regional military officers who shared the perspective of their local civilian counterparts toward the center and who often had grievances of their own related to the declining welfare of their troops. Having participated in the Revolution, many of these officers also came to feel that they deserved a role — perhaps a substantial role, given parliamentary incompetence — in the governmental process.

The first direct, open challenges to central authority by regional military officers were the December 1956 takeovers of provincial governments in Central Sumatra, North Sumatra, and South Sumatra by their respective territorial army commanders. The North Sumatra coup was quickly reversed, but the others held firm and were soon joined by a similar takeover in East Indonesia. The movement reached its peak a year later, when a Revolutionary Government of the Republic of Indonesia was proclaimed in Sumatra.

While these events were taking place, President Sukarno was engaged in a campaign to replace the weak leadership provided by cabinet government with strong leadership of his own. The president had long been frustrated by the limitations of his office, which prevented him from fully utilizing the special position he enjoyed as first leader of the Revolution to pursue his own vision of the kind of society Indonesia might become. As a first step, Sukarno in February 1957 called for the creation of a National Council, responsible directly to himself and made up primarily of representatives of functional groups, which would bypass parliament and legitimize Sukarno's claim to speak for the whole Indonesian nation. A second step was to fan the flames of the Irian question, the kind of issue for which he was superbly equipped to rally enthusiastic mass support. In late 1957, after the United Nations General Assembly failed to vote in support of the Indonesian position on Irian, there was a wave of worker-initiated expropriations of Dutch firms, followed by the hasty departure of most Dutch nationals.

The ultimate consequences of these and other activities by the president and the regional army commanders were profound. The central army leadership and loyal territorial commands were prime beneficiaries, strengthened first by a nationwide declaration of war and seige in March 1957, following the collapse of the second Ali Sastroamidjojo cabinet, then by the army's assumption of administrative responsibilities for the former Dutch firms, and finally by their military successes in March-May 1958, which broke the back of the regional rebellions. Most political parties suffered a loss in power and influence from these events, declining as parliament and civilian government in general declined, but Masyumi — the major party of the Outer Islands — and PSI were hit especially hard. Several national leaders of both parties defected to the rebels, and there was much congruence between the policy views of the regionalists and those of the Masyumi and PSI leaders who remained loyal to the center. In 1960 both parties were formally banned and thereafter played a largely behind-the-scenes role in national politics.

The one party which managed to improve its situation through these events was PKI. In contrast to the expectations of most observers, the Communists had done well in the 1955 elections. In 1957 provincial and county (*kabupaten*) elections were held in Java, and PKI improved its position in every county (mostly at the expense of PNI), becoming the largest party on Java (Lev 1966: 84). As the fear of Islam began to recede with Masyumi's failure in 1955 to win its widely predicted majority, fear of communism took its place. Opposition to PKI from both central army leaders and the regional rebels, one of whose demands was typically for a harsher government policy toward communism, pushed the party closer toward the one force which could and would protect it — President Sukarno.

If the first participation system, 1949-1953, was relatively closed in terms of the degree of participation of popular forces in national political life, its successor — the election period — represented a classic liberal democratic response to the problem of how to bring the widely accepted value of popular sovereignty into line with the actual distribution of power. But the attempt to create a relatively open liberal democratic system — with parliamentary government, regular elections, a party leadership accountable in some degree to members and supporters — was, as I have noted, forestalled by the passage of political power out of parliamentary hands even as the first elections were being organized. President Sukarno's response to these events was to argue that the fault lay in Indonesia's failure to be true to her own identity and traditions, in her reliance on Western solutions to Indonesian problems. What Indonesia needed was the unity of the revolutionary spirit and of devotion to the interests of the people as a whole, not the divisiveness of competition among narrowly based parties and of regional hostility. To achieve this unity he proposed a participation system which in its fullest elaboration had two major characteristics: the formal incorporation into decision-making institutions of all loyal political currents and other groupings in society, together with adoption of such quasi-traditional attitudes and practices as *gotong-royong* (working together for the common good) and the replacement of voting by *musyawarah* (discussion) leading to *mufakat* (consensus, unanimity); and reliance on himself as the supreme embodiment of the aspirations of the Indonesian people, in both their diversity and their essential unity.

In the first phase of Guided Democracy, 1959-1962, the president was obliged to share power with the army (see Feith 1963; Hindley 1962; Lev 1963). The events of 1957-1959 had brought the army new powers (in particular over regional government and nationalized industries, but also in central government policy-making), autonomy from parliamentary control, and a new sense of the appropriateness of its expanded political role. Many officers felt strongly that the army had both a duty and a right — deriving from its revolutionary role and the political, technical, and managerial capacities of its personnel — to be a legitimate and permanent participant in the political system, including those aspects of government that had no direct bearing on its institutional responsibilities. But few army leaders saw a military regime as the successor to parliamentary government; rather, like many civilian politicians, journalists, and others in those difficult times, they accepted much of Sukarno's critique of liberal democracy and his prescription for improvement. They also recognized that a coalition with the president would legitimize, for many outside the military, the exercise of their newly acquired powers.

The participation system of early Guided Democracy thus consisted of two major forces which were participants and contenders for power in their own right, with particular interests to pursue and defend and broader conceptions of the good society to promote. In the absence or weakness of other institutions they also became the major arenas of participation, the decision-making centers toward which all other would-be political actors were drawn. As such, they tended to develop separate clienteles and some areas of separate responsibilities, although there was much overlap and competition as well. The president's principal spheres of influence were in the formulation of ideology (defining the nation's identity and sense of purpose, the goals worth striving for and the means with which they could be achieved), in the mobilizational aspects of popular politics, and in the conduct of foreign policy. Closest to the president, protected by him and pursuing their interests through him, were PNI, PKI, and at times NU and Parkindo, some elements of the central government bureaucracy, and some Chinese business interests. The army's spheres of influence were in the areas mentioned previously — its own internal affairs, regional government outside Java, and management of former Dutch industries and plantations. Working through it, often at a level which kept them out of the national political arena, were regional autonomists, ex-Masyumi and ex-PSI interests, Partai Katolik and sometimes Parkindo and NU, and a large proportion of those who wanted the government to attend more to problems of economic stabilization and development than it had in recent years. Guided Democracy was thus to some extent a continuation of the PNI-Masyumi conflict of the early and mid-1950s, but other forces were at work as well and the army in particular more or less accurately reflected (or at least contained within it) the whole political spectrum, including Java and the outer islands, entrepreneurs and bureaucrats, pro-communists and anti-communists, and so on.

The second phase of Guided Democracy, 1963-1965, was marked by the centrality of PKI in political life (Feith 1964; Mortimer 1974). The initiative seemed to have shifted from the army, which after 1960 was engaged mostly in consolidating its gains and maintaining its position, to President Sukarno, whose ideological formulations and policy positions increasingly paralleled those of PKI, and to PKI itself, which engaged in bolder policies of confronting its opponents than it had before. As in the earlier election period, popular forces were destabilizing a relatively limited and conservative (in accomplishments, if not in projected image) participation system.

Although many events combined to create the sense of PKI success and forward movement, it was primarily the party's grassroots activities (and the mystique those activities created) which gave it its leverage with Sukarno and made it a serious contender, together with the army, for Indonesia's future. In the countryside, especially in East and Central Java but also in the other areas of serious social dislocation such as the plantation region of East Sumatra, no party could match PKI for organizational ability or level of activity. From the early 1950s the party had pioneered the development of special-purpose party affiliates designed to obtain the support of workers, farmers, youth, women, and so on, and by 1965 these organizations claimed over 23 million members (Mortimer 1974: 366).[1] By contrast, most other parties, after a spurt of organizational development in the mid-1950s, tended to neglect the cultivation of their mass bases in favor of the more immediately rewarding activity of obtaining the support of powerful civilian and military bureaucrats. In addition, PKI's leaders had a reputation for a minimum of *embourgeoisement* and a maximum of commitment to the cause and willingness to accept discipline. Again by contrast, most other parties were split into warring factions and had many leaders known not to be above the buying and selling of influence. In 1964 and 1965, through a series of *aksi sepihak* (unilateral actions by branches of its farmers' organization against landlords alleged to have refused to conform to the requirements of the 1960 land reform law) and other mass agitational activities, PKI seemed determined to demonstrate – to the other parties, to Sukarno, and most pointedly to the army – its right to speak for the Indonesian people.

The New Order

In sharp contrast to Guided Democracy, and indeed to all previous participation systems, the New Order of President Suharto contains only one major power center, the armed forces. As the single dominating group, the military – or more precisely the central leadership whose power derives primarily

1. The party's claimed membership at this time was 3.5 million. There is no way of checking these figures, and the reader is forewarned that membership inflation has been a common tactic in Indonesian party politics. My own observation of PKI organizational activity in East Sumatra from 1962 to 1964 confirms the general argument of great organizational skill and energy, and an impression among the elite of mass sympathy toward PKI fully as important in terms of the atmosphere it created as actual membership figures.

from the army, the core of the armed forces – is a good deal more powerful than any of its predecessors. It is also less of an arena in which other political actors may seek to influence the outcome of events than previous governing institutions, itself included, have been.

The transition from Guided Democracy to the New Order began in the early morning of October 1, 1965, when six army generals were taken from their homes and murdered. The circumstances surrounding this event – in particular whether it was essentially an internal army affair or a PKI attempt to weaken anti-Communist elements in the army – are still the subject of heated controversy, and likely to remain so (see Mortimer 1974: app. *A, B*; Lev 1966*a*; Notosusanto and Saleh, n.d.; Anderson and McVey 1971). But there is little disagreement concerning what happened next. Leadership of the army was assumed by Major General Suharto, commander of the army's strategic reserve forces, and the back of the coup was broken within a few hours. Suharto and other army leaders from the outset took the position that PKI was deeply involved in the murders, and almost immediately launched a purge against it that quickly spread to the villages. By the end of 1965, although killings and arrests continued long afterward, the party no longer existed as an organized force.

In its first years, nothing shaped the emerging regime – in its attitude toward President Sukarno, its relationships with other social groups, and its internal power dynamics – more than the decision to destroy PKI (see Paget 1967; Hindley 1970; Feith 1968). The president's support for the party, after as well as before October 1, and his rumored complicity in the murder plot made it extremely difficult for his supporters within the armed forces and elsewhere in the society to defend his continuation in office. In March 1966, in an atmosphere of increasing political tension and declining presidential authority, Sukarno signed an order giving extensive executive powers to General Suharto, by then army chief-of-staff. In March 1967 Suharto was named acting president by the People's Consultative Assembly, a kind of super-parliament charged by the 1945 constitution with responsibility for selecting the president and for setting the basic guidelines of state policy, and Sukarno was prohibited from engaging in political activity. In March 1968, by vote of the same body, Suharto became full president.

The new president's rise to power involved the active participation of a number of social groups and forces from which little had been heard in recent years. In Jakarta, new student and youth organizations were formed for the specific purpose of opposition first to communism and then to President Sukarno, and immediately attracted thousands of supporters. Many of these groups had a strongly Islamic orientation and were built on organizations affiliated with NU or formerly associated with Masyumi, but some had Catholic or Protestant origins and still others were organized by student leaders of no pronounced religious affiliation whose political views had much in common with the old PSI. These groups played an independent (though parallel) role of considerable importance in the political process, often moving ahead of the army leadership in defining issues and then using the technique of the mass demonstration to apply pressure on the government. In the villages, too, there was new political activity, as NU, Masyumi, and other party leaders and youth groups mobilized in opposition to the Communist party, usually working closely with local military officers in the arrest and/or execution of PKI leaders, members, and sympathizers. In some areas PNI groups also cooperated in the anti-Communist drive, but at the national level and in many regions as well PNI was unwilling or unable to extricate itself from its close association with President Sukarno and through him with PKI. In 1966 an extraordinary PNI congress, held in Bandung under army protection and with army intervention, replaced the old national leadership with one more in tune with the new government, but most PNI activists continued to withhold their support (see Rocamora 1970; McIntyre 1972).

Divisions within the armed forces, some inherited from the past, others a product of the circumstances of the period, were pronounced during the early New Order. Although the most prominent military defenders of PKI and of Sukarno were either removed from office or in other ways rendered ineffectual, there was still much support for the former president among lower ranking officers and their troops, especially in East and Central Java. More importantly, at least in the short run, the New Order army leadership itself was divided into two groups identified by Donald Hindley as "army radicals" and "Suharto centrists" (Hindley 1970: 55). The army radicals were associated primarily with the Siliwangi division of West Java, the army's most ethnically comprehensive and thus "national" division, the source of many prominent officers since the Revolution, and strategically situated near the national capital. The radicals wanted the government to move more decisively not only against Sukarno but against the whole civilian political class of the Guided Democracy period, and they were in favor of a thoroughgoing restructuring of the political system designed to remove all obstacles to rapid economic development. President Suharto and the men around him, a large proportion of them from the Central Java Diponegoro division which Suharto had once commanded, were said to share many of the radicals' objectives but to want to move more slowly and to bring a larger proportion of the nation along with them in a process of consensual change. The Suharto centrists also had to take into account the potential political strength of the army's most senior officer, General A. H. Nasution. The only target of the October 1 conspirators who had escaped with his life, General Nasution was in 1968 chairman of the important People's Consultative Assembly. As an Outer Islander and a devout Muslim he was a symbolic rallying point for those opposed to the leadership of the Javanese and nominally Islamic Suharto.

As late as 1969 the emerging pattern of New Order politics seemed comparable in some of its essential characteristics to the limited participation systems of the early parliamentary and Guided Democracy periods. Though the army was clearly in power and had no serious rivals, there were still important differences within it, differences which reflected the views of broader groups in society. Other political forces continued to exist as well, and in 1968 presidential permission was given for the formation of a new Muslim party, Parmusi, albeit on condition that no former Masyumi leader at any level be given a leadership position. There continued to be much talk of who was ahead in the competition for the role of "partner" in governmental positions and on whom the success of the government's economic program depended; one or more of the political parties, with their acknowledged mass followings; or the civilian counterparts of the army radicals, who wanted a major revamping of the party system in which the old "ideological" parties would be replaced by "programmatic" organizations more attuned to the needs of a modernizing society (see Liddle 1973).

The limited participation systems of 1950-1953 and 1959-1963 were both followed by periods of high levels of participatory demands, and then breakdown, as previously less powerful forces tried to gain access to decision-making centers or otherwise to improve their position in the overall struggle for power. In the 1953-1956 period, Sukarno, the military, and popular groups mobilized by the political parties were all extraparliamentary forces ultimately not incorporable within the parliamentary framework; in the 1963-1965 period PKI's demands — and the mass support and agitation behind them — had a similarly destabilizing effect on the Sukarno-army coalition of early Guided Democracy. The limited participation system of 1966-1969, on the other hand, was replaced by an authoritarian regime in which power is concentrated rather than diffused as in the previous periods and in which breakdown, if it comes, will be more a product of internal struggles (which may, to be sure, reflect broader social divisions) than of conflict among groups whose limited resources make them no match for a unified military.

Two events in 1969 signaled the shift toward a more centralized and authoritarian regime: the armed forces reorganization, announced in October, and the passage of an election law by Parliament in November. The reorganization of the armed forces was designed explicitly to minimize conflict and the possibility of coup attempts by taking power away from the four service chiefs (army, navy, air force, and police) and from the regional commanders, and concentrating it in the army-dominated Ministry of Defense and Security, at whose head was President/Minister Suharto (*Current Data* 1970). This unprecedented concentration of power made it possible for the armed forces to prepare and implement a more concerted policy toward other political actors, which they proceeded to do in the election campaign of 1970/71.

Almost from the beginning of the New Order the idea of national elections had received support from a variety of sources (Liddle 1973a; Ward 1974). Political party leaders saw in elections an opportunity to restore their position as representatives of the people and to make Parliament once again a major governmental institution, and some student groups and other pro-New Order forces, civilian and military, wanted to use elections as a means of beginning a total restructuring of the party system. But to President Suharto and the men closest to him the purpose of elections was not to destabilize the political system, either by letting the parties compete for popular allegiance as in 1955 or by creating new channels of elite-mass communication, but rather to secure unchallengeable control of parliament, the People's Consultative Assembly, and regional legislative bodies. For this purpose a new political organization, GOLKAR (an acronym for *golongan karya,* functional groups), was created under the leadership of generals Sumitro, Amir Moertono, and Darjatmo of the Ministry of Defense, Major General Amir Machmud of the Ministry of Home Affairs (with responsibility for the territorial civil service), and Brigadier General Ali Moertopo, personal assistant to President Suharto and an experienced political operative and manipulator of political parties.[2]

Although the election itself was conducted with scrupulous honesty, GOLKAR's campaign tactics were heavy-handed on the extreme. Most civil servants and village officials were prohibited from campaigning for parties of their own choice and were instead obliged to join and work for GOLKAR. Military officers became local GOLKAR chairmen or supervised closely those who were. Party candidate lists were screened and many names were removed from the ballot. Party leaders considered insufficiently sympathetic to military rule were forced out of their party positions. Voters were required in some areas to register as GOLKAR members, were told that a vote against GOLKAR was a vote against the regime (or against the nation), that there would be no jobs or government services for opponents of GOLKAR, or that if the parties won the chaos of the massacre period of 1965-1966 would return. Of the major parties only Nahdatul Ulama was able to withstand this onslaught, obtaining about the same percentage of total vote as in 1955 (18.7 percent compared with 18.4 percent). PNI, the largest party in 1955, won only 6.9 percent. Parmusi, with Masyumi's star-and-crescent electoral symbol but without its old leadership (or spirit), was well below the 1955 Masyumi vote with 5.3 percent. Parkindo and Partai Katolik barely managed to stay alive with 1.3 percent and 1.1 percent respectively. GOLKAR was the first party in every province-level electoral district, with an absolute majority in all but two provinces and an overall vote of 62.8 percent.

Despite its overwhelming victory, GOLKAR since 1971 has been largely inactive, especially at the several administrative levels below the center. In evaluating its potential importance as a channel for popular demands on government, or as a reshaper of demands in the manner of mobilization regimes, it is well to bear in mind that it was created for the purpose of weakening rather than replacing the old parties. Only a few intellectuals, concentrated in Jakarta, wanted to use the organization for more positive purposes, and they had limited

2. Strictly speaking, GOLKAR was a reshaping of an already existing parliamentary group, Sekber GOLKAR (Joint Secretariat of Functional Groups), created in 1964 under army auspices to control and mobilize those members who had been appointed to Parliament by President Sukarno to represent various "functional groups" in Indonesian society, such as labor, farmers, youth, women, the armed forces, and so on. During Guided Democracy the army supported functionalism as a means of legitimizing its own political participation (see Lev 1963).

influence in the making of most important decisions. Nominations for GOLKAR seats in Parliament and the regional legislatures, for example, were controlled by government officials and given to other government officials (and, in many cases, their wives). GOLKAR legislators today are thus not only overwhelmingly bureaucratic in social background but more important are accountable only to the ministers, governors, military commanders, and other high officials who appointed them. It is a self-contained system, with almost no constituency outside itself.

In post-1971 self-characterizations of the New Order a constantly recurring theme has been the image of the national community as a family, with President Suharto or the government as a whole in the role of father and the people, or organized groups, as the children. The metaphor reflects closely the president's conception of the kind of participation system he would like to create: a public that is deferential, a government that speaks with a single voice, and an interaction pattern in which the government provides guidance and is attentive to group and public opinion but obligated to grant only those requests which in its judgment contribute to the well-being both of those directly concerned and of the whole community. The probability, never very high, that the New Order reality might approach this paternalistic model has been sharply reduced since 1971 by events in three major areas of political activity – political party reorganization and party demands, student demands, and internal military conflict.

In its dealings with the political parties the New Order's touch has been both heavy and light. Having virtually hand-picked major party leaders and then soundly defeated them in the 1971 elections, the government was expected by most observers to ease the pressure. Instead, it moved ahead on several fronts, coercing the parties to coalesce into two new parties, the Indonesian Democratic party and the Development Unity party,[3] creating new GOLKAR-affiliated mass organizations to challenge the parties' role as spokesmen for the interest of civil servants, workers, farmers, and youth (without much apparent success beyond the establishment of formal structures), limiting the range of issues which could be discussed publicly, and exerting heavy pressure on party leaders in the Supreme Consultative Assembly to support the government's draft "Broad Outlines of State Policy." A disbanding of village party branches, intended to create a "floating mass" isolated from partisan conflict except during election periods, has also been a continuing threat. But as if to confound its critics, in the

3. The Indonesian Democratic party is a fusion of the old PNI, Parkindo, Partai Katolik, IPKI (a small nationalist party founded by the army in 1952 which has tended to be a spokesman for regional interests), and Murba (a pale reflection of what was once a national Communist party), and the Development Unity party is made up of NU, Parmusi, and the small Islamic parties PSII and Perti. The government's reasoning in forcing the fusions is not entirely clear – it may have been a fairly subtle attempt to read Muslims qua Muslims out of political life, as the new Development Unity party was required to declare itself an open membership party. Or it may have been intended primarily for its symbolic value, in that systems with few parties are thought to be more stable than those with many. Or it may have been the last act in a drama staged to satisfy – also symbolically – the wishes of army radicals who had vigorously promoted party simplification in the late 1960s.

latter part of 1973 the government (in an attempt to avert a new Muslim-student alliance) dealt more gently with Development Unity party (Muslim) leaders who opposed its draft marriage bill, finally acceding to Muslim demands for changes. In mid-1975, the government again agreed to Muslim demands, this time for changes in its proposed election bill, but it is uncertain how much practical effect these revisions will have on the conduct of the next elections, scheduled for 1977.

Student dissatisfaction with government policies and personnel has been a regular feature of New Order politics. In recent years the pattern has been one of quiescence followed by opinions respectfully offered in campus seminars and discussions, then unproductive meetings between students and the relevant government officials, followed by charges angrily hurled in public meetings and demonstrations, and ending with strongly worded government warnings to desist from further protest and the temporary detention of a few leaders. The first major post-election student protests, against a project sponsored by Mrs. Tien Suharto to build an Indonesia-in-miniature village for tourists, roughly followed this pattern, ending in January 1972 when President Suharto in a public speech threatened (more harshly than most observers felt necessary) to use his emergency powers if demonstrations continued.

The next cycle of protests, which began in October 1973 and ended in violence in January 1974, followed the usual pattern only in part. To student protest was added two additional and highly inflammable ingredients – conflict among powerful generals and the spontaneous participation of urban masses – not included in the New Order's paternalistic model of a proper participation system. The effects of the government's reaction to these events – the arrests of dozens of students and intellectuals (and the temporary detention of hundreds of others), the closing of several Jakarta newspapers, and a much more repressive atmosphere – had eased only slightly by the end of 1976.

Nineteen seventy-three was to have been a year of triumph, the first meeting of an elected People's Consultative Assembly in the history of independent Indonesia. By March, when the assembly session began, there was already an atmosphere of tension in Jakarta. In the economic sphere there had been a serious rice shortage in late 1972 and prices of basic commodities had risen nearly 50 percent over the previous year and were expected to continue to rise. Despite a widely publicized intelligence estimate predicting no serious disturbances, security precautions for the assembly meeting – including warnings to newspapers, bans on public discussion of issues, and so on – were extreme. In April there was fighting between university students and trishaw drivers in Jogjakarta, and in August a serious anti-Chinese riot erupted in Bandung, both weather vanes of popular unrest in a political system in which there are few instruments available for the expression of mass discontent. As they have done frequently in the past several years, government officials blamed the Bandung riot on the underground PKI. In September a near-riot occurred in Parliament, as Muslim youths protested the marriage bill and had to be forcibly removed.

On October 24, a national holiday commemorating the 1928 commitment of Indonesian youth to the nationalist cause, members of the student council of the University of Indonesia read a petition at the Kalibata Heroes' Cemetery, precipitating an avalanche of similar statements from student councils and ad hoc groups in Jakarta, Bandung, Jogjakarta, Surabaya, Medan, and Ujung Pandang. The complaints were both general and sharply focused – against authoritarianism, the monopolization of government positions by military officers, the flagrant corruption of many generals, the failure of the regime's development policies to effect changes in the villages, the favoritism shown to Chinese businessmen and foreign investors, the lack of government control over its major entrepreneur, General Ibnu Sutowo of the state oil company PERTAMINA, and so on. When the chairman of the Inter-Governmental Group on Indonesia, a group of Western countries plus Japan created to coordinate foreign assistance, visited Indonesia in November, he was beseiged by students who wanted to use his reputation for radicalism to further legitimize and publicize their case.

On November 15 General Sumitro, deputy commander of the armed forces and commander of the politically important Operational Command for the Restoration of Order and Security (KOPKAMTIB), announced in Jogjakarta that by April 1, 1974, Indonesia would have a "new pattern of leadership" in which two-way communication between the people and the government would be restored.[4] Previously regarded as the second most powerful man in the armed forces, but also as close to President Suharto, General Sumitro was now perceived as an opponent, laying down the gauntlet not only to Suharto's powerful personal assistant Major General Ali Moertopo (as had been rumored for some time) but to the president himself. Whatever the accuracy of this perception, in the next few weeks General Sumitro put on a remarkable performance – speaking to student groups, consulting with Muslims on the marriage bill, and flying to Jogjakarta to approve the performance of an antimilitarist play by the Javanese poet and playwright W. S. Rendra.

The tensions generated by student demonstrations, conflict within the military and its extension into student politics (Ali Moertopo was believed to have attempted the overthrow of the University of Indonesia student council at the end of December), and continuing price inflation erupted on January 14,

---

4. General Sumitro's KOPKAMTIB, originally an adminstrative device created to give territorial military commanders special emergency powers to be used against PKI, had become increasingly involved in other matters since the election. The general himself, however, maintained a relatively low profile until 1973. In October he condemned long hair among Indonesian youth as a sign of decadence, arousing an angry reaction from university campuses. In the same month he traveled with a group of Jakarta reporters to the island of Buru, where he had long talks with exiled PKI prisoners, among them leading writers and intellectuals, and was quoted as telling them, "We are the remnants of the revolution. We are the remnants of the state." And further "Power and authority have no meaning" (*Pedoman*, October 26, 1973).

General Sumitro was also reported to be observing the Muslim fasting month during his Buru trip. Although one should be careful not to read too much back into these and subsequent events, it is possible to interpret them as a very Javanese attempt to get in touch with the aspirations of the people and to restore harmony to a society deeply divided by class and religious differences.

when Japanese Prime Minister Tanaka arrived in Jakarta on an official visit. Student demonstrators opposing Japan's role in the Indonesian economy were joined by the Jakarta poor, mobs roamed the streets, and incidents of burning and looting occurred in widely separated sections of the city during the next two days. When the smoke cleared, Sumitro was on his way to retirement, Ali Moertopo was still in power, the universities were closed, and most of the student leaders and others thought to be behind them were in jail. On January 21 Ali Moertopo said in a news interview that the ringleaders of the "Affair of 15 January" (now called Malari, the "January Disaster") were clearly ex-PSI and ex-Masyumi elements, an interpretation which remained the official position nearly three years later.

INDONESIAN SOCIETY AND POLITICS:
SOME EXPLANATIONS OF CONTINUITY AND CHANGE

It is hard to miss the familiar faces in the events leading up to the January Disaster. In the controversy over the marriage law, Nahdatul Ulama, old Masyumi, new Parmusi, and an assortment of Islamic youth groups made their voices heard. In the student protests the 1965-1966 combination of Muslim, Christian, and secular modernization-oriented youth, itself a renewal of the Muslim-Socialist alliance of the 1950s, was once again revived, though not, one suspects, in the conspiratorial form charged by the government. PNI leaders and their organizations were only minimally involved, but the party's Javanese populism was represented by General Sumitro. Even PKI, in spectral form as a scapegoat but more corporeally on the island of Buru visited by General Sumitro and as the putative party of urban mobs, lent its presence to the affair.

If the faces are familiar, some of the forms are very different. What is it exactly that has persisted, and how does one account for it? In my opinion it is not so much to the parties as organizations that one should look for answers, but rather to the distinctive visions of polity or conceptions of the good political order which parties and other political forces have pursued during the past quarter century, and to the kind and extent of support those visions have received within Indonesian society.

Although the major point that I shall make has to do with deeply rooted and perhaps unresolvable conflict, it must first be said that for all their archipelagic diversity Indonesians do have a sense of common national commitment, a desire to live together as Indonesians. For the generation now in power, the central experiences forming this commitment took place a long time ago, during the Revolution and the Japanese occupation; for Indonesians under forty or forty-five, the common experience has been one of coping with the promises and frustrations of independence, of attempting to interpret and implement values formulated during and before the Revolution. To be sure, it has been — and continues to be — a relatively small minority of Indonesians — urban or urban-linked, educated, fluent, and at ease in the national language — who are directly and more or less consciously engaged in this process, but they are a far-flung minority and control the channels of access to nearly all major social institutions from the county to the national level.

Common commitment to Indonesian nationality has not, however, precluded profound disagreement over the content of that nationality. Such central symbols as the Revolution have had quite different meanings attached to them by different groups, and some of the differences over the kind of society and polity Indonesia should be have come close to being questions of whether ultimately Indonesia can be a single society and polity after all. The most important disagreements may be summarized in three interlinked patterns of polar opposition, each of which is itself a complex of issues and subject to more than one interpretation: center versus region, or Java versus the Outer Islands; Islamic state versus secular state, or *santri* versus *abangan*; and a broadly "upper versus lower" pattern which contains four overlapping but quite distinct perspectives — nationalism versus communism, rich versus poor, hierarchy versus equality, and "for the people" versus "against the people" (see Feith and Castles 1970; Alfian 1971).

When labeled center versus region, the first pair of opposing poles describes an essentially political disagreement related to the amount of power that ought to be exercised by the central government over the regions (or conversely the degree of autonomy that ought to be enjoyed by the regions). The difference is in part one of administrative efficiency, in which arguments can be made both ways — that centralization results in greater efficiency, because national plans can be implemented nationwide, or that decentralization results in greater efficiency, in that national plans can be adjusted to local conditions. It is also in part a question of democratic theory, in which it is argued by regionalists that local democracy as well as national democracy is a good thing and that for local democratic processes to be meaningful there must be a substantial devolution of authority.

When labeled Java versus the Outer Islands, this controversy takes on ethnic and religious dimensions. The ethnic Javanese, who inhabit mainly the central and eastern provinces of Java, constitute about half of the total Indonesian population. Their culture has for centuries been among the most complex and highly elaborated in the archipelago, and although it has incorporated elements of Islam since the fourteenth century, Java has not become a predominantly Muslim culture. (This is particularly true of those Javanese — like Sukarno and Suharto — who have led the central government since independence.) Most other groups — the Sundanese of West Java, the Acehnese, Bataks, and Minangkabaus of Sumatra, the Madurese and Balinese, the Dyaks of Kalimantan, the Makassarese, Buginese, and Toraja of Sulawesi, the Timorese and Ambonese, the many small groups in Irian Jaya — are thoroughly Muslim or Christian or have their own religious traditions which add to their ethnic distinctiveness. In general, these Outer Islanders have tended to see the Javanese as a threat to their cultural autonomy, their material prosperity, and their political control over their own internal affairs as distinctive communities within the larger nation.

In the early and mid-1950s, the center-region/Java-Outer Islands conflict was mediated primarily through the party system, with the large Masyumi and the small PSI, Parkindo, and Partai Katolik expressing the regional point of view, and PNI, PKI, and Nahdatul Ulama, all East and Central Java-based parties, expressing the perspective of the center. With the regional rebellions in 1956 came a de facto decentralization that continued after central government authority had been restored. Through the 1960s regional military officers had a relatively free hand in the administration of their regions as long as they adhered to the central ideology. The value to the regions of this autonomy was limited, however, by the frequent appointment of Javanese as regional commanders and by limited access of government in most regions to resources which might have made power more productive of social goods. The 1969 armed forces reorganization appears to have reduced considerably the power of the territorial commanders, except perhaps on Java, and the Parmusi segment of the Development Unity party, having been badly defeated in the 1971 elections, was in no position to play Masyumi's former role. GOLKAR's members of Parliament from the Outer Islands, most of whom were originally nominated by and now represent their military commander and/or governor (and are thus not directly accountable to any broader regional population groups) may be playing a limited role, but the basic pattern appears to be one of severe regional underrepresentation in central government decision-making processes.

Islam was the great ideological issue of the 1950s. In its most extreme form — never declared the platform of a major party — an Indonesian Islamic state would have elevated the *ulama* (religious teachers and scholars) to the position of final arbiter of the constitutionality of legislation passed by Parliament, required all Indonesians who had declared themselves Muslims to practice their religion fully (for example, the five daily prayers, observance of the fasting month, payment of a religious tax), prevented Muslims from converting to any other religion, and made Christians and Jews (but probably not Hindu Balinese) a special category of citizens, protected against forced conversion to Islam but unable to spread their faith or to hold the office of head of state.

Part of what made the Islamic state issue so divisive was its close correspondence to the Java-Outer Islands conflict and the unacceptability to Javanese of a government run by Outer Islanders. But the core of the problem — and the reason for its continuing force in the 1960s and 1970s — lies in Java itself, in the self-conscious division of the Javanese people into a devoutly Muslim minority, the santri, and a syncretistic, part Muslim, part Hindu, part animist majority, the *abangan* (see C. Geertz 1960, 1959; Jay 1963).

Most of the people of East and Central Java are abangan Javanese, inheritors of an ancient indigenous religious tradition altered but never obliterated by the waves of religious change that have periodically swept over the island. Intermittently exposed during the past few centuries to Islam, they have come to consider themselves Muslims for many purposes – life-crisis ceremonies, for example, have a substantial Islamic component – but consider total commitment a denial of their identity as Javanese. The santri are people who take their Islamic religion very seriously. Since the early part of the twentieth century, they have been divided into two groups: the reformists or modernists, who have wanted to cleanse Javanese and Indonesian Islam of post-Muhammad additions to the religion originating both from Javanese tradition and from the historical development of the religion in the Middle East; and conservatives or traditionalists, who have maintained that Islam as they and their fathers have known it – including strict adherence to the Syafi'i legal school and also incorporation of many Javanese beliefs and interpretations – is the true religion. In the eyes of the abangan, the santri is an extremist, almost a non-Javanese; to the santri, especially the more aggressive, proselytizing reformist, the abangan is a man of weak, little, or false faith.

In the early 1950s the division between abangan and santri, and the further division between modernist and traditionalist santri, was the principal basis of political party organization in Central and East Java. Nahdatul Ulama became the party of traditional Islam, Masyumi (largely through Muhammadiyah) the party of reformist Islam, and PNI and PKI competed for the allegiance of the abangan. There was also some competition between Masyumi and NU within the santri community. For many Muslims, especially rural villagers, the doctrinal distinction is not sharp, and prominent village Muslims with substantial personal followings could sometimes be enticed to one or the other party with promises of position or financial assistance. But between the two worlds of santri and abangan there was virtually no partisan competition.

In the period of greatest party activity in the countryside, 1953-1955, the parties (according to Clifford Geertz) were "a fertile new source of social forms on the basis of which the underorganized village could finally be reshaped," with each party and its affiliated organizations "a comprehensive focus of social integration" and the party system as a whole a network linking the villages to the national political and social system (C. Geertz 1959: 36-37; C. Geertz 1965). After 1955 these hopes were dashed by the ups and downs of individual party fortunes in Jakarta, which were also felt in the villages, and by the general decline of party power in government. Party leaders from the village to the province and Jakarta continued to speak in the legislatures of Java and the national parliament on behalf of their santri and abangan constituencies, but as decision-making power shifted they were obliged to rely more heavily on their allies in officialdom. By the early 1960s governors, county heads, territorial military commanders, and their subordinates in the provinces and counties, bureaucratic factions in the civilian and military administrative departments of the center, and President Sukarno had become the principal exponents of the religious cleavages of Java. In the New Order some of this pattern has remained. President Suharto, in particular, is as much an abangan as his predecessor, and political party leaders below the national level continue to work with civilian and military bureaucratic sympathizers. But their opportunities for collaboration have been substantially reduced by the GOLKARization not only of the legislatures but of the *pamong praja* (a particular blow to PNI) and by the appointment of a nonparty man as minister of religion (a post held by NU from 1953 to 1971). Perhaps of greatest importance, santri influence within the military seems at its lowest ebb in independent Indonesian history.

From one perspective, the third pattern of opposed poles describes the most narrowly focused of the major conflicts in Indonesian society, the competition between PNI and PKI for the support of the abangan Javanese. PNI took great pride in its closeness to the personification of Indonesian nationalism, President Sukarno, laid claim to the role of most vigorous opponent of Dutch colonialism, and developed its own ideology of Marhaenism, a term originated by Sukarno to characterize the average Indonesian, a man who owned his own tools and a small plot of land but was nonetheless exploited by colonialism and capitalism. PKI was excoriated (in public by more conservative PNI leaders, in private by more radical ones) as an opponent of nationalism, a part of the international Communist movement led from Moscow and/or Peking, and, in its emphasis on the proletarian rather than the *marhaen,* as ideologically irrelevant to Indonesian conditions.

At the level of competition for mass support the differences between PNI and PKI were more complex than this simple nationalist-Communist ideological dichotomy suggests. For one things, there were some true PNI radicals, particularly in the youth organizations and also in the party outside Java, where conditions were somewhat different (see Rocamora 1973; Liddle 1970). Also, like other parties in the 1950s and 1960s PKI played several games simultaneously and was not always able to play its primary game well. But the basic pattern was one of opposition between rich and poor or between elite and mass, with PNI as champion of the former and PKI as defender of the latter.

From the early 1950s PNI and its brand of nationalism were (and, more in spirit than in body, still are) the first choice of Indonesia's chief social elite, abangan officialdom. In Jakarta civil servants of all sorts, excepting only those in the Ministry of Religion, were disproportionately attracted to PNI. In the provincial capitals, the county and subdistrict towns, and the villages it was the *pamong praja*, the schoolteachers, and the *pamong desa* (village officials) who built PNI. To many abangan villagers, the incumbents of these positions merit respect and deference in the natural order of things; to others, they control sufficient quantities of scarce resources — land to be tilled, crops to be harvested, day laborer jobs, money to be lent, the authority to collect taxes and to process needed government documents — to make them valuable as patrons and dangerous as enemies. The combination of these variables with the party's special claim to speak for Indonesian nationalism and its relationship to Sukarno are probably sufficient to account for its 1955 election victory.

Until 1965 virtually the only political organization defending the interests of the urban and rural poor was PKI. At the national level the party sought the support and protection of Sukarno, PNI, and accessible elements within the armed forces, and reformulated its doctrines to conform with nationalist dogma, but in the villages of Java it often stood alone. Its leaders typically came from the ranks of small landowners, the landless, or the teachers in local elementary and secondary schools.[5] Financial support for local party branches came for the most part from outside the locality itself, which made it possible for PKI leaders to maintain their autonomy from the larger landowners and village officials who led PNI, NU, and Masyumi (often in de facto coalition against PKI). In the last years of Guided Democracy Sukarno's protection was also an important condition underlying PKI's aggressiveness and occasional ability to win a battle. As the slaughter of its adherents in 1965 and 1966 demonstrated, however, PKI never became a party of militants prepared to fight a war. Its mass strength, such as it was, was based instead on the general recognition that PKI was willing and able to pursue the socioeconomic ends of the poorest strata of the population, to defend the interests of the *wong cilik* (little man) against those on whom he always been dependent in the past. When such help was available, the villager showed himself willing and able to make use of it.

The opposition of rich and poor has another connotation in Indonesian political life — the attempt of modernizing intellectuals to create a democratic socialist Indonesia through the utilization of Western technology and methods of industrial organization. This group was once represented chiefly by PSI and some elements in Masyumi, but it extends today to a much larger group of educated Indonesians without direct or indirect ties to any party. The modernizing intellecturals identify themselves with the cause of the poor but have no actual mass base, even in GOLKAR, with which a number of them are affiliated. Their solutions to Indonesia's economic problems tend to be either growth- (as opposed to distribution-) oriented or require administrative and political capabilities which the Indonesian bureaucracy has not shown that it possesses. Despite these deficiencies, the modernizers have often had a significant impact on events. The most technically capable among them have held high governmental positions during both the parliamentary and New Order periods. More important, the university students, in their attacks on corruption and the monopolization of power in the hands of the few and the rich, have tried to be a moral force, the conscience of the New Order. The number of their leaders jailed after the January Affair is an indication of the seriousness with which they take their role as well as of the government's attitude toward their participation.

Third, in this general category of horizontal divisions in Indonesian society there is also a profound dispute over the most basic principles of social integration. This conflict pits the hierarchical, ordered, introspective values of the

5. There is unfortunately little hard data on village leadership. Mortimer writes that "in multi-party villages, PKI support tended to come from unaccommodated youth and other radicalized elements; in single party villages, by contrast, the leading Communists were often those who had the most prestige and could command the greatest patronage in traditional terms" (Mortimer 1974: 278-79). My own observations in East Sumatra in 1962-1964 and interviews in Kulon Progo regency, Jogjakarta, in 1971 indicated that PKI leaders were of distinctly simpler origins and status than their counterparts (although in East Sumatra both PNI and PKI leaders came for the most part from non-elite backgrounds).

traditional Javanese governing class, the *priai,* against the egalitarian, spontaneous, action-oriented stance of the *pemuda* (revolutionary youth) (see Anderson 1972). In the 1950s and 1960s PKI was the chief exponent of egalitarian
values, although in rather more disciplined fashion than the pemuda guerrilla
bands of the revolutionary period, and PNI, though containing both radical and
conservative wings, was more identified with order and the priai. PSI and
modernizing intellectuals in general have attempted to place themselves outside
the framework of this dichotomy by emphasizing rationalism and democratic
socialism, but their elitism and sense that the Western educated must guide the
traditional and uneducated place them solidly with the forces of order. In the
1970s it is hierarchy and the "priai mentality" which predominate, but the
pemuda spirit may still be found in the abangan villages of East and Central Java,
in some PNI quarters, and indeed wherever revolutionary experience played a
fundamental role in shaping political consciousness.

Finally, the populist distinction between those who are "for the people"
versus those who are "against the people" has some of its roots in the pemuda
experience and in PKI-style egalitarianism, but also partakes of the priai tradition of service and of Javanese mystical conceptions, in particular, the idea of the
essential oneness of humanity.[6] This sort of thinking has been most characteristic of PNI politicians (also of President Sukarno) and of some army circles
(especially in Central Java) but also affected PKI, whose concept of equality
derived in part from European Marxism and in part from traditional Javanese
messianism. Its importance lies not so much in the political groups which it
differentiates (there are few who would admit to being against the people) but in
the moral foundation and justification it provides to those opposed to a
prevailing regime or social order.[7]

PARTICIPATION AND THE FUTURE

If the measure of continuity in the history of political participation in
Indonesia is the persistence of distinct conceptions of the good political system,
then the changes in patterns of participation may be explained by the depth of
commitment to those conceptions and by the determination with which they
have been pursued on all sides. Today it is abangan Javanese generals who value

6. See C. Geertz 1960: chap. 20. "[S]ince the devine in each person is identical,
at the ultimate level of experience there is no individuality because the more
advanced one is spiritually, the more one has a genuine fellow-feeling for others, a
comprehensive sympathy." Geertz also argues that this belief, combined with the
organic theory of social organization that I have simplified here as "hierarchy,"
constitutes a normative social theory "congruent with the needs of a rank-conscious
class of white-collar administrators with idealistic pretensions" (p. 333).

7. On political thinking in the Diponegoro division, see the brief but insightful
treatment in Anderson and McVey 1971: 1-6. My own experience with the Diponegoro division, in particular an extended series of conversations in 1971 with a
middle-ranking, politically active officer, has also contributed to my sense of this
particular type of mystical populism and the self-denying, ascetic leadership associated with it.

concentrated rather than decentralized authority, a hierarchical rather than egalitarian social order, and a deferential rather than participant population who are in power in Indonesia. What is the probability that they will be there tomorrow?

In their present organizational form the political parties do not seem to be serious contenders for power. PKI, of course, is proscribed. PNI, Parkindo, and Partai Katolik no longer exist, and their successor the Indonesian Democratic party is under close supervision, its leadership subject to government approval and its financial viability dependent on government handouts. The Development Unity party is in a similar condition, although its constituents Nahdatul Ulama, the modernist organizations like Muhammadiyah which have been the heart of Masyumi/Parmusi support, and the smaller Muslim parties PSII and Perti have been able to declare themselves nonpolitical, social and educational organizations and thus retain their legal existence. GOLKAR is essentially the parliamentary voice of the government, the legitimator in the name of popular sovereignty of policies made in the presidential office, the circle of Ali Moertopo, or the Ministry of Defense and Security. It has also been to a limited extent an arena in which there has been some policy conflict, produced mainly by modernizing intellectuals trying to push the government further than it has been willing to go on some issues. But GOLKAR'S legislators, at both the national and lower levels, are men and women whose political roots go no deeper than the central and regional officials who nominated them. Outside the legislative bodies, GOLKAR does not seem to be making a serious effort to develop a mass base, despite the recent formation of labor, farmer, and youth affiliates.

If the political parties and other social groups do play a role in the next system change, it will almost certainly be as contributors to conflict within the armed forces. Unfortunately for outside observers and Indonesian political actors alike, this makes prediction extremely difficult, for there are many variables at work within the military — including the presence in the wings of a politically untested postrevolutionary generation of officers — and few serious studies which illuminate their relative importance (see McVey 1971; McVey 1972; Sundhaussen 1972). But the weight of evidence presented in this essay suggests first that such conflict is likely and second that it will involve matters of principle.

Among the various alternatives to this view — including the simple dismissal of the force of ideas in Indonesian politics, the presumed stability of the developmental model of the economists of the paternalistic image put forward by some regime spokesmen — perhaps the most persuasive case can be made for a highly personalized political system, an Indonesia, Inc., made stable by the satisfaction of the personal drives for wealth, status, and power of the higher levels of the officer corps, and in which conflict is limited to a tightly contained competition among self-seeking individuals. There is, indeed, little doubt that since 1957 the Indonesian armed forces in general and the officer corps in particular have benefited handsomely from involvement in the economy and political system. There are today many wealthy and powerful officers, a few of them extremely wealthy and powerful. Individual aspirations are not likely to diminish, and competition for scarce goods and positions — among the present leaders and between them and the next generation — may well intensify. At the same time, given the vital force of collective values throughout the postindependence period, both in Indonesian society generally and within the armed forces, the long-term stability of such an amoral polity is difficult to imagine.

To predict the specific character of the next system change, even when the focus is narrowed to conflict within the military, is of course much more difficult than to predict that it will involve a confrontation of values. Throughout its history since the early days of the Revolution, the Indonesian military has had to contend with the cleavages of Indonesian society as well as with its own internal contradictions, and the latter inevitably have become entangled in complex ways with the former. Today, to be sure, some sources of conflict within the military appear less pronounced (or less easy to activate) than others — santri coups and regional rebellions, for example, are probably not in the cards in the near future. The impulse to forced, rapid, root-and-branch modernization which once motivated some army radicals is a possibility, although the protagonists of that view were quieted and dispersed in the late 1960s. A better argument can perhaps be made for a resurgence of Javanese abangan-based populism in opposition to a ruling group that has been seen by too many for too long as "against the people." But if one takes a slightly longer time perspective than the immediate future, say the next twenty years, then it is possible that almost any of the sources of conflict described in this essay will once again have a major impact on the course of political change.

7 Conceptions of Politics, Power, and Ideology in Contemporary Indonesian Islam

ALLAN A. SAMSON

AN OVERVIEW

THE RELIGIOUS tradition of any society possesses an undeniable author-itative role in the formulation and maintenance of broad societal ethics and values. To what extent, however, does religious belief influence political behavior? Under what circumstances is religious affirmation likely to be immedi-ately transformed into political action? The dimensions of the relationship between religion and politics will of course vary according to the religion and culture. They will also vary within a given religious tradition where a diversity of political views may prevail. For some believers, religious faith inspires all worldly action and clearly exceeds in importance pragmatic interests and materialistic concerns. For others, no less personally devout, belief is maintained in a less holistic and more subdued public sense. Religious belief can impel a broad range of political choices, from the certitude that religious values provide the sole legitimate criterion of political choice, through the perception of religion as a broad, unifying sociopolitical symbol, to an acknowledgment of the legitimacy of the separation, or at least compartmentalization, of religion from politics.

Of the world religions, Islam is perhaps the most comprehensive in its insistence on the appropriateness of a direct relationship between religion and political power. The tenets of classical Islam, as enunciated in the Qur'an and Sunnah (Traditions of the Prophet) and elaborated on by the theologians and jurists of early Islam, acknowledged no legitimate distinction between religion and secular activity. Classical Islamic theology and social theory envisaged a society which was thoroughly regulated according to the tenets of Shari'ah (divine law). Politics, in particular, was encompassed within the overarching authority of the religious imperative. Sovereignty belonged only to God, while spiritual authority was exercised by the caliph, the vice-regent of Muhammad, whose duty it was to implement Shari'ah, defend the faith, and dispense justice.

Classical Islamic theory possessed both an ideal and a pragmatic view of power. The ideal view posited the indissoluble unity of religion and political power within the framework of the caliphate — a relationship in which political power was clearly subordinate to religion. Power unaccountable to prophetic law was felt to be illegitimate; the theoretical primacy of religion over politics was unquestioned. The political concepts of classical Islam were, however, honored in theory rather than implemented in practice. The influence of the caliphate declined and Shari'ah came to be restricted more and more to the symbolic and the realm of personal and family law. Diluted and curtailed almost from its inception, the concept of the ideal Islamic polity stood more as a utopian symbol of religious solidarity than as a pragmatic institutional basis around which to organize a Muslim state. Although the concept came to bear diminishing resemblance to the political reality developing in the Islamic world with the weakening of the caliphate and the rise of the nonreligious authority of the sultans and emirs, its theoretical hold was not diminished. Succeeding classical theorists compromised; though they were forced to acknowledge the de facto power of nonreligious authority, they constructed an elaborate theoretical structure of compromise-cum-expediency while clinging to the ideal concept of a unified religious power structure.

The classical Islamic pragmatic view acknowledged, though it did not approve of, power unattached to religion. This view, combining pragmatism with theological concern, was formulated by Ibn Khaldun (perhaps Islam's first social scientist) who, though sincerely committed to Islam and the ideal of the caliphate, nonetheless recognized the reality of autonomous power. His realistic view of man and sober view of power impelled him to recognize the will to power and domination as man's principal driving force. The "power-state," he maintained, that is, government by authority based on power rather than revelation, was natural to man's needs as a rational being. *Siyasa aqliya,* or government founded on human reason, was less preferable than *siyasa diniya* (government based on Shari'ah) but was appropriate for certain times and conditions (see Khaldun 1958: vols. 1-3). Purely political authority was necessary and legitimate if it sought to promote the well-being of the populace, even if religious concerns were subordinated to the political and social needs of the state. Religion and power no longer formed an indissoluble unity; other factors were operative as well.

The Islamic experience in Indonesia produced a diversity of political perceptions as it has developed over the past three centuries. Central to such diversity has been the division of Indonesian society along religious-cultural-political lines ranging from the strongly Islamic to the nominally or even non-Islamic. The strongly Islamic-nominally Islamic dichotomy is especially pronounced in Java, where Islamic culture, after its introduction in the sixteenth century, interacted with a highly eclectic Javanese culture comprised of animist, Hindu, and Buddhist elements. What resulted was a checkered pattern of exclusivity and syncretism, in which the Islamic and Indic-influenced civilizations warily interacted with each other — neither being able fully to subjugate or absorb the other. Many Islamic practices were incorporated into Hindu-Javanese ceremonies and rituals, while much that was syncretically Javanese found its way into Islamic practice.

During the colonial period, much of Indonesian Islamic behavior in an institutional sense (especially in Java) was assimilative in nature and accommodative to colonial and traditional Javanese court authority. The participation of Islamic officialdom (mosque administrators and judicial officials) in positions subordinate to Dutch and Javanese aristocratic administrative superiors reflected its acquiescence to nonreligious authority. The accommodation of the traditional Islamic bureaucracy to nonreligious rule was of the order of a *quid pro quo* in which the legitimacy of non-Islamic power was acknowledged in exchange for the retention by the Islamic bureaucracy of various perquisites of office and symbols of authority (Lev 1972: 12). In contrast to the accommodative style of the religious bureaucracy stood a more autonomous religious figure – the *kiyayi* – a well-known Islamic teacher or notable who usually headed his own Qur'anic school. Although the Islamic bureaucracy was perceived as an appendage to Dutch and Javanese aristocratic authority, the kiyayi was perceived by his followers, as well as by colonial authority, as an independent religious and social force (see Sartono Kartodirdjo 1966). For the kiyayi, only religiously grounded power was truly legitimate, but if the practice of Islam was not hindered, the economy sufficient, and interference by central authority minimal, he also accepted the reality and limited legitimacy of secular rule.

Diversity exists as well within Indonesian Islam, which essentially is divided between modernist and traditionalist orientations. Islamic modernism, introduced into Indonesia at the end of the nineteenth century, has received social and political expression through the activities of several organizations: the first modernist organizations, Muhammadiyah, established in 1912; the avowedly political Partai Sarekat Islam Indonesia (PSII), which was especially influential among Islamic circles in the 1920s and 1930s; the politically assertive Masyumi, the most influential Islamic party in the 1950s before its dissolution in 1960 by presidential decree; and Partai Muslimin Indonesia (Parmusi), established in 1966, and for a time envisioned as Masyumi's successor. Modernists contended that traditionalist Islam had for too long been mired in a world of stagnation and superstition and that a return to the purity of the Qur'an and Hadith and an extended acceptance of the right of individual interpretation in religious matters would demonstrate that Islam was consonant with material and scientific progress. Modernist thought and organizations developed most rapidly in the urban areas of Java and Sumatra – areas known for their cosmopolitan, urban, and commercial character, developed through centuries of cultural contact and trade.

Islamic traditionalism has received political and social expression through the existence of Nahdatul Ulama (Renaissance of the Islamic Scholars). Nahdatul Ulama was established in 1926 by a number of East Javanese *ulama* (religious teachers) who united to combat the threat presented to their traditionalist religious beliefs by the rapid growth of Muhammadiyah. Traditionalists scorned modernists for having the audacity to reject long-accepted religious practice and to seek the faddish, false, and amoral values of Western society. The concern of modernists with reconciling Islam to a so-called modernity, traditionalists maintained, was an implied rejection of the eternal truth embodied in the teachings of the great scholars of classical Islam. The gap between traditionalists and modernists, who were bitter enemies throughout much of the 1920s and 1930s, gradually narrowed as points of religious disagreement came to be defined as differences of practice and tactics, rather than of principle. Keenly felt differences of orientation, outlook, and life style remained, however, and they constituted obstacles to sustained cooperation among the coreligionists.

From 1945 until 1951, both Nahdatul Ulama and Muhammadiyah were members of Masyumi. Nahdatul Ulama withdrew in 1952, chagrined and resentful over the declining influence of traditionalists within the party. Masyumi's modernists were able to dominate the party due to their broader national experience, higher level of education, and greater organizational ability.

Nahdatul Ulama's base of support is in rural East Java, where traditional Javanese Hindu-Buddhist and animist practices absorbed elements of the later-arriving Islamic religion and tended to modify its character so that it adjusted to some of the syncretic aspects of Javanese culture. Predominant influence is in the hands of rural ulama, several of whom are associated with the religious schools in Jombang (a small town in East Java, generally considered to be the "birthplace" of Nahdatul Ulama). Their influence is buttressed by a web of marital alliances between leading ulama families and a network of ulama-disciple relationships operative throughout East Java. Nahdatul Ulama represents the religious interests of rural Javanese Muslims, whereas Masyumi and Partai Muslimin Indonesia represent the interests of a largely urban, commercial, Islamic middle class. Nahdatul Ulama's social base of support has expanded, however, to incorporate some elements of a more urban, educated constituency.

Both the two major modernist political parties, Masyumi and Partai Muslimin Indonesia, and the traditionalist Nahdatul Ulama have suffered from internal divisions. Such divisions are perhaps more a reflection of intra-organizational and intra-elite competition than a product of thorough-going "top-to-bottom" schisms within traditionalist and modernist thought. Nonetheless, factions and divisions have continually existed within the parties since their inceptions and have been widely perceived as presenting an obstacle to the fashioning of organizational unity.

In a previous article, I considered the basic political and ideological lines of division in Indonesian Islamic modernism (Samson 1973: 116-142). Briefly recapitulating, I concluded that Masyumi and Partai Muslimin were internally divided by the competitive interaction of three factions characterized by differing conceptions of the appropriate role of a religious party, the importance of ideology, and the mode of interaction between Islamic and non-Islamic groups. These factions I labeled fundamentalists, reformists, and accommodationists. Fundamentalists affirm a strict, *puristic* interpretation of Islam, oppose secular thought and Western influence as well as the syncretism of traditionalist belief, and insist on the primacy of religion over politics. Reformists also theoretically stress the primacy of religion over politics, but they are far more willing than fundamentalists to cooperate with secular groups on a sustained basis. They are also concerned with making the faith relevant for the modern age. Accommodationists value the framework of unity provided by Islam, but maintain that social and economic interests should be given priority by Islamic organizations. They further stress the necessity of acknowledging the legitimate interests of secular groups and cooperating with them on a sustained basis.

Internal divisions within Nahdatul Ulama are predicated more on personal competition than on concerns of ideology or political principle. In this regard, Nahdatul Ulama is not so much a goal-centered political party as it is a religious welfare organization governed by a confederation of religious and political notables. Political leadership in Nahdatul Ulama is operative through the interaction of three partially overlapping elite groups who articulate and aggregate the religious and political interests of the party's mass following and attempt to accommodate those interests to the reality of centralized secular rule. The three elite factions which comprise Nahdatul Ulama's leadership structure are a number of well-known *kiyayis* (Islamic teachers or notables, often possessing a regional or national reputation), national politicians, and religious bureaucrats. The vast majority of Nahdatul Ulama's supporters perceive it primarily as a religious organization and only secondarily as a political party. Their political support is channeled through the actions of the traditional Javanese kiyayi, whose approval provides religious legitimacy to Nahdatul Ulama. So long as their preeminence in local and religious affairs is acknowledged and deference is paid to them by NU's politicians, they are content to legitimize the party's political leadership by their support without demanding a sustained role in party management or the formulation of policy. Such management is carried out by NU's politicians, whose organizational actions were often easily accommodative to secular authority in exchange for noncritical political positions and control of the religious bureaucracy of the Ministry of Religion. The Ministry of Religion provided a source of patronage for thousands of religious teachers and administrators associated with NU. Recipients of the higher positions in the religious bureaucracy offered a source of intellectual leadership for NU and the involvement of the ministry in religious educational institutions and mosque administration throughout Indonesia provided convenient access to potential political support.

CONCEPTIONS OF POWER

Contemporary Indonesian Islamic conceptions of politics and power are derived from both the ideal and pragmatic variants of classical theory, as well as from the historical experience of the Islamic penetration in Indonesia. Although power is no longer felt to be indissolubly tied to religion, it is nonetheless defined in relation to it. Within this framework, it is perceived in several ways: (1) as religiously sanctioned and therefore legitimate, (2) as secular but legitimate, (3) as illegitimate.

The Islamic perception of the legitimacy of power is in large measure based on the power-holder's participation in or treatment of the *ummat Islam* (Islamic community). Religiously sanctioned power is firmly predicated on Islamic norms where the power-holder is himself perceived as a member of the ummat Islam. For some, this may necessitate the implementation of Shari'ah; for others, the perception that societal values and norms are predicated on the ethical values in the Islamic tradition may be enough. This shades off into secular, but legitimate or acceptable power, which is not explicitly predicated on Islamic norms, but where the power-holder is respectful of such norms. This view, acceptant of the nonsacral realities of power, is close to the social theory of Ibn Khaldun. Illegitimate power is not predicated on religious norms and is indeed perceived as distinctly hostile to Islam. It should be noted that Muslim groups frequently differ in their estimations as to whether secular power is being implemented in a legitimate or illegitimate manner. In the estimation of the majority of Indonesian Muslims, the government of the Republic of Indonesia has exercised legitimate political power. For thousands of zealous believers involved in the West Javanese-based Dar'ul Islam revolt, however, only a formal Islamic state could possess legitimacy (see Boland 1971).

In the contemporary Islamic view, religiously legitimate power is derivative. It consists of a relationship not among men, but between God and man. The legitimate power that men possess is granted to them by God, from whom all real power flows (see Anderson 1972a: 54). Political leaders of Islamic parties whose actions are consistently governed by the contours of such a relationship are said to be acting in a legitimate manner, for their deeds are predicated on the consciousness that they are the servants (*abdi*) of Divine Will.

Such a view affirms that the source of wholly legitimate political power and action is God. It is in this sense that the exercise of political power is derivative, originating not with man but with God. The Islamic *tokoh* (political notable) or *pimimpin* (leader) are believed to be acting legitimately in their utilization of power so long as they act for God. The dimensions of such activity can be broadly secular; actions which benefit the political, social, and economic interests of the Islamic groups are usually interpreted as reflecting divine intention. The Islamic tokoh can act in a highly pragmatic manner — seeking accommodation with non-Islamic groups and secular authorities — if this is deemed to benefit the groups he represents. Through all this, the sacral provenance of political legitimacy is manifest.

The Muslim politician possesses influence, status, and prestige to the extent that he is perceived to possess religious knowledge, to be personally devout, and to speak for the sociopolitical interests of his constituency. Within Nahdatul Ulama, it is the kiyayi, rather than the professional politician, whose prestige and influence is highest. Although Nahdatul Ulama's affairs are managed on a daily basis by professional politicians, it is the kiyayis whose approval guarantees popular support for the party (C. Geertz 1960*a*: 228-249). Numerous debates have been carried on within Nahdatul Ulama as to what the appropriate relationship between intellectuals and kiyayis should be, which usually end with the generalized maxim that kiyayis should become "intellectualized" and intellectuals should become "kiyayi-ized." Nonetheless, the role of the kiyayi is clearly pre-eminent. Although such practices as kissing the kiyayi's hand are gradually becoming moribund, intellectuals and politicians are nonetheless expected to *menghormati* (honor) him. This aspect of Nahdatul Ulama's character is spoken of disparagingly by Islamic modernists, who term it "blind faith." Actually, it reflects concepts of a hierarchy of knowledge and devotion within traditionalist Islam, in which knowledge is perceived of as comprehensive scholasticism and esoteric insight, attainable by years of dedicated study and religious devotion. Religious knowledge is held in higher esteem than secular knowledge, and the kiyayi is deemed to possess the *keramat* (charisma) lacking in the *sarjana* (scholar) or the politician. The traditionalist politician is respected for his instrumental competence, if not revered for his erudition or charisma. So long as deference was paid to the rural kiyayi and to the religious fervor of his following, Nahdatul Ulama's national politicians were able to set political policy according to their own proclivities and with a minimal level of accountability. At the national level, they had relatively free rein in their political maneuverings, as the vast majority of Nahdatul Ulama supporters viewed the party primarily as a religious organization, and only secondarily as a political party.

The influence of the tokoh or pimimpin is high in Islamic modernism, for he is deemed to be both religiously knowledgeable and politically capable. In a sense, there is a division among those who are primarily identified as theologians (Hamka, Professor Rasjidi), those who are primarily identified as politicians (Muhammad Roem, Prawoto Mangkusasmito, Kasman Singodimedjo), and those involved in both politics and theology (Muhammad Natsir, Anwar Harjono), but close contact and intellectual interchange make the division somewhat artificial. The modernist tokoh is, in effect, both a political and religious figure. His influence within the Ummat Islam is further heightened by the physical suffering and imprisonment he may have endured during the Guided Democracy period of the Sukarno era. The adjectives used to describe these leaders by their followers are usually *berprincip* (principled), *djudjur* (honest), *konsekwen* (consistent, especially in the sense of practicing what one preaches), and *berpengalaman* (experienced). The tokoh's high prestige may in part be attributable to the Muslim position as a political minority and the difficulty modernist organizations have had in accepting this fact. Within the framework of such an interpretation, the modernist politician's principled behavior may actually be opposition to secular political authority phrased in the grammar of ideological and religious principles.

The Muslim political leader's influence and prestige among his followers are sustained by a network of communication extending from public speeches to published articles to personal contacts. The tokoh will try to visit important regions (usually in Java, but including the Outer Islands as well) every year or so. An itinerary will have been arranged well in advance, scheduling speeches in the larger provincial and district towns. Days before their speeches, it will have been widely publicized that, for example, "Pak Natsir" or "Buya Hamka" would be coming, virtually guaranteeing a large crowd. During election campaigns, the speeches are highly political, the speaker urging the crowd to support one of the Islamic parties. At other times, the tokoh will be the main speaker at a *pengajian* (religious meeting) to which thousands will often come. At such meetings, the tokoh will intermix both religious and political elements — emphasizing the importance of a moral life and supporting one of the numerous Islamic organizations. Pengajians can be large or small affairs, addressed by local *muballighin* (preachers), regional political or religious leaders, or national figures. What is politically important about them is that they are one of the major vehicles for channeling religious faith into political mobilization. Even when politics are mentioned only sporadically, the pengajian stresses the religious, social, and political solidarity of believers. Pengajians commonly connote traditionalist Islamic activity, implying a rural milieu — a large field, a hastily constructed public address system, an enthusiastic crowd which responds easily to the jokes, double entendres, and fervor of the speaker. Modernist meetings also seek to evoke religious solidarity, but they are usually more formal, taking the form of a *pidato* (speech), *sidang* (meeting), or *chotbah* (sermon following Friday prayers).

Another vehicle of interaction between tokohs and their followers is provided by the participation of the leaders in *da'wah* (missionary) activities. Da'wah is religious activity carried out among Muslims which is intended to enlarge the believer's commitment to and understanding of Islam. To this effect, numerous da'wah organizations have been established to disseminate and promote Islamic ideas via speeches, sermons, and pamphlets. Although da'wah is not confined to any one group, modernists have been most active in promoting such efforts on a sustained and institutionalized basis. The best-known of the da'wah organizations, Dewan Da'wah Islamiyah (Islamic Missionary Council), was founded and continues to be directed by Muhammad Natsir. Another, Pendidikan Tinggi Da'wah Islam (PTDI, Organization of Islamic Missionary Higher Education), is associated with well-known senior army officers (generals Sarbini and Sudirman) considered close to modernist thought. In most instances, the "big names" of a few well-known leaders are considered necessary to attract public attention and popular support.

Ties between Islamic leaders and their followers are also maintained by the voluminous articles and books written by the tokohs. Religious, moral, and political ideas are articulated in a rapid stream of publications. Instrumental in this are the numerous newspapers, magazines, journals, and publishing houses identified as "Islamic." Jakarta publishing firms such as Bulan Bintang, Tintamas, and Tamaddun publish in book or pamphlet form much of the writings of the well-known modernist leaders, including those that first appear in newspapers and magazines such as *Abadi, Pelita, Panji Masyarakat, Kiblat, Pembina,* and *Assiyasah.* Their combined circulation is sufficient to disseminate modernist ideas widely throughout Indonesia. Modernists are far more active in writing than traditionalists. NU leaders, for example, rarely articulate their views on religion and politics in intellectual journals or the public forum, whereas modernist leaders speak formally and publish frequently.[1]

One particular pattern of personal contact exists between leader and follower which demonstrates the influence of the tokoh and the reverence in which they are held by their followers. What I term the "five o'clock meeting" establishes a direct contact between a national leader and his followers, adds to the leader's already existent supply of charisma, and takes on many of the attributes of symbolic ritual.

On awakening from their afternoon nap, Islamic religious and political leaders are wont to grant appointments and receive various groups or delegations. The meeting is an "event" which provides a link of continuity and intimacy between leader and followers. Political or da'wah strategy may be discussed, the sentiments of the faithful in Sumatra or Kalimantan appraised, or an opportunity merely to be in the presence of the tokoh provided. The ostensible purpose of the visit is to *minta nasehat* (request advice) on a course of religious or political action to follow. The request may pertain to the appropriate strategy to follow toward the local army commander, the seeking of assistance in mediating a fractional dispute, or the proposed participation of the tokoh in an upcoming conference or *chotbah* (sermon). The meeting also serves the function of solidifying the cohesion and religious solidarity of the visitors. After a brief discussion, the group will leave, and when it later returns to its

1. Only one Jakarta newspaper, *Duta Masjarakat,* is associated with Nahdatul Ulama, and it is frequently closed down for periods of time due to financial problems. The only Nahdatul Ulama journal I have come across is *Risalah Islamyah.* It should be noted that most analyses of traditionalist-modernist political and doctrinal differences are written from a modernist point of view. In this sense, the terms of the debate are defined by modernists. Most sources and interpretive material that non-Indonesian scholars rely on for their analyses are modernist in origin which, although not necessarily predisposing them to a modernist view, certainly results in more being written about modernists than about traditionalists. The greater frequency of contact between modernist leader and foreign scholar than between kiyayi and foreign scholar also adds to this state of affairs. Geertz's dichotomy of *kolot* versus *moderen* Muslims provides an example: *kolot* is defined as "old-fashioned," implying a stick-in-the-mud quality, when in fact the nuance of the term is closer to traditionalist (see C. Geertz 1960). Interpretation of doctrinal differences provides another example: modernists affirm the right of (*ijtihad* or individual autonomy in interpreting the wisdom of the Qur'an and Hadith, whereas traditionalists counsel *taqlid* or obedience to one of the four orthodox *madzhabs* (schools of Islamic jurisprudence) of Sunni Islam in doctrinal matters. The disputation between *ijtihad* and *taqlid* came to be interpreted by many (relying as they were on modernist material) as one of reason and logic versus "blind faith" and "superstition." Such unfortunate misinterpretation of doctrinal and behavioral differences grossly and perjoratively oversimplifies existing differences and ignores the subtleties, intricacies, and contradictions present in the characters of both reformist and traditionalist thought. These descriptive terms have acquired a connotation which has inaccurately placed Nahdatul Ulama on the negative side of a supposed "backward-progressive" dichotomy and has masked an adaptability and flexibility lacking among many reformist organizations.

region and relates to its full membership just how *djudjur* (honest) and *ber-prinsip* (principled) Pak Natsir and Pak Roem are, their religious and social solidarity will have been further strengthened.[2]

On any late afternoon, several unrelated groups and individuals may arrive and patiently wait their turn, often speaking in solemn tones, mindful of the specialness and seriousness of the occasion. The visitors sit on the verandah, sipping tea while waiting to see the tokoh. When the schedule is especially crowded, each group may be placed in a different area (for example, verandah, living room, study) and the tokoh will go from one group to another, speaking briefly with each, occasionally urging the individual or group to remain longer, until the other groups have departed.

> I sat on the verandah of Natsir's house in Menteng, a desirable section of Jakarta. Seated on my right were two regional leaders of Partai Muslimin Indonesia from Central Sulawesi. They told me they had briefly met Natsir twice before. Why had they come to visit Pak Natsir on this occasion? To *minta nasehat* on Partai Muslimin's affairs in their region. On my left was Osman Raliby, a former political leader in Masjumi and currently a writer and lecturer on Islamic and international affairs. Raliby was active in Dewan Da'wah Islamiyah and a well-known figure in modernist circles in his own right. The Sulawesi delegates were also pleased to see him; they were familiar with several of his articles and considered him to be a close confidant of Natsir's. Natsir came out and greeted his seated guests. Upon shaking hands, the two Sulawesi guests were invited inside. Shortly thereafter, three Muhammadijah members came and sat down. Their purpose was, they stated, to take back to their fellow members Natsir's opinion of the new leadership of Partai Muslimin. This pattern, *terima tamu* (receiving guests), often lasted until 8:00 P.M. [Source: Personal meeting].

The same process occurs with other major leaders as well, though to a lesser extent among traditionalist figures. This may be attributable to the fact that the most revered figures in traditionalist circles are ulama, who head *pesantrens* (traditionalist religious schools), usually located far from Jakarta, Surabaya, or other major urban areas. Visits made to the pesantren to see the ulama are likely to take on highly ritualized symbolic patterns. On meeting the ulama, the visitor will bow, grasp the ulama's hand, and attempt to kiss it or press it to his forehead as a sign of obeisance and devotion. The ulama will pull his hand away as if in disapproval of this inegalitarian ritual, but usually not before the gesture has been made. This ritual reflects the perceived *keramat*

---

2. This personal exchange should not be confused with patron-client ties, which have received some attention in Southeast Asia (see Scott 1972: 91-112). A patron-client relationship involves an instrumental friendship in which the patron provides protection or other benefits for his clients while they, in turn, offer general support and assistance, including personal services, to the patron. In Indonesian Islam, the relationship between well-known religious and political figures and their followers is not primarily an instrumental one, but one based on religious solidarity, symbolic ties, and the perceived charismatic qualities (often referred to as *sakti*) of the tokoh.

(charisma) of the ulama in the eyes of his followers at the same time that it acknowledges the equality of all believers in the eyes of God. For his largely rural following, the ulama is deemed to possess holy power and mystical knowledge and the ability to perceive within himself the essence of God – all attributes which sustain his charismatic power (C. Geertz 1960a: 239).

The *minta nasehat* aspect of this meeting is also present. However, it extends far beyond the bounds of religious and political strategy. The ulama's advice is sought on a wide range of issues, including personal problems, marital counseling, curing, and mystical endeavors. Middle-level figures may visit Nahdatul Ulama's national leaders on their trips to the capital, but the sense of occasion and awe is decidedly absent.

UMMAT ISLAM

Central to Islamic identity is the concept of the ummat Islam, the worldwide community of believers of which all Muslims feel themselves members. For Indonesian Muslims, this sense of religious community is central, providing a solidarity which transcends in importance ethnic or national differences. The ummat is a universal community, uniting Muslims of all races and cultures. The world is perceived in somewhat of an exclusivist fashion, divided between those who affirm Islam (and are hence part of the ummat Islam) and those who are *kafir* (nonbelievers). Islamic practice stipulates no lengthy conversion process; the convert need only repeat the confession of the faith, "*La ilaha illa'llah*" ("There is no God but Allah"), and he is at once part of the ummat. As Geertz notes, the sense of worldwide community is primary:

> Islam is seen as a set of concentric social circles, wider and wider communities – Modjokuto, Java, Indonesia, the whole of the Islamic world – spreading away from the individual santri where he stands: a great society of equal believers constantly repeating the name of the Prophet, going through the prayers, chanting the Koran [C. Geertz 1960].

The concept of the ummat Islam is all-encompassing; the existence of intermediate groups between the individual and the ummat is not countenanced. Theoretically, no justification exists for the actions of any groups which interfere with or dilute the totalistic concerns of the faith or its temporal expression within the universal religious community of Islam. It may be asked whether the religious exclusivism of Islam produces an exclusivism in contemporary political strategy and action. Benedict Anderson contends that attempts to cooperate with or accommodate to non-Islamic groups on a sustained or institutionalized basis tend to blur the boundaries between the "we" of the ummat and the "they" of everyone else (Anderson 1972a: 62). Speaking of the modernist Islamic politician, Anderson writes, "To the extent that he authentically represents the claims of Islam, he will have high prestige within his own community, but little purchase on the nation as a whole; to the degree that he succeeds in working out relationships with non-Ummat groups and spreading his effective influence in the society at large, his prestige within his own community may be weakened (Anderson 1972*a*: 62). As I have argued elsewhere, however, such dichotomization need not occur if the political goals of modernist Islam are perceived as being fairly considered (Samson 1973). Under such conditions, political cooperation with secular groups is indeed countenanced, while at the same time a predominant Islamic political identity is still maintained. The reformist mainstream of Masyumi, led by Natsir, Roem, and Prawoto, maintained close ties with the secular-intellectual Partai Sosialis Indonesia (PSI) before both were dissolved in 1960 by order of Sukarno. The accommodationist wing of Masyumi in turn held close ties with the secular Partai Nasionalis Indonesia (PNI). These leaders long had dealings with non-ummat politicians and groups with no noticeable decline in their intra-ummat prestige. It would appear, then, that the religious exclusiveness of the modernists only partially results in political exclusiveness, that is, in times of great crisis, when the social fabric of the faith is perceived as endangered.

To be sure, Islam has long been on the political defensive in Indonesia, a fact which has tended to exacerbate and politicize the exclusivity of an ummat/non-ummat division. The sense of worldwide religious solidarity implied by the concept of ummat has become politically intensified in recent years by the perception of a beleaguered, defensive Islam limited by secular authority, ideological antagonists, and Christian proselytization efforts. Denoting religious identity, the ummat Islam has come to signify political community as well, such community entailing support for a Muslim political party. But need political community entail political exclusiveness? In the estimation of Anderson, it would indeed appear to for modernist Islam. This interpretation equates religious exclusivism with political exclusivism, a confluence which Anderson assumes arises from Islam's sense of political community. I would maintain that no such "natural" confluence exists and that the political defensiveness evinced by many modernist leaders was a reaction to long-perceived thwarting by secular authority of Masyumi's and Parmusi's political goals. Modernist Muslim leaders usually were willing to cooperate with secular groups to attain pragmatic ends. They attempted to influence public policy through alliance with secular forces, but ultimately draped themselves in the mantle of ummat solidarity when they perceived the political system to be threatening Islamic integrity. Increasing frustration at the inability of modernist Islam to achieve its political goals in the face of non-Islamic opposition has been the primary cause of the religiopolitical exclusiveness of modernist Indonesian Islam.

Muslim leaders publicly affirm that the ummat includes even the most nominal adherents of Islam, those whose religious orientations are a complex synthesis of animism, Hindu-Buddhism, Brahmanism, and Islam. They need only to be shown the truth of Islam, persuaded of its all-embracing nature, and they will become seriously committed to their religious obligations, including support for Muslim social and political organizations. This interpretation maintains that the ummat comprises 90 percent of Indonesia's populations. To reach these millions of ummat Islam who are not yet fully "enlightened" as to their religious obligations and sociopolitical interests, da'wah (missionary) activity is proposed. This expansive view of the ummat has, however, ironically been one contribution to the religiopolitical exclusivism of modernist Islam. There has been a tendency on the part of Muslim leaders to interpret the failure of Islamic parties to achieve their ideological and political goals as a result of anti-Islamic plots by small secular groups, an interpretation which blends with their belief that Indonesia is 90 percent Muslim. How else could the demands of the "numerical" Muslim majority be subverted if not by conspiracy? Frustrations inevitably ensue as the failure to achieve political goals comes to be interpreted as a religious threat. What may have commenced as political competition takes on the character of religious defense — rigid, absolutist, and exclusivist.

Somewhat related to the concept of ummat is that of *keluarga* (literally, family, but in this context connoting a religious family). The term refers especially to supporters of Masyumi and to the Masyumi-supporting faction of Partai Muslimin Indonesia. Whereas ummat Islam refers to the world community of all believers, keluarga connotes a cohesiveness forged by modernist religious orientation and political commitment. In particular, the Keluarga Bulan Bintang (Family of the Cresent and Star) signifies the "religious family" consisting of the mainstream Masyumi leadership and its large following. It is a solidarity based on the spirit of Islamic reformism and the years of shared suffering during the period of Sukarno's Guided Democracy (1960-1965) in which much of Masyumi's top leadership was imprisoned in response to the involvement of several Masyumi figures, including Muhammad Natsir, in the anti-PERI revolt of 1958-1959. But keluarga is a term which is more encompassing than membership in Masyumi or support for the Masyumi-leaning faction of Partai Muslimin Indonesia. It also connotes membership in reformist social, religious, and youth organizations such as HMI (Himpunan Mahasisiva Islam, Islamic University Students' Association) and PII (Pemuda Islam Indonesia, Movement of Indonesian Islamic Youth). Continual reference is made to the spiritual ties of the keluarga, which are said to be more indicative of modernist strength than formal membership.

The self-image projected by Nahdatul Ulama plays an important role in strengthening its sense of religious belongingness and cohesion. Whereas modernist supporters of the Masyumi tradition utilized the symbol of the keluarga, traditionalist supporters of Nahdatul Ulama perceived themselves as being within the established Islamic tradition of *Ahlu Sunnah Wal Jama'ah* (the doctrine of Sunni Islam). Traditionalists interpret Ahlu Sunnah Wal Jama'ah as involving the acceptance of the teachings of the eminent theologians of Islam's classical period and adherence to one of the four madzhabs. Nahdatul Ulama has utilized the term *Ahlu Sunnah Wal Jama'ah* as a party system — especially to differentiate their faithfulness to tradition from the impertinences of Masyumi and Parmusi. "We follow Ahlu Sunnah Wal Jama'ah," one old kiyayi affirmed, "while Muhammadiyah and Masyumi emulate the deviations of Wahhabism." Such an image of themselves contributes to a strengthening of the bonds of affiliation that comprise Nahdatul Ulama. It may be that the bonds of affiliation were most gripping when traditionalism was felt to be threatened by modernist thought. As traditionalist and modernist Islam have learned to live with each other, Ahlu Sunnah Wal Jama'ah has come to imply more a self-pride than a traditionalist battle cry. Adherence to Ahlu Sunnah Wal Jama'ah also connotes membership in traditionalist *onderbouw* (subsidiary) organizations affiliated with Nahdatul Ulama, such as Gerakan Pealdjar Islam Indonesia (Movement of Indonesian Islamic University Students) and Ansor (the Nahdatul Ulama youth organization).

PERJUANGAN UMMAT ISLAM

The contemporary Indonesian Islamic view of politics has been influenced by the concept of *Perjuangan Ummat Islam* (struggle of the Islamic community), a term which is frequently referred to in the speeches and articles of traditionalist and modernist figures and which often appears in everyday political conversation. *Perjuangan* broadly connotes the political struggle and aspirations of the ummat Islam — the political effort to be endured (or the burden to be borne) in order to achieve an Islamic society. Varying interpretations are proffered by Islamic leaders as to just what exactly the perjuangan is. "Struggle" is defined by some in a metaphorical, by others in a literal, sense. The field of "struggle" alternately concerns religious belief, social development, political success, or a combination of all.

For Islamic fundamentalists (Isa Anshary of Masyumi; Muttaquien of GPII; and, in a far more extreme sense, Kartosoewirjo of the fanatical Dar'ul Islam movement) who desire the establishment of a Negara Islam (Islamic state), perjuangan is likely to be interpreted in a militantly political manner, in the sense of unceasing struggle against non-Islamic forces for control of the state. For the traditionalist leadership of Nahdatul Ulama, an Islamic state exists as a future goal, but long-established accommodation with the civil state in exchange for administrative and political security has moderated the tenor of perjuangan to a metaphorical, though sincerely held, affirmation of religiopolitical solidarity. The reformist figures of Masyumi-Partai Muslimin Indonesia (Muhammad Natsir, Muhammad Roem, Hamka, Anwar Harjono, Hasan Basri) interpret perjuangan in a religiopolitical sense, as a striving to achieve an Islamic society (though not necessarily an Islamic state) and a politically influential role for Islamic parties. Reformists maintain that the Perjaungan Ummat Islam can succeed only through formal political victory.[3] The accommodationist leadership of Partai Muslim Indonesia (H. M. Mintaredja, Djaelani Naro, Agus Sudono)

3. During the process of establishing Partai Muslimin Indonesia in 1967 and during its first few months of formal existence, there was much controversy as to its composition. It was apparent that the government did not want a new Islamic party in Masyumi's image and would discourage the old Masyumi leaders from exercising positions of leadership in the new party. A deep internal split developed between those who insisted on an active role for Natsir, Prawoto, and Roem, and those who contended that if the new party was to get off the ground, it had to temporarily acquiesce to the government. During this period, the old leaders continually urged that the unity of the keluarga must remain firm, that fissiparous tendencies not become ingrained in Partai Muslimin Indonesia.

interpret perjuangan in a socioeconomic sense, as articulating the social interests and improving the economic position of Muslim organizations and individuals. Accommodationists emphasize the importance of flexibility and the need to cooperate with stronger secular and military forces and criticize the reformist and fundamentalist stress on perjuangan as political struggle. H. M. Mintaredja, as chairman of Partai Muslimin, has written,

> Is the politics in which we have been active in the past wrong? The answer is clear! Yes.... What and where is it wrong? What we have carried out until now is too much political battling, just politics, without concerning ourselves with matters which are needed to bring us to national prosperity, national economic justice....

> It is clear that what we have implemented until now has been a political approach striving for formal victory.... It is important that we must carry out now and in the future a political approach leading to material victory, stressing development in all fields (economy, food and clothes... etc.) [Mintaredja 1971: 46-47].

The current leadership of both Nahdatul Ulama and Partai Muslimin are accommodationist — supported by Indonesia's military power-holders who desire a pragmatic, "program-oriented" Islam, free from the religiopolitical desires and ideological demands of the past. Military pressure and manipulation eliminated the initial neo-Masyumi character of Partai Muslimin — first by refusing "clearance" for well-known Masyumi figures to exercise positions of leadership in Partai Muslimin, then by fomenting an internal party "coup" which catapulted accommodationist figures into party power.

The normally accommodationist character of Nahdatul Ulama has always been supported by the government, both under Sukarno and Suharto. The one serious challenge to accommodationist primacy in Nahdatul Ulama was neatly disposed of when Subchan, Nahdul Ulama's vice-chairman, was questionably removed from his position with the clear approval of the government. In January 1973, all political parties were "fused" into two new political parties with the prodding of the government. These two parties were to serve the government. The four Islamic parties were fused to form the PPP (Partai Persatuan Pemban-gunan, Development Unity party). Governmental policy provides support for accommodationist leaders such as Idham Chalid (Nahdatul Ulama's general chairman for over fifteen years) and H. M. Mintaredja of Partai Muslimin in exchange for their acquiescence in the authority of the New Order.

This relationship has clearly resulted in a depoliticization of the Perjuan-gan Ummat Islam, relegating religiopolitical competition to the background while emphasizing Islam as a broad, nonpolitical framework of solidarity and moral precepts. Such emphasis is in line with Nahdatul Ulama's priorities, but may create some difficulty for pro-Masyumi reformists, whose frustration at political exclusion is bitter and who still are the largest political element in Islamic modernism. Accommodationists have been on the political periphery of Islamic modernism, and whether they can convince the reformist mainstream that the Perjuangan Ummat Islam must take a new form still remains conjectural.[4] The memory of the Keluarga Bulan Bintang persecuted by Sukarno from without, but united from within because of this, and motivated by the requisites of a militant perjuangan bulks large in the vision of most modernists. The continued political defeats suffered by Indonesian Islamic modernism produced frustration which intensified the militancy of the "struggle." If a depoliticized perjuangan is to be acceptable to the reformists and fundamentalists, the accommodationism of the newly "fused" PPP must bring about definite socio-economic gains for Muslim groups. Their chances for doing so will be considered in the concluding chapter.

RELIGIOUS BELIEF AND POLITICAL BEHAVIOR

A close relationship between religion and politics is explicitly stated in an Islamic party. A political state of affairs is perceived as good or bad depending on its congruence with Qur'anic intentions. For many, the Qur'an thus becomes the arbiter of appropriate public policy. In such circumstances, religious terms are applied to assess a political situation for which they were not initially intended. What this means is that a particular political policy may be legitimized by how closely it is felt to fulfill Qur'anic intention, or a Qur'anic injunction may be said "morally" to demand a political response. In such a manner, political action may take on militant dimensions, as when *jihad* (holy war) is urged against political opponents, or exegesis of Qur'anic intention may encourage political moderation, as when the Qur'anic injunction to "do good and avoid evil" is used to support a policy accommodative to secular authority. As Coulson has demonstrated, Qur'anic approval can be construed for a variety of public policies, several of which appear to be at odds with Qur'anic intention (Coulson 1965: 88). By such refashioning and reinterpretation, numerous contemporary civil actions can be religiously legitimized. Thus, for example, the Tunisian law of personal status interpreted the Qur'anic injunction pertaining to the permissibility of polygamy so long as all wives were treated impartially to mean that in the circumstances of modern society it was impossible for a husband to treat several wives impartially to their mutual satisfaction. Hence, polygamy, which is sanctioned by the Qur'an, was prohibited in Tunisia in the light of contemporary Qur'anic reinterpretation.

In politics, also, religious commitment need not predetermine a single oppositionist course of action. Certainly in Indonesia, widely varying political views (both accommodative to and critical of secular authority) have been held by Islamic coreligionists. Doctrinal, ideological, social, and educational differences between and within Muslim parties have made a united Islamic political stand the exception rather than the rule. The Qur'an has been used to legitimize

4. Such revered Masyumi figures as Haji Agus Salim, Sukiman Wirjosandjojo, and Muhammad Natsir were at one time in their political careers considered to be accommodationists.

or oppose divergent courses of political action, while politics, for many, is defined in terms of religious commitment — social, political, and economic interests matter as well. What is declared to be religiously "imperative" according to Qur'anic interpretation may basically serve to provide religious legitimacy to the material and political interests of specific groups.

Although certain generalizations about the effect of religious belief on political action can be made, I contend that religious belief is not a sufficient determinant of political behavior. What is one to make, for example, of the apparent anomaly between the religious traditionalism of Nahdatul Ulama (which is religiously totalistic, consummatory, and prescribes stringent limitations on the autonomy of individual reason) and its political flexibility, adaptbility, and ease of accommodation to secular authority? Conversely, what is one to make of the religious modernism of the Masyumi tradition (which encourages rationalism, pragmatic behavior, and holds a more limited view of the purview of religion in secular life) with its rigidity and inflexibility in matters of political ideology and principle, and its tendency to interpret political defeat as religious threat. (Once again, it should be noted that reformists in Masyumi and Partai Muslimin were willing to cooperate with secular political forces so long as they felt their political interests were being fairly considered.) With regard to Islamic traditionalism, religion has legitimized political accommodation. With regard to Islamic modernism, religion has exacerbated political defeat. In neither circumstance can it be demonstrated that political behavior has been unalterably determined by religious belief.

Both traditionalists and modernists justify their political behavior in terms of religious belief and draw on scripture to "prove" or legitimize their stands. In this manner, both the political accommodationism of Nahdatul Ulama and the opposition of Masyumi could be articulated in the context of Qur'anic terms. Traditionalists often use Qur'anic injunctions which counsel moderation, fundamentalists seek militant verses, while reformists rely on both (depending on whether they feel their political demands are being equitably considered).[5]

Islamic fundamentalists often refer to *jihad* (holy war) — evoking the imagery of struggle and fervor in defense of the faith. The spirit of jihad has been described by fundamentalist Masyumi and Persatuan Islam (Islamic Union) figure, Isa Anshary, in the oath of the Islamic soldier:

> I promise God that I will surely die!
> Surely die in order to destroy the enemy of God and my enemy!
> Throw me into it! So that I may open the door! [Anshary 1949: 90].

In the Qur'an, jihad clearly connotes martial endeavors and defense of the faith against the enemies of Islam, but its meaning has been stretched to include

5. In this regard Ward notes a traditionalist informant's comment that while Masyumi and Partai Muslimin deliberately sought Qur'anic verses (*dalil*) that were *keras* (hard, militant), Nahdatul Ulama looked for easier verses, such as the one which states that "struggle must be carried on slowly, because what is slow comes from God, what is in haste comes from the Devil" (Ward, n.d.: chap. 4, p. 8).

struggle against immorality within Islam and political competition with non-Islamic groups.[6]

The same Qur'anic verse has been used both to counsel moderation and to urge militance. The injunction *amar ma'ruf nahi munkar* (do good and avoid evil) has been used by (1) a council of ulamas to stress the religious duty of Muslims to support an Islamic political party (GPII, n.d.); (2) Nahdatul Ulama leaders to justify their silence at Sukarno's dissolution of the Constituent Assembly in 1959 (Nahdatul Ulama 1959: 117); (3) H. M. S. Mintaredja, Partai Muslimin chairman, to criticize emphasis given to political competition by Islamic leaders at the expense of economic improvement (Mintaredja 1971: 47).

In this manner, religion provides legitimacy for already existing political interests. Both traditionalists and modernists draw on Islamic precepts and symbols to validate their actions after their political interests are determined. The limited political and economic benefits which Nahdatul Ulama's leadership gained from accommodation with civil government gave it a stake in a policy of moderation. The numerous political defeats suffered by pro-Masyumi reformists highlighted Islam's position as a political minority and evoked an ideological response articulated in the tenor of religious defense. Throughout all of this religion appears to be as much a legitimizing as a motivating force. Throughout the 1950s and 1960s, political concern at the national level was reflected in the ideological demands of the Islamic parties. It is this ideological aspect of the Islamic conception of politics which will be considered next.

THE QUEST FOR IDEOLOGY

If someone is able to separate sugar from its sweetness, he will be able to separate Islamic religion from politics [K. H. A. Wahab Chasbullah, quoted Ahmad 1956: 6].

Committed Muslims claim that the relationship between religion and politics is an intimate one, extending not merely to the immediacy of sacral themes to mobilize political support, but to the establishment of Islamic standards and symbols as the prime foci of societal identity. It is the goal of most Muslims to see the values encompassed in Islam predicate the norms of society. This commitment has been expressed at varying times through revolts against the central government launched by fanatical movements proclaiming an Islamic state, debates over the appropriate ideological basis of the state between the proponents of Islam and secular nationalism, and sustained but unsuccessful attempts by Islamic organizations to have the Islamic context of law widened

6. Referring to the general election of 1955, Isa Anshary termed it a *Jihad Akbar* (great holy war) against the Communists. Conversely, the war of independence against the Dutch was termed a *Jihad Ashqar* (small holy war) (quoted in Sidjabat 1965: 66).

For many, the frequent use of the term *jihad* implied a fervor and fanaticism that aroused fear and hostility on the part of non-Muslims and left even many Muslims apprehensive.

beyond the registration of marriage and divorce. All behavior, for some, is interpreted within the totality of a fervent religious commitment; for others, Islam is more of a loose unifying framework — a symbol of solidarity rather than the fulcrum of their being. A common denominator, however, is the desire to provide a place of recognized importance for Islam in government and society.

A strand of continuity has been evident in modernist and traditionalist thought which affirms the desirability and necessity of Islamic ideals as a source of inspiration for secular behavior. The ideals embodied in Islam should not be separated from other aspects of life. As Muhammad Natsir stated,

> Islam is a philosophy of life, an ideology, a system of living for the victory of man now and in the hereafter. . . . Because of this, we as Muslims cannot detach ourselves from politics. And as political persons we cannot detach ourselves from our ideology, namely Islam. For us, to construct Islam cannot be separated from constructing society, constructing the state, constructing freedom. . . . Concerning the relationship of man with his fellow man, the function of religion is to defend that connection in all aspects of life. Here we should notice the function of politics in defending the relationship. Does politics cover one aspect of life or all aspects? Politics only includes one aspect of the relationship between man with his fellow man, while the function of religion is to defend this relationship in all aspects of life. So how is it possible that religion, which is inclusive of all aspects, can be separated from politics, which only includes one aspect? [Natsir 1961: 106, 157].

Political activity without religious norms to guide it was felt to be amoral, susceptible to manipulation by opportunists and demagogues. Even a so-called technological meritocracy, infused with rational and material values, could lose sight of moral considerations (Natsir, n.d.: 18-19). Only Islam, Islamic leaders stressed, could provide a guide for all temporal action — individual and political.

For the state to exist separately from religious concern was to replace morality with expediency, to substitute temporary interests for permanent principles. Governmental regulation was deemed necessary to ensure that Islamic obligations were fulfilled. Non-Muslims need have no fear of Islamic tolerance, Muslim leaders stated. Islam's liberality had been proved many times in the past, during its classical age. But if the majority of the population of a state were Muslim, that state should be regulated by Shari'ah (Islamic law). If 90 percent of the population of a state were Muslim, Persatuan Islam leader Ahmad Hassan asked, "Is it fitting that we blot out the importance of the 90 percent majority because of the 10 percent minority? Would such a settlement be fair? (Hassan 1941: 41).

A noticeable vagueness has been evident on the part of Muslim leaders, whether traditionalist or modernist, in their conceptualization of the character of an Islamic state. Before the ideological defeat of the Islamic forces in the 1957 Constituent Assembly debates there was widespread sentiment among Islamic groups in favor of an Islamic state, but only slight speculation, analysis, or planning as to its capabilities of supporting a modern legal structure and social system. Even modernists, who faulted traditionalists for their blind adherence to the pronouncements of medieval scholars and historical orientation, did little investigation into the compatibility of the legal tenets of Shari'ah with a developing, urbanizing society, beyond repeated apologetical assurances that the Qur'an and Hadith were valid for all times and places.

Traditionalists were even less specific. They were disposed to conceive of an Islamic state along the lines of a theocracy in which the most eminent kiyayis would govern — guided by the wisdom of the religious code of conduct embodied in the four madzhabs. If the kiyayis did not govern directly, many stated, they would have veto power over legislation that was deemed irreligious or immoral.

Differing gradations of support were given to the concept of an Islamic role in politics by traditionalists and modernists. Traditionalists within Nahdatul Ulama (both ulama and politicians) gave pro forma support to the establishment of an Islamic state, but their dependence on and consequent accommodation to secular political authority belied their religious pronouncements. The religious fervor of Nahdatul Ulama's kiyayis and traditional following was clearly balanced by the caution of its political leadership, though Nahdatul Ulama officially espoused the view that the declaration of an Islamic state should come before the creation of an Islamic society (Federspiel 1970: 165).

Within Masyumi, fundamentalists and reformists supported an Islamic state, albeit with differing levels of intensity. Fundamentalist thought, as expressed by Ahmad Hassan and Isa Anshary of Persatuan Islam, stressed that the establishment of an Islamic state was mandatory. Cooperation with secular forces was accepted only as a temporary expedient. Fundamentalist zeal in seeking the establishment of a state based on Islam and their often intemperate style opened them to accusations of intolerance. Reformists also supported an Islamic state, but were disposed to cooperate with secular forces so long as they felt they had a stake in the political order. The religio-ideological issue was not held to be an obstacle to participation in secular politics until Masyumi's failure to achieve its major political goals throughout the 1950s forced it to the ideological ramparts. These political goals were the establishment of a state based on Islamic tenets, decentralization with consequent devolution of power from a Javanese-dominated unitary government to one of wide local and regional autonomy, and the recognition of Islam as an influential and legitimate political force with a degree of political power commensurate with its numbers. Masyumi's reformist mainstream theoretically favored an Islamic state, but its urbanized, pragmatic character ensured it an influential role in secular politics and made it a moderating influence within Islam. Its continued defeats on matters of moment to it was to change this.

Accommodationists were little concerned with enunciating an exclusivist, ideological stance. They perceived Islam as a framework of unity rather than as the pursuit of the Absolute. The issue of an Islamic state was of slight importance to them, though Islam as a symbol retained its importance. They were more concerned with social and economic goals than with Islamic doctrine.

How literally should the Islamic stress on the importance of ideology be interpreted? Is ideology an issue of great moment in Indonesian Islam? Are the Islamic political parties so based on an overarching ideological conception that immediate political goals are little more than way stations to the achievement of an Islamic society and its legal or symbolic expression in a state based on Islam? Admittedly, I may be posing these questions in such a leading (and even skewed) manner that simple equity and moderation may invite a response that is somewhat deprecatory of the power of ideology to determine political behavior. This is, nonetheless, an interesting (and even relevant) question. It is such because reformist Islamic leaders have defined politics in just these terms. Islam's expressed political goals have, in fact, been highly ideological. Its well-articulated raison d'être is predicated on an idealized conception of society — a desired spiritual-temporal state, rather than a more prosaic quest for influence, seats, and the perquisites of power. The question is still a relevant one, even if ideology turns out to be of relatively minor importance to Islam, for this may indicate a contradiction (conscious or unconscious) between Islam's professed and actual goals, or an accommodation to actual societal conditions.

At times the political response of the major Islamic parties has been highly ideological and militant, whereas at other times it has been pragmatic and interest-seeking. I have posited here that the ideological response of the Islamic parties was in large measure determined by whether their important political interests and goals had been met. If this interpretation is correct, can it mean that the professed emphasis on ideology is little more than an inverse reflection of the nonsatisfaction of distinctly political goals? Is ideology, then, some last resort — a tactic to be utilized when pragmatic action has failed? Is it, in the final measure, an autonomous and constant concern, or a response to cumulative failure and frustration?

At the risk of appearing to dispose too neatly of unwieldy divergent interpretations, I would contend that ideology is both. For the Indonesian Islamic leader (and for many of his followers) it possesses two levels of significance, not so much clashing or blending as layered. It is, first of all, a unifying symbol and needs no political success to maintain its appeal or relevance (see Lev 1966: 126). At this level, Islam's professed ideological goals are symbolically rather than literally interpreted by all but fundamentalists. Pronouncements in favor of an Islamic state come to mean a state whose tenets are motivated by Islamic norms. An Islamic society where Shari'ah must be implemented becomes a society "inspired" by Islamic principles. Ideological concern remains, but is less intensively stressed.

In this situation, ideological goals serve as an instrument of identity and solidarity, and are to some extent interchangeable with political goals (see Apter 1965: 328). For Islamic modernists, especially, the achievement or nonachievement of political goals has direct bearing on religious self-perception. If political goals are realized, religious self-assurance is maintained. Under these circumstances, the sense of identity ordinarily provided by ideology is equaled by the confidence and self-assuredness resultant from political success. For both Islamic reformists and traditionalists, ideological compromise can therefore be agreed to in exchange for political concession. If the political goals or interest of Islamic parties are met, the larger political system is perceived as legitimate and an accommodative strategy is pursued. Ideological goals are interpreted as broadly symbolic rather than religiously imperative. Although ideology plays a part in politics, politics is not ideologized.

At the second level of significance, ideological concern becomes more intensive. At first, just as ideology can be compromised for political concessions, so the failure to achieve political goals can be assuaged by slight ideological concession on the part of non-Muslim political forces. In these circumstances, ideology is still more of a unifying symbol than an explicit demand to make official a connection between Islam and the state. When there is a continuing failure to achieve political goals, however, and symbolic concessions are not agreed to by secular forces, Islamic ideological demands take on intense proportions in response to the discernible frustration felt by the Islamic groups. Ideology is then a series of imperative demands, becoming increasingly rigidified as previous demands remain unmet.

The rigidity of ideological response is in this instance a defensive reaction against continued failure to realize strongly held political goals. The demands of Islamic reformists in Masyumi and Partai Muslimin have been more comprehensive in nature than the basic interest orientation of Nahdatul Ulama, and failure to achieve these demands has provoked a greater commitment to ideology on their part — though failure is often perceived as a religious threat by traditionalists as well. Ideology under such circumstances is equated with the defense of Islam and the response of the Islamic parties becomes defensive, rigid, and single-minded.

The ideological response of Islam has been similar to both the Constitutional Democracy period (1945-1959) and the early years of the New Order (1965-1971). In both periods, Islamic parties were initially accommodative to non-Islamic authority, which was perceived as legitimate. Politics was viewed as a pragmatic process and ideology was loosely symbolic. Reformists and fundamentalists came to feel, however, that their political and religious demands were constantly ignored and ideology became a focal point of direct and immediate contention.

Since Indonesia proclaimed its independence in 1945, its official ideology has been Pancasila. First formulated in a June 1945 speech by Sukarno, Pancasila, or Five Principles, became part of the official ideology of the Republic (Sukarno 1952). The five principles — nationalism, humanitarianism, democracy, social welfare, and belief in One God — were intended to provide a unifying framework for Indonesia's diverse population. Highly influenced by Hindu-Javanese cosmological conceptions, Pancasila was a compromise within the Javanese tradition — an attempt to achieve national unity through synthesis. Sukarno felt that in Pancasila he had captured *tata,* the traditional mystical harmony and world order (see Dahm 1969: 347). Intended by its proponents to promote harmony through the syncretic conciliation of diverse orientations, it was hoped that Pancasila would enable a modus vivendi to be achieved among the major cleavages in Indonesian society: Islam and Christian, aristocracy and peasantry, nationalist and Communist, commercial and agrarian, Javanese and Outer Island groups (C. Geertz 1964: 68). Each *sila* symbolized some desired condition for one of the preceding groups: Muslims emphasized belief in One God; Communists stressed social welfare; nationalists emphasized nationalism. By this process, it was hoped that the entire ideology would be accepted as legitimate.

As a symbol of national unity, Pancasila was at first acceptable to much of the Islamic community, which supported its position as official state ideology. Dissatisfaction became apparent when a number of its political goals and interests were not achieved, and by 1953 Islamic sentiment had begun to turn. In January of that year, Sukarno spoke at Amuntai, South Kalimantan, where he criticized the concept of an Islamic state, stating that many non-Muslims would secede from the republic if Indonesia became a state based on Islam (Compton 1953). Islamic response was initially restrained; only fundamentalists such as Isa Anshary responded sharply and, in turn, received criticism from Masyumi's moderate majority for intensifying a potential conflict (Feith 1962: 281-83). In general, however, the proponents of Islam and Pancasila increasingly came to view these concepts as polar opposites. Pancasila was no longer seen as a symbol of national unity but as a non-Islamic ideology of slight depth and comprehensiveness when compared to Islamic principles. Neither side desired ideological conflict, but as Masyumi failed to achieve its major political goals, it increasingly evinced an ideologically rigid stance, phrased in the symbolic terms of religious struggle.

Ideological polemics received direct expression in the 1957 Constituent Assembly debates on the appropriate ideological basis of the Indonesian state. Both Masyumi and Nahdatul Ulama supported the concept of an Islamic state while at the same time participating in Indonesia's essentially secular political system. Had Masyumi been satisfied that its political interests were being fairly considered, ideology need not have become an issue of such acrimonious dimensions. Its increasing sense of impotence, however, contributed to the intensity of ideological debate, which came to be seen as the point of final defense.

The Constituent Assembly debates were insurmountably split between proponents of Islam and Pancasila (see *Tentang Dasar Negara Republik Indonesia dalam Konstiuante*). Nahdatul Ulama retained hopes for the possibility of ideological compromise, but joined Masyumi in actively speaking for an Islamic state. Whether or not compromise was generally anticipated, the debates provide a clear view of just how sincerely the opposing ideological positions were held. In the estimation of many nationalists, Islam would divide the nation along religious lines. Muslim leaders contended that only Islam offered a moral guide to all action — secular and religious.

The public pronouncements of Islamic leaders favoring an Islamic state adequately reflected the feelings of most of their followers. The Islamic parties, however, possessed distinct political interests which were as important to them as ideology. In a sense, their ideological stand was similar to the opening demands of antagonists in contract negotiations. They did not anticipate the attainment of all they desired, but expected some compromise wherein many of their major interests would be met. Both Masyumi and Nahdatul Ulama, Lev notes, were interested more "in a favorable resolution of political issues than in ideological purity" (Lev 1972: 126). Ideological polemics could have been toned down once compromise, either in ideology or politics, appeared likely. This never came to pass, however, as Masyumi was continually frustrated in its opposition to the government's federal, regional, and economic policies, and increasingly came to view politics in the metaphor of religious defense. Masyumi's reformist and accommodationist factions were on the defensive by this time, and further conciliatory gestures on their part would have totally discredited them in the estimation of the party's constituency. The debates ended inconclusively with no vote taken, both sides eschewing compromise. An ideological last stand was made a year and a half later in the Constituent Assembly debates concerning Sukarno's proposal to return to the 1945 constitution and lay the groundwork for his concept of Guided Democracy. Masyumi led the struggle of all Islamic parties to reject the proposal unless a phrase (deleted from the Jakarta charter of 1945) obligating all Muslims to follow Islamic law was reinserted and made part of the constitution. Secular forces objected to this because the phrase was interpreted by Islamic leaders not as a permissive rule but as one which must be enforced by the state (Lev 1972: 267).[7] This interpretation seems to imply the placement of civil codes and customary law by Shari'ah.

The issue was perceived as the final line of defense by Masyumi reformers and fundamentalists. Constant previous political failure had intensified this issue to the dimensions of the ultimate defense of Islam. The vote in the Constituent Assembly was a recapitulation of the inconclusive results of two years earlier. The opposition of the Islamic parties was sufficient to prevent a two-thirds majority from being realized. On July 5, 1959, Sukarno abolished the Constituent Assembly and declared the 1945 constitution in effect. He stated in the decree that the Jakarta charter (with the phrase obligating all Muslims to follow Islamic law) "inspires the 1945 constitution and comprises a framework of unity with the constitution." This was meant to be slight concession to Islam but, on the whole, one that was not overly significant, for it did not change the fact that the Jakarta charter was not made a part of the constitution or of legislation. As a symbolic nod, it apparently satisfied Nahdatul Ulama, which was only too pleased to regain its place on the periphery of political influence. Masyumi's impotence as an effective political force was clearly demonstrated by this defeat, and no conciliatory phrase could evoke any other illusion. It was dissolved in August 1960 on the order of Sukarno, and its major leaders were arrested and

7. Islamic speakers emphasized the necessity of incorporating the Jakarta charter as the preamble of the constitution or as article 29 (see Bajasut 1966).

imprisoned. The period of Guided Democracy was a grim one for the political
fortunes of the Islamic groups.

IDEOLOGY IN THE NEW ORDER: 1965-1970

Cooperation among the army, student organizations, and Islamic groups in
decimating the Communist party in the aftermath of the attempted coup of
September 30, 1965, indicated to many that Islam would gain a legitimate place
of political importance in the New Order. Indeed, many Islamic leaders came to
feel that Islam was the most important civil force in society. Its major antagonists, the PKI and Sukarno, had been eliminated. With the destruction of the
Communist party and its millions of supporters, the Islamic parties comprised
the largest single political force. Such cooperation was short-lived, however, as
non-Islamic groups and much of the military believed that the Islamic parties
still clung tenaciously to their goal of an Islamic state, and remained on guard
against any attempt to rekindle ideological disputation.

Although Islamic figures affirmed their support for Pancasila, secular
groups criticized such support as being based on political expediency. "The
Muslim parties still want an Islamic state," a secular leader emphasized. "Make
no mistake! They can't oppose the armed forces openly on this, but they're
waiting for the right moment to bring up the issue again" (this quotation comes
from a personal interview). Muslim leaders claimed the issue was dead. Pancasila,
they claimed, could be accepted and supported according to the norms of Islam.
In this regard, it was particularly stressed by Muslim leaders that the first sila,
belief in Almighty God, inspired the four other silas. Nonetheless, suspicion on
the part of non-Islamic groups toward Muslim intentions was often intensified
by phrases such as *"Pancasila yang diridhoi Tuhan"* ("Pancasila which is blessed
by God"). Secular groups interpreted such statements as attempts to introduce
the Jakarta charter in a covert manner (see *Pedoman,* August 6, 1969).

Ideological debate continued in the post-1965 period, albeit on a plane of
lower comprehensiveness and immediacy. In part, this was a reflection of
ideological concern operating at both the levels of unifying symbol and imperative demand. At the first level, Islamic concern with ideology in the New Order
was broadly symbolic, providing identity and solidarity. At the second level, it
was also a reaction against military determination not to allow the rehabilitation
of Masyumi (which had been dissolved by order of Sukarno in 1960) nor to
allow the participation of the major Masyumi figures in the newly established
Partai Muslimin Indonesia. At this level, ideological concern took on more
intense proportions, reflecting the frustration felt by many modernist supporters
of Masyumi. It did not reach the level of imperative demand, as was the case in
the 1959 Constituent Assembly debates, but was in its own way a defensive
reaction against clear military hegemony and the frustration engendered by the
political weakness of Islamic modernism. Nahdatul Ulama's ideological concerns
were broadly symbolic; it could affirm its theological dedication to an Islamic
state, Shari'ah, or the Jakarta charter without sacrificing its accommodative

policy and the limited influence it had gained at the periphery of political influence. Similarly, for the accommodationists in Partai Muslimin (Mintaredja, Agus Sudono, H. M. Sansui, Djaelani Naro, Imron Kadir), ideology was interpreted in a broadly symbolic manner as pertaining to a loose, personal religious identity.[8] Ideology was far more important for the reformists and fundamentalists in Partai Muslimin, for whom it possessed both symbolic and political importance. Consequently, when the political goals of the Masyumi-supporting majority of Partai Muslimin were thwarted and obstructed, their reaction was phrased in the meter of religio-ideological demands.

Post-1965 debate revolved around the demand of the Muslim parties that a statement emphasizing the obligation of Muslims to follow Islamic law be given legal force. This obligation was stated in the Jakarta charter of June 22, 1945, which, with the exclusion of the Islamic law statement, was made the preamble of the 1945 constitution. The Islamic parties demanded that this statement be reinserted and given legal force. They expressed this view in the March 1968 meeting of the Peoples' Deliberative Assembly in which the ideological direction of the state was discussed. Their proposal would make it incumbent on all Muslims (be they nominal or intense adherents) to follow Islamic law and would link the state to religious observance and practice. The state would then have the responsibility of enforcing Islamic law. It was this topic which aroused such strong feeling during the 1959 Constituent Assembly debates on the return to the 1945 constitution. With the state responsible for the enforcement of religious observation, many feared that the Islamic political parties and their affiliated organizations would be catapulted to predominant political influence. Muslim religious and political leaders interpreted the Jakarta charter not as a permissive rule, but as one which must be enforced by the state (*Api Pantja Sila*, April 15, 1968). Such an eventuality left even many Muslims apprehensive.

Throughout 1968 and 1969, the Islamic parties sponsored "Jakarta charter Commemoration Day" programs to be held each June 22. Fanfare and wide press coverage accompanied preparation for the event during the preceding month. Organizational impetus was held by Partai Muslimin associated groups, but Nahdatul Ulama also supported the effort, which served to tighten ideological solidarity (albeit temporarily) among the generally divided Islamic ranks.

Three views of the Jakarta charter were expressed by Islamic groups:

1. The statement that the Jakarta charter "inspires" the 1945 constitution could be accepted without attempting to further define or modify it. With this, the issue would be deliberately downplayed, possibly avoiding a renewal of acrimonious debate. Symbolic satisfaction would thus be provided for some but not for all.

2. The Jakarta charter should be made the preamble to the 1945 constitution (which would essentially mean reinserting the deleted phrase into the text

8. Nahdatul Ulama's view of ideology differed from that held by Partai Muslimin's accommodationists in that it was felt to pertain to a social, as well as to a personal, identity.

of the document). This would signify a symbolic victory for Islam in that Shari'ah would officially be recognized by the state.

3. The Jakarta charter should be made a part of legislation in article 29 of the constitution, thereby giving Shari'ah legal force and designating the state as being responsible for its implementation. This option was feared most by nominally and non-Islamic groups who opposed any attempt to force implementation of Islamic law.

The first view was acceptable to the political leadership of Nahdatul Ulama, for whom the retention of minor political influence and control of the religious bureaucracy was preferable to ideological confrontation. Once the expression of symbolic concern was made, Nahdatul Ulama was content to continue its accommodationist policy. Masyumi-Partai Muslimin reformists favored the second or third options which implied state recognition, and possible enforcement, of Islamic law. As in 1959, their ideological demands were intensified by the political obstruction they encountered at the hands of the government. Whether governmental agreement to the participation of the Masyumi figures in Partai Muslimin would have diluted the ideological demands of the reformists in the Jakarta charter debates is conjectural. That Partai Muslimin was not permitted to develop in this direction clearly makes the question an academic one. Military determination to "domesticate" Partai Muslimin, however, was predicated on the interpretation that a vigorous, politicized Islamic modernism writ in the image of Masyumi would itself evince an ideological concern far exceeding the realm of the broadly symbolic. Governmental strategy was to encourage Partai Muslimin's accommodationists while obstructing its reformists and fundamentalists. To this effect, the military-fomented internal coup within Partai Muslimin in October 1970 resulted in the leadership of H. M. Mintaredja, who urged accommodation to secular authority and a devolution of religious concern from the political to the personal.

In effect, the government was following the policy of Snouck Hurgronje, the eminent Dutch Islamologist of the late nineteenth and early twentieth century, who urged that Islamic religious activities be encouraged and political activities restricted. Nahdatul Ulama's leadership could accept these restrictions, but the situation was a frustrating one for reformists, who argued that the political weakness of Islam was attributable only to external obstruction and did not reflect Islam's actual numerical strength in society. The disparity between Islam's political weakness and the tendency of reformists leaders to overestimate their numerical and social strength intensified the political dimensions of the Perjuanagan Ummat Islam. By 1971, all of this served to intensify a perception of politics which defined political participation as unremitting struggle, ideology as imperative demand, the "Islamic struggle" as a zero-sum political competition, secular political power as only semilegitimate, and the ummat Islam as a politically exclusivist concept.

INDONESIAN ISLAM SINCE THE ELECTION

The decisive victory of government-sponsored GOLKAR in the 1971 national election, in which the Islamic parties received 27 percent of the votes cast, gives further evidence of Islam's minority position in politics. This total represents a noticeable decline from the 43 percent of the vote Islamic parties received in the 1955 national election. The Islamic parties sustained a political defeat, a fact which may finally indicate to the Islamic parties and leaders that Islam is but one of several political forces in Indonesia, and by no means the largest one. If so, the failure to achieve political goals can no longer be attributed to "behind-the-scenes" machinations of secular groups, and a more pragmatic assessment of Islam's actual political strength may therefore curb unrealistic expectations and demands.

Ideology as imperative demand was of immediate concern when political failure was attributed to manipulation by non-Islamic groups who were deemed unrepresentative of Indonesia's supposed Islamic majority (the "myth of the numerical majority"). However, an election which shows Islam to be no more than a political minority may change political self-perception within the ummat Islam and perhaps lay the groundwork for an internal reassessment. Could such a realization lead to a diminution of ideological expectations and demands on the part of the ummat Islam? Ideology has been of immediate concern to Islamic parties — both as symbolic unity and imperative demand — and the response of Islamic modernism to political failure has been couched in terms of ideological defense. Is it plausible to anticipate a reassessment in which religious defense is eschewed for the more prosaic articulation of definite social and economic interests? More generally, the question could be asked whether a politicized Islam is capable of relinquishing religio-ideological demands. Are Islam and ideology so inextricably linked that — paraphrasing the Qur'an — each is as close to the other as man is to the vein in his neck, or can political problems be faced in political terms? If secular political authority is perceived as legitimate, the political demands and expectations of Islamic organizations may be readjusted downward and the incidence of ideology as imperative demand in response to political failure may also diminish. To predict, however, with any degree of certainty that this will occur is clearly impossible; politicized Islam has been on the defensive and frustrated for too long to be able to posit a calculated response on its part. What is evident, however, is that for the first time in this century, Islam has been shown by the results of a national election to be a distinct political minority — a fact which cannot help but be a sobering experience for Muslim leaders, and one which may call for a readjustment of strategy.[9]

> 9. Although Islamic organizations lost out to secular leaders for control of the nationalist movement due to the greater skill and expertise of the latter, the claim to societal primacy could still be maintained so long as a majority of the population was felt to be Islam-oriented. The results of the recent election would appear to weaken this conviction.

Such a readjustment has been made most easily by Nahdatul Ulama's accommodationist leadership and by the accommodationist faction of Partai Muslimin — the very groups which currently exercise leadership. Partai Muslimin's accommodationist faction, which was the least disposed to a rigid ideological stance, was always on the defensive in internal party debate. Its perception of politics as the attainment of definite social and economic interests, rather than the expression of religious demands, received slight welcome from fundamentalists and reformists. With the accommodationists on the defensive within the party, diminution of ideological intensity remained unrealized. The Indonesian military's frank interference in Partai Muslimin's affairs has greatly altered this political equation. The thrust of both Sukarno's and Suharto's restrictive policies toward Islam, however coercive they may have been, appear to have succeeded in preventing the reification of Islamic symbols at the expense of national symbols. Islamic political parties were weakened by Sukarno but could maintain a political confidence based on belief in their comprising a numerical majority. Given the results of the 1971 election, this confidence is no longer merited.

Ideology will certainly retain its relevance as a unifying symbol so long as the Islamic and Javanese *weltanschauungen* remain counterpoised. Ideology as imperative demand, however, may decline in importance, for it is the response to the frustration engendered by perceiving one's own groups as a natural majority, beset by covert, unethical forces.

For Partai Muslimin's military-supported accommodationists, the results of the election demonstrated what they had long suspected — that the expanse of Islam's political goals had to be reduced. I have previously noted that reformist policy was pragmatic and realistic if many of the important political goals and demands of the Islamic parties were achieved. However, given reformist leaders' overestimation of Islam's actual social strength, failure to achieve political goals was attributed to plots by a well-placed anti-Islamic minority rather than to Islam's own minority status. Accommodationists urged a reassessment of Islam's actual social and political strength and a new strategy to follow therefrom. The ideal Islamic society could not be achieved through political means. Politics was not the pursuit of the ideal but the art of the possible, and the clear political primacy of military and secular political power made accommodation necessary. This necessitated, they contended, a relinquishing of Islam's ideological goals, its dreams of political victory, and the emphasis of Islamic groups on perjuangan as religiopolitical struggle.

This sentiment was expressed by Mintaredja in a criticism of the "formal political approach" previously carried out by the Islamic political parties. An approach which emphasized ideological struggle, he maintained, was "out of date." Politics was a worldly concern and could be differentiated from religion; material advantage should be sought:

Where is the proof of the Perjuanan Ummat Islam during the twenty-five years we have been free? It seems the public is already bored waiting for the results of the struggle which have been promised by leaders who only consider formal ideological struggle important. This [formal political approach] is empty; what is awaited by the public and the Ummat Islam especially are the [material] results of the political struggle. To achieve this result . . . we need to implement development in all fields, especially in the field of the economy. . . .

Partai Muslimin Indonesia does not desire to carry out the formal political approach as formerly. Partai Muslimin Indonesia has already decided . . . to cooperate with the armed forces and get in line with the development group [program-oriented order]. In other words, Partai Muslimin Indonesia will carry out a political material approach without forgetting its base, namely Islam [Mintaredja 1971: 48].

If it is to overcome reformist and fundamentalist suspicions of religious laxity and political opportunism, such a policy would have to bring noticeable benefits in its wake. In particular, this would connote economic improvement, in view of the fact that the social base of support for Indonesian Islamic modernism continues to lie in the commercial and trading strata of Indonesia's cities and towns. A quid pro quo between the government and modernist groups would necessitate governmental policies that benefit (or at least do not harm) Islamic entrepreneurial groups. Only such development might promote a willingness on the part of many reformists to reassess strategy and agree to accommodation.

In early 1973, the government ordered the nine existing political parties (excluding GOLKAR) to "fuse" into two basic parties which were to serve as an issue-oriented "loyal opposition" matched against GOLKAR. This plan was intended to curtail the influence of the ideologically based party system. The four Islamic parties fused to form the PPP (Partai Persatuan Pembangunan, Development Unity party). Idham Chalid of Nahdatul Ulama and H. M. Mintaredja of Partai Muslimin became chairman and vice-chairman respectively of the PPP. The four Islamic "component parties" were then instructed to divest themselves of their political identity and revert back to a more basic socioreligious orientation. Although this was unpopular with the Islamic rank and file, it would appear to have the effect of successfully depoliticizing Islamic activities, so long as governmental policy is not perceived as threatening or injurious to religious and material interests.

Another potentially important consequence of the election may be a cultural reflorescence within Islam in which faith may come to be defined in terms of a religious and cultural rather than a political commitment. In this sense, the belief that Islam is on the political decline may, as Lev notes, "effect a kind of cultural liberation" (Lev 1972: 262). Even before the election, a number of younger Islamic figures formerly associated with Himpunan Mahasiswa Indonesia opened a serious social and theological debate among knowledgeable Muslims by contending that the personal affirmation of Islamic faith need not imply support for an Islamic political party. Led by the former chairman of HMI, Nurcholish Madjid, this group posited compartmentalization of religious belief from political affairs — one in which Islamic norms would influence the broad ethical values of society but remain within the purview of personal, as opposed to political, commitment. Such a model affirmed the concept of an ummat united by religious sentiment, but deliberately eschewing a political identity. These ideas were first articulated publicly in 1970, but have received considerable attention since the 1971 election.[10] These younger figures have by no means won the established Islamic political leaders over to their side; even within their own organizations, they have generated much opposition to their position. What they have done, however, is to propose a rethinking, a re-examination, of the Islamic religiopolitical traditions and its relevance to modern society.

All of the preceding, then, may serve to rechannel the Islamic emphasis on politics into religious and cultural directions. The policies desired by figures as diverse as Snouck Hurgronje and Sukarno may now be realized by the actions of the Suharto government. The irony presented by its restrictive actions is that in the long run they may have the unintended consequence of promoting a rethinking on the part of Islam's younger generation, a generation which is not committed to the religiopolitical issues and struggles of the 1950s that so mobilized their elders. The critical variable was the result of the election. Whereas governmental restrictiveness was perceived as anti-Islamic repression when Islam was felt to comprise a "natural political majority," the elections demonstrated that Islam did not comprise such a majority. The committed struggles of the 1950s still bulk large in the memories of many, but as younger figures increasingly come to articulate their views, an Islamic consciousness may develop which "derives moral guidance from Islam, but faces political problems in political terms" (Bellah 1970: 161). Such a development need not necessarily mean the loss of religious importance; indeed, it could ultimately strengthen the ethical and moral influence of the faith.

10. See Madjid 1970. See also the journal *Arena* on the speech by Madjid, "Menyegarkan Faham di Kalangan Ummat Islam Indonesia," October 30, 1972, given at Taman Ismail Marzuki. For critical comments, see Rasjidi 1972 and Anshari 1973.

PART III: Communications and Integration

8 The Mass Communications System in Indonesia

ASTRID SUSANTO

DEVELOPING COUNTRIES have two systems of communication, namely, the modern mass media and the traditional communications system (Schramm 1964). To have a political impact in a developing country the communicator must use the correct medium or, more precisely, the appropriate mixture of several different media required to reach several, quite distinct audiences. For instance, as I will show, modern mass media's influence in Indonesia is limited largely to the towns. Political communication on matters of national importance using the modern mass media will not contact the vast majority of Indonesians because most of them live in villages where mass media exposure remains extremely low. To be successful in communicating with the villages, communication strategy must utilize the local traditional communication system which is interpersonal in nature and very much dependent on the cooperation of local opinion leaders. But the policy dialogue conducted in the mass media is important because it affects political decision-making at the elite level. When and if development plans require significant levels of peasant participation, the traditional, interpersonal communication networks must be employed simultaneously with the mass media.

Rural people are less active in macropolitics but are very much involved in efforts to improve daily living conditions by breaking out of the subsistence economy that has characterized village life. These efforts have increased since the first national development plan (REPELITA, 1969-1974) and especially since the introduction of the BIMAS.[1] As a result of the development program, the rural population has been drawn more closely into the orbit of macropolitics, but progress has not been as fast as expected. The effort of the mass media to spread information and stimulate the participation of the rural sector has proved that although the mass media can spread information effectively, wholehearted participation in development can be achieved only if the interpersonal traditional communication system is also used. In a predominantly rural country like Indonesia, mass communications experts must always be aware of the two-step

1. BIMAS is the acronym for Pembimbingan Massal, which means "guidance of the masses," and is used not only in agricultural extension programs but also for other governmental programs such as family planning.

flow mechanism by which local opinion leaders act as gate-keepers, filtering the information that is eventually received by the vast majority of citizens.

Any realistic analysis of the political impact of mass communications on Indonesian development must, therefore, stress how difficult it is for the mass media alone to influence the behavior and deeply held attitudes of large audiences. The mass media's influence will depend on how relevant each medium is to daily life in the diverse kinds of communities it seeks to influence. One must analyze the function played by each medium in each community by asking questions such as the following: Is the radio an important source of development information for peasant farmers, or is it merely a cheaper means of access to traditional entertainment, or alternately is the radio only a status symbol whose possession fulfills a personal social need?

In this chapter I analyze the nature of the mass communications system in general, along with its relevance to political decision-making. I identify the different mass communications publics and emphasize the different functions fulfilled by a medium when it is applied to different social groups or regions. The first section describes Indonesia's multiple audiences in the most general terms. The second and third sections describe the development of radio, television, film, and the press and try to gauge the relative impact of these media on different audiences and regions in Indonesia. The final section considers the traditional communications networks, which are perhaps the most important medium for stimulating mass participation in Indonesian development.

INDONESIA'S MULTIPLE AUDIENCES

In Indonesia each mass medium tends to have a distinct audience defined by sociological variables such as urbanization, literacy, and age. According to 1971 census data 64 percent of the nearly 120 million Indonesians are concentrated on a single island, Java, while the remaining 42 million persons are scattered across approximately 3,000 islands stretching on a 3,500-mile arc which extends southeastward from the northern tip of Sumatra all the way to West Irian (see Table 1). Not only are the audiences separated by geographic factors, in addition, though there is a national language, *bahasa Indonesia*, each region also has a separate mother tongue as well as a distinct cultural heritage.

In addition to the audience fragmentation imposed by geography and culture, the census of 1971 indicated that 82.5 percent of the total population lives in rural areas. Because the rural sector constitutes the vast majority of the Indonesian public, the government in 1973 suggested that the Indonesian press should become more rurally oriented (Departemen Penerangan 1973: 3). However, the difficulty with such an aim is that newspaper readership is almost entirely restricted to the urban areas because only in the urban areas do large numbers of people have the interest, time, literacy, and economic surplus that would motivate them to purchase newspapers.

Data given by the Department of Information in June 1972 indicated that 776,154 newspaper copies were available throughout Indonesia in 1971. The

TABLE 1

The Indonesian Population by Island and Urban-Rural

	Town population as percentage of total population	Village population as percentage of total population	Percentages of total population
Java and Madura	11.6%	52.6%	64.2%
Sumatra	3.1	14.5	17.6
Kalimantan	1.0	3.4	4.4
Sulawesi	1.2	6.0	7.2
Other Islands	0.7	5.9	6.6
	17.6%	82.4%	100.0%

UNESCO standards mention as ideal the situation in which there is one newspaper for 10 persons. In Indonesia there is only one newspaper for 154 persons (Atmadi; 1972). The size of the potential newspaper audience in Indonesia does not exceed 9.4 percent of the entire national population and, in fact, it is probably considerably less. This figure is based on the assumption that newspaper readership in Indonesia is largely restricted to those who are both adult and urban. If urban adults who are illiterate are subtracted, this further decreases the size of the potential newspaper-reading audience. Thus the political messages or policy directives carried by the press at best influence considerably less than 10 percent of the total Indonesian population.

Radio is much more widely distributed among the common people than newspapers. The population tends to resist registering their radios, thus making it difficult to estimate the potential radio audience for the whole nation. Current estimates range from 2.5 million (official estimates, 1971) to 5 million (Sumadi 1972) radio sets for the whole country.[2] Recent evidence from two surveys covering 100 different villages in West Java in 1969 and 1971-1972 would counsel caution before accepting the higher figure. The two surveys respectively estimated the number of radios at 27 radios and 25 radios per 1,000 persons (Jackson forthcoming; Direktorat Jenderal Pembangunan Masyarakat Desa 1972). Radios are probably not more plentiful in other provinces, and if the number of radios per 1,000 in West Java is extrapolated to the entire national population, this would mean that there were less than 3.2 million sets in Indonesia in 1971. In any case, it is generally accepted that the number of radios is expanding rapidly in rural areas, because utilizing radio in the age of the transistor requires neither village electrification nor a high level of literacy.

The dearth of newspapers in the country is amply attested to by a survey held in nine villages in West Java, where 50 to 80 percent of the rural population

2. The official estimate includes all registered radios plus an addition of 25 percent to account for unregistered radios.

had never read a newspaper. Furthermore, between 1 percent and 4 percent of the very same population claimed to own a radio, which is considerably lower than the 5 percent standard set by UNESCO for developing countries (Fakultas Publisistik Universitas Padgadjaran 1973). Not only is the mass media audience for both print and radio quite low for all villages, but the audience contacted by any broadcast will depend substantially on the type of village. In the survey in West Java six of the villages were predominantly agricultural while the remaining three were fishing villages. The fishing villages were substantially lower in radio ownership, with only 1.2 percent owning radios.

Thus, although there are relatively few radios by world standards, radio is still the most important modern medium entering village life. The data presented in Table 2 are from the West Javanese village of Indihiang, which at the time of the study in 1970 had known radio for just one year. They show that newspapers and radios reach quite different audiences. Of those who say newspapers are their priority source of information 48.5 percent are government officials, whereas only 16 percent of those giving newspapers top priority are farmers, even though farmers constitute the vast majority of the population. The majority of those who list radio as the most important source of information are farmers. A study conducted in the villages of Lampung (South Sumatra) in 1973 also showed that radio was the first source of information.

TABLE 2

Occupation, by Percentage, Designating a Mass Medium
as the First Priority Source of Information:
Rural West Java
(n = 540)

Occupation	Daily newspaper	Network radio	Transistor radio
Farmer	16%	34%	71%
Government official	49	11	8
Teacher	26	46	16
Army and retired people	10	9	5
	101%	100%	100%

SOURCE: Suhandang 1970.

The situation differs substantially for the towns. In a thesis on advertising effects in Bandung, newspapers were much more frequently listed as the most important source of information than were radios (see Table 3). In a recent study conducted in Jakarta television appeared to be an increasingly important source of information (Navy 1974). However, television sets are expensive and therefore are limited to a small elite who have reached a relatively high level of income. In 1972 the National Post Office reported that there were 200,091 sets

TABLE 3

Respondents Designating a Medium
as the Most Important Source of
Information: City of Bandung
(*n* = 619)

Newspaper	37%
Television	27%
Film	11%
Radio	4%
Friends	15%

SOURCE: Boediawan 1971: 53.

registered throughout Indonesia, with over 74 percent concentrated in the cities of Jakarta and Bandung, which respectively had 119,982 and 29,252 television sets.

Although further research is required, the studies presently available indicate that a community's level of modernization substantially determines which mass media it will consider as most important. Villagers prefer radio because of their high illiteracy and the poor distribution of newspapers. Towns have a larger reading audience than the villages, and in the cities of Bandung and Jakarta television is becoming an increasingly important medium for spreading information. If the mass media expert wants to reach ordinary townsmen, he must use a combination of radio and newspapers; and if he wants his message to have maximum effect on the political elite he should use newsprint plus television. In short, Indonesia is an archipelago with different audiences for different media, and rational information planning must take this fact into account.

RADIO, TELEVISION, AND FILM

Radio

The RRI (Radio Republik Indonesia) has as its date of birth Indonesia's Independence Day, Radio Jakarta having broadcast the Proclamation of Independence at ten o'clock in the morning on August 17, 1945. From the days of the Revolution to the present, RRI has sought to keep its pledge of TRIPRA-SETKA by being nationalist but nonpartisan, fighting to keep the country independent, but standing above all political currents and party interests for the sake of national unity (Department of Information 1972: 15).

Radio Republik Indonesia falls under the jurisdiction of the Ministry of Information. It owns forty-six stations with the central studio in Jakarta. To serve the needs of the forty-six stations there are coordinating studios in Ujung Pandang (Makassar), Jogjakarta, and Medan. Studio Ujung Pandang, also known as Studio Nusantara I, coordinates the stations of Kalimantan, Nusa Tenggara, Sulawesi, Maluku, and West Irian. Studio Jogjakarta, known as Studio Nusantara II, coordinates the stations on Java and Madura. Studio Medan, Studio Nusantara III, coordinates the stations in Sumatra. Each Nusantara studio consists of five main divisions: programming, news service, administration, engineering, and public relations. At a higher level the Directorate General of Radio, Television, and Film is divided into eight divisions: home service, overseas service, news service, engineering planning and development, transmission service, Jakarta transmitters unit, administration, and development of internal cooperation (Department of Information 1972: 3, 1). These forty-six stations owned by the government – according to 1971 estimates – serve the 2.5 million registered radio owners.[3] The Home Service division is in charge of development programs and disseminaton of development information together with the Ministry for Agriculture (Sumadi 1972: 1-2). Another main task of the Home Service is to strengthen social integration and the five principles of the State, Pancasila.

In addition to supervising the forty-six RRI stations, Home Service is responsible for regulating the operations of the nongovernment radio stations (Department of Information 1972: 1). The number of the non-RRI radio stations is increasing. Atmadi noted that between 1970 and 1972 the number of stations increased to forty-two stations in Jakarta, twenty-eight in Central Java, forty-two in West Java, and twenty in East Java (Atmadi 1972). Government regulations no. 55/1970 and no. 25/1971 stipulate the wavelengths and organization of the non-RRI stations and regulation no. 39/Kep/MenPen1971 regulates the content of the programs. Programs must stress education and information, adhere to the state's philosophy (the Pancasila), shall *not* be involved in political activities, and shall relay some RRI programs such as the news and other important events of the day. Although the non-RRI stations live on advertising as their source of income, government regulation no. 39/1971 monitors advertising activities, eliminating "unfair competition" and requiring that 10 percent of all broadcasting must be public service programming in the interest of the community. Government regulation of private stations reflects the philosophy that mass media not only disseminate information and shape political opinion but can also act as an agent of social change and modernization (Soegito 1973: 14-16). The government is sensitive to radio's potential for shaping culture, especially since the spread of transistor radios in the villages. The radio is perceived as a mechanism for bridging the physical and psychological gap between town and country, strengthening social integration by spreading not only information but also common forms of entertainment (Soegito 1973: 24-25).

One final technological development should be noted here. There is now a ground satellite station at Jatiluhur, West Java, and Indonesia has seven relay stations with four additional ones under construction. The radio, unlike tele-

---

3. See preceding section for discussions of estimates of radio owners.

vision, the press, or even the telephone, can cover the entire Indonesian nation simultaneously.

As to the radio broadcast content of RRI, broadcasts are usually 60 percent music and 40 percent the spoken word. The programs reflecting government policy are as follows (Soegito 1973*a*: 34):

Radio and television

1. Nondramatic	— news
	— discussion
	— panel and quiz
	— women's programs
	— children's programs
	— teens' programs
	— education
	— information
	— religion
	— variety and music
2. Dramatic	— serials
	— drama
	— comedy
	— others

Film

1. Entertainment

2. Features and documentary films

3. Educational films	— teaching
	— trade
	— documentary
	— religion
	— advertisements

4. Newsreels

Table 4 gives the results of a survey conducted in Jakarta to determine the public response to various programs. In Jakarta 63.2 percent of the respondents listened to the Radio Republik Indonesia station, whereas 36 percent were classified as non-RRI listeners. Outside the capital city of Jakarta the percentage of non-RRI listeners may be slightly higher. For example, in East Java according to a survey conducted in 1970-1971, 45 percent of the respondents classified themselves as primarily non-RRI listeners (Radio Republik Indonesia 1972: 94).

If Jakarta's respondents listen to radio mainly for news, respondents from East Java, and perhaps other regions, use radio mainly for entertainment (compare Tables 4 and 5). The top entertainment program broadcast by Studio Jogjakarta (Nusantara II), the coordinating studio for Java and Madura, are listed in Table 6. Once one moves outside metropolitan Jakarta, the most popular

TABLE 4
Reason for Listening to Radio
Programs among Jakarta Respondents

News	42%
Government programs	11
Town news	2
Commentary	2
Culture	5%
Wayang	1
Religion	4
Sports	0
Popular music	11
Cabaret	2
Education	2
General knowledge	1
Family news	1%
Economics	2
Women's programs	0
Broadcasting technique	14%
Radio signal	0.6

SOURCE: Departemen Penerangan 1972.

TABLE 5

Reasons for Listening to Radio
Programs among East Javanese
Respondents

Shadow plays (Wayang)	24%
(Ludruk)	21
Popular opera (Ketoprak)	15
Radio cabaret	7

SOURCE: Radio Republik Indonesia 1972: 94.

radio shows are clearly traditional entertainment, such as the Wayang, rather than news or development information.

The data from Table 6 indicate that there is a motivational difference between radio audiences in the capital and the regions: whereas Jakarta listeners turn to radio for news, audiences in the regions stress traditional entertainment with a preference for the local tradition. The audiences in the regions benefit from an average of fifteen hours each day of broadcasting by Nusantara II, with an average of 57 percent music and 43 percent spoken word. One may then conclude that for the rural areas and even for the cities and towns (with the exception of Jakarta), the primary function fulfilled by radio is providing entertainment, especially traditional entertainment programs tailored to the local cultural tastes of each region.

TABLE 6
Most Popular Programs

Studio		Kind of entertainment
Bogor		Wayang golek
Bandung	West Java	Wayang golek
Cirebon		Tarling
Purwokerto		Klenengan Banyumasan
Jogjakarta	Central Java	Ketoprak Mataran RRI-Jogjakarta
Surakarta		Wayang Orang RRI-Surakarta
Madiun		Wayang Krucil
Malang	East Java	Wayang Kulit
Surabaya		Ludruk RRI-Surabaya
Jember		Topeng Madura
Sumenep	Madura	Ludruk Madura

SOURCE: Radio Republik Indonesia 1972: 96.

In addition to variations in content to match different radio audiences, there are differences in listening habits. In the rural areas most listeners are peasant farmers by occupation. Because they are at work in the fields from sun-up until sundown, the early morning audience will be dominated by farmers. Whereas the mid-day listeners are almost entirely tradesmen, afternoon is the favored listening time among the military (see Table 7).

There are also differences in listening habits between villages and the semirural areas composed of small market towns (see Table 8). Like the

TABLE 7
Occupation by Listening Habits
in a West Javanese Village

	Listening Time			
Occupation	Morning	Noon	Afternoon	Evening
Farmer	88%	0%	62%	66%
Government official	4	0	2	9
Tradesman	3	96	22	20
Military	2	0	9	2
Retired	3	5	5	4
	100%	101%	100%	101%

NOTE: These data were collected in Cijeunjing, a village in West Java that had known radio for only one year when the study was made. Therefore, they can be looked on only as typical of similar, very isolated villages rather than typical of all West Javanese villages.

SOURCE: Suhandang 1970.

TABLE 8
Occupation by Listening Habits
for a Semirural Population
(n = 80)

	Listening Time				
Occupation	Morning	Noon	Afternoon	Evening	Blank
Government official	1%	0%	1%	8%	5%
Tradesman	0	0	0	4	2
Worker	1	0	2	12	5
Student	3	0	4	33	10
Housewife	1	0	0	4	1
	6%	0%	7%	61%	23%

SOURCE: Sulaiman Mohamed 1972.

city-dwellers, the semirural residents depend less exclusively on the radio than the peasants do. Time of listening also changes with the alteration of occupational structure implied by being a townsman. Most respondents living in semirural areas listen to the radio at night, whereas the early morning hours tend to be favored by peasants.

This is why the agricultural extension programs are broadcast during the early morning. According to government information, there were forty-two studios broadcasting community development radio programs in May 1972 with a total broadcast time equaling over ninety hours per week. Official information also indicated that there were 5,367 radio discussion forums, but studies conducted by several university communications departments proved that most radio discussion groups never met and that listening to extension programs was a matter of individual initiative. The importance of local languages for broadcasting to farmers is indicated by a survey of listeners to agricultural extension programs. Nearly 90 percent said they preferred the local language whereas only 3 percent preferred Indonesian alone, with the remainder choosing a combination of Indonesian and the local language (Departemen Penerangan 1972: 3). Optional communications contact with the village is most easily obtained by utilizing the local language rather than the national one, even though this may conflict with the long-range goal of conducting all national business in bahasa Indonesia.

Any discussion of the political impact of mass media would be incomplete if special attention were not paid to the students. Students are an active and attentive public and have played an important role in the political history of Indonesia, and it is important to know their media habits as well as the sources of information utilized by student radio stations. First of all, laws prohibit non-RRI stations from engaging in political activities, and this applies to the student stations even though these were born as a result of the political events of 1965-1966.

According to a 1974 study, the sources used by Bandung's IPMI radio station are primarily organizations and sources exclusively concerned with student as opposed to national affairs (see Table 9).

To learn the influence of student radio on its listeners the same study conducted two separate surveys: one broadcast questions over the air and received answers by mail from 542 listeners, and the other interviewed 350

TABLE 9
Sources of Information for the Student
Radio Station in Bandung

Campus news	30%
Own reporter	30
Student government	20
Extra-university student organizations	10
Listeners	5
Newspapers	5
	100%

SOURCE: Suhada 1974.

students from three universities in Bandung. The questions broadcast over the air attracted respondents living in Bandung but hailing originally from all over Indonesia, thus indicating that the radio station had an appeal that was not restricted to locally born students.[4] Classifying the respondents by occupation also showed that the student radio station's appeal transcended the immediate student community (see Table 10).

TABLE 10
Occupation of Persons Responding to the
Broadcast Questionnaire in Bandung
(n = 542)

Student	24%
Teacher or government official	24
No work	23
Military	3
Housewife	3
Farmer	1
Retired	1
	100%

SOURCE: Suhada 1974.

Few major differences exist between the responses of the students interviewed at the university and the responses of a wider spectrum of the population who mailed in their replies. Those replying by mail to the broadcast questionnaire were probably a bit more affluent, as evidenced by the fact that 91 percent of them owned their own radios as opposed to 80 percent of those directly interviewed (Suhada 1974: 82, 89). The two samples differ by only one or two percentage points on each of the questions reported here and hence the samples have been combined. This is because the most interesting aspect is not the difference between the two samples but the implicit comparison with other non-Jakarta audiences.

The majority of listeners to the student radio stations attend quite frequently (see Table 11). Only among the students who were directly interviewed does one find a small minority, 8 percent, who never listen to the student radio station. In addition, most of the listeners in the two samples, 53 percent, tend to listen to whole programs rather than just parts of programs (Suhada 1974: 83, 90). At least by this measure, intensity of attention to the student radio by their listeners seems moderate.

4. Approximately 20 percent of the respondents were drawn from each of the provinces of West, Central, and East Java, while an additional 20 percent came from the island of Sumatra.

TABLE 11
Frequency of Listening to Student
Radio Station in Bandung
($n = 792$)

Often	54%
Sometimes	42
Never	3
Blank	1
	100%

SOURCE: Suhada 1974.

With regard to the time of listening the audience of student radio differs, although only slightly, from the semirural respondents previously reported (compare Table 8 and Table 12). Most of the student radio station's audience listens during the evening, but the concentration in the evening hours is not as heavy as among the semirural population. More listeners tune in the student radio station in the morning and afternoon than appears to be the case among semirural listeners.

TABLE 12
Average Listening Time for Student
Radio Station Audience

Morning	15%
Noon	3
Afternoon	18
Evening	52
No fixed times	45

SOURCE: Suhada 1974.

Table 13 shows that the listeners to the student radio station are most interested in gaining information and increasing their general knowledge. The student radio audience in Bandung is probably more cosmopolitan than the general provincial audience described by the data in Table 5. The students and their listeners are distinct because radio for them fulfills an informational rather than an entertainment function. The student radio audience is similar to the more news-oriented Jakarta audience than it is to the typical provincial radio audience that attends more closely to traditional forms of entertainment (compare Table 13 with Tables 4 and 5).

TABLE 13

Reasons for Listening to Bandung Student
Radio Station (Radio IPMI)
(*n* = 792)

Information	65%
Education	38
Entertainment	33
Increasing knowledge	81
Topics and hobbies	15
Blank	7

SOURCE: Suhada 1974.

It would be a mistake, however, to assume that the student audience is not parochial in its own way. Just because the student radio station audience listens to obtain information and knowledge does not mean they attend heavily to national affairs on a daily basis. In a probe question the respondents were asked which programs they evaluated most highly. In Table 14 the results from both samples are reported separately because, unlike previous questions, there are substantial differences between the mailed responses to the broadcast interview and the direct interview. The topics of highest interest for both samples were university news, student activities, and science. However, the wholly student sample in the direct interviews is more interested in university news and science than the more general audience encompassed by the mailed questionnaire (see Table 14).

TABLE 14

Topics of Greatest Interest to Listeners of Bandung
Student Radio (IPMI) by Broadcast Interview
and Direct Interview Samples

Program items	Broadcast interviews	Direct interviews
Special topics and Editorials	18%	11%
University news	57	73
Science	36	45
Student activities	41	36
Commentary	14	0

SOURCE: Suhada 1974.

The listeners to Radio IPMI are only marginally interested in editorials and commentary. Although it is generally believed that students take an active part in politics on a day-to-day basis, this impression is misleading because in "normal" times their interest in political news is rather small. When political "explosions" have taken place between 1949 and 1970 the students turn avidly to newspaper reading for political news, but in more quiet times their interest is concentrated on campus news, science, and events connected with university life (Lembaga Pers Dan Pendapat Umum, n.d.). Basically non-RRI stations, like student radio, supply entertainment and local news of interest to a special group, leaving political and development communications in the hands of the government radio stations.

One can conclude that radio is the most widely dispersed medium in Indonesia's mass communications arsenal. For the rural population radio is first of all a means of entertainment, especially traditional music and cultural features. For peasants living in remote areas the radio also serves as an instructor in agricultural modernization. The function performed by radio changes for different groups or individuals as they become increasingly remote from village life. For the semirural the entertainment function is gradually being replaced by the information function, and this coincides with the tendency of semirural people to depend less exclusively on radio while increasingly attending to newspapers and television for information and entertainment. This trend is also found among the listeners to student radio in Bandung, and it culminates among the news- and information-oriented inhabitants of metropolitan Jakarta.

Television

On August 17, 1962, Indonesia's television, TVRI, was on the air for the first time, with a trial broadcast from the Fourth Asian Games taking place in Jakarta. This first transmission was carried on nine channels, each with a capacity of 10 kilowatts, and channel 5, a special channel with a 100-watt capacity for use in emergency cases. Over the years the number of television stations has grown to twelve. The number of television stations is still increasing with the use of seven relay stations on Java (as of 1972) and the four other relay stations nearing completion. Although television transmission capacity has recently been extended beyond Java (with stations in Medan, Ujung Pandang, Palembang, and Balikpapan), transmission capacity limits television contact chiefly to approximately 30 percent of the land area of Java where 50 percent of the population lives (see Figure 1).

TVRI benefits from the ground satellite station at Jatiluhur, West Java, but the high costs of television transmission restrict its use to very important events such as an international sports match or President Suharto's visit to Europe. Usually use of the Jatiluhur ground station services for television programs is sponsored by many large firms in order to enable the viewer to enjoy the special program. An example was the Thomas Cup final match in Kuala Lumpur (1970) which cost U.S. $40,000 (excluding service costs which were

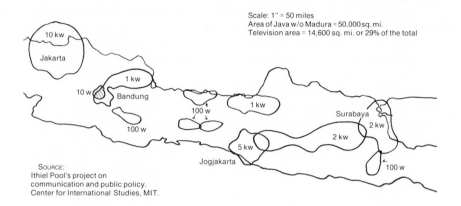

FIG. 1. Java Television Coverage

borne by Malaysian TV) and was sponsored by three large firms, the Jakarta municipality, and Malaysian TV.

TVRI began its transmission in 1962 with a single hour of broadcasting each day, but the amount has increased with its growth in technical as well as personnel capabilities. Today TVRI transmits news, information, educational, and entertainment programs between six o'clock and ten o'clock in the evening; it had a total transmission of 167 hours and 24 minutes in 1971 and 164 hours and 35 minutes in 1972. The broadcast day begins with a children's program followed by the news of the regions, usually featuring economic development projects. In 1962 the percentage distribution of the several programs was: education, 15 percent; indoctrination, 15 percent; culture, 25 percent; serious entertainment, 30 percent; sports, 5 percent; advertising, 10 percent. By 1971 and 1972 the variety of programs available to television had increased substantially (see Table 15). Recent trends in program offerings include increased use of films and a decrease in entertainment (mostly musical programs) and advertisements.

A study in 1973 proved that the percentage of ads had decreased to 10 percent of total programming. TVRI charges different prices for transmitted advertisement according to time of broadcasting, namely, U.S. $750 for class *A* advertisements (broadcast for twenty-six weeks as either two-minute spots or sixty-minute sponsored serials), and U.S. $600 for class *B* (two-minute spots or serials of thirty minutes). Class *A* advertisements are transmitted between seven and eight o'clock in the evening, the peak hours, and class *B* advertisements are transmitted either before seven or after eight o'clock.

One study of the use of television in Bandung provides an indication of the

TABLE 15
Program Offerings of TVRI
in 1971 and 1972

Program Type	% in 1971	% in 1972
Education	13%	12%
Sports	3	2
Culture and religion	5	5
Drama	3	2
News/information	20	20
Entertainment	15	11
Film serials	17	26
Sponsored films	4	5
Documentary	2	3
Advertisements	18	13

SOURCE: Departemen Penerangan 1972.

social distribution of television viewers. Table 16 gives the occupational distribution of television ownership in the households of a sample of 360 children in five elementary schools in Bandung. From these data it is clear that television ownership is limited to the official, professional, and trading elites of the city of Bandung.

Another study sought to determine why viewers watch television. Ninety percent of television viewers watched their sets daily, and television, in contrast to radio, seems to serve almost entirely an entertainment function (see Table 17).

TABLE 16
Occupation of Television-Owning Parents
of Bandung Elementary School Students

Government official	32%
Businessman	20
Tradesman	19
Military	14
University lecturer	4
School teacher	4
Physician	1
Tailor/rickshaw driver	1
Blank	7

SOURCE: Gunawan 1973.

TABLE 17
Reasons for Watching Television
in Bandung

Entertainment	80%
News	10
General knowledge	10

SOURCE: Gunawan 1972.

Film

The Indonesian film industry has only one studio, located in Jakarta. The government allows the import of foreign films as long as they do not clash with Indonesian standards. For this reason the Indonesian government maintains censorship, although it must be admitted that in many ways the Indonesian films do not hesitate to show horror, crime, and sex. The government has one studio and laboratory where the films are processed; films by the government include documentaries, newsreels, and story films.

Private film producers have increased their production recently. It is the government's policy to support national producers in order to decrease the import of foreign films. The government carries out its policy by asking the film importers to pay more attention to educational films, science fiction, and films for children, as films are considered a medium for adult and nonformal education as well as a medium for entertainment. Government regulations stipulated that for the years 1971 and 1972 the total number of imported films had to be limited to six hundred with a specified ratio for each importer: five action films three nonaction films, one film on arts, and one film for children. Yet in 1971 imported films surpassed the fixed quota. The country of origin of films imported in 1971 is given in Table 18. The Second National Development Plan states that the national film industry and especially the state film agency. Perusahaan Film Negara (PFN), will be upgraded in technical equipment and production quality. National film producers will enjoy priorities, and film importation will be adjusted accordingly. The PFN will eventually be equipped with a more modern laboratory and studio to permit increased newsreel and documentary film production.

THE PRESS IN INDONESIA

In the 1950s most Indonesian newspapers rarely exceeded circulations of 5,000 copies; in the 1970s, though the number of Indonesian newspapers is decreasing, their average circulation is higher. According to figures in the Second Development Plan, total newspaper circulation reached 1.5 million copies in 1973, with two-thirds of these belonging to the 122 daily newspapers scattered

TABLE 18
Country of Origin of Films
Imported During 1971

Asia
India	50 films
Japan	20
Philippines	10
China (Taiwan and Hong Kong)	100
Korea	10
Other countries	10
	200 films

Europe
Germany	20 films
England	15
France	25
Italy	100
Greece	5
Sweden	10
Other countries	25
	200 films

North and South America
U.S.A.	135 films
Latin American countries	10
Other countries	5
	150 films

Other countries	50 films
	600 films

all over the country. The capital city of Jakarta absorbed 56 percent of the total national circulation.

As part of a study of the national and local press, inquiries were sent in mid-1973 to thirty-three Jakarta newspapers and four Bandung papers. The questionnaires were returned by the Jakarta dailies *Berita Buana, Harian Kami, Abadi, Suara Karya, Kompas, Merdeka, Nusantara,* and *Sinar Harapan. Gala* and *Pikiran Rakyat* of Bandung also returned questionnaires. Of these newspapers *Harian Kami, Abadi,* and *Nusantara* had their publishing licenses revoked by the government in the political aftermath of the riots of January 1974 (*Tempo,* June 1, 1974: 37).

The Indonesian press today faces difficulties stemming from the absence of performance standards. Considerable controversy has surrounded the publication of "off-the-record news" obtained from government officials. In 1973 a major Jakarta daily was closed temporarily for printing off-the-record news in its headlines. Of the ten newspapers responding to the survey, nine thought the "off-the-record" or news "embargo" restrictions were binding on the editor. The one newspaper that felt the restrictions were not binding no longer exists. The newspapers considering the restrictions as binding still felt free to use off-the-record materials informally as part of general news coverage. Several of the newspapers felt the off-the-record and news embargo restrictions ceased to be valid when such news proved to be untrue. Many of the clashes between government and press have their source in the press's dependency on the government and its officials for all political news.

Another source of government-press tensions is that although 100 percent of the respondents to a survey of working journalists thought the Code of Ethics of the Press was most important, only 60 percent thought it necessary to observe and obey government regulations, and only 50 percent thought the law of the country was binding on them (Ruslan 1973: 74). That 50 percent of the journalists felt the law of the country was not necessarily binding on them can probably be traced to a belief in the "supremacy of the press" or in the role of the press "as a watchdog."

All of this proves that the Indonesian press badly needs a more modern press law. Social change has altered the relationship between the media and political institutions in Indonesia. The nature of the relationship between journalism and politics has been transformed into an interaction between "two separate but related social systems" (Prosser 1973: 346). Efforts to tackle such problems on behalf of the press are the responsibility of the Indonesian Journalists' Association (Persatuan Wartawan Indonesia) and the Newspaper Publishers' Association (Serikat Penerbit Suratkabar), which were founded simultaneously February 9, 1946. The Students' Press Association (Ikatan Pers Mahasiswa Indonesia) is responsible for the activities of the student press. Although the Publishers' Association was called into existence to tackle newsprint problems, its function is decisive in lobbying between the government and the press to secure the continuation of press publications. The Publishers' Association is not so much an association of newspaper owners as the coordinating body of the publishing firms. The Journalists' Association was designed to maintain the standards of Indonesian journalism through its Court of Honor (Dewan Kehormatan). In addition, according to Press Law no. 11, 1966, and Government Regulation no. 19, 1970, a press advisory body exists to advise the Minister of Information on matters concerning the press and its future development. The minister is the chairman of this advisory body.

Studies made by Fakultas Publisistik Universitas Padjadjaran (Bandung) have shown that newspaper readers belong to the elite and middle to upper class. These readers generally read more than one newspaper, namely, one national and one local newspaper. A study of the effects of advertising in Bandung indicated that newspapers were the primary source of information about new products, television was an important secondary source, and radio lagged far behind (see Table 19).

TABLE 19

Percentage of Respondents Selecting Various
Media as the Most Important Source of
Information about New Products in
the City of Bandung

Newspapers	39%
Television	27
Film	11
Radio	4
Outdoor advertising	3
Visitors and friends	15
Mobile advertising	1
While shopping	4

SOURCE: Boediawan 1971.

In Bandung a study of the items leading people to read the newspaper indicated that readers turn to it first to increase their general knowledge, second to follow the daily serials, and third for sports information (see Table 20). Thus, two of the three most frequently attended items concern entertainment rather than the information function. Overtly political items such as home news, foreign affairs, and editorials are less frequently mentioned as reasons for reading the press.

These findings are corroborated by data concerning Bandung students. Although the students are more information-oriented than the general readership, they manifest no significant interest in the interpretive activities of the press.

To determine the relative effectiveness of capital city and provincial dailies for transmitting political communications a comparative study was conducted of the content of *Kompas* and *Pikiran Rakyat*, respectively the leading Jakarta and Bandung city newspapers. Both papers are considered to be politically independent although they each endorsed the government party, GOLKAR, during the course of the election campaign. The content of each newspaper was studied for the three months preceding the general elections of June 1971. The analysis followed two separate procedures. The first counted the frequency of election news stories and computed the average for each month for each paper. The second method counted the percentage of column centimeters devoted to election news relative to other types of news. Tables 21 and 22 report the results. The data indicate that the local newspaper, *Pikiran Rakyat*, covered the

TABLE 20

Why People Read the Newspaper in Bandung
(*n* = 160)

Newspaper item	
Home affairs	19%
Foreign affairs	19
Home economic news	19
Foreign economic news	14
National literature	15
Foreign literature	13
Prose	18
Poetry	20
Humorous (serial) stories	30
Serious (serial) stories	24
Moral writings	21
Indonesian arts and culture	17
Foreign arts and culture	13
Social events	18
Foreign social events	15
Science and general knowledge	31
Editorial	20
Sports	28

SOURCE: Ruslan 1973: 54.

TABLE 21

Percentage of the Total Number of News Items Devoted to
Election News, Domestic News, and Foreign News
by *Kompas* and *Pikiran Rakyat*, April-June 1971

Month	Election News		Domestic News		Foreign News	
	Kompas	*Pikiran Rakyat*	*Kompas*	*Pikiran Rakyat*	*Kompas*	*Pikiran Rakyat*
April	6%	11%	7%	7%	7%	8%
May	8%	14%	6%	6%	10%	10%
June	11%	14%	5%	6%	10%	9%

SOURCE: Humas Lembaga Pemilu Pusat, Jakarta, September 1971. Cited by Aminuddin 1972: 90, 104.

NOTE: For coding purposes election news was separated from other domestic news and not included in the domestic news category.

TABLE 22

Percentage of the Total Column Centimeters Used for
Election News, Domestic News, and Foreign News
by *Kompas* and *Pikiran Rakyat*, April-June 1971

	Election News		Domestic News		Foreign News	
Month	Kompas	Pikiran Rakyat	Kompas	Pikiran Rakyat	Kompas	Pikiran Rakyat
April	4%	8%	4%	6%	4%	4%
May	3%	8%	7%	4%	4%	4%
June	5%	10%	3%	5%	5%	5%

SOURCE: Humas Lembaga Pemilu Pusat, Jakarta, September 1974. Cited by Aminuddin 1972: 106, 140.

election more frequently than the Jakarta newspaper, *Kompas*. Both newspapers devoted nearly identical portions of their coverage to domestic and foreign news.

The study also revealed that the capital city and provincial dailies differed in sources used for their election coverage (see Table 23). *Kompas* used its own staff more frequently as the source of its coverage, whereas *Pikiran Rakyat* depended nearly twice as heavily on the news agencies. The newspapers also differed in the types of stories used to report election coverage. The Jakarta newspaper concentrated more heavily on feature and lead articles, whereas the more frequent coverage of the Bandung paper consisted almost entirely of straight news stories (see Table 24).

A parallel study endeavored to determine the effectiveness of news presentation among a sample of adults in the city of Bandung. The administrative unit R. W. XIII in east Bandung was chosen because the election had gone smoothly

TABLE 23

Source Used by Newspapers for
Election News Stories

	Own Staff		News Agencies	
Month	Kompas	Pikiran Rakyat	Kompas	Pikiran Rakyat
April	95%	85%	5%	15%
May	94%	89%	6%	11%
June	98%	93%	2%	7%

SOURCE: Aminuddin 1972.

TABLE 24
Percentage of Total Column Centimeters of Election Coverage Devoted to Different Types of Stories by *Kompas* and *Pikiran Rakyat*, April-June 1971

Month	Straight News		Campaign		Picture		Feature Article		Lead Article	
	Kompas	*Pikiran Rakyat*	*Kompas*	*Pikiran Rakyat*	*Kompas*	*Pikiran Rakyat*	*Kompas*	*Pikiran Rakyat*	*Kompas*	*Pikiran Rakyat*
April	48%	89%	3%	2%	9%	7%	29%	1%	11%	1%
May	62%	77%	0	13%	7%	9%	14%	1%	16%	1%
June	67%	85%	0	8%	9%	6%	16%	0	8%	0

SOURCE: Aminuddin 1972: 90, 124.

there and a high level of participation had been achieved. The population was composed of government officials, military personnel, traders, and students in addition to the lower income strata of the population; hence, the area could be expected to yield newspaper readers who would attend to both the capital city and provincial press. Questionnaires were sent to the 582 adults in the population, but only 242 respondents returned completed questionnaires, 98 women and 144 men. The questions covered such matters as frequency of newspaper reading, preferred form of news presentation, and media source used for information about the election campaign.

One of the primary findings was that newspapers were by far the most important source of general information as well as election news (see Table 25). Ninety-seven percent of the respondents listed newspapers as their source of information, whereas radio and television were selected by only 13 percent and 14 percent of the respondents. Magazines, films, and interpersonal communication were not important sources of information according to the responses to this question.

Table 26 compares *Kompas* and *Pikiran Rakyat* as sources of general information as well as election news. *Kompas* was more frequently mentioned as a source of information by the entire sample. Although the majority of female respondents read either *Kompas* or both papers, the tendency to read only *Pikiran Rakyat* was higher among women than men.

When asked to compare the clarity of election news in the two newspapers, the capital city paper received much more favorable ratings. Eighty-four percent of the respondents characterized *Kompas's* election coverage as clear, whereas only 61 percent were equally complimentary about the coverage of *Pikiran Rakyat* (see Table 27). Thus, even though the local newspaper devoted a larger part of its coverage to the national election, the readers evaluated its coverage less favorably and hence sought out the capital city paper more frequently for general as well as election news (see Tables 21 and 27).

The reliability of this finding is reinforced by the respondents' endorsement of feature articles as the most comprehensive type of newspaper coverage (see Table 28). The more positive evaluation of *Kompas* as a source of information is correlated with *Kompas's* more pronounced tendency to run feature articles (see Table 24).

Finally the study of Bandung newspaper readers indicated that only a small fraction of people read and are influenced by editorials. This finding is corroborated by another study which indicated that editorial readership was limited almost entirely to the few individuals who had attended a university, academy, or senior high school (Ruslan 1973).

In sum, the coverage of national news in a provincial paper such as *Pikiran Rakyat* is not sought as avidly as the same coverage would be in a capital city newspaper such as *Kompas*. Each paper serves a different function for the reader, the capital press serving for national events while the provincial press provides local news and information. Regardless of the provincial press's investment in covering national events, it will continue to be evaluated as a secondary source for such information.

TABLE 25

Sources of General Information and Election News
among Bandung Adults

($n = 242$)

Sex	Newspaper	Magazine	Radio	T.V.	Film	Family/ Friends
Female	95% (93)	1% (1)	10% (10)	10% (10)	1% (1)	3% (3)
Male	98% (141)	4% (6)	15% (21)	17% (25)	1% (2)	5% (7)
Total	97% (234)	3% (7)	13% (31)	14% (35)	1% (3)	4% (10)

SOURCE: Aminuddin 1972: 147.

NOTES: The respondents were all above eighteen years of age, had the right to vote, and were readers of either the national or provincial press.

The raw percentages exceed 100 percent because respondents often listed more than one medium as the source of election information.

TABLE 26

Which Newspaper Was Used as the Source of
General Information and Election News?
(*n* = 242)

Sex	Kompas	Pikiran Rakyat	Both Kompas and Pikiran Rakyat	No Response
Female	48% (47)	37% (36)	14% (14)	1% (1)
Male	59% (85)	22% (31)	15% (21)	5% (7)
Total	55% (132)	28% (67)	14% (35)	3% (8)

SOURCE: Aminuddin 1972: 148.

TABLE 27

Was the Election News Clear Enough in
Kompas and *Pikiran Rakyat*?
(*n* = 242)

Election News Clear	Kompas	Pikiran Rakyat
Yes	84%	61%
No	15%	30%
Incomprehensible	1%	0
No Reply	0	8%

SOURCE: Aminuddin 1972: 90.

TRADITIONAL INTERPERSONAL COMMUNICATIONS

Illiteracy is high in Indonesia, and therefore traditional forms of inter-personal communication play an important role in both developmental and political communications. Nearly 83 percent of the Indonesian population resides in the rural areas where traditional forms of communication remain much more important than the mass media. The village headman (*lurah*) plays a decisive role in the collective decision-making process that dominates village life. Soedjito characterizes the village communication system, comparing it to a broom — tightly bound together at the top but widely dispersed at the bottom (Soedjito 1974). The village headman binds the population together and oversees communication with the outside world. Out of deference to the lurah's position, daily discussions rarely touch on village matters except for routine work chores.

TABLE 28

Type of Article Most Comprehensible
to Respondents
(*n* = 242)

Sex	Feature Article	Straight News	Lead Article	No Response
Female	66% (65)	19% (19)	8% (8)	4% (4)
Male	58% (84)	31% (45)	22% (32)	0
Total	62% (149)	26% (64)	17% (40)	2% (4)

SOURCE: Aminuddin 1972: 124.

NOTE: The raw percentages exceed 100 percent because respondents often consult more than one type of article to obtain election information.

Several studies have indicated that fishing villages are more traditional than agricultural villages and that the poorer the village the more traditional the people. In such villages individual decision-making is rare. Wihara Gumelar used formal interviews in a study of five villages near Cirebon on the border between West and Central Java. Initially he discovered that almost every respondent gave identical, nearly stereotyped answers to his questions. To avoid the seemingly pervasive influence of the village opinion leader, Gumelar changed his research tactics by collecting his data through the *anyangsana* technique of interviewing each respondent informally in the respondent's living quarters. With this more culturally apt technique he discovered just how dependent the fishermen were on the boat owners. The boat owners were the fishermen's chief source of advice on matters having nothing to do with fishing. Table 29 shows that the boat owners are the most frequent source of opinion leadership on both general problems and trade-related matters. In these villages the boat or fish-net owners (*juragan*) are the critical opinion leaders consulted on all manner of village problems. Fellow fishermen are the next most important group whereas the *lugu blok*, a village official, is seldom consulted on solutions to general village problems. Although the lugu blok has been chosen by the fishermen to act as a village official, he remains subordinate to the juragan in economic, social, and political decision-making.

The importance of traditional interpersonal communications networks is emphasized by the dearth of mass media exposure in these villages. Radio usage in these five villages is extremely low because although the transistor radio may be within reach of the rice farmer it is still beyond the economic means of poor fishermen. In the five villages from which the sample of 147 individuals was drawn, the proportion utilizing radio varied between 3 percent and 7 percent (Gumelar 1973: 71). With such low exposure, not even the radio can realistically

TABLE 29

Opinion Leadership in Five West Java
Fishing Villages

	Fishing matters	General problems
Boat owner (*juragan*)	45% (66)	55% (80)
Fellow fishermen	25% (37)	15% (22)
Elder (*sesepuh*)	15% (22)	(0)
Local leader (*lugu blok*)	10% (15)	10% (15)
No reply	5% (7)	20% (29)
Total	100% (147)	100% (147)

SOURCE: Gumelar 1973.

be expected to be a useful medium for spreading development information or political messages. For political communications especially the traditional interpersonal linkages must be used.

Yet finding the right traditional channel is not always easy. Many studies have described the traditional communications process transpiring at village meetings. According to local tradition in Central Java these meetings, known as *lapanan,* were held every thirty-five days. With time they have been transformed into official meetings where the headman meets with other village officials and decides what actions should be taken on village problems. According to tradition all decisions must be taken by acclamation. However, participation of the villagers is obtained beforehand by visiting the farmers in their homes, using the *kenduri* (*selamatan* or village get-togethers) as a means of spreading information by word-of-mouth. Another means of traditional political communication is the *botoh,* a respected villager who acts as the public relations representative of a particular candidate for the office of headman. The botoh is not himself a candidate but is a close friend or relative of the candidate. The botoh must be a rich man, owning substantial rice acreage, because during his visits he is expected to give gifts on behalf of the future lurah. During the campaign the houses of the botohs backing separate candidates are usually open night and day to supply food and drink to any guest. A study of botohs in a village in Kebumen in Central Java indicated that a botoh must be rich, influential, and an opinion leader (Supardjo 1973).

The same study in Central Java investigated motives for selecting a headman. In addition to being backed by an influential botoh the successful candidate must be well known in the village, experienced in village affairs, and a dedicated village leader. The communications that are most important to the election do not take place through the mass media but rather through anjangsana or home visiting (Supardjo 1973). Although the constant round of visitations might not be favored by modern city people, the villagers prefer personal meetings in their homes to mass meetings conducted at the *bale desa* (village meeting hall). These findings from Central Java corroborate findings mentioned earlier from West Java which indicated the importance of home visits (Gumelar 1973).

The West Java survey also showed that places for exchanging information and media habits in general were constrained by the daily routine inherent in particular occupations. Fishermen, as compared to rice farmers, evince lower interest in attending village meetings. Places preferred for interpersonal communication also change from region to region. *Warung kopi* (coffee shops) that would seem to be a natural meeting place are seldom frequented by fishermen and villagers because they involve the expenditure of cash rather than kind. The tendency to select *langgar* (small mosques) varies widely. In the nine fishing villages near Cirebon the proportion of respondents indicating a preference for the langgar was 31 percent, whereas in three villages in the West Java district of Sukabumi nearly two-thirds of the respondents identified the langgar as a favorite place for exchanging information. Thus, before an analyst could confidently identify the mosque as the most important location for information exchange, he must possess substantial information about the religious behavior of particular villages or groups of villages.

CONCLUSION

The major conclusion to be drawn from this chapter is that predicting the effectiveness of a particular mode of communication in Indonesia requires extensive information about the target audience and its location within the society. Whether mass media or interpersonal communication will be more effective depends on the audience's standard of living, its occupationally determined daily routine, and whether it is in a village or located in the heart of the Jakarta metropolis. Indonesia is composed of many separate and distinct audiences, each requiring a unique media mixture, and by far the largest portion of the total audience remains profoundly traditional in its communications habits. Everything presently known about the Indonesian media system supports Suhendra Kushwaha's generalization "that for developing countries mass media are in fact *not yet* media for the masses but should still be looked upon as elite media" (Kushwaha 1974: 4).

9

The Indonesian Press:
An Editor's Perspective

NONO ANWAR MAKARIM

THE GENERALIZATION contained in the chapter title needs to be qualified before proceeding to the treatment of a very specific subject. What is proposed for discussion here is concerned more with the men "behind" the press, and less with newspapers as such; more with the press in the capital city as distinguished from that of the provinces; and ultimately more with soft data than hard facts, for the simple reason that hard facts in government-press relations seldom emerge in an environment where a feeling for subtle hints and signals has proved more important for the continuation of a functioning press than open and formal statements, or even written law.

The following essay deals with an "imperfect" triangular relationship. It is triangular because it is concerned with differing perceptions of the role of the press emanating from the ruling elite, society at large, and the newsman himself; it is imperfect because the newsman involuntarily finds himself part of both the elite and the general reading public. Keeping the delicate balance between the two has always been the most strenuous task of the editor. A tipping of the balance in the rulers' favor runs the risk of widespread suspicion of having been bought by the powers that be; a too fervent crusade for the public interest would soon create inaccessibility to sources of news, an overwhelmingly large number of which are under government control. Both conditions can have adverse effects on a newspaper. The benefits drawn and sacrifices made in this unique triangular relationship would be an interesting study in itself.

Another aspect to be treated is what bearing the close government-press relations have on the change of outlook of newspapers from a preoccupation with "national prestige and national identity" during the period of Guided Democracy, to a concern with a clean and efficient government for economic growth under the "New Order" administration. Finally, it is proposed to deal with the influence, if any, that the press has on the process of government as well as on its reading audience.

I

A "conventional" assessment of benefits accruing to the Indonesian press as a result of its privileged position in society would invariably render it suspect of not functioning as a free and independent agent of information and opinion. Ranking undoubtedly among the most poorly paid in Southeast Asia, the Indonesian newsman is generously compensated by a whole range of privileges and special treatment.

In the capital city of Jakarta, where real estate prices are prohibitive even for the upper-middle-income bracket among the population, the governor has dedicated a large ready-to-build plot of land to be allotted to members of the Indonesian Journalists' Association, besides furnishing an air-conditioned secretariat for the organization on one of the city's main avenues surrounding Merdeka Square. Houses for the journalists were built as part of a pilot project of economy homes by the Ministry of Public Works and Power. The financing of the project was arranged through a very soft and long-term loan from the State Commercial Bank.

A reporter being assigned to cover activities of government departments will soon find it difficult to decline favors such as a monthly allotment of rice, a weekly distribution of transport fees, discreetly called "the envelope," to meet the rising cost of living. Sometimes there are arrangements for special coverage for extended periods of time of activities in certain government institutions, rationalized under the professional term of "development support communication," in exchange for which the institution underwrites the subscription to a sizable number of copies of the newspaper. A state corporation, resorting under the Directorate General of Sea Communications, in charge of transporting pilgrims to Mecca, annually distributes a free ticket to newspapers in Jakarta in order to enable a member of the newspaper's staff to make the pilgrimage.

Through an arrangement between the Journalists' Association and the Directorate General of Immigration, a trip abroad is tremendously facilitated for the newspaperman. The formalities for acquiring a passport and an exit permit, requiring days and many documents to arrange even for a government employee to be sent abroad on official business, take for the journalist only a few hours and one formal letter by the chairman of the Journalists' Association stating that the person mentioned is indeed a reporter or editor of a newspaper and that the person needs to go abroad to perform professional duties.

In the heavily congested streets of Jakarta, where numerous on-the-spot checks are made by traffic police on the widely popular practice of motor vehicle tax evasion, the newsman's car with a press tag on its windshield is exempted from scrutiny most of the time. Some have even reported the policeman saluting the driver in deference and going out of his way to arrange traffic in such a way as to make the journalist's passage as speedy as possible.

This pattern of deference tends to be more apparent the farther a newspaperman travels from the capital. Outside the capital, the Jakarta editor is almost accorded the honor due to a representative of the central government, with whom it is always safe to have the best of relations.

Great though the temptation may be to consider these benefits from a purely favor-trading viewpoint, it would be a serious mistake to detach this pattern of government-press interaction from the prevailing mode of social intercourse among the elite. It is no exaggeration to say that to refuse an offer of a favor is extremely difficult, if not altogether impossible, if one is committed to remaining within the web of intricate social relationships. The refusal or acceptance of a favor determines one's identity, one's extent of cohesion with the prevailing social fabric. The extension of a gift or a favor is first and foremost a token of kindness, affection, and respect; its acceptance a matter of courtesy and breeding. Only then, almost as an afterthought and a by-product, the relationship forged by a favor transaction is expected to generate a mutual regard for feelings on the part of the parties concerned. This concern for feelings finds a unique and sometimes very personal expression in newspaper content as well as in the day-to-day relations between the editor and the man of authority.

The national discussion of a code of conduct for the Indonesian press must of necessity take careful note of at least three maxims firmly embedded in the Javanese culture. The first concerns a self-imposed duty of circumspection, and a self-introspection preceding the act of criticizing a policy or a person. The Indonesian term most frequently used for such a quality is *mawas diri.* Another directive for self-restraint is found in the Javanese maxim *tepa selira,* an autochthonous version of the commandment "Do unto others. . . !" Both of these ethical prescriptions are strengthened by a widespread practice of saying the truth gently, indirectly, and with as little purpose to hurt as possible.

The frequent reminders from the Honorary Press Council, a nongovernmental body set up to address itself to the "conscience" of the press, and the numerous statements of ministers of information urging the press to self-restraint in the coverage of controversial issues, are but too clear proof that the ethical standards prescribed for the press by society at large, by the ruling elite, and by the press itself are more easily preached than practiced. To appreciate the difficulties involved, one has to visualize clearly the media of mass communication, a tool born, bred, and developed in the industrialized West, being transplanted into what is popularly called a transitional society, and being handled by men with a multileveled awareness of their identity. The appearance of the newspaper can almost be considered a harsh intrusion in the delicately structured networks of communication at different planes in Javanese social life. The strain that this situation creates can be monitored daily between the lines of lead articles and in the frequent intimate meetings between the press and government officials. Editorials have sometimes shown a proclivity toward the most baffling obscurantist language, the most personal and restricted conversation with strong undercurrents of self-withdrawal and abstract pontifications.

Readers conclude what they want to conclude, and if they lack sufficient "inside" knowledge of a specific situation, their conclusions may very well be the complete opposite from the editor's intentions. This is not considered important, as long as the public figure to whom the message was directed "registers" it. Most of the time the message is "on target," communication is established, and the function of a media is fulfilled, though perhaps not in as wide a circle as had been intended in the culture of its origin.

As has been concluded elsewhere in this book, for developing countries mass media are not yet media for the masses, but still to be looked on as media for the elite.[1] Indonesia is no exception.

The day-to-day contacts between the press and the government are equally marked by unique situations and moods. The usual forums for these contacts are either a large press conference or a more intimate luncheon or dinner.

The structure of these meetings has become very familiar by now. Seating varies according to the "rank" of those present; a luncheon or dinner in which chief editors and cabinet ministers are present would have seating arrangements around a dining table or in the livingroom of a designated dignitary's home. Reporters are usually seated across the table from government officials. Most of the time at such meetings is taken up by the government representative expounding the outlines of his program. This is followed by proper and polite questioning. The presence and questions of foreign correspondents at press conferences, if ever mixed meetings are held, usually evokes a strange blend of envy and disapproval among Indonesian newsmen. They are envied because of their incisive and unrestrained way of getting to the core of problems; they are, however, reproached for the lack of tact and aggressiveness in their straight, inconsiderate ways of "information grabbing." Editors usually have the privilege of addressing top-government executives as *"Saudara Menteri,"* or "Brother Minister"; younger editors, however, feel uneasy with this form of address and prefer the neutral *"Pak Menteri"* or "Father Minister."

The mood in these meetings is one of informality, both cordial and intimate. The "gentlemen" of the press are made to share information long before public knowledge and kindly requested to postpone or even refrain from publishing certain sensitive aspects of government policy. Here again the favor transaction is expected to generate a certain feeling of solidarity and mutual concern for a common goal. Genuine disappointment and even deeply injured feelings result from a breach of the unexpressed commitment. Not being invited to several sessions of this kind is a certain sign of failure to abide by the unwritten rules of the game. It must be very strange for a foreign ear to hear one of the top members of the ruling military elite, a general widely considered a prototype of "the man on horseback," exclaim his disapproval and regret at what he considered a breach of confidence committed by a leading newspaper in terms of "How could they have the heart to do this. . . !"

Another illustration of this intimate and personal relationship is the time when another top army officer put his arm around an editor's shoulder, slowly walking him to a corner of the room and seriously discussing a recent editorial on a political leader of a neighboring country in the mood of "That was an absolutely correct assessment . . . I had trouble on my way back from Europe when their men intercepted me and pleaded for the neutralization of what you wrote . . . let us meet for coffee to solve this. . . !"

Again, there was the time when a startled editorial writer received a personal telephone call from a highly placed military officer pleading with him

---

1. See Chapter 8, "The Mass Communication System in Indonesia," by Astrid Susanto.

not to write on a specific issue the editor already pledged to do through a previous editorial. When the editor politely explained why he could not accept the "advice," the general sadly informed him that he would be forced to take drastic action, but that he wanted the editor to know that the measure was not intended to hurt, it was to be merely a "face-saving" device. The following day the newspaper was closed down for two days, after which there was a marked increase in circulation of the newspaper.

The preceding is but a broad outline of the intricate web of relations between the press and the Indonesian government. It is a very personal relationship, and one in which symbols, signals, and half-messages count as the loudest transmission of ideas and feelings. This pattern has been disturbed somewhat, particularly since 1966 when the Jakarta press received a strong infusion of university dropouts among its journalists and editors. The initial period of adjustment for both the young pressmen and the government must have been a very destabilizing interim. When the mood gets too uncomfortably hot, and tempers become unstuck, however, a defusing current comes from the direction of a good-humored Javanese version of "Forgive them, for they know not . . . !" Seldom is the paternalistic attitude of the government allowed to deteriorate into open confrontation.

The overwhelming attention given to tensions arising from government-press relations tends to overshadow the frictions occurring within the press itself between the more tradition-oriented newsman and his "modernized" colleagues. Long exposure to social interaction within urban elites, frequent participation in international conferences, and the command of foreign languages seem to have predisposed a few editors to the use of more analytical tools in the assessment of their environment. Their coverage of events tends to be more descriptive and less "normative," their by-line stories and editorial comments have that "harsh" and incisive element so carefully avoided by those who still adhere to form and circumstance in the communication of news and ideas. Defense of this open, direct, and analytical approach on the part of some editors by invoking ethnic cultural tolerance proclaimed by the republic's emblem of "unity in diversity" has aroused amused response rather than acceptance.[2]

The attitude of the average Indonesian newsman to journalists of such predispositions is one of benevolent condescendence. They view this "new" breed of editors in much the same way as, for instance, a veteran of many wars would look upon a "green" conscript. Occasionally frictions occur between the two when the "new" editor, driven by impatience with the complacent treatment of a serious public issue in another newspaper, directs merciless and derisive editorials on the topic to such publications. Polemics of this nature occurred frequently in the Jakarta press of the late 1960s.

This rather sharp distinction between a "cosmopolitan" small group of

2. One editor went so far as to draw parallels between the "soft" Javanese way of communication and Java's structure of densely populated villages, as opposed to the "shouts" a Sumatran would have to resort to in order to make himself heard in the sparsely populated villages of Sumatra with its plantations and widely scattered location of houses.

journalists and the majority of less "urbanized" newsmen cuts across age and newspaper delineations. The "modernizing" assertiveness of this new type of journalist is expressed in his relations with others among a newspaper's staff. He is concerned with "crisp" reports and clear and concise editorials. His relations with others are more businesslike, showing a preference for efficiency in work rather than a pleasant and too easy-going atmosphere. To this kind of man is accorded a great respect and admiration by other members of the editorial staff. He rises much faster to positions of prominence in the newspaper. Seldom, however, is he made aware of the affection and personal loyalty due the editor who exudes a father image so deeply appreciated in Java's culture.

II

The widely held belief that the press is a mighty generator of influence on the general course of events in the nation has sometimes caused it to become an overvalued object on which influence is imposed by both government and the reading public. Time and time again the Indonesian press finds itself "sandwiched" between opposing pressures of interests.

The myth of the press as the "fourth estate" has been a source of both despair and pride for the press in Indonesia. Through this myth the press has had to sustain an ever-alternating current of admiration and respect, pressures and pleadings for support of tenable as well as untenable positions taken by either government or segments of the public, requests for help and cooperation which at times turn into outright impositions of influence, closures of editorial offices at the hands of angry mobs, and termination of publication by government measure. The average newspaper office in Jakarta may not be cluttered so much with IBM composers or wire tickers, but it is certainly alive with "visiting delegations" from all walks of life. The envoy of an outlying region's governor will, for instance, plead with a reporter, who happens to have been born in the same region, that the newspaper would do well in supporting pressures on the central government to extend the present governor's term of office. In another corner of the newsroom, patiently awaiting their turn to be heard will be a delegation of indigenous vendors from a local market who have been evicted from their stalls because of the Jakarta governor's decision to upgrade and "modernize" the site, with the consequence that the rent to be paid for new stalls would be considerably higher and thus prohibitive for the poor vendors. This delegation will skillfully argue their case before the chief reporter along the "charged" line of protection of indigenous businesses against unfair competition from "foreign" economic interests, meaning of course the local Chinese.

In the meantime, the chief editor may be forced to explain to a group of agitated young men why his recent editorial stand on merely understanding the terror activities of the Palestinian freedom fighters does not necessarily constitute becoming an agent of Zionism. Or, as the case may be, the chief editor is busily engaged in the exchange of courtesies on the telephone with a highly placed government official inviting the editor to come over for lunch or dinner. After the usual acceptance of such invitations, the chief editor will consult with his senior editors on what possible critical appraisal the newspaper may have published about either the official in question or his department. The topic will eventually be brought up in the course of the prospective luncheon, and the editor had better be briefed on its details to meet the occasion.

The intensity of the sociopolitcal pulls and pushes which the Indonesian editor has to absorb or reject would be difficult to evaluate without placing him in the proper perspective of the Indonesian elite, its sense of community and loyalties.[3] The difficulty in describing an Indonesian sense of community stems mainly from the country's multicommunal structure. The numerous ethnic groups, each of which commands varying degrees of clearness of image and loyalty among its members, are interlinked in a configuration roughly called Indonesian. Thus, the Indonesian individual experiences a sense of community at different levels, and the intensity of this at each level depends on his perception of personal interests and commitments. Ethnic ties of loyalty generally take precedence over the more abstract sense of being part of the national community, although these traditional ties are sometimes shed when more direct personal interests of a material nature are at stake.

On the other hand, religious sentiment, which is a strong cross-ethnic cohesive factor, at times tends to be sensitive to divisions along sociocultural lines. The difficulty in sorting out this fluid and interlinked pattern of loyalties is compounded by the fact that the upholding of the matrix of mores and rules of conduct is vaguely attributed to a multi-interpretable reference group, the *masyarakat,* which can be construed to mean either the religious community, the ethnic entity, a social class, or simply the public at large. This complex structure of the Indonesian sense of community can in large measure be explained by its historical background.

Preindependent Indonesia was loosely administered by the Dutch colonial regime. Ruling indirectly through local elites, the Dutch left much of the existing cultural pattern intact. A lingua franca of Malay origin initially served trade purposes along the archipelago's extended coastline; it later became convenient for the Dutch to use this language as the medium of colonial administration. Command of this language, however, diminishes the farther one lives from coastal areas. Farther inland, people speak their own languages, which cannot even be considered dialects of what is now known as the Indonesian language. The coexistence of an oppressive alien ruler and a lingua franca, coupled with the rapid twentieth-century development of the mass media, provided a new educated elite with the necessary setting and tools to launch an intensive and largely successful national politicization process. It is the resulting deeply entrenched idea of a unitary Indonesian sovereign nation, so vital during the national liberation struggle, which after independence has proved difficult to translate into a day-to-day working pattern of social life.

Contending conceptions of what ideology should be the base of the young

3. The following is taken from "The Indonesian Sense of Community," a text written by the author for the purpose of a series of radio broadcasts by the Australian Broadcasting Commission entitled "The Indonesian Gift" (summer 1974).

nation-state and conflicting views on how best to govern keep harassing the orderly conduct of state affairs. Sociocultural groups, of which the political party is but one manifestation, continue vying for political domination. Each contends it has the right answers and solutions, each claims to be the genuine representative of the *masyarakat.*

An "internal" view of the Indonesian sense of community would be marked by the prevalence of an ongoing basic conflict between two sociocultural mainstreams, the *abangan* and the *santri,* which is sometimes complacently referred to as a conflict between nominal and practicing Muslims. Its relevance goes much deeper than such placid terms as "nominal" and "practicing" would imply.

Islam came to Southeast Asia quite late into an already established Hindu or Buddhist civilization. The introduction of Islam through trade rather than conquest compelled it to adjust to local custom; it evolved into a spongelike system, accommodating a myriad of Hindu-Buddhist beliefs already firmly entrenched. As only the trading class could afford the trip to Mecca, they became the only group able to maintain contact with the wider Muslim world and more closely aligned with doctrinaire Islam. It was these traders who in the mid-nineteenth century zealously carried out the ideas of Islamic reform origi-nating from the great Madrasah of Al Azhar. They preached a radical return to pure religion as it was practiced in the days of the prophet Muhammad and attacked the breaking up of Islam into mystical brotherhoods. This was the pure religion, and their community was called pious, or santri. On the other hand, the native ruling elite and the peasants continued embracing their own version of Islam, syncretic and philosophical with animistic traits at the grassroots level. These were the abangan (C. Geertz 1968).

A conflict between the two was unavoidable. The old hierarchically structured system collided with the egalitatarian and quasipolitical ideas of the "new" Islam; a syncretic and "passive" way of life aspiring to harmony and moderation clashed with the activistic central concern to preserve only those religious and moral obligations explicitly legalized by the sacred law of the Qur'an.

In modern Indonesia part of these conflicts were fought out in the jungles of West Java, Central Java, and South Sulawesi, while another part resulted in the predisposition of the political system to more or less coercive administra-tions. It is a remarkable fact, though, that whatever confrontations took place, they were always conceived as ones in which the masyarakat strongly opposed unjust treatment by "certain groups," and never in the name of the specific groups engaged in the conflict. Each cultural mainstream fashions itself the true Indonesian community oppressed by an ill-willed minority.

A great many social and political events in Indonesia can be fruitfully explained by projection against this abangan-santri confrontation. In this larger perspective must also be seen the microweb of social relationships, group interests, and aspirations in semiurban Indonesia, those big villages called cities. It is this perspective, also, that gives the newspaper editor a useful manual on how to "read" the hidden purposes of statements, the numerous, seemingly unintelligible positions taken on issues by various groups, and the apparently senseless physical actions resorted to by others. For instance, a too-frequent use of the term *Pancasila*[4] in a strongly worded statement directed to nobody in particular would connote that the source has an abangan frame of reference and is anxious to deflate a santri political build-up.

In the unsolved controversy in the Indonesian Constituent Assembly in 1958 on the subject of the ideological basis for the nation, the santri's stand on the theocratic Muslim state was confronted with the abangan's insistence on Pancasila, which ever since has become the symbol *par excellence* of agangan opposition toward Muslim assertiveness. Only in this context is an identification of the group or person issuing the statement feasible, being either part of the large abangan sociopolitical force, or a minority group seeking the protection of abangans against a perceived santri threat by invoking Pancasila as the solidarity-making symbol of the abangans.

Strong opposition in parliament on the part of abangans and non-Muslims against a proposed marriage bill purportedly to protect the rights of Muslim women against polygamy would be incomprehensible without realizing the political import of its clauses. The rule, for instance, that a marriage is legal only after a religious ceremony, and only then open to the state's secular sanction, would result in the strengthening of the positions of Muslim courts and institutions through the possibility of appealing for the state's assistance to uphold Islamic law. Moreover, the rule would render a marriage between partners of different religious denominations almost impossible unless either party formally and openly switches religion, a practice frowned upon even among the syncretic abangans. It would also seem that for the non-Muslim minority an unobtrusive channel of proselytization would be closed.

A call for law and order could be easily identified as originating from the predominantly abangan government, whereas an impassioned appeal for fundamental human rights and freedom of expression would be more "appropriate" coming from either urbanized and university-educated groups or the santri youth. Violent demonstrations, the ransacking of gambling casinos, nightclubs, and steambath parlors are a characteristic last resort, a typical fundamentalist reaction of Muslim youth frustrated by the feeling of being constantly refused accommodation in the Indonesian body politic.

The stirring of latent extreme-nationalist and xenophobic sentiment through statements and speeches by a member of the ruling elite most of the time indicates an intra-elite power struggle, with which the editor is wise not to chime in lest he is willing to suffer the consequences of betting on the losing side. It seems that resorting to nationalistic agitation comes almost as a reflex to a member of the ruling elite engaged in a struggle for power within the bureaucracy. It would appear that an elite-mass link-up for the mobilization of

4. The five basic principles on which the Indonesian state is based being democracy, nationalism, social justice, belief in God, and humanism.

popular support is considered an absolute necessity for supplementing the intrabureaucratic build-up of forces and securing maximum success in the achievement of desired positions in the power structure. This link-up is invariably done through whipping up dormant xenophobia among the masses.

Aligning editorial policy with an ongoing power struggle has not only proved a risky venture but also a difficult one, due to the fact that the issues at stake tend to relate more to personal power and less to policy alternatives. How the editor reacts to this kaleidoscopic pattern of social interrelations depends very much on his cultural and educational background and his perception of the different loyalties due ideas, groups, and persons.

The editor is a prominent member of the national elite and that national elite is drawn from a society characterized by sociocultural and political cleavages. Being a member of the elite, the editor reacts in much the same fashion as others in his "class." There is the tendency toward "philosophic" paternalism as he overlooks the national scene from behind his editorial desk. At times, however, a slight irritation can be discerned in editorial comments on the yet-unmastered mystery of economic analysis, exposing an "imperfection" in his much-cherished image as an omniscient opinion leader. For that matter, the Indonesian editor is still very much a product of the period of the grand gestures of politics and the far sweep of great ideas. Painstaking analysis of news and events are still for the "dull" few. Although there is undeniably a strong identification with the one-nation idea, at times the somewhat parochial interests of sociocultural or ethnic groups most closely affiliated with the editor are taken to heart. He stands up for positions taken by a specific group more readily and argues their case more convincingly than he would for other groups. Years of grappling with national issues have sharpened his skills to deal with these "particularistic" issues from the national viewpoint. In taking up a cause for the santri or abangan groups he would, for instance, call forth such arguments as the necessity of participation in politics to all sociocultural groups in order to avoid cultural impediments to economic development or the need to harness latent progressive elements in traditional cultural patterns for the sake of a successful completion of government programs.

Arguments for the necessity of mobilizing foreign and nonindigenous capital resources for rapid economic growth may be issued by the editor most closely aligned with wealthy urban elites or minority groups most actively engaged in trade and finance. The championing of the idea of forging a national entrepreneurial class as a prerequisite for economic development based on national self-reliance may indicate an editor's affiliation with indigenous entrepreneurs who have benefited from government's patronage in the 1950s.

A few newspapers consciously try to present relationships and problems as they are, which would amount to a policy of adhering more to principles than to groups or men. In these cases, the ruling elite complain about the "blurred" policy line of the newspaper, while a public finding itself incapable of profiting from such an unbiased editorial policy accuses the editor of being "wishy-washy" and simply stops reading that particular newspaper.

III

It would now seem possible to construct a configuration of the varying functions of the press as perceived by government, the reading public, and the press itself.

A bitterly frustrated editorial describing the role of the New Order press as a government information "conveyor belt" may be overstating a case, but it certainly gave a correct assessment of opinion trends among government executives. Government considers the press an ally, a kind of outside "insider" to whom the giving of special privileges and status in society comes naturally in the context of a Javanese version of a corporate state. The social responsibility attributed to the Indonesian press finds a different interpretation than in the West. In the Javanese "central court" concept of the corporate state, social responsibility is vested in the president and his government. The press is expected to support and promote the carrying out of this social responsibility of the state. In this conceptual framework there is not much place for open dissent and criticism, let alone the denunciation of policies or public figures. A theme much publicized by Indonesian government officials in reprimanding either student demonstrators or press critics is the so-called *pe-pe*[5] practice in old Java. Tradition prescribes the expression of discontent, complaints, or demands by persons or groups of persons through silently standing or sitting in the heat of the sun, in the middle of the traditional *alun-alun* or square in front of the king's court, until the ruler deigns to grant audience. Another tradition has it that criticism aimed at the ruler has to be channeled through the court jester, who occupies a unique position of immunity from the king's scorn. Indonesian transitional society finds it difficult to reconcile these traditions with day-to-day events, and the continued existence of dissident elements in the press as well as among university students is a source of bewilderment and irritation for the Javanese executive.

Except for one or two national newspapers, which, due to their neutrality, have managed to acquire a cross-cultural readership, the readers of Jakarta newspapers and magazines are small in number, grow very slowly, and are easily recognized by their separate cultural patterns. There are substantial groups of people who feel that it is only natural for them to read newspapers known to be aligned with an institutionalized religion. There are those politicized readers, very small in number, who abhor the "blandness" of the larger newspapers and subscribe to the more lively newspapers with small circulations. Although newspapers such as *Kompas* and *Sinar Harapan* have what has just been described as a cross-cultural readership, one would still find most Catholics and Protestants subscribing to these dailies. A newspaper like *Abadi,* for instance, would be avidly read by the very politicized urban Muslims, whereas *Duta Masyarakat* finds its majority of readers among Muslims educated at the *pesantren* or

5. Pronounced as "pay-pay," and literally meaning "to bask in the heat of the sun."

rural religious school. *Merdeka,* on the other hand, would be favored by the more radically nationalist abangan segments among the reading audience.

The loyalty of readers to certain publications tends to be strengthened by admiration for individual editors. This admiration finds expression in the many invitations that the editor receives, and is expected to accept, to speak to a great variety of audiences, ranging from women's organizations to groups of university lecturers and pesantren students. It is on these occasions that an editor is offered the opportunity to establish a personal relationship with his audience, a factor not to be overlooked if the newspaper is serious about acquiring a hard-core readership. The following illustration, though indicative of the small total press circulation, to a certain extent also denotes a loyalty of readers to certain kinds of publications. A successful publisher of several entertainment magazines was once asked why he kept publishing new magazines instead of simply raising the circulation of his first magazine, which alone had managed to reach a quite large circulation. The reply was that in the past his readers bought only one magazine; now they buy three. The publisher sells more magazines to the same number of people.

For the editor this environment conditions a subtle keeping of a balance between what he thinks his readers need and what he perceives as the nation's cultural pattern of communication. The scale seldom behaves as he would like it to.

An editor must identify himself squarely with the existing system to be given the opportunity to work at all. And as a rule he is basically in support of stands taken and objectives pursued by the powers that be. His critical appraisals are directed most of the time to marginal aspects of policy and rarely touch the basic tenets of the regime. There is a vividly clear framework of ideological trends and style within which he can move more or less freely and with which he also measures government policy and its outcomes. He did not speak about cost-benefit analysis of prestige projects during the Guided Democracy period, nor does he elaborate on the contradiction between the old established forces and the newly emerging nations under the New Order administration.

This is not to say, however, that dissenting elements are completely absent from the Indonesian press at all times. In the Sukarno era a sizable number of newspapers directed a barrage of editorial attacks toward the nationalist-Communist symbiosis of political organizations and their presses, accusing them of subverting "Sukarnoism" by making it appear as a pseudo-Maoism. These newspapers formed a united front, dubiously calling themselves promotors of "Sukarnoism," when in essence the informed public, the adversaries, and Sukarno himself realized that this was a crystallization of the opposition to Sukarno's efforts to merge nationalist, Communist, and Islamic forces in a single Sukarno-led political force. Although the organization was eventually dissolved by presidential decree, and the majority of its member newspapers were closed down, a few were allowed to continue publication under a new name, a new management, and "new" protectors from among the power elite.

Ideological dissent was not restricted to the period of Sukarno's rule. Under the New Order government there remain a few newspapers which continue the old editorial policy of aspiring to national identity and prestige, the pursuit of development based on national self-reliance, and latent distrust of foreign involvement in the national task of economic development either through aid, credits, or investments. The convenient target of their criticism is the small group of economists educated in American universities, presently occupying key positions in the Suharto government. As was the case with the opposition newspapers during Guided Democracy, which "used" Sukarnoism as a protective shield behind which to wage the controversy, newspapers opposed to Suharto's open-door policy toward foreign investment, and the New Order's curtailment of patronage of indigenous businessmen, "use" Pancasila democracy as the framework within which they launch their editorial attacks.

The looseness and the grand sweep with which the concepts of both Pancasila and Guided Democracy have been formulated make varying, and even contradictory, interpretations possible, supplying thereby a welcome protection for those aspiring to opposition.

The close and frequent interaction between the Indonesian press and the government has at times created very intimate relationships between editors and members of the ruling elite. Such relations entail mutual support, solidarity, and the usual exchange of favors. In the case of a minister having close relations with an editor-in-chief, it is invariably expected that the editor often accompany the minister on his "field trips." It is also assumed that the editor be consulted, or at least notified, about impending regulations and briefed about what goes on in closed cabinet sessions. In exchange the editor gives ample coverage of the minister's activities as well as the progress made by the minister's department. The editor enjoys a "hot-line" to the minister's desk and has direct access to the minister's time and attention. The forging of such relationships does not go unnoticed by other members of the ruling elite or the observant political public, including other editors. The particular editor is then known to have a special tie with the minister. People having difficulties in breaking through the numerous layers of bureaucratic procedure in order to request the minister's attention or approval now approach the editor. And word gets around that if one has problems with a certain ministry, one would do well to approach a particular editor, because the editor "dines weekly at the minister's home, writes the minister's speeches," or in the case of youthful journalists, because the reporter is a "favorite son of the minister."

This relationship with either individual cabinet members or the government as a whole has occasionally become so close that government posts are known to have been offered to and accepted by editors. Sukarno's ambassadors in Peking, Moscow, and Algiers were journalists. Suharto's first ambassador to Washington was an intellectual with some newspaper affiliations, while the Indonesian foreign minister and Suharto's first information minister were both editors. In 1972 the ambassadorial post to Pnompenh was offered to one of Jakarta's most respected editors, although the man eventually declined to accept.

Thus, the editor's position among the elite is certainly one of political actor. He is considered as such by both the public at large and the ruling elite. A popular story among journalists in Jakarta concerns a young reporter being asked why he remained with one newspaper noted for paying very low salaries. The reporter's answer is typical of the editor's image in the eyes of those around him: it always pays to stay close to a future minister or ambassador.

Although this esteem and status considered to be due leaders in the developing countries may compensate for the meager income of editors, it also has its drawbacks. In assessing policy formulations and implementation too critically, the editor runs the risk of having to meet allegations that he is after a particular government post, rather than being interested in constructive policy appraisal, and that he is after power rather than truth. More disastrously, in periods of great social and political upheavals, such as was experienced in Indonesia in the mid-1960s, the editor may have to bow out altogether or, as was often the case, face arrest and confinement for extended periods of time. And because his newspaper bears his ineffaceable stamp, it too may be compelled to close down.

This is why the much-publicized change of content in Indonesian newspapers, from an overwhelming preoccupation with issues of national prestige and identity assertion in the period of Guided Democracy to a concern with economic growth and sound administration after 1965, first and foremost relates to a change of personnel and cultural outlook, which subsequently would be reflected in altered editorial policy. When in 1965 General Suharto started taking over control of the government, a score of newspapers were closed down and previously prominent editors were reduced to dignitaries-in-exile in socialist countries or had to face long prison terms. The change of persons was not confined to the "private" media; all leadership positions and senior posts in the government press agency *Antara* underwent a New Order purge. "Politicians" were replaced by "professionals." As one ruling group passes away to be replaced by another, so also disappears that segment of the elite most closely identified with it.

The eventful and rapidly fluctuating course of an Indonesian editor's career has often been glamorized as one encompassing exciting contrasts. His is a career most often likened to the dichotomous behavior of cork and lead in water; his is either a ministerial portfolio or a prison term.

As a profession, journalism draws many idealists and many more opportunistic "adventurers." Seldom does it draw the solid "backbone-of-the-nation" type of person who has had the privilege of an outstanding higher education and a life of opulence. The latter rather become practicing physicians or lawyers, research economists or consultants, businessmen, junior government executives, or minister's assistants. Even the equally low-salaried job of university lecturer is preferred over and above journalism. As a matter of fact, university dropouts and "free" intellectuals now make up the bulk of a newspaper's editorial staff. One gets the impression that, no matter how tempting the benefits, journalism is not seen by many as a really "serious" profession. It has the public image of having too many attributes of an interim occupation, a kind of a stepping-stone to a more lucrative and stable career. Journalism is frequently seen as the short-cut to prominence and influence, an avenue taken by those who aspire to high positions but decline to climb the arduous and slippery bureaucratic ladder.

This image, however, is changing. The "political" type of journalistic venture frequently found in the period of the first and second wave of nationalism in Indonesia is slowly, but surely, making way for the venture in which information will be more and more considered an industrial commodity to be merchandised.

And as the change takes place, no doubt, the profession will be placed on more solid bases and in more stable environments. A publishing venture in which large amounts of capital and technical and organizational skills have been invested can hardly be expected to indulge in daring campaigns or deal with politically controversial issues. Such a venture, as would befit a large organization, will be too much engaged in the absorbing task of securing its continued growth and eventual establishment as a strong social institution.

It was not long ago that the publication of a newspaper merely required a meeting and consensus between two types of persons: a man of ideas who had a "pen" and a man of means who had a "heart." For a considerable period in the history of the Indonesian press these two kinds of men were the mind and soul of the newspaper, the former very much in the center of things, the latter much more in the background. "Little" matters such as the news page, the managing editor, a circulation manager, the subeditor were problems that were treated as they arose, almost as an unpleasant interruption of the important and concentration-demanding cultivation of the editorial page.

What was important was the idea behind the newspaper; the technicalities of the business side must not be allowed to overshadow the original purpose of the newspaper, which was politics. And as politics during the colonial period consisted mainly of opposing the alien ruler, the Indonesian press of necessity took on a decidedly oppositionist character, a trait which it found difficult to shed long after independence was achieved. Such was the Indonesian press when Sukarno was leading the nationalist movement against the Dutch; such was, though to a lesser extent, the situation in the years 1966-1968, when Jakarta was overwhelmed by the profusion of newspapers. Of course, there were important exceptions in the early 1950s and during Sukarno's rule, when a few newspapers managed to achieve solid standards of professionalism, both in business and editorial aspects. But in general, newspapers had a short life span; their editorial temper was shorter still.

Mention must be made of one important aspect of Guided Democracy policy of assistance to the press. A heavily subsidized press, benefiting from very low-priced newsprint sold by the government, soon tempted the emergence of "ghost" newspapers. A few pro forma copies were printed as proof of the existence of the publication in order to qualify for the much-desired distribution of cheap newsprint. Apparently, some editors found it more profitable at the time to sell newsprint in the open market than publish newspapers. As for the others, a strictly controlled "Sukarnoist" editorial policy was the price paid for financial dependence on the government. As a result, the contents of most newspapers published at that time, excepting the few engaged in a real power game, abounded with political speeches, statements, and slogans.

The New Order ended this policy of giving subsidies. Continued assistance to publishing enterprises the market was incapable of supporting could not be reconciled with the anti-inflation measures and the strictly balanced budget policy of the new government. Moreover, it was the time of widespread reaction against involvement of the state in private business. Reversing the subsidy policy had the beneficial result of throwing the newspaper market open for competition among the numerous publications. A great many were forced to close down early, some terminated publication much later, only a few prospered. Much more attention had to be given to managerial matters, to layout, to editorial management, and to the procurement of aggressive advertisement executives. Chief editors began to sense the presence of other authorities and nonpolitical priorities in managing their newspapers.

Changes have also occurred in the relations between newspaper and printing plant. Whereas in the past most newspapers subcontracted the printing of their dailies to independent printers, now great effort has been exerted in purchasing old linotype machines and prewar Heidelberg presses. Some papers have even made the switch to the expensive offset process, laying out huge sums of money. It is clear that an irreversible change was taking place in the Indonesian press. If in the past the reading public was taken for granted, now conducting readership surveys, if only for the purpose of formulating an advertising pitch, has become a common feature of Jakarta newspapers. Whereas in the earlier stages in the history of the Indonesian press great stress was laid on selling ideas, now newspapers are sold. More and more pages are added to the conventional four-page Indonesian newspaper; salaries of reporters and editors are raised to "respectable" levels, "face lifts" are frequently administered to front pages. Although the editorial page is still not taken lightly by the successful newspaper, the news page is now given much more weight than was considered its due until recently.

It seems logical to deduce from this trend to "industrialize" in the Indonesian press that the consequence must be a depersonalization of the triangular relationships among the press, the government, and the reading audience, and especially among the newspaper's staff. Competition among publishers to sell the newspaper as "merchandise" will soon prompt publications to seek as large a circulation as possible in an effort to pursue the cost-reducing and profit-generating economies of scale. To achieve this the merchandise has at least to be produced in such a form as to arouse as little disapproval as possible among as wide an audience as possible. The "commodity" cannot contain controversial elements and would thus simultaneously avoid collision with the government, while submitting "straight and neutral" information to the public. Competition would also involve the recruitment of newspaper staff, in the sense of creating a market for skills where the best professional skills are "sold" to the newspaper bidding the highest price. This was once brought up by an editor in one of the regularly held discussions sponsored by the Indonesian Journalists' Association. The response was characteristic of the deeply ingrained journalistic ethos in Indonesia. None spared the most strenuous argument to contradict, and everyone pledged the utmost effort to prevent, the emergence of such a "materialistic" condition. It was remarkable indeed that the most vehement critic of the idea of a market for journalistic skills was the chief editor of the largest circulating newspaper in Indonesia, one that has successfully switched to the offset process, completely rationalized its management, and counts the most highly paid journalists among its staff.

IV

The process of influencing policy in a closed political system is made very difficult because in essence it consists of a particular conditioning of the executive's frame of mind, as well as preventing the implementation of an undesired policy from becoming a matter of personal prestige for the power-holder. On the other hand, the process is facilitated by the presence of a continuing intra-elite struggle for power, which in most cases amounts to "jockeying" for positions closest to the apex of power, the presidency.

The problem for the editor seeking to influence government policy is one of finding the correct balance between steady insistence and the submissive withdrawal required to allow "face saving," without which there can be no policy change. The importance of losing face, which is a superficial translation of the Javanese word *wirang*,[6] cannot be overstressed in a culture where form and formality connote a state of excellence. This striving for excellence through form is a widely and firmly embedded aspiration. Huge debts are contracted by the peasant while marrying off his daughter or circumcising his son in a *pantas* or proper form.

It would render the Javanese wirang if he finds himself incapable of adhering to traditionally prescribed propriety. A wirang man in the village would either leave his community or conduct a desperate act which is called *amok* by Western authors. If, however, one belongs to the elite, particularly if one considers oneself a *satria* or warrior-nobility, the ultimate recourse can be withdrawal from worldly affairs into a life of seclusion and meditation, or even, though rarely so, suicide. An acknowledgedly rare case in point was the suicide of a Javanese military officer after being recalled from a diplomatic post abroad in order to be interrogated on his alleged involvement in the 1965 Communist-inspired coup attempt. The ways in which the summons was transmitted and the questioning conducted presumably did not conform to the officer's concept of propriety for a man of his rank. After the fatal incident, both interrogators and colleagues of the deceased respectfully muttered, "He is a satria!" He could not endure wirang and with his act reached a state of excellence. The respect

---

6. *Wirang* is a cohesive blend of humiliation, shame before the community, inadequacy, loss of self-worth and dignity, the robbing of self-respect.

accorded a satria who purportedly committed suicide in order to avoid having to bear the burden of wirang is the more pronounced against a background of the frequently expressed concern about the loss of all but a very fragmented, and often self-serving, creed of "Javanism" among the present generation Javanese ruling elite.

Most of the time the working editor fails to reach the balance between getting desired policy changes and preventing wirang. Restrained insistence may fail to create attention to the problem at issue, whereas a full-scale campaign usually invites strong rebuttal and inflexibility on the part of the government. The aggressiveness with which denunciations of critics are made, the pledges that no attention shall be due disruptive parties who "have lost objectivity and are out to topple the government or reach positions of power from which they have been barred," usually have the effect of stifling criticism or student protests. It is usually not apparent until much later that the government denunciations were not the end of the affair.

Usually a certain "cooling off" period is allowed to lapse, after which, taking the appearance of an initiative taken by government, the desired changes are effected. The influence process is completed, faces are saved, and everybody had better forget the original conflict. The following serves as an illustration of the evolvement of a process of influencing government conduct.

A very influential group in the government had contracted the services of an American business research company to conduct a poll on the popularity of national leaders in Central Java, including the president's standing in this densely populated province. A rival faction saw this as an opportunity to disqualify the other group in the ongoing struggle for influence by discrediting the polling activity. This was done through a much-publicized speech given by a key central government executive before a group of local government officials in a town in East Java. In this speech the polling activity was described as a foreign subversive operation aimed at disclosing the unpopularity of the central government and undermining the prestige of President Suharto. Note must be taken of the fact that the assault was not aimed at those who hired the company, but rather directed against the foreign company itself.

It appeared that in the fervor of stressing the dangers of foreign subversion the top executive transgressed the boundaries of his original "instructions." While not forgetting to mention universities as hotbeds for subversive activities, he included foreign aid, grants, and credits among the sources of subversion. The publication of the speech in newspapers was met by a hail of student protests and editorial criticism. Initially the government flatly denied the alleged content of the speech, a few editors were even summoned by the attorney general and interrogated as to the source and correctness of the newspapers' "interpretations." After a recorded tape was produced, however, government statements took on an apologetic tone, explaining that there was a misunderstanding, that the government executive in question did not agree with the interpretation so far given to his words, and that continued insistence on a "literal" interpretation would only cloud the matter, a clear hint to stop editorial comment.

The ensuing process was typical of the workings of internal corrective mechanisms of the bureaucracy. The American business research company was forced to terminate by order of the attorney general, and the director was given a few days to leave the country. But the top government executive was also barred from giving off-the-cuff speeches. Editorial criticism had proved influential in censuring the conduct of a highly placed government official, but a price had to be paid to save a face, a very important one at that, and the foreign company was sacrificed.

Another case concerns criticism by the press and some radical university student groups of a lavishly budgeted project for the purpose of attracting tourists. It should be noted that the First Lady was one of the venture's promoters and that some of the criticism had at times become too personally reprehensive of the First Lady's preoccupations. The president, taking the criticism as a personal affront, in a rare display of loss of temper publicly threatened to use armed force against his detractors. The immediate impact of the president's anger was that all public discussion on the topic of the proposed project ceased. However, notwithstanding the president's stated determination to go ahead with the project, it was on his personal directive that the project be kept burning on a very low flame with the expressed intention of preventing its funding from interfering with the government's overall economic program and scale of national priorities.

All appearances had pointed to governmental defiance of the criticism offered by the press and student groups, but ultimately the waste of much-needed financial resources was thwarted. These are among the most noteworthy examples of instances in which the press has been able to exert some influence on government conduct in the capital city. However, the influence of the Jakarta press at times tends to be felt in the provinces too. Here one finds a popular practice of what is jokingly called by regional journalists the "ping-pong" game. Grievances on the part of the public or the press which are felt to be too risky to air in the provincial presses are first transmitted to a sympathizing Jakarta newspaper. The appearance of an item of concern to the regional government in the capital press can then "safely" be quoted by the local press, thereby creating anxiety among local officials which is but too easy to understand in view of the central government's overwhelming and frequently used authority in the appointments and replacement of government personnel serving in the region. The appearance of critical coverage in the Jakarta press set off a frantic scramble to write a report explaining the "true" position to the central government to counteract the potential unfavorable influence the newspaper stories have on powerful government executives in Jakarta. The "ping-pong" game just described is a clear indication that, at least in the eyes of provincial officials, the capital city's press is influential. The image of influence is sufficiently widespread in the provinces that even the regional newspapers share its "halo."

The instances of misuse of this prestige by journalists are as numerous as the occasions when local problems through coverage in national newspapers were more speedily solved than would otherwise have been the case. Another channel of influence would of course be the one based on personal relations between editors and members of the ruling elite, creating a two-way traffic of privileges and support already touched upon in the initial part of this article.

Concerning the impact of the Indonesian press on its reading public, not much can be asserted in support of the widely held belief that the newspaper has a strong influence on public opinion, and thus on the course of social events in the nation. One should add that opinion thus created, irrespective of what organized form is achieved in the process, in only individual cases implies the logical consequence of organized pressure. Although the distance between thought and expression in Indonesia may be covered in a relatively short time, especially through a newspaper, the gap between the spoken or written word and action based on opinion has always proved difficult to bridge. Unless an influential and powerful member of the ruling elite clearly appeals for it, action among the Indonesian public is extremely difficult to bring about. Even the turbulent university student population has need of ruling elite gestures of encouragement before venturing to stage a demonstration.

It is true that the powerful member of government may eventually lose control of the course of the movement that he himself instigated, much to the detriment of the objectives that he may be pursuing, but without his initial, albeit covered, consent the demonstration may not have taken place at all. In the restraint of such "runaway" movements, however, the newspaper may have a much more decisive role than rulers, unless of course a regime decides to resort to physical suppression.

This is mainly because the Indonesian press, as has been pointed out previously, has a much more intimate relationship with its reading public than would perhaps be the case elsewhere. This close relationship is the more vital in times of massive controversy, when an intense relationship of mutual influence is forged between the newspaper and segments of its reading public engaged in the conflict.

An outstanding illustration would be the case of a newspaper considered to represent the voice of youth during the turbulent years of the middle and late 1960s. The editors were as a rule told in advance of an impending demonstration, of the targets of such mass action, of the high point in the massive display of force, and of the political composition of the demonstrators. The basic purpose of giving the editors this preview was, of course, to obtain one of the most valuable commodities for the "authors" of the demonstration: extensive coverage and editorial support. The securing of this commodity would first of all amplify the demands voiced by the group and open the possibility that what started as a local movement would soon take on national dimensions, not only by drawing the nation's attention but, more important still, by encouraging similar movements in other major university towns in Java.

It is at this point that the bargaining position of editors grow to great proportions, becoming suddenly a function of the poor organization and communication network of political movements in general. It is at this point also that the slightest editorial disapproval becomes a major concern for the movement's leadership and another bargaining point for the editor in demanding concessions from the rulers on behalf of the movement. Other newspapers with a less distinct "following" enjoy this influence too, though probably in a lesser degree. But theirs is the exertion of a greater influence on their cross-cultural readership, that of transmitting an alternative frame of reference to the one provided by the mass media controlled by the government. As the Indonesian in general is not a book reader, the newspapers, though limited in total circulation, nevertheless function almost exclusively as the single reading source for the public in big cities.

V

The Indonesian press reflects the structure and composition of the public it communicates with. The composition of agents in the triangular web of communication between the press, society, and government can almost be considered fluid, a condition which makes the gauging of the influence process a not too easy task.

The government, looming so overwhelmingly large over almost every aspect of social life in Indonesia, cannot but impose on the national press a sensitivity to the rulers' approval or disapproval conveyed through an intricate and culturally conditioned network of subtle gestures and signals. Positive responses to the host of government "messages" are amply rewarded by privileges and special treatment; failure to comply, on the other hand, is met with paternalistic reproach most of the time. It is at this juncture that the closing down in 1974 of a number of newspapers of distinct urban sociocultural denominations raises the relevant question about the validity of such close and intimate relations and the casting of doubts as to the effectiveness of the informal network of communication between editors and the power elite.

What could have been the causes of its breakdown? The only plausible explanation would be that "abnormal" situations beget "abnormal" actions on the part of otherwise gentle and reasonable people. At least two hypotheses can be offered to an inquiry into the government's frame of mind leading to such drastic action as the closure of newspapers.

The few months toward the end of 1973 in Jakarta were rampant with protesting student groups. Alleged misappropriation of foreign aid and credits, the heavy corruption and lavish display of wealth among key government officials, accompanied by heavy inflation, fed student unrest. The huge windfall profits accruing to the state due to the oil-boom created simultaneously high expectations and anxiety about its proper appropriation. Posters with messages such as "On this place we started selling out the Republic" and "We are condemned to be the generation of the state-debt payers" were conspicuously displayed on the square facing the splendid Japanese-built Nusantara office building on Jakarta's miracle mile, a location of foreign investors' offices. The August 1973 anti-Chinese riots in the West Javanese town of Bandung stirred a responsive chord among Jakarta students. They denounced the Chinese for "bribing government officials and tempting military officers into close business cooperation with them." A group of university youth peacefully standing in line to welcome the Dutch chairman of the Inter-Governmental Group on Indonesia (IGGI), a consortium of aid-giving countries, unexpectedly turned into a demonstration, unfurling banners and releasing a previously prepared statement to the effect that foreign aid was being used in Indonesia to widen the gap between the rich and the poor.

Weak reprimands aside, the government's reaction, in particular on the part of the military authorities, was remarkably docile. Deducing from various government statements expressing an understanding of the student protests, there was reason to believe that there was even support for the daring student actions. Moreover, one of the most powerful military officers was touring the country propagating the government's new approach toward solving the nation's problems; it was now to be a two-way communication between the people and the government. Talking to student groups in the university town of Jogjakarta, he even lent his personal approval to the previously banned performance of a play considered to be highly critical of the military in power.

Encouraged by these indications of a liberalizing trend, the press gave heavy coverage of the students' activities and their often not-too-polite statements. The government's indecisiveness in the face of widespread displays of discontent, its hesitation to act when the sporadic student protests were growing into huge demonstrations on the eve of the Japanese prime minister's visit to Jakarta, were clear signs that heavy infighting was taking place among the most powerful factions in the government. With one of the adversaries clearly supporting the protest movement in a bid for popular support, a fatal choosing of sides by student leaders as well as some editors was inevitable.

The solution of the struggle for power took a much shorter time than the build-up of forces for the showdown. A massive wave of arrests was followed by the deposition of the second most powerful man in the country, and with him an awe-inspiring power-bloc "mysteriously" disappeared. With the demise of one of the contending groups, of necessity came the time for reckoning with its supporters. The fact that the power struggle was carried on too close to the center was the more reason for quick measures. And only later people recalled the popular analogy of the fighting elephants and the grass.

Another hypothesis, though less convincing than the previous, in explaining the government's heavy-handedness would be to see the student demonstrations, particularly those meeting the chairman of the IGGI and the Japanese prime minister, as flagrant breaches of a host's code of conduct. As is most proper in a corporate state, the chief executive bears the brunt of shame. Punishment of the guilty was but one way of meeting the obligation of appeasing the insulted guests.

The closure of newspapers in Jakarta is cause for deep concern. Some have appraised these measures as basically a part of the two-faceted cultural attitude of rulers toward its critics, an alternating urge to guide and discipline. Others have seen this simply as but another step along the course of increasingly authoritarian control over all social institutions in Indonesia, a step preceded by the imposed reduction of the number of political parties in 1972. It would seem, however, that more compelling indications in Indonesia's government-press relations need to be displayed in order to conclude that the present trend is toward more stringent government control.

10

Cartoons and Monuments: The Evolution of Political Communication under the New Order

BENEDICT R. O'G. ANDERSON

WITH THE APPEARANCE in 1970 of *Indonesian Political Thinking,* students of Indonesian society and politics were for the first time presented with a wide-ranging collection of writings and speeches by important Indonesian politicians and intellectuals in the post-1945 period (Feith and Castles 1970; see also Alfian 1971). The timing of its publication was not fortuitous: it clearly reflected a growing scholarly interest in Indonesian ideology and political discourse (see the following translations of important individual texts by Indonesian political leaders: Sjahrir 1949, 1968; Hatta 1960; Sukarno 1960, 1970; Aidit 1961; Nasution 1964, 1965; Simatupang 1972). Recent work by Weatherbee (1966), Dahm (1969), Legge (1972), Mrázek (1972), Mortimer (1974), and Scherer (1975) has been devoted to thoughtful, pioneering analysis of important segments of Indonesian political thought. Their studies show not only how rich this field of enquiry is, but also how much more research still needs to be done.

At the same time one should recognize that the materials used in this genre of research have a specialized character. In general, they take the form of more or less studied, quasi-literary, and *printed* statements of positions — whether they reach the scholar as printed speeches, printed articles, or printed books. Almost invariably, they are exegetic in character, addressed to particular audiences to combat alternative exegeses, arguments, and appeals. In such circumstances, it is understandable that in his introduction to *Indonesian Political Thinking,* Herbert Feith tentatively characterized the overall body of Indonesian political thought as "diffusely moral," "optimistic," and marked by "a tendency to see society as undifferentiated" (Feith and Castles 1970: 18). Yet although these traits may well be characteristic of the political communications with which he was concerned, it could be argued that they are less "typically Indonesian" (or typically "Asian" or "Third World," as Feith proposed) than typical of a certain genre of utterance. In such a perspective these traits may seem no more surprising than moralism in sermons or irony in satire. One could also suggest that scholars have focused their attention so exclusively on a particular type of political communication that by unconscious synecdoche the part has literally been taken for the whole. Other important modes of political

FIG. 1. Roadside village between Malang and Selecta

communication and expression have been neglected, which, if analyzed, would throw a different light on Indonesians' conceptions of their politics. Two such modes, which for convenience I shall call "direct speech" and "symbolic speech," will be discussed here, though, owing to the nature of the material at hand, only the second will be analyzed at length.

DIRECT SPEECH

"Direct speech" in reality forms the overwhelming bulk of political communication in any society: gossip, rumors, discussions, arguments, interrogations, and intrigues. Yet despite its vast quantity, almost all such communication escapes the scholarly eye. What is observed is seldom reported directly, but rather is congealed into indirect speech: "rumors circulated in Jakarta that . . . ," "the interviewee told the author that at the party conference . . . ," and so forth. In the process, the live ephemeral communication is transmuted into an illustration or symbolic representation. Only rarely is it accorded the status of speech *qua* speech, capable *in itself* of speaking directly to Indonesian political concerns. Yet even the most marginal observation of or participation in Indonesian political life shows that such utterance is simply another mode of political communication – as it were, playing *ngoko* to the *krama* of *Indonesian Political Thinking*. (*Krama* and *ngoko* are respectively the "high" [polite, formal] and "low" [intimate, informal] levels of Javanese speech.)[1] As might be expected from a ngoko mode, this type of speech is rarely "moralistic" or "optimistic"; nor does it present Indonesian society as an "undifferentiated whole."

In part, neglect of this type of communication has its roots in scholarly convention. Krama communication, organized and printed, appears more permanent, more replicable, and thus more credible. Different scholars can at least read the same texts if they can rarely hear the same argument or witness the same conference or intrigue. Analysis based on unreplicable interviews, overheard chat, or whatever, seems tenuous and problematic. Unless checked by krama sources, therefore, ngoko messages are of dubious value. Most often, they are either aggregated and used to describe a political force or reality ("rumors circulated that . . .") or introduced raw into the analysis as "quotations from field notes" – colorful illustrations of themes derived from the study of krama documents.

The problem is more than one of etiquette. Scholars, particularly if they are foreigners, are disadvantaged in gaining effective access to many types of ngoko communication. The spoken word is ephemeral, and this fact in itself imposes high linguistic and mnemonic demands on the observer-analyst. Beyond that, much ngoko speech cannot take place if the foreigner is looking on – he tends to kramanize things with his alien presence. Even in the intimacy of the private interview, the "subject" usually suspects that what he says will end up as printed exegesis, and thus confides in krama to his recording angel.

1. For a discussion of krama and ngoko forms in contemporary Indonesian political discourse, see Anderson 1966.

Yet some ngoko discourse is available in more or less untransmuted form. In them, aliens can observe, *at any time*, Indonesians talking not to the world or to the faithful, but to and against one another, sometimes even to themselves. Rare as they may be, these utterances, by taking printed form, have lost their ephemerality and come to assume documentary status. Some notable examples are the stenographic records of the discussions of the Sanyō Kaigi (Council of Advisors), the Badan Penjelidik (Investigation Committee), and the Panitia Persiapan Kemerdekaan Indonesia (Committee for the Preparation of Indonesian Independence) in the late Japanese period;[2] and the records of the DPR (Parliament) and Konstituante (Constituent Assembly) in the period after independence. In all these texts ngoko and krama speech are mixed — the talk varying widely in spontaneity and informality — but the ngoko element is important and often even preponderant. (In most of these cases, Indonesians are in real dialogue with one another, and foreigners are not present as sympathetic censors.) Most voluminous of all are the stenographic proceedings of the Extraordinary Military Tribunals which, since 1966, have judged and condemned some dozens of left-wing military officers and civilian politicians.[3] Although many of these documents have long been available, the tendency has been to mine them for content (historical fact) rather than for form and meaning (political thought).

SYMBOLIC SPEECH

If direct speech often eludes the academic eye because of its fluid and ephemeral nature, symbolic speech escapes attention for rather different reasons. We understand that public monuments and rituals, cartoons, films, and advertisements represent a mode of political communication. But the grammar may be perplexing, the relation of form and content at once more salient and more ambiguous. More than printed speech, these visual condensations of significance find their meanings shift, deepen, invert, or drain away with time. As their audiences are necessarily fleeting and anonymous, context is all-important, yet singularly problematic to the would-be interpreter. For example, on August 17, 1945, a new-made Red-White national flag was flown at Sukarno's side as he read the historic proclamation of Indonesian independence. Twenty-three years later, on August 17, 1968, the same flag was flown again for the last time. In the meantime, it had become a *pusaka* (heirloom). The red had faded to the color of dried blood, the white to ashen gray. On all sides there fluttered hundreds of new-made flags, brilliant in the morning sun. In 1945 — can one doubt it? — the flag had expressed an extraordinary hope and promise. In 1968, who could be sure what its flying meant, amidst the hundred replicas, either to those who flew it or those who watched it fly?

2. A partial translation of one extended Sanyō Kaigi discussion is contained in Anderson 1966*a*. A somewhat tampered-with version of the debates of the other two bodies is contained in Yamin 1959.

3. It is sad that it should be such records of judicial interrogations, where the stakes, at least for the accused, are so high, and where all parties, for their own reasons, are deeply concerned to question, justify, and accuse, that bring the alien his keenest sense of ngoko exchange.

In what follows, I will try to explore some of the meanings of different elements in the symbolic speech of the New Order era, both to illustrate, however tentatively, a method of interpretation and to suggest how such interpretation throws light on the "political thinking" of the period. In a number of instances, I will be making explicit contrasts with the symbolic speech of the pre-1965 era, not only to highlight certain characteristic features of New Order symbolic speech, but also to show how the latter in many ways developed out of, or against, the former.

CARTOONS

Of all the forms of visual political communication, cartoons are perhaps the most readily decipherable. As they frequently make use of written words, they seem closest to conventional printed documents. As they are usually responses to particular historical events, they can, on one level at least, be mined for their "factual" content.[4] A book of Herblock cartoons, for example, tells the reader a great deal that is concrete and specific about American politics in various phases of the postwar era. But one would miss something, I think, if one were to study the cartoons from this perspective alone. Form may tell as much as content. To demonstrate this point, let us look at the work of two very successful Indonesian cartoonists and observe not only the targets of their attacks, but also the way in which the form of their cartoons communicates another type of meaning altogether.

The elder of the two cartoonists is Sibarani, who made his reputation as editorial cartoonist for the sensationalist left-wing daily *Bintang Timur* in the late 1950s and early 1960s. The younger is Johnny Hidajat, perhaps the most popular of New Order cartoonists, working for *Pos Kota,* a sensationalist right-wing paper sponsored by the Jakarta municipal authorities, and for a variety of weeklies, particularly the very successful *Stop* (partly modeled on *Mad* magazine).[5] Before attempting an analysis of some of the two artists' typical cartoons, a brief explanation of each may be useful.

Cartoon 2*a*. John Foster Dulles is flying a political kite – the PRRI prime minister, Sjafrudin Prawiranegara. But the kite is immobile, hopelessly entangled in the Rakjat (People) tree.

Cartoon 2*b*. As the dollar sun shines, Foreign Capital greedily swallows up the produce of Indonesian soil, digests it, and excretes. Indonesian capitalists feed on the excrement, digest it, and excrete in turn. An unnamed figure, presumably representing the common people, feeds on what is left.

Cartoon 2*c*. The caption tells us that the sinister face labeled Anti-Communist is that of former Vice-President Hatta. In the brain bubble the

4. A good example of this approach is Henderson 1912.
5. I have found no written accounts of Sibarani or his work, but there is an informative article on Hidajat in *Tempo,* January 31, 1976. It is a curious fact that both men belong to Indonesia's small Protestant minority.

FIG. 2a

FIG. 2b

FIG. 2d

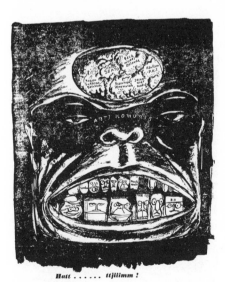

FIG. 2c

FIG. 2e

FIG. 2. Sibarani Cartoons

following ideas: Defend Dutch Capital! Smash the PKI! Overthrow the
Sukarno regime! Join SEATO! Bring down the government! Irian *niet
nodig*! (Dutch for "Isn't necessary!"). Hatta's teeth are caricatures of
leading PRRI figures. One can identify (top row): Major Somba, Des Alwi,
Lt. Col. Saleh Lahade, Col. Zulkifli Lubis, Col. Dahlan Djambek, and
Runturambi; (bottom row): Lt. Col. Achmad Husein (as a pig), Col.
Simbolon, Lt. Col. Ventje Sumual, Sjafrudin Prawiranegara, Sumitro
Djojohadikusumo (?), and Burhanuddin Harahap.

Cartoon 2*d*. Outside the concentration camp at Ladang Lawas (in West
Sumatra, where the PRRI forces held many left-wing militants prisoner in
1958), the Masyumi leader Mohammad Natsir (identified as Himmler/
Natzir) goose-steps. Both his body and the Masyumi emblem (crescent
moon and star) have been turned into swastikas. His sword is labeled Holy
War.

Cartoon 2*e*. The Statue of Liberty, in the guise of President Eisenhower,
brandishes the severed head of Jimmy Wilson, a young black sentenced to
death for stealing $1.95 in the summer of 1958 (the sentence was com-
muted by Eisenhower shortly after the appearance of this cartoon). The
torch of freedom has become a bleeding head, the aura glitters with
dollars, and the book has been replaced by a blood-stained sword.

FIG. 2f   FIG. 2g

Cartoon 2f. The PRRI cart is drawn by a donkey named Sjafrudin Prawiranegara. On it ride Allan Pope (the CIA operative and pilot shot down by central government forces near Ambon in May 1958), Tasrif (alleged mastermind of the attempted assassination of President Sukarno in November 1957), and the executioners of Situjuh and Ladang Lawas (two prison camps in West Sumatra).

Cartoon 2g. A memorial to the militants who died at the hands of the PRRI. The caption reads: Rise up!

Cartoon 3a. Djon Domino sings *pantun* (folk quatrains) at an expensive restaurant to earn money. The lyrics go,

> In Krawang market work the pickpockets —
> They take the train, alight at Bekasi.
> The people starve, they cannot pay their debts —
> Bigshots enrich themselves illegally!

With a sour expression, the company director turns and says, "That's enough! Here's a dime!" Djon accepts with a grin.

Cartoon 3b. Djon and his friend are playing cards. Friend: "Arbitrary officials...?" Djon: "We crush!" Friend: "Lazy officials...?" Djon: "We dismiss!" Friend: "Corrupt officials...?" Djon: "We get friendly with, they're well-heeled!" Friend: "Shhh!"

Cartoon 3c. Djon calls on a prospective father-in-law. Father-in-law: "Djon! Are you serious about Ida?" Djon: "Of course I'm serious, *pak*! Only I need three years first to finish my studies!" Father-in-law: "In that case, give me a down payment of half a million, so I don't give her to someone else!"

Cartoon 3d. Djon and his friend watch a luxurious official limousine roar by. Djon: "Hey there, bigshot, have a thought for the fate of the people! Don't just think of 'commissions' and young concubines!" Friend: "How can he possibly hear you, Djon?" Djon: "Think I'm crazy? If he could hear me, he'd clout me a good one! I'm a relative (*masih famili*) of his!"

Cartoon 3e. Djon and his girlfriend Ida are out riding on his motorbike. Ida: "Do you really love me, Djon?" Djon: "100%, Ida!" Ida: "Suppose I killed myself, Djon?" Djon: "I'd kill myself too!" Ida: "Suppose I sold myself, Djon?" Djon: "Then I'd be your tout so long as I got a cut!"

Cartoon 3f. Djon is teaching some children about the meaning of Sanskritized words. Djon: "Bina Marga?" First boy: "Bina means erect, build; marga means road, so Bina Marga means roadbuilding." Djon: "Bina Ria?" Second boy: "Bina means erect, make; ria means happy, so Bina Ria means something that makes you happy!" [The reference is to the Bina Ria amusement park in Jakarta, much patronized by lovers and prostitutes.] Djon: "Binatu?" [Binatu (launderer) is an ordinary Malay word, not a Sanskritized honorific — but it happens to begin with Bina, and so is used for comic effect here.] Third boy: "Bina means erect; 'tu means you-know-what, so binatu means you-know-what is erect!"

FIG. 3a

FIG. 3b

FIG. 3c

FIG. 3. Johnny Hidajat Cartoons

FIG. 3d

FIG. 3e

FIG. 3f

Although satirical or comic art is very old in Indonesia, it would be a mistake not to recognize the novelty of the cartoon form. The cartoon, as we know it, is dependent on a sophisticated printing technology as well as on a partly monetarized economy creating a public able and willing to purchase this type of industrial commodity. But beyond that, the cartoon appears to correspond historically to the development of a certain type of consciousness — one which conceives of politics secularly as a separate, half-autonomous realm of human interaction, and one in which mass publics share. It seems plausible that the normally oppositionist aspect of the cartooning tradition derives less from the lampooning instinct than from the historial fact that mass publics had access to modern political communication long before they had access to power. Cartoons were a way of creating collective consciences by people without access to bureaucratic or other institutionalized forms of political control.[6] In Indonesia, the conditions outlined here did not come into being until the early part of the twentieth century, and therefore, although I have no data on the dates of the first Indonesian cartoons or comic strips, it would seem unlikely that they appeared much earlier than the 1930s.

In formal terms, then, Sibarani and Hidajat have a common ancestry in the great British cartoonists of the eighteenth century, James Gillray and Thomas Rowlandson, and in the fertile caricaturists of the French Revolution, mediated through the tradition of Dutch cartooning and the later corpus of the American comic strip.[7] But although this perhaps tells us something about the adoption of the cartoon/comic strip *format,* it tells us little about the individual artists' personal style and message.

It would not be hard to find an indigenous ancestry for Sibarani's powerful and rough-hewn style. In the immediate past one thinks of the cartoon and poster art that developed so rapidly under official sponsorship during the Japanese occupation, and less officially in the subsequent national revolution.[8]

6. This may account for the relative rarity and late appearance of cartoons as instruments of official political propaganda. Perhaps the best-known example of this minority group is the Soviet official humor magazine *Krokodil.* A nice collection of *Krokodil* cartoons is contained in Swearingen 1961.

7. For some interesting material on the history of cartooning, see Reitberger and Fuchs 1971, especially pp. 7, 11, 29, 174-75. Though the authors declare that "from political caricature to comic strip was but a short step," they point out that "comics have [only] existed for the last seventy-five years." They note, too, that historically the prime audience for comic strips has been the lower middle class. The first "indigenous" comic strips (that is, not American imports) did not appear even in Europe until the 1920s, and really flourished only after World War II.

8. For some examples, see various issues of *Djawa Baroe*; Anonymous 1945; Departemen Penerangan, n.d. Some distinctions need to be made here, though their interpretation will be left to later in this essay. Under the Occupation, cartoons and posters were widely used, but they appeared exclusively under the aegis of the military authorities. The targets of the cartoons were typically outside society — the Dutch, the British, and the Americans. During the Revolution, posters and graffiti were the most common and most popular forms of visual speech, whereas cartoons became a relative rarity. Of forty newspapers and magazines I have checked from that period, only eight carried cartoons at all; even these cartoons appeared irregularly, and at rare intervals. Doubtless part of the explanation lies in the technical problems caused by the shortages and disorder of those years. But the fact

Further back in time, the sharply humorous and eerily monumental art of Sibarani's Batak ancestors comes to mind (see de Lorm and Tichelman 1941; Tichelman 1937; de Boer 1920). For many Indonesians the Batak have a reputation for being *serem* (sinister, frightening) in terms of physiognomy and character, and Sibarani's cartoons could also well be described this way. But even indigenous tradition in itself sheds little light on the historical meaning of an artist's work; to explore this more coherently, we must turn to the specifics of his style.

Many of Sibarani's best cartoons depend for their emotional effect on a stark chiaroscuro. Executioners, embezzlers, imperialists, and spies appear as somber figures in a twilight landscape. Moral and pictorial darkness complement each other. The artist does not simply label Natsir or Tasrif a butcher, but reinforces the judgment with a simple element of design. At first sight Sibarani seems merely to be exploiting a standard cartooning technique for "blackening" the objects of his enmity. Yet at the same time, by looking at the landscape of the cartoons as well as the central figures, one can learn something more about the meaning of this lighting. Sibarani's readers lived and read his cartoons in a physical landscape drenched in sunlight, dust, and color. The actions he describes and condemns took place in daylight, more or less in public, often in the crowded rough-and-tumble of urban politics. Yet one sees none of this in his designs. This suggests that the chiaroscuro is less political expressionism used as a pillorying device than a means of political education. Sunlight in the world and darkness within the image is a contrast which shows Sibarani's readers something about the everyday opacity of the social-political order and the reality of the forces that move it. Sibarani's chiaroscuro is thus a tool for political demystification.[9]

Another key element in Sibarani's style is its iconographic density, exemplified by the conscious layering of symbolic emblems. Again, this is in itself a traditional aspect of a certain type of editorial cartooning.[10] But it is instructive to see how Sibarani employs the device, and for what purposes. Cartoon *2d* is a good example of his method. Sibarani seizes on the fortuitous assonance of Natsir and Nazi as the basis for an intricately constructed icon.[11] The point

---

that the bulk of these cartoons were printed in papers published in Dutch-occupied Jakarta, not in towns held by the Republic, suggests that the full answer lies as much in the political-cultural as in the technical realm.

9. One could argue that even the personal caricatures are deployed to the same ends. If Husein becomes a pig and Sjafrudin a donkey, it is less because their physiognomies lend themselves to "animalization" (note that in cartoon *2c* only Husein is so transformed, and in cartoon *2f* only Sjafrudin) than that the particular animals are chosen and used only when the animal is *verbally* associated with particular moral qualities. Put crudely, it is as if Sibarani were saying, "Sjafrudin may have a law degree, but he is an ass; Husein may be an army officer, but he is a dirty pig."

10. The caricaturists of the French Revolution were particularly ingenious builders of elaborate cartoon emblems. See Henderson 1912.

11. I have found no satisfactory explanation of the contemporary Indonesian fascination with the Third Reich. In the early 1960s bookshops did a flourishing trade in cheap and lurid booklets on Nazi cruelties, espionage, and terror. One finds frequent references to Nazism, by no means always horror-struck, in the writings of

made explicitly on Natsir's cap — Himmler-Natzir — is picked up in the enswastikaed Masyumi crescent moon and star and the very shape of Natsir's goose-stepping body. The sign at the entrance to the Ladang Lawas camp identifies it with Nazism by the use of German rather than Indonesian words; and as a final emblematic detail, instead of the "correct" ending to *Konzentrationslager* (concentration camp), Sibarani ingeniously substitutes, not *kamp* but *kampf,* a deft reference to Hitler's *Mein Kampf.* In cartoon 2e the same method is employed to dismantle the formal iconography of the Statue of Liberty and reassemble it for educational purposes. I have already observed that the torch has become a severed head, the book a bloody sword, the aura a dollar glow, and the placid female face a caricature of Eisenhower. Again one finds Sibarani's characteristic use of language for iconographic point. The Indonesian words on the label attached to the head, "Jimmy Wilson, pentjuri $1.95," stand outside the icon, acting as an explanatory footnote. But "Statue of Liberty" remains in English, inside the icon. American "liberty" is being pilloried, not *merdeka* or *kemerdekaan*: indeed *merdeka* and liberty are implicitly contrasted by this device. In cartoon 2g, too, the significance of the death of left-wing militants is condensed onto the image of the Crucifixion, while the caption alludes to the Resurrection.

In all these instances, the dense, meticulous iconography serves the same purpose as the chiaroscuro: by distortion and designing artifice to reveal the artificial nature of perceived, received reality and thereby to demonstrate the really real. (The contrast is between the violently emblematic and "artificial" style of Sibarani and the naturalism of Hidajat. Where Hidajat says, "Look, my pictures are like life," in a way Sibarani says, "Only my cartoons will show you what appearances conceal.")

A third notable element in Sibarani's style is the use of foreign languages and symbols. In some cases the point is clear. For example, in cartoon 2c, he deliberately uses the hybrid *Irian niet nodig* rather than the Indonesian *Irian tidak perlu* or even the Dutch *Nieuw-Guinea niet nodig* to pillory the mestizo Dutch-mindedness of Hatta and his anti-Communist associates. In other cases, the meaning is more obscure. In cartoon 2f, for example, Sjafrudin is depicted as a donkey. To understand the point of the cartoon, one almost has to know the European stereotype of the donkey, and the use in Dutch and English of *ezel* or "ass" to describe stupidity and obstinacy. For the animal itself is rarely found in Indonesia, and the Indonesian word for donkey, *keledai,* seems only recently, under Dutch influence, to have acquired such connotations. How far is Sibarani aware of how European this cartoon's point has become? In cartoon 2g, he clearly uses the theme of crucifixion and resurrection in a quite unself-conscious manner: Christian symbols have become fully assimilated into the contemporary

---

the political elite. A notable example is Sukarno 1963. See also Parlindungan 1964. One of the most effective instruments of the psychological warfare campaign waged against the Left after the 1965 "coup" was the coining of the acronym GESTAPU (from Gerakan Tiga Puluh September, September 30th Movement), which linked the coup conspirators with the cruelty of the Gestapo.

style and identity of Toba Batak like himself. On the other hand, in numerous cartoons not reproduced here, Sibarani deftly uses scenes from Western Westerns playing in Jakarta movie-houses to satirize Western imperialist intrigues and menaces. One gets the strong impression that this ambiguous jousting with foreign signs and symbols shows Sibarani precisely as a "nationalist" – a man who sees the nation as an *enterprise*. For such men, defining what is national can only be a complex project of juxtapositions and separations between the "foreign" and the "indigenous."[12]

This judgment is reinforced by the "national" quality of Sibarani's work. If the landscape of his cartoons is dark and threatening, it is nonetheless a national landscape peopled by national figures. Murder is done in Ladang Lawas in rural West Sumatra, but Ladang Lawas appears as a place in the moral-political geography of Indonesia, not of Sumatra and not of Alam Minangkabau. Eisenhower stands at the gates of both New York and Jakarta. Dulles's mishap is caused by the tree of the entire Indonesian people. Irian is "nodig." And names are named – men who, if they acted on provincial and local stages, nonetheless drew their significance for Sibarani from the parts they played in the national drama. They are named, not simply because Sibarani wanted, and dared, to do so, but because names assign responsibility, reveal reality, and place cartoonist, reader, and target in a clear relationship in political space. This in turn is linked to the presence of the cartoonist himself. He never appears in his own cartoons, rather it is as if he stood beside or behind them, proffering them to his readers with index finger pointed. The significance of this posture will only become clear, however, when contrasted with the role that Hidajat plays with respect to his cartoons.

If Hidajat's work seems so different from Sibarani's, it may be tempting to attribute this to differences in ancestry and genre. Hidajat's forms appear to derive from a comic strip tradition going back at least as far as the Japanese occupation. The comic strip genre has its own conventions to which Hidajat strictly adheres: the strip explores situations and actions where the cartoon "summarizes" a condition.[13] Rather than elaborating on space to explore meaning, the strip moves rapidly through time toward a denouement. The printed word is "in the picture" and carries the movement of the strip, only rarely performing an iconographic function. In part, then, one can perhaps account for the rudimentary drawing, the absence of landscape, and the symbolic poverty in terms of genre conventions – though this does not tell us why the conventions are adopted in the first place. Nor do the conventions help to explain Hidajat's popularity. Even the jokes themselves, good as they usually are, do not adequately account for the strip's success. The interpreter is inclined, therefore, to turn to style and, ultimately, context.

It may be useful to start with the central figure of Hidajat's cartoons – the

---

12. This was a central theme in the intellectual tradition of the prewar *pergerakan*. For a sophisticated treatment, see McVey 1967.

13. There is probably an analogy here with the relationship between editorials and *pojok* (corner columns) in Indonesian newspapers.

long-nosed, canvas-capped, T-shirted Djon Domino. The long nose, a physiog-
nomical rarity among Indonesians, suggests at once an iconographic allusion to
the long-nosed *wayang* clown (*punakawan*) Petruk (see Figure 4).[14] Why this
particular clown figure should have been selected from the wide variety of such
punakawan is a question that will be taken up later on. For the moment what is
important is that, *qua* punakawan, Petruk has a dual role to play. In wayang of
whatever sort, the punakawan appear both as comic characters *within the line* of
the drama, embedded in its space and time, and as mouthpieces for contempo-
raneous satire and criticism directed straight at the audience, so to speak *at right
angles* to the drama and outside its space and time.[15] So here one sees Petruk
playing his part *in the strips,* but there is also, as it were, a *dalang* behind the
paper screen or a player behind the mask. Djon Domino, as Petruk here is
termed, is a rebus that can be deciphered as: Djon equals Johnny (Hidajat) plus
Domino equals mask, or better half-mask.[16] Djon Domino is Hidajat behind his

FIG. 4. Petruk

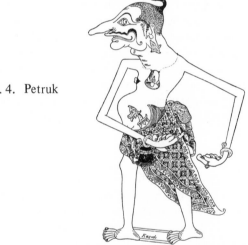

14. This connection is explicitly made in the *Tempo* article cited in footnote 5.

15. This applies to both of the most popular contemporary forms of wayang —
wayang wong and *wayang kulit.* In the older wayang kulit shadow-play, highly stylized and iconographically specialized leather puppets are deployed and vocally
animated by a single puppeteer (*dalang*) seated behind a lighted screen. For much of
the audience the dalang is invisible, yet his personal presence is manifested through
all the puppets, above all through the sallies of the punakawan. In the newer wayang
wong, a stage drama in which the older puppet-roles are taken by human actors, the
punakawan-players wear heavily stylized facial make-up modeled on wayang kulit
iconography and on the wooden masks of the largely obsolescent *topèng* dance
drama. From behind these "masks" the players — often the stars of the troupe —
direct their sardonic, anachronistic asides to the delighted audience.

16. Domino may also refer to the game of dominoes, very popular with
itinerant vendors and other poor people with a lot of time on their hands. In any
case, the accuracy of my rebus interpretation is marginal to the main argument
outlined here.

mask. Yet there are further ambiguities, as befits the relationship between player and mask. Djon Domino appears in the strips dressed identically (it is his iconographically conventionalized *costume* one observes) as singer in a restaurant, roadside lay-about, student, motorcyclist, teacher, and relative of a high government official. These roles have no particular connection with one another — in "real life" they would be, in many cases, mutually exclusive. In an obvious way they are created in the service of particular jokes and satirical observations. But one notes that Djon Domino not only has no clearcut social role or status, but that he has no friends or enemies, even no identifiable associates, unlike many stock characters in American strips. Only his mask links Djon Domino's protean and elusive appearances. It becomes evident that the mask mediates its creator's dalang consciousness.

This relates directly to another half-hidden element of order and continuity in the strips. Almost all of them reveal a symmetrical relationship between Djon Domino and the "target" of his creator's satire. Thus, in cartoon 3*a*, Djon is cadger-petty blackmailer to the embezzling director; in 3*b* he is would-be accomplice to a corrupt official; in 3*c* he is the loser in a cynical game of wits with a prospective father-in-law; in 3*d* he is "masih famili" with the opulent minister; in 3*e* he plays pimp to his girlfriend's prostitute; in 3*f* he pretends shock while egging on the sexually precocious and knowing children. In effect, in almost every strip, Djon appears as a less successful version of the target pilloried, as an accomplice, almost as a hanger-on. The key phrase is "masih famili" — which implies both a kin relationship, but also a subordinate or dependent form of that relationship. This in turn is connected to both the traditional and contemporary meanings of the Petruk-Djon Domino figure.

The punakawan in the wayang drama are servants, followers, and dependents; they follow where their *satria* or other masters lead them. They are both closely intimate with their masters (as it were "masih famili"), and yet permanently consigned to their subordination. They both know their masters completely, and yet are destined to continue serving them. Their jokes are often sly digs at their masters' pretensions, but these digs are without subversive intent: the nature of the wayang world — a world of masters and servants — is not called into question. As we have seen, however, the punakawan also play a direct role vis-à-vis the audience. In traditional milieux, it is precisely subordinate elements among the audience to whom they speak and who appreciate them most: servants, children, women. Indeed, responding to the jokes at all involves, for any member of the audience, an identification, if only temporary, with the subordinate and dominated. Thus, in the performance of wayang, a complex net of intimacies, dependencies, and solidarities is created. And it is the punakawan's iconography that links them all. Hidajat's Domino serves largely the same function. Yet there is one key difference from the wayang world: in even modern forms of the ancient drama, subordination is not complicity. The satria may be laughed at — at the appropriate time — but his moral universe is separate, autonomous, and recognized by punakawan and audiences as such (Anderson 1965). The satria is a different order of man, not just a man of higher power and status.

The punakawan are not and cannot be satria. When they on occasion try, the result is chaos and anarchy. The best-known play (*lakon*) on this theme is *Petruk Dadi Ratu* (Petruk Becomes King), a wild farce in which Petruk "masks" himself as a king, holds temporary sway, causes tremendous comic disorder, and is finally "unmasked" (resumes his mask) — at which point the drama closes in renewed serenity and order. But in modern times the words "Petruk Dadi Ratu" have become a proverbial commonplace to describe real social and political conditions of disorder, corruption, and black farce.[17] One might be inclined to view Hidajat's strips as a variant on this theme: Each authority figure that appears could be seen as a Petruk playing a role that is not in him. But a closer look at the universe of the cartoons suggests that their theme may rather be "Ratu Dadi Petruk," an idea unimaginable in the traditional world. Moral statuses are indistinct, everyone is a clown, and subordinate and master are linked not in complementarity but complicity. Petruk is not unmasked in each denouement, rather it is the king.[18]

Another stylistic element in Hidajat's strips which relates both to the Javanese past and the Indonesian present is the use of obscenity; and again the contrast with Sibarani is instructive. Many of Hidajat's cartoons are sexually explicit in a manner inconceivable a few years ago. In part this reflects the fact that in contemporary Jakarta sex and sexual jokes are much more publicly acceptable than hitherto. The nightclub and the "massage parlor" are now well-established institutions of metropolitan life. In Sukarno's day, the one arena where sex and sexual jokes were publicly permitted was the traditional theater, whether wayang, *ludruk,* or *ketoprak.* In wayang, at least, they were above all the province of the punakawan.[19] It is therefore not surprising, if one accepts Djon

17. There are comparable lakon about other punakawan becoming king — all in the same vein. But none has the popularity of Petruk's temporary elevation. One suspects that the answer to the question of why Hidajat picked Petruk as the model for Djon Domino lies precisely in his peculiar proverbial association with disorder and reversal.

18. It would be interesting to learn more about the way in which the phrase "Petruk Dadi Ratu" began to acquire new political meanings. Traditional usage refers to a temporary period of disorder, after which Petruk and ratu return to well-defined complementary roles and statuses. Petruk is well and good — *in his place.* During the Revolution, one finds instances of a sharp shift in meaning. In *Penghela Rakjat,* May 9, 1947, for example, the prominent pro-Dutch Sundanese collaborator Kartalegawa is denounced as a Petruk Dadi Ratu. But now the implications are that there is no correct stable role to which Kartalegawa could return. He can neither be a true Petruk in the old sense, nor a real ratu. Ratu-ship has lost its meaning, become hollowed out: It is an empty title conferred as a reward for puppetry and collaboration. A further irony is that everyone knows that Kartalegawa in fact comes from the Sundanese upper (as it were satria) class from which traditional ratu were drawn. So we have a ratu who behaves like a clown but who is pretending to be a ratu. The nexus with traditional usage lies only in the continuity of the idea of disorder, which now, however, is sinister rather than comic. In Hidajat's cartoon world the implications of the *Penghela Rakjat* article have been pushed even further. The Petruk have multiplied to become the permanent norm rather than the temporary and pilloried exception. There are no ratu left or possible.

19. To the disgust of some traditionalists, this has been slowly changing in the commercial wayang wong. One finds satria-class women, such as Banowati and Srikandi, occasionally engaging in sexual banter and risqué jokes.

Domino as Petruk, to find Hidajat's strips a natural outlet for such jokes. But the style of the jokes and the context in which they are made suggest new meanings for such humor.

One of the odd, yet logical aspects of sexuality in wayang is its rigid social stratification. Though sexual gossip in traditionalist areas of Java focuses continually on cross-status sex (masters sleeping with servants, aristocrats with prostitutes, officials with actors), on-stage sexual relations are confined within status groups — or at least the servant-master (punakawan-satria) separation is rigidly maintained. Aristocrats mate with aristocrats, servants with servants. Demons and giants are often shown lusting after aristocratic women, to the audience's great amusement, but with a few very special exceptions, they never succeed in getting them. This *sexual invulnerability* is an important element in the prestige of the satria group, both in itself and because in some respects it is a sign of self-control and thus of power (Anderson 1972a: 9-10, 27). In Hidajat's strips, by contrast, no one is "invulnerable." In 3c, sex is a matter of commercial bargaining between Djon and his prospective father-in-law; in 3e Djon and Ida are both lovers and pimp-and-whore-in-the-making; in 3f teacher Djon eggs on his pupils to answer questions with sexual repartee. It seems clear that sex is being used here not to make separations, or to show the complementarity of opposites, but to reveal vulnerabilities and complicities. Lovers, teachers, and fathers-in-law are "just like everyone else." Gossip has become form.

Sex as such is largely absent from Sibarani's cartoons, but he uses obscenity for his own very different purposes. Cartoon 2b is a good example of this. It has none of Sibarani's typical chiaroscuro, perhaps because the artist is here dealing not with the nature of particular men or specific events, but rather with a basic social condition. The plain penlines have almost the character of a diagram or equation rather than of an emblem or icon. The second half of the cartoon's theme is well described by *New York Times* correspondent James Sterba as follows:

> The people in the *kampong* ... along the canal ... make their living by picking through the trash bins of the wealthy residents of Menteng, Jakarta's prosperous residential section, which begins on the other side of the railroad tracks. Everything of value is taken from the bins, mostly at night or in the early morning hours, just after the trash is thrown away by maids and houseboys. The salvage is carted in baskets back to the canal for sorting and sale. Most of the dirt-floor shacks are made of cardboard picked from trash. Five soft-drink or beer cans are worth a penny. Broken glass and broken dishes bring a cent a kilogram ... as do old bones. Assorted broken plastic sells for four cents a kilogram. Unbroken bottles, all reusable, can bring from half a cent to a nickel, depending on the size and color; clear white glass is worth more than green or brown. A quart beer bottle, a small treasure, is worth a nickel. An average trash picker makes about 100 Rupiahs, or 25 cents a day ... [*New York Times*, March 20, 1973].

The first half of the cartoon's theme depicts a symmetrical relationship between powerful foreign capitalists (wealthy foreigners in general) and a dependent, parasitic Indonesian urban middle class. The metaphor of coprophagy is used to bring out the humiliation Sibarani saw in the political and economic relationships prevailing in Indonesia at the time. Obscenity is a way of talking about domination and subordination. Thus, whereas Hidajat uses sexual imagery to describe intimacy and complicity, Sibarani employs excrement to depict alienation and degradation. (Only the foreign capitalists "eat no shit.")

Lastly, the question of locale. There is no landscape in Hidajat's pictures. The empty white space recalls the cotton *kelir* (screen) against which the wayang lakon are played out. Nonetheless, just as the kelir encloses and delimits a world, the universe of wayang, so Hidajat's strips define a particular milieu, that of Jakarta in the early 1970s. This is not Old Jakarta, the colonial city whose Indonesian population was largely composed of pious Muslim *orang Betawi,* but the new city that grew up after independence, dominated by migrants from all over Indonesia, and particularly from the Javanese hinterland. Language and costume make this clear. The speech in Hidajat's balloons is *bahasa Jakarta,* but laced with the Javanisms that the flood of migrants brought to the old metropolitan argot. Djon Domino's prospective father-in-law, with his *surdjan* (*lurik* jacket), *djarik* (wrap-around skirt), and particularly his "egg"-tailed *blangkon* (headcloth) is unmistakably from Jogjakarta, but he speaks in the same bahasa Jakarta as Djon himself. This points up one of the most interesting aspects of Hidajat's strips — their linguistic homogeneity. Whereas Sibarani uses different languages quite self-consciously to build his iconography and to talk in different ways about the national project, Hidajat is consistently monoglot — foreign words almost never appear and all parties use the same "level" of language, the ngoko of bahasa Jakarta. Why this should be so is not altogether clear. It could be argued that Hidajat, a younger man than Sibarani, grew to maturity within what Hildred Geertz has called the "metropolitan superculture of Indonesia"; [20] and that accordingly language is simply less problematic and political a matter than it was for Sibarani (see Anderson 1966: 105-16). Or, in different words, that national-ness for Hidajat is no longer a self-conscious project but a received reality. Although this may well be true, it also seems plausible to see the use of the bahasa Jakarta in the strips as analogous to the use of sex. Both are devices for talking about the contemporary relationship between ruler and ruled (or at least a certain segment of the ruled). Just as no one is sexually invulnerable, so no one is linguistically impregnable. Like sexual innuendo, resolute use of the vulgar and familiar bahasa Jakarta points to an acknowledgment of power

20. See H. Geertz 1963: 35-37. She writes, "The Indonesian metropolitan superculture is still in the process of formation, and is at most only two or three generations old.... It is in the areas of political ideology, artistic styles, and material culture that the content of the metropolitan superculture has been most elaborated. The foremost characteristic of the superculture is the colloquial everyday use of the Indonesian language.... The prime external symbols of adherence to the superculture are the acquisition of higher education, facility with foreign languages, travel experience abroad, and Western luxury goods such as automobiles.... It is the intellectual and political elite and the wealthy of the great cities who are bearers of the full metropolitan superculture."

combined with a refusal of any moral status. This in turn ties in with something I shall be returning to at the end of this chapter – why it is that, though Hidajat's Jakarta is being deluged with foreign influences (far more than that of Sibarani), and foreigners are in constant contact with Djon Domino's world of prostitutes, cab drivers, hawkers, students, and so forth, they are so absolutely excluded from the cartoons.

MONUMENTS

In the days of Sukarno's ascendancy under Guided Democracy, Indonesia saw a great deal of monumental construction. Visitors to Jakarta since the early 1960s would find it difficult to overlook the National Monument, the Freedom Monument, the Liberation of West Irian Monument, the Gelora stadium, the Istiqlal mosque, and other more utilitarian structures which have come to dominate the skyline in the city's center. It would be an error, however, to imagine that monument-building was a peculiarity of the Sukarno years. As we shall see, the New Order has in some ways been even more monument-minded, though the type and style of the monuments have changed, and their locations are more widely dispersed. Although the political intent of Sukarno's constructions has often been noted by journalists and scholars, analysis has rarely gone further than formulations of the type "X was a prestige project, designed to impress Indonesians and foreigners with Sukarno's domestic and international political successes," or "Y was essentially a monument symbolizing Indonesia's new-found self-confidence [or lack of confidence]." In effect, the monuments were treated as manipulative devices or as psychological "symptoms": Either way, the approach was purely diagnostic. Few observers have recognized that monuments are a type of *speech*, or tried to discern concretely *what* is being said, why form and content are specifically what they are.

It may be useful to begin a discussion of monumental styles by drawing a schematic contrast between the periods of Guided Democracy and the New Order – in part because the politics of the two periods were very different, but also because certain themes apparent in New Order building were there in embryo under the previous regime, and these themes have something to do with the longer-term transformation of "Indonesian political thinking." In what follows I will be discussing above all nonutilitarian monuments, that is, those in which iconography clearly prevails over functionality.

It is a peculiarity of monuments of this type that, by and large, they face two ways in time. Normally they commemorate events or experiences in the past, but at the same time they are intended, in their all-weather durability, for posterity. Most are expected to outlive their constructors, and so partly take on the aspect of a bequest or testament. This means that monuments are really ways of mediating between particular types of pasts and futures.

Two of the best-known monuments of the Sukarno era stand in the center of Jakarta: the Liberation of West Irian Monument on Lapangan Banteng (see Figure 5) and the National Monument on Medan Merdeka (see Figure 6). The

FIG. 5. West Irian Monument

FIG. 6. Mock-Up of National
           Monument

first consists of a rugged human figure, standing on top of two vertical concrete steles, his arms flung up to the sky, and broken chains at his feet. The style of the figure is "realist," or better "Jogja socialist realist" (see Holt 1967: chap. 9). The National Monument is conceived more abstractly: a tall stele crowned with a sculpted golden flame, implanted in a flat-topped base large enough to contain within it chambers for the exhibition of patriotic reliefs and tableaux as well as certain "national heirlooms." The style of the Irian Monument is both modern and, as it were, "individual." It does not obviously evoke traditional Indonesian monumental art, and the form itself has evidently been created for a specific historical event. The statue symbolizes directly the liberation of the Irianese from Dutch colonial rule.[21] Innovation and uniqueness remind the observer of the final completion of a historic task — the reunification of Indonesia under Indonesian rule — launched more than half a century before. Paradoxically, therefore, novelty of form emphasizes the achievements of the past, but at the same time commemorates a project in which the constructor and his audience all in different ways participated directly (and thus points back to the future they once shared). Even if the modern statuary is mediocre, it nonetheless is a *traditional* monument in the sense that it is part of the real movement of Indonesian history, not a gloss upon it.[22]

The National Monument is more ambiguous in character and seems to foreshadow the monuments of the New Order in some interesting respects. In terms of formal style the monument is mestizo: It borrows from the conventions of European patriotic obelisks, while at the same time evoking the *lingga-yoni* of ancient Javanese art (compare, for example, Kempers 1959: 19 and plate 166; and Holt 1967: plate 18). The lingga-yoni motif was self-consciously chosen (Sukarno reportedly joked that the monument testified both to his own and Indonesia's inexhaustible virility): It was to be "national" because it was "traditional," not, as it were, "traditional" because it was "national." The monument, in fact, commemorates no specific event or achievement but is rather in the nature of a summary of or commentary on the Indonesian past. Thus, the implicit movement of the form lies in the opposite direction to that of the Irian Monument: conventional iconography appears to use the past to express Indonesia's triumphant modernity, but in fact it points backward, in that it is no more than a gloss on that past. To put it another way, whereas the ancient Javanese built lingga-yoni monuments because they meant something *in themselves* (Kempers says they stood for "the Duality . . . which is dissolved into the Supreme Unity or Totality of all existence") and were part of the ancient present and future, Sukarno built his to show that the present Indonesia is connected to the past. The National Monument is thus less part of tradition than a way of claiming it. The lingga-yoni on Medan Merdeka means nothing in itself, but is a sign for "continuity."

The monuments of the New Order exhibit this pattern far more clearly. The most celebrated is the so-called Proyek Miniatur Indonesia Indah (Beautiful Indonesia in Miniature Project), popularly known as "Mini," planned and eventually constructed by the Our Hope Foundation chaired by President Suharto's wife. Whether the initial inspiration for the project came from her March 1970

21. It is thus analogous to the well-known melancholy statue of General Sudirman on Malioboro in Jogjakarta, which commemorates the last heroic years of his life as guerrilla leader in the Revolution.

22. In this respect it resembles the first national monument of the newborn Republic: the stele-cum-plaque erected in 1946 at Pegangsaan Timur 56, Jakarta, to commemorate the proclamation of independence a year earlier (see *Ra'jat,* August 19-20, 1946, for a picture with a descriptive article). What is noticeable about both monuments is that their construction followed very closely in time the event or circumstance that they commemorated. The contrast is striking with the monuments now to be discussed.

visit to Bangkok (where an analogous project, Timland, had already been completed) (*Tempo*, June 5, 1971) or from the contemporary vogue for beautification work by presidential wives, as described to the public in the fall of 1971, Mini was to consist of a fenced-in 100-hectare compound containing an 8-hectare artificial lake in which little islands representing the archipelago would be placed. In addition, there would be twenty-six *adat* (traditional) houses from each of Indonesia's twenty-six provinces (1 hectare apiece), a 1,000-room tourist hotel, an imitation waterfall, a cable car, a revolving and an outdoor theater, and so forth (*Tempo*, November 27, 1971). The adat houses would contain appropriate handicrafts from the various regions.

For reasons which need not detain us here, Mini was unpopular from the start, causing a wave of student protests in a number of cities and some strongly critical editorials in the metropolitan press.[23] The controversy, however, did have the effect of goading the project's sponsors into clarifying the purposes of their undertaking. Speaking to the Working Conference of Provincial Governors on December 1, 1971, Mrs. Suharto urged them to contribute financially to the project on the grounds that it would serve to "project" their regional cultures onto the Jakarta stage for the international tourist. But she also went on to say that "if, in the olden days, our ancestors worked cooperatively together [*bergotong-royong*] to create the Borobudur, which now commands the attention of the whole world [it is not clear whether this reference was to the Borobudur's beauty or its disastrous state of disrepair], today we too can work cooperatively to build the Beautiful Indonesia in Miniature Project" (*Sinar Harapan*, December 1, 1971). In response to what she felt was intemperate criticism, the president's wife told reporters on December 15,

> Whatever happens, I won't retreat an inch! This project must go through! Its implementation won't retreat a single step! For this project is not a prestige project — some of its purposes are to be of service to the People. The timing of its construction is also just right — so long as I'm alive — for someone's conception cannot possibly be carried out by someone else, only by the conceiver herself — unless I am summoned by God in the meantime![24]

The opposition continued, however, and the head of state was finally forced to take matters in hand. In the well-known "PERTAMINA" speech of

23. As early as May 1971 some of the people who had been evicted to make room for the project complained to the Lembaga Bantuan Hukum (Legal Aid Institute) that they were being compelled to sell their land to Our Hope at prices less than half their real market value and that the land they were being given in compensation was of much lower quality (for details, see *Tempo,* May 20, 1971). The student protests began on December 16, 1971, in Jakarta, spread to Bandung by December 23 and to Jogjakarta by December 28 (for details see *Sinar Harapan,* December 16, 22, and 28, 1971).

24. *Harian Kami,* December 16, 1971. It was in this context that Ms. Suharto used the Javanese term *mumpung,* which has subsequently become something of a byword in Indonesian political parlance. Mumpung means, more or less, "so long as I have the opportunity." For more on mumpung, see footnote 36.

January 6, 1972, he said; "Quite frankly, I'll deal with them! No matter who they are! Anyone who refuses to understand this warning, frankly I'll deal with them! If they go on making trouble, it's no problem for me! I'll use SUPER-SEMAR!"[25] He went on to reveal that the project was intended to make Indonesia known to tourists and to raise national consciousness. As he put it, since there were so few remains of Madjapahit and Sriwidjaja, new things were needed to raise national consciousness and pride.

To get a fuller sense of the meaning of Mini, it may be useful to look at some other New Order monuments, noting for the moment only the way the president and his wife linked it to the glories of the ancient Indonesian past. The traveler returning to East Java in recent years will have been struck by the extraordinary proliferation of monuments in that region, which, not wholly coincidentally, contains the surviving ruins of Madjapahit. These constructions take a variety of shapes. One finds, for example, on the outskirts of Ponorogo, a large concrete replica of a major temple in the Panataran complex near Blitar (for the "original," see Kempers 1959: plates 271 and 274; and Holt 1967: plate 65). The main entranceways to the town of Tulungagung are flanked by yellow-painted guardian *raksasa*, reduced versions of the great statues that guard the gateway to Tjandi Singhasari, and similar to the little giant-demons found at the entrances of royal palaces of Central Java (Kempers 1959: plate 239). Across the main road leading into the mountain resort of Selecta a permanent archway has been constructed, consisting of two "East Java"-style *meru* linked over the motorists' heads by a horizontal cat's cradle of metal trellis-work (see Figure 8).[26] And in countless villages along the highways throughout the province the eye is caught by strange new portals at village entrances and in front of the doors of the more prosperous wayside houses: strange, because they consist of man-sized concrete numbers, painted red — 1 and 9 to the left, 4 and 5 to the right (see frontispiece to this chapter, Figure 1).

The cumulative effect of these innumerable constructions is impressive: They represent a sustained program of monument construction and distribution far surpassing the efforts of the Sukarno years, and possibly without precedent in Indonesian history since precolonial times. Yet one asks oneself, why these forms? What is being said? One notes, first of all, that many of the monuments appear at first sight to be replicas of ancient ruins. But closer inspection shows that the ruins are at once copied and not copied. What is typically replicated is the "general shape" of the ruin, so that, as it were, the passerby immediately understands the *reference* ("Of course, the temple at Panataran!"). At the same

25. *Harian Kami,* January 7, 1972. SUPERSEMAR is an acronym for Surat Perintah Sebelas Maret (Order of March 11), the document signed by Sukarno on March 11, 1966, transferring all executive authority to the then General Suharto. The acronym is also a *wayang rebus*: super = super, Semar is the all-powerful senior punakawan and elder brother of Batara Guru (Shiva).

26. Holt 1967; see Figure 7 for a Madjapahit period meru portal (at Trawulan). The emblem of the East Javanese Brawijaja army division consists of this type of meru with a star on top. (Most of the East Java construction has been done under its auspices.)

FIG. 7. Sketch of Tjandi Sumberdjati,
Fourteenth-Century Burial
Temple
(Photo: Claire Holt)

FIG. 8. Gateway at Selecta

time, though funds were clearly not lacking for the program of construction and East Java has no lack of talented artisans, little attempt has been made to reproduce the gracefully executed reliefs and ornamentation of the ancient model. The workmanship often seems clumsy and hurried. The replicas begin to look more like signposts than reproductions. And indeed, as we shall see, in a way they are.

Another interesting monument, in the same vein, is the Tegalrejo complex under construction outside Jogjakarta. The site is believed to have been that of Pangeran Diponegoro's *puri* (palace/quarters) during the Java War (1825-1830), though all that survives seems to be a blasted mangosteen tree. Inaugurated by General Surono in August 1969 and financed by the Rumpun Diponegoro ("Family" of the Diponegoro Division of Central Java), the monument consists of a large 150-by-60-meter fenced-in compound containing a large *pendapa* (Javanese traditional audience hall) decorated with reliefs of Diponegoro's exploits, two *gamelan* from the Jogjakarta *kraton,* and some antique Japara chairs; a museum; a library; an administrative office; and a mosque. The shape of the structures is traditional — "to stir people's memories of ancient days." A special inscription (*prasasti*) has been put up which reads, "All the members of the Diponegoro Division Family, Inheritors of the Heroic Fighting Spirit of Pangeran Diponegoro, have built this Diponegoro Monument on the site of the Pangeran's former puri in order to venerate and record the Fighting Spirit of the Hero Pangeran Diponegoro for eternity."[27]

One is reminded of the curious episode in which Prince Norodom Sihanouk had a sizable miniature replica of the Bayon constructed and put on display in the national sports stadium at Phnom Penh as part of the celebrations

27. For details, see *Tempo,* February 26, 1972. For all the self-conscious archaism of this inscription, the Rumpun Diponegoro is very much aware of the needs of the times. A guesthouse is to be built behind the *pendapa* for tourists wishing to see performances or to meditate (*njepi*). Plans are afoot for the later construction of a proper modern tourist hotel and a shopping plaza.

There is an interesting comparison to be made with a curious painting done in the mid-1950s by the artist Oesman Effendi, part of a series commissioned for reproduction in Indonesian classrooms to give schoolchildren a picture of the progress of their history. The work shows the Borobudur "as it might once have looked," plastered gleaming white, undamaged, upright, symmetrical, and grand. There are two odd things, however, about the picture. First, the immediate glory of the Borobudur, its incomparable reliefs, are not even blurredly represented. Second, *there are no people at the shrine,* though the painting is supposed to convey to children the actuality of the glorious Shailéndra age. All that one sees, then, is a brilliant, deserted shape: not a re-creation of the past, but a sign for it. That the singular character of this painting is not accidental is demonstrated by others in the series, not painted by Oesman Effendi. The greatness of the seventeenth-century empire of Mataram, for example, is depicted in two works by Trisno Sumardjo and Zaini: One shows the deserted *tomb* of Sénopati in Kuta Gedé, the other the equally deserted *mausoleum* of his grandson Sultan Agung at Imogiri. It is strange enough that glory should be represented by tombs: But these tombs are neither shown as they appear to tourists and pilgrims today, nor depicted in any historically accurate manner. The simplicity, emptiness, and sheen show that what one has here is again a *sign.* Perhaps it is not coincidental that these three "mortuary" artists of the 1950s ended as strong adherents of the New Order in the 1960s. (See Figure 9).

commemorating the fifteenth anniversary of Cambodia's independence, November 9, 1968 (see figure 10). The replica was used for the particular part of the celebrations in which the Royal Khmer Socialist Youth "paid tribute to Samdech 'Father of Independence.' "[28] The Cambodian leader's construction is peculiarly apposite in this context, for the Bayon was constructed by Jayavarman VII to be the center of the city of Angkor, a city which was in its own way a "Mini" of the abode of the gods (Heine-Geldern 1956: 3-4). But Jayavarman, his sculptors, and his architects built their "Mini" from the mind's eye, creating a monument of awesome grandeur and beauty, as it were, "on the model" of an unseen heavenly city. Sihanouk's portable Bayon was not only, then, a "Mini" of a "Mini," but meant something quite different from its model: it was a claim to the national past, not a creative elaboration of it. As in the case of the Indonesian monuments I have been describing, Bayon II is a gloss, produced by a changed consciousness; and in a secondary sense, like the Indonesian monuments, it is an advertisement for the legitimacy of the ruler: a legitimacy, however, conceived less in terms of legal-biological than of cultural genealogy. [29]

We can now return to the Mini project and interpret it as in many ways analogous to Bayon II, Tegalrejo, and the rest. Traditional Javanese, Batak, Minangkabau, or Toraja houses, like Jayavarman's masterpiece, drew their authentic power from their generation in contemporary and living cultures. All were, in a sense, built for the present and the future. Even when they are constructed today, in the landscapes which gave their forms birth, many continue to embody long-standing meanings. The general forms are firmly established, but there are always countless small, personal variations of ornament, texture, and proportion. For the inhabitants and their neighbors they are unproblematic and represent nothing beyond themselves. In other cases, however, these houses are becoming monuments, in the sense that they are no longer lived in, have become museums, or are mechanically reconstructed to advertise the essence of tradition. In Jakarta, Surabaya, Medan, and Makasar, new urban dwellings are being built which provide a clear stylistic link between the *rumah adat* and Mini's "rumah adat." One may find, for example, a successful Minangkabau businessman erecting for himself not a Minangkabau adat house, but rather a "Minangkabau-style" house, identified as such by an adventitious agglomeration of Minangkabau decoration or by an abstracted motif (the typical winged roof, for example). These formal elements enable the owner to signal to his neighbors and passers-by that here lives a successful Minangkabau: Minangkabau by the winged roof, successful by the Dutch colonial, Singapore-modern,

28. See *Kambuja* 45 (December 15, 1968). I am indebted to Mr. Dieter Bartels for this reference.

29. On the Javanese way of using a special type of genealogy as a sign of power, see Anderson 1972*a*: 25-28. In contrast to Western emphasis on genealogical descent as a legal concept, the Javanese stress is on "cultural" linkage. The contemporary variation on this tradition is that, aside from claiming power on the basis of possession of, say, a *kris* that once belonged to Sultan Agung, one constructs a replica of the kris, as a "power-less" sign of power.

FIG. 9. "Barabudur" by Oesman Effendi (Photo: Claire Holt)

FIG. 10. Bayon II (Photo: *Kambuja* 45, December 15, 1968)

or other "modern" living space.[30] Motif in such cases has been wholly separated from function and serves only to communicate a message of Minangkabauity. In the completed Mini all this has gone one step further, for the houses are "pure adat" and *no one lives in them*. Warehouses of regional artifacts, they are in effect icons of ethnicity and Mini as a whole an icon of "Indonesian-ness" generated by the formal juxtaposition of these ethnicities. Its significance is all the more salient, indeed, to the extent that concrete and immediate life is drained from its architectural components. There is nothing more poignant, in a way, than that this sign-for-Indonesia should be located in the living heart of the metropolis where Indonesia is so much in becoming; indeed, that living Indonesians should have been required to make way for Indonesian-ness.

To sum up, then, it seems that a common element in many of the New Order's public monuments lies in a style of "replication," designed to reveal essence and continuity rather than to record existence and change. But to show that this idea need not express itself solely in archaism and replication, one very different monument should be mentioned. This is the Yani Museum, which has been established in memory of the former commander of the Indonesian army who was murdered during the October 1, 1965, Affair. It can hardly be said that the museum is housed in General Yani's well-appointed home, for the museum really is the home, which has been turned into a monument by two contrary types of alterations. First, a few specific mementos of the Affair have been lodged in it: the gun with which the Communist leader, D. N. Aidit, was executed lies in a glass cabinet above Yani's bed; the site where Yani fell has a plaque embedded in the marble flooring; and so forth. Second, almost anything that might have been peculiarly and personally Yani's has been removed. The walls of the house are lined with signed photographs of visiting dignitaries, gifts conferred on Yani on his trips abroad, tokens and insignia of various Indonesian military units, army uniforms, a few conventional Indisch landscapes, some trophies, and so forth. The house is Yani's house, and yet it already has the feeling of a "rumah adat." Yani's life has been almost completely drained away. One would guess nothing of his reputed charm and intelligence, his meteoric career, his conspicuous life-style, or even his habits and beliefs. Though the events commemorated are less than a decade old, and the monument is in every way modern and untraditional in form, one sees the link with the archaism of Tegalrejo: both are *signs for tradition*. One could easily imagine the museum being decorated with a prasasti of its own: "All the members of the Family of the Indonesian Army, Inheritors of the Heroic Fighting Spirit of Achmad Yani have built this Yani Museum on the site of Yani's former *puri* in order to venerate and record the Fighting Spirit of the Hero General Yani for eternity."

30. Compare the discussion of Basque architectural motifs in Parisian suburban housing in Barthes 1972: 124-25. The difference between Paris and Jakarta, however, seems to be that whereas Parisians affect Basqueness without being in any way Basque, in Jakarta it is unlikely that any but Minangkabau would build "Minang-kabau" houses or any but Batak "Batak."

BEQUESTS AND INHERITANCES:
QUESTIONS OF TRADITION

Finally, I turn to the immediate historical interpretation of the style I have been trying to identify. On March 2, 1972, General Djamin Gintings announced to the public, after conferring with the president, that he had received from Suharto some guidelines on how "the spirit and soul of '45 might be passed on to the younger generation."[31] A week later, General Jasin, deputy army chief of staff, revealed that the forthcoming army seminar would discuss the integration of the Army Younger Generation and the Ordinary Younger Generation, to achieve harmony between them and to implant in both a love of country. Thereby the object of "drawing society closer to the armed forces" would be achieved.[32] On March 13 the seminar was convened. Opening the seminar, President Suharto observed that although scientific and technological knowledge could be acquired from abroad, "the source of leadership, character, and determination as a people building its future must continue to be drawn from the history of our own struggle and our own identity." The present grave danger was "indications of an estrangement of the younger generation precisely from the history of the national struggle and the national identity. . . . The consequence is that they tend to orient themselves toward an alien culture, not their own." If this process were not halted, in one generation their own culture and identity would be irretrievably lost. He warned the members of the 1945 Generation to take cognizance of their own actions and style of life and see how far they themselves lived up to their own values. Otherwise, their example would only alienate the young still further. "We need to arm ourselves with the philosophy of devoted service to state and nation taught by Mangkunegoro I in his *Tri Darma*. The first Darma is *rumongso handuwèni* – to feel that one has a share of something which is the property or interest, the property or interest of the state and nation. From this feeling there arises the second Darma – *wadjib mèlu hangrukebi* – meaning to share responsibility for defending and sustaining this common property or interest. To carry out this first and second Darma, a third is needed, in other words, *mulat sariro hangrosowani*, meaning to have the courage constantly to examine ourselves to see how far we have really acted to defend the common property or interest" (*Harian Kami*, March 14, 1972).

Other officers expressed themselves in less philosophical terms. The "army intellectual" General Sajidiman remarked, "The problem is how to convince the younger generation of the truth of the values of '45 as the Generation of '45 is itself convinced." Only during the Revolution, fighting and suffering with the people, realizing that if one deviated from the Pancasila one was destroyed, did his generation truly understand the truth of these values. General Darjatmo

31. *Harian Kami*, March 3, 1972. Gintings was a prominent leader of the so-called Musyawarah Angkatan '45 (Consultative Council of the 1945 Generation), formed in the Guided Democracy period to bring together veterans of the revolution of 1945.
32. *Harian Kami*, March 10, 1972. It was specified that the seminar would be attended by about five hundred people, including army chiefs, alumni of the Army Staff and Command College, some civilian intellectuals, but no "*pejuang diluar ABRI*" (freedom-fighters outside the Indonesian armed forces).

observed that the values of 1945 were "steadfastness of heart to struggle for the interests of the people, an unconquerable spirit, the basic principles contained in the prologue to the 1945 constitution and the Pancasila . . . all of these values infuse the New Order at the present time." Finally, General Sumitro spoke directly to the younger generation in the following terms: "There is no good reason why the younger generation should not have full confidence in the older generation, for the older generation *has bequeathed to them its doctrines*, which are the products of its experience, although the younger generation will always have the right to test the truth of these doctrines in institutions of education."[33]

Old themes undoubtedly, at least at first sight. Suharto is not the first leader tó quote Javanese adages, or Sumitro a pioneer in transforming values into *doktrin*. One recalls Sukarno appealing to Indonesians to "return to our Revolution," to go back to the "track of our Revolution," and "never abandon history." But there is also an obvious difference. Sukarno made his appeals to people who had been "in the Revolution," had once been on its "track" and had "made history." He spoke to the memories and conscience of a community which had *shared* a climactic historical experience, but which, as he saw it, had allowed itself to become divided, corrupted, and demoralized. Suharto and his generals, however, are more and more speaking to groups who do not share that experience, except in the most tangential way. The links are now less those of a shared political enterprise than those of kinship, in all its ambiguity. Hence, a new language of "inheritance" and "bequest."

Kinship, however, is thought of and used in two different ways. In one sense, it is a metaphor for the overall relationship between generations in Indonesian history, and for what links the present to the Revolution.[34] Whatever conflicts may exist between old and young in Indonesia, all the same they are conflicts "within the family," as the concept of generation in itself implies. Young and old, rulers and opposition, are "masih famili," as Djon Domino would put it. In another sense, kinship has a more direct sociological significance. Only a very small, urban, and privileged minority of Indonesian youth can

33. *Harian Kami,* March 16, 1972. Italics added. Not all of the seminar participants seem to have shared Sumitro's self-satisfaction. Shortly afterward, General A. H. Nasution was quoted as saying that at the Bandung Commanders' Call (a meeting of territorial commanders which immediately preceded the seminar) he had observed many generals whose bellies protruded above the tables at which they were sitting. "When I was army chief of staff, this sort of thing never occurred" (*Indonesia Raya*, March 28, 1972). Nasution was chief of staff, 1950-1952 and 1955-1962.

34. It has long been a tradition to periodize Indonesian political and cultural history by generation. There is a rough correspondence between the political sequence Angkatan '28 (the year of the celebrated Oath of Youth), Angkatan '45 (the year of the proclamation of independence), Angkatan '66 (the year of Sukarno's overthrow) and Pudjangga Baru (writers of the 1930s), Angkatan '45 (writers of the Japanese occupation and revolutionary years), Angkatan '66 (writers of the post-revolutionary years). There are a number of interesting polemical pieces on this theme, particularly in the literary field (where divisions by generation are especially problematic). For some articles on the controversy surrounding the concept of the Generation of '66, see Jassin 1966; Hoerip 1966; Hamidjaja 1967; Djoko Pradopo 1967.

reasonably be regarded as so oriented to foreign culture as to be in danger of losing "its culture and identity." And this minority is largely composed of the extended families of Indonesia's contemporary power-holders. In many ways, then, the generals are speaking to their own children within an all-Indonesian symbology.

For there is a real and painful paradox in the position of Indonesia's rulers. They wield vast power over the political life of the nation, but find the culture, morals, and values of their younger kinfolk increasingly out of their control.[35] There is a prevailing feeling that established values are rapidly disappearing in certain youth circles. This is less a matter of such *causes célèbres* as the Sum Kuning gang-rape case (which involved children of the Jogjakarta elite and was therefore never properly cleared up) than of general style. Two scandalous episodes may serve to illustrate this concern. In Surabaya the 1972 New Year celebrations were the occasion for holding a contest to select a "king" and "queen" of freaks (*orang eksentrik*). The competition seems to have been fierce. All kinds of outré clothes were displayed; some youths simulated sexual intercourse with a group of young transvestites; and a certain Udjang went so far as to strip nude and exhibit himself before the crowd (see Figure 11). The irony of the episode lay in the choice of the arena for the contest: Tambaksari Stadium, entitled Flaming Spirit of November 10, in memory of the tragic and heroic battle of the Surabayans against the British, which opened on November 10, 1945 (see *Tempo,* January 29, 1972). The second scandal occurred in May 1972 in Jogjakarta, traditionally a conservative and respectable center of Javanese culture (compare Figure 12), the Revolutionary capital between 1946 and 1949, and President Suharto's place of provenance. The authorities had given permission for eight local bands to perform on a local football field. When these bands finally wished to pack up and go home, the audience protested violently. As the national weekly *Tempo* described it,

> Buttons were torn open. People pushed forward to the dais. One boy climbed the collapsible ladder by the stage, exposed his genitals and rubbed them against the metal. Another opened his underpants and caressed "himself" openly before the public. Another leapt onto the dais and began kissing the drummer who was wearing half-female costume. It was then that the police made their appearance on the stage. On the orders [of the police commander], the performance was then closed [*Tempo,* May 20, 1972].

What was scandalous here, of course, was the public display of sexuality by upper- or middle-class people, not their private sexual behavior (about which traditional Java has generally been tolerant).

35. People in Jakarta frequently comment on how few children of well-known *pejuang* have "*jadi orang*" (made respectable careers for themselves). They shake their heads at the numbers who have become bandleaders, fashion models, criminals, tourist agents, PR-men, call-girls, and what not. The facts are usually attributed to parental spoiling or to the great opportunities for social mobility which independence has offered, such that "outsiders" have been able to reach the positions that these children would have inherited automatically in an earlier age. There is probably an element of truth in both suggestions.

FIG. 11. Udjang (Photo: *Tempo*,
January 29, 1972)

Such events suggest to Indonesia's rulers that the future threatens to elude them and so the past is summoned to their aid. Most of them are deeply aware of the far journey they have made in their lives from the rural townships of late colonial Java to the metropolitan opulence of the "cosmopolitan" Jakarta they now enjoy. Given this abrupt, almost fortuitous transition, it is not surprising that their present power at times feels adventitious. In part, this is the basis for that mumpung psychology to which I have previously referred.[36] (Another part, as can be seen from Ms. Suharto's remarks, is middle-aged intimations of mortality.) But there is more to it than adventitiousness of power. Their past has also not prepared them morally for the lives that they now lead. Most of them grew up in the sphere of provincial Javanese society, and the norms and values of that society have left powerful residues at the core of their consciousness. For such provincials tags drawn from the *Tri Darma* or from Mangkunegoro IV's *Tripama* do represent the real and solid basis of Javanese tradition. When Suharto quotes Mangkunegoro I, his words are not a gloss on tradition, like Mini, but a real expression of it. Furthermore, for most of the men and women of Suharto's political generation, the Revolution of 1945 *was* a profound moral experience and a creative act of fundamental value. The egalitarian solidarity to

36. It is instructive to read a section of the defense speech of senior PKI leader Sudisman before the Extraordinary Military Tribunal on July 21, 1967: "To make us conscious of our limitations and keep our feet on the ground, we Javanese use the phrase *odjo dumèh* – a phrase I find very hard to translate exactly into Indonesian. If one analyzes why this should be so, it is because people who *dumèh kuasa* or 'let power go to their heads' are usually politely warned with the words 'odjo dumèh' " (Sudisman 1975: 14). *Dumèh* is very close to mumpung: thus dumèh kuasa means "just because (I) happen to have the power"; and odja dumèh "don't, just because you happen to (have the power) . . .".

FIG. 12. The youthful Sultan Hamengku-
         buwono IX of Jogjakarta (Photo:
         Tempo, December 11, 1971)

which General Sajidiman referred at the army seminar was not a rhetorical fiction, but was a basic element of the revolutionary ethos (Anderson 1972: chaps. 2, 3, 7, 8, 15). Yet that experience is now a quarter of a century in the past; General Sajidiman and his colleagues now live in opulence far away from the people. At the same time, little in their postrevolutionary experience has allowed for the creation of a new moral stance which would permit them to deal with their present circumstances with inner tranquility. *Pembangunan* (development) has no more than instrumental implications, and derives whatever moral thrust it has from the revolutionary ethos of the past. Accordingly, the contrast between circumstance and ethos has led to the congealing of the values of 1945 into the Doktrin of the Values of 1945; Pancasila Democracy and Pancasila Economy, phrases which evoke the memory of Sukarno's historic 1945 speech proclaiming the moral basis of the independent Indonesian state, are doktrin too, icons attesting to the coherence of present and past, or the life of the past in the present, though they are experienced by many as their fundamental negation — military authoritarianism and an economy subjected to foreign capital.

Their children, however, have grown up in the sphere where their fathers' journeys ended. They are not provincials come to the metropolis, but natural denizens of the new urban centers. The lives they observe and lead themselves are not clearly linked to the ethos either of the Revolution or of *Tri Darma*. For them the moral tensions which underlie their parents' lives — Pancasila life versus Pancasila doktrin, wadjib mèlu hangrukebi versus mumpung — have little meaning. Their link to their parents' generation is less a moral or political link (they have their own city-bred ethos of competition, individualism, self-expression, and so forth) than one of kinship. They are, after all, masih famili. One begins to see part of the meaning of that multitude of scarlet numbers scattered across the East Java countryside. The numbers, in their own way, are like Tegalrejo, the Monumen Nasional, and even Mini — attenuated glosses on historical experience. By a flattening of time, it is almost as if 1945 were as remote as 1830. As the Diponegoro Family is "heir" to Diponegoro, so the younger generation is to be "heir" to the Revolution. The numbers are signs for continuity with tradition.

The motifs outlined here are well delineated in a curious film which had its Jakarta premiere a few weeks after the army seminar closed. *Lewat Tengah Malam* (Past Midnight) is the story of a former pejuang (freedom-fighter) of the revolutionary period, who, disgusted with the corruption and opportunism he sees around him in contemporary Jakarta, becomes a skilled professional burglar. Exploiting the entrée which his revolutionary experience gives him to the fashionable homes of the capital's new rich — he is, as Jakartans say, *binnen* ("in") — he robs their safes and jewelry boxes. Together with faithful comrades from the old days, he uses the loot to establish a productive factory in a poverty-stricken area of rural Java, treating the workers with paternal solicitude and care. Under his managerial alias he wins the loyalty and admiration of the local population by his unselfish efforts to involve them in genuine development. His downfall comes when he falls in love with a beautiful policewoman employed as an undercover agent by his elder brother, an incorruptible commissioner of the metropolitan police. The brothers finally confront each other. Each recognizes the sincerity of the other's motives. The hero agrees to surrender and serve his legally ordained prison term, with the police-agent promising to wait for him in patience.

What is most striking about the film is the counterpoint between its ethos and the movement of the plot. The moral leitmotiv is commitment to pejuang ideals, the ideals of 1945; but the plot *requires* the hero — who is frequently referred to early in the film as a mysterious *bandit intelèk* (intellectual [educated] bandit) — to pretend to be a member of the corrupt and wealthy ruling class by dressing, drinking, driving, and holidaying in a suitably ostentatious and luxurious manner. (If the hero pretends to be decadently corrupt in order to fool his victims, the policewoman also pretends to be a liberated woman of high fashion in order to fool the hero!) The hero's basic concern for the welfare of the people is thus consistently juxtaposed to his mod clothes and sleek sports-cars. Only his melancholy expression signifies his real values, and is thereby a genuine mask of the traditional sort. On the other hand, if the contemporary situation makes the product of the bandit's robberies a development project, the moral impulse is not so much a drive to achieve "accelerated modernization," but rather a continuation of the spirit of '45. The characters in the bandit's group even ruminate on the Sajidiman theme of the pejuang's dependence on the people in the Revolution and the need to repay the moral debt thereby incurred. Beyond that, another typical "traditional" theme is sounded in a romantic flashback in which the hero recalls his village boyhood, remembering himself splashing carefree in the ponds and running through the shimmering ricefields. It is no coincidence that this flashback occurs to the hero while he is on holiday in Bali, staying at a luxurious beach hotel with the undercover policewoman.

Finally, one notes the recurrence of the kinship motif. Burglar and police commissioner are, after all, real brothers. The tie that links them is that of family. But the hero's success in his criminal profession also depends on his close social ties with Jakarta's nouveaux riches. He can steal from them with impunity because he is invited to their parties. So to speak, he is "masih famili".[37] Paradoxically, the link between kinship and 1945 is crime-*cum*-development. It is as if the film were saying, "Yes, indeed, there are many rich and ostentatious ex-pejuang in Jakarta, and yes, there is a lot of crime in high places, but don't be misled! The old revolutionary and traditional values are still there. Just look at the mask! Watch the development! In any case, be patient, wait and see how it all turns out!"

---

37. Yet the hero has no children, though he must be close to middle age, and has little immediate prospect of having them. The issue of legacies therefore does not arise, perhaps not accidentally.

CONCLUSION

In a way, all the different visual political communications that I have been examining are related to the career, history, and consciousness of what can broadly be termed the "revolutionary generation." In Indonesia today, a major social and cultural turning point is approaching: the passing of this generation. Scarcely a month goes by without the newspapers recording the death of yet another well-known pejuang. The proximate eclipse of this generation, in conjunction with the present absence of dramatic political conflict in Indonesia, makes one reflect on the vast changes that have taken place in the twenty-five years that this generation has dominated the scene. On the social level, one observes the articulation of a fully Indonesian class structure both in the countryside (with the abandonment of land reform and agrarian redistribution since 1965, landlordism and debt bondage have notably increased) and in the larger cities (where a weak but visibly prosperous indigenous middle class has emerged).[38] On the political level, power has been concentrated and stabilized in the hands of a moderately unified military elite (McVey 1971, 1972). On the cultural level, a mestizo metropolitan culture has developed and spread, which is no longer adopted but grown up in. This is the reality of what the successors of the "revolutionary generation" will inherit. At the same time, as the 1972 army seminar shows, this is far from what the "revolutionary generation" sees (publicly, at any rate) as its bequests.

The evident discrepancy between such bequests and such inheritances, between history as conceived by legators and history experienced by legatees, brings us back to the cartoonists with whom we started. Sibarani belonged (perhaps still belongs) to the "revolutionary generation." Partly because of his left-wing sympathies, partly because of the period in which he did his best-known work, there is no question in his cartoons of legacies and bequests. Though the drawings are often full of darkness and horror, paradoxically they have an optimistic base. Real conflict was taking place in Indonesian society, and the future was not foreclosed. The promise of 1945, in other words its continuity, was real though it remained to be fulfilled. The Revolution was by no means over. His cartoons were directly political, indeed educational, precisely for this reason. They showed intellectuals who were "really" bandits, not bandits who were "really" intellectuals. The spirit and values of '45 were things to be acted on, not encoded and bequeathed. If his cartoons' impulses came from the past, they pointed directly into the future. They were, to put it another way, quite traditional, in that they were submerged in history rather than glosses on it.

38. Classes are in part defined over time by marriages. The consolidation of a ruling class is typically marked by endogamy. The society pages of the Indonesian press make interesting reading in this regard. "Family" power seems to function socially as economic and bureaucratic power do in the economic and political realms. For indications of increasing class differentiation and oppression in rural areas, especially since 1965, see, for example, Mubyarto 1969; Duester 1971; Franke 1971, 1972; Penny and Singarimbun 1972; Montgomery 1974.

By the middle years of Guided Democracy things had begun to change, and after 1965 the direction of that change was finally determined for the "revolutionary generation." With Sukarno it was still a question of "returning to" the Revolution as a real political act and possibility. Under the New Order, there is nothing to return to, and the spirit of 1945 is less to be acted on than to be bequeathed. Monuments, films, and doktrin attest to this changing consciousness. *Lewat Tengah Malam* is a form for showing that whatever the present is, it is really the past. And the archaism of Mini, Tegalrejo, and the East Java monuments communicates the same message in different ways; essentially, nothing has changed: Diponegoro's spirit, the 1945 spirit, Madjapahit's spirit are always with us. There is no need to return to them, because they are, by definition, here.

In Hidajat, one sees the lineaments of the revolutionary generation's legatees. The white light of his cartoons reveals a fundamental pessimism under the comedy and farce. Nothing in his drawings suggests the possibility of change. The world it encloses is without real conflict, and thus without a force within it which could alter it at all. If older characters appear one would not guess that they are pejuang or even ex-pejuang. The generations are linked together in a homogenous moral bond. Though there is no explicit conflict or argument between generations in his strips, this should not conceal the fact that "no argument" itself distills a fundamental argument. The Revolution, the National Struggle, the Spirit of '45 are not part of real experience or lived tradition and so must now appear as gleaming, depopulated Borobudur at best, or riddling doktrin at worst.

This brings us to a question raised earlier on: How is one to explain the absence of foreigners in Hidajat's cartoons, when Hidajat's Jakarta is so conspicuously filled with their dominating presence? The answer, I think, is that at bottom the foreigners make no difference. Including them in the world of the cartoons would not change its character, but merely extend it further into space. Sibarani drew his Americans because their presence and actions were major contributing elements to the conflict he saw working itself out in his generation in his society. Dulles and Pope were counterposed to the Rakjat; together they represented two fundamentally antagonistic political forces and moral universes. In Hidajat's work, Johnson, Nixon, Kissinger, or better, in keeping with his Jakarta style, local American diplomats and businessmen, can be counterposed to nothing: they would merely be a further ramification of an indefinitely extended *famili.*[39] For there are no more kings, only a world of Petruk. What

39. Lest it be thought that this absence is simply a matter of discretion, given the present intimate relationship between Indonesia's rulers and the United States, it should be pointed out that even the enemies of the state — the Communists (domestic, Russian, Chinese, or whatever) — also never appear in the strips, whether in their own form, or in the guise of saboteurs and spies. If the inhabitants of Hidajat's cartoons are aware of the Indonesian government's constant warnings of subversive threats to the world they inhabit, they give no sign of it whatever.

Jakarta is like today is in reality what the world is like: the city is in its own way an authentic "Mini." One discerns here a new perspective — pragmatism it has often been called, though it seems, in Hidajat's work, to be a more complex blend of irony and resignation. What one observes, however, is that with Hidajat, one is back in the flow of history. His work has, in its own way, all of Sibarani's immediacy, and in style and content is thereby just as authentically traditional.

11

Bureaucratic Linkages and Policy-Making in Indonesia: BIMAS Revisited

GARY E. HANSEN

THE ECONOMY OF Java essentially rests on an agricultural base with the large plantation and the small rice farm constituting the basic foci of productive activity.[1] The plantations, a legacy of colonial investment, were largely foreign owned until the late 1950s, when most were nationalized. Although plantation crops, both in diversity and volume, constitute an important component of Java's economy, the small rice-holding sector still remains by far the dominant source of income and employment for most of the island's rural inhabitants. Approximately 65 percent of all households in Java are involved in farming and the 1963 agricultural census revealed that of Java's 10.1 million farmers, 6.25 million were holding an average farm size of a half hectare or less. Current evidence suggests that income from a farm of less than half a hectare is insufficient for meeting basic family needs. But farm size cannot be expanded, as most agricultural land on Java was under cultivation by the turn of this century. For lack of modern technological inputs, the peasant has not been able to expand his production at a pace equal to population growth. Thus, in the past forty years peasant income and welfare have declined to a point where many of the island's 80 million people consume less than a minimal intake of calorie and animal protein.

By the year 2000 another 30 to 40 million people will be added to Java's population, and the most simple prognosis would suggest that in order to make way for these additional numbers measures should be undertaken immediately to increase Java's food supply. Indeed, in the past twenty-five years the Indonesian government has initiated a number of programs to alleviate the food situation on Java. Nevertheless, attempts to increase peasant productivity have met with only partial success, and the rate of progress has been much slower than expected. This essay will examine the issue of rice production from the perspective of policy formulation and administrative execution, with particular

1. Research on the dynamics of agricultural development in Java has been extremely limited. Standard references include Pelzer 1963; C. Geertz 1963; Penny 1969, 1966; Sajogyo 1973; Franke 1972; Bowers 1973; Affif and Timmer 1971; Soen 1968.

concern being directed at the flow of power and communication between the government and the peasant. The analysis will focus primarily on the first five-year plan launched in 1969 with the intent of achieving a Green Revolution on Java by 1974. The Green Revolution campaign has been identified as the BIMAS program, a commonly used word in Indonesia and one that evokes in peasants and officials alike a complex and at times mutually opposing set of images and reactions.[2] Hopefully, this essay will provide some understanding of the BIMAS program and the diverse perceptions and evaluations of its performance in the past five years.

RICE PRODUCTION AND THE GREEN REVOLUTION

Beginning in the early 1950s, it became increasingly difficult to meet consumer demand for rice from domestic production, and with greater frequency the government found itself expending scarce foreign exchange for rice imports from the world market. Various attempts were made to increase rice production, and in 1952 the Kasimo plan was launched with the intention of achieving self-sufficiency in rice production by 1956. An effort was made to promote the distribution of fertilizer and improved seeds, but the plan was abandoned in 1952 when floods damaged a substantial portion of the rice crop on Java. Domestic supplies continued to remain inadequate, and in 1956 the government was compelled to import 824,000 tons of rice, the largest amount in the history of rice imports to Indonesia. In 1959 the government again launched a national campaign to achieve self-sufficiency in rice production, this time by 1962. The distribution of fertilizer and improved seeds was again intensified and a great deal of administrative energy was expended in its implementation. Nevertheless, an excessive period of drought in 1961 brought the program to a halt, and from the years 1961 to 1964 annual rice imports exceeded one million tons.

In 1966 the Suharto government faced the enormous task of trying to rehabilitate an economy devastated by long years of political and economic instability. On Java rice production had failed to increase since 1954, and the government now found itself with no existing rice reserves and no foreign exchange with which to purchase needed imports from the world market. During the next several years a policy of economic retrenchment coupled with massive foreign aid enabled the government to wage a fairly successful effort in maintaining an adequate supply of rice. Nevertheless, its influence over Java's rice economy remained tenuous at best, a fact driven home in 1967 when a substantial decline in harvest yields, occasioned by an excessively long dry season, suddenly forced rice prices up by a margin of 100 percent. These price increases dealt a serious blow to the government's stabilization program, and in the eyes of many this temporary setback seemed to foreshadow a further

2. BIMAS is an acronym meaning "Bimbingan massal" or "mass guidance," and is used to identify the government's program in the distribution of high-yield seeds, fertilizer, and pesticides.

gathering of the clouds. Fluctuations in domestic production, a growing dependency on imports, and a rapidly increasing population, all these forces seemed to be converging on the government with greater force and immediacy, demonstrating in bold relief that, barring some form of drastic action, the country faced a turbulent and uncertain future in meeting its basic food needs.

The growing sense of urgency and concern in finding a solution to Java's rice problem was, in its timing, coincidental with the country's first contact with the high-yielding rice varieties developed at the International Rice Research Institute in Los Banos, Philippines. The superb showing of the new rice technology in other areas of Asia provided a hard-pressed government with what seemed to be foolproof weaponry for attacking what heretofore had been an intractable problem. Thus in 1969 the government mounted with unprecedented determination an ambitious program designed to bring off a Green Revolution in the rice *sawahs* of Java. In many respects the magnitude of this effort was in some measure equivalent to a great leap forward. The first five-year plan was initiated in 1969, and it was stated in no uncertain terms that the government intended to achieve self-sufficiency in rice production by 1974, a goal which would entail raising rice production by over 50 percent from the 1968 base figure. Java, Indonesia's rice bowl, was to bear the full brunt of this campaign, and the rural bureaucracy was set in motion to mobilize farmer support in accepting the new high-yielding varieties (HYVs).

Since its inception in 1969, in any one rice-growing season nearly 25 percent of all farmers on Java have been participants in the government's program, and by 1974, the last year of the five-year plan, practically every farmer in the irrigated regions of Java had had some knowledge or experience with HYVs. Nevertheless, despite an enormous outpouring of energy and resources, the results have been less than expected. By 1974 production had increased by a margin of 20 to 30 percent, a total significantly below the plan target, and Indonesia again found itself having to supplement domestic production with annual imports exceeding one million tons.[3]

In effect, the Green Revolution has turned out to be something less than revolutionary in yielding major production gains, and for many the euphoria of 1968, when it was thought that a once-and-for-all breakthrough could be achieved in rice production, has now faded into a condition of vague discomfort in having to face a persisting and long-term dependency on foreign imports. This mood is associated also with a feeling of disenchantment among some of those who have participated in the program. In the first five-year plan the government staked a great deal of its credibility on pulling off the revolution and was prepared to support this effort with large expenditures of financial and adminis-

---

3. The most accurate data on production increases as a result of the Green Revolution are available in the reports of the Agro-Economic Survey. Their data indicate that HYVs have outperformed (per hectare yields) local varieties by an average of 20 to 30 percent. For a summary of these reports and others, see Hansen 1974.

trative resources. Indeed, most of the programs of the five-year plan were focused either on rice production itself or on the development of those services and infrastructure related to its cultivation. Most members of the rural bureaucracy were forcefully pressed into service in implementing this effort, and likewise peasants were frequently compelled to accept the HYVs. Yet the shortfall in production remains, and not because of an absence of further opportunities for increasing rice production in Java.

The potential of the high-yielding technology has yet to be fully exploited, largely because administrative structures are not performing at a level consistent with the sophistication of the technology itself. Given the timely delivery and the proper mix of production factors (water, seeds, pesticides, and fertilizer), further advances could be made in raising the productivity of the Javanese rice farmer. Nevertheless, major administrative deficiencies still remain in the provision of these resources and in their adaptation to peasant needs. Finally, major obstacles have been encountered in devising strategies and institutional mechanisms for mobilizing peasant support behind the effort to achieve self-sufficiency. This problem transcends the technical issues of rice production and entails an examination of the form or pattern of interaction which structures the relationship between the peasant and the government. More succinctly, a system of power and communication linkages has yet to be worked out which, if effected, would enable both the government and peasant to pursue a mutually satisfactory and productive course of action. The exercise of power and the initiation of communication has been largely a one-way process and at times almost totally preempted by the government. Avenues have not been open that would facilitate the passage of policy-correcting feedback from the farmers to the frequently misinformed planners. This condition reflects the fact that the government has been inclined to place a greater premium on self-sufficiency as the ultimate solution than developing the mixture of incentives and procedures necessary for achieving the solution. As a consequence, they frequently find the peasant in opposition to what seems like, in the perceptions of policy-makers, a rational strategy for improving his welfare.

A typical scenario in the first five-year plan was one of an official acting with determination to implement a program and a peasant either passively resisting or directly aborting his intention. The motives that lie behind peasant opposition to government development efforts are frequently complex, but at times they simply represent an effort to avoid the adverse impact of poorly conceived and inappropriate policies, policies which in fact, when put into application, may be in conflict with their stated objectives. Thus, a typical cycle has been one of introducing a new policy and then discovering after a prolonged period of confusion and peasant resistance that the policy suffers from basic deficiencies; a making of appropriate revisions but then discovering much later that conditions have changed or were never in fact as the government perceived them and that indeed the modified policy was from the beginning off base; the formulation of a new policy and then a repetition of the preceding process. In time, the government may break out of this pattern, but it will be seen that the rice program in the first five-year plan has been both the cause and effect of its perpetuation.

THE BIMAS GOTONG ROJONG CAMPAIGN

In 1969, what seemed like an easy task to some policy-makers, inducing farmers to accept the new HYVs, soon developed into a major bone of contention with peasant and government alike working at cross purposes, and with each perceiving the intent of the other as adverse to its own interest. In that same year the government launched a massive program for distribution of HYVs, fertilizers, and pesticides throughout Java. This program came to be identified as BIMAS Gotong Rojong (or BIMAS GR) and was unique in that it relied in great part on foreign assistance both in the provision of inputs and as well in their distribution at the village level. The Indonesian government engaged in contractual arrangements with a number of large private firms from Europe and Japan, with the companies agreeing to provide predetermined amounts of fertilizers and pesticides and to assist in the logistics of their distribution throughout Java.[4] This mode of operation seemed appealing at that time in that the companies agreed to advance the inputs on short-term credit, thereby alleviating a possible drain on the country's limited supply of foreign exchange. More importantly, the government was not certain that its bureaucratic structures could single-handedly undertake such a vast program. Its past performance in administering projects of more modest scope was less than impressive, and therefore it was anticipated that these deficiencies could be rectified by employing the foreign firms to assist in the distribution of inputs.

In brief the BIMAS GR formula seemed like an easy and quick method for getting under way a major program which, if successful, would hopefully precipitate a breakthrough in rice production. This optimistic vision was soon dispelled, however, as BIMAS GR immediately became a symbol of government inefficiency and coercion, with its name arousing the misgivings and at times the animosity of both peasant and local official alike. To the dismay of many, particularly those in higher levels of government, BIMAS GR became an unwanted and burdensome incumbrance, from which the government had finally to disassociate itself. In June 1970, only a year and a half after its inception, a brief press release conveyed President Suharto's decision to abolish BIMAS GR and to terminate the government's contractural arrangement with the foreign firms.

A postmortem analysis of BIMAS GR would reveal that basic deficiencies in the policy itself and in the manner of its administration accounted for its abrupt demise in 1970 (see Hansen 1973). The magnitude of the program was

4. Contracts were made with the following companies: Ciba (Switzerland), Hoechst (West Germany), Mitsubishi (Japan), and Coopa, a company registered in Europe but with considerable involvement on the part of Indonesian entrepreneurs.

such as to overwhelm local organs of administration. During any one wet season the program covered over one million hectares on Java and thereby entailed organizing approximately two to three million farmers. The extension service, numbering only 2,000 on Java, was unable to provide to such a large number of farmers adequate instruction and supervision on the application of the new technology. Likewise, production inputs frequently arrived late at village sites. It was intended that the farmer would pay for the BIMAS inputs by returning in kind one-sixth of his harvest yield to the government, but the logistics of collecting rice as credit repayment was more than the bureaucracy could handle. Nevertheless, local administrative agencies were compelled to shoulder these burdens just as the farmers were expected to participate in the program. Actual targets on the number of hectares to be included in the program for any one harvest season were negotiated by representatives of the central government with the foreign farms in Jakarta. Targets were then parceled out to the three provinces of Java, with each province dividing up the target among the approximately eighty district (*kabupaten*) governments on Java, and then down the line the district government dividing its targets up among the subdistricts (*kecamatan*), and at the end each village headman (*lurah*) receiving a target obliging him to enroll a certain number of hectares in the program. Although some degree of negotiation in target setting occurred between provincial authorities and the central government, administrative units below the provincial level seldom had an opportunity to participate in this process. Moreover, as the central government was paying the foreign firms for their inputs and services, laxity on the part of the officials in fulfilling their targets was more than frowned on. Regional officials were simply uncompromising when instructing their subordinates to achieve the targets, and subordinates were equally unyielding when mobilizing peasant participation.

In the early days of BIMAS GR, peasants were relatively unconcerned over the fact that the program was forced on them without their consent, for in the final analysis the balance of power was tipped unintentionally in their favor. This apparent advantage emerged from the government's stipulation holding each peasant responsible for handing over one-sixth of his harvest, an amount which according to government calculation would equal the cost of the BIMAS fertilizer, seeds, and pesticides. In practice, however, it became almost impossible to secure compliance with this provision, for the bureaucracy had neither the manpower nor the organizational muscle to undertake the formidable task of verifying yield estimates and then extracting payments from a multitude of small farmers. Again, the critical institutional innovation missing in this situation was a channel for relaying early feedback on policy inadequacy from local officials up through the provincial level to the national planners. As official reports began filtering in from the field, it became apparent that collection rates were falling far short of the anticipated targets. In effect the government was having to foot a large part of the bill for what was to have been a self-financing program. In order to rectify these deficiencies and improve the repayment rate, the government announced in September 1969 that henceforth all peasants would be required to repay the credit in a cash amount at a rate fixed by the government, and presumably equal to the value of one-sixth of the harvest yield.

The decision to alter the repayment schedule from a sliding one-sixth formula to a fixed cash payment spelled doom for the first stage of Indonesia's Green Revolution offensive. In effect, this subtle change in policy constituted a major and abrupt shift in power, with the government rather than the peasant now holding the upper hand, and the modification produced a major change in the peasants' perception of BIMAS GR. Many peasants had been willing to tolerate deficiencies in the policy and administration of this program as long as they were able to exercise control over the amount of repayment. With the changeover to a fixed payment they lost this control, and for many peasants the cost now of participating in the program simply exceeded its benefits. All of the policy and administrative shortcomings which heretofore had remained relatively unimportant now emerged as major issues of contention between the peasantry and the government. Thus, peasants were more prone to express their displeasure over the late delivery of inputs and the fact that the extension service provided little educational assistance in the application of the new technology. More important, discontent was growing over the fact that the peasant had little opportunity to exercise a choice in tailoring the program to meet his own needs. The government's package approach entailed the provision of a standard and fixed input mix, and in kind or amount it frequently fell short of the peasant expectations. And although the preceding problems aroused strong resentment, the peasant's most basic grievance centered on the fact that he had no choice on whether to participate; government officials were making it quite clear that participation was mandatory. Entire villages were simply enrolled, and peasants were expected to queue up and follow instructions in compliance with program directives.

From September 1969 well on into the following year a struggle ensued, with peasants either trying to avoid the program or modify it to meet their own needs, and officialdom trying to hold the line and insisting on peasant participation and compliance with government expectations. That the peasant seemed hedged in on all sides did not preclude his being able to exercise some leverage over local officials, and the same officials were not all that unresponsive in trying to tailor the program to meet peasant needs. In fact, the bureaucracy was sufficiently flexible in allowing peasants to frequently exact concessions and/or exemptions on the finer points of regulatory enforcement. In general, however, officials were unbending in insisting that peasants not resist participating in the program. Civil servants were constrained by instructions from their superiors to achieve the allotted targets, and the usual *perintah halus* or "gentle pressure" was applied in securing the appropriate peasant response. The crass and overt use of force was seldom warranted, for peasants knew that noncompliance would not be looked on with leniency. Either by direct or indirect communication most officials were careful to inform peasants of the risks inherent in any act which could be construed as an outright refusal to participate in the program.

Although peasants were not prepared to mount a direct and overt challenge against BIMAS GR, they were disposed to employ a strategy of passive resistance, a posture which gradually sapped the strength of the bureaucracy, as many officials simply became overextended in trying to fill the void left by peasant indifference and tired of having to single-handedly supervise and manage all the details of an enormously complex program. Indeed, peasants were quick to read these signs and played the situation to their advantage. Thus, by early 1970 there was a growing number of reports concerning unused BIMAS inputs piling up at village sites, of farmers selling their subsidized BIMAS fertilizer to black-market dealers, and finally of delays in securing peasant repayment of BIMAS credits. In part, the peasant could exercise these options because the bureaucracy lacked the manpower and penetration at the village level necessary to effectively hold peasants in line. In addition, rural officials were becoming more inclined to accept peasant noncompliance largely because they were having second thoughts about the efficacy of BIMAS GR.

Growing skepticism within the rural bureaucracy was in part a reaction to the program's excessive administrative burdens and the distasteful aspects of having to browbeat peasants into accepting the inputs. In great part, however, officials were beginning to recognize that despite the best of their intentions and efforts the program still suffered from major administrative shortcomings, and that it frequently produced a negligible and, at times, adverse impact on peasant welfare. Thus, villages were being indiscriminately chosen to participate in the program, even though on closer examination, they lacked proper irrigation and soil conditions. In these situations the HYVs usually performed at a level below the yields attained from traditional varieties. Even in those villages where appropriate irrigation and soil conditions prevailed, inputs frequently would arrive too late for fully maximizing their use, and the government's highly touted aerial spraying of pesticides proved to be a fiasco. With so many more farmers planting at such diverse intervals, it proved impossible to effectively regulate and time the application of pesticides from the air. Thus, pesticides became just one more input or service for which the peasant paid out cash and yet failed to receive an equivalent return in production gains.

Although there appeared to be an emerging coalescence of peasant-civil service sentiment against BIMAS GR, within the formal lines of bureaucratic communication many of these problems remained below the surface. Indeed, the content of informal bureaucratic discussion definitely indicated a basic disenchantment with BIMAS GR, yet most officials were not prepared to convey this in formal and written communication. Nevertheless, informal channels of reporting functioned relatively well in informing most levels of the bureaucracy that the program was in need of basic reform. Initially, some high-level policy-makers were not prepared to give much credence to fragmentary press reports and rumblings in the bureaucracy that BIMAS GR was floundering, and rather doggedly persevered in insisting that "hard evidence" would be needed before making any judgments about the effectiveness of the government's rice program. Acquiring such information, however, proved to be a formidable task. By early 1970 press accounts were indicating that BIMAS GR had failed to significantly increase production and that peasants were opposed to its continuation. Information generated within the bureaucracy was so inconclusive as to neither confirm nor negate these reports. The entire information process seemed to be submerged within a vast web of confusion, with no particular institutional source being able to establish its preeminence as a credible source of information.

By early 1970 the hard evidence, or at least traces to that effect, began to emerge from West Java, thereby lifting the veil of confusion which had shrouded the program since its inception in 1969. West Java is the largest rice-growing area in Java, and in any one season 40 to 50 percent of the BIMAS GR effort was concentrated in this province. Failure or success in West Java would in great part determine the fate of the entire program, and thus considerable pressure was applied from Jakarta to assure that the provincial administration adequately performed its responsibilities. The governor was the object of frequent visits by high-level BIMAS officials and was more than occasionally called on to meet with cabinet ministers in Jakarta.

Nevertheless, despite the watchful eye of the central government and the best efforts by the governor to achieve the assigned BIMAS targets, West Java was unable to bear up under the pressure of having to absorb the major brunt of the government's rice program. By early 1970 it was apparent that the provincial administration was encountering serious difficulties in its implementation of the program. In part West Java's administration was floundering because peasants were more inclined to resist compliance with government regulations. In contrast to the more entrenched and penetrating structures of rural government in East and Central Java, in West Java a less ascendant and more loosely structured bureaucracy has seldom been in a position of holding uncontested sway over a submissive peasantry. Unlike their counterparts in other areas of Java, peasants in West Java have been able to retain more of the traditional vestiges of village autonomy and thereby have been in a much better position to resist and subvert the intrusion of unwanted government programs. BIMAS GR was no exception to this rule. In time it became apparent that rural officials were rapidly losing ground in their effort to win peasant acceptance of the government's rice program. Corruption, the selling of BIMAS fertilizer in the black market, and nonpayment of the BIMAS credits had become common practice in many areas, and officials were inclined with greater frequency to either modify the program to meet peasant needs or provide only token and passive support of its administration. The press in West Java was particularly aggressive in pursuing the program and reporting on cases of maladministration and peasant discontent. These reports enabled members of the district legislative assemblies and the provincial legislative body to assume a more informed stance in their inquiries and criticisms of the bureaucracy, and it also permitted some officials to ease up in their administration of the program when they discovered via the press that their colleagues were taking a more relaxed approach to the problem. In this respect the contribution of the press cannot be overestimated, as it played an extraordinarily critical role in opinion formation among local and provincial elites.

By the spring of 1970 five districts of the twenty-two districts in West Java had decided to completely withdraw from the BIMAS GR program. Such rejection of a major central government development program constituted a course of action which few local officials were willing to initiate, but in the upper echelons of the regional bureaucracy a district head or governor could afford to take such a risk, particularly in case of an unpopular effort like BIMAS GR, where the central government was already under a great deal of pressure to modify or abandon the program. The defection of these districts, mounting press criticism, and growing confusion and dissension within its own bureaucracy, all these events were sufficient to move the central government from a wait-and-see posture. In April 1970 the president and several of his aides journeyed incognito to the rice fields of West and Central Java, where in discussions with peasants they were able to accumulate some hard evidence. Two weeks later it was announced that the president had decided to terminate BIMAS GR.

THE IMPROVED BIMAS PROGRAM
AND THE BUUD MOVEMENT

The second phase of Indonesia's Green Revolution was initiated in the fall of 1970, and a new program entitled Improved BIMAS became the successor to the now infamous BIMAS GR effort. In magnitude, Improved BIMAS was roughly similar to its predecessor, covering in any one season approximately 25 percent of Java's rice farmers. In content, however, the new policy constituted a distinct and basic change in the government's approach to rural development. The most obvious modification was evident in the fact that the foreign firms had been totally removed from the scene, with the government now shouldering the entire range of financial and administrative tasks involved in sustaining its rice program. The second major innovation concerned the government's effort to return to the peasant some degree of decision-making opportunity in the selection and utilization of production inputs. Thus, aerial spraying was abandoned in preference for hand spraying, and the formula for the input package was made more flexible in order to allow the individual peasant an opportunity to combine inputs in a manner consistent with his needs. In brief, whereas the balance of power in the BIMAS GR effort had shifted from one side to the other, with the peasantry initially holding sway and later the government acquiring supremacy, the new program seemed to strike a balance between these extremes. The peasant could exercise some discretion over the contents of the input package, and at the same time the government still imposed certain minimum and maximum constraints in guiding this selection. In theory the new program seemed to accommodate the interests of both parties.

As the Improved BIMAS program evolved, practice seemed to vindicate theory, as peasant and official seemingly operated in a more mutually compatible and responsive manner. There were fewer cases of corruption and the program was less enfettered with bureaucratic regulations. Fertilizer distribution was given over to the private sector, and the government banking system began to streamline the process of dispensing credit to farmers. There were still many cases of administrative inefficiency, with inputs either being undersupplied or arriving late in village sites. Profit margins on fertilizer distribution were by regulation tipped heavily in favor of the importer and wholesaler, and therefore provided little incentive for retailers to improve their sales at the village level. Nevertheless, these deficiencies were offset by the fact that officials were much less prone to commandeer peasant participation. This less coercive approach stemmed from the fact that the block or group credit system had been eliminated and banks were giving out credit on an individual basis, with rather stringent stipulation governing its dispensation. Likewise, local administrative units were under much less pressure to achieve certain allotted targets, although this was not the case in some areas such as East Java, where the administration pressed ahead with an ambitious program insisting that district and subdistrict officials achieve their assigned targets.[5]

Despite the persistence of logistical bottlenecks and an occasional display of heavy-handed administration, the new BIMAS program constituted a definite improvement over BIMAS GR. By early 1972 it seemed that the first skirmish had been won: A growing number of peasants were accepting HYVs, and the government could now turn its attention to some of the more long-term problems associated with the Green Revolution and its impact on peasant welfare. In particular, it was felt that some kind of institutional device would need to be created in order to extend the channels of communication and power downward to the village level. The link between the government and the village was tenuous at best, and in order to fill this vacuum some intermediary structure would need to be introduced with a mandate for performing a major role in village development, but with particular emphasis on improving the inward flow of production inputs to the farmer and the outward flow of his products to the market. It was envisaged that this organization would perform a wide range of tasks including the distribution of credit and fertilizer, the processing and storing of rice and other crops, and finally their transport to nearby market towns.

In response to this perceived need, in 1971 the government set about introducing, on a limited and selective basis, a new organizational structure identified as the BUUD (an Indonesian acronym, the translation rendered as "Badan Usaha Unit Desa" or "village working unit"). This effort usually was confined to one particular subdistrict, an area inhabited by 20,000 to 35,000 people, and entailed the grouping of peasant cooperatives, many of them dormant or nearly inactive, into one subdistrict federation. The subdistrict federation became thereby a BUUD. Control of this organization was supposed

5. In September, 1972, press reports revealed that the governor of East Java had announced his intention of dismissing those lurahs and camats who failed to achieve their BIMAS targets. See *Kompas,* September 18, 1972. The issue of forcing farmers to enter the BIMAS program was discussed at a symposium on agricultural and village development in Jakarta, December 1972. Several of the delegates touched on the fact that too much emphasis was being placed on achieving production targets and that farmers were frequently being forced to plant the high-yield seeds. See *Kompas,* December 2, 1972.

to rest in the hands of farmers themselves, with each member cooperative joining together in appointing a manager and director to preside over BUUD activities. The government moved with caution in the establishment of the BUUDs, and by mid-1972 in any one district one usually could find three to five functioning BUUDs. In accordance with the government's intention these organizations gradually were assuming a major role in the production and marketing of rice. Thus, many of the BUUDs were allowed to purchase modern rice hullers on low-interest credit from government banks. In time they also came to acquire a monopoly hold over the distribution of BIMAS fertilizer. They also were empowered to buy and sell rice in local markets and to act as a purchasing agent in supplying the government's rice stock (see Hadisapoetro 1973).

The initial emphasis on processing and marketing represented an effort by the government to redistribute control over these functions, in the hope that their performance could be accomplished in a manner more consistent with the interest of peasant and government alike. In the past twenty years the government frequently has followed policies, the underlying assumptions of which indicate a basic lack of confidence in private rice trade. Rice millers and traders have been under constant suspicion of unfairly appropriating large profit margins in their purchases from farmers and then accumulating large rice stocks, and thereafter acquiring windfall profits by selling their rice in a market suffering from artificially induced high rice prices. Although there has been little research undertaken to either support or refute government claims against private rice traders, the creation of the BUUD was an obvious effort to make the private sector more competitive and responsive to market forces. Presumably the BUUD, being under the control of the farmer, would buy rice at a fair price. The BUUDs were also tied directly to the government's procurement policy in that if prices fell below a certain minimum floor, the government was willing to advance credit to the BUUDs to buy rice, thereby hopefully preventing prices from falling below the floor. In turn the BUUD was expected to repay the credit by transferring the purchased rice to government stocks. In theory this relationship seemed beneficial to both parties in that the BUUD, with government credit, could assist the farmer in maintaining prices from falling below the floor price, and the government in turn would add to its rice stocks with the BUUD purchases. In practice, however, it was soon to be demonstrated that the government and the BUUDs had much less in common than anticipated, and in fact that their interests sharply diverged in the area of rice procurement.

In mid-1972 the gradual expansion of BUUDs throughout Java was progressing fairly well, and it appeared that the government finally had brought some degree of order and direction to the BIMAS effort, a program which only two years before was deeply mired in a morass of administrative confusion and bureaucratic turmoil. The painful memories of the BIMAS GR debacle had faded, and government officials seemed confident in their capacities to sustain the new BIMAS effort. Indeed, it appeared that the last bend in the road had been rounded and that the government was well into the long road ahead.

The tranquil period of the early 1970s was unfortunately short-lived, and the prevailing sense of confidence was shattered suddenly when in December 1972 the government found itself in the midst of a major rice crisis. An excessively long dry season had reduced the fall harvest, leaving the government and private traders without adequate reserves for carry-over to the spring 1973 harvest. This condition suddenly manifested itself in December 1972 when prices rapidly soared, rising by 100 percent within a few weeks and thereby unleashing a powerful inflationary effect throughout the entire economy. An emergency import program was immediately undertaken, and as with the 1970 BIMAS GR program high-level policy-makers suddenly found themselves totally immersed in the day-to-day tasks of trying to prop up a faltering rice economy. By early 1973 the crisis had been weathered, but at a significant economic cost in the expenditure of foreign exchange for emergency rice imports and at the expense of having to temporarily neglect other major policy concerns of equal and pressing priority. The crisis constituted a setback in the government's development effort and served to dispel any notion that it had gained the upper hand in the long-run task of mastering Java's rice problem.

When called to task because some precautionary measures should have been taken to avert the rice crisis, high-level officials were quick to attribute the problem to unfavorable weather conditions, and yet there was an element of truth in these criticisms in that the rice shortage simply demonstrated how out of touch government was with agricultural conditions in Java.[6] The formal lines of communication within the bureaucracy had failed to reveal any clear signals that such a situation was about to befall the government. Yet the evidence of lower yields was there to be seen, but many officials, seemingly more confident that the situation was in hand, simply ignored these warning signals. This laxity was most notably evident in the indifference with which the government had administered its domestic purchasing policy. In the nine months preceding the crisis, the bureaucracy has been less than resolute in building up reserves from domestic sources and thus, when December came, the government had no recourse but to purchase at much higher prices large volumes of rice from an already food-deficient world market.

Although the government was unprepared to admit to these errors, the lessons from this experience were not to be forgotten. Immediately thereafter, revisions were made in the government's rice program, changes primarily directed at acquiring more control over rice marketing. In this regard the government was relatively satisfied with the performance of the BIMAS program and its contribution in raising rice production. Indeed, there had been a production shortfall, but this was rightly attributed to unfavorable weather rather than to any basic imperfections within the program itself. More importantly it was

6. BULOG, an Indonesian acronym for Biro Urusan Logistik or Bureau of Logistics, is a government agency responsible for the purchasing and storage of domestically acquired and imported rice for government stocks. This agency has long been under criticism and suspicion for intentionally failing to anticipate shortages in the supply of rice and allegedly reaping profits from inflated prices of rice imports and the selling of rice locally.

the government's suspicion that in some measure the rice crisis had been exacerbated by private traders holding back their stocks and riding the crest of rapidly increasing rice prices to gather in windfall profits. The obvious solution to the problem of private sector price manipulation seemed to be one of expanding public sector involvement in rice marketing, and a major move was made in this direction in early 1973. Still smarting from the embarrassment of the December crisis and intent on avoiding any repetition of such a calamitous event, the government launched a major offensive to capture 10 percent of the impending spring rice harvest. In the past the government had established ambitious targets for its domestic rice procurement program, but for lack of tenacity in administration it usually had fallen short by a wide margin of achieving these goals. This time, however, it moved with unprecedented determination to corner its share of the market.

Evidence of the government's resolve in this matter was immediately made clear when it abandoned its usual policy of purchasing rice indirectly through private mills and rather assigned a large portion of the procurement effort over to the BUUDs. The government's procurement policy was essentially tied to a floor price and thus, when rice prices fell below the floor, it was intended the BUUDs would act on behalf of the government in buying rice, thereby maintaining the floor and turning over the procured rice to replenish government stocks. This arrangement was clouded, however, when it became apparent that the government might try to collect the 10 percent goal irrespective of whether prices fell below the floor. Indeed, there was a very real danger that prices would not fall below the floor simply because the government's floor price had remained relatively static since 1970, whereas rice prices had steadily increased over this time. As the harvest began in the spring of 1973, reports indicated that in most instances prices were remaining above the floor and thus, if market forces continued to prevail, it appeared that the government's share in the harvest would be marginal. It soon became apparent, however, that the government intended to replenish its depleted rice reserves and that it would not be put at the beck and call of the market. Rather, the impersonal forces of supply and demand were eschewed, and domestic procurement became a pendant of administrative fiat with decision on the amount and time of purchasing being subject to bureaucratic discretion. In brief, there seemed to be a very real possibility that farmers would be forced to sell to the government 10 percent of the crop at the floor price despite prevailing higher prices in the open market.

What seemed like a possibility in fact became a reality; free market prices did not fall below the floor and yet the government was prepared to commandeer a portion of the peasants' rice on its own terms. It is unclear whether high-level policy-makers were simply unaware of these price differentials and the fact that its procurement program would therefore represent a loss in income for the farmer, or whether they were simply taking the farmer for granted in assuming that out of good will he was prepared to accept the lower government price. It was clear, however, that the government intended to achieve its 10 percent target. Thus each province on Java was assigned a target, and in turn the province divided its target among the districts and on down the line to a point where each village was given its own quota. The BUUD was responsible for collecting a major share of the target, and in practically every subdistrict a BUUD had been established. Although these were frequently just paper organizations, with a village or subdistrict official hastily appointed to oversee its activities, they were expected to collect an amount of rice equal to the quota assigned to the subdistrict.

Once the spring harvest was under way, it became apparent that a major conflict was in the making, as peasants immediately resisted underselling their rice to the BUUD. Local officials were therefore burdened with the predicament of trying to fulfill the expectations of their superiors in the achievement of the assigned targets, and yet having at the same time to face a peasantry steadfastly opposed to the government's policy. There were a number of alternative courses of action which individual officials could employ in resolving this problem, and in any one province there seemed to be a distinct pattern in the manner in which the procurement policy was implemented. These differences in style and form of local administration simply reflected the fact that in regional affairs the authority of the governor is paramount, and the weight of his intentions and expectations generally sets the tone for the entire region. Indeed, in his capacity as governor, wide discretionary powers can be exercised in the interpretation and implementation of central government directives, a feature of his office which enables him to deflect central government policies in a direction consistent with his own interest. This attribute of provincial administration was immediately made evident in the case of the government's procurement policy. Early on in its administration, wide variation began to appear between the provinces with respect to their commitment and compliance with Jakarta's intentions (see *Tempo,* June 9, 1973; Arndt 1973*a*; McCawley 1973; *Kompas,* May 19, 24 and June 11, 1973).

In West Java the governor attempted to blunt the cutting edge of what seemed to be an unrealistic policy, and local officials were encouraged to seek some form of accommodation in avoiding the use of force in acquiring the peasant's rice. Although there were many instances where force was used, it was frequently the case that less coercive measures were applied. Thus, some BUUDs simply bought rice at the higher price, reselling it then to the government for the lower floor price, and thereby having to absorb a significant loss in the price differential. Some BUUDs simply refused to buy rice, whereas others bought lower grades of rice which in quality fell below the government's procurement standards. As a consequence of these practices, collection rates on the government's procurement program ran very low in West Java, and in great part this poor showing can be attributed to the governor's lack of enthusiasm in trying to force compliance with a highly unpopular policy.

In contrast to West Java where local authorities were frequently quite adaptable, in Central and East Java a much more aggressive and unyielding attempt was made in meeting Jakarta's expectations. This was particularly the case in East Java. Unlike his counterpart in West Java where the governor underplayed the procurement effort, in East Java the governor moved in the exact opposite direction, administering the policy with a vigor and forcefulness which far exceeded the intentions of Jakarta. Prior to the harvest the governor raised the procurement target assigned to him by Jakarta and announced that if the target were not achieved, he would resign and his district heads would in turn be expected to do likewise. It appears that the governor's ambitious effort in this regard was in part a reflection of his lack of confidence in the private sector. In the past, government contracts with rice traders to procure rice and maintain the floor price had been only moderately effective, and there were frequent reports that farmers were having to sell their rice at levels below the floor price. Suspicions lingered that traders were deliberately deflating prices and thereby defeating the intent of the government's effort to protect the farmer. In the context of this background it now appears the governor intended to use the new procurement policy to weaken the private sector's hold over rice marketing, and in March 1973 he journeyed through the province meeting with assembled village chiefs and instructed them that the BUUD would now be the only agent permitted to purchase rice from farmers. Private traders would be forbidden to engage in such transactions, and they could buy rice only indirectly from the BUUDs if they would agree in advance to selling a portion of their rice for the government's procurement program. The ramifications of these instructions were profound, for in content they represented an entirely new approach to rice marketing which put the province immediately at odds with Jakarta. The central government had stipulated that except for giving over 10 percent of his harvest to the BUUD, the farmer would be allowed to sell his rice at will in the open market. Forbidding farmers to sell their rice to private traders constituted a direct contravention of these regulations, and in April a meeting of high-level officials in Jakarta resulted in a special directive instructing the governor to comply with central government regulations allowing farmers to sell rice on the free market.

The governor was slow in responding to these instructions and, moreover, the regional bureaucracy had been set in motion with such determination that it was difficult to change course in midstream. As evidence unfolded in the early harvest months of April and May, it became apparent that officials in East Java were prepared to enforce in spirit what already had been stated in fact by the governor. Farmers were pressed to give over 10 percent of their rice to the government's procurement program and when reluctant to do so, military and police authorities were frequently called in to assure their compliance. Likewise, private traders were prevented from buying rice directly from farmers. The administration of this policy occasioned the perpetration of major inequities, as local officials apparently under great pressure to achieve their procurement targets were at times unwavering in burdening the farmer with inordinant and excessive demands. Incidents were reported from villages where for reasons of crop failure peasants were forced to sell property and possessions, and then pay the BUUD a cash amount equal to their 10 percent rice quota. Equally distressing were reports that some peasants were being obliged to sell up to 25 percent of their harvest to the BUUDs at times when the BUUD floor price was only half the free market price. This seems to have occurred in areas where BUUDs were set up after the harvest was well under way, with those farmers who had yet to harvest their crop having to shoulder the entire burden of meeting the BUUD quota.

The fact that the bureaucracy of East Java had a near monopoly hold over all rice transactions constituted an irresistible enticement for some officials to profit from this situation. Thus many officials became just another middle-man, acting as a go-between in the delivery of rice from the farmer to the trader, but from each exacting his own illegal tariff. In time it was found that significant amounts of rice were leaking into the hands of private traders, and as a consequence collections were on the decrease with respect to fulfilling the government's procurement target. In June the central government imposed a ban on the movement of rice between provinces in Java, a policy designed to further discourage private traders from engaging in rice commerce. This policy in turn triggered a series of unanticipated actions in which district and subdistrict heads, realizing that leakages to the free market were growing and thereby reducing their collection rate for the government's procurement program, began to prohibit the flow of rice beyond their territorial jurisdictions.[7] Border check-points were set up and if by chance a trader was found with rice in his possession, he was simply forced to sell at the floor price, a price considerably lower than what he had put out for its purchase.

It was the unexpected emergence of these local trade barriers which broke the back of the government's procurement program. By late June restrictions on local trade were so effective as to considerably reduce the flow of rice to urban markets, a phenomenon which served to further depress prices in oversupplied rural areas and to occasion their sudden and persistent increase in undersupplied cities. Widening price distortions, along with mounting criticism of the government's attempt to burden farmers with mandatory rice deliveries and rapidly accumulating reports that many BUUDs were failing by a wide margin in meeting their quotas (by July the government had succeeded in collecting only 30 percent of its procurement target), all these trends looked ominous and the government was moved to act (*Kompas,* July 26, 1973). In July it was announced that all procurement targets were being abolished. Likewise the government instructed local authorities to lift all barriers to trade and to curb all practices which constrained the farmer from being able to sell his rice in the open market. This major turnabout in policy, a shift welcomed by farmers and many officials alike, was easier said than done, as many local authorities were inclined to simply ignore Jakarta's change in direction and persevere in their attempt to extract rice from an unwilling peasantry. Because of high consumer prices in the cities, it is probable that some local authorities were hesitant to lift trade barriers for fear that the outflow of rice to the cities would leave their

7. Similar incidents occurred during the Sukarno years (1958-1965), when rice shortages prompted local authorities to forbid the export of rice from within their jurisdiction.

areas rice poor. In order to wind down what seemed to be an irreversible drift, several cabinet ministers were assigned to meet with regional officials in reiterating the central government's unequivocal commitment to abolish the old procurement program.

By August 1973 Jakarta seemed to have the situation under control, and as events progressed it seemed that all trends pointed to a decided upturn. The bureaucracy appeared to have BIMAS well in hand, with no major points of dissatisfaction discernible in peasant reactions to its performance, and to the relief of the government, rice production seemed to be recovering from the drought of a year before. No major campaigns were launched, as Jakarta saw fit not to saddle a weary peasantry and officialdom with a major policy change or new program, and the first five-year plan ended its term in March 1974 without further incident. To the comfort of all it seemed like a welcome return to normalcy.

ENDURING PROBLEMS AND THE LIMITS OF ACTION

For policy-makers, rural officials, and peasants alike, the years of the first five-year plan were at times both climactic and confusing, and all have been sobered by the experience. The BIMAS program, an enormous effort involving a large expenditure of resources and conveying the most advanced of modern technology, failed to produce a production miracle on Java. Indeed production has gone up, and yet in 1974 the government had to import rice in amounts which approximate 10 percent of the country's consumer needs, and most of this went to feed Java's inhabitants. As noted in Glassburner's chapter in this book, rising per capita consumption of rice has further heightened the need to increase imports. The failure in achieving a major production breakthrough on Java has prompted the government to look elsewhere, and now the Outer Islands are looming as major candidates for shoring up the country's still distant dream of someday attaining self-sufficiency in rice production. Negotiations have been under way for some time with a number of foreign firms in Japan, the U.S., and elsewhere, to undertake the development and management of large mechanized rice plantations in Sumatra and Sulawesi. These discussions have moved ahead more slowly than anticipated, and it appears that the enormous outlays required for infrastructure development constitute a major obstacle in their progress.[8] The government's turning away from Java represents at least a temporary respite from what has been a prolonged and at times heavy-handed effort to squeeze self-sufficiency from its overtaxed soil. Java always has been considered the country's rice bowl, and this tiny island has had to bear the full brunt of most of the BIMAS program. The development of interisland markets and transport for the exploitation of rice surplus areas in the Outer Islands has been neglected.

8. A contract was signed recently between Brewer Pacific Agronomics, an Hawaii-based firm, and PERTAMINA for the development of a 15,000-hectare mechanized rice plantation near Palembang. Negotiations are nearly completed for a similar venture involving Brewer and Caltex for a rice plantation near Pakanbaru.

Conversely, the government's excessive concern with rice production on Java has led it to neglect the provision of incentives for Javanese farmers to develop a more diversified range of agricultural crops. Ample market opportunities are available in urban Java for fruit and garden vegetables, and the farming of these crops would be much more lucrative than traditional investment in rice sawahs. These opportunities have been neglected largely because rice programs like the BIMAS effort have monopolized the government's attention.

In summary, the turn to the Outer Islands could augur well for Java. Nevertheless, investment plans for the rice plantations have yet to materialize. For the time being, the government is content to ride the crest of its burgeoning oil revenues and will continue to purchase foreign rice imports to make up for deficiencies in domestic supply. Reliance on foreign imports at a time when world food reserves are in short supply could expose Indonesia to the peril of having its external food sources cut off on short notice. Should external import sources suddenly dry up, it is possible that the Javanese peasant will have to again shoulder the yoke of another major campaign to increase domestic supplies. Likewise, the events of the first five-year plan would probably find their repetition in the resumption of an effort to refashion Java's rice economy.

A repeat performance of past events would not be welcomed by many members of the Indonesian bureaucracy. Administration of the government's rice program at times proved to be more than the bureaucracy could handle, and their frequent failure to execute without incident central level directives only served as a frustrating reminder to Jakarta that its exercise of power at the local level was subject to a great many contingencies, and at times its authority seemed to dissipate rapidly as it filtered down the bureaucratic line. Administrative breakdown and failure to acknowledge instructions from above can be attributed to more than mere communication gaps and bureaucratic inertia. What appeared as poor administrative performance was frequently a symptom or smoke screen behind which officials were engaged in adapting policy to local conditions. Indeed, in the final analysis, it was the local official who shouldered the difficult task of trying to secure peasant acceptance of an unpalatable and poorly conceived policy, and he had frequently no recourse but to enforce regulations in an uncompromising manner. Where a governor or district head was prepared to eschew a hard-line approach, then lower officials were in a position to soften and accommodate programs to local conditions. In this respect regional administrative organs have been quite effective in selectively modifying or transforming the policies and intentions of Jakarta. Administrative flexibility, however, really adds up to being a two-edged sword, inviting either a slackening of effort or indiscriminate and headlong plunges ahead. The exercising of either of these options can serve to sabotage the best of Jakarta's programs. Thus, paradoxically, it was West Java's underplaying of Jakarta's efforts which rang down the curtain on BIMAS GR, and it was East Java's overamplification of central level policies which brought a halt to the government's procurement program. Thus, whether by under- or overcommitment, the regional bureaucracy managed to undo a major national program.

For the peasant the experience with the first five-year plan served at times to demonstrate just how vulnerable he is to intrusions or what seems like a capricious and cumbersome bureaucracy. Major programs and campaigns were suddenly announced, and without forewarning the officialdom set in motion obliging the peasant to make the appropriate accommodations on behalf of a presumed contribution to village and national development. Programs came and went in quick succession and the best that most peasants could do was to acquiesce, thereby making a virtue of necessity, hoping at best that their condition would not shift from bad to worse. When the burden became unbearable, the most likely recourse was either to exercise a posture of passive resistance or one of individually seeking reprieve at the sufferance of a receptive official. The peasant is unable to register or defend his interests in the organized articulation of demands and grievances, for in the post-1966 era the government has cast a wary eye on any activity which promised to result in the organized aggregation of village claims. Indeed, deliberate attempts have been made to shield the village from penetration by outside organizations, and the political parties and their offshoot organizations have lost much of their former influence over village affairs. Not even those organizations closely associated with government sponsorship have been allowed to fill this vacuum.

The one organization which had some potential for emerging as a vehicle for the expression of peasant interests was the BUUD. In theory the BUUD was to serve as a catalytic agent in the structure of village development, and some of its promoters had envisaged its flowering into a full-fledged farmers' association, an organization capable of exercising influence over the formulation and administration of agricultural policies. Indeed, the possible makings of such a structure are evident in the current effort to build provincial federations of member BUUDs.[9] If properly managed, these federations would be in a position to exercise leverage over such concerns as rice policy, the pricing of agricultural inputs, and the procedure for their wholesale and retail marketing in the rural sector. It will be an enormously difficult task to move these embryonic federations to a point where they can genuinely act on behalf of peasant interest in areas of important policy concerns. At the moment the federations are largely staffed by government employees, and past experience would indicate that they can end up as a mere appendage of a self-serving bureaucracy, or in trying to bring in outside leadership they can become prey to personal and opportunistic interests. In either instance, however, they remain isolated and out of touch with village conditions.

In company with the long-term problem of moving the BUUDs to a position where they can effectively articulate peasant interests, there is also the issue of building the kind of trust and confidence which enables a peasant to perceive his interests as consonant with those of the BUUD. The fact that this organization was pressed into service in the recent effort to procure 10 percent

9. One federation of BUUDs is being developed in the special district of Jogjakarta, and plans are under way for a similar effort in other areas of Java.

of the harvest only serves to reinforce suspicions that the BUUD is really an adversary rather than an advocate of peasant interests. This organization was proffered by the government as a farmers' organization and yet its performance has contravened this very purpose, and for this reason alone peasants have ample reason for harboring serious misgivings about linking their fate with the BUUD. It, therefore, remains to be seen whether the government will assist or at least allow the BUUD to emerge as an autonomous and active proponent of issues and interests that relate to village welfare.

CONCLUSION

In summary, during the first five-year plan the government's ability to generate a more dynamic response to its BIMAS program, the bureaucracy's rather erratic record of performance in its administration, and the peasants' sometimes jaundiced and skeptical view of its avowed benefits, all these problems derived in great part from the asymmetrical structure of power and communication on Java. The government has held a near monopoly control over the channels of power and communication, and the peasant was relegated to a position of being buffeted about by a usually well-intentioned but clumsy and uninformed bureaucracy. Unless some effort is made in making these structures more symmetrical, with the peasant acquiring a more dynamic role in the process of policy formulation and administrative action, the prospects of rapidly improving rural conditions in Java would seem to be relatively limited. In the absence of such structural changes, agricultural development runs the risk of proceeding in a hit-and-miss fashion with both the peasant and the government trying to second-guess the other, but neither being able to arrive at a long-term workable solution in improving peasant welfare. A basic shift in the direction of providing more opportunity for organized peasant participation in policy-making will depend in great part on how the current elite views the process of development. Until now a more open-ended approach to development has been ruled out for fear that it would rekindle the still-burning embers of peasant unrest and ferment in rural Java. The turbulence and turmoil of the strife-torn Sukarno years still serves as a painful reminder that embedded within rural Java are forces, which if left uncontained, could possibly overpower any government, military or otherwise. The current regime has therefore opted to keep the lid on, rather than running the risk of setting it ajar by an overzealous and artless attempt at participatory development. As new elites come to the fore and as old memories fade, it is possible that greater confidence will emerge to allow for a more pluralistic and organized sharing of power and communication among various levels of Indonesian society.

12

Urbanization and the Rise of Patron-Client Relations: The Changing Quality of Interpersonal Communications in the Neighborhoods of Bandung and the Villages of West Java

KARL D. JACKSON

THIS CHAPTER describes how interpersonal communication networks change during the urbanization process in West Java. The central focus will be on comparing interview data collected on this subject from three villages in the regency of Garut, southeast of Bandung, with interviews conducted with first-generation migrants to Bandung from villages in the same area, and a small subsample of urban residents who were born either in the city of Bandung or in nearby district towns.

Elsewhere I have written that the politics of rural West Java are the politics of traditional authority relationships (Jackson and Moeliono 1973). My subsequent research in the poorer *kampungs* of the city of Bandung leads me to hypothesize that traditional authority relationships to a large extent give way to patron-client relationships as the most frequent and efficacious type of power

The thoughts and efforts of Dr. Johannes Moeliono of the Institute of Technology of Bandung everywhere are writ large in this paper. Only the vagaries of the international mail and the press of time have precluded his being listed as co-author.

Several institutions and many individuals contributed to this research. The Center for International Studies and the Department of Political Science at MIT financed the field research carried out in 1968-1969. Three Indonesian universities in Bandung, Padjadjaran, Pasundan, and Parahiangan helped by contributing facilities and students. The urban sample was coded and data analysis begun at the East-West Population Institute of the East-West Center during the summer of 1972. The Center for South and Southeast Asia Studies and the Committee on Research at the University of California, Berkeley, contributed to the project's completion. Credit must be given to Virginia H. Jackson, Mary Ellen Nordyke, and Bella Z. Bell, who together with the author expended approximately 3,000 hours coding the urban and rural materials. Thanks are also due to Jim Modeke and Mary Ruggie, who performed the laborious task of submitting the computer runs on the urban data. Finally, Suchitra Bhakdi, Graeme Hugo, Lucian W. Pye, and Robert Wessing supplied helpful suggestions for revising an earlier draft of this chapter.

relationship.[1] By comparing village residents, village-born urbanites, and town-born urbanites, a trend appears in which traditional authority bonds are broken and replaced by patron-client linkages. This change in the quality of inter-personal communications characterizing migrants to Bandung represents a step, albeit a limited one, in the direction of modernization. To the extent that urban patron-client relations are relatively more limited, instrumental, opportunistic, specialized, achievement-based, and focused on the recent present rather than the distant past, the rise of patron-client relations is taken as evidence of gradual modernization rather than retraditionalization.

From the data reported in this chapter no prognostications can be offered about whether this modernizing trend will continue with patronage in turn being replaced by another method of mobilizing power. However, the nonindustrial character of Bandung and many other Southeast Asian cities probably will function as a brake on the development of a more participant polity based on powerful, stable, mass political organizations capable of enforcing their eco-nomic and ideological demands on the governing elite.[2]

Distinguishing between these two types of power relationships and illus-trating that one tends to be dominant in the rural and the other in the urban sector should sensitize us to the ways in which the mobilization and participa-tion processes vary across the urban-rural divide. The distinction should lessen the confusion about the ways in which patron-client relations in the villages differ from those found in the city. In doing so, the distinction will make clear how different the "urban villager" is from his rural brethren, especially with regard to the informal groupings underpinning mass political behavior in both villages and cities.

In the search for general, cross-culturally applicable propositions social scientists are sometimes wont to bring already completed conceptual frame-works to the foreign field setting. In cultures such as Indonesia's, where the existing store of systematic attitude research is small, this can result in the collection of data about concepts that are essentially irrelevant to the culture and its polity. The research reported here has taken the opposite course. The concepts of traditional authority and patronage are derived from the research experience itself. However, because of the complex nature of the differences between these two types of power, they will be summarized in the opening section of this chapter before they are confronted in their full empirical detail.

1. This chapter is the first fragment of an on-going study comparing an urban and rural data set gathered in West Java in 1969. At this point in time analysis of the urban data set is far from complete, and hence I cannot present definitive proof that alternative variables such as religious values, ethnic stereotypes, and socioeconomic conditions are less important to politics than patronage. Although I can show clearly how traditional authority gives way to patronage in the city at this juncture, I cannot test its effectiveness relative to other types of power in the city as I have done else-where in regard to the village data set. For consideration of alternative hypotheses on the rural data, see Jackson 1971: 303-529.

2. For the relatively greater impact on modernization and political participation of involvement in industrial work as opposed to urbanization per se, see Inkeles 1969 and Inkeles and Smith 1974.

Although the order of reporting moves from concepts to data, it should be remembered that the research process followed exactly the opposite order.

DEFINITIONS: TRADITIONAL AUTHORITY AND PATRONAGE

Power is defined behaviorally as an interaction between persons or groups in which at a particular moment in time one actor (the influencer, R) changes the behavior of a second actor (the influencee, E) (Frey 1970; see also Easton 1958). Traditional authority is an interaction with the following characteristics: R sends a message to E, and E adopts it as the basis of his behavior, (1) without evaluating the request of R in terms of his own standards or (2) in spite of his initial evaluation of the request in terms of his own standards and interests; E adopts the message as the basis of his behavior because of his perception of the existence of a diffuse, long-standing, affect-laden, binding mutual obligation between R and himself. Traditional authority is the exercise of personalistic power accumulated through the past and present role of the influencer as provider, protector, educator, source of values, and status superior of those who have an established dependency relationship with him. Once established, the traditional authority figure need not threaten, offer material or symbolic rewards, attempt to persuade, or refer to rules regulating roles; his commands are accepted solely on the basis of who he is and the particular personal, diffuse relationship that he has cultivated with each of his followers.

Unlike persuasion, a second type of power, traditional authority does not require opinion change prior to behavior change. In traditional authority, obedient behavior is *not* based on agreement with the leader's ideological stance; the followers adhere to the leader's position regardless of the ideologically contradictory turns that he may take. The traditional leader may espouse a political or religious ideology or appeal to communal sentiments such as ethnicity but, although these appeals may serve a psychological function for the leader in connecting him with other segments of society, the part played by the content of these appeals is probably marginal as far as his followers are concerned. This is because the traditional leader is probably addressing his ideological, religious, or communal appeals to a village audience that is politically ignorant, insensitive to differences in religious beliefs, and almost totally unaware of the existence of other ethnic groups.

This is not to deny that discussions utilizing political, religious, and ethnic symbols take place between leaders and followers. In fact, just prior to climactic events like elections, such discussions are rife. However, the function of the discussion for the follower is different from persuasion. The follower does not ask himself, "Do I agree with what my leader has proposed?" or "Does it agree with my opinions and beliefs?" Instead, such discussions with the leader are a means of determining where the follower should stand on the issue. The discussion is an educative process in which superior informs subordinate rather than a negotiation for the follower's support as a result of the views put forward by the leader. In a fundamental sense, the opinions of the follower were determined long ago, perhaps twenty years previously when he entered into a dependency relationship with the particular leader. The discussion communicates commands rather than attempting to sway opinions. Traditional authority, in its pure form, is not vitally dependent on ideological and communal appeals.

Traditional authority also differs from a third form of power called reward-deprivation. Unlike reward-deprivation, traditional authority does not involve calculation of immediate personal interests by the follower. Nor does the follower perceive it as a contract in which he supplies a specific service in return for a predetermined level of compensation. Although the leader may have done many things for his followers in time past, and even though he may be obligated to continue dispensing favors in the future, the pattern of power is not simply one of exchanging rewards for services. The concept of the follower deciding whether or not to support his leader politically on the basis of careful calculation of the excess of benefits over costs is foreign to the system of traditional authority.

Why is this type of power labeled traditional? Chiefly this is because its possession almost always depends on the passage of time and because it is often legitimized by inheritance across generations. First, the endurance of traditional authority relations is counted in decades rather than in years. When the habit of obedience to a particular leader has existed for more than twenty-five years, and when this relationship was inherited from one's father, to change leaders over trifles as ephemeral as party labels and political issues would be a dysfunctional breach of time-honored wisdom as well as etiquette. Traditional authority relationships are not mere alliances of opportunity and convenience but are viewed as bonds binding both leader and follower to former generations. The traditional authority bonds establish the continuity of the individual's place in the closed community of the past as well as the more open community of the present. These relations are legitimate not only because they are efficient and prosperous but because they transcend time in ways sanctioned by the customs of the elders (see Weber 1947: 341-58; Hagen 1962: 55-75).

Second, "traditional" implies that leadership is more likely to devolve on those possessing inherited rather than achieved status. For instance, the holders of traditional authority in a village often belong to the same family or group of higher status families. Although it is not unthinkable for a village to confer such authority on a person from outside the traditional ruling families, usually selection devolves on a stable set of families possessing unique sacred or secular knowledge or a distinct role in the historical evolution of the community. Rather than asking, "Who is the most efficient leader?" or "What are his achievements?" traditional authority emphasizes questions such as "Who is he?" "Who was his father?" and "Did his family treat my father well?" [3]

3. For examples of traditional authority and patronage and their influence on Indonesian political behavior, see Anderson 1972a; Chabot 1950: 101-10, 134-35; Chabot 1967: 203-04; Compton, n.d.: 2-3; Fagg 1958: 233-34, 239-40, 275-76, 282-83; Feith 1962: 115, 127; H. Geertz 1959: 25-29; Goethals 1959: 12-23;

Traditional authority and patronage are power relations that share many qualities but which also may be distinguished analytically and empirically. To begin with the similarities, both types of relationships are vertical, dyadic, and asymmetric.[4] The critical bond is the personal, face-to-face relationship between the leader and follower with few, if any, strong horizontal linkages existing between those of equal status even among individuals owing fealty to the same leader. The successful patron or traditional authority figure is one who establishes himself as the indispensable intermediary between a group of individuals having heterogeneous but complementary skills. The whole is thus able to satisfy the needs of its parts only through the personal intervention of the leader, who sends the follower in need to another follower previously obligated to the leader and hence willing to supply the sought-after service. It is for this reason that coalitions mobilized through the use of traditional authority and patronage may be marked by heterogeneity of ethnic composition, values, and interest.[5] The critical aspect of affiliation is identification with the leader rather than identification of followers with one another because of similar economic status, ideological viewpoint, or even primordial characteristics.[6]

Both patrons and traditional authority figures relate to their followers through asymmetric exchanges. Thus the economically hard-pressed follower will obtain sustenance from his leader, but in return he will volunteer his labor, his vote, and in some cases even his life, although these obligations are never made explicit at the time of the original favor. Maintenance at the subsistence level, crisis insurance, physical protection, brokerage, specialized knowledge, and the psychological reassurance of having a protector are provided by the leader in return for amplifying the leader's status, magnifying his power and prestige in the community, placing one's skills at his disposal, contributing to his financial support, and, in some instances, mobilizing militarily or politically on his behalf. The asymmetric quality of the exchange is expressed in the perception held by leaders and followers alike that a debt in money is seldom repaid in either money or kind. Instead, the obligation incurred is left unstated and unclear and often, therefore, open-ended. The asymmetric quality of the items being exchanged to some extent accounts for why patron-client and traditional authority relationships are unions of opposites uniting the "haves" with the

---

Goethals 1967: 56-62; de Haan 1912; Koentjaraningrat 1967: 279; Palmer 1959: 43, 49-51; Palmer 1967; Soedjatmoko 1956: 131-33; Selosoemardjan 1962: 138-39; Willner 1963; Willner 1967: 515.

4. For an excellent article on patron-client relations, see Scott 1972.

5. See Milne 1973. In Milne's case study, patron-client relations supply vertical integration all the way up to the cabinet level of the state government. He also shows instances where patron-client bonds cut across ethnic divisions and describes the changes brought about by the advent of party politics and the expansion of government expenditure.

6. For many similar points describing Burmese and Thai politics, see Hanks 1968: 32-36, 41-46; Hanks 1968a; Hanks 1962; Nash 1963: 197-202; Phillips 1958; Phillips 1965; Riggs 1966. For the Philippines, see Lande 1965 and Nowak and Snyder 1974. For the best description available on the effects of interpersonal communication networks on village social life, see Wiser and Wiser 1971.

"have nots," the knowledgeable with the ignorant, and the powerful with the politically impotent.

Both types of power are noncontractual, diffuse, whole-person relationships. The same leader may be called on to provide institutional entrée, to find his follower a bride, to pay hospital bills, and to decide how the follower should vote. In some cases, the leader may also be responsible for the spiritual progress of his flock, being expected to "teach them to do right in this world and the next."

Predictably such personal relationships tend to supersede institutional arrangements. The patron or traditional authority figure can dictate that followers join a political organization and likewise he can lead them out of it en masse and on short notice. Even within bureaucracies under patron-client or traditional authority systems, loyalty flows to persons rather than to offices or institutions, and the ability to manage effectively is restricted to those whose formal subordinates are also their dependent followers. Paradoxically the adminstrator who is "able to get things done" may be the one who allows the official car to be used as a taxi during office hours in order to earn money to support his subordinates and thereby ensure their obedience to his will in official matters.

Finally, the social conditions bringing forth both patronage and traditional authority as types of power are similar. These types of power thrive in conditions of gross income inequality, restricted social mobility, government paralysis or bankruptcy, declining respect for law and order, and even civil war. Social chaos generally increases the salience of the informal protective shield offered by patron-client and traditional authority relations.

The major differences between traditional authority and patronage are qualitative ones. Patronage is primarily instrumental, responsive to changing opportunities, and more attuned to material facets of life. As such, these relationships have a shorter duration and entail less extensive feelings of binding, affect-laden reciprocity. Reciprocity exists but is more limited in scope and more ephemeral in duration. The power interaction between a patron and client has the following characteristics: the patron (or influencer, R) sends a message to the client (or influencee, E), and the client adopts it as the basis for his actions to the extent that the following conditions are met:

   a. The client clearly acknowledges the patron as the superior partner in the dyadic relationship;

   b. The patron and client must have sustained a mutually rewarding, respect-filled relationship over at least a few years;

   c. The patron and client must have sufficient trust in the reciprocal nature of their relationship, enabling it to transcend exchanges disproportionately benefiting only one of them;

   d. The patron and client, although not sharing identical interests, knowledge, skill, and power, must possess a general complementarity of interests, especially within the economic realm;

   e. The patron's requests must be moderate, rather than unlimited, and tailored in magnitude to relatively recent services performed by the patron.

Patronage stresses the material qualities of the interaction between the leader and his followers. The ability of the patron to assert power flows more directly from his monopolistic or oligopolistic control over resources vital to the client. Although neither patronage nor traditional authority is a short-term contractual relationship, instrumental and material aspects are more important to the former than the latter. The traditional authority relationship is endowed with a strongly affective quality such that once the relationship has been firmly established, the follower will be bound to obey almost without regard for the pecuniary content of the leader's immediate request. In contrast, in patronage the balance between affective and instrumental bonds tips decidedly in favor of the latter. The client's perception of his interests plays a much more prominent role in deciding whether to accede to the patron's request. His willingness to obey the patron is no longer as predictable; the aura of absolutism surrounding the traditional authority figure's call for support is partially replaced by a calculation of medium- and long-term cost and gain.

The variation between the two kinds of power is clarified by the way in which each handles the moral and ethical obligations arising from a debtor-creditor relationship with a patron or traditional authority figure. In both cases, the follower feels a debt of moral obligation, *hutang budi*, extending beyond the purely monetary aspect of the debt. However, the lengths to which the individual will go to pay back hutang budi are much more limited in the patron-client relationship than in traditional authority. In the patron-client relationship, repayment is envisioned as more defined and likely to take the form of labor service or merely the honoring of the patron "as a second father," whereas in the case of traditional authority the Indonesian maxim is more readily applied that "debts in money are easily paid but debts in hutang budi endure 'til the grave."

In general, patronage has a more abbreviated time horizon than traditional authority, being measured in years, not decades. Patron-client unions are more opportunistic. The patron acquires clients to enhance the size and self-sufficiency of his entourage, and he gives due regard to his present preoccupations rather than inheriting the followers of his father or father's father simply because such relations existed in a former generation. Patronage is oriented toward the present and immediate past and does not concern itself with defining the individual's relationship to past generations and to the entire, all-encompassing local community.

Whereas the traditional authority relationship deals extensively in deferred gratifications, patronage bonds have a foreshortened time perspective. Clients switch patrons and patrons abandon clients according to changing circumstances and opportunities, whereas the relationship to the traditional authority figure endures. One of the reasons why patronage is more characteristic of city life than traditional authority is that the rational quality of investment in life-long relationships is vitally dependent on the stability provided by village social, economic, and political relations. In urban areas the rising merchant suddenly loses his business or the office manager is transferred, whereas in the village the primary landed families are more stable and the future of political leadership is more predictable.

The patron-client relationship, with its greater emphasis on the instrumental quality of the relationship, places more weight on the achieved characteristics of the patron. Although such traditional marks of status as noble birth and good family remain important supplementary traits of the patron, his most important characteristics are his own resources, official position, or his hold over specialized knowledge. Although traditional authority tends to be inherited across generations, the patron is selected largely because his own achievements have marked him as a man to whom it would be desirable to be attached.

Patronage is a type of power that falls between traditional authority and reward-deprivation. Although the instrumental and material assets and liabilities are more important to patronage than they are to traditional authority, patronage remains quite separate from the explicit, impersonal, and completely opportunistic interaction defined as reward-deprivation. Patronage remains a personal relationship extending over time with qualities of friendship that are not central to reward-deprivation. The importance of patronage as a power type in the analysis of migration and urbanization is that it forms a particularly attractive way station for those who have abandoned traditional authority but as yet show no sign of entering horizontal interest groups based on homogeneity of economic and social interests. Although patronage marks a definite movement in the direction of more opportunistic, instrumental, and short-term power relations, it maintains the vertical, leader-led format familiar in traditional society.

In Indonesia, both traditional authority and patronage are referred to as *bapak-anak buah* relationships. The father (*bapak*) accumulates authority by building what is, in effect, an extended family for which he must assume diffuse responsibilities. The bapak forms relations with his *anak buah* (children) by assuming responsibility for their spiritual, material, and social needs. The primary characteristic of bapak-anak buah relations is that the bonds are diffuse, personal, nonideological, and in their genesis apolitical.

RESEARCH PROCEDURES

The data reported here were collected with an extensive interview schedule originally designed and pretested in the village context and subsequently modified for use among the urban poor. The interview covered a large variety of subjects, consisted of 229 separate questions, and required an average of 3½ to 4 hours to complete. The interviews were conducted in the Sundanese language by eight male and two female university students who had been trained in interviewing techniques for two months prior to entering the field. In addition to being trained formally, these interviewers were peculiarly well fitted to study the process of migration from village to city because each had been born in a

Sundanese village and lived, at the time of the study, in a kampung not unlike those being studied. The most impressive quality of the interviewing team was the ease with which it carried out its task, creating minimum disturbance to the lifeways of the respondents. The spontaneous quality of many interviews is especially apparent in the long literal replies to open-ended questions, and the ease manifested by many respondents probably resulted from their perception of being interviewed by one of their own kind, by a person with whom they shared a similar life experience.

The rural sample reported here was drawn from three villages in the regency of Garut, a district one hour southeast of Bandung by car. The villages were representative of a larger set of nineteen villages utilized in a preliminary survey. The village study concerned the subject of integration into the nation-state, with particular reference to the Dar'ul Islam rebellion that raged across West Java from 1948 to 1962. Each village was selected because it represented a particular portion of a political variable of importance throughout West Java, namely village behavior toward the rebellion. The three villages used in the study were one village that had fought hard for the rebellion to found an Islamic state, a second village that was equally active in its opposition, and a third village that assumed a neutral position between the contending forces. Although the villages were selected purposively for the study of national integration, nothing in the extensive study of them or in subsequent analysis of aggregate data from other villages in West Java indicates that the three villages were in any way atypical of the villages in the geographic area southeast of the city of Bandung.[7] Given that the political variable sampled was of great pertinence to most villages in the area, that the most important parts of the spectrum of political choice were covered by the three villages, and that striking homogeneity existed among the three villages on all of the variables that will be compared here with the urban sample (Jackson 1971: 120-531), it can reasonably be assumed that the findings can be generalized to the larger group of villages in southeastern West Java that faced the same political problem between 1948 and 1962. Of course, there are villages in West Java that are probably quite different from the ones sampled, for example, villages on the outskirts of Jakarta that are more suburban than rural, or villages in the northern coastal lowland plain with their higher population densities supported by even more intense rice cultivation.[8] However, our experience and contacts with many villages in West Java gives the research team

7. The subsequent studies referred to are those undertaken by Dr. Moeliono in conjunction with Dr. G. Hill which required extensive travels in West Java and an analysis of the data collected by the Indonesian Department of the Interior and published in 1972. See chapter 3 of the forthcoming *Traditional Authority and National Integration: The Dar'ul Islam Rebellion in West Java* or the original Indonesian data source, Direktorat Jenderal Pembanguanan Masyarakat Desa, Departemen Dalam Negri, *Desa: Data 7 Contoh Kecamatan Di Jawa Barat Sehubungan Dengan Survey Pedesaan, 1971-72* (Jakarta, 1972).

8. Unfortunately I am aware of no studies that would cast light on whether the village findings concerning interpersonal communication networks apply with equal validity to the *pasisir* area of coastal West Java.

confidence in our ability to generalize the findings on interpersonal communication variables to many other Sundanese villages not included in this study.

In the three villages, a disproportionately stratified sampling frame was employed to select the 199 respondents whose completed interviews are reported here.[9] Approximately twenty community leaders, ten religious leaders, ten economic leaders, ten elite women, and twenty members of the village poor were picked for interviews in each village.[10] Four out of five sampling categories were taken from the village elite. In essence, the rural sample, like the urban one, was an elite sample, although the inclusion of a small sample of the village poor allows one to make certain judgments about the contribution of social status differences to the variation on particular variables.[11]

During the closing stages of the village research it became increasingly apparent that interpersonal communications were an extremely important aspect of village social and political life. Because I was concerned with integration

9. The total number of completed and partially completed interviews in the three villages was 206, but the partially completed interviews have been dropped from this analysis.

10. The community leaders were the most heterogeneous subelite sampled and thus received the largest sampling fraction. The community leader strata included all the general leaders of the village, all the holders of village offices, the political party leaders, and the leaders of nonpolitical organizations in the villages. If a religious leader was reputed to be both a general leader and a religious leader, he was included on the sampling lists for both strata.

Religious leaders as a category included religious teachers at the village religious schools in addition to those referred to as *tokoh agama* (religious leaders). The economic leaders of the village included the large landowners, the petty tradesmen, and the shop-owners of the village. In addition, persons reputed to be the most innovative farmers in the village were included in this sampling list. The elite women were selected from among the wives of the community leaders who already had been chosen to be interviewed.

The village poor were selected by randomly drawing from the tax records respondents whose total land holdings were between 0.02 and 0.3 hectares of land. This would be enough land on which to build a house, but not enough to raise crops sufficient to support a family. In addition, it was specified that the persons in this category must be male and less than sixty-five years old. From the village land records it was clear that the village poor were in the lower half of the village social structure, but that there remained another still poorer stratum of the village population – the landless – from which no interviews were drawn. According to Graeme Hugo's 1973 field work on demographic change in fourteen villages in West Java, 31 percent of the households owned no rice fields whatever. This figure approximates the estimate used in drawing our samples. Hence, although I have no reason to suppose that there would be sharp differences between our sample of the village poor and their still poorer brethren, our rural sample cannot tell anything directly about bapak-anak buah relations attaching the lowest one-third of village life to the social ladder.

11. Interview mortality was high among the village poor: Only two-thirds of the desired number of interviews were completed. This decreases the confidence one can place in the village poor as a randomly selected subsample. The chief reason for high interview mortality is that the poor are less well known and harder to find. Also, because they work for others from morning until night, they often do not have the surplus time and energy to be interviewed. In spite of the large number of interviews that were not begun or were not completed, the subsample of village poor still supplies a valuable counterweight to the otherwise wholly elite character of the rural sample.

between the urban and rural areas, in addition to integration in the context of armed rebellion, I decided to investigate how the variables would be affected by movement to the city. Given that the research budget had already been exhausted and that the character of Bandung's 1 to 1.5 million persons was uncharted, there was no possibility of taking a small sample that would be representative of the entire city in the way that the village samples represented each village. I selected three quite different neighborhoods (*rukun kampung*), each of which contained 3,000 to 4,000 persons. All of the neighborhoods were poor, but substantial variation was deliberately included to ensure at least a rough cross-section of the variety of poor neighborhoods existing in the city. One neighborhood, nestled behind a movie theater in the southeastern quarter of the city on the main road to Garut, was as poor, densely housed, filthy, and disease-ridden as any neighborhood in the city. It supplied shelter for many of the most recent migrants to the city and included several kampungs populated almost entirely by beggars. These beggars' kampungs had to be excluded from the research project because smallpox killed fifteen residents during the five days we interviewed there.[12] In contrast, another neighborhood farther south in the city had an almost rustic atmosphere, with green grass, low population density, and good housing. It was situated on the edge of the city within sight of rice paddies. The third neighborhood was located in the northwestern quarter of the city. Although it was densely populated and had to be entered through a hole in the wall, it was well organized, relatively clean, and disease free, and it housed a more established population.

From these three neighborhoods I sought an urban sample of migrants to the city from the same geographic area in which the villages were located. An urban sample was selected to match the rural sample, that is, the proportion of persons playing each social role (for example, religious leader) should be identical in each sample. Operationally this meant composing lists of each type of person in each neighborhood and selecting randomly from these lists the number of respondents of each type that were necessary to make the proportion identical and hence comparable to that found in the rural sample. Moderate success was achieved with regard to this goal, although too few urban community leaders and too many urban poor were selected (compare columns *A* and *B* of Table 1). In order to correct for this deficiency, a weighting system was devised to bring the larger rural sample into line with the urban sample.[13]

12. A portion of the research budget was used to buy smallpox vaccine in hope of short-circuiting the agonizingly slow bureaucratic process. Public health officials waited for the arrival of the single modern injection gun supplied to the province of West Java by the World Health Organization, while children died or were pockmarked for life in the kampung. Our attempt was unsuccessful, but the epidemic confined itself to the beggars' kampungs until the injection gun arrived.

13. Rather than throwing out interviews in order to make the samples correspond, the weightings make the answers of some respondents more important than others, for instance, when all four types of leaders are summed for analytical purposes to supply a combined elite or when the elite and poor are added together to compare the total urban and rural samples. In general the differences induced by the

There were two other changes in sampling criteria that were applied in the urban sample. First, Indonesian Chinese, regardless of whether they had become naturalized citizens, were excluded from the urban sample to preserve comparability within the villages where there were no Chinese Indonesian residents. Also, land records had been used as a means of selecting the rural poor. No such reliable device for discriminating among levels of poverty was at my disposal in the urban context; hence, I was forced to use the less precise method of selecting them randomly from the population rolls after excluding all local elite members. The result is that the urban poor as a group represent the whole nonelite, whereas the rural poor are limited to those individuals owning some land but not enough to support themselves.

In urban neighborhoods, information about individuals required for sampling was often inaccurate or unobtainable. Either no comprehensive set of records containing date and place of birth existed, or the type of record existing varied greatly between neighborhoods. From the records it was impossible to determine whether a prospective respondent listed as having come from Garut actually hailed from the town of Garut or from a village within the regency of Garut. This anomaly in the population records created a subsample of nine respondents who had been born in Bandung itself as well as thirteen born in one of the district towns. This unintended subsample of twenty-two respondents allows us to consider differences between town-born and village-born urbanites, and this new dichotomy turns out to be as interesting as the original one that sought differences between village-born immigrants and village residents. The subsample of town-born urbanites, unfortunately, is almost completely lacking in poor people, and hence, in the analysis that follows, comparisons between town-born urbanites, village-born urbanites, and village residents are restricted largely to the elite samples.[14]

One final caveat is in order. For the samples just described, methodological soundness prohibits phrasing the urban-rural comparisons in terms of whole social units, for example, "the villages," "the neighborhoods," or "the city of Bandung." This is because the samples consist of types of respondents rather than representing whole social units. Therefore, any comparisons made here should be taken as generalizable to the types of people found in both samples, but the comparisons can say nothing with confidence about the distribution of these types within the whole urban and rural populations. This research compares types of villagers with their urban social equivalents, but it can supply no

---

weighting are marginal, with the possible exception of the rural poor who were positively weighted to bring them up to the same proportion as the poor in the urban sample (compare column C with column B of Table 1). This was done for each cross-tabulation. For details on the weighting procedure used for combining the substrata, see Jackson 1971: 114-24.

14. The temporary migrants between village and city, though probably small in number, are an interesting group because their life-ways may encapsulate the beginning of the transition from traditional authority to patronage. Unfortunately resource limitations precluded sampling the semi-urbanized, temporary migrants to the city of Bandung.

hard data comparing whole village populations with entire neighborhoods in the city.[15]

INTERPERSONAL COMMUNICATION PATTERNS AMONG VILLAGERS AND URBANITES

To ascertain whether a change in the pattern of interpersonal communication is actually taking place with urbanization requires a base line from which to measure. The pattern of communication among the village residents supplies the base line with which to compare the samples of village and town-born urbanites. Taken together the samples of village residents, village-born urbanites, and town-born respondents supply a continuum of urbanization along which to appraise the amplitude and direction of the changes in interpersonal relations.

The evidence for the thesis that traditional authority relations decline

TABLE 1

Completed Interviews as Percentage of Total

	Urban sample A	Rural sample before weighting B	Rural sample after weighting C	Urban sample + rural sample after weighting D
Community leaders	27% (16)	33% (66)	26% (53)	27% (69)
Religious leaders	15% (9)	15% (29)	15% (30)	15% (39)
Economic leaders	17% (10)	15% (29)	17% (33)	17% (43)
Elite women	15% (9)	17% (34)	15% (30)	15% (39)
Poor	27% (16)	21% (41)	26% (53)	27% (69)
Total	101% (60)	101% (199)	99% (199)	101% (259)

15. The present design studies change by using cross-sectional samples rather than by repeatedly interviewing a panel of migrants over the course of decades to chronicle individual adaptation to city life. Therefore, it is entirely possible that the differences between village residents, village-born urbanites, and town-born urbanites may be the product of contaminating influences which have affected one group but not the others, and which may have little but coincidence in common with differing degrees of urbanization. It is hoped that this exploratory research will provoke others to study the processes of change outlined here.

while patron-client bonds increase during urbanization is derived from a battery of sixty-seven separate open-ended and closed questions. No single question or series of questions tells the complete story, and only after analyzing a large number of these replies does the trend of change become apparent.

The sixty-seven questions fall into ten different groups. The first inquired into the respondent's perception of himself as advisor or patron. The next four groups of questions asked whether the respondent had a general advisor, a financial backer, a local informant on political matters, and an outsider to whom he could go for advice on politics. The remaining five sets of questions were largely projective and attempted to cement the connection between political mobilization and interpersonal communications. Sensitivity to the subject of politics and the risk of alienating respondents led us to eschew directly political questions and to phrase the questions about *bapakism* in terms of advisor-advisee relations. The relationship to political mobilization was only subsequently established in the final section of projective questions.

Prevalence of the Role of Advisor

For the urban and rural samples alike there are no differences in the tendency to perceive oneself as an advisor; the vast majority (85 percent or more) in the village and urban samples perceive themselves as persons to whom people come for advice, help, or just to pay respect. Urbanites, regardless of birthplace, are almost unanimous in reporting that they are advisors (see Figure 1). There are considerable differences in both the urban and rural cases between the combined elite of community leaders, religious leaders, economic leaders, and elite women on the one hand, and the poor on the other. However, even among the poor in each case, 75 percent state they are subject to the visitations which are so characteristic of bapak-anak buah relations. The practice spreads throughout the social structure in both the villages and the urban neighborhoods.

The presence or absence of persons coming for advice is, however, too crude an indicator for determining whether or not change has taken place in the character and content of interpersonal communications during urbanization. Therefore, one needs to look at how large the patron-client cliques are, how often clients seek a patron's advice, the type of advice sought, whether the clients call the advisor *bapak*, and how many clients the advisor believes would defend him if he were in danger.

The number of clients in personal entourages remains stable during the first generation after leaving the village, but declines sharply among those who were born and reared within an urban milieu (see Figure 2).[16] Of those responding, 44 percent of elite villagers and nearly half of the village-born

16. To test the proposition that clique size declines only after the first generation of urbanization, columns 1 and 2 of Figure 2 were collapsed, and clique size was dichotomized into 1-10 persons and 11-60 persons. This resulted in a relationship that does not quite reach statistical significance but moves in that direction; chi-square for the collapsed, four-cell table attains a confidence level of 0.08, uncertainty reduction is 4.2 percent, and gamma is 0.56.

Figure 1

Perception of Self as Advisor in Response to the Question,
"Do People Come to You for Advice or Help or
To Pay Respect?": Whole Samples

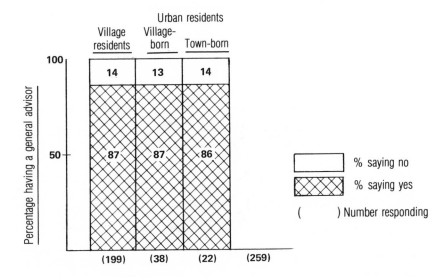

NOTE: Whole samples are reported here even though combined elites are the most legitimate way of comparing differences between village residents, village-born urbanites, and town-born. The whole samples are presented here in the interests of completeness and because the table for elites alone was almost identical.
   If just elites are considered, no differences appear. The percentages of elite members perceiving themselves as advisors among village residents, village-born urbanites, and town-born urbanites respectively are 90 percent, 92 percent, and 89 percent.

urbanites claim that from eleven to "more than sixty" persons come to them for advice or help, only 19 percent of town-born elite members say they are surrounded by cliques of this size, and a full 50 percent report they have very small cliques of less than five persons.

Rather than declining either during or after urbanization, the communication networks connecting an advisor to his followers continue to be used with at least the same frequency that was found in the villages. The high frequency of interaction probably signifies that the act of mixing itself is perceived as rewarding. Through the frequent interchanges both the advisor and the advisee are assured of their respective positions in the local social hierarchy. Both giving and receiving help and advice add to the warmth and security of the relationship.

With urbanization comes increased exposure to mass media, particularly radio, newspapers, and pulp magazines. Both village-born and town-born urbanites score significantly higher than the village elites on a scale of modern mass

Figure 2

Number of Persons Coming for Advice or Help:
Elites Only [a]

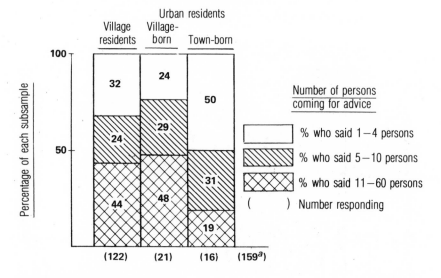

---

[a]The literal wording of the question was, "How many of these are there?" and it directly followed the question reported in Figure 1.

The *N* here falls to 159 because the urban and village poor have been eliminated along with those stating in the previous question that no one came to them for advice or help. Also, the 14 respondents answering with uncodeable replies or saying "don't know," 8 percent, 9 percent, and 6 percent of each respective sample, are not included in the figure. In this as well as other figures the uncodeable and "don't know" responses are eliminated only when the percentages are small and evenly distributed between the subsamples.

The differences reported in the figure do not reach statistical significance. Chi-square reaches only the 0.31 level of confidence and uncertainty reduction is only 2.3 percent.

To test the proposition that clique size declines only after the first generation of urbanization, columns 1 and 2 of Figure 2 were collapsed, and clique size was dichotomized into 1–10 persons and 11–60 persons. The Fisher's exact probability test was applied to the fourfold table yielding a statistically significant relationship at the 0.03 level. In addition uncertainty reduction is 4.2 percent and gamma is 0.56.

media exposure.[17] However, although exposure to mass media increases sharply, mass media are no substitute for the tradition of interpersonal communication that was so prominent in the villages. The leader-follower communication links fail to decline in frequency of usage because they perform important functions extending beyond merely spreading information; they provide services as diverse as social entertainment, financial aid, opinion leadership, and the validation of individual social status in the community. These services are an important reason why the leader-follower connections endure despite the advent of high mass media exposure at the outset of the urbanization process.

17. The scale measuring modern mass media usage combined the scores for cinema, radio, newspapers, magazines, and pulp magazines (*buku carios*).

Figure 3

Response to the Question, "How Often Do You [the Advisor]
Meet with Them?": Elites Only

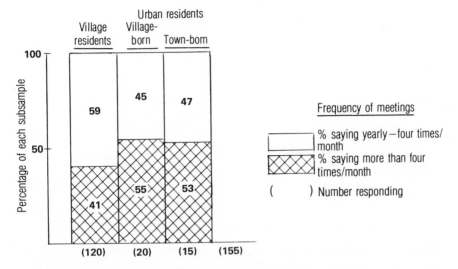

NOTE: The confidence level reached by chi-square is only 0.37, with uncertainty reduction and gamma respectively being 0.9 percent and 0.25. The N here is 155 due to the elimination of the poor, those filtered out by previous questions, and the eighteen respondents giving uncodeable or "don't know" replies. Those giving un-codeable and "don't know" replies account for 10 percent, 9 percent, and 12 percent of the respective sub-samples. If the "don't know" and uncodeable responses are included, chi-square is further reduced to the 0.72 level.

Table 2 indicates that the meetings between advisors and their entourages are not limited to a specific kind of expertise. Many respondents say that people come to them for several or even all of the types of advice enumerated in the question. The meetings are diffuse ones involving the whole person of both advisor and advisee, and the multifunctional character does not change either after peasants come to the city or even when persons have resided outside villages for generations. When the multifunctional nature of the advice is combined with the high frequency of usage and the pervasiveness of these networks within the social structure, a picture emerges of an engrossing social phenomenon removed from the mere contractual exchange of goods for services. Although the table contains a hint of the increasingly material content of the urban relationship, for leader and follower alike the interaction itself remains important because through it each party assures his protection against the dangers inherent in being an isolated individual in a basically corporate society.

These communication networks are not without important political implications. Figure 4 shows that in the perceptions of village elite members the networks can be used for paramilitary mobilization. The social networks are

TABLE 2

Response to the Question, "Do These People Come for
Financial Advice Only, Personal Advice, Political
Advice, Religious Advice, or All Kinds?":
Whole Samples

Kind of advice sought	*Village residents*	*Urban residents*		*Number responding*
		Village-born	*Town-born*	
Personal advice, paying respect, or all kinds of advice	55% (133)	53% (25)	52% (17)	175
Financial advice	17% (41)	23% (11)	27% (9)	61
Religious advice	20% (49)	13% (6)	15% (5)	60
Political or official advice	7% (18)	11% (5)	6% (2)	25
Total	99% (241)	100% (47)	100% (33)	321[a]

a. The N for this table is 321 because many respondents gave answers that were coded in more than one category. The percentages are of the total number of replies given by each subsample. Again whole samples are used here to show the generality of the perceptions, and because virtually no differences appear between subsamples.

perceived as a means for mobilizing very considerable groups for the physical protection of the advisor. The image of a readily available and perhaps even armed retinue is a prominent aspect of the traditional authority relationship between villagers, but this image begins to fade among village-born urbanites and especially among town-born urban residents. Thirty-six percent of village elite members perceive themselves as being able to raise between twenty-one and more than a hundred persons to defend them in time of danger, and the paramilitary aspect of bapakism is almost as prevalent among the village-born urbanites. However, among the town-born elite respondents the decline started among the village-born urbanites becomes statistically significant with only 11 percent believing that they could call up more than twenty men to defend them.

The further removed one becomes from the village context, the lower the confidence in being able to raise a set group for one's own self-protection. Mobilizing for violence may be quite different in the urban social context, because the ability to call up defendants is no longer within the purview of the second-generation bapak, who, after all, is less important in the urban constellation of events than the local elite member is in the smaller village political world. Patron-client networks may still be used for raising political violence in the urban areas, as will be shown in Figure 12, but with the passage of time this

Figure 4

Response to the Question, "If You Need Help from a Considerable Number of
People because You Are in Danger from Those Who Want to Do You Harm,
How Many People Could You Call Up Who Consider You Their
Advisor-Patron [*Panasehat Sareng Panangtajungan*]?": Elites Only

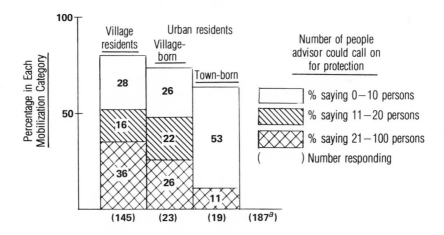

^aThe *N* on this question is higher than on some previous ones because the interviewers were instructed to
ask it of all respondents, ignoring earlier questions that would tend to filter out those denying that people came to
them for advice or help. "Don't know" responses for the village residents, village-born urbanites, and town-born
urbanites are 20 percent, 26 percent, and 37 percent of each subsample. The "don't know" responses were included
in the statistical computations.

Chi-square for this figure is significant at the 0.04 level and the amount of uncertainty reduction (*H*) is
substantial, 6.2 percent.

The expected frequency for three of the cells is less than 5, thus violating the Mann rule concerning the
legitimacy of calculating chi-square. In addition, the troublesome cells contribute substantially to chi-square. This
problem can be dealt with by considering the village-residents and village-born urbanites as a single category. In
this case the figure is statistically significant without a substantial contribution from the remaining pair of troublesome cells. Thus the differences in the mobilization process only become substantial quite late in the urbanization
process.

ability becomes increasingly rare and restricted to citywide elite members of
high social status and position who live beyond the confines of the local
neighborhood. The self-defense mechanism inherent in village bapakism becomes
increasingly restricted, although not until the sons of peasant immigrants
become settled urban residents.

Inquiring directly about bapakism is an invitation to dissimulation for two
reasons. The Sukarno regime in one of its innumerable campaigns attacked
bapakism as feudal, opposed to the nationalistic spirit, and beneath the dignity
of free Indonesians. In addition, there may be a natural reluctance to identify
oneself formally as a power-holder for fear of seeming *kasar* (crude) by boasting

about one's power. As a result, there is a reluctance to admit to being a bapak or anak-buah when the terms are openly used, and hence it seems legitimate to speculate that the number of respondents actually thinking of themselves as bapaks is higher for all subsamples than is indicated in Figure 5. Nonetheless, most advisors state they are bapaks, and, most interestingly, applying the term to oneself initially increases significantly among first-generation urban dwellers compared to village residents. The respect form is reinvigorated in the urban environment and only subsequently declines among the town-born to a level lower than that in the villages.

Figure 5

Response to the Question, "Could You Say that You Are
Their Bapak?":   Elite Only

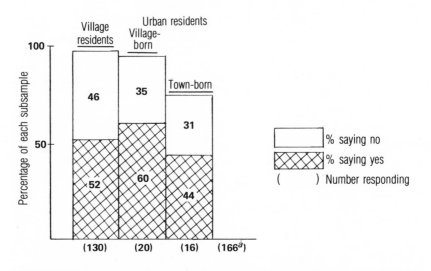

[a]The N here is 166 because respondents were filtered out by previous questions. "Don't know" responses account for 2 percent, 5 percent, and 25 percent of the samples of village residents, village-born urbanites, and town-born urbanites, and they have been included in the statistical computations.

The differences in this figure attained a confidence level of better than 0.01 and uncertainty reduction was 4.7 percent. The same relationships hold true if whole samples are run rather than just the elites. In calculating chi-square, the Mann rule has been ignored because the two cells with expected frequencies of less than 5 do not change the outcome of the statistical test.

What is meant by the use of the term *bapak* can be inferred from a follow-up question inquiring why the term did *not* seem appropriate to those reluctant to apply it to their relationship with followers. The most frequent reply for all types of respondents was that the term *bapak* was not applicable because the particular relationship was one between those of equal status, age, education, or knowledge. The second most frequent reply stated the term was inappropriate for just neighbors, friends, or family. The nay-sayers in both the urban and rural samples in effect define being a bapak as more than just being a family member, friend, or neighbor; being a bapak implies differences in education, knowledge, age, social status, and perhaps office. The qualifications for being termed a bapak do not seem to change, even though, as we shall see, the underlying content of such relationships is changing with urbanization.

The final aspect of the advisor's role is its relationship to organizational membership. Here one sees another clear instance of change through urbanization. In town and country alike a majority of advisors do not perceive their advisees as belonging to the same organization to which they belong or support. However, among the village elite, 45 percent state that there is a connection between organization membership and bapakism. In response to the urban environment, and especially to its wider variety of organizational opportunities, the percentage of village-born and town-born urbanites saying that their advisees follow their lead in membership questions decreases to 20 percent and 11 percent respectively (see Figure 6).

Conclusions About the Role of Advisor

The preceding replies describe the perceptions of the role of advisor recorded in the three subsamples. There are aspects of both stability and change, indications that the respondents are, indeed, urban villagers in some respects but that in others they are being transformed significantly by the urban experience. The pattern that emerges, and one that will be reinforced by analysis of the respondents' perceptions of the role of advisee, is one in which vertical, dyadic, asymmetric, personal, face-to-face relations do not vanish with urbanization. Instead they are modified, and this transformation is in the direction of more limited patron-client linkages.

It would be a mistake, however, to lose sight of the core of interpersonal relations that remains unchanged. The overwhelming majority still perceive themselves as being advisors who are frequently asked to give guidance on the widest assortment of problems besetting their clients. The personal character of the patron is still at least as important to the relationship as the value of the services sought, and the relationship remains a basically noncontractual one between persons of highly unequal status, wealth, knowledge, and position.

Several aspects of traditional authority decline significantly either during or after the conclusion of the urbanization process. These changes mark a slow stripping away of the functions of the system of traditional authority, and the eventual result is a more limited, material, and opportunistic set of patron-client ties. The first transformation is in the size of the cliques surrounding patrons. This probably occurs because the economic context of the relationships is altered by urbanization. In the urban context, the competition for clients changes; there are more patrons to choose from than there were in the relatively closed world of the village. Much of the monopolistic quality of the village leader's sway evaporates with his movement into the city's larger arena. Moreover, patrons and clients alike are less bound by inheritance. They do not retain

Figure 6

Response to the Question, "Are the People Who Come to You Members or
Ex-Members of Organizations You Have Supported or Been a Member of?":
Elites Only

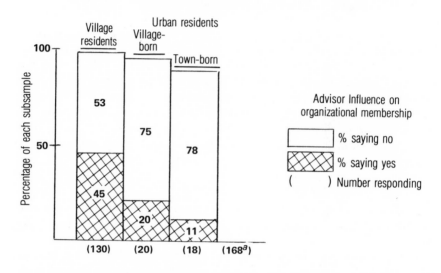

a The *N* here is 168 because of previous filter questions. "Don't know" responses account for 2 percent, 5 percent, and 11 percent of the village residents, village-born urbanites, and town-born urbanites respectively, and have been included in the statistical computations.

The differences in the figure are significant at the 0.01 level; undertainty reduction is 5.8 percent, and gamma is 0.5849. The same relationship is even stronger as whole samples, including the poor, are used; the amount of uncertainty reduction rises to a very respectable 9.2 percent and gamma is 0.6707. Small cell entries create a problem for the legitimacy of statistical testing; if this is resolved by running the affirmative responses against the nonaffirmative ones (no plus "don't know"), the relationship remains significant at better than the 0.01 level.

the relationships of their forefathers, because the act of moving to the city physically severs the face-to-face character of most of these old relationships. Rather than dying out, however, replacement relationships are sought, but the incidence of life-long ascriptive bonds, of necessity, declines.[18] Because relationships by birthright are less frequent, patron and client alike search for connections that are more opportune. The urban patron in his quest to accumulate clients must offer more favors with greater frequency than his rural counterpart. Also, the patron in the city lacks recourse to gifts in kind which ease the cash burdens of the village traditional authority figure who maintains a large entourage with a fairly minimal cash outlay. Being a bapak in the city is simply more expensive, and hence the number of clients surrounding the local patron eventually declines because he cannot support them all. Also, the urban patron does

18. For evidence on the duration of relationships, see Table 5.

not have as many uses for large numbers of followers. The city, unlike the village, is protected by the police and army from large-scale attack, and the urban patron does not tend to be as involved in economic functions that are as labor intensive as rice planting and harvesting. In fact, large numbers of clients may become an intolerable financial liability, especially if the patron is a businessman forced by domestic and international competition to limit his labor costs. The military and economic requirements of bapak and anak-buah alike change with the move to the city, and hence, after the passage of a generation, both the number of men that can be mobilized for protection and the size of the cliques surrounding patrons decline.

The direct connection between being an anak-buah and belonging to the same organization as one's patron declines immediately at the onset of urbanization. The rapid decline of the connection between bapak-anak buah relations and membership in formal organizations represents an adaptation of these personalistic relationships to the complexity of the urban environment, and the result of this adaptation is that formal organizations become less stable in membership and probably less effective than they were in the rural context. Just as the duration of the relationship between leader and follower declines with urbanization, stability of organizational membership through time also declines. In villages, limited organizational stability is guaranteed by the overlapping and reinforcing nature of informal personal bonds and formal organizational relationships. One's protector and provider is also the local political and perhaps even religious leader. Few organizations exist, but they are more frequently backstopped by the traditional authority system as well as by common religion, ethnic group, local heritage, and kinship. Even if the village dramatically changes its political course from, for instance, an NU village to a GOLKAR village, the continuity of the village coalition often remains stable, the affiliation of the entire corporate group having changed en masse at the direction of the village elders.[19]

With movement to the city, the available crop of organizational forms is transformed from famine to feast with a resulting decline in the monopolistic or oligopolistic position of any single organization. Whereas in the village only one or two political parties may have had a significant presence, in the city the individual is exposed to a whole panorama of symbols and ideologies competing for his attention.

In villages I have observed individuals accepting membership who have little or no knowledge of the intent or activities of the organization (for other instances, see Van Niel 1960; Willner 1967). Those proudly displaying membership cards from an Islamic youth organization may have passed their sixth decade in age, and I have repeatedly been told of staunch Sundanese Muslims joining the PKI (Partai Komunis Indonesia) thinking the initials stood for Partai Kiyayi Indonesia (that is, a nonexistent religious party). Modern organizations

19. See three sketches of village politics contained in Jackson and Moeliono 1973: 42-51.

provide virtually no benefits and likewise make demands only rarely. Affiliation may be a largely symbolic act devoid of necessary behavioral outcomes such as paying dues or attending meetings. Like betting on the lottery or buying an amulet, affiliating with a political party or joining the POM (the Parent-Teachers' Association) may be an insurance against the daily exigencies of the unknown or a seemingly costfree chance to feel a part of the new and modern Indonesia represented by formal organizations. Such nearly random affiliation with outside organizations is kept in check in the villages because the common villagers take their membership cues more often from the few village elders, the traditional authority figures who reach a community consensus on how to deal with organizations intruding from the world beyond the village gate.

In the urban context organizational membership becomes ever more distracted from its personalistic foundations. The plethora of organizations and the absence of a defined geographic boundary to the organizational field make control of the anak-buah's memberships more difficult. Organizational life is ephemeral. Some organizations exist in name but not in membership whereas others have members but hold no meetings. Still others have members and carry out activities, but their continued existence always remains perilous. They have no financial backbone because they collect no dues from individual members and are able to extract only minimal contributions in time and kind from their poor, urban rank-and-file. Patrons, realizing the general instability of organizational ties and knowing full well the uncertain life span of many organizations, forge patron-client bonds that cut across organizational lines. The patron's clients will be useful in any organizational context that he elects to enter, but they will remain affiliated to his person and thus independent of the continued existence or well-being of the organization.

None of the preceding should be taken as evidence of a belief that men and resources cannot be mobilized rapidly and effectively in urban areas. The student demonstrations of 1965-1966 and the disturbances in Bandung and Jakarta in 1973 and 1974 would contradict such a thesis. When substantial and concerted economic or political mobilization is required, the vertical, diffuse, largely issue-free patron-client bonds are capable of amassing and directing it. These informal, highly personal bonds are the key to mobilization, at least among the lower part of the urban social structure, in the same way that the more absolute and automatic deference to the village traditional authority figure is fundamental to understanding village political life. Both traditional authority and patron-client relations endure independent of organizational expression. Hence, it is quite rational for both patrons and clients in the urban context to manifest little concern for formal membership because if the client's membership card of yesterday contradicts the patron's political course of tomorrow, there can be little doubt which will prevail. This is one reason why membership may be a poor predictor of individual political behavior at any particular point in time. Implications for action contained in acquiring a membership card are subject to the continued control of the patron in his advice to his client. For example, in the months prior to the September 30 coup, an impoverished resident on the outskirts of Bandung who was a member of a PKI front group was called to demonstrate in the town square, but instead of going directly to the demonstration he asked the advice of the chief man in his neighborhood who was a known anti-Communist. As a result, the card-carrying organization member did not attend the party rally. Such instances amply illustrate why formal membership is an inadequate predictor of political behavior unless the formal organization's demands are reinforced by the advice flowing through informal patron-client channels.

Changing Perceptions of the Role of Advisee

The perceptions of the role of advisor demonstrate certain limited ways in which the rural institution of traditional authority is gradually modified by the urban experience. These changes are primarily those of dropping functions no longer practical or necessary in the urban context. By exploring the respondent's perception of himself in the role of advisee, one can begin to see the ways in which the urban challenge adds new aspects, and how accretions and deletions together create patronage, a type of power more apt for the urban environment.

The role of advisee was explored through four sets of questions covering different kinds of leader-follower interchanges in which the respondent is an advisee. The first probed the advisee role at its most general level by asking whether there were "people here whom you go to in order to ask their advice or opinions." The second set was concerned with the financial aspect, for example, "If your son needs a *hajat* [a religious festival] for which you don't have the money, is there a man who can give you help?" The third and fourth sets touch on political matters by inquiring whether there is a local person knowledgeable on political matters and whether the respondent discusses the "problems of the region or state" with a man who lives outside the village or local neighborhood.

The completeness of coverage of the advisor-advisee networks is signified by the fact that 80 percent or more of the respondents analyzed here play both the role of advisor and the role of advisee, whereas less than 5 percent of each subsample perceive themselves as being excluded from the system of mutual consultation (see Table 3). Most respondents in both town and country are sources of advice and help in addition to being recipients of said same.

If one combines the data on all four types of advisee relations, as has been done in Table 3, there are no apparent differences between the village resident, the village-born urban dweller, and the town-born. However, scrutinizing each type of advisee relationship reveals important distinctions illustrating the scope and direction of social change. The major change running through all four advisee relations is that the village-born urbanites are less likely to have advisors than either the village residents or the town-born urban dwellers. When one compares the village residents with the village-born urbanites, there is a distinct decline in the tendency of these first-generation immigrants to have a general advisor, a financial patron, a local political advisor, or an advisor on politics living outside the local neighborhood. Without the subsample of town-born urbanites one might jump to the wholly unwarranted conclusion that bapakism

TABLE 3

Overlap Between Role of Advisor and Advisee:
Elites Only

Advisor/ advisee roles	Village residents	Urban residents		Number responding
		Village-born	Town-born	
Both roles	87% (127)	80% (20)	84% (16)	163
Just advisor	2% (3)	12% (3)	5% (1)	7
Just advisee	10% (14)	4% (1)	5% (1)	16
Neither role	1% (2)	4% (1)	5% (1)	4
Total	100% (146)	100% (25)	99% (19)	190

fades away rapidly with the onset of urbanization. However, this is certainly not the case, because the decline is only temporary. For each different type of relationship, the town-born respondents return to, and in some cases exceed, the level of participation in bapak-anak buah networks manifest among villagers. This trend is illustrated in Figure 7, regarding whether the respondent has a general advisor, and the trend is consistent throughout all four types of advisor relationships (see Figure 9 and Table 4).

The disengagement of first-generation urban dwellers from bapak-anak buah networks is a manifestation of the disorientation produced by being uprooted from the village and moved to the city. Time, energy, and a capacity for taking initiative are required before the new urbanite either seeks out a new patron or is sought out by one. Rather than advisor-advisee relations being established at birth or during childhood as they often were in the village, the city advisor and advisee must seek out each other or be thrown together by circumstances resulting from employment or settlement patterns.

Temporarily declining participation in the role of advisee plays an important part in the transformation from traditional authority to patron-client relationships. Traditional authority derives much of its mystique from the fact that many of its ties are inherited ones. The participant, through these traditional ties, is linked not only with a provider and protector of today but with his forebears in a continuous stream of social interaction in which roles are sanctified by the passage of time. Once put asunder, these bonds arise again only in a distinctly modified form. With movement to the city the continuity of the individual's sense of his position in a single community spanning several generations is broken. The first-generation migrant, to a greater extent than ever before, must "go solo." He lives with a kinsman or among people drawn from the same cluster of villages, but as a result of having opted out of relationships that were his by birth or from childhood he is, at least initially, without an advisor-protector. That time passes before he rebuilds his complete network of

Figure 7

Response to the Question, "Are There People Here You Go to for Advice, Opinions, Help, or Just To Pay Respect?": Elites Only

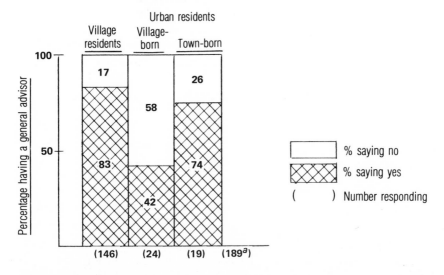

^aA single case of interviewer error among the village-born urbanites is not included in the figure. The differences are statistically significant. Chi-square reaches better than the 0.01 level of confidence and 6.5 percent of uncertainty is reduced.

advisors is evidence that he does not attach himself to the first bapak who comes along. Instead, he either deliberately chooses a patron or waits until circumstances of employment or some other activity expose him to a man in search of a client. In either case, the decision is one taken by an adult who is selecting from among a considerable group of potential patrons, and as such the selection process is less ascriptive and more deliberate, less traditional and more opportunistic, and laden more with instrument and less with affect than the process of attachment was in the village.

Further evidence of the disorganizing effect of urbanization on bapak-anak buah networks is found in replies to questions about the number of general advisors possessed by each respondent. Again, there are no significant differences between village residents and those who have resided in urban areas since birth. Both, however, are quite distinct from the first-generation city dwellers. Whereas 41 percent of the village residents and 44 percent of the town-born urbanites say they have between three and more than five general advisors, only 24 percent of the village-born urbanites have three or more such bapaks.

Not only do bapak-anak buah networks temporarily decline with the first generation of urbanization, but when they appear again at full strength their content is fundamentally altered. The connections most frequently affirmed in

TABLE 4

Percentage Affirming That They Have a
General Advisor, Financial Advisor, Local Political
Advisor, or Outside Political Advisor:
Elites Only

Type of advisor	Village residents	Urban residents		Number responding
		Village-born	Town-born	
General advisor	83% (121)	42% (10)	74% (14)	145
Financial advisor	75% (110)	63% (15)	84% (16)	141
Political advisor (local)	60% (88)	36% (9)	53% (10)	107
Political advisor (outsider)	32% (47)	16% (4)	42% (8)	59

NOTE: The percentages exceed 100 percent because I am reporting the affirmative replies for four separate questions for the three subsamples. A significance test would be inappropriate for the whole table. The differences among the subsamples are significant at the 0.01 level for the general advisor, at the 0.04 level for the local political advisor, and reach only 0.08 level for political advisors living outside the local community.

the urban context are material ones rather than the more general and diffuse connections most prevalent in the village.

We asked both urban and rural respondents the question, "If your son needs a hajat [a religious festival] for which you don't have the money, is there a man who can give you help?" The responses follow the same U-shaped curve found for the questions about general advisors (see Figure 9). The presence of such a financial patron is affirmed by three-quarters of the rural elite, and this proportion becomes even greater — 84 percent — among the town-born unbanites. But it falls to 63 percent among the village-born urban dwellers. Here there is further confirmation of the thesis that time is required before bapak-anak buah networks can be restored to the full prominence they held among villagers.

However, the single most interesting aspect of the data on financial patronship is that although it was the second most frequently affirmed kind of advisor-advisee relationship in the villages, it is found more frequently than any other type of relationship in the city (see Table 4). Although only 42 percent of the village-born urbanites say they have a general advisor, 63 percent say they have a person to whom they can go for financial assistance. The same upward trend appears among the town-born urbanites where the proportion having a financial patron is 10 percent greater than the proportion having a general advisor. Moreover, among village-born urbanites whose interpersonal networks

Figure 8

Number of General Advisors as Indicated by Response to the Question:
"How Many People Could You Go to for Advice?": Elites Only

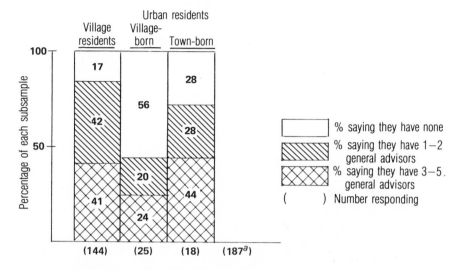

^aIn order to include the whole range of possibilities extending from having no general advisor to having more than five such advisors, the negative replies from Figure 7 have also been included in Figure 8.

The differences in the table are statistically significant at a confidence level higher than 0.01 and 6.3 percent of total uncertainty is reduced.

have been disorganized by urbanization, it is the only type of advisor-advisee relationship possessed by the majority.

An additional indication of the increased importance of the financial advisor-advisee relationship is that its local character decreases with urbanization. While 81 percent of the village elite respondents answering the question said they had only a local benefactor, the percentage decreases sharply among urbanites, to 67 percent and 44 percent for village-born and town-born city dwellers respectively. Naturally enough, with urbanization financial patronship breaks out of the geographic confines imposed by the community of residence. This opens up the closed nature of economic life by making wider geographic and social areas available for the solution of the recurrent problem of personal financial shortage. Because the individual can and does go for help to persons who live in other parts of the city, financial patron-client relations become less local and more cosmopolitan.

The increasingly cosmopolitan nature of the financial advisor-advisee relationship does not extend equally to political advisor-advisee relationships. When respondents were asked if they had a political advisor living outside the immediate local community, the first-generation urban dweller appeared to be even more isolated than his counterpart in the village. Only 16 percent of the

Figure 9

Response to the Question, "If Your Son Needs a *Hajat* [Religious Festival]
for which You Don't Have the Money, Is there a Man Who Can Give
You Help?":   Elites Only

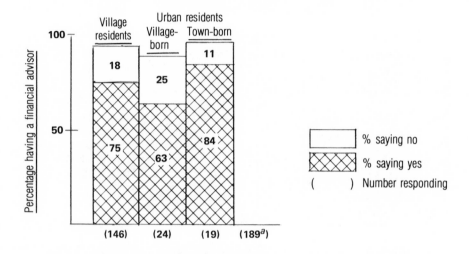

---

[a]"Don't know" responses account for 6 percent, 13 percent, and 5 percent of the village residents, village-born urbanites, and town-born urbanites respectively, and the "don't know responses" have been included in the statistical calculations.

The differences reported in the figure are *not* statistically significant, although they follow the same trend as the significant ones reported for other types of advisor-advisee relationships.

village-born urban elite respondents had an advisor on political matters residing outside the immediate local community.[20] This compares with 32 percent of the village elite respondents who had a political advisor living beyond the village gate. Forty-two percent of the town-born urbanites possessed an outside advisor on political affairs. In financial and political matters, the urban environment eventually leads to less geographically constricted relationships; however, it is perhaps a sign of the increasing importance of financial relations that the financial advisor-advisee relationship is the first to become geographically cosmopolitan, whereas political patronship evolves beyond the community of residence only among those who have been familiar with urban life from birth.

20. Unfortunately no data were collected regarding village residents who continue to function as the bapaks of recently urbanized clients. Although improved transport might make it physically possible to sustain relationships with rural traditional authority figures, the changed requirements of city life would probably lead to eventual abandonment in favor of new patrons capable of satisfying uniquely urban wants.

Figure 10

Residence of Financial Benefactor: Elites Only[a]

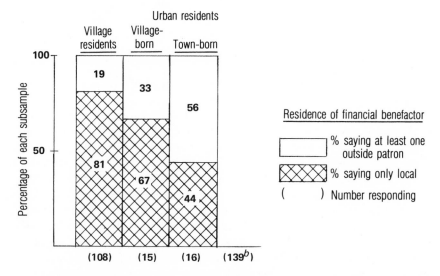

------

[a] Residence indicated by response to the question, "Is that man [who supplies money for the *hajat*] a member of this community here or from outside this neighborhood?" The word neighborhood (*babakan*) was substituted for the word village (*desa*) in the urban questionnaire.

[b] The *N* here is 139 because it was asked only if the respondent had a financial patron. The differences in the figure are significant at better than the 0.01 level; the amount of uncertainty reduction is 5 percent and gamma is 0.5388. The same relationship remains significant at the 0.01 level for whole samples (including the poor).

   Calculating chi-square for the elite samples violates the Mann rule because one-third of the cells have expected frequencies of less than 5. In addition these cells contribute heavily to the total chi-square; hence, the confidence placed in the differences should be less, although the low expected frequencies probably result as much from the large size of the rural sample as they do from the small size of the urban samples.

The Changing Obligations of Leader and Follower

What is being discussed here is more than a structural change, more than an altered frequency of network use. I am concerned with the ways in which the favors being exchanged are altered by urbanization and the more limited sense of reciprocity that patron and client alike come to expect of the relationship.

The financial aspects of village traditional authority relations consist of supplying access to land, employment of the client as either sharecropper or wage laborer, insurance against unpredictable calamities such as drought, and loans to pay off money-lenders. In each case the transaction differs from the commercial ones that many peasants simultaneously maintain with money-lenders. Although the goods proffered by the patron have an economic value, there is no binding obligation to pay them back in a set amount of money or labor. In the perceptions of the participants, repayment is not a simple matter of principle plus interest; instead the debt in money is viewed as a debt in moral obligation (hutang budi) which in some instances may never be fully discharged by the client. The patron realizes that the cash value of his favors to clients will probably never return to his coffers, but the accompanying realization is that he has a follower who can be called to do labor, to pay respect, to attend at family ceremonials, to frequent the bapak's home for advice to vote for the leader's choice, and if necessary to defend the bapak's life should military operations be mounted in the village.

With movement to the city, the elements being exchanged and the extent of mutual obligation incurred are necessarily changed. The primary source of material aid in the urban context is finding employment for the client in either the bloated national bureaucracy, the nationalized enterprises, or private business. Urban employment is high and receipt of a job, even a part-time job, is a favor that compels reciprocal action. The job-holder becomes the client of both the man who found him the opening and his immediate superior in the office or business. Most jobs do not pay nearly enough to support a family; hence, multiple jobs and multiple patrons are the rule rather than the exception.

In the bureaucracy and private business several distinct forms have evolved by which the office patron supplies material aid for his subordinates. The first and most obvious is *korupsi*. The office manager, in return for certain services, receives substantial extra payments which he subsequently shares unequally with his subordinates, thus maintaining them and making them more dependent on him. A second form of corruption is the petty corruption, *catut*, often encountered among minor bureaucrats. With the connivance of their superiors, office workers often tease out extra income by charging more than the legal tariff for official services, for example, charging 400 Rps. while giving an official receipt for only 250 Rps. The superior may or may not receive a share of the proceeds, but he remains the ultimate power figure implicitly sanctioning these means of supplementing income.

The third method for supplementing unreasonably low salaries is the practice of *ngompreng*. The superior permits official equipment to be used during office hours to supply nonofficial services. Examples range from allowing the mimeographing pool to run off circulars for outsiders to giving a subordinate use of the office car during the work day. The subordinate then rents the car either as a taxi or for hauling goods in the town, and the proceeds are used to increase the take-home pay of staff members. The superior's permission to raise extra income through ngompreng often is sought directly, with the clear implication being that he could arbitrarily forbid the use of office equipment for unofficial purposes. In some instances the superior requires that payments be channeled through his hands. In korupsi, *catut*, the ngompreng, the superior uses the perquisites of official position to enable his subordinates to increase their incomes through their personal relationship with him (see Oostingh 1970: 134-42, 206-09; Hanna 1971: 1-8).

Another business-related way in which the urban patron cares for his client is called *ngobyek,* literally, a piece of a deal. The patron, especially if he is a businessman, will subdivide work among his clients asking each to do part of the work, thereby supplying employment and income through his personal intervention. The patron often sets the price, and the client almost always agrees, even in instances when he knows that the price offered is not sufficient to cover his costs. The patron as the receptacle of both knowledge and virtue is expected to know minutely the assets and needs of his client, and if the latter gets in financial trouble while doing his benefactor's bidding, the patron is expected to come to his aid. Hence, the client will almost always say *mangga* (yes) when asked directly whether he can provide a product or service at a set price, and the piece of a deal given by the patron may require supplementary benefactions for the client if the original arrangement proves too onerous.

Another service commonly supplied by the urban patron is emergency loans. If the client is ill, in jail, or simply cannot meet the terms of an inexpertly negotiated business deal, the patron will bail out the client. Hospital bills will be taken care of or money will appear to satisfy a debt. Again, the quality distinguishing the patron's favor from a business matter is that repayment is usually left inexplicit, with the clear possibility that repayment in cash may never be required.

Still another important resource of the urban patron is his central position in a network of diverse reciprocal service relations. Over time he establishes relations with persons in many walks of life, and these obligations can be called due in services rendered to his clients. The proficient urban patron is the leader of a heterogeneous entourage capable of caring internally for most of the needs of its members. If the son of client X needs treatment for tuberculosis, the patron is expected to detect the fact that something is wrong and to tell the client where he can get care. Often a note is carried by the client to the patron's medical contact who may provide the service at a reduced cost, or more often, with no charge whatever. The doctor may be repaying a past debt or investing in his relationship with the client's patron, but in any case the agreement is implicit and noncontractual.

The primary benefits for the urban patron are emotional, social, and political. The patron is, first and foremost, a man respected and revered by his followers. His advice is often asked and for the most part followed. On the street and in the office, behavioral signs of respect flow his way. It is he who is approached to mobilize workers to electrify a kampung or to fix the mosque. It is he who is flattered daily by his followers' expectations that he is so powerful that he can, in a seemingly effortless manner, solve all of their problems. Further, the client's practice of frequently visiting his home is an act of respect publicly acknowledging the client's dependence on him. Clients will vote his wishes, and, if asked, they will join or leave an organization on his bidding. Furthermore, they will magnify the grandeur of any social occasion by swelling the numbers from a small private gathering to a semipublic ceremony testifying to the power and prestige of the patron. All of these add to the patron's stature and power in the community. Of course, each client adds skills and assets to the patron's networks. The patron in need of service knows where he can obtain it at little or no cost. As a result, the obligations to the patron, while being partially paid off by one client, are being reinvested in another.

Another asset obtained by the patron is efficiency of operation. Without an entourage, be he bureaucrat or businessman, it is difficult, if not impossible, to work his will with speed and assurance. The superior who is not also the bapak cannot expect wholehearted compliance with his orders. The businessman whose employees are not also his personal clients will find that the work does not get done, that the materials are diverted, and that the product is often stolen. By making himself the center of the informal as well as the formal group structure the businessman will obtain greater diligence, and in addition will be able to trust his employees not to divert his machines or products to the service of others without his prior approval.

Finally, the patron may obtain cash contributions and labor service from his personal entourage. If he is adding to his house or holding a party, voluntary contributions of labor by male or female members of the client household will be forthcoming. Also, the bureaucrat's garden may be tended by a client from the office, or the client's wife may serve in the household for little or no cash compensation.

In many ways the essence of traditional authority was the sense of open-ended, binding moral obligation felt by the follower toward the leader and vice versa. If traditional authority relations are giving way to patron-client bonds in the city, *hutang budi* (moral obligation) should also be changing. At first glance, this does not seem to be the case. As part of the series of questions about financial assitance, residents were asked, "As a result of his help in the form of money, do you feel morally indebted [*hutang budi*] toward him?" There is virtually no discernible difference between the urban and rural respondents, with more than 90 percent of each sample stating that they would feel a moral obligation. If inquiry halted here, one might conclude that the urban respondents were indeed "urban villagers" indistinguishable in social custom from their rural counterparts.

The appearance of no-change evaporates when one scrutinizes the replies to a follow-up question inquiring how far the respondent would go to repay a debt of moral obligation. The replies to this open-ended question reveal substantial differences, but these appear only at the later stages of the urbanization process. Whereas villagers and first-generation urbanites frequently view hutang budi as an unlimited obligation, the majority of those born in towns perceive hutang budi as requiring the more limited acts of reciprocity due to a patron (see Figure 11).

The distinction between traditional authority and patron-client relations is captured by the words of the respondents themselves as they define their obligations. Responses *A-G* are the high hutang budi responses typical of the majority of village elite members as well as village-born urbanites.

Respondent *A*: Repaying an obligation to a wealthy man is superfluous, but of course, when he is in trouble, I will help him as much as is in my power.

Figure 11

Feelings of Moral Obligation toward a Financial Benefactor Indicated by Response
to the Question, "If You Felt *Hutang Budi* How Far Would You Go To
Repay It?":   Elites Only

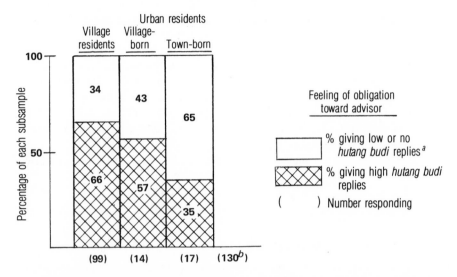

[a] The "No *hutang budi*" replies were included in the "low" category. Those denying they felt *hutang budi* comprised 2 percent, 7 percent, and 6 percent of the village residents, village-born urbanites, and town-born urbanites respectively.

[b] The differences in the Figure 9 reach a confidence level of 0.06 for chi-square, and 3 percent of the uncertainty is reduced. However, the major differences are between the village residents and village-born urbanites on the one hand and the town-born urbanites on the other. To test this hypothesis the first two columns were combined and run against the town-born urbanites. The fourfold table yielded a chi-square that was statistically significant at the 0.04 level.

Respondent *B*: If possible, until I die, wherever possible by labor or advice — as for money — where should I get it?

Respondent *C*: Even in situations of physical violence I will help him when he is in trouble.

Respondent *D*: When it comes to blows, I will come to his aid when he is in trouble.

Respondent *E*: Not only my earthly goods, but I will give my last drops of blood . . .

Respondent *F*: Help his sons and daughters either materially or spiritually if he leaves them behind.

Respondent *G*: Till my dying breath and the end of time I'll love him.

Several aspects are worth noting here. First, the obligation is diffuse and open-ended, extending beyond the money debt itself. In fact, for respondents *A* and *B* the thought of repaying the money itself seems a side issue. The transaction is not a commercial one but an asymmetric dependency bond in which both parties find emotional rewards far beyond the value of the goods or money exchanged. Second, the respondents spontaneously mention violence as part of the repayment obligation involved in hutang budi. The surplus wealth of the bapak has been converted into the ability to mobilize men for action at some future date for some as yet undisclosed political course.

The low hutang budi replies illustrated by respondents *H-K* predominate among the town-born city dwellers. As a result of the transformation occurring in social relations, replies such as "anything I have," "my life," and "I will remember as long as I live," are replaced by "help him when he needs help," and "by showing him my respect." The replies of urban respondents are devoid of references to physical combat, mention limited obligations, and envision a shorter time-frame than the high hutang budi replies of the villagers.

Respondent *H*: It is only a loan and I should pay it off.

Respondent *I*: Tit for tat, according to my ability, physically or spiritually, and also in material goods.

Respondent *J*: It's mutual. Whatever he needs, I'll give if I happen to have it.

Respondent *K*: As to paying back budi, although not in goods, the main thing is in your behavior toward him (you show it).

The Duration of Relationships between Advisor and Advisee

The concept of traditional authority was predicated on the assumption that the leader-follower bonds were of long duration and that this characteristic provided evidence, albeit not conclusive evidence, that these bonds and not the rapidly changing political issues themselves determined the followers' political choices in the villages. If leader-follower bonds endure across long periods fraught with the rapid rise and fall of issues, ideologies, parties, governments, and constitutions, these traditional authority bonds may be more important to politics than transient ideologies and issue orientations.

In villages the data support this interpretation. Not only are most bonds of long duration but they frequently began before the advent of Indonesian independence. Among villagers the most frequent single reply to the question, "How long have you had this relationship?" was "more than twenty-five years." The political implications are readily apparent if one realizes that an advisor-advisee relationship of "more than twenty-five years" at the time of the interviewing in 1969 would have begun in the early 1940s. Although the content of political discourse repeatedly has been changed, the personal bonds among villagers have remained truly traditional.

All of this changes with urbanization, and the change is critical to the transformation from traditional authority to patronage as the most important type of power. With urbanization, power relationships become de-traditionalized and more opportunistic because the interpersonal bonds themselves no longer reflect a life-long stability capable of bridging all manner of short-term differences in interest between leader and follower.[21] Not only are the long-term bonds fractured for first-generation urbanites, but linkages of the same duration do not reappear among the town-born urbanites. Rather than following the now familiar pattern of temporary decline among the village-born and subsequent resuscitation among the town-born, lengthy leader-follower bonds become as uncommon in the city as they were common in the village. The strength and persistence of the change is evident from Table 5, which summarizes the data on duration for three kinds of advisor-advisee relationships. Because there are no differences between village-born and town-born urbanites, these categories have been combined and contrasted with elite village residents.

Most urbanites have known their general advisor a scant five years or less, and a full 50 percent fall into this shortened time-frame in their connection with

TABLE 5

Percentage Possessing an Advisor-Advisee Relationship
of 6 to 25 Years' Duration for the General Advisor,
Financial Advisor, and Local Political Advisor
by Rural and Urban: Elites Only

	Village residents	Urban residents
General advisor	75% (91)	35% (18)
Financial advisor	79% (89)	65% (20)
Local political advisor	76% (68)	50% (9)

NOTE: This table summarizes the results of three tables in which durations of five years or less and six years to more than twenty-five years were run against rural and urban elite respondents for each of the three types of advisor-advisee relationships. All three tables yield statistically significant or nearly significant differences. For the general advisor, the rural-urban difference yields a chi-square significance at better than the 0.01 level and reduces 10.8 percent of the total uncertainty. For financial advisor-advisee bonds, the differences are significant at better than the 0.01 level and 10.8 percent of the uncertainty is reduced. The duration of relations for local political advisors does not quite reach statistical significance, the level of confidence in chi-square being only 0.06 with 4.6 percent of the total uncertainty being reduced.

21. The urban and rural elite samples do not differ significantly on the age variable. Although we did not collect data on exact ages but instead collected group data, for example, 20-29 years, 30-39 years, the urban elite sample averaged forty-one years of age and the mean for the rural elite was forty-two years. Furthermore, when we control for age differences between the rural and urban samples with regard to the questions concerning differences in duration of relationships, the differences do not wash out. Hence, the differences in duration of relationships cannot be a spurious result caused by age differences between the samples.

local political advisors. Only in regard to the financial patron do a clear majority of the urban elite respondents say they have had a relationship of from six to more than twenty-five years. As previously noted, financial advisor-advisee bonds are the most frequently affirmed ones in the city, and in addition they are of longest duration and spread most rapidly beyond the kampung's confines. In combination, these findings supply evidence that among leader-follower bonds those with the financial patron have adapted most readily to the demands of the urban environment.

Endurance across decades endows village leader-led relations with a legitimacy, trust, and sense of personal security enabling the traditional authority figure to obtain nearly automatic adherence to his wishes, even when these wishes abridge the immediate interests of his followers. The bonds of affection nurtured from childhood and adolescence through adulthood are not to be frittered away for some passing promise by another leader, or some dimly perceived ambiguity dramatized by the issue of today. The passage of decades facilitates the development of a vernacular of intimacy between leader and follower which assumes the continuing goodwill of the leader as well as the unswerving loyalty of the follower. The follower believes that his interests will be taken care of and that therefore there is no need to extract an explicit quid pro quo. Likewise, from the traditional authority figure's viewpoint, there is no question that his anak buah of twenty-five years will adopt his position with regard to some national political issue. The time-tied vernacular of intimacy allows most things to be understood without being said, thus largely freeing the traditional leader from the task of cajoling and convincing his followers.

When the time-frame of the relationship is shortened with urbanization, the unquestioned, pervasive authority of the person of the leader decreases. The assumptions of a time-tested solidity underpinning the traditional authority relationship disappear. The relationship between leader and follower becomes increasingly calculated with reference to short- and medium-run gains as well as alternative opportunities. With urbanization, the follower no longer asks of a leader, "What did he do for my father?" and "Who was his father?" because the stability of the social world has been permanently altered, and hence in judging a leader emphasis on the distant past is quite naturally displaced by questions such as "What can I expect in the next few years?" or even "What have you done for me lately?"[22]

22. Of course, some proportion of the change in duration of relationships could result from migration from one village to another rather than from the particular form of migration called urbanization. Unfortunately, the present research design lacks a sample of rural migrants and cannot speak directly to this question. However, if mere physical movement causes the change (as might be argued by the migration hypothesis) it would be difficult to explain why duration does not differ substantially between the more settled town-born urbanites and their counterparts who have experienced the much more substantial movement from villages to the metropolis. While many other aspects of bapakism return to vitality among the town-born urbanites, why is it that duration remains at a uniformly low level for the entire urban sample?

Organizational Membership

Figure 6 demonstrates, from the perspective of the patron, the increasingly limited influence of advisor-advisee relations on the pattern of formal organizational membership. Table 6 corroborates Figure 6 but from the client's vantage point, indicating that the direct connection between bapakism and organizational membership fades rapidly with urbanization. This change is probably permanent because there are no differences between village-born and town-born urbanites; a heavy majority say they do not belong to the same organizations as their advisors, regardless of whether it is the general advisor, the financial patron, or the local political confidant. Taken together, Figure 6 and Table 6 form a consistent pattern of significant or near significant differences on four widely separated questions. Urban respondents are clearly less prone to being members of the same organizations as their patrons.

As will be seen in the next section, this does not mean that the patron cannot use his clients to exert organizational power. It only means that urban organizations cannot expect the same stable support from bapakism that they enjoyed in the villages. Therefore urban organizations with their more fluid and unstable memberships must find other forms of social cement with which to bind their followers. Although urban patrons can use their power to bring clients

TABLE 6

Percentage Affirming a Direct Connection between
Having an Advisor and Membership in an Organization:
Elites Only

Organizational membership influenced by	Village residents	Urban residents
General advisor	55% (66)	5% (1)
Financial advisor	47% (48)	9% (3)
Local political advisor	53% (48)	28% (5)

NOTE: This table summarizes three tables in which the presence or absence of organizational memberships identical with one's advisor is run against the rural and urban elite samples. The differences between country and town are significant for the first two kinds of leader-follower relations and approach significance for the local political advisor-advisee relation. The rural-urban differences for the general advisor reach a confidence level of better than 0.01 and the total uncertainty reduced is 18.6 percent. For the financial advisor, chi-square reaches a confidence level of better than 0.01 and 11.4 percent of total uncertainty is reduced. The differences for the local political advisor yield a chi-square with a confidence level of only 0.09, while 4.2 percent of the total uncertainty is reduced.

into an organization, there is no tendency to do this on a routine basis, hence, modern organizations in urban areas are deprived of the fillip that could be provided by patron-client relations.

BAPAKISM AND POLITICS IN THE CITY

Thus far I have established that certain aspects of the form and content of interpersonal relationships are changing in the urban setting in the first or subsequent generation of acculturation to city life. However, nothing has yet demonstrated that interpersonal relationships continue to have the same pertinence to politics that they enjoyed in the village. Does the political impact of bapakism decline with urbanization, or do the patron-client relations replacing traditional authority bonds have a pervasive influence on political participation in urban neighborhoods? The simple answer is that patron-client relations have a substantial effect and that the influence of these interpersonal communication networks on political decisions may even increase during the first generation of residence in the city.

Opinion Leadership

The influence of interpersonal communication networks on opinion formation is felt equally in town and country alike. Almost by definition, the advisee's opinions seem to be those of the advisor. "Going to a knowledgeable man for advice" in the village context means going to him to acquire his stand on the issues of the day, and this does not change substantially as traditional authority gives way to patronage in the city's poorer neighborhoods. Respondents seem to acquire the entire belief set of their advisors. This impression is confirmed by the responses to the question, "Does the advice given by this man [a local political advisor] concerning the problems of the region or country correspond with your opinions?" and "Do you usually agree with his opinions [those of a political advisor living outside the community]?" With regard to both questions, in the city and village alike, the overwhelming majority of those answering the question affirm the powerful sway exerted by traditional authority figures and patrons alike over opinion formation. In the villages, affirmative responses are given by 95 percent of those responding to the questions. In the city, all twenty-one of the respondents stating that they have a local political advisor say they agree with his opinions, and twelve of the sixteen persons having a nonlocal political advisor state they usually agree with his opinions. Although the numbers are small because of filter questions, the lopsided distribution of responses remains impressive.

Physical Mobilization to Protect a Bapak

If it is correct that the bond between leader and led is the most important factor in politics in the poor urban neighborhoods and villages alike, influence over opinions is less important than influence on manpower mobilization, affiliation with religious currents (*aliran*), and membership in political groups.

Dealing with mobilization and affiliation through questionnaire data pushes survey research to the outer limits of its capabilities in the Indonesian cultural context. To ask individuals directly whether they joined or withdrew from political or religous groups because their patrons wanted them to would yield quite unreliable results. Therefore, the questions in this section are projective, asking the respondent to predict what other actors might do in situations involving bapakism and political affiliation.

The first projective question concerns physical mobilization, in particular whether the anak buah will rush to aid their leader in a quasi-insurrectionary situation. The most important elements in the essay are (1) the diffuse, personal relationship between the leader and the follower, (2) the long duration of the relationship, (3) the allusion to a situation involving violence, and (4) the absence in the essay of any mention of the nature of the cause being fought for. The projective essay read,

> Here is a story concerning a man called Pa Dadap. After I have read this story to you, I would like to ask you a few questions concerning this story. You don't mind, do you?
>
> Pa Dadap has incurred a debt which also involved his son, and which would make the future difficult. Pa Dadap's ex-commander, whom he hasn't seen for ten years, hears of his difficulty and immediately sends money to the sum of about 100,000 Rupiahs without any strings attached. Therefore, Pa Dadap can look forward again to the future. But six months later, there is a disturbance in the region where the commander lives, and Pa Dadap hears that his ex-commander's life may be in danger. Pa Dadap has four alternatives for action. Which of them do you think is best?
>
> 1. Wait for more information about the ex-commander's difficulties.
> 2. Wait until his ex-commander asks for help.
> 3. Immediately send the money.
> 4. Go off and try to see the ex-commander, even if many dangers would thereby be involved.
>
> What do you think Pa Dadap will do?
>
> [Instruction to Interviewer: Repeat once more the four alternatives.]

Figure 12 supplies the responses for the elite samples. Even though the leader-follower relationship has been transformed by the urbanization experience, there is certainly no deterioration in willingness to aid a genuine patron of long standing. Urban dwellers are at least as willing as their village counterparts to aid their bapak even if physical risks are involved. Moreover, among the recent migrants to Bandung, there is a statistically significant rise in the willingness to go to the patron's aid. Far from losing political potency through urbanization, the bapak-anak buah networks have a more intense influence among the recent migrants; this is true in spite of the substantial disarray into which each individual's advisor-advisee network is thrown by movement to the city. Clearly, having fewer advisors because of the social shock of moving to the city does not preclude mobilizing or even doing violence on behalf of the patron. Though the

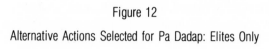

Figure 12

Alternative Actions Selected for Pa Dadap: Elites Only

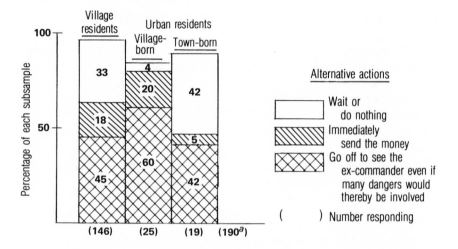

[a]"Don't know" responses account for 4 percent, 16 percent, and 11 percent of the village residents, village-born urbanites, and town-born urbanites respectively, and these responses have been included in the statistical calculations.
     The differences are statistically significant at the 0.02 level, and the amount of uncertainty reduction is 6.8 percent. Four of the cells have expected frequencies of less than 5 in violation of the Mann rule on chi-square. The problem with regard to this figure is caused by the much larger size of the rural sample. Thus, if one generates a hypothetical sample with the village N reduced by two-thirds, but with the proportions maintained, the chi-square remains significant and the contributions of the low expected frequency cells is reduced to unimportance.
     A more orthodox method for alleviating this problem is by collapsing the first and third columns of the original table, thus yielding a significant chi-square at above the 0.01 level. In this case, if the remaining two cells with low expected frequencies are not allowed to contribute to the sum of chi square, the table still remains statistically significant at above the 0.05 level.

individual lacks the complete network of advisors that he possessed in the village, the first-generation urban dweller seems to value his relationship with his patron even more highly than those who remained behind in the villages.
     It should also be noted that among the town-born, the willingness to wait or do nothing is much higher than among the village-born urbanites and slightly higher than among the villagers. This is probably an indication that with the conversion from traditional authority to the more limited patron-client system, the willingness to enter combat for the bapak declines. This supports my earlier contention that mobilization for violence is a function of the leader-follower bond that begins to wither away after the first generation of city life (see Figure 4).
     Yet Figure 12 shows that there are some bapak-anak buah relations even at the close of the urbanization process that can incite urbanites to violence. This

slight anomaly in the data is explained by the differences between the situations depicted in the two questions. Figure 4 reports that urban advisors perceive themselves to be less able to raise large numbers of clients to defend them than their rural counterparts, whereas Figure 12 shows that urban clients will still come to the defense of a very special patron. Unlike the earlier question, the projective essay depicts a special situation where the leader-follower relationship has endured for approximately twenty years, and in which the leader has unselfishly cared for the most vital interests of his follower. Clearly the fires of traditional authority can be rekindled in the city if certain conditions are met, but these conditions are no longer characteristic of the typical patron-client relationship in the city. The ex-commander's relationship to Pa Dadap is of decades duration, whereas the typical urban patron-client relationship has a much briefer tenure. Figure 12 depicts an extraordinary man of very high status who is in trouble, whereas Figure 4 reports how many clients could be raised in everyday life by an ordinary patron.

Affiliation with an Aliran

The second projective question regards a situation more typical of urban political life than mobilization to protect a patron's person. It depicts circumstances in which the respondent is forced to choose between loyalty to his patron and loyalty to an *aliran* (religious current). The projective question read,

> Haji Hasan and Haji Memed are leaders of a religious current [*aliran*] counting many members because the current is led by a famous Kiyayi [religious teacher]. Although it is unclear how it came about, those two men fell out with each other and broke their relationship. Do you think that if one of them left this religious group, he would be followed by the people who were considered his followers [anak-buah]?[23]

As shown in Figure 13, the proportion of persons stating that the anak buah will follow the patron out of the aliran increases sharply among first-generation city-dwellers. Although only a tiny minority, 5 percent of the village elite, think the patron will be followed out of the aliran, among the village-born

23. This question was modified slightly in the urban context by being broken into two parts. The first asked whether the anak buah would follow their leader if he formed a committee to represent his truth within the organization. The data reported here are for the follow-up question, "In the case of the leader who founded the committee, if after a sufficient length of time he decided to go out of the aliran, would his anak buah follow him?" The question used in the urban interviews more closely approximates a set of tactics commonly found in the politics of factionalization. Rather than immediately taking his followers out of the aliran or political party, the leader first forms a committee claiming to be the true representative of the old organization. Only after time has elapsed does he abandon the old organization's name completely. As expected, the number of respondents who could conceive of the anak buah joining a committee to represent his truth within the organization was higher than the number who could conceive of leaving the aliran immediately. Fifty-three percent of all urban dwellers could conceive of joining the bapak's committee, but only 25 percent thought the anak buah would follow their leader directly out of the aliran.

Figure 13

Willingness of *Anak-Buah* To Follow Their *Haji* out of an *Aliran:* Elites Only

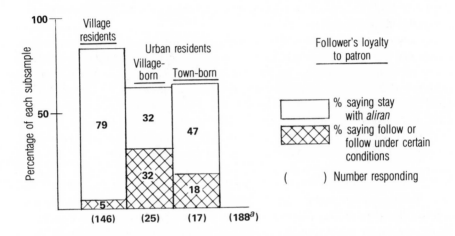

---

[a] "Don't know" responses account for 16 percent, 36 percent, and 35 percent of the village residents, village-born urbanites, and town-born urbanites respectively, and these responses have been included in the statistical calculations.

The differences in this figure are significant at better than the 0.01 level and 11.2 percent of the total uncertainty is reduced. Three of the expected frequencies in the table violate the Mann rule; however, the table would continue to be significant at the 0.01 level if the contribution of these troublesome cells was entirely excluded from the total chi-square. Hence, violating the Mann rule does not change the outcome of the test.

urbanites those stating that the followers will leave the aliran increases by 27 percent, while the proportion stating that the anak buah will stay with the aliran drops by 47 percent. The town-born urbanites, most interestingly, manifest a different pattern from the one displayed in the ex-commander story. They are less willing than the village-born urbanites to consider following a patron out of an aliran, but they remain more willing to do so than their village counterparts. Willingness to follow the patron is higher in the city than it was in the villages, although the increase levels off with those most accustomed to city life.

Only a minority of each of the three subsamples evince a willingness to abandon the aliran to stay with their leader. This could be interpreted as evidence that neither traditional authority nor patronage are very important to affiliation. My experience in both the urban and rural context leads me to reject such an inference. There are limits to survey research as an instrument for divining social reality, especially when it blatantly juxtaposes two highly valued symbols such as affection for the leader and loyalty to religion, and forces the respondent to choose between them. The successful bapak would never be so kasar or crude. Instead, he might avoid placing his respondents in a dissonant situation by forming a committee within the aliran to "support his truth." Doing so would allow his followers to remain steadfast in their loyalty to him, while initially blurring the extent to which they were separating themselves from the mother organization. S. M. Kartosoewirjo, who later led the Dar'ul Islam rebellion, used precisely these tactics in 1940 when he broke with the leadership of the Partai Sarekat Islam Indonesia (PSII) by founding the Komite Pembela Kebenaran PSII, literally the committee for the defense of the true PSII (Pinardi 1964: 24-29). He eventually led his adherents out of the PSII but avoided placing them in a position, such as the one in this question, where respondents were forced immediately to choose between loyalty to religious party and loyalty to their bapak.

Party Loyalty versus Financial Reward

From the evidence on opinion formation, mobilization for violence, and willingness to change alirans, it is clear that leader-follower relations remain at least as important to decision-making in the city as they were in the village. Although the character of the bonds has changed from traditional authority to patronage, the bonds continue to exert a considerable, and perhaps even a rising influence among poor urbanites. That the character of the linkages is steadily changing in the direction of the more material and opportunistic relations is illustrated by the final projective story that involves the application of crass material enticement to alter political affiliation. The projective question read as follows:

> Now I'll tell you a story. I'll first read a story about a man in a village. After I've finished, I should like to ask you some questions about that man. This is the story.
>
> Pa Waru has been a member of political party *A* for ten years. He goes to every meeting and get-together of his party, because, so he says, he believes in the ideal of the party. Also, a representative of Party *A* has helped his son to become a civil servant in town. Because of party affiliation, he can obtain a better price for his rice.
>
> One day a representative of Party *B* came to the village, and Pa Waru was aware that this party was in opposition to his party, although both parties were legal. The representative of Party *B* offered Pa Waru a higher price for his rice on the condition that Pa Waru should become a member of Party *B*. Now Pa Waru has to decide whether he should change parties or not, hasn't he?
>
> Now I would like to ask some questions which are connected with the story.

The responses manifest a steady decline in resistance to material enticement with urbanization. Among the village elite the vast majority resist material temptation and stay with the old party. However, among urban dwellers the respondents perceiving loyalty to the old party as most important decline by nearly 30 percent, and the number who can conceive of Pa Waru switching parties for monetary gain increases substantially.

Figure 14

Changing Parties for Financial Reward: Elites Only

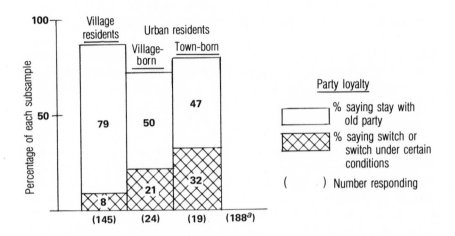

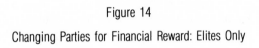

---

[a]"Don't know" responses account for 13 percent, 29 percent, and 21 percent of the village residents, village-born urbanites, and town-born urbanites respectively, and these are included in the statistical calculations.

The differences in this figure are significant at above the 0.01 level and 5.7 percent of the total uncertainty is reduced. Four of the expected cell entries violate the Mann rule, and they contribute more than half the total chi-square. However, the problem is easily resolved if the village-born and town-born urbanites are combined into a single category. The major differences in the figure are basically urban-rural and are significant at above the 0.01 level.

In essence, the pattern encountered here is a movement toward shorter, more limited, more material relationships which still maintain an essentially personal and noncontractual form. The meaning and content of bapak-anak buah relationships in the urban context is summed up in the words of a successful Indonesian trade union organizer who admitted his inability to mobilize his countrymen until he understood the dynamics of the system: "When I came back from Holland and began my work in labor organization, I just couldn't figure it all out . . ." He then offered the following explanation of the relationship of bapakism to organizational activity in West Java:

> The organizational structure of all organizations, including political ones such as the PKI, can be described as following a network of personal ties cemented by past favors which are mostly material in nature, but also consisting of the rewards of status conferred by association with a person of higher status. The networks tend to be fairly permanent as long as no strain is placed on the network. In signing up for a national organization the individuals are merely following the lead of a bapak who is connected by ties of personal loyalty to a higher bapak. Ideology is almost totally irrelevant. The striking thing about Indonesian organizational behavior is

that individuals still bother to sign up as members of organizations rather than just voting or carrying out whatever behaviour [is] required of them by the bapak.[24]

CONCLUSIONS AND IMPLICATIONS

The political and social world of village East Priangan and kampung Bandung remain fundamentally a setting in which authority flows from personal rather than institutional, group, or ideological resources. Power is derived from the constellation of loyal followers surrounding and acknowledging the superiority of particular leaders as a result of each follower's own personal, face-to-face, reciprocal relationship with his leader. The bonds are animated not so much by similarities between leader and led as by profound differences in social status, education, knowledge, wealth, and official position. The resulting coalitions are markedly heterogeneous ones in which the "have nots" on each quality are led by the "haves" in the hope that individual improvement will result from the successful leader whose fruits will then be distributed unequally among his loyal followers. Improvement in personal conditions is sought in the individual's link to his bapak rather than through alliance with those in the wider social world who suffer identical deprivations.

Among the village-born and town-born citizens of the poor neighborhoods of Bandung, one sees evolving substantial changes either with the first or subsequent generation of assimilation into the city. The more open-ended and unlimited personal linkages of the traditional authority figure with his followers give way to a more limited, material, and opportunistic set of patron-client links.[25] Thus, traditional authority in passing away is giving birth to patronage, and patronage continues to exert heavy influence on opinion formation, group affiliation, and patterns of social and political communication.

24. From an informal interview conducted on February 24, 1969, in Bandung.

25. Urbanization is not the only way in which this transition can take place. Traditional authority can decline in a rural setting through either economic change or the forces of civil war or revolution. Commercialization of agriculture, especially when combined with the growth of law and order, may lead the rural traditional authority figure to shed many of his followers. When the landowner becomes increasingly concerned with extracting economic value from his tenants and sharecroppers rather than with providing and protecting the subordinates who give him social status and protection, traditional authority gives way to patronage and maybe even to reward-deprivation. Graeme Hugo indicates in a personal communication that the phenomenon of landowners shedding their followers is becoming more frequent in Central and parts of West Java. However, on the basis of his field work in 1973 this phenomenon does not seem to have had a substantial impact, as yet, in Priangan.

Civil war, plague, and invasion offer other means by which the transition to shorter, more limited relationships may be affected. Executing all the chief patrons along with a significant proportion of the wealthier landowners will probably destroy traditional authority in a village, and the destruction will be permanent if the central government is able to perform the functions formerly supplied by traditional authority figures working in alliance with their followers. See Scott 1972a for an excellent description of the transition from traditional authority to patronage to reward-deprivation in rural areas of Southeast Asia.

The most important demographic change expected in Indonesia during the next decade is *not* the high birth rate, but the much higher rate of growth projected for the urban areas. Although the population is expected to grow at 2.5 percent per annum until at least 1980, between 1970 and 1985 the rate of increase in the urban population is expected to vary between 4.22 percent and 4.62 percent per annum (Population Division, Department of Economic and Social Affairs of the U.N. Secretariat 1970). Given the as yet limited trickle-down effects of Indonesian economic growth and the example supplied by the urban riots of 1974, the political implications of this study must now be explored, even though these implications are not based directly on hard data.

The most probable consequence of the vast influx of village-born into the cities will be increased social and political disorientation combined with a potential for short-term, concerted, but extra-organizational political action such as urban riots.

Disorientation and disorganization result because patron-client relations are less directly tied to organizational membership patterns than they were in the villages. The density of modern organizational forms is much greater in the city but the loyalty of the rank and file is, if anything, more tenuous than it was in the villages because organizational membership is no longer directly supported by bapak-anak buah and other ascriptive relationships. As in most transitional or post-traditional societies there is nothing as fictitious as a modern organization that has lost the backing of fictive kinship and other ascriptive ties.

Furthermore, the declining duration of leader-follower bonds in the city provides a destabilizing force. Patrons drop clients and clients switch patrons, adding an element of uncertainty that would be foreign to the stable and traditional linkages animating village politics. Also, the reciprocal obligations binding patron to client are no longer as unlimited and absolute as they were in the village, and hence the urban patron can be less confident than his rural counterpart in estimating what his clients will do for him in a crucial situation. To the degree that politics remains predominantly personal but becomes more short range and opportunistic, it becomes more unpredictable than it was in the village context.

Uncertainty is also added by the tendency of first-generation urbanites to be less completely involved in the leader-led networks than either established urban-dwellers or village residents. In effect, the recently urbanized are a floating mass set adrift from their social system of birth while being only partially integrated into city social life. The existence of a substantial, only partially integrated mass of migrants makes politics more volatile than it was in the villages. Whereas a few village elders could confidently swing the entire village vote, urban patrons cannot hope to obtain such unanimity within their neighbor-hoods because a substantial proportion of the patron-client links extend beyond the geographic boundary lines, thus allowing many neighbors to be affiliated with unknown outsiders. A final element adding to this instability is the size of the political unit. City life is so complex that the patrons do not have the kind of reliable information about political trends within their social unit that the village elders possessed for their much smaller social world. Hence, miscalculation becomes more likely for the urban patron than it was for the rural traditional authority figure.

From the government planner's perspective, the disorganization of social leadership patterns during the first generation of urbanization creates a problem. Information can be spread more easily because of the higher mass media exposure rates in the city, but changing behavior and deeply ingrained attitudes requires more than merely making information available. Research in many cultures has shown that if mass media messages are not reinforced by supportive interpersonal communications, the messages, no matter how cleverly devised and distributed, are likely to fall on deaf ears and be ineffective for inducing basic changes (Pool 1963). If future research in Indonesian cities confirms my findings, the planner's communication problems are even more difficult among first-generation urbanites than among villagers because a complete, stable set of interpersonal communication networks is temporarily unavailable. In the village context the planner might have confidence in his ability to induce change if he could obtain the wholehearted support of the chief traditional authority figures controlling the highly integrated and largely closed village communication system, but in the urban context the planner has a much more difficult time locating vital network nodules, and a substantial number of individuals may not yet be completely connected to the network.

Although the village-born urbanite perceives himself as less regularly involved in bapak-anak buah networks as an advisee than either the town-born urbanite or the village resident, certain aspects of the village-born urbanite's perception of himself as an advisor convince me that he has a potential for short-run, extra-organizational political volatility which probably includes violence. Although the size of the cliques surrounding patrons declines during urbanization, this does not occur immediately. In fact, the village-born urban patrons claim groups of clients that are just as large as any in the villages. Likewise, though the unlimited, open-ended aspects of hutang budi decline with the tendency to perceive oneself as a bapak is actually higher during the first generation in the city than it was in the village. Paramilitary aspects of bapakism also decline but only after the first generation; newcomers to the city are only slightly less likely than villagers to perceive themselves as capable of raising large numbers of men to defend them, and as a subsample they are more willing than any other to go to the aid of a major patron, the ex-commander, even in an insurrectionary situation. Given these qualities, I would predict that first-generation migrants will be the most amenable to mobilization, though somewhat paradoxically they are least integrated into the full panorama of patron-client networks. The paradox partially accounts for the essentially short-run character of the political actions to be expected from this group, because lack of integration precludes sustained political activity.

Furthermore, even when an individual becomes fully integrated into the system of patron-client relations, the inherently particularistic cast of such attachments precludes mobilization of large numbers of groups for sustained, citywide political activity. A patron-client group seeks improvements for itself rather than for all socioeconomically similar groups, and the inner-directed focus of each group makes it difficult to organize multigroup, semipermanent political organizations (see Cornelius 1974). To the extent that first generation migrants increase disproportionately in Indonesian cities, they will provide manpower for volatile, often chaotic, and extra-organizational political activity. Contagions, panics, and riots rather than sustained, organized violence will characterize the participation of migrants to the limited extent that they are involved (at all) in violent forms of urban political participation.

Like most stages, this too shall pass as village-born urbanites are assimilated into the city and as they give birth to a new generation of established urbanites more wholly divorced from rural habits and forms. The alteration from traditional authority to patronage haltingly begun in the first generation will be concluded in the second. Change is clearly taking place, when one compares the social relations of the village with those evolving among urban residents. Grasping the pace, direction, and political meaning of the changes has required scrutinizing interpersonal communications networks in minute detail. Through such a detailed examination one finds neither retraditionalized urban villagers nor fully modern urban participants but instead an intermediate political form, namely, patronage, that is being used in Indonesian society, as it has previously been in many other societies, to cushion the transition from rural to urban. The types of power and kinds of communications binding the poorer neighborhoods together and connecting them with the city will remain fundamentally transitional until the long process of assimilation has been completed for the waves of immigrants that will continue to roll into cities such as Bandung during the hurricane of urban growth marking the remainder of the century.

Conclusion

13

The Prospects for Bureaucratic Polity in Indonesia

KARL D. JACKSON

AT THE OUTSET of this study it was suggested that the Indonesian political system is best understood as a bureaucratic polity with political power and participation monopolized by the highest levels of the civil and military bureaucracies. Political life revolves around a small number of key decision-makers responding primarily, although not exclusively, to the values and interests of the small, capital-city elite. The system was termed a bureaucratic polity because sucessive regimes have been products of internal competition within the civil and military bureaucracies rather than responses to mass movements mobilized by ideological, class, or primordial sentiments. Interest groups, political parties, and horizontal groupings of all kinds remain weak and incapable of consistently influencing the basic political decisions determining Indonesian domestic and foreign policies.

The main arena for political competition is not the country at large but the bureaucratic, technocratic, and military elite circle in closest physical proximity to the president of the republic. Political parties exist and elections are held but both serve to legitimize, through democratic symbolism, the power arrangements already determined through the maneuvering of competing elite circles in Jakarta. The Indonesian bureaucratic polity favors neither democratic nor totalitarian forms of mass participation, and parties are incapable of either controlling the central bureaucracy or mobilizing the masses behind a single set of ideologically defined social goals. Neither the very substantial gap between the ostentatiously wealthy Jakarta elite and the miserably poor villagers of Java nor the primordial differences found among Indonesian Muslims have been effectively mobilized into politics. With the partial exception of the PKI, class differences have not supplied a compelling principle for mobilizing the masses into politics; similarly, the religious beliefs of the masses have not been translated into organizations capable of enforcing the wishes of the *ummat Islam* on the Jakarta elite.

The Indonesian bureaucratic polity has dressed itself over time in varying ideological guises. Yet, in spite of these changes in surface appearance, the realities of power have remained remarkably constant. The flamboyant Sukarno and the ideologically austere Suharto have both presided over a structure of politics limited to a few key institutions, hierarchial in nature, dependent on an ultimate authority at the center, and largely immune to popular pressures or autonomous political interests. The geography of the country, its pattern of communications, its economic system, and above all its deeply engrained cultural attitudes have all conspired to maintain and reinforce a model of bureaucratic polity. A political earthquake, such as followed the attempted Communist coup of 1965, can briefly level the distribution of power in the country, but the tendencies toward bureaucratic polity soon re-emerge. And even though there are new men in authority committed to new ideals and new programs, the basic structure of power persists.

Neither the president of the Republic nor the bureaucratic elite he represents has great impact on the daily lives of most Indonesian citizens. The bureaucracy neither penetrates the society deeply nor mobilizes its far-flung citizenry with a decisive ideology. The New Order has resuscitated the export sector, brought in foreign capital, and controlled rampant inflation, but all of these laudable and vital policy objectives were obtained without the mobilization of the general population. The regime has failed to reach its goals in agricultural productivity and population growth: effectiveness has declined directly to the extent that goal-fulfillment has required the mobilization or participation of the general population. In Indonesia much needs to be done if there is to be significant modernization and any genuine improvement in the lot of the people; however, the projects most likely to provide dramatic improvement require mass mobilization or participation, and the Indonesian bureaucratic polity has shown itself unwilling or unable to mobilize the required segments of its citizenry. Isolating the peasantry from party politics and fostering a one-way communication system have ensured the short-term survival of bureaucratic polity, but also have made it difficult to energize the peasantry for economic and social development. Further, the social structure emphasizing predominantly vertical rather than horizontal affiliations and the political culture emphasizing deference, self-control, and indirectness have been similarly well adapted to maintaining a bureaucratic polity but less well suited to developing a strong, modern state.

The present Indonesian bureaucratic polity is stable but weak, easy to rule, but difficult to modernize. Economic changes will occur, but the most likely successes will involve foreign capital monopolizing limited skills and expertise in capital-intensive enterprises directed toward the international marketplace. Capital formation and trickle-down effects will occur, but conspicuously modern enclaves will grow richer while the economic and social problems of the rural and urban poor become increasingly intractable and hence unattractive to hard-pressed policy-makers.

Although bureaucratic polity is the most probable form of government in Indonesia for the next several decades, with bureaucratic polities nothing fails like success. To the extent that the ruling elite is able to maintain a rate of GNP expansion exceeding 5 percent per capita per annum over the next twenty years, it will breed its own opposition. To the extent that education, mass media, and modern organizational forms involve an increasing proportion of the population, personal efficacy, horizontal affiliations, and the desire for political participation will increase. At such a juncture the salience of primordial and class differences probably will increase, providing the combustible material for disjunctive political change. Whether substantial political change occurs, its character, and its social and economic costs for Indonesian society will be determined by the wisdom of elite choices presently being made to channel the energies released by the modernization process. The choices taken by the Indonesian political elite over the next decade will affect long-term economic and political stability and the prospect for Indonesia becoming a modern nation with the advent of the twenty-first century. The available alternatives fall into three categories: (1) movement toward a more open, competitive democratic system, expanding the power of the government by sharing control more widely; (2) foundation of an ideologically based, single-party mobilization regime (of Right or Left), extending government organization and political mobilization into every town and village in the society; and (3) the continuation of bureaucratic polity under conditions of increasing challenge from social elements generated by economic expansion. Although all three alternatives are within the purview of the current elite, the third choice remains the most probable. Although President Suharto and his advisors or the ruling circle that follows them may elect to pursue democratic participation or single-party mobilization, selecting either would mark a radical departure from the political history of the past two decades. Rather than adopting either of the alternatives entailing the expansion of participation and mobilization, the bureaucratic and military elites probably will continue to limit participation, and increased coercion will be the most likely response to participatory energies released by the modernization process. The most likely outcome in Indonesia over the next several decades is a hardening of the bureaucratic polity, a harsher use of power, and increasingly authoritarian practices. Pressing social and economic problems may not be solved, the national patrimony of oil and other natural resources may be ineffectually used or wasted, but the traditions of power underpinning the Indonesian bureaucratic polity are unlikely to yield readily to change.

In any case, the primary purpose of this study has not been to foresee the future of Indonesia but rather to understand more fully its present and past. Instead of assuming that Indonesia, as a developing country, is on the verge of moving either toward liberal democracy or totalitarian mobilization, for the time being it is enough to say that Indonesia is a model bureaucratic polity, with all its strengths and weaknesses, and is likely to remain so.

Bibliography

INDONESIAN NEWSPAPERS AND PERIODICALS

Abadi (Jakarta)
Angkatan Bersenjata (Jakarta)
Antara (Jakarta)
Api Pantja Sila (Jakarta)
Bhirawa (Surabaya)
Djawa Baroe (Jakarta)
Djawa Pos (Surabaya)
Harian Kami (Jakarta)
Indonesian Daily News (Surabaya)
Indonesia Raya (Jakarta)
Jakarta Times (Jakarta)
Kompas (Jakarta)

Masa Kini (Jogjakarta)
Merdeka (Jakarta)
Pedoman (Jakarta)
Pikiran Rakyat (Bandung)
Pos Indonesia (Jakarta)
Prisma (Jakarta)
Sinar Harapan (Jakarta)
Surabaya Post (Surabaya)
Tempo (Jakarta)
Topik (Jakarta)
Warta Berita (Jakarta)

BOOKS AND ARTICLES

Adin, A. 1976. Peranan minyak dalam pembangunan ekonomi Indonesia. Prisma. 5(4).

Affif, S., and C. Timmer. 1971. Rice policy in Indonesia. Food Research Institute Studies in Agricultural Economics, Trade, and Development. 10.

Ahmad, Z. 1956. Membentuk negara Islam, Jakarta.

Aidit, D. 1961. The selected works of D. N. Aidit. 2 vols. U.S. Joint Publications Research Service.

Alfian. 1971. Indonesian political thinking: a review. Indonesia. 11.

1971a. Hasil pemilihan umum 1955 untuk Dewan Perwakilan Rakjat (DPR). LEKNAS, Jakarta.

Aminuddin, E. 1972. Partisipasi surat kabar dalam pemilihan umum. Thesis. Universitas Pajajaran, Bandung.

Anderson, B. 1965. Mythology and the tolerance of the Javanese. Cornell Modern Indonesia Project Monograph.

1966. The languages of Indonesian politics. Indonesia. 1.

1966a. The problem of rice. Indonesia. 2.

1972. Java in a time of revolution.

1972a. The idea of power in Javanese culture. In C. Holt et al. 1972.

Anderson, B. and R. McVey. 1971. A preliminary analysis of the October 1, 1965 coup in Indonesia. Cornell Modern Indonesia Project Interim Report.

Anonymous. 1945. Marilah membela tanah air kita dengan darah daging kita!

Anshari, E. 1973. Kritik atas faham dan gerakan "pembaharuan" Drs. Nurcholish Madjid. Bandung.

Anshary, I. 1949. Falsafah perdjuangan Islam. Bandung.

Apter, D. 1964. Editor. Ideology and discontent.
     1965. The politics of modernization.
Army Headquarters. 1972. Dharma Pusaka 45.
Army History Center. 1967. Mengungkap Sapta Marga.
Arndt, H. 1973. Regional income estimates. Bulletin of Indonesian Economic
     Studies. November.
     1973a. Survey of recent developments. Bulletin of Indonesian Economic
     Studies. 9.
     1975. The PERTAMINA crisis. Bulletin of Indonesian Economic Studies.
     11(2).
Arymurthy, S. 1974. Fungsi anggaran pendapatan dan belanja negara dalam
     pelaksanaan pembangunan di Indonesia. Majalah Keuangan. 4(3).
Atmadi, T. 1972. Efforts to communicate for development, the set up and role
     of the Department of Information in Indonesia as one of the agents of mass
     communication. Paper submitted to the 2nd correspondents' meeting to
     AMIC, Singapore, August 1972.
Bachtiar, H. 1972. The function of some institutional arrangements in the
     formation of the Indonesian nation. Fakultas Sastra Universitas Indonesia,
     Jakarta.
Badan Penerbit Almanak Jakarta. 1972. Kabinet Pembangunan Republik
     Indonesia. Jakarta.
     1973. Kabinet Pembangunan II Republik Indonesia. Jakarta.
Bajasut, S. 1966. Facta documenta II: kembali ke UUK 1945, gagasan dan
     tanggapan, 1966.
Bank of Indonesia. Indonesian Financial Statistics. Various dates.
Barthes, R. 1972, Mythologies.
Bartlett, A., et al. 1972. PERTAMINA, Indonesian National Oil. Jakarta.
Bellah, R. 1965. Editor. Religion and progress in modern Asia.
     1970. Beyond belief.
Benda, H. 1965. Decolonization in Indonesia: the problem of continuity and
     change. American Historical Review. 70.
     1966. The pattern of administrative reforms in the closing years of Dutch
     rule in Indonesia. Journal of Asian Studies. 25.
Berman, P., 1974. Revolutionary organization.
Biro Pusat Statistik. 1957. Statistical pocketbook of Indonesia.
     1968. Statistik Indonesia, 1964-1967.
     1972. Sensus penduduk 1971, angka sementara.
     1972a. Statistik Indonesia, 1970-1971.
     1974. Statistik Indonesia, 1972-1973.
     1975. Sensus penduduk 1971.
Boediawan, T. 1971. House-to-house selling sebagai kegiatan periklanan. Thesis.
     Universitas Pajajaran, Bandung.
Boland, B. 1971. The struggle of Islam in modern Indonesia.
Booth, A. 1974. Ipeda — Indonesia's land tax. Bulletin of Indonesia Economic
     Studies. 10(1).
Bowers, I. 1973. Factors influencing village receptivity to agricultural innova-
     tions: a case study in kabupaten Krawang, West Java.
Brugmans, I. 1961. Onderwijspolitiek. In H. Baudet and I. Brugmans, eds.,
     Balans van beleid: terugblik op de laatste halve eeuw van Nederlandsch-Indië.
Budiardjo, C. 1974. Political imprisonment in Indonesia. Bulletin of Concerned
     Asian Scholars. 6(2).
Bulletin of Indonesian Economic Studies. 1975. 11(1).
Chabot, H. 1950. Verwantschap, stand en sexe in zuid-celebes.

1967. Bontoramba: a village of Goa South Sulawesi. In Koentjaraningrat, ed., Villages in Indonesia.

Clapham, M. 1970. Difficulties of foreign investors in Indonesia. Bulletin of Indonesian Economic Studies. March.

Coggin, D. 1975. Tethering the corporate tiger. Far Eastern Economic Review. November 7.

Collier, W., et al. 1973. Recent changes in rice harvesting methods. Bulletin of Indonesian Economic Studies. July.

1973a. Choice of technique in rice milling in Java: a comment. Unpublished.

Compton, B. 1953. President Sukarno and the Islamic state. Newsletter of the Institute of Current World Affairs. March 8. New York.

1955. Letters to the Institute of Current World Affairs. Segan: a word to ponder. A letter from Boyd R. Compton. American Universities Fieldstaff Reports, Southeast Asia Series.

Cornelius, W. 1974. Urbanization and political demand making: cities. American Political Science Review. 68.

Crouch, H. 1971. The army, the parties, and elections. Indonesia. 11.

1972. Military politics under Indonesia's New Order. Pacific Affairs. 45(2).

1974. The "15th January Affair" in Indonesia. Dyason House Papers. 1(1).

1975. The Indonesian army in politics: 1960-1971. Ph.D. thesis. Monash University.

1976. Generals and business in Indonesia. Pacific Affairs. 48(4).

Current data on the Indonesian military elite after the reorganization of 1969-1970. 1970. Indonesia. 10.

Dahm, B. 1969. Sukarno and the struggle for Indonesian independence.

Davies, D. 1974. Indonesia: consensus in the negative. Far Eastern Economic Review. February 25.

Day, C. 1966. The Dutch in Java. Reprint.

de Boer, D. 1920. Het Toba Bataksche huis, Kolff, Batavia.

Defense and Security Staff. 1967. Doktrin Pertahanan-Keamanan Nasional dan Doktrin Perdjuangan Angkatan Bersendjata Republik Indonesia "Tjatur Darma Eka Karma."

de Haan, F. 1912. Priangan: de Preanger-regentschappen onder het Nederlandsch bestuur tot 1811. Vol. 3. Batavia.

de Kat Angelino, A. 1931. Colonial policy. Vol. 2. Trans. G. Renier.

de Lorm, A., and G. Tichelman. 1941. Beeldende kunst der Bataks. Brill. Leiden.

Departemen Penerangan. n.d. [1954?] Lukistan revolusi, 1945-1950. Jakarta.

1972. Jawaban atas pertanyaan komisi I DPR/RI mengenai bidang RRI-TYRI/BSF dilingkungan DitJen Radio-TV-Film.

1973. Pokok-pokok pikiran bahan rancangan terms of reference penyusunan REPELITA II.

Department of Information. 1966. Decisions of the Fourth Plenary Session of the Madjelis Permusjawaratan Rakjat Sementara.

1972. Sound broadcasting in Indonesia.

1974. Rencana Pembangunan Lima Tahun Kedua, 1974/75-1978/79.

Department of Manpower. 1967. Djawaban pemerintah tentang larangan keanggotaan partai politik bagi pegawai negeri Golongan F. Dokumentasi Tenaga Kerdja. August 1.

1967a. Keterangan pemerintah berhubung dengan usul interpelasi anggota[2] jth. Moh. Djazim dkk. tentang pemetjatan massal kaum buruh. Dokumentasi Tenaga Kerdja. September 26.

Deutsch, K. 1953. Nationalism and social communication: an inquiry into the foundations of nationality.
    1961. Social mobilization and political development. American Political Science Review. 60.

Dewan Perwakilan Rakyat. 1974. Rancangan Undang-undang Republik Indonesia nomor___tahun 1974 tentang pokok-pokok pemerintahan di daerah. Jakarta.

de Wit, Y. 1974. The kabupaten program. Bulletin of Indonesian Economic Studies. March.

Direktorat Jenderal Pembangunan Masyarakat Desa, Departemen Dalam Negri. 1972. Desa: data 7 contol kecamatan di Jawa Barat sehubungan dengan survey pedesaan, 1971-1972.

Djoko Pradopo, R. 1967. Penggolongan angkatan dan Angkatan 66 dalam sastra. Horison. 2.

Doktrin Perdjuangan TNI-AD "Tri Ubaya Cakti."

Dorojatun Kuntjoro Jakti. 1971. Strategi ekonomidan beaja^2 sosial-politik. Tempo. April.

Douwes Dekker, E. 1909. The press. Twentieth-century impressions of Netherlands India, its history, people, commerce, industries, and resources.

Duester, P. 1971. Rural consequences of Indonesian inflation: a case study of the Jogjakarta region. Ph.D. thesis. University of Wisconsin.

Easton, D. 1958. The perception of authority and political change. In C. Friedrich, ed., Authority.

Emmerson, D. 1972. Exploring elite political culture: community and change. Ph.D. thesis. Yale University.
    1973. Bureaucratic alienation in Indonesia: "the director general's dilemma." In R. Liddle, ed., Political participation in modern Indonesia.
    1973 a. Students and the establishment in Indonesia: the status-generation gap. In H. Wriggins and J. Guyot, eds., Population, politics and the future of Southern Asia.
    1976. Indonesia's elite: political culture and cultural politics.

Esmara, H. 1975. Regional income disparities. Bulletin of Indonesian Economic Studies. 11(1).

Fagg, D. 1958. Authority and social structure: a study in Javanese bureaucracy. Ph.D. thesis. Harvard University.

Fakultas Publisistik Universitas Pajajaran. 1973. Survey.

Federspiel, H. 1970. Persatuan Islam. Cornell Modern Indonesia Project.

Feith, H. 1957. The Indonesian elections of 1955. Cornell Modern Indonesia Project.
    1958. The Wilopo cabinet, 1952-1953; a turning point in post-revolutionary Indonesia. Cornell Modern Indonesia Project.
    1962. The decline of constitutional democracy in Indonesia.
    1963. Dynamics of Guided Democracy. In R. McVey 1963.
    1964. President Sukarno, the army and the Communists: the triangle changes shape. Asian survey. 4(8).
    1964a. Indonesia. In. G. Kahin, ed., Governments and politics of Southeast Asia.
    1968. Suharto's search for a political format. Indonesia. 6.

Feith, H., and L. Castles. 1970. Editors. Indonesian political thinking 1945-1965.

Feith, H., and D. Lev. 1963. The end of the Indonesian rebellion. Pacific Affairs. 36(1).

Finch, S., and D. Lev. 1965. Editors. Republic of Indonesia cabinets, 1945-1965. Cornell Modern Indonesia Project.

Fisher, C. 1964. Southeast Asia: a social, economic, and political geography.

Franke, R. 1971. The Javanese Kangen family. Draft paper.

    1972. The Green Revolution in a Javanese village. Ph.D. thesis. Harvard University.

Frey, F. 1970. Political science, education, and development. In J. Fischer, ed., The social sciences and the comparative study of educational systems.

Geertz, C. 1956. The development of the Javanese economy: a socio-cultural approach. M.A. thesis. Massachusetts Institute of Technology.

    1956a. The social context of economic change: an Indonesian case study. Massachusetts Institute of Technology.

    1960. The religion of Java.

    1960a. The Javanese kiyayi: the changing role of a cultural broker. Comparitive Studies in Society and History. 2.

    1963. Agricultural involution: the process of ecological change in Indonesia.

    1964. Ideology as a cultural system. In Apter 1964.

    1965. The social history of an Indonesian town.

    1968. Islam observed: religious development in Morocco and Indonesia.

    1972. Religious change and social order in Soeharto's Indonesia. Asia. 27.

    1975. On the nature of anthropological understanding. American Scientist. 63.

Geertz, H. 1959. The Balinese village. In G. Skinner, 1959.

    1961. The Javanese family.

    1963. Indonesian cultures and communities. In R. McVey, 1963.

Glassburner, B. 1970. Pricing of foreign exchange in Indonesia, 1966-1970. Economic Development and Cultural Change. 18(2). Reprinted in B. Glassburner, ed. 1971. The economy of Indonesia.

    1973. The 1973 tariff revision. Bulletin of Indonesian Economic Studies. November.

    1976. In the wake of General Ibnu: crisis in the Indonesian oil industry. Asian Survey. 16(12).

Goethals, P. 1959. The Sumbawan village. In G. Skinner, 1959.

    1967. Rarak: a swidden village of West Sumbawa. In Koentjaraningrat, ed., Villages in Indonesia.

Government of Indonesia. 1975. Financial note and budget plan. Nota Keuangan.

GPII. n.d. Fatwa alim ulama tentang pemilihan umum. Jogjakarta. Mimeographed.

Greenstein, F., and N. Polsby. 1975. Editors. Handbook of political science.

Gumelar, W. 1973. Pengadaan public relations dalam modernisasi. Thesis. Universitas Pajajaran, Bandung.

Gunawan. 1972. Periklanan televisi. Thesis. Universitas Pajajaran, Bandung.

    1973. Tanggapan anak-anak terhadap iklan televisi. Thesis. Universitas Pajajaran, Bandung.

Hadisapoetro, S. 1973. Kelengkapan wilayah unit desa masalah dan prospeknja. Departemen Ekonomi Pertanian, Universitas Gajamada, Jogjakarta.

Hady, H. 1974. Pembangunan daerah dalam REPELITA II. Prisma. 3(2).

Hagen, E. 1962. On the theory of social change.

Hamidjaja, A. 1967. Daerah dan Angkatan 66. Horison. 2.

Hanks, L. 1962. Merit and power in the Thai social order. American Anthropologist. 64.

    1968. Entourage and circle in Burma. Bennington Review. 2.

    1968a. American aid is damaging Thai society. Transaction. 5.

Hanna, W. 1967. The magical mystical syndrome in the Indonesian mentality, part I: signs and seers. American Universities Field Staff Reports, Southeast Asia Series. 15(5).

1967a. The magical mystical syndrome in the Indonesian mentality, part II: Ka'Rachim and the other initiates. American Universities Field Staff Reports, Southeast Asia Series. 15(6).

1971. A primer on korupsi. American Universities Field Staff Reports, Southeast Asia Series. 19(8).

1974. Indonesian projections and the arithmetic of anxiety. American Universities Field Staff Reports, Southeast Asia Series. 22(3).

Hansen, G. 1971. Episodes in rural modernization: problems in the BIMAS program. Indonesia. 11.

1973. The politics and administration of rural development in Indonesia: the case of agriculture. University of California Center for South/ Southeast Asia Studies.

1974. Rural local government and agricultural development in Java, Indonesia. Cornell University Rural Development Committee.

Hardjoprakoso, S. 1969. Conditions in Indonesia for an efficient use of foreign aid. Mimeo, Bangkok.

Hart, H. 1932. De personeelsuitgaven van het land. Koloniale Studien. 16(1).

Harvard Development Advisory Service. 1972. The relative efficiency of the PNP plantations.

Hassan, A 1941. Islam dan kebangsaan.

Hatta, M. 1960. Past and future. Cornell Modern Indonesia Project Translation.

1971. The Putera reports: problems in Indonesian-Japanese wartime cooperation. Trans. W. Frederick. Cornell Modern Indonesia Project.

Heine-Geldern, R. 1956. Conceptions of state and kingship in Southeast Asia. Reprint. Southeast Asia Program Data Paper. Cornell University.

Henderson, E. 1912. Symbol and satire in the French Revolution. Putnam's. London.

Hindley, D. 1962. President Sukarno and the Communists: the politics of domestication. American Political Science Review. 56.

1966. The Communist party of Indonesia 1951-1963.

1967. Political power and the October 1965 coup in Indonesia. Journal of Asian Studies. 26.

1970. Alirans and the fall of the Old Order. Indonesia. 9.

1972. Indonesia 1971: Pantjasila democracy and the second parliamentary elections. Asian Survey. 13(1).

Hoerip, S. 1966. Angkatan 66 dalam kesusasteraan kita. Horison. 1.

Hofsteede, W. 1971. Decision-making processes in four West Javanese villages. Offoetdrukkerij Faculteit der Wiskunde en Natuurwetenschappen.

Holt, C. 1967. Art in Indonesia, continuities and change.

Holt, C., et al., eds. 1972. Culture and politics in Indonesia.

Hughes, J. 1967. Indonesian upheaval.

Humas Lembaga Pemilu Pusat. 1971.

Huntington, S. 1968. Political order in changing societies.

Huntington, S., and J. Nelson. 1976. No easy choice: political participation in developing countries.

Ihalauw, J. 1972. Penggunaan modal asing. Gunung Mulia, Jakarta.

Indonesian Consulate General in Hong Kong. 1975. Business prospects in Indonesia today.

Indonesian Student Press League. 1972. Pemilihan umum 1971. Lembaga Pendidikan dan Konsultasi Pers, Jakarta.

Inkeles, A. 1969. Participant citizenship in six developing countries. American Political Science Review. 63.

Inkeles, A., and D. Smith. 1974. Becoming modern: individual change in six developing countries.

Institute for General Elections. 1971. Daftar pembagian kursi pemilihan umum anggota Dewan Perwakilan Rakjat tahun 1971. Lembaga Pemilihan Umum, Jakarta.

Instruksi Presiden Republik Indonesia. 1967. No. 5. July 26.

Iskandar, N. 1972. Some demographic studies on the population of Indonesia. University of Indonesia. Jakarta.

Isman, M. 1967. The role of the Indonesian armed forces in nurturing democratic life and their relations with the party system in Indonesia.

Jackson, K. 1971. Traditional authority and national integration: the Dar'ul Islam Rebellion in West Java. Ph.D. thesis. M.I.T.
Forthcoming. Description of the village setting. In Traditional authority and national integration: the Dar'ul Islam rebellion in West Java.

Jackson, K., and J. Moeliono. 1972. Communication and national integration in Sundanese villages: implications for communication strategy. East-West Communication Institute. Honolulu.
1973. Participation in rebellion: the Dar'ul Islam in West Java. In R. Liddle, ed., Political participation in modern Indonesia.

Jacob, P., and J. Toscano,. 1964. Editors. The integration of political communities.

Jaspan, M. 1967. Aspects of Indonesian political sociology in the late Soekarno era. University of Western Australian Centre for Asian Studies, Working Paper no. 3.

Jassin, H. 1966. Angkatan 66, bangkitnja satu generasi. Horison. 1.

Jay, R. 1963. Religion and politics in rural central Java. Yale University Southeast Asia Studies Monograph.
1969. Javanese villagers: social relations in rural Modjokuto.

Jenkins, D. 1976. Suharto: a decade of deeds and dilemmas. Far Eastern Economic Review. August 20.

Kahin, G. 1952. Nationalism and revolution in Indonesia.

Kantor Sensus dan Statistik Propinsi Jawa Timur. 1972. Jawa Timur dalam angka. Surabaya.

Kantor Statistik D.C.I. Jakarta. 1973. Jakarta dalam angka 1972.

Kempers, A. 1959. Ancient Indonesian art.

Keputusan Presiden Republik Indonesia no. 79/1969. 1970. Vidya Yudha. 3(10).

Khaldun, I. 1958. The mukaddinah.

King. D. 1974. Social developments in Indonesia: a macro analysis. Asian Survey. 14(10).

King, D., and P. Weldon. 1975. Pembagian pendapatan dan tingkat hidup di Jawa, 1963-1970. Ekonomi dan Keuangan Indonesia. 23(4).

Koentjaraningrat. 1967. Tjelapar: a village in south central Java. In Koentjaraningrat, ed., Villages in Indonesia.

Kushwaha, S. 1974. Zur internationalen dynamik des fernsehens. Entwicklung und Zusammenarbeit. 4(74). Bonn.

Lande, C. 1965. Leaders, factions, and parties: the structure of Philippine politics. Yale University Southeast Asia Studies Monograph.

Laporan Mingguan [Weekly Report]. Bank of Indonesia. Various dates.

Legge, J. 1961. Central authority and regional autonomy in Indonesia: a study in local administration, 1950-1960.

    1972. Sukarno.

Lembaga Pemilihan Umum. 1971.

    Daftar pembagian kursi hasil pemilihan umum anggota Dewan Perwakilan Rakjat tahun 1971. Jakarta.

Lembaga Pers dan Pendapat Umum. n.d. Jakarta.

Lerner, D. 1958. The passing of traditional society.

Lev, D. 1963. The political role of the army in Indonesia. Pacific Affairs. 36(4).

    1966. The transition to guided democracy: Indonesian politics 1957-1959. Cornell Modern Indonesia Project.

    1966a. Indonesia 1965: the year of the coup. Asian Survey. 6(2).

    1967. Political parties in Indonesia. Journal of Southeast Asian History. 8.

    1972. Islamic courts in Indonesia: a study in the political bases of legal institutions.

Liddle, R. 1970. Ethnicity, party, and national integration: an Indonesian case study.

    1973. Modernizing Indonesian politics. In R. Liddle, ed., Political participation in modern Indonesia. Yale University Southeast Asia Studies Monograph.

    1973a. Evolution from above: national leadership and local development in Indonesia. Journal of Asian Studies. 32.

Linz, J. 1975. Totalitarian and authoritarian regimes. In F. Greenstein and N. Polsby, 1975, vol. 3.

Lubis, M. 1969. Mysticism in Indonesian politics. In R. Tilman, ed., Man, state, and society in contemporary Southeast Asia.

McAlister, J., Jr. 1973. Editor. Southeast Asia: the politics of national integration.

McCawley, P. 1973. Survey of Recent Developments. Bulletin of Indonesian Economic Studies. 9.

McDonald, H. 1976. Indonesia: the debt pile rises. Far Eastern Economic Review. July 2.

MacDougall, J. 1975. Technocrats as modernizers: the economists of Indonesia's New Order. Ph.D. thesis. University of Michigan.

McIntyre, A. 1972. Division and power in the Indonesian national party, 1965-1966. Indonesia. 13.

Mackie, J. 1961. Indonesia's government estates and their masters. Pacific Affaris. 34(4).

McNicoll, G., and S. Mamas. 1973. The demographic situation in Indonesia.

McVey, R. 1963. Editor. Indonesia. Rev. 1967.

    1967. Taman Siswa and the Indonesian National Awakening. Indonesia. 4.

    1969. Translator-editor. Nationalism, Islam, and Marxism: the management of ideological conflict in Indonesia. In Sukarno, nationalism, Islam, and Marxism. Cornell Modern Indonesia Project Translation Series.

    1971. The post-revolutionary transformation of the Indonesian army, part I. Indonesia. 11.

    1972. The post-revolutionary transformation of the Indonesian army, part II. Indonesia. 13.

Madjid, N. 1970. Keharusan pembaharusan pemikiran Islam dan masalah integrasi ummat. In Madjid et al. 1970. Pembaharuan pemikiran Islam. Jakarta.

Manihuruk, A. 1973. Pokok-pokok pikiran tentang penyempurnaan pembinaan kepegawaian. Badan Administrasi Kepegawaian Negara. Jakarta.

Maryanov, G. 1958. Decentralization in Indonesia as a political problem. Cornell Modern Indonesia Project.

Marzali, A. 1976. Impak pembangunan pabrik terhadap sikap dan mata pencarian masyarakat: kasus Krakatau Steel. Prisma. 5(3).

Marzuki Arifin, S. 1974. Peristiwa 15 Januari 1974. Publishing House Indonesia, Jakarta.

Mears, L. 1970. A new approach to rice intensification. Bulletin of Indonesian Economic Studies. 6(2).

Milne, R. 1973. Patrons, clients, and ethnicity: the case of Sarawak and Sabah in Malaysia. Asian Survey. 13.

Mintaredja, H. 1971. Masjarakat Islam dan politik di Indonesia. Jakarta.

Mitchell, D. 1970. Wanokalada: a case study in local administration. Bulletin of Indonesian Economic Studies. 6(2).

Moertono, S. 1968. State and statecraft in old Java: a study of the later Mataram period, 16th to 19th century. Cornell Modern Indonesia Project.

Moertopo, A. 1973. Some basic thoughts on the acceleration and modernization of 25 years' development. Center for Strategic and International Studies. Jakarta.

1973a. Indonesia in regional and international cooperation: principles of implementation and construction.

Montgomery, R. 1974. The link between trade and labor absorption in rural Java: an input-output study of Jogjakarta. Ph.D. thesis. Cornell University.

1975. Migration, employment, and unemployment in Java: changes from 1961 to 1971 with particular reference to the green revolution. Asian Survey. 15(3).

Mortimer, R. 1973. Editor. Showcase state: the illusion of Indonesia's "accelerated modernization."

1973a. Indonesia: growth or development? In R. Mortimer, ed., Showcase state.

1974. Indonesian Communism under Sukarno: ideology and politics, 1959-1965.

Mosher, A. 1966. Getting agriculture moving.

Mrázek, R. 1972. Tan Malaka: a political personality's structure of experience. Indonesia. 14.

Mubyarto. 1969. The sugar industry. Bulletin of Indonesian Economic Studies. 5(2).

Myrdal, G. 1963. Asian drama: an inquiry into the poverty of nations. 3 vols.

Nahdatul Ulama. 1959. Buku kenang[2] an mu'tamar ke-XXII Partai NU December.

Nash, M. 1963. Party-building in upper Burma. Asian Survey. 3.

Nasution, A. B. 1976. Minyak dan segi hukum kasus PERTAMINA. Prisma. 5(4)

Nasution, A. H. 1963. Tentara Nasional Indonesia. Vol. 1. Bandung.

1964. Toward a people's army. Jakarta.

1965. Fundamentals of guerilla warfare. London.

1971. Kekarjaan ABRI.

Natsir, M. 1961. Capita selecta.

n.d. Dapatkah dipisahkan politik dan agama?

Navy, M. 1974. Peranan persuasi dan opini publik untuk meningkatkan kepariwisataan. Thesis. Universitas Pajajaran.

Nishihara, M. 1972. GOLKAR and the Indonesian Elections of 1971. Cornell Modern Indonesia Project.

Noel, C. 1965. The concept of progress and Islamic law. In R. Bellah 1965.

Nowak, T., and K. Snyder. 1974. Clientelist politics in the Philippines: integration and instability. American Political Science Review. 68.

Nugroho Notosusanto and I. Saleh. n.d. The coup attempt of the "September 30 Movement" in Indonesia.

Oostingh, R. 1970. The pegawai negri of Bandung: structure and process in Indonesia. Ph.D. thesis. University of Virginia.

Organisasi dan prosedur komand daerah militer. 1972. Circulated in the Army Staff and Command School, Bandung.

Paget, R. 1967. The military in Indonesian politics: the burden of power. Pacific Affairs. 40.

Palmer, A. 1959. The Sundanese village. In G. Skinner, 1959.

1967. Situradja: a village in Highland Priangan. In Koentjaraninggrat, ed., Villages in Indonesia.

Palmer, I. 1972. Textiles in Indonesia: problems of import substitution.

Parlindungan, M. 1964. Pongkinangolngolan Sinambela gelar Tuanku Rao, teror agama Islam mazhab Hambali di tanah Batak 1816-1833. Mazhab. Tandjung Penharapan. Jakarta.

Pauker, G. 1963. The Indonesian doctrine of territorial warfare and territorial management. RAND memorandum.

Pelzer, K. 1963. The agricultural foundation. In R. McVey, 1963.

Penny, D. 1966. The economics of peasant agriculture: the Indonesian case. Bulletin of Indonesian Economic Studies. 5.

1969. Indonesia. In R. Shand, ed., Agricultural development in Asia.

Penny, D., and M. Singarimbun. 1972. A case study of rural poverty. Bulletin of Indonesian Economic Studies. 8(1).

Phillips, H. 1958. The election ritual in a Thai village. Journal of Social Issues. 14.

1965. Thai peasant personality.

Pinardi, 1964. Sekarmadji Maridjan Kartosuwirjo. Jakarta.

Polomka, P. 1971. Indonesia since Sukarno.

1973. A study of Indonesian foreign policy with special reference to the involvement of the military. Ph.D. thesis. University of Melbourne.

1974. Indonesia's future and South-East Asia. Adelphi Paper 104. London.

Pool, I. 1963. The mass media and politics in the modernization process. In L. Pye, ed., Communications and political development.

Population Division, Department of Economic and Social Affairs of the United Nations Secretariat. 1970. Urban and rural population: individual countries 1950-1958 and regions and major areas 1950-1970. U.N. document ESA/P/WP, 33.

Prosser, M. 1973. Intercommunication among nations and peoples.

Radio Republik Indonesia. Various dates.

1972. Buku Evaluasi Nusantara II, 1972-73.

Ransom, D. 1970. The Berkeley mafia and the Indonesian massacre. Ramparts. 9(4).

1973. Ford country: building an elite for Indonesia. In S. Weissman, ed., The Trojan horse: the strange politics of foreign aid.

Rasjidi, H. 1972. Koreksi terhadap Drs. Nurcholis Madjid tentang sekularisasi. Jakarta.

Reitberger, R., and W. Fuchs. 1971. Comics, anatomy of a mass medium.

REPELITA. 1969. Bandung.

Riggs, F. 1966. Thailand: the modernization of a bureaucratic polity.

1969. Organization theory and international development. Carnegie Seminar on Political and Administrative Development.

Rocamora, J. 1970. The partai nasional Indonesia, 1963-65. Indonesia. 10.

1973. Political participation and the party system: the PNI example. In R. Liddle, ed. Political participation in modern Indonesia.

Roeder, O. 1969. The smiling general. Jakarta.

Rouffaer, G. 1931. Vorstenlanden.

Rudner, M. 1976. The Indonesian military and economic policy. Modern Asian Studies. 10(2).

Ruslan, A. 1973. Pelaksanaan kode etik jurnalistik. Thesis. Universitas Pajajaran, Bandung.

Sadli, M. 1970. Difficulties of foreign investors: a comment. Bulletin of Indonesian Economic Studies. March.

Sajidiman Surjohadiprodjo. 1971. Langkah-langkah perdjoangan kita. Department of Defense and Security. Jakarta.

Sajogyo. 1973. Modernization without development in rural Java. Paper contributed to the study on changes in agrarian structures, organized by the FAO and UN, 1972-73.

Saleh, K. 1974. Editor. Himpunan peraturan dan undang-undang tentang perkawinan. Ichtiar Baru-Van Hoeve, Jakarta.

Salim, E. 1965. Politik dan ekonomi pantjasila. In Masalah^2 ekonomi dan faktor^2 ipolsos. Jakarta.

Samson, A.
    1968. Islam in Indonesian politics. Asian Survey. 4.
    1971-1972. Army and Islam in Indonesia. Pacific Affairs. 44.
    1973. Religious belief and political action in Indonesian Islamic modernism. In R. Liddle, ed., Political participation in modern Indonesia.

Sartono Kartodirdjo. 1966. The peasants' revolt in Banten in 1888, its conditions, course, and sequel: a case study of social movements in Indonesia.

Schacht, H. 1952. Report on general economic conditions in Indonesia. Bulletin of the Indian Chamber of Commerce. 5 (4-20). Surabaya.

Schanberg, S. 1974. Indonesia: a success, but not for everyone. New York Times. January 20.

Scherer, S. 1975. Harmony and dissonance: early nationalist thought in Java. M.A. thesis. Cornell University.

Schmitter, P. 1974. Still the century of corporatism? Review of Politics. 36.

Schramm, W. 1964. Mass media and national development.

Schrieke, B. 1955. Indonesian sociological studies. Vol. 1.

Scott, J. 1972. Patron-client politics and political change in Southeast Asia. American Political Science Review. 66.
    1972a. The erosion of patron-client bonds and social change in rural Southeast Asia. Journal of Asian Studies. 32.
    1972b. Comparative political corruption.

Secretariat of the Ampera Cabinet. 1967. Daftar nama-nama pedjabat alamat dan telepon. Jakarta. December 1.

Selosoemardjan. 1962. Social change in Jogjakarta.
    1965. Sifat-sifat panutan dalam masjarakat Indonesia. In Masalah^2 Ekonomi dan Faktor Ipolsos. LEKNAS, Jakarta.

Shaplen, R. 1974. a Letter from Indonesia. The New Yorker. 50(6).

Sidjabat, W. 1965. Religious tolerance and the Christian faith. Jakarta.

Sievers, A. 1974. The mystical world of Indonesia: culture and economic development in conflict.

Simatupang, T. 1972. Report from Banaran. Trans. B. Anderson and E. Graves. Cornell Modern Indonesia Project.

Simkin, C. 1970. Indonesia's unrecorded trade. Bulletin of Indonesian Economic Studies. 6(1).

Sjahrir, S. 1949. Out of exile. Trans. C. Wolf, Jr.

 1956. Problems the country faces. Atlantic Monthly. June.

 1968. Our struggle. Trans. B. Anderson. Cornell Modern Indonesia Project Translation.

Skinner, G. 1959. Editor. Local, ethnic, and national loyalties in village Indonesia: a symposium. Yale Southeast Asia Studies Monograph.

 1973. Change and persistence in Chinese culture overseas: a comparison of Thailand and Java. In J. McAlister, Jr. 1973.

Sloan, S. 1971. A study in political violence.

Smith, T. 1971. Corruption, tradition, and change. Indonesia. 11.

 1971a. The Indonesian bureaucracy. Ph.D. thesis. University of California, Berkeley.

Soedarso, B. 1969. Korupsi di Indonesia. Bhratara, Jakarta.

Soedjatmoko. 1956. The role of political parties in Indonesia. In P. Thayer, ed., Nationalism and progress in free Asia.

Soedjito. 1974. Seminar discussion. Masalah pembangunan social Indonesia. Sponsored by SEADAG and BAPPENAS.

Soegito, S. 1973. Pengamanan negara pancasila, pengamanan haluan negara, pengaman haluan pembangunan; peranan media massa. Rapat kerja, Departemen Penerangan.

 1973a. Status dan struktur media massa masa depan. Directorate General of Radio, Television, and Film.

Soen, S. 1968. Prospects for agricultural development in Indonesia. Centre for Agricultural Publishing and Documentation.

Soendoro, 1974. Setalah komunikasi dua arah. Sinar Harapan. January 15.

Soleiman, A. 1972. Departemen Agama kini paling tadjam disorot. Pikiran Rakyat. June 9. Bandung.

Starner, F. 1974. Indonesia: much on the mind. Far Eastern Economic Review. January 28.

 1974a. Revolt of a thousand faces. Far Eastern Economic Review. February 4.

Stevenson, W. 1963. Birds' nests in their beards.

Stockwin, H. 1973. An ability to lead. Far Eastern Economic Review. April 2.

Sudisman. 1975. Analysis of responsibility. Trans. B. Anderson. Melbourne. The Works Co-operative.

Suhada, I. 1974. Siaran mahasiswa melalui radio. Thesis. Universitas Pajajaran.

Suhandang, K. 1970. Radio transistor dan petani. Thesis. Universitas Pajajaran.

Suharto. 1974. Speech to Parliament on January 7, 1974. Majalah Keuangan. 4(37).

Sukarno. 1952. The birth of Pantjasila.

Sukarno. 1960. Marhaen and proletarian. Trans. C. Holt. Cornell Modern Indonesia Project Translation.

 1963. Ilmu penetahuan sekadar alat mentjapai sesuatu. Departemen Penerangan. Jakarta.

 1970. Nationalism, Islam and Marxism. Trans. K. Warouw and P. Weldon. Cornell Modern Indonesia Project Translation.

Sulaiman Mohamed. 1972. Suara Malaysia dan audience di Indonesia. Thesis. Universitas Pajajaran, Bandung.

Sumadi. 1972. Problems of development information in Indonesia. Paper submitted to the seminar, "The Role of Government Information in National Development," East-West Communication Institute, Honolulu.

Sumbangan fikiran TNI-AD kepada kabinet Ampera. Jakarta.

Sunandar Priyosudarmo. 1973. Penyelenggaraan pemerintahan di Indonesia berdasarkan U.U.D. 1945. SESKDAD. Bandung.

Sundhaussen, U. 1971. The political orientations and political involvement of the Indonesian Officer Corps 1945-1966: The Siliwangi division and the Army Headquarters. Ph.D. Thesis. Monash University.

    1971a. The fashioning of unity in the Indonesian army. Asia Quarterly. 2.

    1972. The military in research on Indonesial politics. Journal of Asian Studies. 31(2).

    1973. The new order of General Soeharto. Internationales Asienforum. 4(1).

    1976. Decision-making within the Indonesian military. In. H. Schiffrin, ed., Military and state in modern Asia.

Supardjo, S. 1973. Komunikasi dalam proses pemilihan kepala desa. Thesis. Universitas Pajajaran, Bandung.

Suryadinata, L. 1976. Indonesian policies toward the Chinese majority under the New Order. Asian Survey. 16(8).

Sutowo, I. 1974. Management perusahaan perminyakan. Paper delivered to a seminar entitled "In search of an Indonesian managerial identity for development." January 21-26. Jakarta.

    1976. Perataan pendapatan itu suatu utopia. Prisma. 5(1).

Swearingen, R. 1961. What's so funny, comrade?

Tambunan, A., 1974. Editor. Undang-undang Republik Indonesia no. 5 tahun 1974 tentang pokok-pokok pemerintahan di daerah. Binacipta, Bandung.

Tan, M. 1971. The social and cultural context of family planning in Indonesia. Paper delivered to the Fifth Asian Congress of Obstetrics and Gynecology. October 8-15. Jakarta.

Taylor, C., and M. Hudson. 1972. Editors. World handbook of political and social indicators. 2nd ed.

Team Penelitian Antar Universitas. 1973. Kebijaksanaan penerangan/komunikasi PELITA II: penelitian komunikasi pedesaan di Indonesia. Jakarta.

Tentang Dasar Negara Republik Indonesia dalam Konstituante. n.d.

Thomas, J. 1968. Rural public works and East Pakistan's development Paper delivered at Harvard Development Advisory Service Conference.

Thomas, R. 1973. A chronicle of Indonesian higher education. Singapore.

Tichelman, G. 1937. Toenggal panaloean, de Bataksche tooverstaf. Tijdschrift voor Indische Taal-, Land- en Volkenkunde. 77.

Tinker, I., and M. Walker. 1973. Planning for regional development in Indonesia. Asian Survey. 13(12).

Tobing, J. 1976. Minyak dan kontrol DPR. Prisma. 5(4).

United Nations. 1970. Urban and rural population: individual countries 1950-1985 and regions and major areas 1950-2000.

    1974. Statistical yearbook 1973.

    1975. Statistical yearbook 1974.

Universitas Padjadjaran. 1973. Hasil survey mengenai strategi komunikasi pembangunan untuk PELITA II. Bandung.

Vandenbosch, A. 1941. The Dutch East Indies: its government, problems, and politics.

van der Kroef, J. 1956. Economic development in Indonesia: some social and cultural impediments. Economic Development and Cultural Change. 4(2).

    1958. Indonesian social evolution: some psychological considerations.

van der Wal, S. 1963. Editor. Het onderwijsbeleid in Nederlandse-Indië 1900-1942.

van Deventer, T. 1899. Een eereschuld. De Gids.

v. D. Veur, P. 1958. E. F. E. Douwes Dekker: evangelist for Indonesian political nationalism. Journal of Asian Studies. 17(4).

van Marle, A. 1956. The first Indonesian parliamentary elections. Indonesië. 9.

Van Niel, R. 1960. The emergence of the modern Indonesian elite.

Wajon, J. 1967. Kedudukan dan tugas pamong pradja. Ichtiar, Jakarta.

Ward, K. 1970. The foundation of the Partai Muslimin Indonesia. Cornell Modern Indonesia Project.

    1972. The Indonesian elections of 1971: an East Javanese perspective. M.A. thesis. Monash University.

    1974. The 1971 election in Indonesia: an East Java case study. n.d. The Nahadatul Ulama in East Java. Monash University Centre of Southeast Asian Studies.

Weatherbee, D. 1966. Ideology in Indonesia: Sukarno's Indonesian revolution. Yale Southeast Asia Studies Monograph.

Weber, M. 1947. The theory of social and economic organization.

Weinstein, F. 1972. The uses of foreign policy in Indonesia. Ph.D. thesis. Cornell University.

    1976. The foreign policy of Indonesia. In J. Rosenau et al., eds., World politics.

Wells, L. 1973. Men and machines in Indonesia's light manufacturing industries. Bulletin of Indonesian Economic Studies. November.

White, B. 1973. Peranan anak dalam ekonomi rumah tangga desa di Jawa. Prisma. 2(4).

White, L. 1970. Indonesia's unrecorded trade – a comment. Bulletin of Indonesian Economic Studies. 6(2).

    1972. Problems and prospects of the Indonesian exchange system. Indonesia. 14.

Widjojo Nitisastro. 1965. Persoalan[2] ekonomis – teknis dan ekonomis – politis dalam menanggulangi Masalah[2] ekonomi. In Masalah[2] ekonomi dan faktor[2] ipoloss. Jakarta.

    1970. Population trends in Indonesia.

Willner, A. 1963. Problems of management and authority in a transitional society: a case study of a Javanese factory. Human Organization. 22.

    1967. The Communist phoenix and the Indonesian garuda: reflections of cyclical history. World Politics. 19.

    1970. The neo-traditional accommodation to political independence: the case of Indonesia. In L. Pye, ed., Cases in comparative politics: Asia.

Wilopo. 1976. Minyak dan hutang. Prisma. 5(4).

Wiryomartono, W. n.d. Trenggalek sekarang. Pemerintah Daerah Kabupaten Trenggalek, Trenggalek.

Wiser, W., and C. Wiser. 1971. Behind mud walls, 1930-1960.

Yamin, M. 1959. Editor. Naskah persiapan Undang-undang Dasar 1945. Vol. 1. Jakarta.

Index

Abadi (Jakarta newspaper), 25, 203, 247, 269
Abangan Muslims, 9, 29, 72
    abangan-santri division, 189-191, 266-267
ABRI, 57, 70. *See also* Military
Advisor-advisee relationships in interpersonal communications, 356-380
Agriculture, 20, 143-149, 322-342. *See also* BIMAS program; Rice production
    BIMAS program, 146-147, 322-342
    labor force, 157, 160-161
    Ministry of, 91-92
    plantation and rice-farm basis of, 322-323
    production growth rate of selected commodities, 149, 150 table
    rice price policy, 147-149
Agus Sudono, 209-210, 211
Ahlusunnah Wal Jama'ah doctrine, 208-209
Aidit, D. N., 311
Air transportation, 24
Akademi Angkatan Bersenjata Republik Indonesia (AKABRI), 57, 79, 80
Akademi Militer Nasional (AMN), 79, 80
Ali Sastroamidjojo, Mr., 46, 47, 177
Anak buah, 35, 36. See also *Bapakism* and *bapak-anak buah* relationships
    and *aliran* affiliation, 385-387, 386 fig.
    party loyalty of, vs. financial reward, 387-389, 388 fig.
    physical mobilization of, to protect *bapak,* 382-385, 384 fig.
Angkatan Bersenjata (military newspaper), 25
Anshary, Isa, 174, 209, 215
    on *jihad* concept, 212, 213n
Ansor (NU youth organization), 209
ANTARA (national news agency), 51
APRI, 57. *See also* Military
Army, Indonesian, 46, 57. *See also* Military
Authority, traditional, 344, 345-350
    advisor-advisee relations and, 378-380
    compared to patronage, 347-349
    defined, 345
    inherited status and, 346
    leader-follower obligations under, 373-378
    and time dimension, 346
    urbanization and, 355-356, 363-367, 382-392
Authority structure
    one-way communication, 127-130, 325, 327-328
    personalized concept of power, 124-125, 135
    top-down nature of, 123-127
    see also Chapter 2

Bali, 7, 27, 91, 120-121, 188
Bandung, 69, 70, 166, 186
    media information sources, in, 232, 233 table
    population growth of, 161 table
    press in, 247
        compared to Jakarta's, 249, 250 table, 251, 251 table, 252 table, 253, 255 table
    urbanization and interpersonal communication network study, 343-392
Bapakism and *bapak-anak buah* relationships, 35, 36, 37
    advisee role, changing perceptions of, 367-372
    advisor role, 356-363
    defined, 350
    difficulty of inquiry about, 361-363
    future perspectives on, 389-392
    organizational identity, urban effect on, 365-366
    and urban politics, 382-389
        aliran affiliation, 385-387, 386 fig.
        opinion leadership, 382
        party loyalty vs. financial reward, 387-389, 388 fig.
        physical mobilization to protect a *bapak,* 382-385, 384 fig.
    urban-rural measure of, 356
BAPPENAS, 79
Bayon replica (Cambodia), 307-308, 310 fig.
Behavior, ideal interpersonal, 36, 37-40

Berita Buana (Jakarta newspaper), 247
Berita Yuda (military newspaper), 25
BIMAS program, 133, 146-147, 229,
　322-342
　BIMAS Gotong Rojong campaign,
　　326-331
　enduring problems and the limits of
　　action, 339-342
　Improved BIMAS and the BUUD move-
　　ment, 331-339
Bintang Timur, Sibarani cartoons in, 286,
　287 fig., 288 fig.
Blitar (Java), temple complex in, 305
Budget, 110-113
　foreign-exchange sales in, 138
　receipts and expenditures, 110-113,
　　138, 139 table
　taxation, 153-156, 154-155 table,
　　158-159 tables
BULOG (Bureau of Logistics), rice prices
　　and, 15, 51, 147-149, 334n
Bureaucracy, 82-136
　activation of, 133-135
　activity of, 109-122
　　in family planning and transmigra-
　　　tion, 120-121
　　in oil, 113-116
　　revenue and expenditure, 110-113
　　in sugar, 117-120
　and coercion, 135-136
　information sources for, 232 table,
　　238 tables
　interministerial cooperation, lack of,
　　127
　loyalty to state of, 93-109
　　"departyization," 99-100
　　military entrenchment in, 51
　　military officers in bureaucracy,
　　　100-105
　　negative allegiance to New Order,
　　　94-100
　　organized to form "monoloyalty,"
　　　105-109
　power and communication in, 123-131
　　administrative reforms, 130-131
　　one-way communication, 127-130
　　top-down authority, 123-127
　priyayi participation in, 29
　rationalization of, 132-133
　in seventeenth century, 82
　size of, 84-93
　Suharto's reform of, 82-84
Bureaucratic linkages and policy-making,
　322-342
　BIMAS Gotong Rojong campaign,
　　326-331
　enduring problems and limits of action,
　　339-342

Green Revolution, administrative fail-
　ures during, 323-326
Improved BIMAS program and BUUD
　movement, 331-339
Bureaucratic polity, xix-xxi, 3-42
　competition for power within ruling
　　circle, 14-17
　concentration of power, 10-12
　concept of, 3-6
　cultural variables of, 34-42
　　ethnic, linguistic, and religious
　　　impediments to participation,
　　　27-32
　　leader-follower relationships, 34-36
　　need dependence, concept of self,
　　　and ideal personal behavior,
　　　36-40
　　predisposition to violence, 40
　　traditional concept of power, 40-42
　future alternatives to, 19-22, 397
　limits of presidential power, 6-10
　mass participation mobilization by, 9
　military polity distinguished from, 12-13
　overturning a ruling circle, 17-19
　political party role in, 5-6
　presidency as central link, 17-18
　structural variables of, 23-24
　　communications media, 24-26
　　ethnic, linguistic, and religious
　　　impediments to participation,
　　　27-32
　　geography, 23
　　Indonesian Chinese, 27-28
　　Indonesian Muslims, 28-32
　　local leadership role, 30-31
　　transportation, 23-24
　　urbanization, 32-34
　　use of coercion, 31-32
Burhanuddin Harahap, Mr., 287 fig., 288
BUUD movement, 332-339

Cartoons, political communication through,
　286-301
　Johnny Hidajat cartoons, 286, 289,
　　290-291 figs., 295-299, 300-301,
　　320-321
　Sibarani cartoons, 286-289, 287 fig.,
　　288 fig., 292-295, 299-301, 319,
　　321
Chinese, Indonesian, 27-28, 33, 164-166
Circles, personal, 34-36. See also *Bapakism*
　　and *bapak-anak buah*
　　relationships
Cirebon (Java), study of traditional com-
　　munications in, 256-57, 257 table
Civil-military relations, 45-56
　and coup of September 30, 1965, 48
　economic role of military, 52-55

Nasution's policies, 47-48
penetration of bureaucracy by military, 51
penetration of diplomatic and consular corps by military, 51
penetration of legislature by military, 51-52
provincial government control by military, 52, 102-103
under Sjahrir, 45-46
under Suharto and New Order, 48-51
under Sukarno and Guided Democracy, 46-48
Clientelism, 34-36. See also *Bapakism* and *bapak-anak buah* relationships; Patron-client relations
Coercion, 135-136
in bureaucratic polity, 31-32
used by KORPRI, 108-109
Communications. *See also* Mass communications
from leadership to population, 122-131
administrative reform, 130-131
one-way communication, 127-130
top-down authority, 123-127
media, 24-26, 229-258
transportation, 23-24
Communications, interpersonal, effect of urbanization on, 343-392
bapakism and urban politics, 382-389
patterns of, among villagers and urbanites, 355-382
advisee role, changing perceptions of, 367-373
advisor-advisee relationships, duration of, 378-380
advisor role prevalent, 356-367
leader-follower obligations, changes in, 373-378
organizational membership, 381-382
and patron-client relations, 343-392
research procedures, 350-355
difficulty of inquiring about *bapakism,* 361-362
exclusion of Indonesian Chinese, 354
interviewers, 350-351
sampling categories, 352-353
Communications, political, under New Order, 282-321
cartoons, 286-301
direct speech, 284-285
monuments, 301-311
symbolic speech, 285-286
traditions preserved through, 312-318
Computerization of administrative processes, 130-132
Constituent Assembly, 6, 172, 218-219, 221, 285

Constitution of 1945, 6, 29, 45-50, 69
reimposition of in 1959, 172, 219
Cooptation, 32
Corruption, 15-16, 54-55, 163-164, 374-375
Coup of September 30, 1965, 4, 31, 40, 48
and bureaucratic reform, 90-93
impact on presidential power, 6-8
Crush Malaysia campaign, 10, 13
Cultural variables. *See* Bureaucratic polity, cultural variables of
Culture. *See* Political culture

Daendels, Gov., 86
Darjatmo, Lt. Gen., 76
Dar'ul Islam revolt, 201, 209, 351, 387
Da'wah (Islamic missionary activities), 203, 208
Decision-making, military, 74-76
Development Unity party. *See* PPP
Dewan Da'wah Islamiyah (Islamic Missionary Council), 203, 205
Dewan kekaryan pusat, 75-76
Dharsono, Gen., 12, 60, 68
Diplomatic and consular corps, military penetration of, 51
Djaelani Naro, Mr., 209-210, 221
Dulles, John Foster, 286, 287 fig.
Duta Masjarakat (Jakarta newspaper), 204n, 269
Dutch East India Company, 53, 85-86

Economic policy, 137-170
budget, 110-113
centralized nature of, 176
pattern of, 1966-75, 138-153
agricultural policy, 143-149
foreign investment, 152-153
kabupaten program, 149-152
restoration of market system, 142-143
stabilization, 138-141
sociopolitical dimensions of, 153-167
Chinese and Pribumi, 27-28, 33, 164-166
conspicuous consumption, 162-163
corruption, 14-16, 54-55, 163-164, 374-375
distribution considerations, 153-163
economic ideology, 166
geographical distribution, 156-157
labor absorption, 157-161
taxation and expenditure, 153-156
technocrats and the military, 166-167
Economy
agricultural base of, 322-323
agricultural-industrial shares of, 20
economic development and growth, 13, 16, 84, 113, 116

economic growth rate, 137
　　geographical distribution of, 156-157
economic rationality, 13
　　military role in, 52-55
　　state administration of, 53-55
Education, literacy and, 20
Eisenhower, Dwight D., 287 fig., 288
Elections
　　election laws (1953; 1959), 174,
　　　　182-183
　　Muslim role in, 30-31, 223-226
　　of 1955, 175
　　of 1971, 9, 11-12, 31, 183
　　　　and military power, 49
　　　　and political party reorganization,
　　　　　　30-31, 99-100, 106-107, 223-226
　　　　press coverage of, 251, 251 table, 252
　　　　　　table, 253, 254 table, 255 tables
　　of 1977, 132
　　role of, in bureaucratic polity, 5
Elite, 4, 13, 15, 31, 33. See also Power
　　　　relationships, power circles
　　elite-military relations, 45-56
　　media controlled by, 25-26, 268
　　and mobilization of mass participation,
　　　　5-6, 20-21, 267-268
　　the press and, 259, 261-262
　　and response to the September 30, 1965
　　　　coup, 6-8
Ethnic variables, as impediments to partici-
　　　　pation, 27-32
Exports. See Trade

Family planning, 120-123
Farmers
　　and BIMAS program, 325-339
　　　　BUUD organization, 332-333,
　　　　　　335-336
　　　　control of payments for, 327-328
　　　　lack of feedback from, 325, 327
　　　　resistance to program, 328-329,
　　　　　　336-339
　　information sources for, 232 table
　　radio listening habits of, 237-239, 238
　　　　table
　　Films, 233 table, 246, 247 table, 317-318,
　　　　320
　　as source of election news, 254 table
Five-year plans. See also REPELITA
　　first (1969-74), 39-40, 110
　　　　agricultural goals of, 143, 143 table,
　　　　　　144 table
　　　　and rice production, 324-326
　　second (1974-79), 107, 110, 167-169,
　　　　169 table
Foreign exchange, sale of, 139, 141, 142
Foreign investment, 152-153, 165
Foreign policy in bureaucratic polity, 9-10
Freedom Monument, 301

Functional Groups. See GOLKAR

GBHN (policy guidelines, 1973), 97-98,
　　　　110-111, 121
Generasi Muda (Young Generation), 70,
　　　　79-81, 317
Generation of 1945, preservation of tradi-
　　　　tions and, 70, 79-81, 312-318
Geographic features, 23
Gerakan Peladjar Islam Indonesia (Move-
　　　　ment of Indonesian Islamic
　　　　University Students), 209
Gintings, Djamin, 312
GKI (Indonesian Freedom Movement),
　　　　129-130
GOLKAR (Functional Groups), 29, 30,
　　　　99-100, 103
　　and hostility toward Islam, 97-98
　　and 1971 elections, 9, 12, 49, 50-51,
　　　　107
　　post-election role, 183-184
　　Outer-Island representation of, 189
　　as top-down organization, 108, 123
Green Revolution, 323-326, 331-339
Guided Democracy
　　budgets of, 112
　　bureaucracy of, 87-89
　　military role in, 6, 13, 47-48, 101
　　monument construction under, 301-303,
　　　　302 figs.
　　and Muslim solidarity, 208
　　political parties under, 172, 175-179
　　　　in phase I (1959-62), 178
　　　　in phase II (1963-65), 179
　　　　region-center conflict, 175-177
　　　　Sukarno imposition of Guided
　　　　　　Democracy participation system,
　　　　　　177-179
　　press under, 272-274
　　Sukarno's concept of, 6, 8, 177-179
Guided Economy, 141-142

Halus concept, 38-39
Hamengkubuwono IX, Sultan of Jogjakarta,
　　　　76, 167, 316 fig.
Hamka, Mr., 202, 209
HANKAM (Dept. of Defense and Security),
　　　　5, 57-59
　　and military decision-making, 74-75
　　Suharto control of personnel, 78-79
HANSIP (Civil Defense Organization), 57n
Harian Kami (Jakarta daily), 247, 251
Harjono, Anwar, 202, 209
Haryono, Piet, 169
Hatta, Mohammad, 87, 286, 287 fig.
Hidajat, Johnny, cartoons by, 286, 289,
　　　　290-291 figs., 295-299, 300-301,
　　　　320-321
Highways, 23-24

HMI (Islamic University Students' Assoc.),
    95, 208, 225-226
HYVs (high-yielding rice varieties), 324,
    325, 332

Ibn Khaldun, 197, 201
Ibnu Sutowo, Gen., 6, 77, 124
    and PERTAMINA, 15-16, 53-54,
        114-116, 122, 169-170, 186
Ideology, 5-6
    Islamic concept of, 196-226
        and consequences of 1971 elections,
            223-226
        ideology as symbol and as tactics,
            216
        and New Order, 220-222
        quest for ideology, 213-220
        and regimes since 1945, 217-220
    and Islamic question, in 1950s, 189-190
    of New Order, and preservation of tradi-
        tions, 312-318
    Pancasila (Sukarno, 1945), 50, 69,
        217-219, 220, 267, 317
    polarizations
        center-region opposition, 188-189
        Islamic vs. secular, 188, 189-191
        upper vs. lower patterns, 188,
            191-193
    and role of the press, 265-268
Idham Chalid, 210, 225
IGGI (Inter-Governmental Group on
    Indonesia), 280
Imports. See Trade
India, 19, 25, 26
Indonesia Raya (newspaper), 25
Indonesian Armed Forces (ABRI), 57. See
    also Military
Indonesian Communist party. See PKI
Indonesian Democratic party. See PDI
Indonesian Freedom Movement (GKI),
    129-130
Indonesian Journalists' Association, 50,
    248, 260
Indonesian language, 27, 230
Indonesian Muslim party (Parmusi). See PMI
Indonesian National Army (TNI), 59. See
    also Military
Indonesian Nationalist party. See PNI
Indonesian Socialist party. See PSI
Integration, national, and power relation-
    ships, 343-392
International Rice Research Institute, 146,
    334
Investment, foreign and private, 152-153,
    165
Ipeda (land tax), 111-112, 154-155 table
Irian, West, 13, 61, 65, 166, 234
    used as issue to mobilize mass participa-
        tion, 176

Islam
    abangan-santri division, 28-32, 189-191,
        266-267
    and bureaucratic loyalty, 95-96
    government depoliticization of, 225-226
    as impediment to participation, 28-32
    Islamic question, in 1950s, 189-191
    Islamic Students' Assoc., 95, 208,
        225-226
    Islamic vs. secular political polarization,
        188, 189-190
    Jakarta Charter, 221-222
    leadership process, 201-206
    Ministry of Religion under control of,
        87, 88, 95-96
    modernist movement
        Masyumi party, 198, 199
        Muhammadiyah organization, 198,
            199
        PMI (Parmusi party), 198, 199
        PSII (Partai Sarekat Islam Indonesia),
            198
        and view of political power, 198-200
    political parties, 6, 11, 12, 49, 50, 187,
        190, 220
        fusion of, 11, 12, 49-50, 96, 99,
            194, 210, 225-226
        and Jakarta Charter, 221-222
        and 1971 elections, 30-31, 97-99,
            107, 223-226
        under New Order, 180-182, 184-185
        under parliamentary democracy,
            173, 174
    politics, power, and ideology, concepts
        of, 196-226
        concepts of power, 200-206
        ideology, quest for, 213-220
        ideology in New Order, 220-222
        Islam since elections of 1971,
            223-226
        Perjuangan Ummat Islam, 209-211
        religious belief and political behav-
            ior, 211-213
        Ummat Islam, 206-209
    press, 25, 203-204
    priyayi Muslims, 29, 40, 55
    social, economic, and political structures
        of, 29-32
    state concept of, 214-215
    traditionalist movement, 29, 198-200

Jakarta, 145 table, 186
    economic development in, 156
    family planning in, 120
    monument construction in, 301-303,
        302 figs.
    population growth of, 161 table
    press, 247
        compared to Bandung press, 249, 250

table, 251, 251 table, 252 table, 253, 255 table
structural characteristics, 32-34
Jasin, Gen., 312
Jatiluhar (Java), satellite station at, 234, 243
Jatiroto, 134
sugar factory, 117-119
Java, 121, 136
armed forces organizations on, 60, 62
bureaucratic expansion on, 84-85, 103
communication on, 128-129
culture of, 34-42
economy of, 23, 322
family planning policy in, 120-123
ethnic makeup of, 27
Java-Outer Islands opposition, 188-189
land-tax collection on, 111-112
media on, 25-26
population concentrated on, 230, 231 table
power and wealth on, 41-42
radio and television coverage on, 234, 244 fig.
and santri-abangan division, 189-190
Java, Central
bureaucratic purge in, 92
and BUUD rice policy, 336-337
and coup of September 30, 1965, 7, 9
Java, East
bureaucratic purge in, 91
and BUUD rice policy, 336-338
and coup of September 30, 1965, 7, 9
sugar production in, 117-120
Java, West
anti-communist rebellions, 47
and BIMAS program, 330, 336
and coup of September 30, 1965, 7-8
economic development in, 156
illiteracy in, 20
Java War, monument to, 307
Jihad (holy war), 7, 211-213
Jogjakarta, 186, 233, 234, 307, 314
Journalism, 259-281. See also Newspapers; Press
Journalists' Association, 50, 248, 260

Kabupaten program, 149-152
KAMI (Indonesian Student Action Alliance), 7, 11
Kartosoewirjo, S. M., 209, 387
Karyawan Management Board (BAPINKAR), 76
Kasimo plan (for rice production), 323
Kasman Singodimedjo, 202
Keluarga (family) concept, 208
Kemal Idris, Gen., 12, 60, 68
Kinship, preservation of tradition of 1945 Generation and, 313-314, 318
Kiyayis, leadership role of, 7, 198, 200-202

KOKARMINDAGRI, 106-107
Kompas (Jakarta daily), 25-26, 247, 269
content study of, 249, 250 table, 251, 251 table, 252 table, 253, 255 tables, 256 table
Konstituante. See Constituent Assembly
KOPKAMTIB (Komando Operasi Pemulihan Keamanan dan Ketertiban — Operations Command for the Restoration of Security and Order), 51, 62, 64, 65, 71, 72, 186n
KORPRI (Corps of Civil Servants of the Indonesian Republic), 105
coercion used by, 108-109
structure of, 107-108
as top-down organization, 107-108, 123
KOWILHANs (Regional Commands), 58-59
geographical distribution of, 60-61
reorganization of, 62, 63 fig.
Krama speech, 284
Krokodil, cartoons in, 292n

Labor force, 157-161
radio listening habits of, 238 table
Land tax (Ipeda), 111-112, 154-155 table
Language, 27, 230
Leader-follower relations, 34-36. See also Authority, traditional; Bapakism and bapak-anak buah relationship; Patron-client relations
and elections, 30-31
Islamic, 201-203
Legislature, military penetration of, 51-52
Lewat Tengah Malam (film), 217-218, 320
Liberation of West Irian Monument, 301-303, 302 fig.
Linguistic variables, as impediments to participation, 27-32
Lubis, Zulkifli, 287 fig., 288

Machmud, Amir, 51, 124-125
and organization of civil service, 100, 105-106
Madjid, Nurcholish, 225
Madura, 60, 62, 188, 231 table, 234
Malaysia, 20, 25, 26
Crush Malaysia campaign, 10, 13, 64, 65
Malik, Adam, 76, 101
Maluku, 234
Manihuruk, A. E., 108, 131, 135
Marhaenism doctrine, 191
Marriage bill (1973), 9, 11, 29, 50, 97, 186-187, 267
Mass communications, 24-26, 229-258. See also Communications
films, 246, 247 table
multiple audiences, 230-233, 232 table, 233 table

press and newspapers, 246-255, 259-281
radio, 233-243
television, 243-246
and traditional interpersonal communications, 255-258, 357-358
urban impact of, 229
Mass participation. *See* Participation, mass
Masyumi party, 6, 29, 172-177, 192, 194, 198-199, 209
  civil servants banned from, 94
  ideology of, 212, 215, 217
  and New Order, 180-181
  and PMI, 11, 182, 220
  and post-coup politics, 95, 96
  regionalist basis of, 177, 189
  and secular politics, 30, 207, 218-219
Medan (Sumatra), 145 table, 161 table, 186, 233, 243
Merdeka (Jakarta daily), 25, 247, 269
Military
  abangan influence in, 96
  army seminars (1966; 1972), 69, 70, 312-313, 317
  and bureaucratic polity, 3, 12-13
  in civil service, 100-105, 166-167
    by branch of armed service, 103
    at cabinet level, 101-102
    competence of, 104-105
    in regional administrations, 102-104
    statistical measures of, 101
  Generasi Muda control of, 79-81
  under Guided Democracy, 6, 178
  ideology of, 68-70
  information sources of, 232 table
  internal organization of, 57-67
    command integration, 59-62, 63 fig.
    KOPKAMTIB control, 62, 64
    merger of cadet schools, 57
    OPSUS, 64-65
    strategy of, 59
  military-civil relations, 45-56
  under New Order, 179-182, 186-187
  power, influence, and communication within, 67-79
    access to president, 76-79
    decision-making, 74-76
    divisiveness and cohesiveness, 67-72
    power relationships, 72-74
  press, 25
  radio listening habits, 238 table
  size of, 15, 65, 67, 104
Mini monument, 185, 303-305, 308, 311
Mintaredja, H. M., 209-210, 213, 221, 222, 224-225
Moertono, Amir, 108
Moertopo, Ali, 50, 51, 70-73, 78, 186-187
  access to Suharto, 77
  and GOLKAR in 1971 elections, 100
  in OPSUS, 64

Monuments
  of Guided Democracy period, 301-303, 302 figs
  of New Order period, 185, 283 fig., 303-311
Muhammadiyah, 29, 198, 199
Muslims. *See* Islam

Nahdatul Ulama. *See* NU
NASAKOM, 38, 41, 90-91
Nasution, A. H., 12, 52, 55, 70, 73, 181
  and increase of army's political role, 47-48, 67-68, 69
  military reorganization by, 59-60
Nationalism, 191-192, 217. *See also*
    NASAKOM; Pancasila; PNI
  and mass mobilization, 267-268
National Monument, 301, 302 fig., 303
National Planning Board (BAPPENAS), 70, 71
Natsir, Muhammad, 202-203, 207-209, 211, 214
  as cartoon subject, 287 fig., 288, 293-294
New Order
  budgetary expenditure of, 112-113
  constitutional basis of, 49-50
  creation of, 48-49
  economic policies of, 142-143
  personalistic nature of, 78
  political communication under, 282-321
    cartoons, 286-301
    direct speech, 284-285
    monuments, 301-311
    symbolic speech, 285-286
    tradition preserved through, 312-318
  political parties under, 49-51, 172, 179-187
    centrality of military, 179-180
    and dissolution of PKI, 180-181
    GOLKAR created, 183
    military reorganization, 186-187
    new parties created, 184-185
    shift to authoritarianism, 182-183
    and student dissatisfaction, 185-187
  power competition under, 14-17
  and the press, 269, 272, 274
Newspapers, 25-26, 246-255. *See also* Press;
    individual newspapers by name
  attitude toward government, 26
  circulation, 246-247
  as first source of information, 232 table, 233 table
  geographical distribution of, 23-32, 232-233
  government control of, 248
  readership of, 248-249
Ngoko speech, 284-285
NU (Nahdatul Ulama) party, 11, 29, 30,

172, 173, 187, 189, 194,
  198-200, 204n, 209
accommodationism of, and elections of
  1971, 12, 49, 224-226
civil-servant membership in, 94
and concept of Islam, 208-209
under Guided Democracy, 9, 178
on Islamic ideology, 217
on Islamic state concept, 215
on Jakarta chapter, 221-222
Ministry of Religion controlled by, 87,
  88, 200
under New Order, 180-181, 183, 184n
political and ideological flexibility of,
  29, 174-175, 192, 210, 212, 213,
  218-221
and post-coup politics, 95
as *santri* party, 190
status and power in, 201-202
Nusantara (Jakarta daily), 247

Oil. *See also* PERTAMINA
  exports of, 138, 140 table, 141
  New Order policy toward, 113-116
  oil boom, 111, 114, 133
Old Order, power competition in, 14
OPEC, 114
OPSUS (Special Operation Division), 64-65
Organizational identity of *bapak* and
  anak-buah, 365-366
Organizational membership, urbanization
  and, 381-382
Outer Islands
  opposition to Center, 188-189
  regionalism and, 175-177, 188-189
  rice production on, 339-342

Pamong praja organizations, 105-109, 173
Panataran temple complex, 305
Pancasila, 50, 69, 217-219, 220, 234, 267,
  317
  in context of *abangan-santri* difference,
  267
Panitia Persiapan Kemerdekaan Indonesia
  (Committee for the Preparation
  of Indonesian Independence), 285
Panggabean, Gen., 61-62, 64, 72-74, 76
Parkindo (Indonesian Christian [Protestant]
  party), 172, 174, 175, 178, 183,
  189, 194
Parliament, 47, 285
  provincial (DPRD), 52
Parliamentary democracy period, 173-175,
  217
  characteristics, 173
  conservatism of party factions, 173-174
  party strength, 173
  polar politics of, 174

two participation systems under, 173,
  174
Parmusi. *See* PMI
Partai Katolik (Catholic party), 172, 174,
  175, 178, 183, 189, 194
Partai Muslimin Indonesia. *See* PMI
Participation, mass
  in bureaucratic polity, 4-6
  cooptation used to prevent, 32
  ethnic, linguistic, and religious impedi-
    ments to, 27-32
  elite-mass linkup and political change,
    267-268
  factors leading to increase in, 19-21
  future of, 193-195
  under New Order, 179-187
  political parties and, 171-195
  and response to coup of September 30,
    1965, 7-8
Parties, political, 171-195. *See also indi-*
    vidual parties by name
  in bureaucratic polity, 4, 5-6, 395-397
  central government control over, 49
  and concentration of power, 10-12
  and "departyization" of bureaucracy,
    94, 99-100
  elements of continuity and change
    187-193
    center-region opposition, 188-189
    Islamic state vs. secular state, 188,
      189-191
    upper vs. lower pattern of polariza-
      tion, 188, 191-193
  fusion of, 11, 12, 49-50, 96, 99, 194,
    210, 225-226
  future perspectives, 193-195
  under Guided Democracy, 175-179
  lack of economic policy initiative from,
    56
  loyalty to, urban, 387-389, 388 fig.
  under New Order, 49-51, 179-187
    centrality of military, 179-180
    and destruction of PKI, 180-181
  organization of, 5-6
  in parliamentary democracy period,
    173-175
Patron-client relations, 14-15, 34-36, 344,
  345-350
  achieved status in, 350
  bapakism, 35, 36, 382-389
  contrasted to Islamic leader-follower ties,
    205n
  future perspectives, 389-392
  leader-follower obligations,
    373-378
  time dimensions of, 349-350
  and traditional authority, 347-349
  urbanization and rise of, 343-392

PDI (Indonesian Democratic party), 12, 49, 99, 184-185, 194-195
Pedoman (newspaper), 25
People's Consultative Assembly (MPR), 97, 185
People's Deliberative Congress (MPRS), 47, 48, 51-52, 69
Personalistic structures, 34-36, 124-125, 135. *See also* Authority, traditional
PERTAMINA, 53-54, 112-116, 122, 124, 186
    crash of, 15-16, 77, 169-170
Perti party, 184n, 194
Petruk (*wayang* clown figure), 296-298
Philippines, Republic of the, 20, 25, 26
Phnom Penh, 271, 307-308
PII (Movement of Islamic Youth), 208
Pikiran Rakyat (Bandung newspaper), 247
    content study of, 249, 250 table, 251, 251 table, 252 table, 253, 255 tables, 256 table
PKI (Indonesian Communist party), 5, 6, 30, 48, 83, 177, 187, 194
    centralist basis of, 189
    in coup of September 1965, 18, 88
    consequences of, 18, 40, 48, 90
    under Guided Democracy, 6-7, 8, 47-48, 175, 178-179
    in nationalist-communist dichotomy, 191-192
    under parliamentary democracy period, 172-175
    size of, 179n
PMI (Parmusi party – Partai Muslimin Indonesia), 6, 11, 29, 30, 32, 187, 194, 198-199, 208-210, 222
    accommodationist character of, 210, 224-226
    formation and merger of, 29, 172, 182, 184
    ideology of, 217, 221
    on Jakarta Charter, 221-222
    in 1972 elections, 12, 183, 189, 224-226
PNI (Indonesian Nationalist party), 9, 30, 32, 187, 194
    centralist basis of, 189
    civil-servant membership of, 94
    under Guided Democracy, 178
    in Ministry of Home Affairs and Information, 88
    Islamic cooperation with, 29, 207
    in nationalist-communist dichotomy, 191-192
    under New Order, 180-181
    in 1971 elections, 12, 107, 183
    under parliamentary democracy period, 172-175

Political culture, bureaucratic polity and, 34-42
    leader-follower relationships, 34-36
    need dependence, concept of self, and ideal personal behavior, 36-40
    predisposition to violence, 40
    traditional concept of power, 40-42
Population
    geographic distribution of, 30, 230, 231 table
Pos Kota (newspaper), 26, 286
Postal service, 26
Power
    contemporary Islamic concepts of, 196-226
    traditional concept of, 41
Power relationships. *See also* Patron-client relations
    bapak-anak buah relationships, 350, 382-389
    defined, 345
    effect of urbanization on, 343-345
        traditional authority and patronage, defined, 345-350
    interpersonal communication patterns among villagers and urbanites, 355-382
        advisee role, changing perceptions of, 367-372
        advisor-advisee relationship, duration of, 378-380
        advisor role, 356-367
        changing obligations of leader and follower, 373-378
        urban effect on, 355-356, 363-367
    Islamic concept of, 200-206
    power circles, 14-17
PPP (Development Unity party), 11, 49, 50, 84-85, 96, 184-185, 194-195, 210-211, 225
Prawoto Mangkusamito, Mr., 202, 207
Presidency
    as central link in bureaucratic polity, 17-18
    ethnic Javanese monopoly on, 73
    limits of presidential power under bureaucratic polity, 6-10
    military access to, 76-79
Press, 259-281. *See also* Newspapers
    colonial, oppositionist nature of, 273
    editor's need to align with system, 270
    editor's status in society, 271-272
    as elite institution, 25-26, 259-260, 268
    functions of, perceived by government and by public, 269-270
    government-press relations, 259, 262-263, 268, 270-271, 272, 276-277, 279-281

under Guided Democracy, 270, 273-274
impact on public of, 278-279
and Indonesian ideology, 265-268
"industrialization" of newspaper production, 274-275
influences on, 32, 84, 262-263, 264-265,
272, 276-277
inter-press friction, 263-264
under New Order, 270-271
policy influenced by, 275-278
Pribumi, 28, 164-166
Priyayi, 29, 40, 55
Provincial governments, military control of,
52, 102-103
PSI (Indonesian Socialist party), 6, 29, 94,
172-175, 187, 207
PSII (Partai Sarekat Islam Indonesia), 99,
184n, 194, 198, 387

Qur'an, 196, 211-213

Radio, 24-25, 233-243
as first priority information source, 232
table, 233 table
geographic distribution of, 231
public response to programs, 235, 236
table, 237-239, 238 table
radios per capita, 25, 231, 232
as source of election news, 254 table
Rapat pimpinan (leadership meeting),
decision-making and, 74-75
Regionalism, 52, 175-177, 188-189
Religion
as impediment to participation, 27-32
Islamic move away from politics,
225-226
political power and, Islamic concept of,
196-200, 213-220
religious belief and political behavior,
211-213
Religion, Ministry of, 87, 88, 95-96, 200
Muslim party control of, 87, 88, 95-96
Rendra, W. S., 186
REPELITA (five-year plan)
I, 39, 40, 143, 143 table, 144, 144
table, 229-230
II, 167-169
Rice production
BIMAS program, 146-147, 322-342
BIMAS Gotong Rojong program,
326-331
Improved BIMAS and BUUD movement, 331-339
enduring problems, and the limits of
action, 339-342
first five-year plan objectives, 143, 143
table, 144 table
and Green Revolution, 323-326

new varieties (HYVs) developed, 324,
325, 332
on Outer Islands, 339-342
rice prices, 145 table, 147-149
size of farm plots, 322
sugar policy effect on, 118-120
and unrest in urban areas, 144, 145
table, 146
Roem, Muhammad, 202, 207, 209
RRI (Radio Republik Indonesia), 233-235
Rural population
attempted development and, 229-230
interpersonal communications patterns of, compared to urban
population, 355-382
motivations for listening to radio,
237-239, 238 tables
traditional communication among,
255-258

Sadli, Mohammad, 138
Sajidiman, Gen., 312-313, 317
Salim, Emil, 138
Santri Muslims, 9, 29
abangan-santri division, 189-191,
266-267
Sanyo Kaigi (Council of Advisors), 285
Sarbini, Gen., 203
Sarwo Edhie, 12, 68
Satria (warrior-nobility essence), 275-276
Selecta (Java), monument archway in, 305,
306 fig.
Self-concept, social status and, 37, 38-39
SESKOAD (military academy, Bandung),
166
Shari'ah (Muslim divine law), 196, 201
Sibarani, Mr., cartoons by, 286-289, 287
fig., 288 fig., 292-295, 298-301,
319, 321
Sihanouk, Prince Norodom, 307-308
Sombolon, Col., 287 fig., 288
Sinar Harapan (Jakarta daily newspaper),
26, 247, 269
Singapore, 20, 25, 26
Sjafrudin Pramiranegara, 286, 287 fig.,
288, 288 fig., 289
Sjahir, Sutan, 45-46, 88
SKDN (Serikat Karyawan Dalam Negeri),
105-106, 107
Snouck Hurgronje, C., 222, 226
Socialist party. *See* PSI
Social life, models of, 34-35
Soedjatmoto, Mr., 12
Soetran, Col., 135
Solihin, Gen., 55
Somba, Maj., 288
Special Operations Service (OPSUS), 64-65
Speech, political communication through,
284-286. *See also* Cartoons,

political communication through;
  Monuments
direct speech, 284-285
symbolic speech, 285-286
State Intelligence Agency (BINEG), 65
Stop, Hidajat cartoons in, 286
Structural variables. *See under* Bureau-
  cratic polity
Students and student movements, 11,
  122-123, 125
  and *bapakism* concept, 36
  cooptation used against, 32
  and coup of September 30, 1965, 7
  Islamic, 208-209
  under New Order, 185-187
  radio listening habits of, 238 table,
    239-242, 239 table, 240 table,
    241 table, 242 tables
Suara Karya (Jakarta daily newspaper), 247
Subchan, Mr., 210
Subroto, Prof., 138
Sudarmono, Air Marshal, 62
Sudharmono, Maj. Gen., 77
Sudirman, Gen., 68-69, 203
Sudomo, Admiral, 64, 76
Sugama, Yoga, 65, 78
Sugar, 117-120
Suharto, President, 3, 11, 12, 28, 48, 69, 70
  on communication with population,
    122-123
  and creation of New Order, 48-49,
    178-180
  and depoliticization of Islam, 226
  and destruction of PKI, 6, 90-93
  economic policies of, 138-141
    BIMAS program, 147, 326-339
    economists and, 167
    kabupaten program, 149-152
    rice stabilization, 143, 147-149,
      323-334
    second five-year plan, 167
  and future alternatives to bureaucratic
    polity, 21, 22, 396, 397
  and the military, 13, 48-49
    access of military leaders to Suharto,
      76-79
    choice of military commanders, 72-74
    control exercised by Suharto, 70, 71,
      72
    reduction in size of military, 65, 104
    reorganization of military, 57-58,
      60-62, 64, 65
    and Sumitro "coup," 72-73
  and Mini monument project, 304-305
  press policies of, 271, 272
  relations with bureaucracy
    bureaucratic reforms, 84-131
    civil-military relations, 46
    reward distribution to bureaucrats,
      17

and religious cleavages in Java, 190
and traditions of Generation of 1945,
  312-315, 316
Suharto, Mrs., 185, 303-304
Sujono Humardhani, Maj. Gen., 70, 73, 77,
  78
Sukarno, President, 3, 13, 19, 28, 174, 190
  bapakism attacked by, 361-362
  bureaucracy established by, 82-83, 87-89
  and depoliticization of Islam, 226
  dismisses Constituent Assembly, 6, 219
  economic policies of, 4, 141n, 142
  and Guided Democracy, 6, 176-179
  and Marhaenism doctrine, 191
  monument construction under, 301-303,
    302 figs.
  ouster of, 6-8
  Pancasila ideology articulated by,
    217-218
  and political parties, 6, 29, 41, 226
  press policy of, 271
  and religious cleavages on Java, 190
Sukiman Wirjosandjojo, Mr., 211n
Sulawesi, 24, 103, 176
  armed forces organization on, 60, 62
  communications on, 129, 234
  population composition of, 27, 231
    table
  rebellions on, 47, 59
Sumatra, 23, 103, 234
  armed forces organization on, 60
  bureaucratic purges on, 91, 92
  challenge to central authority on, 176
  military role in bureaucracy, 103
  population composition of, 27, 231
    table
  rebellions on, 47, 59
Sumitro, Gen., 6, 62, 64, 73, 76, 78
  dismissal of, 12, 19, 71
  on freedom of communication, 129-130
  Sumitro "coup," 70-72, 186-187
  and traditions of Generation of 1945, 313
Sumitro Djojohadikusumo, 287 fig., 288
SUPERSEMAR, 305
Surabaya, 120, 145 table, 186
  population of, 33, 161 table
Surono Reksodimejo, Gen., 76, 307
Suryo, R., 70, 77
Sutopo Yuwono, Gen., 12, 15, 72
  dismissed from BAKIN, 71, 78
Sutowo, Gen. *See* Ibnu Sutowo
Symbols, 41. *See also* New order, political
  communication under

Tanaka Kakeui, demonstrations against, 12,
  71, 187
Tasril, Mr., 288 fig., 289
Taxation, 153-156, 154-155 table, 158-159
  tables
  direct taxes, 153

in government revenue, 139 table, 141
income tax collection, 163-164
land tax (Ipeda), 111-112, 154-155 table
sumptuary taxation, 162-163
tax structure, 153
Technocrats
    in bureaucratic polity, 3, 101
    and economic ideology of New Order,
        166
    PERTAMINA crisis and, 169-170
    and relations with military, 166-167
Tegalrego complex monument (Jogjakarta),
    307
Telephone service, 26
Television, 25, 132, 243-246
    as first source of information, 232-233,
        233 table
    motivation for watching, 245, 246 table
    social distribution of viewers, 244-245,
        245 table
    as source of election news, 254 table
Thailand, 18, 20, 25, 26
Tjandi Singhasari, statues at, 305, 306 fig.
Tokaido Line, 131, 135
Tokoh (Islamic notable), role of, 201-203
Trade
    foreign, 138, 140 table, 141
    interisland, 24
Tradesmen, radio listening habits of, 238
    tables
Traditional authority. See Authority,
    traditional
Transportation, 23-24, 121
Tri Darma, 315, 317
Tulungagung, (Java) monuments in, 305
TVRI television station, 243-246

Ujung Pandang, 157, 161 table, 186
    price of rice in, 145 table
    radio and television in, 233-234

Ummat Islam concept, 201, 206-211
Untung, Lt. Col., and coup of September
    30, 1965, 48, 62, 68, 69
Urban population and urbanization, 32-34,
    355-392
    bapakism and, 382-389
    interpersonal communication patterns
        of, compared to rural population,
        355-382
    advisee perceptions, changes in,
        367-372
    advisor-advisee relationships, dura-
        tion of, 378-380
    advisor role in, 356-367
    organizational membership, 381-382
    shift from traditional to patron-
        client authority structure,
        355-356
    labor force, 157, 160-161
    mass communications and, 229
    trends in, political implications of,
        390-392
Utojo, Bambang, 46

Values, political communication and
        restoration of, 312-318
Villages, Islamic influence in, 30-31. See
        also Rural population
Violence, predisposition to, 40

Waluyo, Iman, 129-130
Wardhana, Ali, 138, 167
West Irian. See Irian, West
Widjojo Nitisastro, Prof., 138, 166, 167, 169
Wilopo, Mr., 46
Wirang concept, 275

Yani, Achmad, 48, 67, 311
Young Generation (Generasi Muda), 70, 79-81